CONFLICT AFTER THE COLD WAR

CONFLICT AFTER THE COLD WAR

ARGUMENTS ON CAUSES OF WAR AND PEACE

UPDATED SECOND EDITION

Edited by

Richard K. Betts

Columbia University
The Saltzman Institute of War and Peace Studies

New York   San Francisco   Boston
London   Toronto   Sydney   Tokyo   Singapore   Madrid
Mexico City   Munich   Paris   Cape Town   Hong Kong   Montreal

Vice President and Publisher: Priscilla McGeehon
Executive Editor: Eric Stano
Acquisitions Editor: Edward Costello
Senior Marketing Manager: Elizabeth Fogarty
Production Manager: Denise Phillip
Project Coordination, Text Design, and Electronic Page Makeup; WestWords, Inc.
Cover Designer/Manager: John Callahan
Cover Photo: © Pedro Lobo/Photonica
Senior Manufacturing Buyer: Dennis J. Para
Printer and Binder: R. R. Donnelley and Sons
Cover Printer: Coral Graphic Services

Library of Congress Cataloging-in-Publication Data

Conflict after the Cold War : arguments on causes of war and peace / edited by Richard K.
Betts.—Updated 2nd ed.
    p. cm.
  ISBN 0-321-20946-X
1. World politics—1989– 2. War. 3. Peace. I. Betts, Richard K., 1947–

  D2009.C66 2004
  303.6'6—dc22

                                                           2004007332

Please visit our website at http://www.ablongman.com

ISBN 0-321-20946-X

1 2 3 4 5 6 7 8 9 10—DOC—07 06 05 04

CONTENTS

Part V Economics: Interests and Interdependence   219

Part VI Politics: Ideology and Identity   287

Part VII Strategy, I: Military Technology, Doctrine, and Stability   357

Part VIII Strategy, II: Terrorism and Unconventional Warfare   445

Part IX Transnational Tensions: Migration, Resources, and Environment   537

Part X Conclusion: The Future Between Contending Forces 583

PREFACE

In the last decade of the twentieth century the opening of the Berlin Wall and the collapse of the Soviet Union led many to herald a new era of peace and cooperation, in which war would be relegated to the margins of international politics. In the first decade of the twenty-first century terrorist attacks on the World Trade Center led many to proclaim a new titanic struggle for the future of the world, and the return of war to the front burner of foreign policy. Theorists known as realists, who had dominated thinking about international affairs during much of the Cold War, went on the defensive in the 1990s as happy events made the ideas of liberal theorists ascendant. After September 11, 2001, however, theorists who emphasized the importance of cultural conflict, who had been a distant third in academic conceptualizations of the prospects for peace, became equal contenders in the theoretical debate—a debate that the powerful crosscurrents of international life has now made close to a free-for-all among the three ways of looking at the world.

Do these theoretical disputes have much significance beyond the ivory tower, and is it really necessary to inflict them on students, few of whom will wind up in the obsessive contemplation of their intellectual navels that their professors find so compelling? Yes. Do any of the three main approaches to estimating the probability of war or peace in the future have a lock on good sense about the problem, and can any of them be safely ignored? No.

On the first point, policymakers and practical observers of international affairs may care little about theoretical matters, but they all operate on the basis of theories about what causes tend to produce which effects. The difference is that academics do so explicitly while practitioners usually do so unconsciously—and therefore without full recognition of what they take for granted, how much of what they believe to be self-evident is really unexamined common sense, assumed and unproved, and how much of what they think they know comes from instinct and hope or from hard-eyed analysis grounded in history. Presidents and prime ministers, diplomats and generals, senators and journalists have strong opinions on what causes wars, and how to avoid them, but most draw those opinions, often subconsciously, from suppositions outlined and debated in the entries in this book.

On the second point, it would be a mistake to adopt the spineless position that all contending theories have enough good and bad points to make them equally respectable. To figure out which makes the best sense, however, it is necessary to dig deep, stack the arguments against each other, and compare the fine print. Because real life is always more complicated than theorists like, none of these contending arguments can be dispatched as easily as shooting fish in a barrel. Any who think seriously about war and peace need to confront the logic and evidence behind contending views if they are to come to reasoned conclusions, whatever school of thought may ultimately convince them most.

People generally tend to be most impressed and convinced by the apparent lessons of experience, and of events observed most recently. But what do the events that are most familiar to students really indicate? The rapid collapse of Soviet power and communist ideology coincided with a burst of democratization around the world. Could euphoria about permanent peace ever have been better justified? The following decade witnessed the continuing dominance of Western liberalism as a global ideology, increasing international economic integration, and the absence of military conflict among the world's great powers. At the same time, though, political violence and disorder spread widely in poorer regions, major war broke out in the Persian Gulf, dormant cleavages based on religion and ethnicity reopened violently in many countries, war returned to the European continent for the first time since 1945, Russia's reform faltered, and tension between the United States and China began to grow. After September 11, in turn, many saw globalization as faltering, or even, indeed, as causing the rise of large-scale terrorism, and questioned the inevitable triumph of social Westernization and liberal political values throughout the world.

This volume helps students to sort out the main debates about whether war is likely to remain a major problem in international life, or in what forms violent conflict will be most significant. Because assumptions about what causes war or peace are often unconscious, the book was originally designed to put current issues in intellectual historical context. Organized in many of its parts as, in effect, a dialogue, the collection juxtaposes competing views that have been influential at different times over the years. The basic aim is to make students aware that there are powerful arguments for both optimism and pessimism, to make them grapple with the reasoning behind those arguments, and to keep them from letting their own unexamined assumptions lead them to premature certainty that war is either obsolete or just around the corner.

In the years after the first edition was published a few of the readings became dated or less useful, and were not included in the second edition. Most of the original selections, however, remained thoroughly relevant, and were retained, while many new ones were added, including an additional section of readings on psychological and cultural theories of conflict. The original second edition grew from thirty-five authors covering eight topic areas in the first, to forty-five authors and nine subject sections. The present update of the second edition, in turn, has added yet a tenth section with six new entries on unconventional warfare and terrorism, to provide more material on forms of conflict that have grown as concerns since September 11.

For the push to provide this reader I am grateful to my own students, to colleagues in Columbia's Saltzman Institute of War and Peace Studies, and to other friends in the field of security studies—some of whose writings are included in the pages that follow. For the push to revise and then again to update the second edition I thank Eric Stano of Longman. Most of all I am grateful for the patience of my wife Adela M. Bolet and our children Elena Christine, Michael Francis, and Diego Fitzpatrick Betts, who let Dad do one more project without complaint. Since my own views are pessimistic on the question of whether war has a future, the four of them make me hope that history will prove me wrong.

Richard K. Betts
Teaneck, New Jersey

PART I

INTRODUCTION: DOES WAR HAVE A FUTURE?

International conflict in the twentieth century was unusually intense. The first half of the century was an unparalleled catastrophe: two world wars killed well over 60 million people, and ruined the lives of countless others—hundreds of millions maimed, traumatized, displaced, or impoverished. The second half of the century witnessed the Cold War, a titanic struggle between two global superpowers and two transnational ideologies. The Cold War kept conflict within bounds, not least because the nuclear revolution meant that a World War III would dwarf the earlier world wars in destructiveness. Nevertheless, the Cold War was punctuated by "proxy" wars in Korea, Vietnam, and Afghanistan, and numerous revolts and other outbreaks of political violence. In terms of total destruction and constant levels of military mobilization, the past century ranks as one of the most warlike in history.

To some, this dismal record closed decisively in the last decade of the century. Optimism bloomed as the Cold War ended, Western liberalism found new security as the only remaining world-spanning ideology, and growing trade and modern communications brought nations closer together than ever before. To others, the good news of the 1990s suggested only a temporary respite from an eternal cycle of conflict and calm. After all, the nineteenth century had witnessed relatively little large-scale international violence. And while global competition between great powers ended with the Cold War, innumerable local disputes burst out and horrific small wars spread in the wake of communism's collapse and Third World states' disintegration. Then on September 11, terrorist attacks that appeared to declare war on the whole global tide of westernization raised the specter of a future frighteningly violent but different in political and military dynamics from the main wars of the past.

Will the refreshing new wave of international civility that rose when the Berlin Wall opened be limited to the developed "core" of Western Europe, Japan, and North America, while the poor countries of the "periphery" continue to wallow in force and fury?[1] Or is the prospect even worse? Some worry that the durability of the new peace is doubtful in

---

[1] See James M. Goldgeier and Michael McFaul, "A Tale of Two Worlds: Core and Periphery in the Post-Cold War Era," *International Organization* 46, no. 2 (spring 1992).

Europe too, despite the demise of the Soviet threat. The Cold War standoff between the superpowers had imposed a cautionary discipline on the traditional self-assertion of nations and forced them to cooperate in the interests of alliance security.[2] Removal of the threat reduces the incentives for caution and cooperation, making it easier for states of the continent to rediscover old frictions and ambitions. Will the end of the standoff bring the "end of history" and a world of unprecedented peace? or the return of history and old patterns of violence?[3] or a new chapter in history in which social identity, conflicts between cultures, and unconventional threats from transnational or religious groups replace interstate combat as the main danger? To figure out whether international relations in the next millennium will be fundamentally different from the past, we need to understand what forces made for war or peace in the past,[4] which of those forces are more important in the new world and which less, and what novel forces may push events in uncharted directions.

Excessive optimism overlooks the fact that some current explanations of why international relations have become naturally and permanently peaceful are actually similar to old explanations, ones that have been jolted if not discredited by the catastrophes of the first half of the past century (the two world wars) or by the reinvigoration of the Cold War after the detente of the early 1970s. More than once, analysts have discovered decisive shifts in the world, only to find that less had changed than meets the eye.

Pessimists, on the other hand, overlook how much *has* changed. The demise of Marxism-Leninism everywhere but in a few puny enclaves is even more significant an elimination of ideological conflict than the destruction of fascism in 1945. Even traditional dictatorships have been declining as an alternative to the global primacy of Western liberal norms. Can political and economic change on this scale be irrelevant to the prospects for peace or war?

The readings in this volume explore competing ideas about present trends in the light of historic debates about the causes of war and peace. The Introduction presents three stark arguments, one generally optimistic, the others more pessimistic. The subsequent two sections sample the main arguments that have animated debate about whether the threat of war is inevitable or can be made obsolete. The two overarching theoretical traditions that subsume most of the arguments are realism (see Part II) and liberalism (see Part III), both of which cover a wide variety of ideas.

Not long ago, Marxism would have been considered a competing paradigm on a level with the other two, but except to the degree that it shares some assumptions with realism,[5] it has fallen by the wayside intellectually as well as politically. A third

---

[2]See John L. Gaddis, *The Long Peace* (New York: Oxford University Press, 1987).

[3]See Robert Jervis, "The Future of World Politics: Will It Resemble the Past?" *International Security* 16, no. 3 (winter 1991/92).

[4]For a comprehensive survey see Jack S. Levy, "The Causes of War: A Review of Theories and Evidence," in Philip E. Tetlock *et al.,* eds., *Behavior, Society, and Nuclear War* (New York: Oxford University Press, 1989), vol. I.

[5]If we substitute classes for states as the essential units in competition for power, Marxism has much of the materialist and determinist logic of realism. Both assert, in contrast to liberalism, that conflict rather than harmony is the natural condition of human relations. In opposition to realism, classical Marxism sees the state as only the superstructure of class interests, so transnational social alliances should have proved to be more significant than conflict between states. This idea was thoroughly knocked out by World War I. When Leninism came to dominate Marxism, and married it to Russian and Chinese nationalism, Communist statesmanship became eminently realist.

school of thought about international relations that has been prominent recently—"constructivism"—is not as thoroughly represented here.[6] Some of the causes and concerns that figure in constructivist challenges to realism and liberalism, however, can be seen in the Huntington essay in Part I, and in Part IV, and underlie some assessments of global terrorism.

Whereas Parts II and III focus on dynamics in the relations among governments, Part IV illustrates arguments about how human nature or cultural differences affect tendencies toward war or peace. Parts V to VIII present contending views of how political, economic, and military factors may encourage, suppress, or channel decisions to resort to force. Most of these entries reflect variations of the realist and liberal perspectives. (As editor I have tried to keep a balance between the two strands of argument, and I personally do not have complete faith in either one. Honesty, however, requires that I admit a tilt in favor of realism.) Part IX, which briefly considers potential sources of conflict that transcend borders, shows the extent to which newly salient issues may also cut across traditional lines of theoretical explanation. The Conclusion surveys some new trends and issues that may dominate strategic interactions in the future.

This collection does not represent all relevant perspectives. One problem is that like all too much of international relations theory, ideas in this volume are drawn primarily from the experience and interests of Europe and the developed industrial world. A selection of theories must draw from the best of those that have been made available. While there is ample literature on the history of war and peace on other continents, most attempts at rigorous theory (at least those written in English) have drawn their inspiration from European history. Also, most people in the West who are interested in war are not worried about war in general, but about big, potentially cataclysmic wars, or about small ones that could escalate into a big one like World War I or II. Thus attention still tends to focus attention on the great powers and areas where the concentrations of high-tech military capability, gross national product, and per capita wealth are highest, even though these areas have been far more peaceful in recent decades than the so-called Third World. Even the most optimistic arguments about a new era of peace restrict themselves to the Northern Hemisphere.

Another omission is the perspective of game theory or "rational choice" analysis. This volume is not meant to be a sampler, representative of all important strands of scholarship. In deciding what to fit within the limited number of selections that can be included, I chose to expose a few important intellectual traditions and debates in depth, and to strive for some cohesion among the selections, rather than include something of everything. Moreover, while the emphasis in the selections is on theory, it is important to maintain as close a link as possible to evidence from history and current topics, so I have minimized selections that are purely deductive and abstract.

Some of the selections in the volume are reprinted in their entirety. The others have been edited to avoid repetition or discussion of matters not germane to the theme of the collection. Standard ellipses indicate where passages have been deleted. Some footnotes have also been deleted from passages that remain.

---

[6]For a proper exposure see Alexander Wendt, *Social Theory of International Politics* (Cambridge, UK: Cambridge University Press, 1999) or Peter Katzenstein, ed., *The Culture of National Security* (New York: Columbia University Press, 1996).

* * * * * * * *

The selections in the Introduction present the pithiest views about whether traditional international conflict is obsolete. Two of those views bracket more moderate and conditional versions of liberal and realist predictions. Francis Fukuyama argues that the developed world has evolved toward a liberal consensus that is effectively close to ending the bases for violent contention of the past.[7] Fukuyama's argument is particularly remarkable because it was first written before the opening of the Berlin Wall, and was prescient in anticipating the irrelevance of Marxism. At the other extreme, John Mearsheimer[8] challenges optimistic conventional wisdom with a pure distillation of the realist tradition represented in the readings that follow in Part II. To him, the intellectual developments that Fukuyama sees as decisive forces actually matter very little. When push comes to shove, ideas give way to interests. Mearsheimer asserts not only that the new era of peace is a mirage, but that the future will be worse than the recent past. The Cold War, not the new world, represents the most stable and peaceful order we are likely to see. Samuel Huntington's essay, extremely controversial when it appeared in the early post-Cold War period, strikes many as more compelling after September 11.[9] Like liberals, he accords more importance to motives and values as sources of conflict than do realists. Unlike liberals, he does not see westernization as an irresistible tide that overwhelms world politics. Like realists, he sees conflict as natural rather than aberrant, and though not inevitable in the future, quite probable. Unlike realists, he places less emphasis on states as the sources of war in the future, and more on cleavages between major culture areas.

All three of these arguments are arresting, but most observers, even if they gravitate toward one, will have more conditional diagnoses and predictions. Fukuyama, Mearsheimer, and others who argue in the same veins reflect philosophical assumptions rooted in earlier and well-developed schools of thought. Huntington reflects a respect for the causal importance of identity and culture that anthropologists, or constructivists in political science, have long recognized—although most of them would be shocked to find themselves placed in the same boat with Huntington! Roots of all these approaches to argument about war and peace are traced in more detail in the subsequent selections.

—RKB

---

[7]For the full-length version of these arguments see Francis Fukuyama, *The End of History and the Last Man* (New York: Free Press, 1992). Responses to early attacks on the argument can be found in Fukuyama's "A Reply to My Critics," *The National Interest* No. 18 (winter 1989/90). See also Fukuyama, "Second Thoughts: The Last Man in a Bottle," *The National Interest* No. 56 (summer 1999).
[8]A more academic and detailed version of the argument can be found in John J. Mearsheimer, "Back to the Future: Instability in Europe After the Cold War," *International Security* 15, No. 4 (spring 1990).
[9]Huntington himself regards the article reprinted here as a rough preliminary version of his argument, and prefers readers to look to the more thorough and refined development of the argument in his book *The Clash of Civilizations and the Remaking of World Order* (New York: Simon & Schuster, 1996). The article is included in this volume simply because of constraints on the space that can be allocated to the argument.

THE END OF HISTORY?

Francis Fukuyama

In watching the flow of events over the past decade or so, it is hard to avoid the feeling that something very fundamental has happened in world history. The past year has seen a flood of articles commemorating the end of the Cold War, and the fact that "peace" seems to be breaking out in many regions of the world. Most of these analyses lack any larger conceptual framework for distinguishing between what is essential and what is contingent or accidental in world history, and are predictably superficial. If Mr. Gorbachev were ousted from the Kremlin or a new Ayatollah proclaimed the millennium from a desolate Middle Eastern capital, these same commentators would scramble to announce the rebirth of a new era of conflict.

And yet, all of these people sense dimly that there is some larger process at work, a process that gives coherence and order to the daily headlines. The twentieth century saw the developed world descend into a paroxysm of ideological violence, as liberalism contended first with the remnants of absolutism, then bolshevism and fascism, and finally an updated Marxism that threatened to lead to the ultimate apocalypse of nuclear war. But the century that began full of self-confidence in the ultimate triumph of Western liberal democracy seems at its close to be returning full circle to where it started: not to an "end of ideology" or a convergence between capitalism and socialism, as earlier predicted, but to an unabashed victory of economic and political liberalism.

The triumph of the West, of the Western *idea,* is evident first of all in the total exhaustion of viable systematic alternatives to Western liberalism. In the past decade, there have been unmistakable changes in the intellectual climate of the world's two largest communist countries, and the beginnings of significant reform movements in both. But this phenomenon extends beyond high politics and it can be seen also in the ineluctable spread of consumerist Western culture in such diverse contexts as the peasants' markets and color television sets now omnipresent throughout China, the cooperative restaurants and clothing stores opened in the past year in Moscow, the Beethoven piped into Japanese department stores, and the rock music enjoyed alike in Prague, Rangoon, and Tehran.

What we may be witnessing is not just the end of the Cold War, or the passing of a particular period of postwar history, but the end of history as such: that is, the end point of mankind's ideological evolution and the universalization of Western liberal democracy as the final form of human government. This is not to say that there will no longer be events to fill the pages of *Foreign Affairs's* yearly summaries of international relations, for the victory of liberalism has occurred primarily in the realm of ideas or con-

Francis Fukuyama, "The End of History?" *The National Interest* No. 16 (summer 1989). Copyright © 1989 by Francis Fukuyama.

sciousness and is as yet incomplete in the real or material world. But there are powerful reasons for believing that it is the ideal that will govern the material world *in the long run*. To understand how this is so, we must first consider some theoretical issues concerning the nature of historical change.

I

The notion of the end of history is not an original one. Its best known propagator was Karl Marx, who believed that the direction of historical development was a purposeful one determined by the interplay of material forces, and would come to an end only with the achievement of a communist utopia that would finally resolve all prior contradictions. But the concept of history as a dialectical process with a beginning, a middle, and an end was borrowed by Marx from his great German predecessor, Georg Wilhelm Friedrich Hegel.

For better or worse, much of Hegel's historicism has become part of our contemporary intellectual baggage. The notion that mankind has progressed through a series of primitive stages of consciousness on his path to the present, and that these stages corresponded to concrete forms of social organization, such as tribal, slave-owning, theocratic, and finally democratic-egalitarian societies, has become inseparable from the modern understanding of man. Hegel was the first philosopher to speak the language of modern social science, insofar as man for him was the product of his concrete historical and social environment and not, as earlier natural right theorists would have it, a collection of more or less fixed "natural" attributes. The mastery and transformation of man's natural environment through the application of science and technology was originally not a Marxist concept, but a Hegelian one. Unlike later historicists whose historical relativism degenerated into relativism *tout court,* however, Hegel believed that history culminated in an absolute moment—a moment in which a final, rational form of society and state became victorious.

It is Hegel's misfortune to be known now primarily as Marx's precursor, and it is our misfortune that few of us are familiar with Hegel's work from direct study, but only as it has been filtered through the distorting lens of Marxism. In France, however, there has been an effort to save Hegel from his Marxist interpreters and to resurrect him as the philosopher who most correctly speaks to our time. Among those modern French interpreters of Hegel, the greatest was certainly Alexandre Kojève, a brilliant Russian emigre who taught a highly influential series of seminars in Paris in the 1930s at the *Ecole Practique des Hautes Etudes.*[1] While largely unknown in the United States, Kojève had a major impact on the intellectual life of the continent. Among his students ranged such future luminaries as Jean-Paul Sartre on the Left and Raymond Aron on the Right; postwar existentialism borrowed many of its basic categories from Hegel via Kojève.

---

[1]Kojève's best-known work is his *Introduction à la lecture de Hegel* (Paris: Editions Gallimard, 1947), which is a transcript of the *Ecole Practique* lectures from the 1930s. This book is available in English entitled *Introduction to the Reading of Hegel* arranged by Raymond Queneau, edited by Allan Bloom, and translated by James Nichols (New York: Basic Books, 1969).

Kojève sought to resurrect the Hegel of the *Phenomenology of Mind,* the Hegel who proclaimed history to be at an end in 1806. For as early as this Hegel saw in Napoleon's defeat of the Prussian monarchy at the Battle of Jena the victory of the ideals of the French Revolution, and the imminent universalization of the state incorporating the principles of liberty and equality. Kojève, far from rejecting Hegel in light of the turbulent events of the next century and a half, insisted that the latter had been essentially correct. The Battle of Jena marked the end of history because it was at that point that the *vanguard* of humanity (a term quite familiar to Marxists) actualized the principles of the French Revolution. While there was considerable work to be done after 1806—abolishing slavery and the slave trade, extending the franchise to workers, women, blacks, and other racial minorities, etc.—the basic *principles* of the liberal democratic state could not be improved upon. The two world wars in this century and their attendant revolutions and upheavals simply had the effect of extending those principles spatially, such that the various provinces of human civilization were brought up to the level of its most advanced outposts, and of forcing those societies in Europe and North America at the vanguard of civilization to implement their liberalism more fully. . . .

II

For Hegel, the contradictions that drive history exist first of all in the realm of human consciousness, i.e. on the level of ideas—not the trivial election year proposals of American politicians, but ideas in the sense of large unifying world views that might best be understood under the rubric of ideology. Ideology in this sense is not restricted to the secular and explicit political doctrines we usually associate with the term, but can include religion, culture, and the complex of moral values underlying any society as well.

Hegel's view of the relationship between the ideal and the real or material worlds was an extremely complicated one, beginning with the fact that for him the distinction between the two was only apparent. He did not believe that the real world conformed or could be made to conform to ideological preconceptions of philosophy professors in any simple-minded way, or that the "material" world could not impinge on the ideal. Indeed, Hegel the professor was temporarily thrown out of work as a result of a very material event, the Battle of Jena. But while Hegel's writing and thinking could be stopped by a bullet from the material world, the hand on the trigger of the gun was motivated in turn by the ideas of liberty and equality that had driven the French Revolution.

For Hegel, all human behavior in the material world, and hence all human history, is rooted in a prior state of consciousness—an idea similar to the one expressed by John Maynard Keynes when he said that the views of men of affairs were usually derived from defunct economists and academic scribblers of earlier generations. This consciousness may not be explicit and self-aware, as are modern political doctrines, but may rather take the form of religion or simple cultural or moral habits. And yet this realm of consciousness *in the long run* necessarily becomes manifest in the material world, indeed creates the material world in its own image. Consciousness is cause and not effect, and can develop autonomously from the material world; hence the real subtext underlying the apparent jumble of current events is the history of ideology.

Hegel's idealism has fared poorly at the hands of later thinkers. Marx reversed the priority of the real and the ideal completely, relegating the entire realm of consciousness—religion, art, culture, philosophy itself—to a "superstructure" that was determined entirely by the prevailing material mode of production. Yet another unfortunate legacy of Marxism is our tendency to retreat into materialist or utilitarian explanations of political or historical phenomena, and our disinclination to believe in the autonomous power of ideas. A recent example of this is Paul Kennedy's hugely successful *The Rise and Fall of the Great Powers,* which ascribes the decline of great powers to simple economic overextension. Obviously, this is true on some level: an empire whose economy is barely above the level of subsistence cannot bankrupt its treasury indefinitely. But whether a highly productive modern industrial society chooses to spend 3 or 7 percent of its GNP on defense rather than consumption is entirely a matter of that society's political priorities, which are in turn determined in the realm of consciousness.

The materialist bias of modern thought is characteristic not only of people on the Left who may be sympathetic to Marxism, but of many passionate anti-Marxists as well. Indeed, there is on the Right what one might label the *Wall Street Journal* school of deterministic materialism that discounts the importance of ideology and culture and sees man as essentially a rational, profit-maximizing individual. It is precisely this kind of individual and his pursuit of material incentives that is posited as the basis for economic life as such in economic textbooks. One small example will illustrate the problematic character of such materialist views.

Max Weber begins his famous book, *The Protestant Ethic and the Spirit of Capitalism,* by noting the different economic performance of Protestant and Catholic communities throughout Europe and America, summed up in the proverb that Protestants eat well while Catholics sleep well. Weber notes that according to any economic theory that posited man as a rational profit-maximizer, raising the piece-work rate should increase labor productivity. But in fact, in many traditional peasant communities, raising the piece-work rate actually had the opposite effect of *lowering* labor productivity: at the higher rate, a peasant accustomed to earning two and one-half marks per day found he could earn the same amount by working less, and did so because he valued leisure more than income. The choices of leisure over income, or of the militaristic life of the Spartan hoplite over the wealth of the Athenian trader, or even the ascetic life of the early capitalist entrepreneur over that of a traditional leisured aristocrat, cannot possibly be explained by the impersonal working of material forces, but come preeminently out of the sphere of consciousness—what we have labeled here broadly as ideology. And indeed, a central theme of Weber's work was to prove that contrary to Marx, the material mode of production, far from being the "base," was itself a "superstructure" with roots in religion and culture, and that to understand the emergence of modern capitalism and the profit motive one had to study their antecedents in the realm of the spirit.

As we look around the contemporary world, the poverty of materialist theories of economic development is all too apparent. The *Wall Street Journal* school of deterministic materialism habitually points to the stunning economic success of Asia in the past few decades as evidence of the viability of free market economics, with the implication that all societies would see similar development were they simply to allow their populations to pursue their material self-interest freely. Surely free markets and stable political systems are a necessary precondition to capitalist economic growth. But just as surely the cultural heritage of those Far Eastern societies, the ethic of work and saving and family, a religious heritage that does not, like Islam, place restrictions on certain forms of economic behavior, and other deeply ingrained moral qualities, are equally important in explaining their economic performance.[2] And yet the intellectual weight of materialism is such that not a single respectable contemporary theory of economic development addresses consciousness and culture seriously as the matrix within which economic behavior is formed.

Failure to understand that the roots of economic behavior lie in the realm of consciousness and culture leads to the common mistake of attributing material causes to phenomena that are essentially ideal in nature. For example, it is commonplace in the West to interpret the reform movements first in China and most recently in the Soviet Union as the victory of the material over the ideal—that is, a recognition that ideological incentives could not replace material ones in stimulating a highly productive modern economy, and that if one wanted to prosper one had to appeal to baser forms of self-interest. But the deep defects of socialist economies were evident thirty or forty years ago to anyone who chose to look. Why was it that these countries moved away from central planning only in the 1980s? The answer must be found in the consciousness of the elites and leaders ruling them, who decided to opt for the "Protestant" life of wealth and risk over the "Catholic" path of poverty and security. That change was in no way made inevitable by the material conditions in which either country found itself on the eve of the reform, but instead came about as the result of the victory of one idea over another. . . .

III

. . . In the past century, there have been two major challenges to liberalism, those of fascism and of communism. The former[3] saw the political weakness, materialism, anomie, and lack of community of the West as fundamental contradictions in liberal societies that could only be resolved by a strong state that forged a new "people" on the basis of national exclusiveness. Fascism was destroyed as a living ideology by World War II. This was a defeat, of course, on a very material level, but it amounted to a defeat

---

[2]One need look no further than the recent performance of Vietnamese immigrants in the U.S. school system when compared to their black or Hispanic classmates to realize that culture and consciousness are absolutely crucial to explain not only economic behavior but virtually every other important aspect of life as well.

[3]I am not using the term "fascism" here in its most precise sense, fully aware of the frequent misuse of this term to denounce anyone to the right of the user. "Fascism" here denotes any organized ultra-nationalist movement with universalistic pretensions—not universalistic with regard to its nationalism, of course, since the latter is exclusive by definition, but with regard to the movement's belief in its right to rule other people. Hence Imperial Japan would qualify as fascist while former strongman Stoessner's Paraguay or Pinochet's Chile would not. Obviously fascist ideologies cannot be universalistic in the sense of Marxism or liberalism, but the structure of the doctrine can be transferred from country to country.

of the idea as well. What destroyed fascism as an idea was not universal moral revulsion against it, since plenty of people were willing to endorse the idea as long as it seemed the wave of the future, but its lack of success. After the war, it seemed to most people that German fascism as well as its other European and Asian variants were bound to self-destruct. There was no material reason why new fascist movements could not have sprung up again after the war in other locales, but for the fact that expansionist ultrana-tionalism, with its promise of unending conflict leading to disastrous military defeat, had completely lost its appeal. The ruins of the Reich chancellory as well as the atomic bombs dropped on Hiroshima and Nagasaki killed this ideology on the level of con-sciousness as well as materially, and all of the proto-fascist movements spawned by the German and Japanese examples like the Peronist movement in Argentina or Subhas Chandra Bose's Indian National Army withered after the war.

The ideological challenge mounted by the other great alternative to liberalism, communism, was far more serious. Marx, speaking Hegel's language, asserted that lib-eral society contained a fundamental contradiction that could not be resolved within its context, that between capital and labor, and this contradiction has constituted the chief accusation against liberalism ever since. But surely, the class issue has actually been successfully resolved in the West. . . .

But the power of the liberal idea would seem much less impressive if it had not in-fected the largest and oldest culture in Asia, China. The simple existence of communist China created an alternative pole of ideological attraction, and as such constituted a threat to liberalism. But the past fifteen years have seen an almost total discrediting of Marxism-Leninism as an economic system. Beginning with the famous third plenum of the Tenth Central Committee in 1978, the Chinese Communist party set about decollec-tivizing agriculture for the 800 million Chinese who still lived in the countryside. The role of the state in agriculture was reduced to that of a tax collector, while production of consumer goods was sharply increased in order to give peasants a taste of the universal homogenous state and thereby an incentive to work. The reform doubled Chinese grain output in only five years, and in the process created for Deng Xiao-ping a solid political base from which he was able to extend the reform to other parts of the economy. Economic statistics do not begin to describe the dynamism, initiative, and openness, evident in China since the reform began.

China could not now be described in any way as a liberal democracy. At present, no more than 20 percent of its economy has been marketized, and most importantly it con-tinues to be ruled by a self-appointed Communist party which has given no hint of wanting to devolve power. Deng has made none of Gorbachev's promises regarding de-mocratization of the political system and there is no Chinese equivalent of *glasnost*. The Chinese leadership has in fact been much more circumspect in criticizing Mao and Maoism than Gorbachev with respect to Brezhnev and Stalin, and the regime continues to pay lip service to Marxism-Leninism as its ideological underpinning. But anyone fa-miliar with the outlook and behavior of the new technocratic elite now governing China knows that Marxism and ideological principle have become virtually irrelevant as guides to policy, and that bourgeois consumerism has a real meaning in that country for the first time since the revolution. The various slowdowns in the pace of reform, the campaigns against "spiritual pollution" and crackdowns on political dissent are more properly seen as tactical adjustments made in the process of managing what is an extraordinarily difficult political transition. By ducking the question of political reform while putting the economy on a new footing, Deng has managed to avoid the breakdown of authority that has accompanied Gorbachev's *perestroika.* Yet the pull of the liberal idea continues to be very strong as economic power devolves and the economy becomes more open to the outside world. There are currently over 20,000 Chinese students studying in the U.S. and other Western countries, almost all of them the children of the Chinese elite. It is hard to believe that when they return home to run the country they will be content for China to be the only country in Asia unaffected by the larger democratizing trend. The student demonstrations in Beijing that broke out first in December 1986 and recurred recently on the occasion of Hu Yao-bang's death were only the beginning of what will inevitably be mounting pressure for change in the political system as well.

What is important about China from the standpoint of world history is not the present state of the reform or even its future prospects. The central issue is the fact that the People's Republic of China can no longer act as a beacon for illiberal forces around the world, whether they be guerrillas in some Asian jungle or middle class students in Paris. Maoism, rather than being the pattern for Asia's future, became an anachronism. . . .

If we admit for the moment that the fascist and communist challenges to liberalism are dead, are there any other ideological competitors left? Or put another way, are there contradictions in liberal society beyond that of class that are not resolvable? Two possibilities suggest themselves, those of religion and nationalism.

The rise of religious fundamentalism in recent years within the Christian, Jewish, and Muslim traditions has been widely noted. One is inclined to say that the revival of religion in some way attests to a broad unhappiness with the impersonality and spiritual vacuity of liberal consumerist societies. Yet while the emptiness at the core of liberalism is most certainly a defect in the ideology—indeed, a flaw that one does not need the perspective of religion to recognize—it is not at all clear that it is remediable through politics. Modern liberalism itself was historically a consequence of the weakness of religiously-based societies which, failing to agree on the nature of the good life, could not provide even the minimal preconditions of peace and stability. In the contemporary world only Islam has offered a theocratic state as a political alternative to both liberalism and communism. But the doctrine has little appeal for non-Muslims, and it is hard to believe that the movement will take on any universal significance. Other less organized religious impulses have been successfully satisfied within the sphere of personal life that is permitted in liberal societies.

The other major "contradiction" potentially unresolvable by liberalism is the one posed by nationalism and other forms of racial and ethnic consciousness. It is certainly true that a very large degree of conflict since the Battle of Jena has had its roots in nationalism. Two cataclysmic world wars in this century have been spawned by the nationalism of the developed world in various guises, and if those passions have been muted to a certain extent in post-war Europe, they are still extremely powerful in the Third World. Nationalism has been a threat to liberalism historically in Germany, and continues to be one in isolated parts of "post-historical" Europe like Northern Ireland.

But it is not clear that nationalism represents an irreconcilable contradiction in the heart of liberalism. In the first place, nationalism is not one single phenomenon but several, ranging from mild cultural nostalgia to the highly organized and elaborately articulated doctrine of National Socialism. Only systematic nationalisms of the latter sort can qualify as a formal ideology on the level of liberalism or communism. The vast majority of the world's nationalist movements do not have a political program beyond the negative desire of independence *from* some other group or people, and do not offer anything like a comprehensive agenda for socio-economic organization. As such, they are compatible with doctrines and ideologies that do offer such agendas. While they may constitute a source of conflict for liberal societies, this conflict does not arise from liberalism itself so much as from the fact that the liberalism in question is incomplete. Certainly a great deal of the world's ethnic and nationalist tension can be explained in terms of peoples who are forced to live in unrepresentative political systems that they have not chosen.

While it is impossible to rule out the sudden appearance of new ideologies or previously unrecognized contradictions in liberal societies, then, the present world seems to confirm that the fundamental principles of socio-political organization have not advanced terribly far since 1806. Many of the wars and revolutions fought since that time have been undertaken in the name of ideologies which claimed to be more advanced than liberalism, but whose pretensions were ultimately unmasked by history. In the meantime, they have helped to spread the universal homogenous state to the point where it could have a significant effect on the overall character of international relations. ✓

IV

What are the implications of the end of history for international relations? Clearly, the vast bulk of the Third World remains very much mired in history, and will be a terrain of conflict for many years to come. But let us focus for the time being on the larger and more developed states of the world who after all account for the greater part of world politics. Russia and China are not likely to join the developed nations of the West as liberal societies any time in the foreseeable future, but suppose for a moment that Marxism-Leninism ceases to be a factor driving the foreign policies of these states—a prospect which, if not yet here, the last few years have made a real possibility. How will the overall characteristics of a de-ideologized world differ from those of the one with which we are familiar at such a hypothetical juncture?

The most common answer is—not very much. For there is a very widespread belief among many observers of international relations that underneath the skin of ideology is a hard core of great power national interest that guarantees a fairly high level of competition and conflict between nations. Indeed, according to one academically popular school of international relations theory, conflict inheres in the international system as such, and to understand the prospects for conflict one must look at the shape of the system—for example, whether it is bipolar or multipolar—rather than at the specific character of the nations and regimes that constitute it. This school in effect applies a

Hobbesian view of politics to international relations, and assumes that aggression and insecurity are universal characteristics of human societies rather than the product of specific historical circumstances.

Believers in this line of thought take the relations that existed between the participants in the classical nineteenth century European balance of power as a model for what a deideologized contemporary world would look like. Charles Krauthammer, for example, recently explained that if as a result of Gorbachev's reforms the USSR is shorn of Marxist-Leninist ideology, its behavior will revert to that of nineteenth century imperial Russia.[4] While he finds this more reassuring than the threat posed by a communist Russia, he implies that there will still be a substantial degree of competition and conflict in the international system, just as there was say between Russia and Britain or Wilhelmine Germany in the last century. This is, of course, a convenient point of view for people who want to admit that something major is changing in the Soviet Union, but do not want to accept responsibility for recommending the radical policy redirection implicit in such a view. But is it true?

In fact, the notion that ideology is a superstructure imposed on a substratum of permanent great power interest is a highly questionable proposition. For the way in which any state defines its national interest is not universal but rests on some kind of prior ideological basis, just as we saw that economic behavior is determined by a prior state of consciousness. In this century, states have adopted highly articulated doctrines with explicit foreign policy agendas legitimizing expansionism, like Marxism-Leninism or National Socialism.

The expansionist and competitive behavior of nineteenth-century European states rested on no less ideal a basis; it just so happened that the ideology driving it was less explicit than the doctrines of the twentieth century. For one thing, most "liberal" European societies were illiberal insofar as they believed in the legitimacy of imperialism, that is, the right of one nation to rule over other nations without regard for the wishes of the ruled. The justifications for imperialism varied from nation to nation, from a crude belief in the legitimacy of force, particularly when applied to non-Europeans, to the White Man's Burden and Europe's Christianizing mission, to the desire to give people of color access to the culture of Rabelais and Molière. But whatever the particular ideological basis, every "developed" country believed in the acceptability of higher civilizations ruling lower ones—including, incidentally, the United States with regard to the Philippines. This led to a drive for pure territorial aggrandizement in the latter half of the century and played no small role in causing the Great War.

The radical and deformed outgrowth of nineteenth-century imperialism was German fascism, an ideology which justified Germany's right not only to rule over non-European peoples, but over *all* non-German ones. But in retrospect it seems that Hitler represented a diseased bypath in the general course of European development, and since his fiery defeat, the legitimacy of any kind of territorial aggrandizement has been

---

[4]See his article, "Beyond the Cold War," *New Republic,* December 19, 1988.

thoroughly discredited.[5] Since the Second World War, European nationalism has been defanged and shorn of any real relevance to foreign policy, with the consequence that the nineteenth-century model of great power behavior has become a serious anachronism. The most extreme form of nationalism that any Western European state has mustered since 1945 has been Gaullism, whose self-assertion has been confined largely to the realm of nuisance politics and culture. International life for the part of the world that has reached the end of history is far more preoccupied with economics than with politics or strategy.

The developed states of the West do maintain defense establishments and in the post-war period have competed vigorously for influence to meet a worldwide communist threat. This behavior has been driven, however, by an external threat from states that possess overtly expansionist ideologies, and would not exist in their absence. To take the "neo-realist" theory seriously, one would have to believe that "natural" competitive behavior would reassert itself among the OECD states were Russia and China to disappear from the face of the earth. That is, West Germany and France would arm themselves against each other as they did in the 1930s, Australia and New Zealand would send military advisers to block each others' advances in Africa, and the U.S.-Canadian border would become fortified. Such a prospect is, of course, ludicrous: minus Marxist-Leninist ideology, we are far more likely to see the "Common Marketization" of world politics than the disintegration of the EEC into nineteenth-century competitiveness. Indeed, as our experience in dealing with Europe on matters such as terrorism or Libya prove, they are much further gone than we down the road that denies the legitimacy of the use of force in international politics, even in self-defense.

The automatic assumption that Russia shorn of its expansionist communist ideology should pick up where the czars left off just prior to the Bolshevik Revolution is therefore a curious one. It assumes that the evolution of human consciousness has stood still in the meantime, and that the Soviets, while picking up currently fashionable ideas in the realm of economics, will return to foreign policy views a century out of date in the rest of Europe. This is certainly not what happened to China after it began its reform process. Chinese competitiveness and expansionism on the world scene have virtually disappeared: Beijing no longer sponsors Maoist insurgencies or tries to cultivate influence in distant African countries as it did in the 1960s. This is not to say that there are not troublesome aspects to contemporary Chinese foreign policy, such as the reckless sale of ballistic missile technology in the Middle East; and the PRC continues to manifest traditional great power behavior in its sponsorship of the Khmer Rouge against Vietnam. But the former is explained by commercial motives and the latter is a vestige of earlier ideologically-based rivalries. The new China far more resembles Gaullist France than pre-World War I Germany.

---

[5]It took European colonial powers like France several years after the war to admit the illegitimacy of their empires, but decolonialization was an inevitable consequence of the Allied victory which had been based on the promise of a restoration of democratic freedoms.

The real question for the future, however, is the degree to which Soviet elites have assimilated the consciousness of the universal homogenous state that is post-Hitler Europe. From their writings and from my own personal contacts with them, there is no question in my mind that the liberal Soviet intelligentsia rallying around Gorbachev has arrived at the end-of-history view in a remarkably short time, due in no small measure to the contacts they have had since the Brezhnev era with the larger European civilization around them. "New political thinking," the general rubric for their views, describes a world dominated by economic concerns, in which there are no ideological grounds for major conflict beween nations, and in which, consequently, the use of military force becomes less legitimate. As Foreign Minister Shevardnadze put it in mid-1988:

> The struggle between two opposing systems is no longer a determining tendency of the present-day era. At the modern stage, the ability to build up material wealth at an accelerated rate on the basis of front-ranking science and high-level techniques and technology, and to distribute it fairly, and through joint efforts to restore and protect the resources necessary for mankind's survival acquires decisive importance.

The post-historical consciousness represented by "new thinking" is only one possible future for the Soviet Union, however. There has always been a very strong current of great Russian chauvinism in the Soviet Union, which has found freer expression since the advent of *glasnost.* It may be possible to return to traditional Marxism-Leninism for a while as a simple rallying point for those who want to restore the authority that Gorbachev has dissipated. But as in Poland, Marxism-Leninism is dead as a mobilizing ideology: under its banner people cannot be made to work harder, and its adherents have lost confidence in themselves. Unlike the propagators of traditional Marxism-Leninism, however, ultra-nationalists in the USSR believe in their Slavophile cause passionately, and one gets the sense that the fascist alternative is not one that has played itself out entirely there.

The Soviet Union, then, is at a fork in the road: it can start down the path that was staked out by Western Europe forty-five years ago, a path that most of Asia has followed, or it can realize its own uniqueness and remain stuck in history. The choice it makes will be highly important for us, given the Soviet Union's size and military strength, for that power will continue to preoccupy us and slow our realization that we have already emerged on the other side of history.

V

The passing of Marxism-Leninism first from China and then from the Soviet Union will mean its death as a living ideology of world historical significance. For while there may be some isolated true believers left in places like Managua, Pyongyang, or Cambridge, Massachusetts, the fact that there is not a single large state in which it is a going concern undermines completely its pretensions to being in the vanguard of human history. And the death of this ideology means the growing "Common Marketization" of international relations, and the diminution of the likelihood of large-scale conflict between states.

This does not by any means imply the end of international conflict *per se*. For the world at that point would be divided between a part that was historical and a part that was post-historical. Conflict between states still in history, and between those states and those at the end of history, would still be possible. There would still be a high and perhaps rising level of ethnic and nationalist violence, since those are impulses incompletely played out, even in parts of the post-historical world. Palestinians and Kurds, Sikhs and Tamils, Irish Catholics and Walloons, Armenians and Azeris, will continue to have their unresolved grievances. This implies that terrorism and wars of national liberation will continue to be an important item on the international agenda. But large-scale conflict must involve large states still caught in the grip of history, and they are what appear to be passing from the scene.

The end of history will be a very sad time. The struggle for recognition, the willingness to risk one's life for a purely abstract goal, the worldwide ideological struggle that called forth daring, courage, imagination, and idealism, will be replaced by economic calculation, the endless solving of technical problems, environmental concerns, and the satisfaction of sophisticated consumer demands. In the post-historical period there will be neither art nor philosophy, just the perpetual caretaking of the museum of human history. I can feel in myself, and see in others around me, a powerful nostalgia for the time when history existed. Such nostalgia, in fact, will continue to fuel competition and conflict even in the post-historical world for some time to come. Even though I recognize its inevitability, I have the most ambivalent feelings for the civilization that has been created in Europe since 1945, with its North Atlantic and Asian offshoots. Perhaps this very prospect of centuries of boredom at the end of history will serve to get history started once again.

WHY WE WILL SOON MISS THE COLD WAR

John J. Mearsheimer

Peace: It's wonderful. I like it as much as the next man, and have no wish to be willfully gloomy at a moment when optimism about the future shape of the world abounds. Nevertheless, my thesis in this essay is that we are likely soon to regret the passing of the Cold War.

To be sure, no one will miss such by-products of the Cold War as the Korean and Vietnam conflicts. No one will want to replay the U–2 affair, the Cuban missile crisis, or the building of the Berlin Wall. And no one will want to revisit the domestic Cold War, with its purges and loyalty oaths, its xenophobia and stifling of dissent. We will not wake up one day to discover fresh wisdom in the collected fulminations of John Foster Dulles.

We may, however, wake up one day lamenting the loss of the order that the Cold War gave to the anarchy of international relations. For untamed anarchy is what Europe knew in the forty-five years of this century before the Cold War, and untamed anarchy—Hobbes's war of all against all—is a prime cause of armed conflict. Those who think that armed conflicts among the European states are now out of the question, that the two world wars burned all the war out of Europe, are projecting unwarranted optimism onto the future. The theories of peace that implicitly undergird this optimism are notably shallow constructs. They stand up to neither logical nor historical analysis. You would not want to bet the farm on their prophetic accuracy.

The world is about to conduct a vast test of the theories of war and peace put forward by social scientists, who never dreamed that their ideas would be tested by the world-historic events announced almost daily in newspaper headlines. This social scientist is willing to put his theoretical cards on the table as he ventures predictions about the future of Europe. In the process, I hope to put alternative theories of war and peace under as much intellectual pressure as I can muster. My argument is that the prospect of major crises, even wars, in Europe is likely to increase dramatically now that the Cold War is receding into history. The next forty-five years in Europe are not likely to be so violent as the forty-five years before the Cold War, but they are likely to be substantially more violent than the past forty-five years, the era that we may someday look back upon not as the Cold War but as the Long Peace, in John Lewis Gaddis's phrase.

This pessimistic conclusion rests on the general argument that the distribution and character of military power among states are the root causes of war and peace.

John J. Mearsheimer, "Why We Will Soon Miss the Cold War." © 1990 by John Mearsheimer, as originally published in *The Atlantic,* November 1990. Reprinted by permission.

Specifically, the peace in Europe since 1945—precarious at first, but increasingly robust over time—has flowed from three factors: the bipolar distribution of military power on the Continent; the rough military equality between the polar powers, the United States and the Soviet Union; and the ritualistically deplored fact that each of these superpowers is armed with a large nuclear arsenal.

We don't yet know the entire shape of the new Europe. But we do know some things. We know, for example, that the new Europe will involve a return to the multipolar distribution of power that characterized the European state system from its founding, with the Peace of Westphalia, in 1648, until 1945. We know that this multipolar European state system was plagued by war from first to last. We know that from 1900 to 1945 some 50 million Europeans were killed in wars that were caused in great part by the instability of this state system. We also know that since 1945 only some 15,000 Europeans have been killed in wars; roughly 10,000 Hungarians and Russians, in what we might call the Russo-Hungarian War of October and November, 1956, and somewhere between 1,500 and 5,000 Greeks and Turks, in the July and August, 1974, war on Cyprus.

The point is clear: Europe is reverting to a state system that created powerful incentives for aggression in the past. If you believe (as the Realist school of international-relations theory, to which I belong, believes) that the prospects of international peace are not markedly influenced by the domestic political character of states—that it is the character of the state system, not the character of the individual units composing it, that drives states toward war—then it is difficult to share in the widespread elation of the moment about the future of Europe. Last year was repeatedly compared to 1789, the year the French Revolution began, as the Year of Freedom, and so it was. Forgotten in the general exaltation was that the hope-filled events of 1789 signaled the start of an era of war and conquest.

A "HARD" THEORY OF PEACE

What caused the era of violence in Europe before 1945, and why has the postwar era, the period of the Cold War, been so much more peaceful? The two world wars before 1945 had myriad particular and unrepeatable causes, but to the student of international relations seeking to establish generalizations about the behavior of states in the past which might illuminate their behavior in the future, two fundamental causes stand out. These are the multi-polar distribution of power in Europe, and the imbalances of strength that often developed among the great powers as they jostled for supremacy or advantage.

There is something elementary about the geometry of power in international relations, and so its importance is easy to overlook. "Bipolarity" and "multipolarity" are ungainly but necessary coinages. The Cold War, with two superpowers serving to anchor rival alliances of clearly inferior powers, is our model of bipolarity. Europe in 1914, with France, Germany, Great Britain, Austria-Hungary, and Russia positioned as great powers, is our model of multipolarity.

If the example of 1914 is convincing enough evidence that multipolar systems are the more dangerous geometry of power, then perhaps I should rest my case. Alas for theoretical elegance, there are no empirical studies providing conclusive support for this proposition. From its beginnings until 1945 the European state system was multipolar, so this history is barren of comparisons that would reveal the differing effects of the two systems. Earlier history, to be sure, does furnish scattered examples of bipolar systems, including some—Athens and Sparta, Rome and Carthage—that were warlike. But this history is inconclusive, because it is incomplete. Lacking a comprehensive survey of history, we can't do much more than offer examples—now on this, now on that side of the debate. As a result, the case made here rests chiefly on deduction.

Deductively, a bipolar system is more peaceful for the simple reason that under it only two major powers are in contention. Moreover, those great powers generally demand allegiance from minor powers in the system, which is likely to produce rigid alliance structures. The smaller states are then secure from each other as well as from attack by the rival great power. Consequently (to make a Dick-and-Jane point with a wellworn social-science term), a bipolar system has only one dyad across which war might break out. A multipolar system is much more fluid and has many such dyads. Therefore, other things being equal, war is statistically more likely in a multipolar system than it is in a bipolar one. Admittedly, wars in a multipolar world that involve only minor powers or only one major power are not likely to be as devastating as a conflict between two major powers. But small wars always have the potential to widen into big wars.

Also, deterrence is difficult to maintain in a multipolar state system, because power imbalances are common-place, and when power asymmetries develop, the strong become hard to deter. Two great powers can join together to attack a third state, as Germany and the Soviet Union did in 1939, when they ganged up on Poland. Furthermore, a major power might simply bully a weaker power in a one-on-one encounter, using its superior strength to coerce or defeat the minor state. Germany's actions against Czechoslovakia in the late 1930s provide a good example of this sort of behavior. Ganging up and bullying are largely unknown in a bipolar system, since with only two great powers dominating center stage, it is impossible to produce the power asymmetries that result in ganging up and bullying.

There is a second reason that deterrence is more problematic under multipolarity. The resolve of opposing states and also the size and strength of opposing coalitions are hard to calculate in this geometry of power, because the shape of the international order tends to remain in flux, owing to the tendency of coalitions to gain and lose partners. This can lead aggressors to conclude falsely that they can coerce others by bluffing war, or even achieve outright victory on the battlefield. For example, Germany was not certain before 1914 that Britain would oppose it if it reached for Continental hegemony, and Germany completely failed to foresee that the United States would eventually move to contain it. In 1939 Germany hoped that France and Britain would stand aside as it conquered Poland, and again failed to foresee the eventual American entry into the war. As a result, Germany exaggerated its prospects for success, which undermined deterrence by encouraging German adventurism.

The prospects for peace, however are not simply a function of the number of great powers in the system. They are also affected by the relative military strength of those major states. Bipolar and multipolar systems both are likely to be more peaceful when power is distributed equally in them. Power inequalities invite war, because they increase an aggressor's prospects for victory on the battlefield. Most of the general wars that have tormented Europe over the past five centuries have involved one particularly powerful state against the other major powers in the system. This pattern characterized the wars that grew from the attempts at hegemony by Charles V, Philip II, Louis XIV, Revolutionary and Napoleonic France, Wilhelmine Germany, and Nazi Germany. Hence the size of the gap in military power between the two leading states in the system is a key determinant of stability. Small gaps foster peace; larger gaps promote war.

Nuclear weapons seem to be in almost everybody's bad book, but the fact is that they are a powerful force for peace. Deterrence is most likely to hold when the costs and risks of going to war are unambiguously stark. The more horrible the prospect of war, the less likely war is. Deterrence is also more robust when conquest is more difficult. Potential aggressor states are given pause by the patent futility of attempts at expansion.

Nuclear weapons favor peace on both counts. They are weapons of mass destruction, and would produce horrendous devastation if used in any numbers. Moreover, they are more useful for self-defense than for aggression. If both sides' nuclear arsenals are secure from attack, creating an arrangement of mutual assured destruction, neither side can employ these weapons to gain a meaningful military advantage. International conflicts then become tests of pure will. Who would dare to use these weapons of unimaginable destructive power? Defenders have the advantage here, because defenders usually value their freedom more than aggressors value new conquests.

Nuclear weapons further bolster peace by moving power relations among states toward equality. States that possess nuclear deterrents can stand up to one another, even if their nuclear arsenals vary greatly in size, as long as both sides have an assured destruction capability. In addition, mutual assured destruction helps alleviate the vexed problem of miscalculation by leaving little doubt about the relative power of states.

No discussion of the causes of peace in the twentieth century would be complete without a word on nationalism. With "nationalism" as a synonym for "love of country" I have no quarrel. But hypernationalism, the belief that other nations or nation-states are both inferior and threatening, is perhaps the single greatest domestic threat to peace, although it is still not a leading force in world politics. Hypernationalism arose in the past among European states because most of them were nation-states—states composed mainly of people from a single ethnic group—that existed in an anarchic world, under constant threat from other states. In such a system people who love their own nation can easily come to be contemptuous of the nationalities inhabiting opposing states. The problem is worsened when domestic elites demonize a rival nation to drum up support for national-security policy.

Hypernationalism finds its most fertile soil under military systems relying on mass armies. These require sacrifices to sustain, and the state is tempted to appeal to nationalist sentiments to mobilize its citizens to make them. The quickening of hypernationalism is least likely when states can rely on small professional armies, or on complex high-technology military organizations that operate without vast manpower. For this reason, nuclear weapons work to dampen nationalism, because they shift the basis of military power away from mass armies and toward smaller, high-technology organizations.

Hypernationalism declined sharply in Europe after 1945, not only because of the nuclear revolution but also because the postwar occupation forces kept it down.

Moreover, the European states, no longer providing their own security, lacked an incentive to whip up nationalism to bolster public support for national defense. But the decisive change came in the shift of the prime locus of European politics to the United States and the Soviet Union—two states made up of peoples of many different ethnic origins which had not exhibited nationalism of the virulent type found in Europe. This welcome absence of hypernationalism has been further helped by the greater stability of the postwar order. With less expectation of war, neither superpower felt compelled to mobilize its citizens for war.

Bipolarity, an equal balance of military power, and nuclear weapons—these, then, are the key elements of my explanation for the Long Peace.

Many thoughtful people have found the bipolar system in Europe odious and have sought to end it by dismantling the Soviet empire in Eastern Europe and diminishing Soviet military power. Many have also lamented the military equality obtaining between the superpowers; some have decried the indecisive stalemate it produced, recommending instead a search for military superiority; others have lamented the investment of hundreds of billions of dollars to deter a war that never happened, proving not that the investment, though expensive, paid off, but rather that it was wasted. As for nuclear weapons, well, they are a certifiable Bad Thing. The odium attached to these props of the postwar order has kept many in the West from recognizing a hard truth: they have kept the peace.

But so much for the past. What will keep the peace in the future? Specifically, what new order is likely to emerge if NATO and the Warsaw Pact dissolve, which they will do if the Cold War is really over, and the Soviets withdraw from Eastern Europe and the Americans quit Western Europe, taking their nuclear weapons with them—and should we welcome or fear it?

One dimension of the new European order is certain: it will be multipolar. Germany, France, Britain, and perhaps Italy will assume major-power status. The Soviet Union will decline from superpower status, not only because its military is sure to shrink in size but also because moving forces out of Eastern Europe will make it more difficult for the Soviets to project power onto the Continent. They will, of course, remain a major European power. The resulting four- or five-power system will suffer the problems endemic to multipolar systems—and will therefore be prone to instability. The other two dimensions—the distribution of power among the major states and the distribution of nuclear weapons—are less certain. Indeed, who gets nuclear weapons is likely to be the most problematic question facing the new Europe. Three scenarios of the nuclear future in Europe are possible.

THE "EUROPE WITHOUT NUCLEAR WEAPONS" SCENARIO

Many Europeans (and some Americans) seek to eliminate nuclear weapons from Europe altogether. Fashioning this nuclear-free Europe would require that Britain, France, and the Soviet Union rid themselves of these talismans of their sovereignty—an improbable eventuality, to say the least. Those who wish for it nevertheless believe that it would be the most peaceful arrangement possible. In fact a nuclear-free Europe has the distinction of being the most dangerous among the envisionable post-Cold War orders. The pacifying effects of nuclear weapons—the caution they generate, the security they provide, the rough equality they impose, and the clarity of the relative power they create—would be lost. Peace would then depend on the other dimensions of the new order—the number of poles and the distribution of power among them. The geometry of power in Europe would look much as it did between the world wars—a design for tension, crisis, and possibly even war.

The Soviet Union and a unified Germany would likely be the most powerful states in a nuclear-free Europe. A band of small independent states in Eastern Europe would lie between them. These minor Eastern European powers would be likely to fear the Soviets as much as the Germans, and thus would probably not be disposed to cooperate with the Soviets to deter possible German aggression. In fact, this very problem arose in the 1930s, and the past forty-five years of Soviet occupation have surely done little to mitigate Eastern European fears of a Soviet military presence. Thus scenarios in which Germany uses force against Poland, Czechoslovakia, or even Austria enter the realm of the possible in a nuclear-free Europe.

Then, too, the Soviet withdrawal from Eastern Europe hardly guarantees a permanent exit. Indeed, the Russian presence in Eastern Europe has surged and ebbed repeatedly over the past few centuries. In a grave warning, a member of President Mikhail Gorbachev's negotiating team at the recent Washington summit said, "You have the same explosive mixture you had in Germany in the 1930s. The humiliation of a great power. Economic troubles. The rise of nationalism. You should not underestimate the danger."

Conflicts between Eastern European states might also threaten the stability of the new European order. Serious tensions already exist between Hungary and Romania over Romania's treatment of the Hungarian minority in Transylvania, a formerly Hungarian region that still contains roughly two million ethnic Hungarians. Absent the Soviet occupation of Eastern Europe, Romania and Hungary might have gone to war over this issue by now, and it might bring them to war in the future. This is not the only potential danger spot in Eastern Europe as the Soviet empire crumbles. The Polish-German border could be a source of trouble. Poland and Czechoslovakia have a border dispute. If the Soviets allow some of their republics to achieve independence, the Poles and the Romanians may lay claim to territory now in Soviet hands which once belonged to them. Looking farther south, civil war in Yugoslavia is a distinct possibility. Yugoslavia and Albania might come to blows over Kosovo, a region of Yugoslavia harboring a nationalistic Albanian majority. Bulgaria has its own quarrel with Yugoslavia over Macedonia, while Turkey resents Bulgaria's treatment of its Turkish minority. The danger that these bitter ethnic and border disputes will erupt into war in a supposedly Edenic nuclear-free Europe is enough to make one nostalgic for the Cold War.

Warfare in Eastern Europe would cause great suffering to Eastern Europeans. It also might widen to include the major powers, especially if disorder created fluid politics that offered opportunities for expanded influence, or threatened defeat for states friendly to one or another of the major powers. During the Cold War both superpowers were drawn into Third World conflicts across the globe, often in distant areas of little strategic importance. Eastern Europe is directly adjacent to both the Soviet Union and Germany, and it has considerable economic and strategic importance. Thus trouble in Eastern Europe would offer even greater temptations to these powers than past conflicts in the Third World offered to the superpowers. Furthermore, Eastern European states would have a strong incentive to drag the major powers into their local conflicts, because the results of such conflicts would be largely determined by the relative success of each party in finding external allies.

It is difficult to predict the precise balance of conventional military power that will emerge in post-Cold War Europe. The Soviet Union might recover its strength soon after withdrawing from Eastern Europe. In that case Soviet power would outmatch German power. But centrifugal national forces might pull the Soviet Union apart, leaving no remnant state that is the equal of a unified Germany. Finally, and probably most likely, Germany and the Soviet Union might emerge as powers of roughly equal strength. The first two geometries of power, with their marked military inequality between the two leading countries, would be especially worrisome, although there would be cause for concern even if Soviet and German power were balanced.

A non-nuclear Europe, to round out this catalogue of dangers, would likely be especially disturbed by hypernationalism, since security in such an order would rest on mass armies, which, as we have seen, often cannot be maintained without a mobilized public. The problem would probably be most acute in Eastern Europe, with its uncertain borders and irredentist minority groups. But there is also potential for trouble in Germany. The Germans have generally done an admirable job of combating hypernationalism over the past forty-five years, and of confronting the dark side of their past. Nevertheless, a portent like the recent call of some prominent Germans for a return to greater nationalism in historical education is disquieting.

For all these reasons, it is perhaps just as well that a nuclear-free Europe, much as it may be longed for by so many Europeans, does not appear to be in the cards.

THE "CURRENT OWNERSHIP" SCENARIO

Under this scenario Britain, France, and the Soviet Union retain their nuclear weapons, but no new nuclear powers emerge in Europe. This vision of a nuclear-free zone in Central Europe, with nuclear weapons remaining on the flanks of the Continent, is also popular in Europe, but it, too, has doubtful prospects.

Germany will prevent it over the long run. The Germans are not likely to be willing to rely on the Poles or the Czechs to provide their forward defense against a possible direct Soviet conventional attack on their homeland. Nor are the Germans likely to trust the Soviet Union to refrain for all time from nuclear blackmail against a non-nuclear Germany. Hence they will eventually look to nuclear weapons as the surest means of security, just as NATO has done.

The small states of Eastern Europe will also have strong incentives to acquire nuclear weapons. Without them they would be open to nuclear blackmail by the Soviet

Union, or by Germany if proliferation stopped there. Even if those major powers did not have nuclear arsenals, no Eastern European state could match German or Soviet conventional strength.

Clearly, then, a scenario in which current ownership continues, without proliferation, seems very unlikely.

THE "NUCLEAR PROLIFERATION" SCENARIO

The most probable scenario in the wake of the Cold War is further nuclear proliferation in Europe. This outcome is laden with dangers, but it also might just provide the best hope for maintaining stability on the Continent. Everything depends on how proliferation is managed. Mismanaged proliferation could produce disaster; well-managed proliferation could produce an order nearly as stable as that of the Long Peace.

The dangers that could arise from mismanaged proliferation are both profound and numerous. There is the danger that the proliferation process itself could give one of the existing nuclear powers a strong incentive to stop a non-nuclear neighbor from joining the club, much as Israel used force to stop Iraq from acquiring a nuclear capability. There is the danger that an unstable nuclear competition would emerge among the new nuclear states. They might lack the resources to make their nuclear forces invulnerable, which could create first-strike fears and incentives—a recipe for disaster in a crisis. Finally, there is the danger that by increasing the number of fingers on the nuclear trigger, proliferation would increase the risk that nuclear weapons would be fired by accident or captured by terrorists or used by madmen.

These and other dangers of proliferation can be lessened if the current nuclear powers take the right steps. To forestall preventive attacks, they can extend security guarantees. To help the new nuclear powers secure their deterrents, they can provide technical assistance. And they can help to socialize nascent nuclear societies to understand the lethal character of the forces they are acquiring. This kind of well-managed proliferation could help bolster peace.

Proliferation should ideally stop with Germany. It has a large economic base, and so could afford to sustain a secure nuclear force. Moreover, Germany would no doubt feel insecure without nuclear weapons, and if it felt insecure its impressive conventional strength would give it a significant capacity to disturb the tranquillity of Europe. But if the broader spread of nuclear weapons proves impossible to prevent without taking extreme steps, the current nuclear powers should let proliferation occur in Eastern Europe while doing all they can to channel it in safe directions.

However, I am pessimistic that proliferation can be well managed. The members of the nuclear club are likely to resist proliferation, but they cannot easily manage this tricky process while at the same time resisting it—and they will have several motives to resist. The established nuclear powers will be exceedingly chary of helping the new nuclear powers build secure deterrents, simply because it goes against the grain of state behavior to share military secrets with other states. After all, knowledge of sensitive military technology could be turned against the donor state if that technology were passed on to adversaries. Furthermore, proliferation in Europe will undermine the legitimacy of the 1968 Nuclear Non-Proliferation Treaty, and this could open the floodgates of proliferation worldwide. The current nuclear powers will not want that to happen, and so they will probably spend their energy trying to thwart proliferation, rather than seeking to manage it.

The best time for proliferation to occur would be during a period of relative international calm. Proliferation in the midst of a crisis would obviously be dangerous, since states in conflict with an emerging nuclear power would then have a powerful incentive to interrupt the process by force. However, the opposition to proliferation by citizens of the potential nuclear powers would be so vociferous, and the external resistance from the nuclear club would be so great, that it might take a crisis to make those powers willing to pay the domestic and international costs of building a nuclear force. All of which means that proliferation is likely to occur under international conditions that virtually ensure it will be mismanaged.

IS WAR OBSOLETE?

Many students of European politics will reject my pessimistic analysis of post-Cold War Europe. They will say that a multipolar Europe, with or without nuclear weapons, will be no less peaceful than the present order. Three specific scenarios for a peaceful future have been advanced, each of which rests on a well-known theory of international relations. However, each of these "soft" theories of peace is flawed.

Under the first optimistic scenario, a non-nuclear Europe would remain peaceful because Europeans recognize that even a conventional war would be horrific. Sobered by history, national leaders will take care to avoid war. This scenario rests on the "obsolescence of war" theory, which posits that modern conventional war had become so deadly by 1945 as to be unthinkable as an instrument of statecraft. War is yesterday's nightmare.

The fact that the Second World War occurred casts doubt on this theory: if any war could have persuaded Europeans to forswear conventional war, it should have been the First World War, with its vast casualties. The key flaw in this theory is the assumption that all conventional wars will be long and bloody wars of attrition. Proponents ignore the evidence of several wars since 1945, as well as several campaign-ending battles of the Second World War, that it is still possible to gain a quick and decisive victory on the conventional battlefield and avoid the devastation of a protracted conflict. Conventional wars can be won rather cheaply; nuclear war cannot be, because neither side can escape devastation by the other, regardless of what happens on the battlefield. Thus the incentives to avoid war are of another order of intensity in a nuclear world than they are in a conventional world.

There are several other flaws in this scenario. There is no systematic evidence demonstrating that Europeans believe war is obsolete. The Romanians and the Hungarians don't seem to have gotten the message. However, even if it were widely believed in Europe that war is no longer thinkable, attitudes could change. Public opinion on national-security issues is notoriously fickle and responsive to manipulation by elites as well as to changes in the international environment. An end to the

Cold War, as we have seen, will be accompanied by a sea change in the geometry of power in Europe, which will surely alter European thinking about questions of war and peace. Is it not possible, for example, that German thinking about the benefits of controlling Eastern Europe will change markedly once American forces are withdrawn from Central Europe and the Germans are left to provide for their own security? Is it not possible that they would countenance a conventional war against a substantially weaker Eastern European state to enhance their position vis-à-vis the Soviet Union? Finally, only one country need decide that war is thinkable to make war possible.

IS PROSPERITY THE PATH TO PEACE?

Proponents of the second optimistic scenario base their optimism about the future of Europe on the unified European market coming in 1992—the realization of the dream of the European Community. A strong EC, they argue, ensures that the European economy will remain open and prosperous, which will keep the European states cooperating with one another. Prosperity will make for peace. The threat of an aggressive Germany will be removed by enclosing the newly unified German state in the benign embrace of the EC. Even Eastern Europe and the Soviet Union can eventually be brought into the EC. Peace and prosperity will then extend their sway from the Atlantic to the Urals.

This scenario is based on the theory of economic liberalism, which assumes that states are primarily motivated by the desire to achieve prosperity and that leaders place the material welfare of their publics above all other considerations, including security. Stability flows not from military power but from the creation of a liberal economic order.

A liberal economic order works in several ways to enhance peace and dampen conflict. In the first place, it requires significant political cooperation to make the trading system work—make states richer. The more prosperous states grow, the greater their incentive for further political cooperation. A benevolent spiral relationship sets in between political cooperation and prosperity. Second, a liberal economic order fosters economic interdependence, a situation in which states are mutually vulnerable in the economic realm. When interdependence is high, the theory holds, there is less temptation to cheat or behave aggressively toward other states, because all states can retaliate economically. Finally, some theorists argue, an international institution like the EC will, with ever-increasing political cooperation, become so powerful that it will take on a life of its own, eventually evolving into a superstate. In short, Mrs. Thatcher's presentiments about the EC are absolutely right.

This theory has one grave flaw: the main assumption underpinning it is wrong. States are not primarily motivated by the desire to achieve prosperity. Although economic calculations are hardly trivial to them, states operate in both an international political and an international economic environment, and the former dominates the latter when the two systems come into conflict. Survival in an anarchic international political system is the highest goal a state can have.

Proponents of economic liberalism largely ignore the effects of anarchy on state behavior and concentrate instead on economic motives. When this omission is corrected, however, their arguments collapse for two reasons.

Competition for security makes it difficult for states to cooperate, which, according to the theory of economic liberalism, they must do. When security is scarce, states become more concerned about relative than about absolute gains. They ask of an exchange not "Will both of us gain?" but "Who will gain more?" They reject even cooperation that will yield an absolute economic gain if the other state will gain more, from fear that the other might convert its gain to military strength, and then use this strength to win by coercion in later rounds. Cooperation is much easier to achieve if states worry only about absolute gains. The goal, then, is simply to ensure that the overall economic pie is expanding and that each state is getting at least some part of the increase. However, anarchy guarantees that security will often be scarce; this heightens states' concerns about relative gains, which makes cooperation difficult unless the pie can be finely sliced to reflect, and thus not disturb, the current balance of power.

Interdependence, moreover, is as likely to lead to conflict as to cooperation, because states will struggle to escape the vulnerability that interdependence creates, in order to bolster their national security. In time of crisis or war, states that depend on others for critical economic supplies will fear cutoff or blackmail; they may well respond by trying to seize the source of supply by force of arms. There are numerous historical examples of states' pursuing aggressive military policies for the purpose of achieving economic autarky. One thinks of both Japan and Germany during the interwar period. And one recalls that during the Arab oil embargo of the early 1970s there was much talk in America about using military force to seize Arab oil fields.

In twentieth-century Europe two periods saw a liberal economic order with high levels of interdependence. According to the theory of economic liberalism, stability should have obtained during those periods. It did not.

The first case clearly contradicts the economic liberals. The years from 1890 to 1914 were probably the time of greatest economic interdependence in Europe's history. Yet those years of prosperity were all the time making hideously for the First World War.

The second case covers the Cold War years, during which there has been much interdependence among the EC states, and relations among them have been very peaceful. This case, not surprisingly, is the centerpiece of the economic liberals' argument.

We certainly see a correlation in this period between interdependence and stability, but that does not mean that interdependence has caused cooperation among the Western democracies. More likely the Cold War was the prime cause of cooperation among the Western democracies, and the main reason that intra-EC relations have flourished.

A powerful and potentially dangerous Soviet Union forced the Western democracies to band together to meet a common threat. This threat muted concerns about relative gains arising from economic cooperation among the EC states by giving each Western democracy a vested interest in seeing its alliance partners grow powerful. Each increment of power helped deter the Soviets. Moreover, they all had a powerful incentive to avoid conflict with one another while the Soviet Union loomed to the East, ready to harvest the grain of Western quarrels.

In addition, America's hegemonic position in NATO, the military counterpart to the EC, mitigated the effects of anarchy on the Western democracies and induced cooperation among them. America not only provided protection against the Soviet threat; it also guaranteed that no EC state would aggress against another. For example, France did not have to fear Germany as it re-armed, because the American presence in

Germany meant that the Germans were contained. With the United States serving as a night watchman, fears about relative gains among the Western European states were mitigated, and furthermore, those states were willing to allow their economies to become tightly interdependent.

Take away the present Soviet threat to Western Europe, send the American forces home, and relations among the EC states will be fundamentally altered. Without a common Soviet threat or an American night watchman, Western European states will do what they did for centuries before the onset of the Cold War—look upon one another with abiding suspicion. Consequently, they will worry about imbalances in gains and about the loss of autonomy that results from cooperation. Cooperation in this new order will be more difficult than it was during the Cold War. Conflict will be more likely.

In sum, there are good reasons for being skeptical about the claim that a more powerful EC can provide the basis for peace in a multipolar Europe.

DO DEMOCRACIES REALLY LOVE PEACE?

Under the third scenario war is avoided because many European states have become democratic since the early twentieth century, and liberal democracies simply do not fight one another. At a minimum, the presence of liberal democracies in Western Europe renders that half of Europe free from armed conflict. At a maximum, democracy spreads to Eastern Europe and the Soviet Union, bolstering peace. The idea that peace is cognate with democracy is a vision of international relations shared by both liberals and neoconservatives.

This scenario rests on the "peace-loving democracies" theory. Two arguments are made for it.

First, some claim that authoritarian leaders are more likely to go to war than leaders of democracies, because authoritarian leaders are not accountable to their publics, which carry the main burdens of war. In a democracy the citizenry, which pays the price of war, has a greater say in what the government does. The people, so the argument goes, are more hesitant to start trouble, because it is they who must pay the bloody price; hence the greater their power, the fewer wars.

The second argument rests on the claim that the citizens of liberal democracies respect popular democratic rights—those of their countrymen, and those of people in other states. They view democratic governments as more legitimate than others, and so are loath to impose a foreign regime on a democratic state by force. Thus an inhibition on war missing from other international relationships is introduced when two democracies face each other.

The first of these arguments is flawed because it is not possible to sustain the claim that the people in a democracy are especially sensitive to the costs of war and therefore less willing than authoritarian leaders to fight wars. In fact the historical record shows that democracies are every bit as likely to fight wars as are authoritarian states, though admittedly, thus far, not with other democracies.

Furthermore, mass publics, whether in a democracy or not, can become deeply imbued with nationalistic or religious fervor, making them prone to support aggression and quite indifferent to costs. The widespread public support in post-Revolutionary France for Napoleon's wars is just one example of this phenomenon. At the same time, authoritarian leaders are often fearful of going to war, because war tends to unleash democratic forces that can undermine the regime. In short, war can impose high costs on authoritarian leaders as well as on their citizenry.

The second argument, which emphasizes the transnational respect for democratic rights among democracies, rests on a secondary factor that is generally overridden by other factors such as nationalism and religious fundamentalism. Moreover, there is another problem with the argument. The possibility always exists that a democracy, especially the kind of fledgling democracy emerging in Eastern Europe, will revert to an authoritarian state. This threat of backsliding means that one democratic state can never be sure that another democratic state will not turn on it sometime in the future. Liberal democracies must therefore worry about relative power among themselves, which is tantamount to saying that each has an incentive to consider aggression against another to forestall trouble. Lamentably, it is not possible for even liberal democracies to transcend anarchy.

Problems with the deductive logic aside, at first glance the historical record seems to offer strong support for the theory of peace-loving democracies. It appears that no liberal democracies have ever fought against each other. Evidentiary problems, however, leave the issue in doubt.

First, democracies have been few in number over the past two centuries, and thus there have not been many cases in which two democracies were in a position to fight with each other. Three prominent cases are usually cited: Britain and the United States (1832 to the present); Britain and France (1832–1849; 1871–1940); and the Western democracies since 1945.

Second, there are other persuasive explanations for why war did not occur in those three cases, and these competing explanations must be ruled out before the theory of peace-loving democracies can be accepted. Whereas relations between the British and the Americans during the nineteenth century were hardly blissful, in the twentieth century they have been quite harmonious, and thus fit closely with the theory's expectations. That harmony, however, can easily be explained by common threats that forced Britain and the United States to work together—a serious German threat in the first part of the century, and later a Soviet threat. The same basic argument applies to relations between France and Britain. Although they were not on the best of terms during most of the nineteenth century, their relations improved significantly around the turn of the century, with the rise of Germany. Finally, as noted above, the Soviet threat goes far in explaining the absence of war among the Western democracies since 1945.

Third, several democracies have come close to fighting each other, suggesting that the absence of war may be due simply to chance. France and Britain approached war during the Fashoda crisis of 1898. France and Weimar Germany might have come to blows over the Rhineland during the 1920s. The United States has clashed with a number of elected governments in the Third World during the Cold War, including the Allende regime in Chile and the Arbenz regime in Guatemala.

Last, some would classify Wilhelmine Germany as a democracy, or at least a quasi-democracy; if so, the First World War becomes a war among democracies.

While the spread of democracy across Europe has great potential benefits for human rights, it will not guarantee peaceful relations among the states of post-Cold War Europe. Most Americans will find this argument counterintuitive. They see the United States as fundamentally peace-loving, and they ascribe this peacefulness to its democratic character. From this they generalize that democracies are more peaceful than authoritarian states, which leads them to conclude that the complete democratization of Europe would largely eliminate the threat of war. This view of international politics is likely to be repudiated by the events of coming years.

MISSING THE COLD WAR

The implications of my analysis are straightforward, if paradoxical. Developments that threaten to end the Cold War are dangerous. The West has an interest in maintaining peace in Europe. It therefore has an interest in maintaining the Cold War order, and hence has an interest in continuing the Cold War confrontation. The Cold War antagonism could be continued at lower levels of East-West tension than have prevailed in the past, but a complete end to the Cold War would create more problems than it would solve.

The fate of the Cold War is mainly in the hands of the Soviet Union. The Soviet Union is the only superpower that can seriously threaten to overrun Europe, and the Soviet threat provides the glue that holds NATO together. Take away that offensive threat and the United States is likely to abandon the Continent; the defensive alliance it has headed for forty years may well then disintegrate, bringing an end to the bipolar order that has kept the peace of Europe for the past forty-five years.

There is little the Americans or the West Europeans can do to perpetuate the Cold War.

For one thing, domestic politics preclude it. Western leaders obviously cannot base national-security policy on the need to maintain forces in Central Europe simply to keep the Soviets there. The idea of deploying large numbers of troops in order to bait the Soviets into an order-keeping competition would be dismissed as bizarre, and contrary to the general belief that ending the Cold War and removing the Soviet yoke from Eastern Europe would make the world safer and better.

For another, the idea of propping up a declining rival runs counter to the basic behavior of states. States are principally concerned about their relative power in the system—hence they look for opportunities to take advantage of one another. If anything, they prefer to see adversaries decline, and invariably do whatever they can to speed up the process and maximize the distance of the fall. States, in other words, do not ask which distribution of power best facilitates stability and then do everything possible to build or maintain such an order. Instead, each pursues the narrower aim of maximizing its power advantage over potential adversaries. The particular international order that results is simply a by-product of that competition.

Consider, for example, the origins of the Cold War order in Europe. No state intended to create it. In fact the United States and the Soviet Union each worked hard in the early years of the Cold War to undermine the other's position in Europe, which would have needed the bipolar order on the Continent. The remarkably stable system that emerged in Europe in the late 1940s was the unintended consequence of an intense competition between the superpowers.

Moreover, even if the Americans and the West Europeans wanted to help the Soviets maintain their status as a superpower, it is not apparent that they could do so. The Soviet Union is leaving Eastern Europe and cutting its military forces largely because its economy is floundering badly. The Soviets don't know how to fix their economy themselves, and there is little that Western governments can do to help them. The West can and should avoid doing malicious mischief to the Soviet economy, but at this juncture it is difficult to see how the West can have a significant positive influence.

The fact that the West cannot sustain the Cold War does not mean that the United States should make no attempt to preserve the current order. It should do what it can to avert a complete mutual withdrawal from Europe. For instance, the American negotiating position at the conventional-arms-control talks should aim toward large mutual force reductions but should not contemplate complete mutual withdrawal. The Soviets may opt to withdraw all their forces unilaterally anyway; if so, there is little the United States can do to stop them.

Should complete Soviet withdrawal from Eastern Europe prove unavoidable, the West would confront the question of how to maintain peace in a multipolar Europe. Three policy prescriptions are in order.

First, the United States should encourage the limited and carefully managed proliferation of nuclear weapons in Europe. The best hope for avoiding war in post-Cold War Europe is nuclear deterrence; hence some nuclear proliferation is necessary, to compensate for the withdrawal of the Soviet and American nuclear arsenals from Central Europe. Ideally, as I have argued, nuclear weapons would spread to Germany but to no other state.

Second, Britain and the United States, as well as the Continental states, will have to counter any emerging aggressor actively and efficiently, in order to offset the ganging up and bullying that are sure to arise in post-Cold War Europe. Balancing in a multipolar system, however, is usually a problem-ridden enterprise, because of either geography or the problems of coordination. Britain and the United States, physically separated from the Continent, may conclude that they have little interest in what happens there. That would be abandoning their responsibilities and, more important, their interests. Both states failed to counter Germany before the two world wars, making war more likely. It is essential for peace in Europe that they not repeat their past mistakes. ✔

Both states must maintain military forces that can be deployed against Continental states that threaten to start a war. To do this they must persuade their citizens to support a policy of continued Continental commitment. This will be more difficult than it once was, because its principal purpose will be to preserve peace, rather than to prevent an imminent hegemony, and the prevention of hegemony is a simpler goal to explain publicly. Furthermore, this prescription asks both countries to take on an unaccustomed task, given that it is the basic nature of states to focus on maximizing relative power, not on bolstering stability. Nevertheless, the British and the Americans have a real stake in peace, especially since there is the risk that a European war might involve the large-scale use of nuclear weapons. Therefore, it should be possible for their governments to lead their publics to recognize this interest and support policies that protect it.

The Soviet Union may eventually return to its past expansionism and threaten to upset the status quo. If so, we are back to the Cold War. However, if the Soviets adhere to status-quo policies, Soviet power could play a key role in countering Germany and in maintaining order in Eastern Europe. It is important in those cases where the Soviets are acting in a balancing capacity that the United States cooperate with its former adversary and not let residual distrust from the Cold War obtrude.

Third, a concerted effort should be made to keep hypernationalism at bay, especially in Eastern Europe. Nationalism has been contained during the Cold War, but it is likely to re-emerge once Soviet and American forces leave the heart of Europe. It will be a force for trouble unless curbed. The teaching of honest national history is especially important, since the teaching of false, chauvinist history is the main vehicle for spreading hypernationalism. States that teach a dishonestly self-exculpating or self-glorifying history should be publicly criticized and sanctioned.

None of these tasks will be easy. In fact, I expect that the bulk of my prescriptions will not be followed; most run contrary to important strains of domestic American and European opinion, and to the basic nature of state behavior. And even if they are followed, peace in Europe will not be guaranteed. If the Cold War is truly behind us, therefore, the stability of the past forty-five years is not likely to be seen again in the coming decades.

THE C
CIVILIZ

Samuel P. Huntington

THE NEXT PATTERN OF CONFLICT

World politics is entering a new phase, and intellectuals have not hesitated to proliferate visions of what it will be—the end of history, the return of traditional rivalries between nation states, and the decline of the nation state from the conflicting pulls of tribalism and globalism, among others. Each of these visions catches aspects of the emerging reality. Yet they all miss a crucial, indeed a central, aspect of what global politics is likely to be in the coming years.

It is my hypothesis that the fundamental source of conflict in this new world will not be primarily ideological or primarily economic. The great divisions among humankind and the dominating source of conflict will be cultural. Nation states will remain the most powerful actors in world affairs, but the principal conflicts of global politics will occur between nations and groups of different civilizations. The clash of civilizations will dominate global politics. The fault lines between civilizations will be the battle lines of the future.

Conflict between civilizations will be the latest phase in the evolution of conflict in the modern world. For a century and a half after the emergence of the modern international system with the Peace of Westphalia, the conflicts of the Western world were largely among princes—emperors, absolute monarchs and constitutional monarchs attempting to expand their bureaucracies, their armies, their mercantilist economic strength and, most important, the territory they ruled. In the process they created nation states, and beginning with the French Revolution the principal lines of conflict were between nations rather than princes. In 1793, as R. R. Palmer put it, "The wars of kings were over; the wars of peoples had begun." This nineteenth-century pattern lasted until the end of World War I. Then, as a result of the Russian Revolution and the reaction against it, the conflict of nations yielded to the conflict of ideologies, first among communism, fascism-Nazism and liberal democracy, and then between communism and liberal democracy. During the Cold War, this latter conflict became embodied in the struggle between the two superpowers, neither of which was a nation state in the classical European sense and each of which defined its identity in terms of its ideology.

These conflicts between princes, nation states and ideologies were primarily conflicts within Western civilization, "Western civil wars," as William Lind has labeled them. This was as true of the Cold War as it was of the world wars and the earlier wars

Samuel P. Huntington, "The Clash of Civilizations?" Reprinted by permission of *Foreign Affairs,* Vol. 72, No. 3 (summer, 1993). Copyright 1993 by the Council on Foreign Relations, Inc.

of the seventeenth, eighteenth and nineteenth centuries. With the end of the Cold War, international politics moves out of its Western phase, and its centerpiece becomes the interaction between the West and non-Western civilizations and among non-Western civilizations. In the politics of civilizations, the peoples and governments of non-Western civilizations no longer remain the objects of history as targets of Western colonialism but join the West as movers and shapers of history.

THE NATURE OF CIVILIZATIONS

During the Cold War the world was divided into the First, Second and Third Worlds. Those divisions are no longer relevant. It is far more meaningful now to group countries not in terms of their political or economic systems or in terms of their level of economic development but rather in terms of their culture and civilization.

What do we mean when we talk of a civilization? A civilization is a cultural entity. Villages, regions, ethnic groups, nationalities, religious groups, all have distinct cultures at different levels of cultural heterogeneity. The culture of a village in southern Italy may be different from that of a village in northern Italy, but both will share in a common Italian culture that distinguishes them from German villages. European communities, in turn, will share cultural features that distinguish them from Arab or Chinese communities. Arabs, Chinese and Westerners, however, are not part of any broader cultural entity. They constitute civilizations. A civilization is thus the highest cultural grouping of people and the broadest level of cultural identity people have short of that which distinguishes humans from other species. It is defined both by common objective elements, such as language, history, religion, customs, institutions, and by the subjective self-identification of people. People have levels of identity: a resident of Rome may define himself with varying degrees of intensity as a Roman, an Italian, a Catholic, a Christian, a European, a Westerner. The civilization to which he belongs is the broadest level of identification with which he intensely identifies. People can and do redefine their identities and, as a result, the composition and boundaries of civilizations change.

Civilizations may involve a large number of people, as with China ("a civilization pretending to be a state," as Lucian Pye put it), or a very small number of people, such as the Anglophone Caribbean. A civilization may include several nation states, as is the case with Western, Latin American and Arab civilizations, or only one, as is the case with Japanese civilization. Civilizations obviously blend and overlap, and may include subcivilizations. Western civilization has two major variants, European and North American, and Islam has its Arab, Turkic and Malay subdivisions. Civilizations are nonetheless meaningful entities, and while the lines between them are seldom sharp, they are real. Civilizations are dynamic; they rise and fall; they divide and merge. And, as any student of history knows, civilizations disappear and are buried in the sands of time.

Westerners tend to think of nation states as the principal actors in global affairs. They have been that, however, for only a few centuries. The broader reaches of human history have been the history of civilizations. In *A Study of History,* Arnold Toynbee identified 21 major civilizations; only six of them exist in the contemporary world.

WHY CIVILIZATIONS WILL CLASH

Civilization identity will be increasingly important in the future, and the world will be shaped in large measure by the interactions among seven or eight major civilizations. These include Western, Confucian, Japanese, Islamic, Hindu, Slavic-Orthodox, Latin American and possibly African civilization. The most important conflicts of the future will occur along the cultural fault lines separating these civilizations from one another.

Why will this be the case?

First, differences among civilizations are not only real; they are basic. Civilizations are differentiated from each other by history, language, culture, tradition and, most important, religion. The people of different civilizations have different views on the relations between God and man, the individual and the group, the citizen and the state, parents and children, husband and wife, as well as differing views of the relative importance of rights and responsibilities, liberty and authority, equality and hierarchy. These differences are the product of centuries. They will not soon disappear. They are far more fundamental than differences among political ideologies and political regimes. Differences do not necessarily mean conflict, and conflict does not necessarily mean violence. Over the centuries, however, differences among civilizations have generated the most prolonged and the most violent conflicts.

Second, the world is becoming a smaller place. The interactions between peoples of different civilizations are increasing; these increasing interactions intensify civilization consciousness and awareness of differences between civilizations and commonalities within civilizations. North African immigration to France generates hostility among Frenchmen and at the same time increased receptivity to immigration by "good" European Catholic Poles. Americans react far more negatively to Japanese investment than to larger investments from Canada and European countries. Similarly, as Donald Horowitz has pointed out, "An Ibo may be . . . an Owerri Ibo or an Onitsha Ibo in what was the Eastern region of Nigeria. In Lagos, he is simply an Ibo. In London, he is a Nigerian. In New York, he is an African." The interactions among peoples of different civilizations enhance the civilization-consciousness of people that, in turn, invigorates differences and animosities stretching or thought to stretch back deep into history.

Third, the processes of economic modernization and social change throughout the world are separating people from longstanding local identities. They also weaken the nation state as a source of identity. In much of the world religion has moved in to fill this gap, often in the form of movements that are labeled "fundamentalist." Such movements are found in Western Christianity, Judaism, Buddhism and Hinduism, as well as in Islam. In most countries and most religions the people active in fundamentalist movements are young, college-educated, middle-class technicians, professionals and business persons. The "unsecularization of the world," George Weigel has remarked, "is one of the dominant social facts of life in the late twentieth century." The revival of religion, "la revanche de Dieu," as Gilles Kepel labeled it, provides a basis for identity and commitment that transcends national boundaries and unites civilizations.

Fourth, the growth of civilization-consciousness is enhanced by the dual role of the West. On the one hand, the West is at a peak of power. At the same time, however, and perhaps as a result, a return to the roots phenomenon is occurring among non-Western civilizations. Increasingly one hears references to trends toward a turning inward and

"Asianization" in Japan, the end of the Nehru legacy and the "Hinduization" of India, the failure of Western ideas of socialism and nationalism and hence "re-Islamization" of the Middle East, and now a debate over Westernization versus Russianization in Boris Yeltsin's country. A West at the peak of its power confronts non-Wests that increasingly have the desire, the will and the resources to shape the world in non-Western ways.

In the past, the elites of non-Western societies were usually the people who were most involved with the West, had been educated at Oxford, the Sorbonne or Sandhurst, and had absorbed Western attitudes and values. At the same time, the populace in non-Western countries often remained deeply imbued with the indigenous culture. Now, however, these relationships are being reversed. A de-Westernization and indigenization of elites is occurring in many non-Western countries at the same time that Western, usually American, cultures, styles and habits become more popular among the mass of the people.

Fifth, cultural characteristics and differences are less mutable and hence less easily compromised and resolved than political and economic ones. In the former Soviet Union, communists can become democrats, the rich can become poor and the poor rich, but Russians cannot become Estonians and Azeris cannot become Armenians. In class and ideological conflicts, the key question was "Which side are you on?" and people could and did choose sides and change sides. In conflicts between civilizations, the question is "What are you?" That is a given that cannot be changed. And as we know, from Bosnia to the Caucasus to the Sudan, the wrong answer to that question can mean a bullet in the head. Even more than ethnicity, religion discriminates sharply and exclusively among people. A person can be half-French and half-Arab and simultaneously even a citizen of two countries. It is more difficult to be half-Catholic and half-Muslim.

Finally, economic regionalism is increasing. The proportions of total trade that were intraregional rose between 1980 and 1989 from 51 percent to 59 percent in Europe, 33 percent to 37 percent in East Asia, and 32 percent to 36 percent in North America. The importance of regional economic blocs is likely to continue to increase in the future. On the one hand, successful economic regionalism will reinforce civilization-consciousness. On the other hand, economic regionalism may succeed only when it is rooted in a common civilization. The European Community rests on the shared foundation of European culture and Western Christianity. The success of the North American Free Trade Area depends on the convergence now underway of Mexican, Canadian and American cultures. Japan, in contrast, faces difficulties in creating a comparable economic entity in East Asia because Japan is a society and civilization unique to itself. However strong the trade and investment links Japan may develop with other East Asian countries, its cultural differences with those countries inhibit and perhaps preclude its promoting regional economic integration like that in Europe and North America.

Common culture, in contrast, is clearly facilitating the rapid expansion of the economic relations between the People's Republic of China and Hong Kong, Taiwan, Singapore and the overseas Chinese communities in other Asian countries. With the Cold War over, cultural commonalities increasingly overcome ideological differences, and mainland China and Taiwan move closer together. If cultural commonality is a prerequisite for economic integration, the principal East Asian economic bloc of the future is likely to be centered on China. This bloc is, in fact, already coming into existence. As Murray Weidenbaum has observed,

> Despite the current Japanese dominance of the region, the Chinese-based economy of Asia is rapidly emerging as a new epicenter for industry, commerce and finance. This strategic area contains substantial amounts of technology and manufacturing capability (Taiwan), outstanding entrepreneurial, marketing and services acumen (Hong Kong), a fine communications network (Singapore), a tremendous pool of financial capital (all three), and very large endowments of land, resources and labor (mainland China). . . . From Guangzhou to Singapore, from Kuala Lumpur to Manila, this influential network—often based on extensions of the traditional clans—has been described as the backbone of the East Asian economy.[1]

Culture and religion also form the basis of the Economic Cooperation Organization, which brings together ten non-Arab Muslim countries: Iran, Pakistan, Turkey, Azerbaijan, Kazakhstan, Kyrgyzstan, Turkmenistan, Tadjikistan, Uzbekistan and Afghanistan. One impetus to the revival and expansion of this organization, founded originally in the 1960s by Turkey, Pakistan and Iran, is the realization by the leaders of several of these countries that they had no chance of admission to the European Community. Similarly, Caricom, the Central American Common Market and Mercosur rest on common cultural foundations. Efforts to build a broader Caribbean-Central American economic entity bridging the Anglo-Latin divide, however, have to date failed.

As people define their identity in ethnic and religious terms, they are likely to see an "us" versus "them" relation existing between themselves and people of different ethnicity or religion. The end of ideologically defined states in Eastern Europe and the former Soviet Union permits traditional ethnic identities and animosities to come to the fore. Differences in culture and religion create differences over policy issues, ranging from human rights to immigration to trade and commerce to the environment. Geographical propinquity gives rise to conflicting territorial claims from Bosnia to Mindanao. Most important, the efforts of the West to promote its values of democracy and liberalism as universal values, to maintain its military predominance and to advance its economic interests engender countering responses from other civilizations. Decreasingly able to mobilize support and form coalitions on the basis of ideology, governments and groups will increasingly attempt to mobilize support by appealing to common religion and civilization identity.

The clash of civilizations thus occurs at two levels. At the microlevel, adjacent groups along the fault lines between civilizations struggle, often violently, over the control of territory and each other. At the macro-level, states from different civilizations

---

[1]Murray Weidenbaum, *Greater China: The Next Economic Superpower?*, St. Louis: Washington University Center for the Study of American Business, Contemporary Issues, Series 57, February 1993, pp. 2–3.

compete for relative military and economic power, struggle over the control of international institutions and third parties, and competitively promote their particular political and religious values.

THE FAULT LINES BETWEEN CIVILIZATIONS

The fault lines between civilizations are replacing the political and ideological boundaries of the Cold War as the flash points for crisis and bloodshed. The Cold War began when the Iron Curtain divided Europe politically and ideologically. The Cold War ended with the end of the Iron Curtain. As the ideological division of Europe has disappeared, the cultural division of Europe between Western Christianity, on the one hand, and Orthodox Christianity and Islam, on the other, has reemerged. The most significant dividing line in Europe, as William Wallace has suggested, may well be the eastern boundary of Western Christianity in the year 1500. This line runs along what are now the boundaries between Finland and Russia and between the Baltic states and Russia, cuts through Belarus and Ukraine separating the more Catholic western Ukraine from Orthodox eastern Ukraine, swings westward separating Transylvania from the rest of Romania, and then goes through Yugoslavia almost exactly along the line now separating Croatia and Slovenia from the rest of Yugoslavia. In the Balkans this line, of course, coincides with the historic boundary between the Hapsburg and Ottoman empires. The peoples to the north and west of this line are Protestant or Catholic; they shared the common experiences of European history—feudalism, the Renaissance, the Reformation, the Enlightenment, the French Revolution, the Industrial Revolution; they are generally economically better off than the peoples to the east; and they may now look forward to increasing involvement in a common European economy and to the consolidation of democratic political systems. The peoples to the east and south of this line are Orthodox or Muslim; they historically belonged to the Ottoman or Tsarist empires and were only lightly touched by the shaping events in the rest of Europe; they are generally less advanced economically; they seem much less likely to develop stable democratic political systems. The Velvet Curtain of culture has replaced the Iron Curtain of ideology as the most significant dividing line in Europe. As the events in Yugoslavia show, it is not only a line of difference; it is also at times a line of bloody conflict.

Conflict along the fault line between Western and Islamic civilizations has been going on for 1,300 years. After the founding of Islam, the Arab and Moorish surge west and north only ended at Tours in 732. From the eleventh to the thirteenth century the Crusaders attempted with temporary success to bring Christianity and Christian rule to the Holy Land. From the fourteenth to the seventeenth century, the Ottoman Turks reversed the balance, extended their sway over the Middle East and the Balkans, captured Constantinople, and twice laid siege to Vienna. In the nineteenth and early twentieth centuries as Ottoman power declined Britain, France, and Italy established Western control over most of North Africa and the Middle East.

After World War II, the West, in turn, began to retreat; the colonial empires disappeared; first Arab nationalism and then Islamic fundamentalism manifested themselves;

the West became heavily dependent on the Persian Gulf countries for its energy; the oil-rich Muslim countries became money-rich and, when they wished to, weapons-rich. Several wars occurred between Arabs and Israel (created by the West). France fought a bloody and ruthless war in Algeria for most of the 1950s; British and French forces invaded Egypt in 1956; American forces went into Lebanon in 1958; subsequently American forces returned to Lebanon, attacked Libya, and engaged in various military encounters with Iran; Arab and Islamic terrorists, supported by at least three Middle Eastern governments, employed the weapon of the weak and bombed Western planes and installations and seized Western hostages. This warfare between Arabs and the West culminated in 1990, when the United States sent a massive army to the Persian Gulf to defend some Arab countries against aggression by another. In its aftermath NATO planning is increasingly directed to potential threats and instability along its "southern tier."

This centuries-old military interaction between the West and Islam is unlikely to decline. It could become more virulent. The Gulf War left some Arabs feeling proud that Saddam Hussein had attacked Israel and stood up to the West. It also left many feeling humiliated and resentful of the West's military presence in the Persian Gulf, the West's overwhelming military dominance, and their apparent inability to shape their own destiny. Many Arab countries, in addition to the oil exporters, are reaching levels of economic and social development where autocratic forms of government become inappropriate and efforts to introduce democracy become stronger. Some openings in Arab political systems have already occurred. The principal beneficiaries of these openings have been Islamist movements. In the Arab world, in short, Western democracy strengthens anti-Western political forces. This may be a passing phenomenon, but it surely complicates relations between Islamic countries and the West.

Those relations are also complicated by demography. The spectacular population growth in Arab countries, particularly in North Africa, has led to increased migration to Western Europe. The movement within Western Europe toward minimizing internal boundaries has sharpened political sensitivities with respect to this development. In Italy, France and Germany, racism is increasingly open, and political reactions and violence against Arab and Turkish migrants have become more intense and more widespread since 1990.

On both sides the interaction between Islam and the West is seen as a clash of civilizations. The West's "next confrontation," observes M. J. Akbar, an Indian Muslim author, "is definitely going to come from the Muslim world. It is in the sweep of the Islamic nations from the Maghreb to Pakistan that the struggle for a new world order will begin." Bernard Lewis comes to a similar conclusion:

> We are facing a mood and a movement far transcending the level of issues and policies and the governments that pursue them. This is no less than a clash of civilizations—the perhaps irrational but surely historic reaction of an ancient rival against our Judeo-Christian heritage, our secular present, and the worldwide expansion of both.[2]

---

[2]Bernard Lewis, "The Roots of Muslim Rage," *The Atlantic Monthly,* vol. 266, September 1990, p. 60; *Time,* June 15, 1992, pp. 24–28.

Historically, the other great antagonistic interaction of Arab Islamic civilization has been with the pagan, animist, and now increasingly Christian black peoples to the south. In the past, this antagonism was epitomized in the image of Arab slave dealers and black slaves. It has been reflected in the on-going civil war in the Sudan between Arabs and blacks, the fighting in Chad between Libyan-supported insurgents and the government, the tensions between Orthodox Christians and Muslims in the Horn of Africa, and the political conflicts, recurring riots and communal violence between Muslims and Christians in Nigeria. The modernization of Africa and the spread of Christianity are likely to enhance the probability of violence along this fault line. Symptomatic of the intensification of this conflict was the Pope John Paul II's speech in Khartoum in February 1993 attacking the actions of the Sudan's Islamist government against the Christian minority there.

On the northern border of Islam, conflict has increasingly erupted between Orthodox and Muslim peoples, including the carnage of Bosnia and Sarajevo, the simmering violence between Serb and Albanian, the tenuous relations between Bulgarians and their Turkish minority, the violence between Ossetians and Ingush, the unremitting slaughter of each other by Armenians and Azeris, the tense relations between Russians and Muslims in Central Asia, and the deployment of Russian troops to protect Russian interests in the Caucasus and Central Asia. Religion reinforces the revival of ethnic identities and restimulates Russian fears about the security of their southern borders. This concern is well captured by Archie Roosevelt:

> Much of Russian history concerns the struggle between the Slavs and the Turkic peoples on their borders, which dates back to the foundation of the Russian state more than a thousand years ago. In the Slavs' millennium-long confrontation with their eastern neighbors lies the key to an understanding not only of Russian history, but Russian character. To understand Russian realities today one has to have a concept of the great Turkic ethnic group that has preoccupied Russians through the centuries.[3]

The conflict of civilizations is deeply rooted elsewhere in Asia. The historic clash between Muslim and Hindu in the subcontinent manifests itself now not only in the rivalry between Pakistan and India but also in intensifying religious strife within India between increasingly militant Hindu groups and India's substantial Muslim minority. The destruction of the Ayodhya mosque in December 1992 brought to the fore the issue of whether India will remain a secular democratic state or become a Hindu one. In East Asia, China has outstanding territorial disputes with most of its neighbors. It has pursued a ruthless policy toward the Buddhist people of Tibet, and it is pursuing an increasingly ruthless policy toward its Turkic-Muslim minority. With the Cold War over, the underlying differences between China and the United States have reasserted themselves in areas such as human rights, trade and weapons proliferation. These differences are unlikely to moderate. A "new cold war," Deng Xaioping reportedly asserted in 1991, is under way between China and America.

---

[3]Archie Roosevelt, *For Lust of Knowing,* Boston: Little, Brown, 1988, pp. 332–333.

The same phrase has been applied to the increasingly difficult relations between Japan and the United States. Here cultural difference exacerbates economic conflict. People on each side allege racism on the other, but at least on the American side the antipathies are not racial but cultural. The basic values, attitudes, behavioral patterns of the two societies could hardly be more different. The economic issues between the United States and Europe are no less serious than those between the United States and Japan, but they do not have the same political salience and emotional intensity because the differences between American culture and European culture are so much less than those between American civilization and Japanese civilization.

The interactions between civilizations vary greatly in the extent to which they are likely to be characterized by violence. Economic competition clearly predominates between the American and European subcivilizations of the West and between both of them and Japan. On the Eurasian continent, however, the proliferation of ethnic conflict, epitomized at the extreme in "ethnic cleansing," has not been totally random. It has been most frequent and most violent between groups belonging to different civilizations. In Eurasia the great historic fault lines between civilizations are once more aflame. This is particularly true along the boundaries of the crescent-shaped Islamic bloc of nations from the bulge of Africa to central Asia. Violence also occurs between Muslims, on the one hand, and Orthodox Serbs in the Balkans, Jews in Israel, Hindus in India, Buddhists in Burma and Catholics in the Philippines. Islam has bloody borders.

CIVILIZATION RALLYING:
THE KIN-COUNTRY SYNDROME

Groups or states belonging to one civilization that become involved in war with people from a different civilization naturally try to rally support from other members of their own civilization. As the post-Cold War world evolves, civilization commonality, what H. D. S. Greenway has termed the "kin-country" syndrome, is replacing political ideology and traditional balance of power considerations as the principal basis for cooperation and coalitions. It can be seen gradually emerging in the post-Cold War conflicts in the Persian Gulf, the Caucasus and Bosnia. None of these was a full-scale war between civilizations, but each involved some elements of civilizational rallying, which seemed to become more important as the conflict continued and which may provide a foretaste of the future.

First, in the Gulf War one Arab state invaded another and then fought a coalition of Arab, Western and other states. While only a few Muslim governments overtly supported Saddam Hussein, many Arab elites privately cheered him on, and he was highly popular among large sections of the Arab publics. Islamic fundamentalist movements universally supported Iraq rather than the Western-backed governments of Kuwait and Saudi Arabia. Forswearing Arab nationalism, Saddam Hussein explicitly invoked an Islamic appeal. He and his supporters attempted to define the war as a war between civilizations. "It is not the world against Iraq," as Safar Al-Hawali, dean of Islamic Studies at the Umm Al-Qura University in Mecca, put it in a widely circulated tape. "It is the West against Islam." Ignoring the rivalry between Iran and Iraq, the chief Iranian religious leader, Ayatollah Ali Khamenei, called for a holy war against the

West: "The struggle against American aggression, greed, plans and policies will be counted as a jihad, and anybody who is killed on that path is a martyr." "This is a war," King Hussein of Jordan argued, "against all Arabs and all Muslims and not against Iraq alone."

The rallying of substantial sections of Arab elites and publics behind Saddam Hussein caused those Arab governments in the anti-Iraq coalition to moderate their activities and temper their public statements. Arab governments opposed or distanced themselves from subsequent Western efforts to apply pressure on Iraq, including enforcement of a no-fly zone in the summer of 1992 and the bombing of Iraq in January 1993. The Western-Soviet-Turkish-Arab anti-Iraq coalition of 1990 had by 1993 become a coalition of almost only the West and Kuwait against Iraq.

Muslims contrasted Western actions against Iraq with the West's failure to protect Bosnians against Serbs and to impose sanctions on Israel for violating U.N. resolutions. The West, they alleged, was using a double standard. A world of clashing civilizations, however, is inevitably a world of double standards: people apply one standard to their kin-countries and a different standard to others.

Second, the kin-country syndrome also appeared in conflicts in the former Soviet Union. Armenian military successes in 1992 and 1993 stimulated Turkey to become increasingly supportive of its religious, ethnic and linguistic brethren in Azerbaijan. "We have a Turkish nation feeling the same sentiments as the Azerbaijanis," said one Turkish official in 1992. "We are under pressure. Our newspapers are full of the photos of atrocities and are asking us if we are still serious about pursuing our neutral policy. Maybe we should show Armenia that there's a big Turkey in the region." President Turgut Özal agreed, remarking that Turkey should at least "scare the Armenians a little bit." Turkey, Özal threatened again in 1993, would "show its fangs." Turkish Air Force jets flew reconnaissance flights along the Armenian border; Turkey suspended food shipments and air flights to Armenia; and Turkey and Iran announced they would not accept dismemberment of Azerbaijan. In the last years of its existence, the Soviet government supported Azerbaijan because its government was dominated by former communists. With the end of the Soviet Union, however, political considerations gave way to religious ones. Russian troops fought on the side of the Armenians, and Azerbaijan accused the "Russian government of turning 180 degrees" toward support for Christian Armenia.

Third, with respect to the fighting in the former Yugoslavia, Western publics manifested sympathy and support for the Bosnian Muslims and the horrors they suffered at the hands of the Serbs. Relatively little concern was expressed, however, over Croatian attacks on Muslims and participation in the dismemberment of Bosnia-Herzegovina. In the early stages of the Yugoslav breakup, Germany, in an unusual display of diplomatic initiative and muscle, induced the other 11 members of the European Community to follow its lead in recognizing Slovenia and Croatia. As a result of the pope's determination to provide strong backing to the two Catholic countries, the Vatican extended recognition even before the Community did. The United States followed the European lead. Thus the leading actors in Western civilization rallied behind their coreligionists. Subsequently Croatia was reported to be receiving substantial quantities of arms from Central European and other Western countries. Boris Yeltsin's government, on the other hand, attempted to pursue a middle course that would be sympathetic to the Orthodox Serbs but not alienate Russia from the West. Russian conservative and nationalist groups, however, including many legislators, attacked the government for not being more forthcoming in its support for the Serbs. By early 1993 several hundred Russians apparently were serving with the Serbian forces, and reports circulated of Russian arms being supplied to Serbia.

Islamic governments and groups, on the other hand, castigated the West for not coming to the defense of the Bosnians. Iranian leaders urged Muslims from all countries to provide help to Bosnia; in violation of the U.N. arms embargo, Iran supplied weapons and men for the Bosnians; Iranian-supported Lebanese groups sent guerrillas to train and organize the Bosnian forces. In 1993 up to 4,000 Muslims from over two dozen Islamic countries were reported to be fighting in Bosnia. The governments of Saudi Arabia and other countries felt under increasing pressure from fundamentalist groups in their own societies to provide more vigorous support for the Bosnians. By the end of 1992, Saudi Arabia had reportedly supplied substantial funding for weapons and supplies for the Bosnians, which significantly increased their military capabilities vis-à-vis the Serbs.

In the 1930s the Spanish Civil War provoked intervention from countries that politically were fascist, communist and democratic. In the 1990s the Yugoslav conflict is provoking intervention from countries that are Muslim, Orthodox and Western Christian. The parallel has not gone unnoticed. "The war in Bosnia-Herzegovina has become the emotional equivalent of the fight against fascism in the Spanish Civil War," one Saudi editor observed. "Those who died there are regarded as martyrs who tried to save their fellow Muslims."

Conflicts and violence will also occur between states and groups within the same civilization. Such conflicts, however, are likely to be less intense and less likely to expand than conflicts between civilizations. Common membership in a civilization reduces the probability of violence in situations where it might otherwise occur. In 1991 and 1992 many people were alarmed by the possibility of violent conflict between Russia and Ukraine over territory, particularly Crimea, the Black Sea fleet, nuclear weapons and economic issues. If civilization is what counts, however, the likelihood of violence between Ukrainians and Russians should be low. They are two Slavic, primarily Orthodox peoples who have had close relationships with each other for centuries. As of early 1993, despite all the reasons for conflict, the leaders of the two countries were effectively negotiating and defusing the issues between the two countries. While there has been serious fighting between Muslims and Christians elsewhere in the former Soviet Union and much tension and some fighting between Western and Orthodox Christians in the Baltic states, there has been virtually no violence between Russians and Ukrainians.

Civilization rallying to date has been limited, but it has been growing, and it clearly has the potential to spread much further. As the conflicts in the Persian Gulf, the Caucasus and Bosnia continued, the positions of nations and the cleavages between them increasingly were along civilizational lines. Populist politicians, religious leaders and the media have found it a potent means of arousing mass support and of pressuring hesitant governments. In the coming years, the local conflicts most likely to escalate into major wars will be those, as in Bosnia and the Caucasus, along the fault lines between civilizations. The next world war, if there is one, will be a war between civilizations.

THE WEST VERSUS THE REST

The West is now at an extraordinary peak of power in relation to other civilizations. Its superpower opponent has disappeared from the map. Military conflict among Western states is unthinkable, and Western military power is unrivaled. Apart from Japan, the West faces no economic challenge. It dominates international political and security institutions and with Japan international economic institutions. Global political and security issues are effectively settled by a directorate of the United States, Britain and France, world economic issues by a directorate of the United States, Germany and Japan, all of which maintain extraordinarily close relations with each other to the exclusion of lesser and largely non-Western countries. Decisions made at the U.N. Security Council or in the International Monetary Fund that reflect the interests of the West are presented to the world as reflecting the desires of the world community. The very phrase "the world community" has become the euphemistic collective noun (replacing "the Free World") to give global legitimacy to actions reflecting the interests of the United States and other Western powers.[4] Through the IMF and other international economic institutions, the West promotes its economic interests and imposes on other nations the economic policies it thinks appropriate. In any poll of non-Western peoples, the IMF undoubtedly would win the support of finance ministers and a few others, but get an overwhelmingly unfavorable rating from just about everyone else, who would agree with Georgy Arbatov's characterization of IMF officials as "neo-Bolsheviks who love expropriating other people's money, imposing undemocratic and alien rules of economic and political conduct and stifling economic freedom."

Western domination of the U.N. Security Council and its decisions, tempered only by occasional abstention by China, produced U.N. legitimation of the West's use of force to drive Iraq out of Kuwait and its elimination of Iraq's sophisticated weapons and capacity to produce such weapons. It also produced the quite unprecedented action by the United States, Britain and France in getting the Security Council to demand that Libya hand over the Pan Am 103 bombing suspects and then to impose sanctions when Libya refused. After defeating the largest Arab army, the West did not hesitate to throw its weight around in the Arab world. The West in effect is using international institutions, military power and economic resources to run the world in ways that will maintain Western predominance, protect Western interests and promote Western political and economic values.

That at least is the way in which non-Westerners see the new world, and there is a significant element of truth in their view. Differences in power and struggles for military, economic and institutional power are thus one source of conflict between the West and other civilizations. Differences in culture, that is basic values and beliefs, are a second source of conflict. V. S. Naipaul has argued that Western civilization is the "universal civilization" that "fits all men." At a superficial level much of Western culture has

---

[4] Almost invariably Western leaders claim they are acting on behalf of "the world community." One minor lapse occurred during the run-up to the Gulf War. In an interview on "Good Morning America," Dec. 21, 1990, British Prime Minister John Major referred to the actions "the West" was taking against Saddam Hussein. He quickly corrected himself and subsequently referred to "the world community." He was, however, right when he erred.

indeed permeated the rest of the world. At a more basic level, however, Western concepts differ fundamentally from those prevalent in other civilizations. Western ideas of
individualism, liberalism, constitutionalism, human rights, equality, liberty, the rule of
law, democracy, free markets, the separation of church and state, often have little resonance in Islamic, Confucian, Japanese, Hindu, Buddhist or Orthodox cultures. Western
efforts to propagate such ideas produce instead a reaction against "human rights imperialism" and a reaffirmation of indigenous values, as can be seen in the support for religious fundamentalism by the younger generation in non-Western cultures. The very notion that there could be a "universal civilization" is a Western idea, directly at odds with
the particularism of most Asian societies and their emphasis on what distinguishes one
people from another. Indeed, the author of a review of 100 comparative studies of values in different societies concluded that "the values that are most important in the West
are least important worldwide."[5] In the political realm, of course, these differences are
most manifest in the efforts of the United States and other Western powers to induce
other peoples to adopt Western ideas concerning democracy and human rights. Modern
democratic government originated in the West. When it has developed in non-Western
societies it has usually been the product of Western colonialism or imposition.

The central axis of world politics in the future is likely to be, in Kishore
Mahbubani's phrase, the conflict between "the West and the Rest" and the responses of
non-Western civilizations to Western power and values.[6] Those responses generally
take one or a combination of three forms. At one extreme, non-Western states can, like
Burma and North Korea, attempt to pursue a course of isolation, to insulate their societies from penetration or "corruption" by the West, and, in effect, to opt out of participation in the Western-dominated global community. The costs of this course, however,
are high, and few states have pursued it exclusively. A second alternative, the equivalent
of "band-wagoning" in international relations theory, is to attempt to join the West and
accept its values and institutions. The third alternative is to attempt to "balance" the
West by developing economic and military power and cooperating with other non-
Western societies against the West, while preserving indigenous values and institutions;
in short, to modernize but not to Westernize.

THE TORN COUNTRIES

In the future, as people differentiate themselves by civilization, countries with large
numbers of peoples of different civilizations, such as the Soviet Union and Yugoslavia,
are candidates for dismemberment. Some other countries have a fair degree of cultural
homogeneity but are divided over whether their society belongs to one civilization or
another. These are torn countries. Their leaders typically wish to pursue a bandwago-
ning strategy and to make their countries members of the West, but the history, culture
and traditions of their countries are non-Western. The most obvious and prototypical
torn country is Turkey. The late twentieth-century leaders of Turkey have followed in
the Attatürk tradition and defined Turkey as a modern, secular, Western nation state.

---

[5]Harry C. Triandis, *The New York Times,* Dec. 25, 1990, p. 41, and "Cross-Cultural Studies of
Individualism and Collectivism," Nebraska Symposium on Motivation, vol. 37, 1989, pp. 41–133.
[6]Kishore Mahbubani, "The West and the Rest," *The National Interest,* summer 1992, pp. 3–13.

They allied Turkey with the West in NATO and in the Gulf War; they applied for membership in the European Community. At the same time, however, elements in Turkish society have supported an Islamic revival and have argued that Turkey is basically a Middle Eastern Muslim society. In addition, while the elite of Turkey has defined Turkey as a Western society, the elite of the West refuses to accept Turkey as such. Turkey will not become a member of the European Community, and the real reason, as President Özal said, "is that we are Muslim and they are Christian and they don't say that." Having rejected Mecca, and then being rejected by Brussels, where does Turkey look? Tashkent may be the answer. The end of the Soviet Union gives Turkey the opportunity to become the leader of a revived Turkic civilization involving seven countries from the borders of Greece to those of China. Encouraged by the West, Turkey is making strenuous efforts to carve out this new identity for itself.

During the past decade Mexico has assumed a position somewhat similar to that of Turkey. Just as Turkey abandoned its historic opposition to Europe and attempted to join Europe, Mexico has stopped defining itself by its opposition to the United States and is instead attempting to imitate the United States and to join it in the North American Free Trade Area. Mexican leaders are engaged in the great task of redefining Mexican identity and have introduced fundamental economic reforms that eventually will lead to fundamental political change. In 1991 a top adviser to President Carlos Salinas de Gortari described at length to me all the changes the Salinas government was making. When he finished, I remarked: "That's most impressive. It seems to me that basically you want to change Mexico from a Latin American country into a North American country." He looked at me with surprise and exclaimed: "Exactly! That's precisely what we are trying to do, but of course we could never say so publicly." As his remark indicates, in Mexico as in Turkey, significant elements in society resist the redefinition of their country's identity. In Turkey, European-oriented leaders have to make gestures to Islam (Özal's pilgrimage to Mecca); so also Mexico's North American-oriented leaders have to make gestures to those who hold Mexico to be a Latin American country (Salinas' Ibero-American Guadalajara summit).

Historically Turkey has been the most profoundly torn country. For the United States, Mexico is the most immediate torn country. Globally the most important torn country is Russia. The question of whether Russia is part of the West or the leader of a distinct Slavic-Orthodox civilization has been a recurring one in Russian history. That issue was obscured by the communist victory in Russia, which imported a Western ideology, adapted it to Russian conditions and then challenged the West in the name of that ideology. The dominance of communism shut off the historic debate over Westernization versus Russification. With communism discredited Russians once again face that question.

President Yeltsin is adopting Western principles and goals and seeking to make Russia a "normal" country and a part of the West. Yet both the Russian elite and the Russian public are divided on this issue. Among the more moderate dissenters, Sergei Stankevich argues that Russia should reject the "Atlanticist" course, which would lead it "to become European, to become a part of the world economy in rapid and organized fashion, to become the eighth member of the Seven, and to put particular emphasis on Germany and the United States as the two dominant members of the Atlantic alliance." While also rejecting an exclusively Eurasian policy, Stankevich nonetheless argues that Russia should give priority to the protection of Russians in other countries, emphasize its Turkic and Muslim connections, and promote "an appreciable redistribution of our resources, our options, our ties, and our interests in favor of Asia, of the eastern direction." People of this persuasion criticize Yeltsin for subordinating Russia's interests to those of the West, for reducing Russian military strength, for failing to support traditional friends such as Serbia, and for pushing economic and political reform in ways injurious to the Russian people. Indicative of this trend is the new popularity of the ideas of Petr Savitsky, who in the 1920s argued that Russia was a unique Eurasian civilization.[7] More extreme dissidents voice much more blatantly nationalist, anti-Western and anti-Semitic views, and urge Russia to redevelop its military strength and to establish closer ties with China and Muslim countries. The people of Russia are as divided as the elite. An opinion survey in European Russia in the spring of 1992 revealed that 40 percent of the public had positive attitudes toward the West and 36 percent had negative attitudes. As it has been for much of its history, Russia in the early 1990s is truly a torn country.

To redefine its civilization identity, a torn country must meet three requirements. First, its political and economic elite has to be generally supportive of and enthusiastic about this move. Second, its public has to be willing to acquiesce in the redefinition. Third, the dominant groups in the recipient civilization have to be willing to embrace the convert. All three requirements in large part exist with respect to Mexico. The first two in large part exist with respect to Turkey. It is not clear that any of them exist with respect to Russia's joining the West. The conflict between liberal democracy and Marxism-Leninism was between ideologies which, despite their major differences, ostensibly shared ultimate goals of freedom, equality and prosperity. A traditional, authoritarian, nationalist Russia could have quite different goals. A Western democrat could carry on an intellectual debate with a Soviet Marxist. It would be virtually impossible for him to do that with a Russian traditionalist. If, as the Russians stop behaving like Marxists, they reject liberal democracy and begin behaving like Russians but not like Westerners, the relations between Russia and the West could again become distant and conflictual.[8]

THE CONFUCIAN-ISLAMIC CONNECTION

The obstacles to non-Western countries joining the West vary considerably. They are least for Latin American and East European countries. They are greater for the Orthodox countries of the former Soviet Union. They are still greater for Muslim,

---

[7]Sergei Stankevich, "Russia in Search of Itself," *The National Interest,* summer 1992, pp. 47–51; Daniel Schneider, "A Russian Movement Rejects Western Tilt," *Christian Science Monitor,* Feb. 5, 1993, pp. 5–7.

[8]Owen Harries has pointed out that Australia is trying (unwisely in his view) to become a torn country in reverse. Although it has been a full member not only of the West but also of the ABCA military and intelligence core of the West, its current leaders are in effect proposing that it defect from the West, redefine itself as an Asian country and cultivate close ties with its neighbors. Australia's future, they argue, is with the dynamic economies of East Asia. But, as I have suggested, close economic cooperation normally requires a common cultural base. In addition, none of the three conditions necessary for a torn country to join another civilization is likely to exist in Australia's case.

Confucian, Hindu and Buddhist societies. Japan has established a unique position for itself as an associate member of the West: it is in the West in some respects but clearly not of the West in important dimensions. Those countries that for reason of culture and power do not wish to, or cannot, join the West compete with the West by developing their own economic, military and political power. They do this by promoting their internal development and by cooperating with other non-Western countries. The most prominent form of this cooperation is the Confucian-Islamic connection that has emerged to challenge Western interests, values and power.

Almost without exception, Western countries are reducing their military power; under Yeltsin's leadership so also is Russia. China, North Korea and several Middle Eastern states, however, are significantly expanding their military capabilities. They are doing this by the import of arms from Western and non-Western sources and by the development of indigenous arms industries. One result is the emergence of what Charles Krauthammer has called "Weapon States," and the Weapon States are not Western states. Another result is the redefinition of arms control, which is a Western concept and a Western goal. During the Cold War the primary purpose of arms control was to establish a stable military balance between the United States and its allies and the Soviet Union and its allies. In the post-Cold War world the primary objective of arms control is to prevent the development by non-Western societies of military capabilities that could threaten Western interests. The West attempts to do this through international agreements, economic pressure and controls on the transfer of arms and weapons technologies.

The conflict between the West and the Confucian-Islamic states focuses largely, although not exclusively, on nuclear, chemical and biological weapons, ballistic missiles and other sophisticated means for delivering them, and the guidance, intelligence and other electronic capabilities for achieving that goal. The West promotes nonproliferation as a universal norm and nonproliferation treaties and inspections as means of realizing that norm. It also threatens a variety of sanctions against those who promote the spread of sophisticated weapons and proposes some benefits for those who do not. The attention of the West focuses, naturally, on nations that are actually or potentially hostile to the West.

The non-Western nations, on the other hand, assert their right to acquire and to deploy whatever weapons they think necessary for their security. They also have absorbed, to the full, the truth of the response of the Indian defense minister when asked what lesson he learned from the Gulf War: "Don't fight the United States unless you have nuclear weapons." Nuclear weapons, chemical weapons and missiles are viewed, probably erroneously, as the potential equalizer of superior Western conventional power. China, of course, already has nuclear weapons; Pakistan and India have the capability to deploy them. North Korea, Iran, Iraq, Libya and Algeria appear to be attempting to acquire them. A top Iranian official has declared that all Muslim states should acquire nuclear weapons, and in 1988 the president of Iran reportedly issued a directive calling for development of "offensive and defensive chemical, biological and radiological weapons."

Centrally important to the development of counter-West military capabilities is the sustained expansion of China's military power and its means to create military power. Buoyed by spectacular economic development, China is rapidly increasing its military spending and vigorously moving forward with the modernization of its armed forces. It is purchasing weapons from the former Soviet states; it is developing long-range missiles; in 1992 it tested a one-megaton nuclear device. It is developing power-projection capabilities, acquiring aerial refueling technology, and trying to purchase an aircraft carrier. Its military buildup and assertion of sovereignty over the South China Sea are provoking a multilateral regional arms race in East Asia. China is also a major exporter of arms and weapons technology. It has exported materials to Libya and Iraq that could be used to manufacture nuclear weapons and nerve gas. It has helped Algeria build a reactor suitable for nuclear weapons research and production. China has sold to Iran nuclear technology that American officials believe could only be used to create weapons and apparently has shipped components of 300-mile-range missiles to Pakistan. North Korea has had a nuclear weapons program under way for some while and has sold advanced missiles and missile technology to Syria and Iran. The flow of weapons and weapons technology is generally from East Asia to the Middle East. There is, however, some movement in the reverse direction; China has received Stinger missiles from Pakistan.

A Confucian-Islamic military connection has thus come into being, designed to promote acquisition by its members of the weapons and weapons technologies needed to counter the military power of the West. It may or may not last. At present, however, it is, as Dave McCurdy has said, "a renegades' mutual support pact, run by the proliferators and their backers." A new form of arms competition is thus occurring between Islamic-Confucian states and the West. In an old-fashioned arms race, each side developed its own arms to balance or to achieve superiority against the other side. In this new form of arms competition, one side is developing its arms and the other side is attempting not to balance but to limit and prevent that arms build-up while at the same time reducing its own military capabilities.

IMPLICATIONS FOR THE WEST

This article does not argue that civilization identities will replace all other identities, that nation states will disappear, that each civilization will become a single coherent political entity, that groups within a civilization will not conflict with and even fight each other. This paper does set forth the hypotheses that differences between civilizations are real and important; civilization-consciousness is increasing; conflict between civilizations will supplant ideological and other forms of conflict as the dominant global form of conflict; international relations, historically a game played out within Western civilization, will increasingly be de-Westernized and become a game in which non-Western civilizations are actors and not simply objects; successful political, security and economic international institutions are more likely to develop within civilizations than across civilizations; conflicts between groups in different civilizations will be more frequent, more sustained and more violent than conflicts between groups in the same civilization; violent conflicts between groups in different civilizations are the most likely and most dangerous source of escalation that could lead to global wars; the paramount axis of world politics will be the relations between "the West and the Rest"; the elites in some torn non-Western countries will try to make their countries part of the West, but in most cases face major obstacles to accomplishing this; a central focus of conflict for the immediate future will be between the West and several Islamic-Confucian states.

This is not to advocate the desirability of conflicts between civilizations. It is to set forth descriptive hypotheses as to what the future may be like. If these are plausible hypotheses, however, it is necessary to consider their implications for Western policy. These implications should be divided between short-term advantage and long-term accommodation. In the short term it is clearly in the interest of the West to promote greater cooperation and unity within its own civilization, particularly between its European and North American components; to incorporate into the West societies in Eastern Europe and Latin America whose cultures are close to those of the West; to promote and maintain cooperative relations with Russia and Japan; to prevent escalation of local inter-civilization conflicts into major inter-civilization wars; to limit the expansion of the military strength of Confucian and Islamic states; to moderate the reduction of Western military capabilities and maintain military superiority in East and Southwest Asia; to exploit differences and conflicts among Confucian and Islamic states; to support in other civilizations groups sympathetic to Western values and interests; to strengthen international institutions that reflect and legitimate Western interests and values and to promote the involvement of non-Western states in those institutions.

In the longer term other measures would be called for. Western civilization is both Western and modern. Non-Western civilizations have attempted to become modern without becoming Western. To date only Japan has fully succeeded in this quest. Non-Western civilizations will continue to attempt to acquire the wealth, technology, skills, machines and weapons that are part of being modern. They will also attempt to reconcile this modernity with their traditional culture and values. Their economic and military strength relative to the West will increase. Hence the West will increasingly have to accommodate these non-Western modern civilizations whose power approaches that of the West but whose values and interests differ significantly from those of the West. This will require the West to maintain the economic and military power necessary to protect its interests in relation to these civilizations. It will also, however, require the West to develop a more profound understanding of the basic religious and philosophical assumptions underlying other civilizations and the ways in which people in those civilizations see their interests. It will require an effort to identify elements of commonality between Western and other civilizations. For the relevant future, there will be no universal civilization, but instead a world of different civilizations, each of which will have to learn to coexist with the others.

PART II

INTERNATIONAL REALISM: ANARCHY AND POWER

The appeal of different schools of thought in international relations tends to vary with developments in the real world. Perhaps because the twentieth century was one of unprecedented catastrophe, the dominant tradition has been what is known colloquially as "power politics." In academic circles this family of ideas is known as "realism." The main themes in this school of thought are that in order to survive, states are driven to seek power, that moral or legal principles that may govern relations among citizens within states cannot control the relations among states, and that wars occur because there is no sovereign in the international system to settle disputes peacefully and enforce judgments. States have no one but themselves to rely on for protection, or to obtain what they believe they are entitled to by right.

Thucydides' *Peloponnesian War,* the history of the conflict between Athens and Sparta two and a half millennia ago, is the classic statement of these ideas. The selection included here—the Melian Dialogue—is perhaps the most extreme and frank discussion of power politics, unclouded by diplomatic niceties, ever recorded. Taken alone, the dialogue can appear a caricature, so readers are encouraged to read more of the original work, which is rich in commentary on various aspects of balance of power politics, strategy, and the role of ideology and domestic conflict in international relations.[1]

The tradition of realism can be traced in various forms through Machiavelli, Hobbes, the German schools of *Realpolitik* and *Machtpolitik,* to E.H. Carr, Reinhold Niebuhr, Hans Morgenthau and others in the mid-twentieth century. The selections from Machiavelli's *The Prince* and Hobbes's *Leviathan* that follow capsulize their views of the roots of political ruthlessness, the similarity of diplomacy and domestic competition to the state of nature, and the need for political leaders who seek to secure their regimes to do things in public life that are condemned in traditional morality.

---

[1]Thucydides also presents examples that differ markedly from the Melian dialogue, such as the Mytilene debate. See Michael Walzer's comparison in *Just and Unjust Wars* (New York: Basic Books, 1977), pp. 5–11.

Students not steeped in political philosophy should avoid the popular misinterpretation of these thinkers as amoral. Rather they should be understood as moral relativists, concerned with the need to secure the prerequisite (power) for achievement of anything moral, a need which may require behavior inconsistent with absolute norms or religious ethics. As Machiavelli argues in the excerpt below, a prince must "not deviate from what is good, if possible, but be able to do evil if constrained."

In the past century, Morgenthau's *Politics Among Nations*[2] was the most prominent textbook of realism in the United States. Carr's *Twenty Years' Crisis,* on the other hand, is distinguished by its pungency, which helps to convey the essence of realism in brief selections. Before pigeon-holing Carr as a strident realist, however, note his eloquent discussion of the serious deficiencies of the theory in the middle of the excerpts that follow.

The most prominent recent writings in the realist school have been dubbed "neo-" or "structural" realism to distinguish their more rigorously scientific formulation of the theory. Neorealists focus less on the questions of human motivation or the nature of political regimes than on the security incentives posed by the structure of the international system. The selection by Kenneth Waltz, the dean of neorealism, is close to a summary of his masterwork, *Theory of International Politics.*[3] Mearsheimer's hyper-realist argument in favor of the Cold War, in Part I above, derives directly from Waltz's reasoning about the stability of a bipolar world (discussed in this selection), and the pacifying effect of nuclear weapons (discussed in the selection by Waltz in Part VII).

The favorable view of bipolarity among neorealists, however, contradicts traditional balance of power theory. In considering whether a world of only two major powers, as opposed to a world of many, should be less likely to lead to war, compare Waltz and Mearsheimer with Thucydides, Blainey, and Gilpin. The competition between Athens and Sparta, for example, unlike that between the United States and the Soviet Union, ended in disaster. Where Waltz sees bipolarity as imposing clarity and stability on the competition, others see it as inherently unstable, a delicate balance between contenders ever striving for primacy. Robert Gilpin sees history as a succession of struggles for hegemony between declining and rising powers, with the struggles normally resolved by a major war. Geoffrey Blainey considers a hierarchical system, in which differences in power are clear, to be most stable. When there is no doubt about who would prevail if disagreements were to lead to combat, there is little chance that the strong will need to resort to combat or that the weak will dare. Blainey sees a world of rough parity, in contrast, as unstable, because it is easier for states to miscalculate the balance of power and their chances of being able to impose their will by either initiating or resisting the use of force. This view is consistent with Gilpin's, since the challenger in a hegemonic transition is usually one whose power is approaching that of the leading state.

---

[2]Hans Morgenthau, *Politics Among Nations,* fifth edition (New York: Knopf, 1973).
[3]Kenneth N. Waltz, *Theory of International Politics* (Reading, Mass.: Addison-Wesley, 1979). See also Waltz, *Man, the State, and War* (New York: Columbia University Press, 1959). For a large collection of recent views on realism see the two special issues in volume 5, numbers 2 and 3 of *Security Studies,* edited by Benjamin Frankel: *Roots of Realism* (winter 1995) and *Realism: Restatements and Renewal* (spring 1996).

How much do the structure of the international balance of power and competition for primacy determine the actions of states? We might ask how one could have predicted the end of the Cold War from realist theories. Was the Soviet Union's voluntary surrender of control over Eastern Europe in 1989, indeed its entire withdrawal from the power struggle with the West, consistent with such explanations of state behavior? Realists understand that statesmen do not always act in accord with realist norms. But the enormity of the Gorbachev revolution is an uncomfortable exception for the theory to have to bear. Nevertheless, realist scholars offer arguments for why the end of the Cold War should confirm their theories rather than revise them.[4]

If readers are not fully convinced that realist theories adequately explain the end of the Cold War they might consider another possibility. The greatest irony might be that the end came from the adoption of liberal ideas about international cooperation by the leadership of the Soviet Union, the superpower that had so tenaciously opposed western liberalism as a model for the world.[5] The readings in Part III will present some tenets of the liberal tradition that offer a very different view of the possibilities of peace from the one presented in this section.

—RKB

---

[4]Kenneth N. Waltz, "Structural Realism After the Cold War," *International Security* 25, no. 1 (summer 2000); William C. Wohlforth, "Realism and the End of the Cold War," *International Security* 19, no. 3 (winter 1994/95).

[5]A further irony would be that if the liberal explanation for Soviet foreign policy at the end of the Cold War is convincing, the results in terms of international politics are still consistent with realism. The Gorbachev revolution contributed to the destruction of the Soviet Union, even if it did not fully cause it. It was not necessarily inevitable that a more ruthless Soviet leadership would have failed to preserve the empire, at least into the twenty-first century. In Waltz's terms, the Soviet Union certainly did "fall by the wayside."

THE MELIAN DIALOGUE

Thucydides

The Melians are a colony of Lacedaemon [Sparta] that would not submit to the Athenians like the other islanders, and at first remained neutral and took no part in the struggle, but afterwards upon the Athenians using violence and plundering their territory, assumed an attitude of open hostility. Cleomedes, son of Lycomedes, and Tisias, son of Tisimachus, the generals, encamping in their territory with the above armament, before doing any harm to their land, sent envoys to negotiate. These the Melians did not bring before the people, but bade them state the object of their mission to the magistrates and the few; upon which the Athenian envoys spoke as follows:—

Athenians: 'Since the negotiations are not to go on before the people, in order that we may not be able to speak straight on without interruption, and deceive the ears of the multitude by seductive arguments which would pass without refutation (for we know that this is the meaning of our being brought before the few), what if you who sit there were to pursue a method more cautious still! Make no set speech yourselves, but take us up at whatever you do not like, and settle that before going any farther. And first tell us if this proposition of ours suits you.'

The Melian commissioners answered:—

Melians: 'To the fairness of quietly instructing each other as you propose there is nothing to object; but your military preparations are too far advanced to agree with what you say, as we see you are come to be judges in your own cause, and that all we can reasonably expect from this negotiation is war, if we prove to have right on our side and refuse to submit, and in the contrary case, slavery.'

Athenians: 'If you have met to reason about presentiments of the future, or for anything else than to consult for the safety of your state upon the facts that you see before you, we will give over; otherwise we will go on.'

Melians: 'It is natural and excusable for men in our position to turn more ways than one both in thought and utterance. However, the question in this conference is, as you say, the safety of our country; and the discussion, if you please, can proceed in the way which you propose.'

Athenians: 'For ourselves, we shall not trouble you with specious pretences— either of how we have a right to our empire because we overthrew the Mede, or are now attacking you because of wrong that you have done us—and make a long speech which would not be believed; and in return we hope that you, instead of thinking to influence

---

Thucydides, *The Peloponnesian War,* Richard Crawley, trans. (New York: The Modern Library, 1934), Book V.

us by saying that you did not join the Lacedaemonians, although their colonists, or that you have done us no wrong, will aim at what is feasible, holding in view the real sentiments of us both; since you know as well as we do that right, as the world goes, is only in question between equals in power, while the strong do what they can and the weak suffer what they must.'

Melians: 'As we think, at any rate, it is expedient—we speak as we are obliged, since you enjoin us to let right alone and talk only of interest—that you should not destroy what is our common protection, the privilege of being allowed in danger to invoke what is fair and right, and even to profit by arguments not strictly valid if they can be got to pass current. And you are as much interested in this as any, as your fall would be a signal for the heaviest vengeance and an example for the world to meditate upon.'

Athenians: 'The end of our empire, if end it should, does not frighten us: a rival empire like Lacedaemon, even if Lacedaemon was our real antagonist, is not so terrible to the vanquished as subjects who by themselves attack and overpower their rulers. This, however, is a risk that we are content to take. We will now proceed to show you that we are come here in the interest of our empire, and that we shall say what we are now going to say, for the preservation of your country; as we would fain exercise that empire over you without trouble, and see you preserved for the good of us both.'

Melians: 'And how, pray, could it turn out as good for us to serve as for you to rule?'

Athenians: 'Because you would have the advantage of submitting before suffering the worst, and we should gain by not destroying you.'

Melians: 'So that you would not consent to our being neutral, friends instead of enemies, but allies of neither side.'

Athenians: 'No; for your hostility cannot so much hurt us as your friendship will be an argument to our subjects of our weakness, and your enmity of our power.'

Melians: 'Is that your subjects' idea of equity, to put those who have nothing to do with you in the same category with peoples that are most of them your own colonists, and some conquered rebels?'

Athenians: 'As far as right goes they think one has as much of it as the other, and that if any maintain their independence it is because they are strong, and that if we do not molest them it is because we are afraid; so that besides extending our empire we should gain in security by your subjection; the fact that you are islanders and weaker than others rendering it all the more important that you should not succeed in baffling the masters of the sea.'

Melians: 'But do you consider that there is no security in the policy which we indicate? For here again if you debar us from talking about justice and invite us to obey your interest, we also must explain ours, and try to persuade you, if the two happen to coincide. How can you avoid making enemies of all existing neutrals who shall look at our case and conclude from it that one day or another you will attack them? And what is this but to make greater the enemies that you have already, and to force others to become so who would otherwise have never thought of it?'

Athenians: 'Why, the fact is that continentals generally give us but little alarm; the liberty which they enjoy will long prevent their taking precautions against us; it is rather islanders like yourselves, outside our empire, and subjects smarting under the yoke, who would be the most likely to take a rash step and lead themselves and us into obvious danger.'

Melians: 'Well then, if you risk so much to retain your empire, and your subjects to get rid of it, it were surely great baseness and cowardice in us who are still free not to try everything that can be tried, before submitting to your yoke.'

Athenians: 'Not if you are well advised, the contest not being an equal one, with honour as the prize and shame as the penalty, but a question of self-preservation and of not resisting those who are far stronger than you are.'

Melians: 'But we know that the fortune of war is sometimes more impartial than the disproportion of numbers might lead one to suppose; to submit is to give ourselves over to despair, while action still preserves for us a hope that we may stand erect.'

Athenians: 'Hope, danger's comforter, may be indulged in by those who have abundant resources, if not without loss at all events without ruin; but its nature is to be extravagant, and those who go so far as to put their all upon the venture see it in its true colours only when they are ruined; but so long as the discovery would enable them to guard against it, it is never found wanting. Let not this be the case with you, who are weak and hang on a single turn of the scale; nor be like the vulgar, who, abandoning such security as human means may still afford, when visible hopes fail them in extremity, turn to invisible, to prophecies and oracles, and other such inventions that delude men with hopes to their destruction.'

Melians: 'You may be sure that we are as well aware as you of the difficulty of contending against your power and fortune, unless the terms be equal. But we trust that the gods may grant us fortune as good as yours, since we are just men fighting against unjust, and that what we want in power will be made up by the alliance of the Lacedaemonians, who are bound if only for very shame, to come to the aid of their kindred. Our confidence, therefore, after all is not so utterly irrational.'

Athenians: 'When you speak of the favour of the gods, we may as fairly hope for that as yourselves; neither our pretensions nor our conduct being in any way contrary to what men believe of the gods, or practise among themselves. Of the gods we believe, and of men we know, that by a necessary law of their nature they rule wherever they can. And it is not as if we were the first to make this law, or to act upon it when made: we found it existing before us, and shall leave it to exist for ever after us; all we do is to make use of it, knowing that you and everybody else, having the same power as we have, would do the same as we do. Thus, as far as the gods are concerned, we have no fear and no reason to fear that we shall be at a disadvantage. But when we come to your notion about the Lacedaemonians, which leads you to believe that shame will make them help you, here we bless your simplicity but do not envy your folly. The Lacedaemonians, when their own interests of their country's laws are in question, are the worthiest men alive; of their conduct towards others much might be said, but no clearer idea of it could be given than by shortly saying that of all the men we know they are most conspicuous in considering what is agreeable honourable, and what is expedient just. Such a way of thinking does not promise much for the safety which you now unreasonably count upon.'

Melians: 'But it is for this very reason that we now trust to their respect for expediency to prevent them from betraying the Melians, their colonists, and thereby losing the confidence of their friends in Hellas and helping their enemies.'

Athenians: 'Then you do not adopt the view that expediency goes with security, while justice and honour cannot be followed without danger; and danger the Lacedaemonians generally court as little as possible.'

Melians: 'But we believe that they would be more likely to face even danger for our sake, and with more confidence than for others, as our nearness to Peloponnese makes it easier for them to act, and our common blood insures our fidelity.'

Athenians: 'Yes, but what an intending ally trusts to, is not the goodwill of those who ask his aid, but a decided superiority of power for action; and the Lacedaemonians look to this even more than others. At least, such is their distrust of their home resources that it is only with numerous allies that they attack a neighbour; now is it likely that while we are masters of the sea they will cross over to an island?'

Melians: 'But they would have others to send. The Cretan sea is a wide one, and it is more difficult for those who command it to intercept others, than for those who wish to elude them to do so safely. And should the Lacedaemonians miscarry in this, they would fall upon your land, and upon those left of your allies whom Brasidas did not reach; and instead of places which are not yours, you will have to fight for your own country and your own confederacy.'

Athenians: 'Some diversion of the kind you speak of you may one day experience, only to learn, as others have done, that the Athenians never once yet withdrew from a siege for fear of any. But we are struck by the fact, that after saying you would consult for the safety of your country, in all this discussion you have mentioned nothing which men might trust in and think to be saved by. Your strongest arguments depend upon hope and the future, and your actual resources are too scanty, as compared with those arrayed against you, for you to come out victorious. You will therefore show great blindness of judgment, unless, after allowing us to retire, you can find some counsel more prudent than this. You will surely not be caught by that idea of disgrace, which in dangers that are disgraceful, and at the same time too plain to be mistaken, proves so fatal to mankind; since in too many cases the very men that have their eyes perfectly open to what they are rushing into, let the thing called disgrace, by the mere influence of a seductive name, lead them on to a point at which they become so enslaved by the phrase as in fact to fall wilfully into hopeless disaster, and incur disgrace more disgraceful as the companion of error, than when it comes as the result of misfortune. This, if you are well advised, you will guard against; and you will not think it dishonourable to submit to the greatest city in Hellas, when it makes you the moderate offer of becoming its tributary ally, without ceasing to enjoy the country that belongs to you; nor when you have the choice given you between war and security, will you be so blinded as to choose the worse. And it is certain that those who do not yield to their equals, who keep terms with their superiors, and are moderate towards their inferiors, on the whole succeed best. Think over the matter, therefore, after our withdrawal, and reflect once and again that it is for your country that you are consulting, that you have not more than one, and that upon this one deliberation depends its prosperity or ruin.'

The Athenians now withdrew from the conference; and the Melians, left to themselves, came to a decision corresponding with what they had maintained in the discussion, and answered, 'Our resolution, Athenians, is the same as it was at first. We will not in a moment deprive of freedom a city that has been inhabited these seven hundred years; but we put our trust in the fortune by which the gods have preserved it until now, and in the help of men, that is, of the Lacedaemonians; and so we will try and save ourselves.

Meanwhile we invite you to allow us to be friends to you and foes to neither party, and to retire from our country after making such a treaty as shall seem fit to us both.'

Such was the answer of the Melians. The Athenians now departing from the conference said, 'Well, you alone, as it seems to us, judging from these resolutions, regard what is future as more certain than what is before your eyes, and what is out of sight, in your eagerness, as already coming to pass; and as you have staked most on, and trusted most in, the Lacedaemonians, your fortune, and your hopes, so will you be most completely deceived.'

The Athenian envoys now returned to the army; and the Melians showing no signs of yielding, the generals at once betook themselves to hostilities, and drew a line of circumvallation round the Melians, dividing the work among the different states. Subsequently the Athenians returned with most of their army, leaving behind them a certain number of their own citizens and of the allies to keep guard by land and sea. The force thus left stayed on and besieged the place. . . .

Summer was now over. The next winter the Lacedaemonians intended to invade the Argive territory, but arriving at the frontier found the sacrifices for crossing unfavourable, and went back again. This intention of theirs gave the Argives suspicions of certain of their fellow-citizens, some of whom they arrested; others, however, escaped them. About the same time the Melians again took another part of the Athenian lines which were but feebly garrisoned. Reinforcements afterwards arriving from Athens in consequence, under the command of Philocrates, son of Demeas, the siege was now pressed vigorously; and some treachery taking place inside, the Melians surrendered at discretion to the Athenians, who put to death all the grown men whom they took, and sold the women and children for slaves, and subsequently sent out five hundred colonists and inhabited the place themselves.

DOING EVIL IN ORDER TO DO GOOD

Niccolò Machiavelli

OF THE THINGS FOR WHICH MEN, AND ESPECIALLY PRINCES, ARE PRAISED OR BLAMED

It now remains to be seen what are the methods and rules for a prince as regards his subjects and friends. And as I know that many have written of this, I fear that my writing about it may be deemed presumptuous, differing as I do, especially in this matter, from the opinions of others. But my intention being to write something of use to those who understand, it appears to me more proper to go to the real truth of the matter than to its imagination; and many have imagined republics and principalities which have never been seen or known to exist in reality; for how we live is so far removed from how we ought to live, that he who abandons what is done for what ought to be done, will rather learn to bring about his own ruin than his preservation. A man who wishes to make a profession of goodness in everything must necessarily come to grief among so many who are not good. Therefore it is necessary for a prince, who wishes to maintain himself, to learn how not to be good, and to use this knowledge and not use it, according to the necessity of the case.

Leaving on one side, then, those things which concern only an imaginary prince, and speaking of those that are real, I state that all men, and especially princes, who are placed at a greater height, are reputed for certain qualities which bring them either praise or blame. Thus one is considered liberal, another *misero* or miserly (using a Tuscan term, seeing that *avaro* with us still means one who is rapaciously acquisitive and *misero* one who makes grudging use of his own); one a free giver, another rapacious; one cruel, another merciful; one a breaker of his word, another trustworthy; one effeminate and pusillanimous, another fierce and high-spirited; one humane, another haughty; one lascivious, another chaste; one frank, another astute; one hard, another easy; one serious, another frivolous; one religious, another an unbeliever, and so on. I know that every one will admit that it would be highly praiseworthy in a prince to possess all the above-named qualities that are reputed good, but as they cannot all be possessed or observed, human conditions not permitting of it, it is necessary that he should be prudent enough to avoid the scandal of those vices which would lose him the state, and guard himself if possible against those which will not lose it him, but if not able to, he can indulge them with less scruple. And yet he must not mind incurring the scandal

Niccolò Machiavelli, *The Prince,* Chapters 15, 17, 18 (Modern Library, 1950). Luigi Ricci and E. R. P. Vincent, trans.

of those vices, without which it would be difficult to save the state, for if one considers well, it will be found that some things which seem virtues would, if followed, lead to one's ruin, and some others which appear vices result in one's greater security and wellbeing. . . .

OF CRUELTY AND CLEMENCY, AND WHETHER IT IS BETTER TO BE LOVED OR FEARED

Proceeding to the other qualities before named, I say that every prince must desire to be considered merciful and not cruel. He must, however, take care not to misuse this mercifulness. Cesare Borgia was considered cruel, but his cruelty had brought order to the Romagna, united it, and reduced it to peace and fealty. If this is considered well, it will be seen that he was really much more merciful than the Florentine people, who, to avoid the name of cruelty, allowed Pistoia to be destroyed. A prince, therefore, must not mind incurring the charge of cruelty for the purpose of keeping his subjects united and faithful; for, with a very few examples, he will be more merciful than those who, from excess of tenderness, allow disorders to arise, from whence spring bloodshed and rapine; for these as a rule injure the whole community, while the executions carried out by the prince injure only individuals. And of all princes, it is impossible for a new prince to escape the reputation of cruelty, new states being always full of dangers. Wherefore Virgil through the mouth of Dido says:

> Res dura, et regni novitas me talia cogunt
> Moliri, et late fines custode tueri.

Nevertheless, he must be cautious in believing and acting, and must not be afraid of his own shadow, and must proceed in a temperate manner with prudence and humanity, so that too much confidence does not render him incautious, and too much diffidence does not render him intolerant.

From this arises the question whether it is better to be loved more than feared, or feared more than loved. The reply is, that one ought to be both feared and loved, but as it is difficult for the two to go together, it is much safer to be feared than loved, if one of the two has to be wanting. For it may be said of men in general that they are ungrateful, voluble, dissemblers, anxious to avoid danger, and covetous of gain; as long as you benefit them, they are entirely yours; they offer you their blood, their goods, their life, and their children, as I have before said, when the necessity is remote; but when it approaches, they revolt. And the prince who has relied solely on their words, without making other preparations, is ruined; for the friendship which is gained by purchase and not through grandeur and nobility of spirit is bought but not secured, and at a pinch is not to be expended in your service. And men have less scruple in offending one who makes himself loved than one who makes himself feared; for love is held by a chain of obligation which, men being selfish, is broken whenever it serves their purpose; but fear is maintained by a dread of punishment which never fails.

Still, a prince should make himself feared in such a way that if he does not gain love, he at any rate avoids hatred; for fear and the absence of hatred may well go together, and will be always attained by one who abstains from interfering with the property of his citizens and subjects or with their women. And when he is obliged to take the life of any one, let him do so when there is a proper justification and manifest reason for it; but above all he must abstain from taking the property of others, for men forget more easily the death of their father than the loss of their patrimony. Then also pretexts for seizing property are never wanting, and one who begins to live by rapine will always find some reason for taking the goods of others, whereas causes for taking life are rarer and more fleeting.

But when the prince is with his army and has a large number of soldiers under his control, then it is extremely necessary that he should not mind being thought cruel; for without this reputation he could not keep an army united or disposed to any duty. Among the noteworthy actions of Hannibal is numbered this, that although he had an enormous army, composed of men of all nations and fighting in foreign countries, there never arose any dissension either among them or against the prince, either in good fortune or in bad. This could not be due to anything but his inhuman cruelty, which together with his infinite other virtues, made him always venerated and terrible in the sight of his soldiers, and without it his other virtues would not have sufficed to produce that effect. Thoughtless writers admire on the one hand his actions, and on the other blame the principal cause of them.

And that it is true that his other virtues would not have sufficed may be seen from the case of Scipio (famous not only in regard to his own times, but all times of which memory remains), whose armies rebelled against him in Spain, which arose from nothing but his excessive kindness, which allowed more licence to the soldiers than was consonant with military discipline. He was reproached with this in the senate by Fabius Maximus, who called him a corrupter of the Roman militia. Locri having been destroyed by one of Scipio's officers was not revenged by him, nor was the insolence of that officer punished, simply by reason of his easy nature; so much so, that some one wishing to excuse him in the senate, said that there were many men who knew rather how not to err, than how to correct the errors of others. This disposition would in time have tarnished the fame and glory of Scipio had he persevered in it under the empire, but living under the rule of the senate this harmful quality was not only concealed but became a glory to him.

I conclude, therefore, with regard to being feared and loved, that men love at their own free will, but fear at the will of the prince, and that a wise prince must rely on what is in his power and not on what is in the power of others, and he must only contrive to avoid incurring hatred, as has been explained.

IN WHAT WAY PRINCES MUST KEEP FAITH

How laudable it is for a prince to keep good faith and live with integrity, and not with astuteness, every one knows. Still the experience of our times shows those princes to have done great things who have had little regard for good faith, and have been able by astuteness to confuse men's brains, and who have ultimately overcome those who have made loyalty their foundation.

You must know, then, that there are two methods of fighting, the one by law, the other by force: the first method is that of men, the second of beasts; but as the first method is often insufficient, one must have recourse to the second. It is therefore necessary for a prince to know well how to use both the beast and the man. This was covertly taught to rulers by ancient writers, who relate how Achilles and many others of those ancient princes were given to Chiron the centaur to be brought up and educated under his discipline. The parable of this semi-animal, semi-human teacher is meant to indicate that a prince must know how to use both natures, and that the one without the other is not durable.

A prince being thus obliged to know well how to act as a beast must imitate the fox and the lion, for the lion cannot protect himself from traps, and the fox cannot defend himself from wolves. One must therefore be a fox to recognise traps, and a lion to frighten wolves. Those that wish to be only lions do not understand this. Therefore, a prudent ruler ought not to keep faith when by so doing it would be against his interest, and when the reasons which made him bind himself no longer exist. If men were all good, this precept would not be a good one; but as they are bad, and would not observe their faith with you, so you are not bound to keep faith with them. Nor have legitimate grounds ever failed a prince who wished to show colourable excuse for the non-fulfilment of his promise. Of this one could furnish an infinite number of modern examples, and show how many times peace has been broken, and how many promises rendered worthless, by the faithlessness of princes, and those that have been best able to imitate the fox have succeeded best. But it is necessary to be able to disguise this character well, and to be a great feigner and dissembler; and men are so simple and so ready to obey present necessities, that one who deceives will always find those who allow themselves to be deceived.

I will only mention one modern instance. Alexander VI did nothing else but deceive men, he thought of nothing else, and found the occasion for it; no man was ever more able to give assurances, or affirmed things with stronger oaths, and no man observed them less; however, he always succeeded in his deceptions, as he well knew this aspect of things.

It is not, therefore, necessary for a prince to have all the above-named qualities, but it is very necessary to seem to have them. I would even be bold to say that to possess them and always to observe them is dangerous, but to appear to possess them is useful. Thus it is well to seem merciful, faithful, humane, sincere, religious, and also to be so; but you must have the mind so disposed that when it is needful to be otherwise you may be able to change to the opposite qualities. And it must be understood that a prince, and especially a new prince, cannot observe all those things which are considered good in men, being often obliged, in order to maintain the state, to act against faith, against charity, against humanity, and against religion. And, therefore, he must have a mind disposed to adapt itself according to the wind, and as the variations of fortune dictate, and, as I said before, not deviate from what is good, if possible, but be able to do evil if constrained.

A prince must take great care that nothing goes out of his mouth which is not full of the above-named five qualities, and, to see and hear him, he should seem to be all mercy, faith, integrity, humanity, and religion. And nothing is more necessary than to seem to have this last quality, for men in general judge more by the eyes than by the hands, for every one can see, but very few have to feel. Everybody sees what you appear to be, few feel what you are, and those few will not dare to oppose themselves to the many, who have the majesty of the state to defend them; and in the actions of men, and especially of princes, from which there is no appeal, the end justifies the means. Let a prince therefore aim at conquering and maintaining the state, and the means will always be judged honourable and praised by every one, for the vulgar is always taken by appearances and the issue of the event; and the world consists only of the vulgar, and the few who are not vulgar are isolated when the many have a rallying point in the prince. A certain prince of the present time, whom it is well not to name, never does anything but preach peace and good faith, but he is really a great enemy to both, and either of them, had he observed them, would have lost him state or reputation on many occasions.

THE STATE OF NATURE
AND THE STATE OF WAR

Thomas Hobbes

OF THE NATURAL CONDITION
OF MANKIND AS CONCERNING
THEIR FELICITY AND MISERY

Men by nature equal. Nature hath made men so equal, in the faculties of the body, and mind; as that though there be found one man sometimes manifestly stronger in body, or of quicker mind than another; yet when all is reckoned together, the difference between man, and man, is not so considerable, as that one man can thereupon claim to himself any benefit, to which another may not pretend, as well as he. For as to the strength of body, the weakest has strength enough to kill the strongest, either by secret machination, or by confederacy with others, that are in the same danger with himself.

And as to the faculties of the mind, setting aside the arts grounded upon words, and especially that skill of proceeding upon general, and infallible rules, called science; which very few have, and but in few things; as being not a native faculty, born with us; nor attained, as prudence, while we look after somewhat else, I find yet a greater equality amongst men, than that of strength. For prudence, is but experience; which equal time, equally bestows on all men, in those things they equally apply themselves unto. That which may perhaps make such equality incredible, is but a vain conceit of one's own wisdom, which almost all men think they have in a greater degree, than the vulgar; that is, than all men but themselves, and a few others, whom by fame, or for concurring with themselves, they approve. For such is the nature of men, that howsoever they may acknowledge many others to be more witty, or more eloquent, or more learned; yet they will hardly believe there be many so wise as themselves; for they see their own wit at hand, and other men's at a distance. But this proveth rather that men are in that point equal, than unequal. For there is not ordinarily a greater sign of the equal distribution of any thing, than that every man is contented with his share.

From equality proceeds diffidence. From this equality of ability, ariseth equality of hope in the attaining of our ends. And therefore if any two men desire the same thing, which nevertheless they cannot both enjoy, they become enemies; and in the way to their end, which is principally their own conservation, and sometimes their delectation only, endeavour to destroy, or subdue one another. And from hence it comes to pass, that where an invader hath no more to fear, than another man's single power; if one plant, sow, build, or possess a convenient seat, others may probably be expected to come prepared with

Reprinted with the permission of Scribner, a Division of Simon & Schuster from *Leviathan* by Thomas Hobbes, edited by Michael Oakeshott. Copyright © 1962 by Macmillan Publishing Company. Originally published in 1651.

forces united, to dispossess, and deprive him, not only of the fruit of his labour, but also of his life, or liberty. And the invader again is in the like danger of another.

From diffidence war. And from this diffidence of one another, there is no way for any man to secure himself, so reasonable, as anticipation; that is, by force, or wiles, to master the persons of all men he can, so long, till he see no other power great enough to endanger him: and this is no more than his own conservation requireth, and is generally allowed. Also because there be some, that taking pleasure in contemplating their own power in the acts of conquest, which they pursue farther than their security requires; if others, that otherwise would be glad to be at ease within modest bounds, should not by invasion increase their power, they would not be able, long time, by standing only on their defence, to subsist. And by consequence, such augmentation of dominion over men being necessary to a man's conservation, it ought to be allowed him.

Again, men have no pleasure, but on the contrary a great deal of grief, in keeping company, where there is no power able to over-awe them all. For every man looketh that his companion should value him, at the same rate he sets upon himself: and upon all signs of contempt, or undervaluing, naturally endeavours, as far as he dares, (which amongst them that have no common power to keep them in quiet, is far enough to make them destroy each other), to extort a greater value from his contemners, by damage; and from others, by the example.

So that in the nature of man, we find three principal causes of quarrel. First, competition; secondly, diffidence; thirdly, glory.

The first, maketh men invade for gain; the second, for safety; and the third, for reputation. The first use violence, to make themselves masters of other men's persons, wives, children, and cattle; the second, to defend them; the third, for trifles, as a word, a smile, a different opinion, and any other sign of undervalue, either direct in their persons, or by reflection in their kindred, their friends, their nation, their profession, or their name.

o *Out of civil states, there is always war of every one against every one.* Hereby it is manifest, that during the time men live without a common power to keep them all in awe, they are in that condition which is called war; and such a war, as is of every man, against every man. For WAR, consisteth not in battle only, or the act of fighting; but in a tract of time, wherein the will to contend by battle is sufficiently known: and therefore the notion of *time,* is to be considered in the nature of war; as it is in the nature of weather. For as the nature of foul weather, lieth not in a shower or two of rain; but in an inclination thereto of many days together: so the nature of war, consisteth not in actual fighting; but in the known disposition thereto, during all the time there is no assurance to the contrary. All other time is PEACE.

❧ *The incommodities of such a war.* Whatsoever therefore is consequent to a time of war, where every man is enemy to every man; the same is consequent to the time, wherein men live without other security, than what their own strength, and their own invention shall furnish them withal. In such condition, there is no place for industry; because the fruit thereof is uncertain: and consequently no culture of the earth; no navigation, nor use of the commodities that may be imported by sea; no commodious building; no instruments of moving, and removing, such things as require much force; no knowledge of the face of the earth; no account of time; no arts; no letters; no society; and which is worst of all, continual fear, and danger of violent death; and the life of man, solitary, poor, nasty, brutish, and short.

It may seem strange to some man, that has not well weighed these things; that nature should thus dissociate, and render men apt to invade, and destroy one another: and he may therefore, not trusting to this inference, made from the passions, desire perhaps to have the same confirmed by experience. Let him therefore consider with himself, when taking a journey, he arms himself, and seeks to go well accompanied; when going to sleep, he locks his doors; when even in his house he locks his chests; and this when he knows there be laws, and public officers, armed, to revenge all injuries shall be done him; what opinion he has of his fellow-subjects, when he rides armed; of his fellow citizens, when he locks his doors; and of his children, and servants, when he locks his chests. Does he not there as much accuse mankind by his actions, as I do by my words? But neither of us accuse man's nature in it. The desires, and other passions of man, are in themselves no sin. No more are the actions, that proceed from those passions, till they know a law that forbids them: which till laws be made they cannot know: nor can any law be made, till they have agreed upon the person that shall make it.

It may peradventure be thought, there was never such a time, nor condition of war as this; and I believe it was never generally so, over all the world: but there are many places, where they live so now. For the savage people in many places of America, except the government of small families, the concord whereof dependeth on natural lust, have no government at all; and live at this day in that brutish manner, as I said before. Howsoever, it may be perceived what manner of life there would be, where there were no common power to fear, by the manner of life, which men that have formerly lived under a peaceful government, use to degenerate into, in a civil war.

But though there had never been any time, wherein particular men were in a condition of war one against another; yet in all times, kings, and persons of sovereign authority, because of their independency, are in continual jealousies, and in the state and posture of gladiators; having their weapons pointing, and their eyes fixed on one another; that is, their forts, garrisons, and guns upon the frontiers of their kingdoms; and continual spies upon their neighbours; which is a posture of war. But because they uphold thereby, the industry of their subjects; there does not follow from it, that misery, which accompanies the liberty of particular men.

☻ *In such a war nothing is unjust.* To this war of every man, against every man, this also is consequent; that nothing can be unjust. The notions of right and wrong, justice and injustice have there no place. Where there is no common power, there is no law: where no law, no injustice. Force, and fraud, are in war the two cardinal virtues. Justice, and injustice are none of the faculties neither of the body, nor mind. If they were, they might be in a man that were alone in the world, as well as his senses, and passions. They are qualities, that relate to men in society, not in solitude. It is consequent also to the same condition, that there be no propriety, no dominion, no *mine* and *thine* distinct; but only that to be every man's, that he can get: and for so long, as he can keep it. And thus much for the ill condition, which man by mere nature is actually placed in; though with a possibility to come out of it, consisting partly in the passions, partly in his reason.

☻ *The passions that incline men to peace.* The passions that incline men to peace, are fear of death; desire of such things as are necessary to commodious living; and a hope by their industry to obtain them. And reason suggesteth convenient articles of peace, upon which men may be drawn to agreement. These articles, are they, which otherwise are called the Laws of Nature: whereof I shall speak more particularly, in the two following chapters. . . .

OF OTHER LAWS OF NATURE

The third law of nature, justice. From that law of nature, by which we are obliged to transfer to another, such rights, as being retained, hinder the peace of mankind, there followeth a third; which is this, *that men perform their covenants made:* without which, covenants are in vain, and but empty words; and the right of all men to all things remaining, we are still in the condition of war.

Justice and injustice what. And in this law of nature, consisteth the fountain and original of JUSTICE. For where no covenant hath preceded, there hath no right been transferred, and every man has right to every thing; and consequently, no action can be unjust. But when a covenant is made, then to break it is *unjust:* and the definition of INJUSTICE, is no other than *the not performance of covenant.* And whatsoever is not unjust, is *just.*

Justice and propriety begin with the constitution of commonwealth. But because covenants of mutual trust, where there is a fear of not performance on either part, as hath been said in the former chapter, are invalid; though the original of justice be the making of covenants; yet injustice actually there can be none, till the cause of such fear be taken away; which while men are in the natural condition of war, cannot be done. Therefore before the names of just, and unjust can have place, there must be some coercive power, to compel men equally to the performance of their covenants, by the terror of some punishment, greater than the benefit they expect by the breach of their covenant; and to make good that propriety, which by mutual contract men acquire, in recompense of the universal right they abandon: and such power there is none before the erection of a commonwealth. And this is also to be gathered out of the ordinary definition of justice in the Schools: for they say, that *justice is the constant will of giving to every man his own.* And therefore where there is no *own,* that is no propriety, there is no injustice; and where there is no coercive power erected, that is, where there is no commonwealth, there is no propriety; all men having right to all things: therefore where there is no commonwealth, there nothing is unjust. So that the nature of justice, consisteth in keeping of valid covenants: but the validity of covenants begins not but with the constitution of a civil power, sufficient to compel men to keep them: and then it is also that propriety begins.

REALISM AND IDEALISM

Edward Hallett Carr

. . . In Europe after 1919, planned economy, which rests on the assumption that no nat-ural harmony of interests exists and that interests must be artificially harmonised by state action, became the practice, if not the theory, of almost every state. In the United States, the persistence of an expanding domestic market staved off this development till after 1929. The natural harmony of interests remained an integral part of the American view of life; and in this as in other respects, current theories of international politics were deeply imbued with the American tradition. Moreover, there was a special reason for the ready acceptance of the doctrine in the international sphere. In domestic affairs it is clearly the business of the state to create harmony if no natural harmony exists. In international politics, there is no organized power charged with the task of creating har-mony; and the temptation to assume a natural harmony is therefore particularly strong. But this is no excuse for burking the issue. To make the harmonisation of interests the goal of political action is not the same thing as to postulate that a natural harmony of interests exist; and it is this latter postulate which has caused so much confusion in in-ternational thinking.

Politically, the doctrine of the identity of interests has commonly taken the form of an assumption that every nation has an identical interest in peace, and that any nation which desires to disturb the peace is therefore both irrational and immoral. This view bears clear marks of its Anglo-Saxon origin. It was easy after 1918 to convince that part of mankind which lives in English-speaking countries that war profits nobody. The ar-gument did not seem particularly convincing to Germans, who had profited largely from the wars of 1866 and 1870, and attributed their more recent sufferings, not to the war of 1914, but to the fact that they had lost it; or to Italians, who blamed not the war, but the treachery of allies who defrauded them in the peace settlement; or to Poles or Czecho-Slovaks who, far from deploring the war, owed their national existence to it; or to Frenchmen, who could not unreservedly regret a war which had restored Alsace-Lorraine to France; or to people of other nationalities who remembered profitable wars waged by Great Britain and the United States in the past. But these people had fortu-nately little influence over the formation of current theories of international relations, which emanated almost exclusively from the English-speaking countries. British and American writers continued to assume that the uselessness of war had been irrefutably demonstrated by the experience of 1914–18, and that an intellectual grasp of this fact was all that was necessary to induce the nations to keep the peace in the future; and

From *The Twenty Year Crisis 1919–1939,* 2nd edition by Edward Hallett Carr. Reprinted by permission of Macmillan, Ltd.

they were sincerely puzzled as well as disappointed at the failure of other countries to share this view.

The confusion was increased by the ostentatious readiness of other countries to flatter the Anglo-Saxon world by repeating its slogans. In the fifteen years after the first world war, every Great Power (except, perhaps, Italy) repeatedly did lip-service to the doctrine by declaring peace to be one of the main objects of its policy.[1] But as Lenin observed long ago, peace in itself is a meaningless aim. "Absolutely everybody is in favour of peace in general", he wrote in 1915, "including Kitchener, Joffre, Hindenburg and Nicholas the Bloody, for everyone of them wishes to end the war."[2] The common interest in peace masks the fact that some nations desire to maintain the *status quo* without having to fight for it, and others to change the *status quo* without having to fight in order to do so. . . .

INTERNATIONAL ECONOMIC HARMONY

. . . We find in the modern period an extraordinary divergence between the theories of economic experts and the practice of those responsible for the economic policies of their respective countries. Analysis will show that this divergence springs from a simple fact. The economic expert, dominated in the main by *laissez-faire* doctrine, considers the hypothetical economic interest of the world as a whole, and is content to assume that this is identical with the interest of each individual country. The politician pursues the concrete interest of his country, and assumes (if he makes any assumption at all) that the interest of the world as a whole is identical with it. Nearly every pronouncement of every international economic conference held between the two world wars was vitiated by this assumption that there was some "solution" or "plan" which, by a judicious balancing of interests, would be equally favourable to all and prejudicial to none. . . .

In the nineteenth century, Germany and the United States, by pursuing a "strictly nationalistic policy", had placed themselves in a position to challenge Great Britain's virtual monopoly of world trade. No conference of economic experts, meeting in 1880,

---

[1]"Peace must prevail, must come before all" (Briand, *League of Nations: Ninth Assembly*, p. 83). "The maintenance of peace is the first objective of British foreign policy" (Eden, *League of Nations: Sixteenth Assembly*, p. 106). "Peace is our dearest treasure" (Hitler, in a speech in the German Reichstag on January 30, 1937, reported in *The Times*, February 1, 1937). "The principal aim of the international policy of the Soviet Union is the preservation of peace" (Chicherin in *The Soviet Union and Peace* (1929), p. 249). "The object of Japan, despite propaganda to the contrary, is peace" (Matsuoka, *League of Nations: Special Assembly 1932–33*, iii. p. 73). The paucity of Italian pronouncements in favour of peace was probably explained by the poor reputation of Italian troops as fighters: Mussolini feared that any emphatic expression of preference for peace would be construed as an admission that Italy had no stomach for war.

[2]Lenin, *Collected Works* (Engl. transl.), xviii. p. 264. Compare Spenser Wilkinson's dictum: "It is not peace but preponderance that is in each case the real object. The truth cannot be too often repeated that peace is never the object of policy: you cannot define peace except by reference to war, which is a means and never an end" (*Government and the War*, p. 121).

could have evolved a "general plan" for "parallel or concerted action" which would have allayed the economic rivalries of the time in a manner equally advantageous to Great Britain, Germany and the United States. It was not less presumptuous to suppose that a conference meeting in 1927 could allay the economic rivalries of the later period by a "plan" beneficial to the interests of everyone. Even the economic crisis of 1930–33 failed to bring home to the economists the true nature of the problem which they had to face. The experts who prepared the "Draft Annotated Agenda" for the World Economic Conference of 1933 condemned the "world-wide adoption of ideals of national self-sufficiency which cut unmistakably athwart the lines of economic development".[3] They did not apparently pause to reflect that those so-called "lines of economic development", which might be beneficial to some countries and even to the world as a whole, would inevitably be detrimental to other countries, which were using weapons of economic nationalism in self-defence. . . . *Laissez-faire,* in international relations as in those between capital and labour, is the paradise of the economically strong. State control, whether in the form of protective legislation or of protective tariffs, is the weapon of self-defence invoked by the economically weak. The clash of interests is real and inevitable; and the whole nature of the problem is distorted by an attempt to disguise it.

THE FOUNDATIONS OF REALISM

. . . The three essential tenets implicit in Machiavelli's doctrine are the foundation-stones of the realist philosophy. In the first place, history is a sequence of cause and effect, whose course can be analysed and understood by intellectual effort, but not (as the utopians believe) directed by "imagination". Secondly, theory does not (as the utopians assume) create practice, but practice theory. In Machiavelli's words, "good counsels, whencesoever they come, are born of the wisdom of the prince, and not the wisdom of the prince from good counsels". Thirdly, politics are not (as the utopians pretend) a function of ethics, but ethics of politics. Men "are kept honest by constraint". Machiavelli recognised the importance of morality, but thought that there could be no effective morality where there was no effective authority. Morality is the product of power.[4]

The extraordinary vigour and vitality of Machiavelli's challenge to orthodoxy may be attested by the fact that, more than four centuries after he wrote, the most conclusive way of discrediting a political opponent is still to describe him as a disciple of Machiavelli. . . .

. . . Theories of social morality are always the product of a dominant group which identifies itself with the community as a whole, and which possesses facilities denied to subordinate groups or individuals for imposing its view of life on the community. Theories of international morality are, for the same reason and in virtue of the same process, the product of dominant nations or groups of nations. For the past hundred years, and more especially since 1918, the English-speaking peoples have formed the

---

[3]*League of Nations:* C.48, M.18, 1933, ii. p. 6.
[4]Machiavelli, *The Prince,* chs. 15 and 23 (Engl. transl., Everyman's Library, pp. 121, 193).

dominant group in the world; and current theories of international morality have been designed to perpetuate their supremacy and expressed in the idiom peculiar to them. France, retaining something of her eighteenth-century tradition and restored to a position of dominance for a short period after 1918, has played a minor part in the creation of current international morality, mainly through her insistence on the role of law in the moral order. Germany, never a dominant Power and reduced to helplessness after 1918, has remained for these reasons outside the charmed circle of creators of international morality. Both the view that the English-speaking peoples are monopolists of international morality and the view that they are consummate international hypocrites may be reduced to the plain fact that the current canons of international virtue have, by a natural and inevitable process, been mainly created by them.

THE REALIST CRITIQUE OF THE HARMONY OF INTERESTS

The doctrine of the harmony of interests yields readily to analysis in terms of this principle. It is the natural assumption of a prosperous and privileged class, whose members have a dominant voice in the community and are therefore naturally prone to identify its interest with their own. In virtue of this identification, any assailant of the interests of the dominant group is made to incur the odium of assailing the alleged common interest of the whole community, and is told that in making this assault he is attacking his own higher interests. The doctrine of the harmony of interests thus serves as an ingenious moral device invoked, in perfect sincerity, by privileged groups in order to justify and maintain their dominant position. But a further point requires notice. The supremacy within the community of the privileged group may be, and often is, so overwhelming that there is, in fact, a sense in which its interests are those of the community, since its well-being necessarily carries with it some measure of well-being for other members of the community, and its collapse would entail the collapse of the community as a whole. In so far, therefore, as the alleged natural harmony of interests has any reality, it is created by the overwhelming power of the privileged group, and is an excellent illustration of the Machiavellian maxim that morality is the product of power.

. . . British nineteenth-century statesmen, having discovered that free trade promoted British prosperity, were sincerely convinced that, in doing so, it also promoted the prosperity of the world as a whole. British predominance in world trade was at that time so overwhelming that there was a certain undeniable harmony between British interests and the interests of the world. British prosperity flowed over into other countries, and a British economic collapse would have meant world-wide ruin. British free traders could and did argue that protectionist countries were not only egotistically damaging the prosperity of the world as a whole, but were stupidly damaging their own, so that their behaviour was both immoral and muddle headed. In British eyes, it was irrefutably proved that international trade was a single whole, and flourished or slumped together. Nevertheless, this alleged international harmony of interests seemed a mockery to those under-privileged nations whose inferior status and insignificant stake in international trade were consecrated by it. The revolt against it destroyed that overwhelming British preponderance which had provided a plausible basis for the theory. Economically, Great Britain in the nineteenth century was dominant enough to make a bold bid to impose on the world her own conception of international economic morality. When competition of all against all replaced the domination of the world market by a single Power, conceptions of international economic morality necessarily became chaotic.

Politically, the alleged community of interest in the maintenance of peace, whose ambiguous character has already been discussed, is capitalised in the same way by a dominant nation or group of nations. Just as the ruling class in a community prays for domestic peace, which guarantees its own security and predominance, and denounces class-war, which might threaten them, so international peace becomes a special vested interest of predominant Powers. In the past, Roman and British imperialism were commended to the world in the guise of the *pax Romana* and the *pax Britannica.* To-day, when no single Power is strong enough to dominate the world, and supremacy is vested in a group of nations, slogans like "collective security" and "resistance to aggression" serve the same purpose of proclaiming an identity of interest between the dominant group and the world as a whole in the maintenance of peace.

. . . It is a familiar tactic of the privileged to throw moral discredit on the under-privileged by depicting them as disturbers of the peace; and this tactic is as readily applied internationally as within the national community. "International law and order", writes Professor Toynbee of a recent crisis, "were in the true interests of the whole of mankind . . . whereas the desire to perpetuate the region of violence in international affairs was an anti-social desire which was not even in the ultimate interests of the citizens of the handful of states that officially professed this benighted and anachronistic creed."[5] This is precisely the argument, compounded of platitude and falsehood in about equal parts, which did duty in every strike in the early days of the British and American Labour movements. It was common form for employers, supported by the whole capitalist press, to denounce the "anti-social" attitude of trade union leaders, to accuse them of attacking law and order and of introducing "the reign of violence", and to declare that "true" and "ultimate" interests of the workers lay in peaceful cooperation with the employers.[6] In the field of social relations, the disingenuous character of this argument has long been recognised. But just as the threat of class-war by the proletarian is "a natural cynical reaction to the sentimental and dishonest efforts of the privileged classes to obscure the conflict of interest between classes by a constant emphasis on the minimum interests which they have in common",[7] so the war-mongering of the dissatisfied Powers was the "natural, cynical reaction" to the sentimental and dishonest platitudinising of the satisfied Powers on the common interest in peace. When Hitler refused to believe "that God has permitted some nations first to acquire a world by force and

---

[5]Toynbee, *Survey of International Affairs, 1935,* ii. p. 46.
[6]"Pray earnestly that right may triumph", said the representative of the Philadelphia coal-owners in an early strike organised by the United Mine Workers, "remembering that the Lord God Omnipotent still reigns, and that His reign is one of law and order, and not of violence and crime" (H. F. Pringle, *Theodore Roosevelt,* p. 267).
[7]R. Niebuhr, *Moral Man and Immoral Society,* p. 153.

then to defend this robbery with moralising theories"[8] he was merely echoing in another context the Marxist denial of a community of interest between "haves" and "have-nots", the Marxist exposure of the interested character of "*bourgeois* morality", and the Marxist demand for the expropriation of the expropriators. . . .

THE LIMITATIONS OF REALISM

The exposure by realist criticism of the hollowness of the utopian edifice is the first task of the political thinker. It is only when the sham has been demolished that there can be any hope of raising a more solid structure in its place. But we cannot ultimately find a resting place in pure realism; for realism, though logically overwhelming, does not provide us with the springs of action which are necessary even to the pursuit of thought. Indeed, realism itself, if we attack it with its own weapons, often turns out in practice to be just as much conditioned as any other mode of thought. In politics, the belief that certain facts are unalterable or certain trends irresistible commonly reflects a lack of desire or lack of interest to change or resist them. The impossibility of being a consistent and thorough-going realist is one of the most certain and most curious lessons of political science. Consistent realism excludes four things which appear to be essential ingredients of all effective political thinking: a finite goal, an emotional appeal, a right of moral judgment and a ground for action. . . .

Consistent realism, as has already been noted, involves acceptance of the whole historical process and precludes moral judgments on it. As we have seen, men are generally prepared to accept the judgment of history on the past, praising success and condemning failure. This test is also widely applied to contemporary politics. Such institutions as the League of Nations, or the Soviet or Fascist regimes, are to a considerable extent judged by their capacity to achieve what they profess to achieve; and the legitimacy of this test is implicitly admitted by their own propaganda, which constantly seeks to exaggerate their successes and minimise their failures. Yet it is clear that mankind as a whole is not prepared to accept this rational test as a universally valid basis of political judgment. The belief that whatever succeeds is right, and has only to be understood to be approved, must, if consistently held, empty thought of purpose, and thereby sterilise and ultimately destroy it. Nor do those whose philosophy appears to exclude the possibility of moral judgments in fact refrain from pronouncing them. Frederick the Great, having explained that treaties should be observed for the reason that "one can trick only once", goes on to call the breaking of treaties "a bad and knavish policy", though there is nothing in his thesis to justify the moral epithet. Marx, whose philosophy appeared to demonstrate that capitalists could only act in a certain way, spends many pages—some of the most effective in *Capital*—in denouncing the wickedness of capitalists for behaving in precisely that way. The necessity, recognised by all politicians, both in domestic and in international affairs, for cloaking interests in a guise of moral principles is in itself a symptom of the inadequacy of realism. Every

---

[8]Speech in the Reichstag, January 30, 1939.

age claims the right to create its own values, and to pass judgments in the light of them; and even if it uses realist weapons to dissolve other values, it still believes in the absolute character of its own. It refuses to accept the implication of realism that the word "ought" is meaningless.

Most of all, consistent realism breaks down because it fails to provide any ground for purposive or meaningful action. If the sequence of cause and effect is sufficiently rigid to permit of the "scientific prediction" of events, if our thought is irrevocably conditioned by our status and our interests, then both action and thought become devoid of purpose. If, as Schopenhauer maintains, "the true philosophy of history consists of the insight that, throughout the jumble of all these ceaseless changes, we have ever before our eyes the same unchanging being, pursuing the same course to-day, yesterday and for ever", then passive contemplation is all that remains to the individual. Such a conclusion is plainly repugnant to the most deep-seated belief of man about himself. That human affairs can be directed and modified by human action and human thought is a postulate so fundamental that its rejection seems scarcely compatible with existence as a human being. Nor is it in fact rejected by those realists who have left their mark on history. Machiavelli, when he exhorted his compatriots to be good Italians, clearly assumed that they were free to follow or ignore his advice. Marx, by birth and training a *bourgeois,* believed himself free to think and act like a proletarian, and regarded it as his mission to persuade others, whom he assumed to be equally free, to think and act likewise. Lenin, who wrote of the imminence of world revolution as a "scientific prediction", admitted elsewhere that "no situations exist from which there is absolutely no way out". In moments of crisis, Lenin appealed to his followers in terms which might equally well have been used by so thorough-going a believer in the power of the human will as Mussolini or by any other leader of any period: "At the decisive moment and in the decisive place, you *must prove* the stronger, you must *be victorious"*. Every realist, whatever his professions, is ultimately compelled to believe not only that there is something which man ought to think and do, but that there is something which he can think and do, and that his thought and action are neither mechanical nor meaningless.

We return therefore to the conclusion that any sound political thought must be based on elements of both utopia and reality. Where utopianism has become a hollow and intolerable sham, which serves merely as a disguise for the interests of the privileged, the realist performs an indispensable service in unmasking it. But pure realism can offer nothing but a naked struggle for power which makes any kind of international society impossible. Having demolished the current utopia with the weapons of realism, we still need to build a new utopia of our own, which will one day fall to the same weapons. The human will continue to seek and escape from the logical consequences of realism in the vision of an international order which, as soon as it crystallizes itself into concrete political form, becomes tainted with self-interest and hypocrisy, and must once more be attacked with the instruments of realism.

Here, then, is the complexity, the fascination and the tragedy of all political life. Politics are made up of two elements—utopia and reality—belonging to two different planes which can never meet. There is no greater barrier to clear political thinking than failure to distinguish between ideals, which are utopia, and institutions, which are reality. The communist who set communism against democracy was usually thinking of

communism as a pure ideal of equality and brotherhood, and of democracy as an institution which existed in Great Britain, France or the United States and which exhibited
the vested interests, the inequalities and the oppression inherent in all political institutions. The democrat who made the same comparison was in fact comparing an ideal
pattern of democracy laid up in heaven with communism as an institution existing in
Soviet Russia with its class-divisions, its heresy-hunts and its concentration camps. The
comparison, made in each case between an ideal and an institution, is irrelevant and
makes no sense. The ideal, once it is embodied in an institution, ceases to be an ideal
and becomes the expression of a selfish interest, which must be destroyed in the name
of a new ideal. This constant interaction of irreconcilable forces is the stuff of politics.
Every political situation contains mutually incompatible elements of utopia and reality,
of morality and power. . . .

Military Power

The supreme importance of the military instrument lies in the fact that the *ultima ratio*
of power in international relations is war. Every act of the state, in its power aspect, is
directed to war, not as a desirable weapon, but as a weapon which it may require in the
last resort to use. Clausewitz's famous aphorism that "war is nothing but the continuation of political relations by other means" has been repeated with approval both by
Lenin and by the Communist International[9] and Hitler meant much the same thing
when he said that "an alliance whose object does not include the intention to fight is
meaningless and useless".[10] In the same sense, Mr. Hawtrey defines diplomacy as "potential war".[11] These are half-truths. But the important thing is to recognise that they
are true. War lurks in the background of international politics just as revolution lurks in
the background of domestic politics. There are few European countries where, at some
time during the past thirty years, potential revolution has not been an important factor
in politics;[12] and the international community has in this respect the closest analogy to
those states where the possibility of revolution is most frequently and most conspicuously present to the mind.

Potential war being thus a dominant factor in international politics, military
strength becomes a recognised standard of political values. Every great civilisation of
the past has enjoyed in its day a superiority of military power. . . .

Military power, being an essential element in the life of the state, becomes not only
an instrument, but an end in itself. Few of the important wars of the last hundred years
seem to have been waged for the deliberate and conscious purpose of increasing either
trade or territory. The most serious wars are fought in order to make one's own country

---

[9]Lenin, *Collected Works* (Engl. transl.), xviii. p. 97; Theses of the Sixth Congress of Comintern quoted
in Taracouzio, *The Soviet Union and International Law,* p. 436.
[10]Hitler, *Mein Kampf,* p. 749.
[11]R. G. Hawtrey, *Economic Aspects of Sovereignty,* p. 107.
[12]It is perhaps necessary to recall the part played in British politics in 1914 by the threat of the
Conservative Party to support revolutionary action in Ulster.

militarily stronger or, more often, to prevent another country from becoming militarily stronger, so that there is much justification for the epigram that "the principal cause of war is war itself".[13] Every stage in the Napoleonic Wars was devised to prepare the way for the next stage: the invasion of Russia was undertaken in order to make Napoleon strong enough to defeat Great Britain. The Crimean War was waged by Great Britain and France in order to prevent Russia from becoming strong enough to attack their Near Eastern possessions and interests at some future time. The origin of the Russo-Japanese War of 1904–5 is described as follows in a note addressed to the League of Nations by the Soviet Government in 1924: "When the Japanese torpedo-boats attacked the Russian fleet at Port Arthur in 1904, it was clearly an act of aggression from a technical point of view, but, politically speaking, it was an act caused by the aggressive policy of the Tsarist Government towards Japan, who, in order to forestall the danger, struck the first blow at her adversary".[14] In 1914, Austria sent an ultimatum to Servia because she believed that Servians were planning the downfall of the Dual Monarchy; Russia feared that Austria-Hungary, if she defeated Servia, would be strong enough to menace her; Germany feared that Russia, if she defeated Austria-Hungary, would be strong enough to menace her; France had long believed that Germany, if she defeated Russia, would be strong enough to menace her, and had therefore concluded the Franco-Russian alliance; and Great Britain feared that Germany, if she defeated France and occupied Belgium, would be strong enough to menace her. Finally, the United States came to fear that Germany, if she won the war would be strong enough to menace them. Thus the war, in the minds of all the principal combatants, had a defensive or preventive character. They fought in order that they might not find themselves in a more unfavourable position in some future war. Even colonial acquisitions have often been prompted by the same motive. The consolidation and formal annexation of the original British settlements in Australia were inspired by fear of Napoleon's alleged design to establish French colonies there. Military, rather than economic, reasons dictated the capture of German colonies during the war of 1914 and afterwards precluded their return to Germany.

It is perhaps for this reason that the exercise of power always appears to beget the appetite for more power. There is, as Dr. Niebuhr says, "no possibility of drawing a sharp line between the will-to-live and the will-to-power".[15] Nationalism, having attained its first objective in the form of national unity and independence, develops almost automatically into imperialism. International politics amply confirm the aphorisms of Machiavelli that "men never appear to themselves to possess securely what they have unless they acquire something further from another",[16] and of Hobbes that man "cannot assure the power and means to live well which he hath present, without the acquisition of more".[17] Wars, begun for motives of security, quickly become wars of aggression and self-seeking. President McKinley invited the United States to intervene

---

[13]R. G. Hawtrey, *Economic Aspects of Sovereignty*, p. 105.
[14]*League of Nations: Official Journal*, May 1924, p. 578.
[15]R. Niebuhr, *Moral Man and Immoral Society*, p. 42.
[16]Machiavelli, *Discorsi*, I. i. ch. v.
[17]Hobbes, *Leviathan*, ch. xi.

in Cuba against Spain in order "to secure a full and final termination of hostilities between the Government of Spain and the people of Cuba and to secure on the island the establishment of a stable government."[18] But by the time the war was over the temptation to self-aggrandisement by the annexation of the Philippines had become irresistible. Nearly every country participating in the first world war regarded it initially as a war of self-defence; and this belief was particularly strong on the Allied side. Yet during the course of the war, every Allied Government in Europe announced war aims which included the acquisition of territory from the enemy Powers. In modern conditions, wars of limited objective have become almost as impossible as wars of limited liability. It is one of the fallacies of the theory of collective security that war can be waged for the specific and disinterested purpose of "resisting aggression". Had the League of Nations in the autumn of 1935, under the leadership of Great Britain, embarked on "military sanctions" against Italy, it would have been impossible to restrict the campaign to the expulsion of Italian troops from Abyssinia. Operations would in all probability have led to the occupation of Italy's East African colonies by Great Britain and France, of Trieste, Fiume and Albania by Yugoslavia, and of the islands of the Dodecanese by Greece or Turkey or both; and war aims would have been announced, precluding on various specious grounds the restoration of these territories to Italy. Territorial ambitions are just as likely to be the product as the cause of war.

Economic Power

Economic strength has always been an instrument of political power, if only through its association with the military instrument. Only the most primitive kinds of warfare are altogether independent of the economic factor. The wealthiest prince or the wealthiest city-state could hire the largest and most efficient army of mercenaries; and every government was therefore compelled to pursue a policy designed to further the acquisition of wealth. The whole progress of civilisation has been so closely bound up with economic development that we are not surprised to trace, throughout modern history, an increasingly intimate association between military and economic power. In the prolonged conflicts which marked the close of the Middle Ages in Western Europe, the merchants of the towns, relying on organised economic power, defeated the feudal barons, who put their trust in individual military prowess. The rise of modern nations has everywhere been marked by the emergence of a new middle class economically based on industry and trade. Trade and finance were the foundation of the short-lived political supremacy of the Italian cities of the Renaissance and later of the Dutch. The principal international wars of the period from the Renaissance to the middle of the eighteenth century were trade wars (some of them were actually so named). Throughout this period, it was universally held that, since wealth is a source of political power, the state should seek actively to promote the acquisition of wealth; and it was believed that the right way to make a country powerful was to stimulate production at home, to buy as little as possible from abroad, and to accumulate wealth in the convenient form of

---

[18]*British and Foreign State Papers,* ed. Hertslet, xc. p. 811.

precious metals. Those who argued in this way afterwards came to be known as mercantilists. Mercantilism was a system of economic policy based on the hitherto unquestioned assumption that to promote the acquisition of wealth was part of the normal function of the state.

THE SEPARATION OF ECONOMICS FROM POLITICS

The *laissez-faire* doctrine of the classical economists made a frontal attack on this assumption. The principal implications of *laissez-faire* have already been discussed. Its significance in the present context is that it brought about a complete theoretical divorce between economics and politics. The classical economists conceived a natural economic order with laws of its own, independent of politics and functioning to the greatest profit of all concerned when political authority interfered least in is automatic operation. This doctrine dominated the economic thought, and to some extent the economic practice (though far more in Great Britain than elsewhere), of the nineteenth century. . . .

Marx was overwhelmingly right when he insisted on the increasing importance of the role played by economic forces in politics; and since Marx, history can never be written again exactly as it was written before him. But Marx believed, just as firmly as did the *laissez-faire* liberal, in an economic system with laws of its own working independently of the state, which was its adjunct and its instrument. In writing as if economics and politics were separate domains, one subordinate to the other, Marx was dominated by nineteenth-century presuppositions in much the same way as his more recent opponents who are equally sure that "the primary laws of history are political laws, economic laws are secondary".[19] Economic forces are in fact political forces. Economics can be treated neither as a minor accessory of history, nor as an independent science in the light of which history can be interpreted. Much confusion would be saved by a general return to the term "political economy", which was given the new science by Adam Smith himself and not abandoned in favour of the abstract "economics", even in Great Britain itself, till the closing years of the nineteenth century.[20] The science of economics presupposes a given political order, and cannot be profitably studied in isolation from politics.

SOME FALLACIES OF THE SEPARATION OF ECONOMICS FROM POLITICS

. . . The most conspicuous practical failure caused by the persistence of this nineteenth-century illusion was the breakdown of League sanctions in 1936. Careful reading of the text of Article 16 of the Covenant acquits its framers of responsibility for the

---

[19]Moeller van den Bruck, *Germany's Third Empire,* p. 50. The idea is a commonplace of National Socialist and Fascist writers.

[20]In Germany, "political economy" was at first translated *Nationalökonomie,* which was tentatively replaced in the present century by *Sozialökonomie.*

mistake. Paragraph 1 prescribes the economic weapons, paragraph 2 the military weapons, to be employed against the violator of the Covenant. Paragraph 2 is clearly complementary to paragraph 1, and assumes as a matter of course that, in the event of an application of sanctions, "armed forces" would be required "to protect the Covenants of the League". The only difference between the two paragraphs is that, whereas all members of the League would have to apply the economic weapons, it would be natural to draw the necessary armed forces from those members which possessed them in sufficient strength and in reasonable geographical proximity to the offender.[21] Subsequent commentators, obsessed with the assumption that economics and politics were separate and separable things, evolved the doctrine that paragraphs 1 and 2 of Article 16 were not complementary, but alternative, the difference being that "economic sanctions" were obligatory and "military sanctions" optional. This doctrine was eagerly seized on by the many who felt that the League might conceivably be worth a few million pounds worth of trade, but not a few million human lives; and in the famous 1934 Peace Ballot in Great Britain, some two million deluded voters expressed simultaneously their approval of economic, and their disapproval of military, sanctions. "One of the many conclusions to which I have been drawn", said Lord Baldwin at this time, "is that there is no such thing as a sanction which will work, which does not mean war."[22] But the bitter lesson of 1935–36 was needed to drive home the truth that in sanctions, as in war, the only motto is "all or nothing", and that economic power is impotent if the military weapon is not held in readiness to support it.[23] Power is indivisible; and the military and economic weapons are merely different instruments of power.[24]

A different, and equally serious, form in which this illusory separation of politics and economics can be traced is the popular phraseology which distinguishes between "power" and "welfare", between "guns" and "butter". "Welfare arguments are 'economic'", remarks an American writer, "power arguments are 'political'."[25] This fallacy

---

[21]This interpretation is confirmed by the report of the Phillimore Committee, on whose proposals the text of Article 16 was based. The Committee "considered financial and economic sanctions as being simply the contribution to the work of preventing aggression which might properly be made by countries which were not in a position to furnish actual military aid" (*International Sanctions: Report by a Group of Members of the Royal Institute of International Affairs,* p. 115 where the relevant texts are examined).

[22]House of Commons, May 18, 1934; *Official Report,* col. 2139.

[23]It is not, of course, suggested that the military weapon must always be used. The British Grand Fleet was little used in the first world war. But it would be rash to assume that the result would have been much the same if the British Government had not been prepared to use it. What paralyzed sanctions in 1935–36 was the common knowledge that the League Powers were not prepared to use the military weapon.

[24]It is worth noting that Stresemann was fully alive to this point when Germany entered the League of Nations. When the Secretary-General argued that Germany, if she contracted out of military sanctions, could still participate in economic sanctions, Stresemann replied: "We cannot do that either; if we take part in an economic boycott of a powerful neighbour, a declaration of war against Germany might be the consequence, since the exclusion of another country from intercourse with a nation of sixty million citizens would be a hostile act" (*Stresemann's Diaries and Papers* (Engl. Transl.), ii. p. 69).

[25]F. L. Schuman, *International Politics,* p. 356.

is particularly difficult to expose because it appears to be deducible from a familiar fact. Every modern government and every parliament is continually faced with the dilemma of spending money on armaments or social services; and this encourages the illusion that the choice really lies between "power" and "welfare", between political guns and economic butter. Reflexion shows, however, that this is not the case. The question asked never takes the form, Do you prefer guns or butter? For everyone (except a handful of pacifists in those Anglo-Saxon countries which have inherited a long tradition of un-contested security) agrees that, in case of need, guns must come before butter. The question asked is always either, Have we already sufficient guns to enable us to afford some butter? or, Granted that we need x guns, can we increase revenue sufficiently to afford more butter as well? But the neatest exposure of this fallacy comes from the pen of Professor Zimmern; and the exposure is none the less effective for being uncon-scious. Having divided existing states on popular lines into those which pursue "wel-fare" and those which pursue "power", Professor Zimmern revealingly adds that "the welfare states, taken together, enjoy a preponderance of power and resources over the power states"[26] thereby leading us infallibly to the correct conclusion that "welfare states" are states which, already enjoying a preponderance of power, are not primarily concerned to increase it, and can therefore afford butter, and "power states" those which, being inferior in power, are primarily concerned to increase it, and devote the major part of their resources to this end. In this popular terminology, "welfare states" are those which possess preponderant power, and "power states" those which do not. Nor is this classification as illogical as it may seem. Every Great Power takes the view that the minimum number of guns necessary to assert the degree of power which it con-siders requisite takes precedence over butter, and that it can only pursue "welfare" when this minimum has been achieved. For many years prior to 1933, Great Britain, be-ing satisfied with her power, was a "welfare state." After 1935, feeling her power con-tested and inadequate, she became a "power state"; and even the Opposition ceased to press with any insistence the prior claim of the social services. The contrast is not one between "power" and "welfare", and still less between "politics" and "economics", but between different degrees of power. In the pursuit of power, military and economic in-struments will both be used. . . .

THE NATURE OF INTERNATIONAL LAW

International law differs from the municipal law of modern states in being the law of an undeveloped and not fully integrated community. It lacks three institutions which are essential parts of any developed system of municipal law: a judicature, an executive and a legislature.

(1) International law recognises no court competent to give on any issue of law or fact decisions recognised as binding by the community as a whole. It has long been the

---

[26]Zimmern, *Quo Vadimus?* p. 41.

habit of some states to make special agreements to submit particular disputes to an international court for judicial settlement. The Permanent Court of International Justice, set up under the Covenant of the League, represents an attempt to extend and generalise this habit. But the institution of the court has not changed international law: it has merely created certain special obligations for states willing to accept them.

(2) International law has no agents competent to enforce observance of the law. In certain cases, it does indeed recognise the right of an aggrieved party, where a breach of the law has occurred, to take reprisals against the offender. But this is the recognition of a right of self-help, not the enforcement of a penalty by an agent of the law. The measures contemplated in Article 16 of the Covenant of the League, in so far as they can be regarded as punitive and not merely preventive, fall within this category.

(3) Of the two main sources of law—custom and legislation—international law knows only the former, resembling in this respect the law of all primitive communities. To trace the stages by which a certain kind of action or behaviour, from being customary, comes to be recognised as obligatory on all members of the community is the task of the social psychologist rather than of the jurist. But it is by some such process that international law has come into being. In advanced communities, the other source of law—direct legislation—is more prolific, and could not possibly be dispensed with in any modern state. So serious does this lack of international legislation appear that, in the view of some authorities, states do on certain occasions constitute themselves a legislative body, and many multilateral agreements between states are in fact "law-making treaties" *(traités-lois)*.[27] This view is open to grave objections. A treaty, whatever its scope and content, lacks the essential quality of law: it is not automatically and unconditionally applicable to all members of the community whether they assent to it or not. Attempts have been made from time to time to embody customary international law in multilateral treaties between states. But the value of such attempts has been largely nullified by the fact that no treaty can bind a state which has not accepted it. The Hague Conventions of 1907 on the rules of war are sometimes treated as an example of international legislation. But these conventions were not only not binding on states which were not parties to them, but were not binding on the parties *vis-à-vis* states which were not parties. The Briand-Kellogg Pact is not, as is sometimes loosely said, a legislative act prohibiting war. It is an agreement between a large number of states "to renounce war as an instrument of national policy in their relations with one another". International agreements are contracts concluded by states with one another in their capacity as subjects of international law, and not laws created by states in the capacity of international legislators. International legislation does not yet exist. . . .

In June 1933, the British Government ceased to pay the regular installments due under its war debt agreement, substituting minor "token payments"; and a year later these token payments came to an end. Yet in 1935 Great Britain and France once more

---

[27]The Carnegie Endowment has, for example, given the title *International Legislation* to a collection published under its auspices of "multipartite instruments of general interest".

joined in a solemn condemnation of Germany for unilaterally repudiating her obligations under the disarmament clauses of the Versailles Treaty. Such inconsistencies are
so common that the realist finds little difficulty in reducing them to a simple rule. The
element of power is inherent in every political treaty. The contents of such a treaty reflect in some degree the relative strength of the contracting parties. Stronger states will
insist on the sanctity of the treaties concluded by them with weaker states. Weaker
states will renounce treaties concluded by them with stronger states so soon as the
power position alters and the weaker state feels itself strong enough to reject or modify
the obligation. Since 1918, the United States have concluded no treaty with a stronger
state, and have therefore unreservedly upheld the sanctity of treaties. Great Britain concluded the war debt agreement with a country financially stronger than herself, and de-
faulted. She concluded no other important treaty with a stronger Power and, with this
single exception, upheld the sanctity of treaties. The countries which had concluded the
largest number of treaties with states stronger than themselves, and subsequently
strengthened their position, were Germany, Italy and Japan; and these are the countries
which renounced or violated the largest number of treaties. But it would be rash to assume any *moral* distinction between these different attitudes. There is no reason to assume that these countries would insist any less strongly than Great Britain or the United
States on the sanctity of treaties favourable to themselves concluded by them with
weaker states.

The case is convincing as far as it goes. The rule *pacta sunt servanda* is not a moral
principle, and its application cannot always be justified on ethical grounds. It is a rule
of international law; and as such it not only is, but is universally recognised to be, necessary to the existence of an international society. But law does not purport to solve
every political problem; and where it fails, the fault often lies with those who seek to
put it to uses for which it was never intended. It is no reproach to law to describe it as a
bulwark of the existing order. The essence of law is to promote stability and maintain
the existing framework of society; and it is perfectly natural everywhere for conservatives to describe themselves as the party of law and order, and to denounce radicals as
disturbers of the peace and enemies of the law. The history of every society reveals a
strong tendency on the part of those who want important changes in the existing order
to commit acts which are illegal and which can plausibly be denounced as such by conservatives. It is true that in highly organised societies, where legally constituted machinery exists for bringing about changes in the law, this tendency to illegal action is
mitigated. But it is never removed altogether. Radicals are always more likely than conservatives to come into conflict with the law.

Before 1914, international law did not condemn as illegal resort to war for the purpose of changing the existing international order; and no legally constituted machinery
existed for bringing about changes in any other way. After 1918 opinion condemning
"aggressive" war became almost universal, and nearly all the nations of the world
signed a pact renouncing resort to war as an instrument of policy. While therefore resort
to war for the purpose of altering the *status quo* now usually involves the breach of a
treaty obligation and is accordingly illegal in international law, no effective international machinery has been constituted for bringing about changes by pacific means. The
rude nineteenth-century system, or lack of system, was logical in recognising as legal

the one effective method of changing the *status quo*. The rejection of the traditional method as illegal and the failure to provide any effective alternative have made contemporary international law a bulwark of the existing order to an extent unknown in previous international law or in the municipal law of any civilised country. This is the most fundamental cause of the recent decline of respect for international law; and those who, in deploring the phenomenon, fail to recognise its origin, not unnaturally expose themselves to the charge of hypocrisy or of obtuseness.

Of all the considerations which render unlikely the general observance of the legal rule of the sanctity of treaties, and which provide a plausible moral justification for the repudiation of treaties, this last is by far the most important. Respect for international law and for the sanctity of treaties will not be increased by the sermons of those who, having most to gain from the maintenance of the existing order, insist most firmly on the morally binding character of the law. Respect for law and treaties will be maintained only in so far as the law recognises effective political machinery through which it can itself be modified and superseded. There must be a clear recognition of that play of political forces which is antecedent to all law. Only when these forces are in stable equilibrium can the law perform its social function without becoming a tool in the hands of the defenders of the *status quo*. The achievement of this equilibrium is not a legal, but a political task. . . .

Peaceful Change

. . . The attempt to make a moral distinction between wars of "aggression" and wars of "defence" is misguided. If a change is necessary and desirable, the use or threatened use of force to maintain the *status quo* may be morally more culpable than the use or threatened use of force to alter it. Few people now believe that the action of the American colonists who attacked the *status quo* by force in 1776, or of the Irish who attacked the *status quo* by force between 1916 and 1920, was necessarily less moral than that of the British who defended it by force. The moral criterion must be not the "aggressive" or "defensive" character of the war, but the nature of the change which is being sought and resisted. . . .

. . . When the change is effected by legislation, the compulsion is that of the state. But where the change is effected by the bargaining procedure, the *force majeure* can only be that of the stronger party. The employer who concedes the strikers' demands pleads inability to resist. The trade union leader who calls off an unsuccessful strike pleads that the union was too weak to continue. "Yielding to threats of force", which is sometimes used as a term of reproach, is therefore a normal part of the process. . . .

The defence of the *status quo* is not a policy which can be lastingly successful. It will end in war as surely as rigid conservatism will end in revolution. "Resistance to aggression", however necessary as a momentary device of national policy, is no solution; for readiness to fight to prevent change is just as unmoral as readiness to fight to enforce it. To establish methods of peaceful change is therefore the fundamental problem of international morality and of international politics. We can discard as purely utopian and muddle-headed plans for a procedure of peaceful change dictated by a world legislature or a world court. We can describe as utopian in the right sense (i.e. performing the proper function of a utopia in proclaiming an ideal to be aimed at, though not wholly attainable) the desire to eliminate the element of power and to base the bargaining process of peaceful change on a common feeling of what is just and reasonable. But we shall also keep in mind the realist view of peaceful change as an adjustment to the changed relations of power; and since the party which is able to bring most power to bear normally emerges successful from operations of peaceful change, we shall do our best to make ourselves as powerful as we can. In practice, we know that peaceful change can only be achieved through a compromise between the utopian conception of a common feeling of right and the realist conception of a mechanical adjustment to a changed equilibrium of forces. That is why a successful foreign policy must oscillate between the apparently opposite poles of force and appeasement. . . .

THE ORIGINS OF WAR IN NEOREALIST THEORY

Kenneth N. Waltz

Like most historians, many students of international politics have been skeptical about the possibility of creating a theory that might help one to understand and explain the international events that interest us. Thus Morgenthau, foremost among traditional realists, was fond of repeating Blaise Pascal's remark that "the history of the world would have been different had Cleopatra's nose been a bit shorter" and then asking "How do you systemize that?"[1] His appreciation of the role of the accidental and the occurrence of the unexpected in politics dampened his theoretical ambition.

The response of neorealists is that, although difficulties abound, some of the obstacles that seem most daunting lie in misapprehensions about theory. Theory obviously cannot explain the accidental or account for unexpected events; it deals in regularities and repetitions and is possible only if these can be identified. A further difficulty is found in the failure of realists to conceive of international politics as a distinct domain about which theories can be fashioned. Morgenthau, for example, insisted on "the autonomy of politics," but he failed to apply the concept to international politics. A theory is a depiction of the organization of a domain and of the connections among its parts. A theory indicates that some factors are more important than others and specifies relations among them. In reality, everything is related to everything else, and one domain cannot be separated from others. But theory isolates one realm from all others in order to deal with it intellectually. By defining the structure of international political systems, neorealism establishes the autonomy of international politics and thus makes a theory about it possible.[2]

In developing a theory of international politics, neorealism retains the main tenets of *realpolitik,* but means and ends are viewed differently, as are causes and effects. Morgenthau, for example, thought of the "rational" statesman as ever striving to accu-

Kenneth N. Waltz, "The Origins of War in Neorealist Theory," *Journal of Interdisciplinary History,* Vol. 18, No. 4 (spring 1988), pp. 615–628. © 1988 by the Massachusetts Institute of Technology and the editors of *The Journal of Interdisciplinary History.*
[1]Hans J. Morgenthau, "International Relations: Quantitative and Qualitative Approaches," in Norman D. Palmer (ed.), *A Design for International Relations Research: Scope, Theory, Methods, and Relevance* (Philadelphia, 1970), 78.
[2]Morgenthau, *Politics among Nations* (New York, 1973; 5th ed.), 11. Ludwig Boltzman (trans. Rudolf Weingartner), "Theories as Representations," excerpted in Arthur Danto and Sidney Morgenbesser (eds.), *Philosophy of Science* (Cleveland, 1960), 245–252. Neorealism is sometimes dubbed structural realism. I use the terms interchangeably and, throughout this article, refer to my own formulation of neorealist theory. See Waltz, *Theory of International Politics* (Reading, Mass., 1979); Robert Keohane (ed.), *Neorealism and its Critics* (New York, 1986).

mulate more and more power. He viewed power as an end in itself. Although he acknowledged that nations at times act out of considerations other than power, Morgenthau insisted that, when they do so, their actions are not "of a political nature."[3] In contrast, neorealism sees power as a possibly useful means, with states running risks if they have either too little or too much of it. Excessive weakness may invite an attack that greater strength would have dissuaded an adversary from launching. Excessive strength may prompt other states to increase their arms and pool their efforts against the dominant state. Because power is a possibly useful means, sensible statesmen try to have an appropriate amount of it. In crucial situations, however, the ultimate concern of states is not for power but for security. This revision is an important one.

An even more important revision is found in a shift of causal relations. The infinite materials of any realm can be organized in endlessly different ways. Realism thinks of causes as moving in only one direction, from the interactions of individuals and states to the outcomes that their acts and interactions produce. Morgenthau recognized that, when there is competition for scarce goods and no one to serve as arbiter, a struggle for power will ensue among the competitors and that consequently the struggle for power can be explained without reference to the evil born in men. The struggle for power arises simply because men want things, not because of the evil in their desires. He labeled man's desire for scarce goods as one of the two roots of conflict, but, even while discussing it, he seemed to pull toward the "other root of conflict and concomitant evil"—"the *animus dominandi,* the desire for power." He often considered that man's drive for power is more basic than the chance conditions under which struggles for power occur. This attitude is seen in his statement that "in a world where power counts, no nation pursuing a rational policy has a choice between renouncing and wanting power; *and, if it could,* the lust for power for the individual's sake would still confront us with its less spectacular yet no less pressing moral defects."[4]

Students of international politics have typically inferred outcomes from salient attributes of the actors producing them. Thus Marxists, like liberals, have linked the outbreak of war or the prevalence of peace to the internal qualities of states. Governmental forms, economic systems, social institutions, political ideologies—these are but a few examples of where the causes of war have been found. Yet, although causes are specifically assigned, we know that states with widely divergent economic institutions, social customs, and political ideologies have all fought wars. More striking still, many different sorts of organizations fight wars, whether those organizations be tribes, petty principalities, empires, nations, or street gangs. If an identified condition seems to have caused a given war, one must wonder why wars occur repeatedly even though their causes vary. Variations in the characteristics of the states are not linked directly to the outcomes that their behaviors produce, nor are variations in their patterns of interaction. Many historians, for example, have claimed that World War I was caused by the interaction of two opposed and closely balanced coalitions. But then many have

---

[3]Morgenthau, *Politics among Nations,* 27.
[4]*Idem, Scientific Man vs. Power Politics* (Chicago, 1946), 192, 200. Italics added.

claimed that World War II was caused by the failure of some states to combine forces in an effort to right an imbalance of power created by an existing alliance.

Neorealism contends that international politics can be understood only if the effects of structure are added to the unit-level explanations of traditional realism. By emphasizing how structures affect actions and outcomes, neorealism rejects the assumption that man's innate lust for power constitutes a sufficient cause of war in the absence of any other. It reconceives the causal link between interacting units and international outcomes. According to the logic of international politics, one must believe that some causes of international outcomes are the result of interactions at the unit level, and, since variations in presumed causes do not correspond very closely to variations in observed outcomes, one must also assume that others are located at the structural level. Causes at the level of units interact with those at the level of structure, and, because they do so, explanation at the unit level alone is bound to be misleading. If an approach allows the consideration of both unit-level and structural-level causes, then it can cope with both the changes and the continuities that occur in a system.

Structural realism presents a systemic portrait of international politics depicting component units according to the manner of their arrangement. For the purpose of developing a theory, states are cast as unitary actors wanting at least to survive, and are taken to be the system's constituent units. The essential structural quality of the system is anarchy—the absence of a central monopoly of legitimate force. Changes of structure and hence of system occur with variations in the number of great powers. The range of expected outcomes is inferred from the assumed motivation of the units and the structure of the system in which they act.

A systems theory of international politics deals with forces at the international, and not at the national, level. With both systems-level and unit-level forces in play, how can one construct a theory of international politics without simultaneously constructing a theory of foreign policy? An international-political theory does not imply or require a theory of foreign policy any more than a market theory implies or requires a theory of the firm. Systems theories, whether political or economic, are theories that explain how the organization of a realm acts as a constraining and disposing force on the interacting units within it. Such theories tell us about the forces to which the units are subjected. From them, we can draw some inferences about the expected behavior and fate of the units: namely, how they will have to compete with and adjust to one another if they are to survive and flourish. To the extent that the dynamics of a system limit the freedom of its units, their behavior and the outcomes of their behavior become predictable. How do we expect firms to respond to differently structured markets, and states to differently structured international-political systems? These theoretical questions require us to take firms as firms, and states as states, without paying attention to differences among them. The questions are then answered by reference to the placement of the units in their system and not by reference to the internal qualities of the units. Systems theories explain why different units behave similarly and, despite their variations, produce outcomes that fall within expected ranges. Conversely, theories at the unit level tell us why different units behave differently despite their similar placement in a system. A theory about foreign policy is a theory at the national level. It leads to expectations about the responses that dissimilar polities will make to external pressures. A theory of international politics bears on the foreign policies of nations although it claims to explain only certain aspects of them. It can tell us what international conditions national policies have to cope with.

From the vantage point of neorealist theory, competition and conflict among states stem directly from the twin facts of life under conditions of anarchy: States in an anarchic order must provide for their own security, and threats or seeming threats to their security abound. Preoccupation with identifying dangers and counteracting them become a way of life. Relations remain tense; the actors are usually suspicious and often hostile even though by nature they may not be given to suspicion and hostility. Individually, states may only be doing what they can to bolster their security. Their individual intentions aside, collectively their actions yield arms races and alliances. The uneasy state of affairs is exacerbated by the familiar "security dilemma," wherein measures that enhance one state's security typically diminish that of others.[5] In an anarchic domain, the source of one's own comfort is the source of another's worry. Hence a state that is amassing instruments of war, even for its own defensive, is cast by others as a threat requiring response. The response itself then serves to confirm the first state's belief that it had reason to worry. Similarly, an alliance that in the interest of defense moves to increase cohesion among its members and add to its ranks inadvertently imperils an opposing alliance and provokes countermeasures.

Some states may hunger for power for power's sake. Neorealist theory, however, shows that it is not necessary to assume an innate lust for power in order to account for the sometimes fierce competition that marks the international arena. In an anarchic domain, a state of war exists if all parties lust for power. But so too will a state of war exist if all states seek only to ensure their own safety.

Although neorealist theory does not explain why particular wars are fought, it does explain war's dismal recurrence through the millennia. Neorealists point not to the ambitions or the intrigues that punctuate the outbreak of individual conflicts but instead to the existing structure within which events, whether by design or accident, can precipitate open clashes of arms. The origins of hot wars lie in cold wars, and the origins of cold wars are found in the anarchic ordering of the international arena.

The recurrence of war is explained by the structure of the international system. Theorists explain what historians know: War is normal. Any given war is explained not by looking at the structure of the international-political system but by looking at the particularities within it: the situations, the characters, and the interactions of states. Although particular explanations are found at the unit level, general explanations are also needed. Wars vary in frequency, and in other ways as well. A central question for a structural theory is this: How do changes of the system affect the expected frequency of war?

KEEPING WARS COLD: THE STRUCTURAL LEVEL

In an anarchic realm, peace is fragile. The prolongation of peace requires that potentially destabilizing developments elicit the interest and the calculated response of some or all of the system's principal actors. In the anarchy of states, the price of inattention or

---

[5]See John H. Herz, "Idealist Internationalism and the Security Dilemma," *World Politics,* II (1950), 157–180.

miscalculation is often paid in blood. An important issue for a structural theory to address is whether destabilizing conditions and events are managed better in multipolar or bipolar systems.

In a system of, say, five great powers, the politics of power turns on the diplomacy by which alliances are made, maintained, and disrupted. Flexibility of alignment means both that the country one is wooing may prefer another suitor and that one's present alliance partner may defect. Flexibility of alignment limits a state's options because, ideally, its strategy must please potential allies and satisfy present partners. Alliances are made by states that have some but not all of their interests in common. The common interest is ordinarily a negative one: fear of other states. Divergence comes when positive interests are at issue. In alliances among near equals, strategies are always the product of compromise since the interests of allies and their notions of how to secure them are never identical.

If competing blocs are seen to be closely balanced, and if competition turns on important matters, then to let one's side down risks one's own destruction. In a moment of crisis the weaker or the more adventurous party is likely to determine its side's policy. Its partners can afford neither to let the weaker member be defeated nor to advertise their disunity by failing to back a venture even while deploring its risks.

The prelude to World War I provides striking examples of such a situation. The approximate equality of partners in both the Triple Alliance and Triple Entente made them closely interdependent. This interdependence, combined with the keen competition between the two camps, meant that, although any country could commit its associates, no one country on either side could exercise control. If Austria-Hungary marched, Germany had to follow; the dissolution of the Austro-Hungarian Empire would have left Germany alone in the middle of Europe. If France marched, Russia had to follow; a German victory over France would be a defeat for Russia. And so the vicious circle continued. Because the defeat or the defection of a major ally would have shaken the balance, each state was constrained to adjust its strategy and the use of its forces to the aims and fears of its partners.

In alliances among equals, the defection of one member threatens the security of the others. In alliances among unequals, the contributions of the lesser members are at once wanted and of relatively small importance. In alliances among unequals, alliance leaders need worry little about the faithfulness of their followers, who usually have little choice anyway. Contrast the situation in 1914 with that of the United States and Britain and France in 1956. The United States could dissociate itself from the Suez adventure of its two principal allies and subject one of them to heavy financial pressure. Like Austria-Hungary in 1914, Britain and France tried to commit or at least immobilize their ally by presenting a fait accompli. Enjoying a position of predominance, the United States could continue to focus its attention on the major adversary while disciplining its two allies. Opposing Britain and France endangered neither the United States nor the alliance because the security of Britain and France depended much more heavily on us than our security depended on them. The ability of the United States, and the inability of Germany, to pay a price measured in intra-alliance terms is striking.

In balance-of-power politics old style, flexibility of alignment led to rigidity of strategy or the limitation of freedom of decision. In balance-of-power politics new style, the obverse is true: Rigidity of alignment in a two-power world results in more flexibility of strategy and greater freedom of decision. In a multipolar world, roughly equal parties engaged in cooperative endeavors must look for the common denominator of their policies. They risk finding the lowest one and easily end up in the worst of all possible worlds. In a bipolar world, alliance leaders can design strategies primarily to advance their own interests and to cope with their main adversary and less to satisfy their own allies.

Neither the United States nor the Soviet Union has to seek the approval of other states, but each has to cope with the other. In the great-power politics of a multipolar world, who is a danger to whom and who can be expected to deal with threats and problems are matters of uncertainty. In the great-power politics of a bipolar world, who is a danger to whom is never in doubt. Any event in the world that involves the fortunes of either of the great powers automatically elicits the interest of the other. President Harry S Truman, at the time of the Korean invasion, could not very well echo Neville Chamberlain's words in the Czechoslovakian crisis by claiming that the Americans knew nothing about the Koreans, a people living far away in the east of Asia. We had to know about them or quickly find out.

In a two-power competition, a loss for one is easily taken to be a gain for the other. As a result, the powers in a bipolar world promptly respond to unsettling events. In a multipolar world, dangers are diffused, responsibilities unclear, and definitions of vital interests easily obscured. Where a number of states are in balance, the skillful foreign policy of a forward power is designed to gain an advantage without antagonizing other states and frightening them into united action. At times in modern Europe, the benefits of possible gains have seemed to outweigh the risks of likely losses. Statesmen have hoped to push an issue to the limit without causing all of the potential opponents to unite. When there are several possible enemies, unity of action among them is difficult to achieve. National leaders could therefore think—or desperately hope, as did Theobald Von Bethmann Hollweg and Adolf Hitler before two world wars—that a united opposition would not form.

If interests and ambitions conflict, the absence of crises is more worrisome than their presence. Crises are produced by the determination of a state to resist a change that another state tries to make. As the leaders in a bipolar system, the United States and the Soviet Union are disposed to do the resisting, for in important matters they cannot hope that their allies will do it for them. Political action in the postwar world has reflected this condition. Communist guerrillas operating in Greece prompted the Truman Doctrine. The tightening of Soviet control over the states of Eastern Europe led to the Marshall Plan and the Atlantic Defense Treaty, and these in turn gave rise to the Cominform and the Warsaw Pact. The plan to create a West German government produced the Berlin blockade. During the past four decades, our responses have been geared to the Soviet Union's actions, and theirs to ours.

Miscalculation by some or all of the great powers is a source of danger in a multipolar world; overreaction by either or both of the great powers is a source of danger in a bipolar world. Which is worse: miscalculation or overreaction? Miscalculation is the greater evil because it is more likely to permit an unfolding of events that finally threatens the status quo and brings the powers to war. Overreaction is the lesser evil because at worst it costs only money for unnecessary arms and possibly the fighting of limited wars. The dynamics of a bipolar system, moreover, provide a measure of correction. In a world in which two states united in their mutual antagonism overshadow any others, the benefits of a calculated response stand out most clearly, and the sanctions against irresponsible behavior achieve their greatest force. Thus two states, isolationist by tradition, untutored in the ways of international politics, and famed for impulsive behavior, have shown themselves—not always and everywhere, but always in crucial cases—to be wary, alert, cautious, flexible, and forbearing. . . .

WARS, HOT AND COLD

Wars, hot and cold, originate in the structure of the international political system. Most Americans blame the Soviet Union for creating the Cold War, by the actions that follow necessarily from the nature of its society and government. Revisionist historians, attacking the dominant view, assign blame to the United States. Some American error, or sinister interest, or faulty assumption about Soviet aims, they argue, is what started the Cold War. Either way, the main point is lost. In a bipolar world, each of the two great powers is bound to focus its fears on the other, to distrust its motives, and to impute offensive intentions to defensive measures. The proper question is what, not who, started the Cold War. Although its content and virulence vary as unit-level forces change and interact, the Cold War continues. It is firmly rooted in the structure of postwar international politics, and will last as long as that structure endures.

HEGEMONIC WAR AND INTERNATIONAL CHANGE

Robert Gilpin

Because of the redistribution of power, the costs to the traditional dominant state of maintaining the international system increase relative to its capacity to pay; this, in turn, produces the severe fiscal crisis. . . . By the same token, the costs to the rising state of changing the system decrease; it begins to appreciate that it can increase its own gains by forcing changes in the nature of the system. Its enhanced power position means that the relative costs of changing the system and securing its interests have decreased. Thus, in accordance with the law of demand, the rising state, as its power increases, will seek to change the status quo as the perceived potential benefits begin to exceed the perceived costs of undertaking a change in the system.

As its relative power increases, a rising state attempts to change the rules governing the international system, the division of the spheres of influence, and, most important of all, the international distribution of territory. In response, the dominant power counters this challenge through changes in its policies that attempt to restore equilibrium in the system. The historical record reveals that if it fails in this attempt, the disequilibrium will be resolved by war. Shepard Clough, in his book *The Rise and Fall of Civilization,* drew on a distinguished career in historical scholarship to make the point: "At least in all the cases which we have passed . . . in review in these pages, cultures with inferior civilization but with growing economic power have always attacked the most civilized cultures during the latters' economic decline" (1970, p. 263). The fundamental task of the challenged dominant state is to solve what Walter Lippmann once characterized as the fundamental problem of foreign policy—the balancing of commitments and resources (Lippmann, 1943, p. 7). An imperial, hegemonic, or great power has essentially two courses of action open to it as it attempts to restore equilibrium in the system. The first and preferred solution is that the challenged power can seek to increase the resources devoted to maintaining its commitments and position in the international system. The second is that it can attempt to reduce its existing commitments (and associated costs) in a way that does not ultimately jeopardize its international position. Although neither response will be followed to the exclusion of the other, they may be considered analytically as separate policies. The logic and the pitfalls of each policy will be considered in turn.

Historically, the most frequently employed devices to generate new resources to meet the increasing costs of dominance and to forestall decline have been to increase

Robert Gilpin, Chapter 5, "Hegemonic War and International Change," in *War and Change in World Politics*. © 1981. Reprinted with the permission of Cambridge University Press.

domestic taxation and to exact tribute from other states. Both of these courses of action have inherent dangers in that they can provoke resistance and rebellion. The French Revolution was triggered in part by the effort of the monarchy to levy the higher taxes required to meet the British challenge (von Ranke, 1950, p. 211). Athens's "allies" revolted against Athenian demands for increased tribute. Because higher taxes (or tribute) mean decreased productive investment and a lowered standard of living, in most instances such expedients can be employed for only relatively short periods of time, such as during a war.

The powerful resistance within a society to higher taxes or tribute encourages the government to employ more indirect methods of generating additional resources to meet a fiscal crisis. Most frequently, a government will resort to inflationary policies or seek to manipulate the terms of trade with other countries. As Carlo Cipolla observed (1970, p. 13), the invariable symptoms of a society's decline are excessive taxation, inflation, and balance-of-payments difficulties as government and society spend beyond their means. But these indirect devices also bring hardship and encounter strong resistance over the long run.

The most satisfactory solution to the problem of increasing costs is increased efficiency in the use of existing resources. Through organizational, technological, and other types of innovations, a state can either economize with respect to the resources at its disposal or increase the total amount of disposable resources. Thus, as Mark Elvin explained, the fundamental reason that imperial China survived intact for so long was its unusually high rate of economic and technological innovation; over long periods China was able to generate sufficient resources to finance the costs of protection against successive invaders (Elvin, 1973). Conversely, the Roman economy stagnated and failed to innovate. Among the reasons for the decline and destruction of Rome was its inability to generate resources sufficient to stave off barbarian invaders. More recently, the calls for greater industrial productivity in contemporary America derive from the realization that technological innovation and more efficient use of existing resources are needed to meet the increasing demands of consumption, investment, and protection.

This innovative solution involves rejuvenation of the society's military, economic, and political institutions. In the case of declining Rome, for example, a recasting of its increasingly inefficient system of agricultural production and a revised system of taxation were required. Unfortunately, social reform and institutional rejuvenation become increasingly difficult as a society ages, because this implies more general changes in customs, attitudes, motivation, and sets of values that constitute a cultural heritage (Cipolla, 1970, p. 11). Vested interests resist the loss of their privileges. Institutional rigidities frustrate abandonment of "tried and true" methods (Downs, 1967, pp. 158–66). One could hardly expect it to be otherwise: "Innovations are important not for their immediate, actual results but for their potential for future development, and potential is very difficult to assess" (Cipolla, 1970, pp. 9–10).

A declining society experiences a vicious cycle of decay and immobility, much as a rising society enjoys a virtuous cycle of growth and expansion. On the one hand, decline is accompanied by lack of social cooperation, by emphasis on rights rather than emphasis on duty, and by decreasing productivity. On the other hand, the frustration and pessimism generated by this gloomy atmosphere inhibit renewal and innovation. The

failure to innovate accentuates the decline and its psychologically debilitating consequences. Once caught up in this cycle, it is difficult for the society to break out (Cipolla,
1970, p. 11). For this reason, a more rational and more efficient use of existing resources to meet increasing military and productive needs is seldom achieved.

There have been societies that have managed their resources with great skill for
hundreds of years and have rejuvenated themselves in response to external challenges,
and this resilience has enabled them to survive for centuries in a hostile environment. In
fact, those states that have been notable for their longevity have been the ones most successful in allocating their scarce resources in an optimal fashion in order to balance,
over a period of centuries, the conflicting demands of consumption, protection, and investment. An outstanding example was the Venetian city-state. Within this aristocratic
republic the governing elite moderated consumption and shifted resources back and
forth between protection and investment as need required over the centuries (Lane,
1973). The Chinese Empire was even more significant. Its longevity and unity were due
to the fact that the Chinese were able to increase their production more rapidly than the
rise in the costs of protection (Elvin, 1973, pp. 92–3, 317). The progressive nature of
the imperial Chinese economy meant that sufficient resources were in most cases available to meet external threats and preserve the integrity of the empire for centuries. In
contrast to the Romans, who were eventually inundated and destroyed by the barbarians, the Chinese "on the whole . . . managed to keep one step ahead of their neighbours in the relevant technical skills, military, economic and organizational" (Elvin,
1973, p. 20).

An example of social rejuvenation intended to meet an external challenge was that
of revolutionary France. The point has already been made that European aristocracies
were reluctant to place firearms in the hands of the lower social orders, preferring to
rely on small professional armies. The French Revolution and the innovation of nationalism made it possible for the French state to tap the energies of the masses of French
citizens. The so-called *levée en masse* greatly increased the human resources available
to the republic and, later, to Napoleon. Although this imperial venture was ultimately
unsuccessful, it does illustrate the potentiality for domestic rejuvenation of a society in
response to decline.

The second type of response to declining fortunes is to bring costs and resources
into balance by reducing costs. This can be attempted in three general ways. The first is
to eliminate the reason for the increasing costs (i.e., to weaken or destroy the rising
challenger). The second is to expand to a more secure and less costly defensive perime-
ter. The third is to reduce international commitments. Each of these alternative strategies has its attractions and its dangers.

The first and most attractive response to a society's decline is to eliminate the
source of the problem. By launching a preventive war the declining power destroys or
weakens the rising challenger while the military advantage is still with the declining
power. Thus, as Thucydides explained, the Spartans initiated the Peloponnesian War in
an attempt to crush the rising Athenian challenger while Sparta still had the power to do
so. When the choice ahead has appeared to be to decline or to fight, statesmen have
most generally fought. However, besides causing unnecessary loss of life, the greatest
danger inherent in preventive war is that it sets in motion a course of events over which
statesmen soon lose control (see the subsequent discussion of hegemonic war).

Second, a state may seek to reduce the costs of maintaining its position by means of further expansion.[1] In effect, the state hopes to reduce its long-term costs by acquiring less costly defensive positions. As Edward Luttwak (1976) demonstrated in his brilliant study of Roman grand strategy, Roman expansion in its later phases was an attempt to find more secure and less costly defensive positions and to eliminate potential challengers. Although this response to declining fortunes can be effective, it can also lead to further overextension of commitments, to increasing costs, and thereby to acceleration of the decline. It is difficult for a successful and expanding state to break the habit of expansion, and it is all too easy to believe that "expand or die" is the imperative of international survival. Perhaps the greatest danger for every imperial or hegemonic power, as it proved eventually to be for Rome, is overextension of commitments that gradually begin to sap its strength (Grant, 1968, p. 246)[2]

The third means of bringing costs and resources into balance is, of course, to reduce foreign-policy commitments. Through political, territorial, or economic retrenchment, a society can reduce the costs of maintaining its international position. However, this strategy is politically difficult, and carrying it out is a delicate matter. Its success is highly uncertain and strongly dependent on timing and circumstances. The problem of retrenchment will be considered first in general terms; then a case of relatively successful retrenchment by a great power will be discussed.

The most direct method of retrenchment is unilateral abandonment of certain of a state's economic, political, or military commitments. For example, a state may withdraw from exposed and costly strategic positions. Venice, as was pointed out, pursued for centuries a conscious policy of alternating advance and retreat. The longevity of the later Roman Empire or Byzantine Empire may be partially explained by its withdrawal from its exposed and difficult-to-defend western provinces and consolidation of its position on a less costly basis in its eastern provinces; its survival for a thousand years was due to the fact that it brought the scale of empire and resources into balance (Cipolla, 1970, p. 82; Rader, 1971, p. 54). In our own time, the so-called Nixon doctrine may be interpreted as an effort on the part of the United States to disengage from vulnerable commitments and to shift part of the burden of defending the international status quo to other powers (Hoffmann, 1978, pp. 46–7).

A second standard technique of retrenchment is to enter into alliances with or seek rapprochement with less threatening powers. In effect, the dominant but declining power makes concessions to another state and agrees to share the benefits of the status quo with that other state in exchange for sharing the costs of preserving the status quo. Thus the Romans brought the Goths into the empire (much to their later regret) in exchange for their assistance in defending the frontiers of the empire. As will be pointed

---

[1]This cause of expansion is frequently explained by the "turbulent-frontier" thesis. A classic example was Britain's steady and incremental conquest of India in order to eliminate threatening political disturbances on the frontier of the empire. Two recent examples are the American invasion of Cambodia during the Vietnam War and the Soviet invasion of Afghanistan.

[2]As Raymond Aron argued (1974), defeat in Vietnam may, in the long run, save the United States from the corrupting and ultimately weakening vice of overexpansion of commitments.

out in a moment, the policy of entente or rapprochement was pursued by the British prior to World War I as they sought to meet the rising German challenge. The American rapprochement with Communist China is a late-twentieth-century example. In exchange for weakening the American commitment to Taiwan, the Americans seek Chinese assistance in containing the expanding power of the Soviet Union.

Unfortunately, there are several dangers associated with this response to decline. First, in an alliance between a great power and a lesser power there is a tendency for the former to overpay in the long run, as has occurred with the United States and the North Atlantic Treaty Organization (NATO); the great power increases its commitments without a commensurate increase in the resources devoted by its allies to finance those commitments. Further, the ally is benefited materially by the alliance, and as its capabilities increase, it may turn against the declining power. Thus the Romans educated the Goths in their military techniques only to have the latter turn these techniques against them. Second, the utility of alliances is limited by Riker's theory of coalitions: An increase in the number of allies decreases the benefits to each. Therefore, as an alliance increases in number, the probability of defection increases (Riker, 1962). Third, the minor ally may involve the major ally in disputes of its own from which the latter cannot disengage itself without heavy costs to its prestige. For these reasons, the utility of an alliance as a response to decline and a means to decrease costs is severely restricted.

The third and most difficult method of retrenchment is to make concessions to the rising power and thereby seek to appease its ambitions. Since the Munich conference in 1938, "appeasement" as a policy has been in disrepute and has been regarded as inappropriate under every conceivable set of circumstances. This is unfortunate, because there are historical examples in which appeasement has succeeded. Contending states have not only avoided conflict but also achieved a relationship satisfactory to both. A notable example was British appeasement of the rising United States in the decades prior to World War I (Perkins, 1968). The two countries ended a century-long hostility and laid the basis for what has come to be known as the "special relationship" of the two Anglo-Saxon powers.

The fundamental problem with a policy of appeasement and accommodation is to find a way to pursue it that does not lead to continuing deterioration in a state's prestige and international position. Retrenchment by its very nature is an indication of relative weakness and declining power, and thus retrenchment can have a deteriorating effect on relations with allies and rivals. Sensing the decline of their protector, allies try to obtain the best deal they can from the rising master of the system. Rivals are stimulated to "close in," and frequently they precipitate a conflict in the process. Thus World War I began as a conflict between Russia and Austria over the disposition of the remnants of the retreating Ottoman Empire (Hawtrey, 1952, pp. 75–81).

Because retrenchment signals waning power, a state seldom retrenches or makes concessions on its own initiative. Yet, not to retrench voluntarily and then to retrench in response to threats or military defeat means an even more severe loss of prestige and weakening of one's diplomatic standing. As a consequence of such defeats, allies defect to the victorious party, opponents press their advantage, and the retrenching society itself becomes demoralized. Moreover, if the forced retrenchment involves the loss of a "vital interest," then the security and integrity of the state are placed in jeopardy. For these reasons, retrenchment is a hazardous course for a state; it is a course seldom pursued by a declining power. However, there have been cases of a retrenchment policy being carried out rather successfully.

An excellent example of a declining hegemon that successfully brought its resources and commitments into balance is provided by Great Britain in the decades just prior to World War I. Following its victory over France in the Napoleonic wars, Great Britain had become the world's most powerful and most prestigious state. It gave its name to a century of relative peace, the Pax Britannica. British naval power was supreme on the high seas, and British industry and commerce were unchallengeable in world markets. An equilibrium had been established on the European continent by the Congress of Vienna (1814), and no military or industrial rivals then existed outside of Europe. By the last decades of the century, however, a profound transformation had taken place. Naval and industrial rivals had risen to challenge British supremacy both on the Continent and overseas. France, Germany, the United States, Japan, and Russia, to various degrees, had become expanding imperial powers. The unification of Germany by Prussia had destroyed the protective Continental equilibrium, and Germany's growing naval might threatened Britain's command of the seas.

As a consequence of these commercial, naval, and imperial challenges, Great Britain began to encounter the problems that face every mature or declining power. On the one hand, external demands were placing steadily increasing strains on the economy; on the other hand, the capacity of the economy to meet these demands had deteriorated. Thus, at the same time that the costs of protection were escalating, both private consumption and public consumption were also increasing because of greater affluence. Superficially the economy appeared strong, but the rates of industrial expansion, technological innovation, and domestic investment had slowed. Thus the rise of foreign challenges and the climacteric of the economy had brought on disequilibrium between British global commitments and British resources.

As the disequilibrium between its global hegemony and its limited resources intensified, Britain faced the dilemma of increasing its resources or reducing its commitments or both. In the national debate on this critical issue the proponents of increasing the available resources proposed two general courses of action. First, they proposed a drawing together of the empire and drawing on these combined resources, as well as the creation of what John Seeley (1905) called Greater Britain, especially the white dominions. This idea, however, did not have sufficient appeal at home or abroad. Second, reformers advocated measures to rejuvenate the declining British economy and to achieve greater efficiency. Unfortunately, as W. Arthur Lewis argued, all the roads that would have led to industrial innovation and a higher rate of economic growth were closed to the British for social, political, or ideological reasons (Lewis, 1978, p. 133). The primary solution to the problem of decline and disequilibrium, therefore, necessarily lay in the reduction of overseas diplomatic and strategic commitments.

The specific diplomatic and strategic issue that faced British leadership was whether to maintain the global position identified with the Pax Britannica or to bring about a retrenchment of its global commitments. By the last decade of the century, Great Britain was confronted by rival land and sea powers on every continent and every sea. European rivals were everywhere: Russia in the Far East, south Asia, and the Middle

East; France in Asia, the Middle East, and north Africa; Germany in the Far East, the Middle East, and Africa. Furthermore, in the Far East, Japan had suddenly emerged as a great power; the United States also was becoming a naval power of consequence and was challenging Great Britain in the Western Hemisphere and the Pacific Ocean.

At the turn of the century, however, the predominant problem was perceived to be the challenge of German naval expansionism. Whereas all the other challenges posed limited and long-term threats, the danger embodied in Germany's decision to build a battle fleet was immediate and portentous. Despite intense negotiations, no compromise of this naval armaments race could be reached. The only course open to the British was retrenchment of their power and commitments around the globe in order to concentrate their total efforts on the German challenge.

Great Britain settled its differences with its other foreign rivals one after another. In the 1890s came the settlement of the Venezuela-British Guiana border dispute in accordance with American desires; in effect, Britain acquiesced in America's primacy in the Caribbean Sea. A century of American-British uneasiness came to an end, and the foundation was laid for the Anglo-American alliance that would prevail in two world wars. Next, in the Anglo-Japanese alliance of 1902, Great Britain gave up its policy of going it alone and took Japan as its partner in the Far East. Accepting Japanese supremacy in the northwestern Pacific as a counterweight to Russia, Great Britain withdrew to the south. This was immediately followed in 1904 by the *entente cordiale,* which settled the Mediterranean and colonial confrontation between France and Great Britain and ended centuries of conflict. In 1907 the Anglo-Russian agreement resolved the British-Russian confrontation in the Far East, turned Russia's interest toward the Balkans, and eventually aligned Russia, Great Britain, and France against Germany and Austria. Thus, by the eve of World War I, British commitments had been retrenched to a point that Britain could employ whatever power it possessed to arrest further decline in the face of expanding German power.

Thus far we have described two alternative sets of strategies that a great power may pursue in order to arrest its decline: to increase resources or to decrease costs. Each of these policies has succeeded to some degree at one time or another. Most frequently, however, the dominant state is unable to generate sufficient additional resources to defend its vital commitments; alternatively, it may be unable to reduce its cost and commitments to some manageable size. In these situations, the disequilibrium in the system becomes increasingly acute as the declining power tries to maintain its position and the rising power attempts to transform the system in ways that will advance its interests. As a consequence of this persisting disequilibrium, the international system is beset by tensions, uncertainties, and crises. However, such a stalemate in the system seldom persists for a long period of time.

Throughout history the primary means of resolving the disequilibrium between the structure of the international system and the redistribution of power has been war, more particularly, what we shall call a hegemonic war. In the words of Raymond Aron, describing World War I, a hegemonic war "is characterized less by its immediate causes or its explicit purposes than by its extent and the stakes involved. It affected all the political units inside one system of relations between sovereign states. Let us call it, for want of a better term, a war of hegemony, hegemony being, if not conscious motive, at any rate the inevitable consequence of the victory of at least one of the states or groups" (Aron, 1964, p. 359). Thus, a hegemonic war is the ultimate test of change in the relative standings of the powers in the existing system.

Every international system that the world has known has been a consequence of the territorial, economic, and diplomatic realignments that have followed such hegemonic struggles. The most important consequence of a hegemonic war is that it changes the system in accordance with the new international distribution of power; it brings about a reordering of the basic components of the system. Victory and defeat reestablish an unambiguous hierarchy of prestige congruent with the new distribution of power in the system. The war determines who will govern the international system and whose interests will be primarily served by the new international order. The war leads to a redistribution of territory among the states in the system, a new set of rules of the system, a revised international division of labor, etc. As a consequence of these changes, a relatively more stable international order and effective governance of the international system are created based on the new realities of the international distribution of power. In short, hegemonic wars have (unfortunately) been functional and integral parts of the evolution and dynamics of international systems.

It is not inevitable, of course, that a hegemonic struggle will give rise immediately to a new hegemonic power and a renovated international order. As has frequently occurred, the combatants may exhaust themselves, and the "victorious" power may be unable to reorder the international system. The destruction of Rome by barbarian hordes led to the chaos of the Dark Ages. The Pax Britannica was not immediately replaced by the Pax Americana; there was a twenty year interregnum, what E. H. Carr called the "twenty years' crisis." Eventually, however, a new power or set of powers emerges to give governance to the international system.

What, then, are the defining characteristics of a hegemonic war? How does it differ from more limited conflicts among states? In the first place, such a war involves a direct contest between the dominant power or powers in an international system and the rising challenger or challengers. The conflict becomes total and in time is characterized by participation of all the major states and most of the minor states in the system. The tendency, in fact, is for every state in the system to be drawn into one or another of the opposing camps. Inflexible bipolar configurations of power (the Delian League versus the Peloponnesian League, the Triple Alliance versus the Triple Entente) frequently presage the outbreak of hegemonic conflict.

Second, the fundamental issue at stake is the nature and governance of the system. The legitimacy of the system may be said to be challenged. For this reason, hegemonic wars are unlimited conflicts; they are at once political, economic, and ideological in terms of significance and consequences. They become directed at the destruction of the offending social, political, or economic system and are usually followed by religious, political, or social transformation of the defeated society. The leveling of Carthage by Rome, the conversion of the Middle East to Islam by the Arabs, and the democratization of contemporary Japan and West Germany by the United States are salient examples. . . .

Third, a hegemonic war is characterized by the unlimited means employed and by the general scope of the warfare. Because all parties are drawn into the war and the stakes involved are high, few limitations, if any, are observed with respect to the means employed; the limitations on violence and treachery tend to be only those necessarily imposed by the state of technology, the available resources, and the fear of retaliation. Similarly, the geographic scope of the war tends to expand to encompass the entire international system; these are "world" wars. Thus, hegemonic wars are characterized by their intensity, scope, and duration.

From the premodern world, the Peloponnesian War between Athens and Sparta and the Second Punic War between Carthage and Rome meet these criteria of hegemonic war. In the modern era, several wars have been hegemonic struggles: the Thirty Years' War (1618–48); the wars of Louis XIV (1667–1713); the wars of the French Revolution and Napoleon (1792–1814); World Wars I and II (1914–18, 1939–45) (Mowat, 1928, pp. 1–2). At issue in each of these great conflicts was the governance of the international system.

In addition to the preceding criteria that define hegemonic war, three preconditions generally appear to be associated with the outbreak of hegemonic war. In the first place, the intensification of conflicts among states is a consequence of the "closing in" of space and opportunities. With the aging of an international system and the expansion of states, the distance between states decreases, thereby causing them increasingly to come into conflict with one another. The once-empty space around the centers of power in the system is appropriated. The exploitable resources begin to be used up, and opportunities for economic growth decline. The system begins to encounter limits to the growth and expansion of member states; states increasingly come into conflict with one another. Interstate relations become more and more a zero-sum game in which one state's gain is another's loss.

Marxists and realists share a sense of the importance of contracting frontiers and their significance for the stability and peace of the system. As long as expansion is possible, the law of uneven growth (or development) can operate with little disturbing effect on the overall stability of the system. In time, however, limits are reached, and the international system enters a period of crisis. The clashes among states for territory, resources, and markets increase in frequency and magnitude and eventually culminate in hegemonic war. Thus, as E. H. Carr told us, the relative peace of nineteenth-century Europe and the belief that a harmony of interest was providing a basis for increasing economic interdependence were due to the existence of "continuously expanding territories and markets" (1951, p. 224). The closing in of political and economic space led to the intensification of conflict and the final collapse of the system in the two world wars.

The second condition preceding hegemonic war is temporal and psychological rather than spatial; it is the perception that a fundamental historical change is taking place and the gnawing fear of one or more of the great powers that time is somehow beginning to work against it and that one should settle matters through preemptive war while the advantage is still on one's side. It was anxiety of this nature that Thucydides had in mind when he wrote that the growth of Athenian power inspired fear on the part of the Lacedaemonians and was the unseen cause of the war. The alternatives open to a state whose relative power is being eclipsed are seldom those of waging war versus promoting peace, but rather waging war while the balance is still in that state's favor or waging war later when the tide may have turned against it. Thus the motive for hegemonic war, at least from the perspective of the dominant power, is to minimize one's losses rather than to maximize one's gains. In effect, a precondition for hegemonic war is the realization that the law of uneven growth has begun to operate to one's disadvantage.

The third precondition of hegemonic war is that the course of events begins to escape human control. Thus far, the argument of this study has proceeded as if mankind controlled its own destiny. The propositions presented and explored in an attempt to understand international political change have been phrased in terms of rational cost/benefit calculations. Up to a point, rationality does appear to apply; statesmen do explicitly or implicitly make rational calculations and then attempt to set the course of the ship of state accordingly. But it is equally true that events, especially those associated with the passions of war, can easily escape from human control.

"What is the force that moves nations?" Tolstoy inquires in the concluding part of *War and Peace,* and he answers that ultimately it is the masses in motion (1961, Vol. II, p. 1404). Leadership, calculation, control over events—these are merely the illusions of statesmen and scholars. The passions of men and the momentum of events take over and propel societies in novel and unanticipated directions. This is especially true during times of war. As the Athenians counseled the Peloponnesians in seeking to forestall war, "consider the vast influence of accident in war, before you engage in it. As it continues, it generally becomes an affair of chances, chances from which neither of us is exempt, and whose event we must risk in the dark. It is a common mistake in going to war to begin at the wrong end, to act first, and wait for disaster to discuss the matter" (Thucydides, 1951, p. 45).

Indeed, men seldom determine or even anticipate the consequences of hegemonic war. Although in going to war they desire to increase their gains or minimize their losses, they do not get the war they want or expect; they fail to recognize the pent-up forces they are unleashing or the larger historical significance of the decisions they are taking. They underestimate the eventual scope and intensity of the conflict on which they are embarking and its implications for their civilization. Hegemonic war arises from the structural conditions and disequilibrium of an international system, but its consequences are seldom predicted by statesmen. As Toynbee suggested, the law governing such conflicts would appear to favor rising states on the periphery of an international system rather than the contending states in the system itself. States directly engaged in hegemonic conflict, by weakening themselves, frequently actually eliminate obstacles to conquest by a peripheral power.

The great turning points in world history have been provided by these hegemonic struggles among political rivals; these periodic conflicts have reordered the international system and propelled history in new and uncharted directions. They resolve the question of which state will govern the system, as well as what ideas and values will predominate, thereby determining the ethos of succeeding ages. The outcomes of these wars affect the economic, social, and ideological structures of individual societies as well as the structure of the larger international system.

In contrast to the emphasis placed here on the role of hegemonic war in changing the international system, it might be argued that domestic revolution can change the international system. This is partially correct. It would be foolish to suggest, for example, that the great revolutions of the twentieth century (the Russian, Chinese, and perhaps Iranian) have not had a profound impact on world politics. However, the primary consequence of these social and political upheavals (at least of the first two) has been to facilitate the mobilization of the society's resources for purposes of national power. In other words, the significance of these revolutions for world politics is that they have served to strengthen (or weaken) their respective states and thereby cause a redistribution of power in the system.

As the distinguished French historian Elie Halévy put it, "all great convulsions in the history of the world, and more particularly in modern Europe, have been at the same time wars and revolutions" (1965, p. 212). Thus the Thirty Years' War was both an international war among Sweden, France, and the Hapsburg Empire and a series of domestic conflicts among Protestant and Catholic parties. The wars of the French Revolution and the Napoleonic period that pitted France against the rest of Europe triggered political upheavals of class and national revolutions throughout Europe. World Wars I and II represented not only the decay of the European international political order but also an onslaught against political liberalism and economic laissez-faire. The triumph of American power in these wars meant not only American governance of the system but also reestablishment of a liberal world order.

REFERENCES

Aron, Raymond. *Peace and War—A Theory of International Relations.* Garden City, N.Y.: Doubleday, 1966.

———. "War and Industrial Society." In *War—Studies from Psychology, Sociology, Anthropology,* edited by Leon Bramson and George W. Goethals, pp. 351–394. New York: Basic Books, 1964.

———. *The Imperial Republic.* Englewood Cliffs, N.J.: Prentice-Hall, 1974.

Beer, Francis A. *Peace Against War—The Ecology of International Violence.* San Francisco: W. H. Freeman, 1981.

Carr, Edward Hallett, *The Twenty Years' Crisis, 1919–1939. An Introduction to the Study of International Relations.* London: Macmillan, 1951.

Cipolla, Carlo M. *Guns, Sails and Empires—Technological Innovation and the Early Phases of European Expansion 1400–1700.* New York: Minerva Press, 1965.

———. ed. *The Economic Decline of Empires.* London: Methuen, 1970.

Clark, George. *War and Society in the Seventeenth Century.* Cambridge University Press, 1958.

Clough, Shepard B. *The Rise and Fall of Civilization.* New York: Columbia University Press, 1970.

Downs, Anthony. *An Economic Theory of Democracy.* New York: Harper & Row, 1957.

———. *Inside Bureaucracy.* Boston: Little, Brown, 1967.

Elvin, Mark. *The Pattern of the Chinese Past.* Stanford: Stanford University Press, 1973.

Grant, Michael. *The Climax of Rome, the Final Achievements of the Ancient World.* London: Weidenfeld and Nicolson, 1968.

Halévy, Elie. *The Era of Tyrannies.* New York: Doubleday, 1965.

Hawtrey, Ralph G. *Economic Aspects of Sovereignty.* London: Longmans, Green, 1952.

Hoffmann, Stanley, ed. *Contemporary Theory in International Relations.* Englewood Cliffs, N.J.: Prentice-Hall, 1960.

———. "International Systems and International Law." In *The State of War—Essays on the Theory and Practice of International Politics,* edited by Stanley Hoffmann, pp. 88–122. New York: Praeger, 1965.

———. "Choices." *Foreign Policy* 12 (1973): 3–42.

———. "An American Social Science: International Relations." *Daedalus* 1 (1977): 41–60.

———. *Primacy or World Order—American Foreign Policy since the Cold War.* New York: McGraw-Hill, 1978.

Lane, Frederic C. "The Economic Meaning of War and Protection." *Journal of Social Philosophy and Jurisprudence* 7 (1942): 254–70.

―――. "Economic Consequences of Organized Violence." *The Journal of Economic History* 18 (1958): 401–17.

―――. *Venice and History: The Collected Papers of Frederic C. Lane.* Baltimore: Johns Hopkins University Press, 1966.

―――. *Venice—A Maritime Republic.* Baltimore: Johns Hopkins University Press, 1973.

Lewis, W. Arthur. *The Theory of Economic Growth.* New York: Harper & Row, 1970.

―――. *Growth and Fluctuations 1870–1913.* London: George Allen and Unwin, 1978.

Lippmann, Walter. *U.S. Foreign Policy: Shield of the Republic.* Boston: Little, Brown, 1943.

Luttwak, Edward. *The Grand Strategy of the Roman Empire—From the First Century A.D. to the Third.* Baltimore: Johns Hopkins University Press, 1976.

Mensch, Gerhard. *Stalemate in Technology—Innovations Overcome the Depression.* Cambridge, Mass.: Ballinger Publishing, 1979.

Modelski, George. "Agraria and Industria: Two Models of the International System." *World Politics* 14 (1961): 118–43.

―――. *Principles of World Politics.* New York: Free Press, 1972.

"The Long Cycle of Global Politics and the Nation-State." *Comparative Studies in Society and History* 20 (1978): 214–35.

Mowat, R. B. *A History of European Diplomacy 1451–1789.* New York: Longmans, Green, 1928.

Perkins, Bradford. *The Great Rapprochement—England and the United States, 1895–1914.* New York: Atheneum, 1968.

Rader, Trout. *The Economics of Feudalism.* New York: Gordon & Breach, 1971.

Riker, William H. *The Theory of Political Coalitions.* New Haven: Yale University Press, 1962.

Rostow, W. W. *Politics and the Stages of Growth.* Cambridge University Press, 1971.

―――. *Getting from Here to There.* New York: McGraw-Hill, 1978.

―――. *Why the Poor Get Richer and the Rich Slow Down: Essays in the Marshallian Long Period.* Austin: University of Texas Press, 1980.

Seeley, John. *The Expansion of England—Two Courses of Lectures.* Boston: Little, Brown, 1905.

Thucydides. *The Peloponnesian War.* New York: Modern Library, 1951.

Tolstoy, L. N. *War and Peace.* 2 vols. Baltimore: Penguin Books, 1961.

Toynbee, Arnold J. *Survey of International Affairs 1930.* London: Oxford University Press, 1931.

―――. *A Study of History.* Vols. 3 and 12. London: Oxford University Press, 1961.

von Ranke, Leopold. "The Great Powers." In *Leopold Ranke—The Formative Years,* edited by Theodore H. von Laue, pp. 181–218. Princeton University Press, 1950.

Walbank, F. W. *The Awful Revolution: The Decline of the Roman Empire in the West.* Liverpool: Liverpool University Press, 1969.

Wright, Quincy. *A Study of War.* 2 vols. Chicago: University of Chicago Press, 1942.

POWER, CULPRITS, AND ARMS

Geoffrey Blainey

THE ABACUS OF POWER

I

The Prussian soldier, Carl von Clausewitz, died of cholera in 1831, while leading an army against Polish rebels. He left behind sealed packets containing manuscripts which his widow published in the following year. The massive dishevelled books, entitled *On War,* could have been called *On War and Peace,* for Clausewitz implied that war and peace had much in common. In his opinion the leisurely siege of the eighteenth century was not much more than a forceful diplomatic note; that kind of war was 'only diplomacy somewhat intensified'.[1] In essence diplomatic despatches breathed deference, but their courtesy was less effective than the silent threats which underwrote them. The threat might not be mentioned, but it was understood. The blunt words of Frederick the Great had similarly summed up the way in which military power influenced diplomacy: 'Diplomacy without armaments is like music without instruments'.[2]

Clausewitz had fought for Prussia in many campaigns against the French but he had more influence on wars in which he did not fight. He is said to have been the talisman of the German general who planned the invasions of France in 1870 and 1914. His books were translated into French just before the Crimean War and into English just after the Franco-Prussian War, and in military academies in many lands the name of this man who had won no great battles became more famous than most of those names inseparably linked with victorious battles. His writings however had less influence outside military circles. He was seen as a ruthless analyst who believed that war should sometimes be 'waged with the whole might of national power'.[3] His views therefore seemed tainted to most civilians; he appeared to be the sinister propagandist of militarism. Those who studied a war's causes, as distinct from its course, ignored him. And yet one of the most dangerous fallacies in the study of war is the belief that the causes of a war and the events of a war belong to separate compartments and reflect completely different principles. This fallacy, translated into medicine, would require the causes and course of an illness to be diagnosed on quite different principles.

Reprinted with permission of The Free Press, a Division of Simon & Schuster, Inc., from *The Causes of War,* Third Edition, by Geoffrey Blainey. Copyright © 1973, 1977, 1988 by Geoffrey Blainey. Chapters 8, 10.

[1]A siege likened to diplomacy: Clausewitz, III 97.
[2]'Diplomacy without armaments': Gooch, *Studies in Diplomacy,* p. 226.
[3]'Waged with the whole might': Leonard, p. 25.

Clausewitz's tumble of words was overwhelmingly on warfare, and the index of the three English volumes of his work points to only one sentence on peace. Nevertheless some of his views on peace can be inferred from lonely sentences. He believed that a clear ladder of international power tended to promote peace. 'A conqueror is always a lover of peace', he wrote.[4] His statement at first sight seems preposterous, but at second sight it commands respect.[5]

II

Power is the crux of many explanations of war and peace, but its effects are not agreed upon. Most observers argue that a nation which is too powerful endangers the peace. A few hint, like Clausewitz, that a dominant nation can preserve the peace simply by its ability to keep inferior nations in order. There must be an answer to the disagreement. The last three centuries are studded with examples of how nations behaved in the face of every extremity of military and economic power.

That a lopsided balance of power will promote war is probably the most popular theory of international relations. It has the merit that it can be turned upside down to serve as an explanation of peace. It is also attractive because it can be applied to wars of many centuries, from the Carthaginian wars to the Second World War. The very phrase, 'balance of power', has the soothing sound of the panacea: it resembles the balance of nature and the balance of trade and other respectable concepts. It therefore suggests that an even balance of power is somehow desirable. The word 'balance', unfortunately, is confusing. Whereas at one time it usually signified a set of weighing scales—in short it formerly signified either equality or inequality—it now usually signifies equality and equilibrium. In modern language the assertion that 'Germany had a favourable balance of power' is not completely clear. It is rather like a teacher who, finding no equality of opportunity in a school, proceeded to denounce the 'unfavourable equality of opportunity'. The verbal confusion may be partly responsible for the million vague and unpersuasive words which have been written around the concept of the balance of power.

The advantages of an even balance of power in Europe have been stressed by scores of historians and specialists in strategy. The grand old theory of international relations, it is still respected though no longer so venerated. According to Hedley Bull, who was a director of a research unit on arms control in the British foreign office before becoming professor of international relations at the Australian National University, 'The alternative to a stable balance of military power is a preponderance of power, which is very much more dangerous'.[6] Likewise, Alastair Buchan, director of London's Institute for Strategic Studies, suggested in his excellent book *War in Modern Society:* 'certainly we know from our experience of the 1930s that the lack of such a balance

---

[4]'A conqueror': Clausewitz, II 155.
[5]Clausewitz on peace: On first reading Clausewitz I noticed no comment on peace. Later, realizing that he must have commented by implication, I skimmed through his work again. As his references to peace seem sparse, I cannot be sure that I have interpreted his views correctly.
[6]Bull: cited in Buchan, p. 34.

creates a clear temptation to aggression'.[7] Many writers of history have culled a similar lesson from past wars.

Most believers in the balance of power think that a world of many powerful states tends to be more peaceful. There an aggressive state can be counterbalanced by a combination of other strong states. Quincy Wright, in his massive book, *A Study of War,* suggested with some reservations that 'the probability of war will decrease in proportion as the number of states in the system increases'.[8] Arnold Toynbee,[9] observing that the world contained eight major powers on the eve of the First World War and only two—the United States and the Soviet Union—at the close of the Second World War, thought the decline was ominous. A chair with only two legs, he argued, had less balance. As the years passed, and the two great powers avoided major war, some specialists on international affairs argued that a balance of terror had replaced the balance of power. In the nuclear age, they argued, two great powers were preferable to eight. The danger of a crisis that slipped from control was diminished if two powers dominated the world.[10] Nevertheless even those who preferred to see two powers dominant in the nuclear age still believed, for the most part, that in the pre-nuclear era a world of many strong powers was safer.[11]

To my knowledge no historian or political scientist produced evidence to confirm that a power system of seven strong states was more conducive to peace than a system of two strong states. The idea relies much on analogies. Sometimes it resembles the kind of argument which old men invoked in European cities when the two-wheeled bicycle began to supersede the tricycle. At other times it resembles a belief in the virtues of free competition within an economic system. It parallels the idea that in business many strong competitors will so function that none can win a preponderance of power; if one seems likely to become predominant, others will temporarily combine to subdue him. It is possibly significant that this doctrine of flexible competition in economic affairs was brilliantly systematised at the time when a similar doctrine was refined in international affairs. While Adam Smith praised the virtues of the free market in economic affairs, the Swiss jurist Emerich de Vattel praised it in international affairs. In one sense both theories were reactions against a Europe in which powerful monarchs hampered economic life with meddlesome regulations and disturbed political life with frequent wars.

It is axiomatic that a world possessing seven nations of comparable strength, each of which values its independence, will be a substantial safeguard against the rise of one world-dominating power. Even two nations of comparable strength will be a useful safeguard. When all this has been said we possess not an axiom for peace but an axiom for national independence. And that in fact was the main virtue of a balance of power in

---

[7]Buchan, p. 177.
[8]Wright, abridged edn., p. 122.
[9]Toynbee, *A Study of History,* IX 244.
[10]The preference for a bi-polar system often seems to hinge on the idea that wars are often the result of situations which go further than either nation intended.
[11]Scholars' preference for a multi-polar system before 1945 and bi-polar system thereafter: G. H. Snyder in Pruitt and Snyder, p. 124.

the eyes of those who originally practiced it. It was not primarily a formula for peace: it was a formula for national independence. Edward Gulick,[12] Massachusetts historian, was adamant that its clearest theorists and practitioners—the Metternichs and Castlereaghs—'all thought of war as an instrument to preserve or restore a balance of power'. In essence a balance of power was simply a formula designed to prevent the rise of a nation to world dominance. It merely masqueraded as a formula for peace.

III

The idea that an even distribution of power promotes peace has gained strength partly because it has never been accompanied by tangible evidence. Like a ghost it has not been captured and examined for pallor and pulse-beat. And yet there is a point of time when the ghost can be captured. The actual distribution of power can be measured at the end of the war.

The military power of rival European alliances was most imbalanced, was distributed most unevenly, at the end of a decisive war. And decisive wars tended to lead to longer periods of international peace. Indecisive wars, in contrast, tended to produce shorter periods of peace. Thus the eighteenth century was characterised by inconclusive wars and by short periods of peace. During the long wars one alliance had great difficulty in defeating the other. Many of the wars ended in virtual deadlock: military power obviously was evenly balanced. Such wars tended to lead to short periods of peace. The War of the Polish Succession—basically an ineffectual war between France and Austria—was followed within five years by the War of the Austrian Succession. That war after eight years was so inconclusive on most fronts that the peace treaty signed in 1748 mainly affirmed the status quo. That ineffectual war was followed only eight years later by another general war, the Seven Years War, which ended with Britain the clear victor in the war at sea and beyond the seas, though on European soil the war was a stalemate. But even the Anglo-French peace which followed the Treaty of Paris in 1763 was not long; it ended after fifteen years. It ended when the revolt of the American colonies against Britain removed Britain's preponderance of power over France.

The French Revolutionary Wars which, beginning in 1792, raged across Europe and over the sea for a decade were more decisive than any major war for more than a century. They ended with France dominant on the continent and with England dominant at sea and in America and the East. They thus failed to solve the crucial question: was England or France the stronger power? The Peace of Amiens, which England and France signed in 1802, lasted little more than a year. So began the Napoleonic Wars which at last produced undisputed victors.

This is not to suggest that a general war which ended in decisive victory was the sole cause of a long period of peace. A decisive general war did not always lead to a long period of peace. This survey of the major wars of the period 1700 to 1815 does suggest however that the traditional theory which equates an even balance of power with peace should be reversed. Instead a clear preponderance of power tended to promote peace.

---

[12]Gulick, p. 36.

Of the general wars fought in Europe in the last three centuries those with the most decisive outcome were the Napoleonic (1815), Franco-Prussian (1871), First World War (1918), and Second World War (1945). The last days of those wars and the early years of the following periods of peace marked the height of the imbalance of power in Europe. At the end of those wars the scales of power were so tilted against the losers that Napoleon Bonaparte was sent as a captive to an island in the South Atlantic, Napoleon III was captured and permitted to live in exile in England, Kaiser Wilhelm II went into exile in Holland and Adolf Hitler committed suicide. Years after the end of those wars, the scales of power were still strongly tilted against the losers. And yet those years of extreme imbalance marked the first stages of perhaps the most pronounced periods of peace known to Europe in the last three or more centuries.

Exponents of the virtues of an even distribution of military power have concentrated entirely on the outbreak of war. They have ignored however the conditions surrounding the outbreak of peace. By ignoring the outbreak of peace they seem to have ignored the very period when the distribution of military power between warring nations can be accurately measured. For warfare is the one convincing way of measuring the distribution of power. The end of a war produces a neat ledger of power which has been duly audited and signed. According to that ledger an agreed preponderance of power tends to foster peace. In contrast the exponents of the orthodox theory examine closely the prelude to a war, but that is a period when power is muffled and much more difficult to measure. It is a period characterised by conflicting estimates of which nation or alliance is the most powerful. Indeed one can almost suggest that war is usually the outcome of a diplomatic crisis which cannot be solved because both sides have conflicting estimates of their bargaining power.

The link between a diplomatic crisis and the outbreak of war seems central to the understanding of war. That link however seems to be misunderstood. Thus many historians, in explaining the outbreak of war, argue that 'the breakdown in diplomacy led to war'. This explanation is rather like the argument that the end of winter led to spring: it is a description masquerading as an explanation. In fact that main influence which led to the breakdown of diplomacy—a contradictory sense of bargaining power—also prompted the nations to fight. At the end of a war the situation was reversed. Although I have not come across the parallel statement—'so the breakdown of war led to diplomacy'—it can be explained in a similar way. In essence the very factor which made the enemies reluctant to continue fighting also persuaded them to negotiate. That factor was their agreement about their relative bargaining position.

It is not the actual distribution or balance of power which is vital: it is rather the way in which national leaders *think* that power is distributed. In contrast orthodox theory assumes that the power of nations can be measured with some objectivity. It assumes that, in the pre-nuclear era, a statesman's knowledge of the balance of international power rested mainly on an 'objective comparison of military capabilities'.[13] I

---

[13]'The objective comparison of military capabilities': G. H. Snyder in Pruitt and Snyder, p. 117. According to Wright, p. 116, the term 'balance of power' implies that fluctuations in power 'can be observed and measured'.

find it difficult however to accept the idea that power could ever be measured with such objectivity. The clear exception was at the end of wars—the points of time which theorists ignore. Indeed, it is the problem of accurately measuring the relative power of nations which goes far to explain why wars occur. War is a dispute about the measurement of power. War marks the choice of a new set of weights and measures.

IV

In peace time the relations between two diplomats are like relations between two merchants. While the merchants trade in copper or transistors, the diplomats' transactions involve boundaries, spheres of influence, commercial concessions and a variety of other issues which they have in common. A foreign minister or diplomat is a merchant who bargains on behalf of his country. He is both buyer and seller, though he buys and sells privileges and obligations rather than commodities. The treaties he signs are simply more courteous versions of commercial contracts.

The difficulty in diplomacy, as in commerce, is to find an acceptable price for the transaction. Just as the price of merchandise such as copper roughly represents the point where the supply of copper balances the demand for it, the price of a transaction in diplomacy roughly marks the point at which one nation's willingness to pay matches the price demanded by the other. The diplomatic market however is not as sophisticated as the mercantile market. Political currency is not so easily measured as economic currency. Buying and selling in the diplomatic market is much closer to barter, and so resembles an ancient bazaar in which the traders have no accepted medium of exchange. In diplomacy each nation has the rough equivalent of a selling price—a price which it accepts when it sells a concession—and the equivalent of a buying price. Sometimes these prices are so far apart that a transaction vital to both nations cannot be completed peacefully; they cannot agree on the price of the transaction. The history of diplomacy is full of such crises. The ministers and diplomats of Russia and Japan could not agree in 1904, on the eve of the Russo-Japanese War; the Germans could not find acceptable terms with British and French ministers on the eve of the Second World War.

A diplomatic crisis is like a crisis in international payments; like a crisis in the English pound or the French franc. In a diplomatic crisis the currency of one nation or alliance is out of alignment with that of the others. These currencies are simply the estimates which each nation nourishes about its relative bargaining power. These estimates are not easy for an outsider to assess or to measure; and yet these estimates exist clearly in the minds of the ministers and diplomats who bargain.

For a crisis in international payments there are ultimate solutions which all nations recognise. If the English pound is the object of the crisis, and if its value is endangered because England is importing too much, the English government usually has to admit that it is living beyond its present means. As a remedy it may try to discourage imports and encourage exports. It may even have to declare that the value of the English pound is too high in relation to the French franc, the German mark and all other currencies, and accordingly it may fix the pound at a lower rate. Whichever solution it follows is not pleasant for the national pride and the people's purse. Fortunately there is less shame and humiliation for a nation which has to confess that its monetary currency is overvalued than for a country which has to confess that its diplomatic currency is overvalued. It is almost as if the detailed statistics which record the currency crisis make it seem anonymous and unemotional. In contrast a diplomatic crisis is personal and emotional. The opponent is not a sheet of statistics representing the sum of payments to and from all nations: the opponent is an armed nation to which aggressive intentions can be attributed and towards whom hatred can be felt.

A nation facing a payments crisis can *measure* the extent to which it is living beyond its means. As the months pass by, moreover, it can measure whether its remedies have been effective, for the statistics of its balance of payments are an accurate guide to the approach of a crisis and the passing of crisis. On the other hand a deficit in international power is not so easy to detect. A nation with an increasing deficit in international power may not even recognise its weaknesses. A nation may so mistake its bargaining power that it may make the ultimate appeal to war, and then learn through defeat in warfare to accept a humbler assessment of its bargaining position.

The death-watch wars of the eighteenth century exemplified such crises. A kingdom which was temporarily weakened by the accession of a new ruler or by the outbreak of civil unrest refused to believe that it was weaker. It usually behaved as if its bargaining position were unaltered. But its position, in the eyes of rival nations, was often drastically weaker. Negotiations were therefore frustrated because each nation demanded far more than the other was prepared to yield. Likewise the appeal to war was favoured because each side believed that it would win.

In diplomacy some nations for a longer period can live far beyond their means: to live beyond their means is to concede much less than they would have to concede if the issue was resolved by force. A government may be unyielding in negotiations because it predicts that its adversary does not want war. It may be unyielding because it has an inflated idea of its own military power. Or it may be unyielding because to yield to an enemy may weaken its standing and grip within its own land. Whereas an endangered nation facing a currency crisis cannot escape some punishment, in a diplomatic crisis it can completely escape punishment so long as the rival nation or alliance does not insist on war. Thus diplomacy may become more unrealistic, crises may become more frequent, and ultimately the tension and confusion may end in war. . . .

War itself provides the most reliable and most objective test of which nation or alliance is the most powerful. After a war which ended decisively, the warring nations agreed on their respective strength. The losers and the winners might have disagreed about the exact margin of superiority; they did agree however that decisive superiority existed. A decisive war was therefore usually followed by an orderly market in political power, or in other words peace. Indeed one vital difference between the eighteenth and nineteenth centuries was that wars tended to become more decisive. This is part of the explanation for the war-studded history of one century and the relative peacefulness of the following century. Whereas the eighteenth century more often had long and inconclusive wars followed by short periods of peace, the century after 1815 more often had short and decisive wars and long periods of peace.

Nevertheless, during both centuries, the agreement about nations' bargaining power rarely lasted as long as one generation. Even when a war had ended decisively the hierarchy of power could not last indefinitely. It was blurred by the fading of memories of the previous war, by the accession of new leaders who blamed the old leaders for the defeat, and by the legends and folklore which glossed over past defeats. It was blurred by the weakening effects of internal unrest or the strengthening effects of military reorganisation, by economic and technical change, by shifts in alliances, and by a variety of other influences. So the defeated nation regained confidence. When important issues arose, war became a possibility. The rival nations believed that each could gain more by fighting than by negotiating. Those contradictory hopes are characteristic of the outbreak of war. . . .

VII

Wars usually end when the fighting nations *agree* on their relative strength, and wars usually begin when fighting nations *disagree* on their relative strength. Agreement or disagreement is shaped by the same set of factors. Thus each factor that is a prominent cause of war can at times be a prominent cause of peace. Each factor can oscillate between war and peace, and the oscillation is most vivid in the history of nations which decided to fight because virtually everything was in their favour and decided to cease fighting because everything was pitted against them. . . .

AIMS AND ARMS

I

A culprit stands in the centre of most generalised explanations of war. While there may be dispute in naming the culprit, it is widely believed that the culprit exists.

In the eighteenth century many philosophers thought that the ambitions of absolute monarchs were the main cause of war: pull down the mighty, and wars would become rare. Another theory contended that many wars came from the Anglo-French rivalry for colonies and commerce: restrain that quest, and peace would be more easily preserved. The wars following the French Revolution fostered an idea that popular revolutions were becoming the main cause of international war. In the nineteenth century, monarchs who sought to unite their troubled country by a glorious foreign war were widely seen as culprits. At the end of that century the capitalists' chase for markets or investment outlets became a popular villain. The First World War convinced many writers that armaments races and arms salesmen had become the villains, and both world wars fostered the idea that militarist regimes were the main disturbers of the peace.

Most of these theories of war have flourished, then fallen away, only to appear again in new dress. The eighteenth-century belief that mercantilism was the main cause of war was re-clothed by the Englishman, J. A. Hobson, and the Russian exile, V. I. Lenin, in the Boer War and in the First World War; and the theme that manufacturers of armaments were the chief plotters of war was revived to explain the widening of the war in Vietnam. The resilience of this type of explanation is probably aided by the fact that it carries its own solution to war. Since it points to a particular culprit, we only have to eliminate the culprit in order to abolish war. By abolishing dictators, capitalists, militarists, manufacturers of armaments or one of the other villains, peace would be preserved. Indeed it is often the passion for the antidote—whether democracy, socialism or free trade—rather than an analysis of the illness that popularises many of these theories of war.

These theories assume that ambitions and motives are the dominant cause of wars. As war is increasingly denounced as the scarlet sin of civilisation, it is understandable that the search for the causes of war should often become a search for villains. The search is aided by the surviving records of war. So many of the documents surrounding the outbreak of every war—whether the War of Spanish Succession or the recent War of the Saigon Succession—are attempts to blame the other side. The surviving records of wars are infected with insinuations and accusations of guilt, and some of that infection is transmitted to the writings of those who, generations or centuries later, study those wars. Since so much research into war is a search for villains, and since the evidence itself is dominated by attempts to apportion blame, it is not surprising that many theories of war and explanations of individual wars are centred on the aims of 'aggressors'.

Most controversies about the causes of particular wars also hinge on the aims of nations. What did France and England hope to gain by aiding the Turks against the Russians in the Crimean War? What were the ambitions of Bismarck and Napoleon III on the eve of the Franco-Prussian War of 1870? Who deserves most blame for the outbreak of the First World War? The evergreen examination-question at schools and universities—were the main causes of a certain war political or economic or religious—reflects the strong tradition that ambitions are the key to understanding war.

The running debate on the causes of the Vietnam War is therefore in a rich tradition. Measured by the mileage of words unrolled it must be the most voluminous which any war has aroused, but it is mainly the traditional debate about ambitions and motives. The war in Vietnam is variously said to have been caused by the desire of United States' capitalists for markets and investment outlets, by the pressures of American military suppliers, by the American hostility to communism, by the crusading ambitions of Moscow and Peking, the aggressive nationalism or communism of Hanoi, the corruption or aggression of Saigon, or the headlong clash of other aims. The kernel of the debate is the assumption that pressures or ambitions are the main causes of the war.

II

The idea that war is caused simply by a clash of aims is intrinsically satisfying. It is easy to believe that historians will ultimately understand the causes of war if only they can unravel the ambitions held on the eve of a war by the relevant monarchs, prime ministers, presidents, chiefs of staff, archbishops, editors, intellectuals and cheering or silent crowds. Explanations based on ambitions however have a hidden weakness. They portray ambitions which were so strong that war was inevitable. It is almost a hallmark of such interpretations to describe ambitions—whether for prestige, ideology, markets or empire—as the fundamental causes, the basic causes, the deepseated, underlying or long-term causes. Such causes merely need the provocation of minor events to produce war. The minor events are usually referred to as the occasion for war as distinct from the causes of war. Sometimes the incidents which immediately precede the war are called the short-term causes: the assumption is that long-term causes are more powerful.

This idea of causation has a distinctive shape. Its exponents see conflict as a volcano which, seeming to slumber, is really approaching the day of terror. They see conflict as water which slowly gathers heat and at last comes to the boil. The events which happen on the eve of a war add the last few degrees of heat to the volcano or kettle. It is a linear kind of argument: the causes of war are like a graph of temperatures and the last upward movement on the graph marks the transition from peace to war. If in fact such a graph were a valid way of depicting the coming of war, one would also expect to see the temperature curve move downwards in the last days of a war. One would also expect that if, on the eve of a war, minor incidents could convert the long-term causes of conflict into war, similar incidents could activate the transition from war to peace. No such explanations however are offered for the end of a war. If one believes that the framework of an explanation of war should also be valid for an explanation of peace, the volcano or kettle theories are suspect.

For any explanation the framework is crucial. In every field of knowledge the accepted explanations depend less on the marshalling of evidence than on preconceptions of what serves as a logical framework for the evidence. The framework dominates the evidence, because it dictates what evidence should be sought or ignored. Our idea of a logical framework is often unconscious, and this elusiveness enhances its grip. One may suggest that the explanations of war which stress ambitions are resting on a persuasive but rickety framework.

The policies of a Frederick the Great, a Napoleon and a President Lincoln were clearly important in understanding wars. So too were the hopes of the inner circles of power in which they moved and the hopes of the people whom they led. Likewise the aims of all the surrounding nations—irrespective of their eagerness or reluctance to fight—were important. It is doubtful however whether a study of the aims of many wars will yield useful patterns. There is scant evidence to suggest that century after century the main aims of nations which went to war could be packaged into a simple economic, religious or political formula. There is no evidence that, over a long period, the desire for territory or markets or the desire to spread an ideology tended to dominate all other war aims. It is even difficult to argue that certain kinds of aims were dominant in one generation. Admittedly it is often said that the main 'causes'—meaning the main aims—of war were religious in the sixteenth century, dynastic or mercantile in various phases of the eighteenth century and nationalist or economic in the nineteenth century. It seems more likely, however, that those who share in a decision to wage war pursued a variety of aims which even fluctuated during the same week and certainly altered during the course of the war.

One generalisation about war aims can be offered with confidence. The aims are simply varieties of power. The vanity of nationalism, the will to spread an ideology, the protection of kinsmen in an adjacent land, the desire for more territory or commerce, the avenging of a defeat or insult, the craving for greater national strength or independence, the wish to impress or cement alliances—all these represent power in different wrappings. The conflicting aims of rival nations are always conflicts of power. Not only is power the issue at stake, but the decision to resolve that issue by peaceful or warlike methods is largely determined by assessments of relative power.

III

The explanations that stress aims are theories of rivalry and animosity and not theories of war. They help to explain increasing rivalry between nations but they do not explain why the rivalry led to war. For a serious rift between nations does not necessarily end in war. It may take other forms: the severing of diplomatic relations; the peaceful intervention of a powerful outside nation; an economic blockade; heavy spending on armaments; the imposing of tariffs; an invasion accomplished without bloodshed; the enlisting of allies; or even the relaxing of tension through a successful conference. Of course these varieties of conflict may merely postpone the coming of war but serious rivalry and animosity can exist for a century without involving warfare. France and Britain were serious rivals who experienced dangerous crises between 1815 and 1900, but the war so often feared did not eventuate.

One may suggest that this kind of interpretation is hazy about the causes of peace as well as war. Its exponents usually ignore the question of why a war came to an end. They thus ignore the event which would force them to revise their analysis of the causes of war. Consider for instance the popular but dubious belief that the main cause of the First World War was Berlin's desire to dominate Europe. Now if such an explanation is valid, what were the main causes of the peace which ensued in 1918? It would be consistent with this interpretation to reply that the crumbling of German ambitions led to peace. And why had those ambitions crumbled? Because by October 1918 Germany's military power—and morale is a vital ingredient of power—was no longer adequate. As the emphasis on aims cannot explain Germany's desire for peace in 1918, it would be surprising if the emphasis on aims could explain Germany's decision for war in 1914. Indeed Germany's aims would not have been high in 1914 if her leaders then had believed that Germany lacked adequate power. Bethmann Hollweg, chancellor of Germany at the outbreak of war, confessed later that Germany in 1914 had overvalued her strength. 'Our people', he said, 'had developed so amazingly in the last twenty years that wide circles succumbed to the temptation of overestimating our enormous forces in relation to those of the rest of the world.'[14]

One conclusion seems clear. It is dangerous to accept any explanation of war which concentrates on ambitions and ignores the means of carrying out those ambitions. A government's aims are strongly influenced by this assessment of whether it has sufficient strength to achieve these aims. Indeed the two factors interact quietly and swiftly. When Hitler won power in 1933 and had long-term hopes of reviving German greatness, his ambitions could not alone produce a forceful foreign policy. Hitler's foreign policy in 1933 was no more forceful than his means, in his judgment, permitted. His military and diplomatic weapons, in his opinion, did not at first permit a bold foreign policy. A. J. P. Taylor's *The Origins of the Second World War,* one of the most masterly books on a particular war, reveals Hitler as an alert opportunist who tempered his objectives to the available means of achieving them. When Hitler began to rearm Germany he was guided not only by ambitions but by his sense of Germany's bargaining position in Europe. He would not have rearmed if he had believed that France or

---

[14]'Our people', Fischer, p. 637.

Russia would forcefully prevent him from building aircraft, submarines and tanks. In the main decisions which Hitler made between 1933 and the beginning of war in 1939, his short-term objectives and his sense of Germany's bargaining position marched so neatly in step that it is impossible to tell whether his aims or his oscillating sense of Germany's strength beat the drum. Opportunity and ambition—or aims and arms—so acted upon one another that they were virtually inseparable. The interaction was not confined to Berlin; it occurred in the 1930s in London, Paris, Warsaw, Moscow, Rome, Prague and all the cities of power. . . .

REFERENCES

Buchan, Alastair. *War in Modern Society: an introduction* (London, 1968).

Clausewitz, Carl von. *On War,* ed. by F. N. Maude, tr. from German, 3 vols. (London, 1940).

Fischer, Fritz. *Germany's Aims in the First World War,* tr. from German (London, 1967).

Gooch, G. P. *Studies in Diplomacy and Statecraft* (London, 1942).

———. *Louis XV: the monarchy in decline* (London, 1956).

Gulick, E. V. *Europe's Classical Balance of Power* (New York, 1967).

Leonard, Roger A., ed. *A Short Guide to Clausewitz on War* (London, 1967).

Pruitt, Dean G. and Snyder, R. C., eds. *Theory and Research on the Causes of War* (Englewood Cliffs, New Jersey, 1969).

Toynbee, Arnold. *Experiences* (London, 1969).

———. *A Study of History,* 12 vols. (London, 1934–61).

Wright, Quincy. *A Study of War,* 2 vols. (Chicago, 1942).

———. *A Study of War,* abridged by Louis L. Wright (Chicago, 1965).

PART III

INTERNATIONAL LIBERALISM: INSTITUTIONS AND COOPERATION

Realist theories sometimes dominate academic thinking about international relations, especially in periods when the world finds itself locked in conflict. But realist theories have never been popular in periods of optimism because they seem so fatalistic and unhopeful, and so oblivious to the power of values and logical alternatives to destructive competition.

In the previous section E. H. Carr presented idealism as the alternative to realism. Many sorts of ideals can drive people toward war or away from it: for example, religious militance (the Crusades or the Thirty Years War); religious pacifism (the Quakers); racist ideology (German fascism); or militarist moral codes (Japanese Bushido). At the moment, however, liberalism—the idealism of the contemporary western world—is the only major challenge to realism. Many theorists also believe that liberal ideas about international life are no less grounded in reality than is realism—that liberalism is not wishful thinking about the "harmony of interests," as Carr presented it, but a description of how the world sometimes does work as well as how it should work.

There are three general variants of liberal theory about international cooperation. The economic strand, based on assumed effects of self-interest and comparative advantage in international trade, is represented in several selections in Part V. The domestic political variant, based on alleged effects of democratic constitutionalism, appears in Part VI. This section focuses more on the third form, "neoliberal institutionalism,"[1] which assumes that pacifying effects flow from the development of international norms and institutions that fall short of full world government.

"Liberal" in the sense used here does not mean left-of-center, the colloquial meaning of the word in U.S. politics. Rather it means the broad philosophical tradition that enshrines the values of individual political and economic liberty, the free market of ideas and enterprise—the basic values that *unite* what passes for left and right in American politics. The United States has been so fundamentally liberal a country in

---

[1]See Robert Keohane, *International Institutions and State Power* (Boulder: Westview Press, 1989).

this general sense that most Americans take the basic principles utterly for granted, and are not even conscious of their liberalism as a distinct ideology. Debates occur only among different positions within liberalism.[2]

Three general points distinguish liberal views of international conflict from realism or, in some respects, Marxism.

First, ideas matter. The pen is mightier than the sword. A society's political and economic values will make it more or less prone to peace, no matter what the structure of the international balance of power may be. "Good" states—liberal republics—are likely to use force only in what they believe to be self-defense, not for the purpose of ruling or exploiting others. Societies devoted to free trade will seek profit through exchange and comparative advantage in production rather than through conquest and plunder.

Second, history is *progress,* a process of development in which the right ideas steadily drive out the wrong, not a cycle in which the fate of nations is to repeat the same follies. With allowances for exceptions and occasional backsliding, the world has been developing from primitive, parochial, and destructive behavior toward modern, cosmopolitan, efficient interchange. This is the conviction that animates Fukuyama's "End of History" and Kant's "Perpetual Peace."

Third, the fact that the international system is anarchic does not bar civility among nations. Under certain conditions, norms of cooperation can help keep countries from each others' throats because governments can recognize their mutual interest in avoiding conflict.[3] To realists, insecurity and the possibility of war are inherent in a system of separate states without an overarching authority. To liberals, anarchy may be a necessary cause of war but not a sufficient one. The proximate cause of war is usually that people who are bad, backward, or deluded decide to start it. The causes can be exposed as unnecessary, inimical to selfish material interests as well as moral ones, and can thus be overcome by the spread of liberal values and institutions.

Kant's "Perpetual Peace" is as classic a statement of some aspects of the liberal paradigm as Thucydides' *Peloponnesian War* is of the realist.[4] Kant claims that the tendency to progress is inherent in nature, and that as men and republics improve themselves they will create perpetual peace. The logic of Kant is the primary ingredient in Michael Doyle's analysis in Part VI of why liberal democracy breeds peace.

Among the contemporary authors in this section, Hedley Bull argues that the international system has become more civil than the state of nature, even without a sovereign to suppress conflict. Keohane and Nye present the case for why modern interdependence among states reduced the utility of force in relations among them, even

---

[2]See Louis Hartz, *The Liberal Tradition in America* (New York: Harcourt, Brace, 1955). The deep roots of liberal assumptions lie behind much of the American behavior that realists criticize as legalistic and moralistic. See George F. Kennan, *American Diplomacy, 1900–1950* (Chicago: University of Chicago Press, 1951).

[3]See Kenneth A. Oye, ed., *Cooperation Under Anarchy* (Princeton: Princeton University Press, 1986) and Robert Axelrod, *The Evolution of Cooperation* (New York: Basic Books, 1984).

[4]For an argument that reconciles Kant with realism see Kenneth N. Waltz, "Kant, Liberalism, and War," *American Political Science Review* 56, no. 2 (June 1962).

before the end of the Cold War.[5] John Mueller argues that major war has become obsolete because it has been recognized as an unnecessary, uncivilized, anachronism, like dueling and slavery.

Liberal arguments of various sorts about the obsolescence of war, declining significance of the nation state, and growing import of cooperative supranational institutions have been popular periodically in the past. Most recent was the resurgence of such ideas in the 1970s, just after the Vietnam War soured many observers on the utility of force and before the collapse of U.S.-Soviet detente made optimism about basic changes in international relations seem premature. With the reinvigoration of the Cold War, realism became the dominant school of thought again. As the end of the Cold War was celebrated and widely seen as a fundamentally new departure in world development, the liberal paradigm was again ascendant in the 1990s.

—RKB

---

[5]For an earlier essay in this vein see Klaus Knorr, *On the Utility of Force in the Nuclear Age* (Princeton: Princeton University Press, 1966). Knorr later had second thoughts about how far the argument was being taken in literature of the early 1970s, and qualified his views. See Knorr, "Is International Coercion Waning or Rising?" *International Security* 1, no. 4 (spring 1977) and "On the International Uses of Force in the Contemporary World," *Orbis* 21, no. 1 (spring 1977).

PERPETUAL PEACE

Immanuel Kant

SECTION II: CONTAINING THE DEFINITIVE ARTICLES FOR PERPETUAL PEACE AMONG STATES

The state of peace among men living side by side is not the natural state *(status naturalis);* the natural state is one of war. This does not always mean open hostilities, but at least an unceasing threat of war. A state of peace, therefore, must be *established,* for in order to be secured against hostility it is not sufficient that hostilities simply be not committed; and, unless this security is pledged to each by his neighbor (a thing that can occur only in a civil state), each may treat his neighbor, from whom he demands this security, as an enemy.

First Definitive Article for Perpetual Peace

"THE CIVIL CONSTITUTION OF EVERY STATE SHOULD BE REPUBLICAN" The only constitution which derives from the idea of the original compact, and on which all juridical legislation of a people must be based, is the republican.

. . . The republican constitution, besides the purity of its origin (having sprung from the pure source of the concept of law), also gives a favorable prospect for the desired consequence, i.e., perpetual peace. The reason is this: if the consent of the citizens is required in order to decide that war should be declared (and in this constitution it cannot but be the case), nothing is more natural than that they would be very cautious in commencing such a poor game, decreeing for themselves all the calamities of war. Among the latter would be: having to fight, having to pay the costs of war from their own resources, having painfully to repair the devastation war leaves behind, and, to fill up the measure of evils, load themselves with a heavy national debt that would embitter peace itself and that can never be liquidated on account of constant wars in the future. But, on the other hand, in a constitution which is not republican, and under which the subjects are not citizens, a declaration of war is the easiest thing in the world to decide upon, because war does not require of the ruler, who is the proprietor and not a member of the state, the least sacrifice of the pleasures of his table, the chase, his country houses, his court functions, and the like. He may, therefore, resolve on war as on a pleasure party for the most trivial reasons, and with perfect indifference leave the justification which decency requires to the diplomatic corps who are ready to provide it. . . .

Second Definitive Article for a Perpetual Peace

"THE LAW OF NATIONS SHALL BE FOUNDED ON A FEDERATION OF FREE STATES" Peoples, as states, like individuals, may be judged to injure one another merely by their coexistence in the state of nature (i.e., while independent of external laws). Each of them may and should for the sake of its own security demand that the others enter with it into a constitution similar to the civil constitution, for under such a constitution each can be secure in his right. This would be a league of nations, but it would not have to be a state consisting of nations. That would be contradictory, since a state implies the relation of a superior (legislating) to an inferior (obeying) i.e., the people, and many nations in one state would then constitute only one nation. This contradicts the presupposition, for here we have to weigh the rights of nations against each other so far as they are distinct states and not amalgamated into one.

When we see the attachment of savages to their lawless freedom, preferring ceaseless combat to subjection to a lawful constraint which they might establish, and thus preferring senseless freedom to rational freedom, we regard it with deep contempt as barbarity, rudeness, and a brutish degradation of humanity. Accordingly, one would think that civilized people (each united in a state) would hasten all the more to escape, the sooner the better, from such a depraved condition. But, instead, each state places its majesty (for it is absurd to speak of the majesty of the people) in being subject to no external juridical restraint, and the splendor of its sovereign consists in the fact that many thousands stand at his command to sacrifice themselves for something that does not concern them and without his needing to place himself in the least danger. The chief difference between European and American savages lies in the fact that many tribes of the latter have been eaten by their enemies, while the former know how to make better use of their conquered enemies than to dine off them; they know better how to use them to increase the number of their subjects and thus the quantity of instruments for even more extensive wars.

When we consider the perverseness of human nature which is nakedly revealed in the uncontrolled relations between nations (this perverseness being veiled in the state of civil law by the constraint exercised by government), we may well be astonished that the word "law" has not yet been banished from war politics as pedantic, and that no state has yet been bold enough to advocate this point of view. Up to the present, Hugo Grotius, Pufendorf, Vattel, and many other irritating comforters have been cited in justification of war, though their code, philosophically or diplomatically formulated, has not and cannot have the least legal force, because states as such do not stand under a common external power. There is no instance on record that a state has ever been moved to desist from its purpose because of arguments backed up by the testimony of such great men. But the homage which each state pays (at least in words) to the concept of law proves that there is slumbering in man an even greater moral disposition to become master of the evil principle in himself (which he cannot disclaim) and to hope for the same from others. Otherwise the word "law" would never be pronounced by states which wish to war upon one another; it would be used only ironically, as a Gallic prince interpreted it when he said, "It is the prerogative which nature has given the stronger that the weaker should obey him."

States do not plead their cause before a tribunal; war alone is their way of bringing suit. But by war and its favorable issue in victory, right is not decided, and though by treaty of peace this particular war is brought to an end, the state of war, of always finding a new pretext to hostilities, is not terminated. Nor can this be declared wrong, considering the fact that in this state each is the judge of his own case. Notwithstanding, the obligation which men in a lawless condition have under the natural law, and which requires them to abandon the state of nature, does not quite apply to states under the law of nations, for as states they already have an internal juridical constitution and have thus outgrown compulsion from others to submit to a more extended lawful constitution according to their ideas of right. This is true in spite of the fact that reason, from its throne of supreme moral legislating authority, absolutely condemns war as a legal recourse and makes a state of peace a direct duty, even though peace cannot be established or secured except by a compact among nations.

For these reasons there must be a league of a particular kind, which can be called a league of peace *(foedus pacificum),* and which would be distinguished from a treaty of peace *(pactum pacis)* by the fact that the latter terminates only one war, while the former seeks to make an end of all wars forever. This league does not tend to any dominion over the power of the state but only to the maintenance and security of the freedom of the state itself and of other states in league with it, without there being any need for them to submit to civil laws and their compulsion, as men in a state of nature must submit.

The practicability (objective reality) of this idea of federation, which should gradually spread to all states and thus lead to perpetual peace, can be proved. For if fortune directs that a powerful and enlightened people can make itself a republic, which by its nature must be inclined to perpetual peace, this gives a fulcrum to the federation with other states so that they may adhere to it and thus secure freedom under the idea of the law of nations. By more and more such associations, the federation may be gradually extended.

We may readily conceive that a people should say, "There ought to be no war among us, for we want to make ourselves into a state; that is, we want to establish a supreme legislative, executive, and judiciary power which will reconcile our differences peaceably." But when this state says, "There ought to be no war between myself and other states, even though I acknowledge no supreme legislative power by which our rights are mutually guaranteed," it is not at all clear on what I can base my confidence in my own rights unless it is the free federation, the surrogate of the civil social order, which reason necessarily associates with the concept of the law of nations—assuming that something is really meant by the latter.

The concept of a law of nations as a right to make war does not really mean anything, because it is then a law of deciding what is right by unilateral maxims through force and not by universally valid public laws which restrict the freedom of each one. The only conceivable meaning of such a law of nations might be that it serves men right who are so inclined that they should destroy each other and thus find perpetual peace in the vast grave that swallows both the atrocities and their perpetrators. For states in their relation to each other, there cannot be any reasonable way out of the lawless condition which entails only war except that they, like individual men, should give up their savage (lawless) freedom, adjust themselves to the constraints of public law, and thus establish a continuously growing state consisting of various nations *(civitas gentium),* which will ultimately include all the nations of the world. But under the idea of the law of nations they do not wish this, and reject in practice what is correct in theory. If all is not to be lost, there can be, then, in place of the positive idea of a world republic, only the negative surrogate of an alliance which averts war, endures, spreads, and holds back the stream of those hostile passions which fear the law though such an alliance is in constant peril of their breaking loose again. *Furor impius intus . . . fremit horridus ore cruento* (Virgil). . . .

FIRST SUPPLEMENT: OF THE GUARANTEE FOR PERPETUAL PEACE

The guarantee of perpetual peace is nothing less than that great artist, nature *(natura daedala rerum).* In her mechanical course we see that her aim is to produce a harmony among men, against their will and indeed through their discord. As a necessity working according to laws we do not know, we call it destiny. But considering its design in world history, we call it "providence," inasmuch as we discern in it the profound wisdom of a higher cause which predetermines the course of nature and directs it to the objective final end of the human race.

. . . Before we more narrowly define the guarantee which nature gives, it is necessary to examine the situation in which she has placed her actors on her vast stage, a situation which finally assures peace among them. Then we shall see how she accomplishes the latter. Her preparatory arrangements are:

1. In every region of the world she has made it possible for men to live.
2. By war she has driven them even into the most inhospitable regions in order to populate them.
3. By the same means, she has forced them into more or less lawful relations with each other. . . .

The first instrument of war among the animals which man learned to tame and to domesticate was the horse (for the elephant belongs to later times, to the luxury of already established states). The art of cultivating certain types of plants (grain) whose original characteristics we do not know, and the increase and improvement of fruits by transplantation and grafting (in Europe perhaps only the crab apple and the wild pear), could arise only under conditions prevailing in already established states where property was secure. Before this could take place, it was necessary that men who had first subsisted in anarchic freedom by hunting, fishing, and sheepherding should have been forced into an agricultural life. Then salt and iron were discovered. These were perhaps the first articles of commerce for the various peoples and were sought far and wide; in this way a peaceful traffic among nations was established, and thus understanding, conventions, and peaceable relations were established among the most distant peoples.

As nature saw to it that men *could* live everywhere in the world, she also despotically willed that they *should* do so, even against their inclination and without this *ought* being based on a concept of duty to which they were bound by a moral law. She chose war as the means to this end. So we see peoples whose common language shows that they have a common origin. For instance, the Samoyeds on the Arctic Ocean and a people with a similar language a thousand miles away in the Altaian Mountains are separated by a Mongolian people adept at horsemanship and hence at war; the latter drove the former into the most inhospitable arctic regions where they certainly would not have spread of their own accord. Again, it is the same with the Finns who in the most northerly part of Europe are called Lapps; Goths and Sarmatians have separated them from the Hungarians to whom they are related in language. What can have driven the Eskimos, a race entirely distinct from all others in America and perhaps descended from primeval European adventurers, so far into the North, or the Pescherais as far south as Tierra del Fuego, if it were not war which nature uses to populate the whole earth? War itself requires no special motive but appears to be engrafted on human nature; it passes even for something noble, to which the love of glory impels men quite apart from any selfish urges. Thus among the American savages, just as much as among those of Europe during the age of chivalry, military valor is held to be of great worth in itself, not only during war (which is natural) but in order that there should be war. Often war is waged only in order to show valor; thus an inner dignity is ascribed to war itself, and even some philosophers have praised it as an ennoblement of humanity, forgetting the pronouncement of the Greek who said, "War is an evil inasmuch as it produces more wicked men than it takes away." So much for the measures nature takes to lead the human race, considered as a class of animals, to her own end.

Now we come to the question concerning that which is most essential in the design of perpetual peace: What has nature done with regard to this end which man's own reason makes his duty? That is, what has nature done to favor man's moral purpose, and how has she guaranteed (by compulsion but without prejudice to his freedom) that he shall do that which he ought to but does not do under the laws of freedom? This question refers to all three phases of public law, namely, civil law, the law of nations, and the law of citizenship. If I say of nature that she wills that this or that occur, I do not mean that she imposes a duty on us to do it, for this can be done only by free practical reason; rather I mean that she herself does it, whether we will or not *(fata volentem ducunt, nolentem trahunt)*.

1. Even if a people were not forced by internal discord to submit to public laws, war would compel them to do so, for we have already seen that nature has placed each people near another which presses upon it, and against this it must form itself into a state in order to defend itself. Now the republican constitution is the only one entirely fitting to the rights of man. But it is the most difficult to establish and even harder to preserve, so that many say a republic would have to be a nation of angels, because men with their selfish inclinations are not capable of a constitution of such sublime form. But precisely with these inclinations nature comes to the aid of the general will established on reason, which is revered even though impotent in practice. Thus it is only a question of a good

organization of the state (which does lie in man's power), whereby the powers of each selfish inclination are so arranged in opposition that one moderates or destroys the ruinous effect of the other. The consequence for reason is the same as if none of them existed, and man is forced to be a good citizen even if not a morally good person.

The problem of organizing a state, however hard it may seem, can be solved even for a race of devils, if only they are intelligent. The problem is: "Given a multitude of rational beings requiring universal laws for their preservation, but each of whom is secretly inclined to exempt himself from them, to establish a constitution in such a way that, although their private intentions conflict, they check each other, with the result that their public conduct is the same as if they had no such intentions."

A problem like this must be capable of solution; it does not require that we know how to attain the moral improvement of men but only that we should know the mechanism of nature in order to use it on men, organizing the conflict of the hostile intentions present in a people in such a way that they must compel themselves to submit to coercive laws. Thus a state of peace is established in which laws have force. We can see, even in actual states, which are far from perfectly organized, that in their foreign relations they approach that which the idea of right prescribes. This is so in spite of the fact that the intrinsic element of morality is certainly not the cause of it. (A good constitution is not to be expected from morality, but, conversely, a good moral condition of a people is to be expected only under a good constitution.) Instead of genuine morality, the mechanism of nature brings it to pass through selfish inclinations, which naturally conflict outwardly but which can be used by reason as a means for its own end, the sovereignty of law, and, as concerns the state, for promoting and securing internal and external peace.

This, then, is the truth of the matter: Nature inexorably wills that the right should finally triumph. What we neglect to do comes about by itself, though with great inconveniences to us. "If you bend the reed too much, you break it; and he who attempts too much attempts nothing" (Bouterwek).

2. The idea of international law presupposes the separate existence of many independent but neighboring states. Although this condition is itself a state of war (unless a federative union prevents the outbreak of hostilities), this is rationally preferable to the amalgamation of states under one superior power, as this would end in one universal monarchy, and laws always lose in vigor what government gains in extent; hence a soulless despotism falls into anarchy after stifling the seeds of the good. Nevertheless, every state, or its ruler, desires to establish lasting peace in this way, aspiring if possible to rule the whole world. But nature wills otherwise. She employs two means to separate peoples and to prevent them from mixing: differences of language and of religion. These differences involve a tendency to mutual hatred and pretexts for war, but the progress of civilization and men's gradual approach to greater harmony in their principles finally leads to peaceful agreement. This is not like that peace which despotism (in the burial ground of freedom) produces through a weakening of all powers; it is, on the contrary, produced and maintained by their equilibrium in liveliest competition.

3. Just as nature wisely separates nations, which the will of every state, sanctioned by the principles of international law, would gladly unite by artifice or force, nations which could not have secured themselves against violence and war by means of the law of world citizenship unite because of mutual interest. The spirit of commerce, which is

incompatible with war, sooner or later gains the upper hand in every state. As the power of money is perhaps the most dependable of all the powers (means) included under the state power, states see themselves forced, without any moral urge, to promote honorable peace and by mediation to prevent war wherever it threatens to break out. They do so exactly as if they stood in perpetual alliances, for great offensive alliances are in the nature of the case rare and even less often successful.

In this manner nature guarantees perpetual peace by the mechanism of human passions. Certainly she does not do so with sufficient certainty for us to predict the future in any theoretical sense, but adequately from a practical point of view, making it our duty to work toward this end, which is not just a chimerical one.

Society and Anarchy in International Relations[1]

Hedley Bull

I

Whereas men within each state are subject to a common government, sovereign states in their mutual relations are not. This anarchy it is possible to regard as the central fact of international life and the starting-point of theorizing about it.[2] A great deal of the most fruitful reflection about international life has been concerned with tracing the consequences in it of this absence of government. We can, indeed, give some account in these terms of what it is that distinguishes the international from the domestic field of politics, morals and law.

One persistent theme in the modern discussion of international relations has been that as a consequence of this anarchy states do not form together any kind of society; and that if they were to do so it could only be by subordinating themselves to a common authority. One of the chief intellectual supports of this doctrine is what may be called the domestic analogy, the argument from the experience of individual men in domestic society to the experience of states, according to which the need of individual men to stand in awe of a common power in order to live in peace is a ground for holding that states must do the same. The conditions of an orderly social life, on this view, are the same among states as they are within them: they require that the institutions of domestic society be reproduced on a universal scale. . . .

The view that anarchy is incompatible with society among nations has been especially prominent in the years since the First World War. It was the First World War that gave currency to the doctrine of a 'fresh start' in international relations and set the habit of disparaging the past. Nineteenth century thought had regarded both the existence of international society and its further consolidation as entirely consistent with the continuation of international anarchy. The ideas of 1919 were in part a mere extension of the liberal, progressive strand of this nineteenth century anarchist view: the strengthening of international law, the creation of new procedures for arbitration, the establishment of

---

Hedley Bull, "Society and Anarchy in International Relations," in Herbert Butterfield and Martin Wight, eds., *Diplomatic Investigations: Essays in the Theory of International Politics* (Cambridge: Harvard University Press, 1968). Reprinted by permission of Allen & Unwin and International Thomson Publishing Services.

[1]A number of the leading ideas in this essay derive, in a process in which they may have lost their original shape, from Martin Wight; and a number of others from C. A. W. Manning.

[2]Anarchy: 'Absence of rule; disorder; confusion' *(O.E.D.).* The term here is used exclusively in the first of these senses. The question with which the essay is concerned is whether in the international context it is to be identified also with the second and the third.

permanent institutions for cooperation among sovereign states, a reduction and limitation of armaments, the pressure of public opinion, the aspiration that states should be popularly based and that their boundaries should coincide with the boundaries of nations. But there was now voiced also a view that is not to be found in Cobden or Gladstone or Mazzini: a rejection of international anarchy itself, expressed on the one hand in the view that the true value of the League and the United Nations lay not in themselves, but in their presumed final cause, a world government; and on the other hand in the endorsement of world government as an immediately valid objective, and a depreciation of the League and its successor as destined to 'failure' on account of their preservation of state sovereignty.

The twentieth century view of international anarchy is not, however, something new. Such a doctrine was stated at the outset of modern international history and has since found a succession of embodiments. The European system of sovereign states did not, of course, arise as a result of the outward growth and collision of hitherto isolated communities. Its origin lay in the disintegration of a single community: the waning on the one hand of central authorities, and on the other hand of local authorities, within Western Christendom, and the exclusion of both from particular territories by the princely power. Throughout its history modern European international society has been conscious of the memory of the theoretical imperium of Pope and Emperor and the actual imperium of Rome. When in the sixteenth and early seventeenth centuries the question was raised of the nature of relationships between sovereign princes and states, order and justice on a universal scale were readily associated with the idea of a universal state: not merely because the supremacy of the prince was observed to be a condition of order within the confines of the state, but also because order throughout Western Christendom as a whole was associated with the vanished authority of the Papacy and the Holy Roman Empire. The idea that international anarchy has as its consequence the absence of society among states, and the associated but opposite idea of the domestic analogy, became and have remained persistent doctrines about the international predicament.

The first of these doctrines describes international relations in terms of a Hobbesian state of nature, which is a state of war. Sovereign states, on this view, find themselves in a situation in which their behavior in relation to one another, although it may be circumscribed by considerations of prudence, is not limited by rules or law or morality. Either, as in the Machiavellian version of this doctrine, moral and legal rules are taken not to impinge on the sphere of action of the state: the political life and the moral life being presented as alternatives, as in the theory of quietism. Or, as in the Hegelian version, moral imperatives are thought to exist in international relations, but are believed to endorse the self-assertion of states in relation to one another, and to be incapable of imposing limits upon it. In this first doctrine the conditions of social life are asserted to be the same for states as they are for individuals. In the case of Hobbes, whose views we shall examine more closely, government is stated to be a necessary condition of social life among men, and the same is said to hold of sovereign princes. But the domestic analogy stops short at this point; it is not the view of Hobbes, or of other thinkers of this school, that a social contract of states that would bring the international anarchy to an end either should or can take place.

The second doctrine accepts the description of international relations embodied in the first, but combines with it the demand that the international anarchy be brought to an end. Where the domestic analogy is employed to buttress this doctrine, it is taken further, to embrace the concept of the social contract as well as that of the state of nature. This search for an alternative to international anarchy may be sustained by the memory of an alternative actually experienced, as in the backward-looking tradition of a return to Roman or to Western Christian unity. The other variety, the forward-looking tradition of which we may take Kant to be representative, finds its sustenance in the belief in human progress, in the possibility of achieving in the future what has not been achieved in the past.

Even as these two doctrines were taking shape there was asserted against them both the third possibility of a society of sovereign states; and along with it the beginnings of the idea that the conditions of order among states were different from what they were among individual men. Like the two doctrines against which it has been directed, this third doctrine consists in part of a description of what is taken to be the actual character of relations between states, and in part of a set of prescriptions. The description is one which sees sovereign states in intercourse with one another as consciously united together for certain purposes, which modify their conduct in relation to one another. The salient fact of international relations is taken to be not that of conflict among states within the international anarchy, as on the Hobbesian view; nor that of the transience of the international anarchy and the availability of materials with which to replace it, as on the Kantian view, but co-operation among sovereign states in a society without government. The prescriptions which accompany this account of the nature of international relations enjoin respect for the legal and moral rules upon which the working of the international society depends. In place of the Hobbesian view that states are not limited by legal or moral rules in their relations with one another, and the Kantian view that the rules to which appeal may be had derive from the higher morality of a cosmopolitan society and enjoin the overthrow of international society, there are asserted the duties and rights attaching to states as members of international society.

ℰ Two traditions, in particular, have advanced this third conception on an international society. One is the body of theory to which modern international law is the heir, which depicts states as constituting a society in the course of showing them to be bound of a system of legal rules: whether these rules are thought to derive from natural law or positive law, whether the subjects of the rules are taken to be states or the men who rule them, and whether the rules are regarded as universally valid or as binding only upon the states of Christendom or Europe. In the system of sixteenth century writers like Vitoria and Suarez, and of seventeenth century thinkers like Grotius and Pufendorf, the idea of the domestic analogy was still strong; the alternative notion of the uniqueness of international society was fully worked out only by the positivist international lawyers of the nineteenth century. The other tradition is that of the analysis of the political relations of states in terms of the system of balance of power. According to such analyses states throughout modern history have been engaged in the operation of a 'political system' or 'states-system', which makes its own demands upon their freedom of action and requires them in particular to act so as to maintain a balance of power as a product of policies consciously directed towards it, and in so far as they have asserted that states are obliged to act so as to maintain it, they must be taken also to embody the idea of international society and of rules binding upon its members. In the sixteenth and seventeenth centuries the predominant theories of the law of nations and of the balance of power were held by different groups of persons and in their respective content were largely antithetical. But in the eighteenth century the two streams converged, as in the writings of Vattel international law came to take account of the balance of power, and in the writings of Burke and later Gentz the political maxim enjoining the preservation of a balance of power came to be defined in a more legalistic way. In the nineteenth century the predominant doctrines moved close together: although it may still be doubted whether either theory can be reconciled to the other without sacrifice of an essential part of its content.

It is the validity of this third conception of an international society, either as a description of the past or as a guide for the present and the future, that is called in question by the doctrine that the international anarchy is, or has become, intolerable.

II

. . . The theorists of international society have been able to question the applicability to relations between states of each of the three elements in Hobbes' account of the state of nature. In the first place they have often remarked that sovereign states do not so exhaust their strength and invention in providing security against one another that industry and other refinements of living do not flourish. States do not as a rule invest resources in war and military preparations to such an extent that their economic fabric is ruined; even if it may be argued that the allocation of resources to war and armaments is not the best allocation from the point of view of economic development. On the contrary the armed forces of the state by providing security against external attack and internal disorder, establish the conditions under which economic improvement may take place within its borders. The absence of universal government and the fragmentation among sovereign states of responsibility for military security is not incompatible, moreover, with economic interdependence. The relative economic self-sufficiency of states as compared with individuals, has often been taken to explain why states are able to tolerate a looser form of social organization than that enjoyed by individuals within the modern state. At the same time, these theorists may point to the mutual advantages which states derive from economic relationships; and argue that trade, symbolic as it is of the existence of overlapping through different interests, is the activity most characteristic of international relationships as a whole.

As regards the second feature of the Hobbesian state of nature, the absence in it of notions of right and wrong, it is a matter of observation that this is not true of modern international relations. The theorist of international society has often begun his inquiries, as Grotius did, by remarking the extent to which states depart from rules of law and morality, and by uttering a protest against this situation in asserting the binding character of the rules. However, he has also been able to draw attention to the recognition of legal and moral rules by statesmen themselves, and to traditions of positive law and morality which have been a continuous feature of international life. International action which, although it is contrary to recognized principles of international law and morality, is accompanied by pretexts stated in terms of those principles, attests the force in international relations of notions of right and wrong, just as does action which conforms to them. By contrast, action which in addition to involving a violation of the legal and moral rules of international society is accompanied by no legal and moral pretext, action which, to use Grotius' terms, is 'not persuasive' as well as 'not justifiable', is widely taken by legal theorists to be quite uncharacteristic of the behavior of member states of modern international society (as well as to be hostile to its working in a way in which illegal behavior accompanied by a pretext is not).

The element in the Hobbesian state of nature which appears most clearly to apply to international relations is the third. It is the fact of war which appears to provide the chief evidence for the view that states do not form a society. On the one hand, if we take the modern state to illustrate the idea of a society, one of its salient features is that in it, apart from certain residual rights of self-defense, the private use of force is proscribed. But on the other hand, it cannot be denied that sovereign states in relation to one another are in a state of war, in Hobbes' sense that they are disposed to it over a period of time. It must be conceded also that this war is one of all against all. At any single moment in the history of the modern states-system, it is true, certain states will not be disposed to war against certain other states. That is to say, certain pairs of states will be pursuing common purposes and will be allied to one another; certain other pairs of states will be pursuing purposes which are different but do not cross, and will therefore treat one another with indifference; and certain pairs of states, although they have purposes which are conflicting, nevertheless share such a sense of community that (as now among the English-speaking states) war is not contemplated as a possible outcome of the conflict. But if we consider the states-system not at a single moment but in motion throughout the whole of its life (say, from 1648) then we shall find that every state that has survived the period has at some point or other been disposed to war with every other one.

The theorist of international society has sought to deal with this difficulty not by denying the ubiquity of war, but by questioning the relevance of the model of the modern state. If sovereign states are understood to form a society of a different sort from that constituted by the modern state—one, in particular, whose operation not merely tolerates certain private uses of force but actually requires them—then the fact of a disposition to war can no longer be regarded as evidence that international society does not exist. Theorists of the law of nations and of the system of balance of power have thus sought to show that war does not indicate the absence of international society, or its break-down, but can occur as a part of its functioning. Thus some international legal writers have seen in war a means by which the law of international society is enforced by individual members; others have seen in it a means of settling political conflicts. Theorists of the balance of power have seen war as the ultimate means by which threats to the international equilibrium are redressed. It may even be argued, in line with these theories, that the element in international relations of a 'war of all against all' so far from being detrimental to the working of international society, is in a certain sense positively favorable to it. For if the enforcement of law depends upon the willingness of particular law-abiding states to undertake war against particular law-breaking ones, then the prospects of law enforcement will be best if every state is willing to take up arms against any state that breaks the law. The fact that at any one time certain states are unwilling to contemplate war with certain other states, either because they are allied to them, or because they are indifferent to one another's policies, or because they are bound by a particular sense of community, is an obstacle to the enforcement of international law. In the same way the balance of power is best preserved if states are willing to take up arms against any state that threatens the balance, to focus their attention upon its recalcitrance in this respect and to disregard all special claims it may have on them.

If, then, we were tempted to compare international relations with a precontractual state of nature among individual men, it might be argued that we should choose not Hobbes' description of that condition, but Locke's. In the conception of a society without government, whose members must themselves judge and enforce the law, which is therefore crude and uncertain, we can recognize the international society of many thinkers in the tradition of international law. And although Locke's speculations about life of men in anarchy will leave us dissatisfied, we may turn to modern anthropological studies of actual societies of this kind, which have been forced to consider what, in the absence of explicit forms of government, could be held to constitute the political structure of a people.[3] Such studies widen our view of the devices for cohesion in a society, and suggest a number of parallels in the international field.

There are a number of these which are worth exploring. One which has received some attention from international lawyers is the principle of the 'hue and cry'. Another is the place of ritual. Another is the principle of loyalty—among kinsmen in primitive society, among allies in international society. International society and certain sorts of primitive society would seem also to be alike in respect of the function performed within them by the principle that might is right. This we are inclined to dismiss as the contrary of a moral principle, a mere way of saying that the question of right does not arise. This, indeed, is what, according to Thucydides, the Athenians said to the Melians: they did not appeal to the principle that might is right, but said that the question of right arose only when the parties were equal, which in this case they were not. Yet in international relations the parties are frequently not equal, and the society of states has had to evolve principles which will take account of this fact and lead to settlements. The rule that the will of the stronger party should be accepted provides a means of going directly to what the outcome of a violent struggle would be, without actually going through that struggle. To say that the principle that might is right fulfills a function in international society is not to provide a justification of it or to regard it as a necessary element in international life; but it is to argue that the working of a social order may be recognized even in a feature of relations between states sometimes taken to demonstrate the absence of any kind of order.[4]

We must, however, at some point abandon the domestic analogy altogether. Not only is this because the attempt to understand something by means of analogies with something else is a sign of infancy in a subject, an indication of lack of familiarity with our own subject matter. But also because international society is unique, and owes its

---

[3]M. Fortes and E. E. Evans-Pritchard, *African Political Systems* (Oxford University Press, 1940), p. 6.
[4]On the functioning of the principle that might is right in primitive and in international society, see Ernest Gellner, 'How to Live in Anarchy', *The Listener,* April 3, 1958, pp. 579–83.

character to qualities that are peculiar to the situation of sovereign states, as well as to those it has in common with the lives of individuals in domestic society. One of the themes that has accompanied the statement of the idea of international society has been that anarchy among states is tolerable to a degree to which among individuals it is not. This has been recognized in some measure even by those who originated the description of international relations in terms of the Hobbesian state of nature.

In the first place, as we have noted, it is not consequent upon the international anarchy that in it there can be no industry or other refinements of living; unlike the individual in Hobbes' state of nature the state does not find its energies so absorbed in the pursuit of security that the life of its activities is that of mere brutes. Hobbes himself recognizes this when having observed that persons of sovereign authority are in 'a posture of war', he goes on to say: 'But because they uphold thereby the industry of their subjects, there does not follow from it that misery which accompanies the liberty of particular men.'[5] The same sovereigns that find themselves in the state of nature in relation to one another have provided with particular territories, the conditions in which the refinements of life can flourish.

In the second place states have not been vulnerable to violent attack to the same degree that individuals are. Spinoza, echoing Hobbes in his assertion that 'two states are in the same relation to one another as two men in the condition of nature,' goes on to add 'with this exception, that a commonwealth can guard itself against being subjugated by another, as a man in the state of nature cannot do. For, of course, a man is overcome by sleep every day, is often afflicted by disease of body or mind, and is finally prostrated by old age; in addition, he is subject to other troubles against which a commonwealth can make itself secure.'[6] One human being in the state of nature cannot make himself secure against violent attack; and this attack carries with it the prospect of sudden death. Groups of human beings organized as states, however, may provide themselves with a means of defense that exists independently of the frailties of any one of them. And armed attack by one state upon another has not brought with it a prospect comparable to the killing of one individual by another. For one man's death may be brought about suddenly, in a single act; and once it has occurred, it cannot be undone. But war has only occasionally resulted in the physical extinction of the vanquished people. In modern history it has been possible to take Clausewitz's view that 'war is never absolute in its results' and that defeat in it may be merely 'a passing evil which can be remedied'. Moreover, war in the past, even if it could in principle lead to the physical extermination of one or both of the belligerent peoples, could not be thought capable of doing so at once in the course of a single act. Clausewitz, in holding that war does not consist of a single instantaneous blow, but always of a succession of separate actions, was drawing attention to something that in the past has always held true and has rendered public violence distinct from private. It is only in the context of recent military

---

[5]Hobbes, *Leviathan* (Everyman ed.), p. 65.
[6]Spinoza, *Tractatus Politicus,* ch. iii, para. 11, *The Political Works,* ed. A. G. Wernham (Clarendon Press, 1958), p. 295).

technology that it has become pertinent to ask whether war could not now both be 'absolute in its results' and 'take the form of a single, instantaneous blow,' in Clausewitz's understanding of these terms; and whether therefore violence does not now confront the state with the same sort of prospect it has always held for the individual.[7]

This second difference, that states have been less vulnerable to violent attack by one another than individual men, is reinforced by a third contingency of great importance; that in so far as states have been vulnerable in this sense they have not been equally so. Hobbes builds his account of the state of nature upon the proposition that 'Nature hath made men so equal, in the faculties of body and mind . . . (that) the weakest has strength enough to kill the strongest.'[8] It is this equal vulnerability of every man to every other that, in Hobbes' view, renders the condition of anarchy intolerable. In modern international society, however, there has been a persistent distinction between Great Powers and small. Great Powers have been secure against the attacks of small Powers; and have had to fear only other Great Powers, and hostile combinations of Powers. We have only to think of the security enjoyed by Great Britain in the nineteenth century to appreciate that the insecurity which is a feature of the Hobbesian state of nature, in so far as it exists in international society, is not distributed equally among all its members. It is interesting to find Gentz writing of 'the European Commonwealth' that 'The original inequality of the parties in such a union as is here described is not an accidental circumstance, much less a casual evil; but is in a certain degree to be considered as the previous condition and foundation of the whole system.'[9] A footnote follows: 'Had the surface of the globe been divided into equal parts, no such union would ever have taken place; and an eternal war of each against the whole is probably the only event we should have heard of.' If Great Powers are relatively safe from attack and do not stand in need of the protection of a central authority, then by the same token they are themselves in a position to attack others and to withstand the pressures which other states may seek to bring to bear upon them. If an even distribution of strength among states would seem unfavorable to the development of international society, it is also true that great discrepancies in strength may obstruct its working or even prove irreconcilable with it. One of the central contentions of theorists of the balance of power has been that if international society is to be maintained, no one state may be in a position to dominate the rest. Other writers have gone beyond this, to assert with Gentz himself, in a doctrine in which the principle of the balance of power becomes difficult to disentangle from that of collective security, 'That if that system is not merely to exist, but to be maintained without constant perils and violent concussions, each member which infringes it must be in a condition to be coerced, not only by the collective strength of the other members, but by any majority of them, if not by one individual.'[10] Ancillon, writing sixteen years later, saw the same principle at work in the early development in Italy

---

[7]I have deliberately excluded from this essay any consideration of how far recent military technology should lead us to alter the answers that have been given to these questions in the past.

[8]Hobbes, *op. cit.*, p. 63.

[9]Friedrich von Gentz, *Fragments upon the Balance of Power in Europe* (London, Peltier, 1806), p. 63.

[10]*Ibid.*, p. 62.

of the principle of equilibrium: 'Le voisinage d'un grand nombre d'états, trop inégaux pour résister l'un à l'autre, y avait fait saisir, suivre et appliquer de bonne heure ces maximes de prudence qui servent de sauvegarde au droit, et qui allaient passer de ce petit théâtre sur un théâtre plus vaste.'[11]

A fourth point of contrast that has often been remarked is that states in their economic lives enjoy a degree of self-sufficiency beyond comparison with that of individual men. Thus while it has been one of the themes of theorists of international society to stress the mutual dependence of states in trade, at the same time their relative economic independence of one another, by contrast with individuals, has provided support for the argument that states are able to tolerate a form of society looser than that which is crowned by a government.

As against the Hobbesian view that states find themselves in a state of nature which is a state of war, it may be argued, therefore, that they constitute a society without a government. This society may be compared with the anarchical society among individual men of Locke's imagining, and also with primitive anarchical societies that have been studied by anthropologists. But although we may employ such analogies, we must in the end abandon them, for the fact that states form a society without a government reflects also the features of their situation that are unique. The working of international society must be understood in terms of its own, distinctive institutions. These include international law, diplomacy and the system of balance of power. There may be others which should be ranked alongside these; it is arguable, for example, that collaboration among the Great Powers to manage the affairs of international society as a whole and impart to them a degree of central direction—seen in operation in the series of conferences from Westphalia to Potsdam, and finding its most perfect embodiment in the Concert of Europe—also represents such an institution, even though it has functioned only intermittently.

III

The idea that sovereign states find themselves in a Hobbesian state of nature, as well as standing on its own as a description of what international politics is like, is also to be found linked to demands for the establishment of a universal state. In doctrines like that of Kant in *Perpetual Peace,* the Hobbesian domestic analogy is applied to international relations, but in this case taken further to embrace not only the idea of the state of nature but also that of the social contract.

The Kantian view of international relations involves a dilemma. If states are indeed in a Hobbesian state of nature, the contract by means of which they are to emerge from it cannot take place. For if covenants without the sword are but words, this will be true of covenants directed towards the establishment of universal government, just as it will hold true of agreements on other subjects. The difficulty with the Kantian position is that the description it contains of the actual condition of international relations, and the

---

[11]J. P. F. Ancillon, *Tableau des Révolutions du Système Politique de l'Europe, depuis la Fin du Quinzième Siècle* (Paris, Anselin et Pochard, 1823), vol. I, pp. 262–3.

prescription it provides for its improvement, are inconsistent with one another. Action within the context of continuing international anarchy is held to be of no avail; but at the same time it is in the international anarchy that the grand solution of the international social contract is held to take place.

The advocate of a universal state can show his scheme to be feasible as well as desirable only by admitting that international relations do not resemble a Hobbesian state of nature; that in it covenants without the sword are more than words and the materials may be found with which to bring about collaboration between sovereign governments. But to make this admission is to weaken the case for bringing the international anarchy to an end. For the establishment of a universal government cannot then be regarded as a *sine qua non* of the world order. If a Hobbesian description of the international state of nature is abandoned for a Lockean one, then the case for a fundamental change is simply that which Locke presents for a contract of government: that to crown the anarchical society with a government would be to render it more efficient.

However, such a case might still be a quite formidable one. It may rest essentially on something which the Lockean description of international society itself admits: that in it the private use of force is tolerated or even in certain circumstances required. The international society described by the international lawyers and the theorists of balance of power is one in which war has a permanent and perhaps even a necessary place. The argument for proceeding from anarchy to government may therefore be stated, as Kant states it, in terms of the possibility and desirability of perpetual peace.

It is a facile view according to which a universal state would abolish war because war is a relationship between sovereign states and sovereign states would have been abolished. Either we may take war to mean any kind of organized violence between large groups of human beings, in which case the statement is false. Or we may understand the term in the narrow sense of a contention between sovereign states, in which case although the statement is true it is misleading. War in this latter sense comprises only one area of the spectrum of possible violence; if the elimination of war in this special sense of public war were to occasion the re-establishment of the various forms of private war, this could not necessarily be counted a gain.

If, however, a universal state should be understood as providing, just as does the system of sovereign states, a particular solution to the problem of the management of violence, rather than a means of transcending it, this is not to say that it is an inferior solution. It may be argued that the propensities for violence that are inherent in any form of political organization on a world-scale, will be better managed through the medium of a single authority entrusted with the legitimate exercise of force, than through many such authorities; just as this is the case in the smaller geographical context of the nation-state. Such an argument might well be sustained; yet the traditional arguments upholding international society against universal government would first have to be met.

These arguments have often rested on a preference for liberty in international relations over order or security: the liberty of states and nations from domination by a central power, and of individuals from the reach of a tyrannical government whose ubiquitous authority must deny them the right of foreign asylum. It may well be replied to this that order or security is the prime need of international society, and that liberty should if necessary be sacrificed to it. International anarchy, however, may be preferred on grounds of order also.

Government, involving as it does a legal monopoly of the use of force, provides a means for maintaining order; but it is also a source of dissension among conflicting groups in society, which compete for its control. If government authority, once it is captured, may be wielded so as to deny the resort to force by private individuals or groups, it is also the case that the existence of the governmental mechanism constitutes a prize in political conflict, which raises the stakes in such conflict to a level above that it would otherwise be. In the typical modern nation-state order is best preserved when conflict takes the form of a competition between the contending forces for control of a single government, rather than that of competition among governments. Yet the political community is also familiar in which the reverse is the case; in which the dangers to order arising from the coexistence of sovereign governments are less than those involved in the attempt to hold hostile communities in the framework of a single polity. The partition of India in 1947 had this *rationale*. It is possible also to view the problem of order in the world community in this way. Formidable though the classic dangers are of a plurality of sovereign states, these have to be reckoned against those inherent in the attempt to contain disparate communities within the framework of a single government. It is an entirely reasonable view of world order at the present time that it is best served by living with the former dangers rather than by attempting to face the latter.

POWER AND
INTERDEPENDENCE

Robert O. Keohane and Joseph S. Nye

. . . For political realists, international politics, like all other politics, is a struggle for power but, unlike domestic politics, a struggle dominated by organized violence. In the words of the most influential postwar textbook, "All history shows that nations active in international politics are continuously preparing for, actively involved in, or recovering from organized violence in the form of war."[1] Three assumptions are integral to the realist vision. First, states as coherent units are the dominant actors in world politics. This is a double assumption: states are predominant; and they act as coherent units. Second, realists assume that force is a usable and effective instrument of policy. Other instruments may also be employed, but using or threatening force is the most effective means of wielding power. Third, partly because of their second assumption, realists assume a hierarchy of issues in world politics, headed by questions of military security: the "high politics" of military security dominates the "low politics" of economic and social affairs.

These realist assumptions define an ideal type of world politics. They allow us to imagine a world in which politics is continually characterized by active or potential conflict among states, with the use of force possible at any time. Each state attempts to defend its territory and interests from real or perceived threats. Political integration among states is slight and lasts only as long as it serves the national interests of the most powerful states. Transnational actors either do not exist or are politically unimportant. Only the adept exercise of force or the threat of force permits states to survive, and only while statesmen succeed in adjusting their interests, as in a well-functioning balance of power, is the system stable.

Each of the realist assumptions can be challenged. If we challenge them all simultaneously, we can imagine a world in which actors other than states participate directly in world politics, in which a clear hierarchy of issues does not exist, and in which force is an ineffective instrument of policy. Under these conditions—which we call the characteristics of complex interdependence—one would expect world politics to be very different than under realist conditions. . . .

We do not argue, however, that complex interdependence faithfully reflects world political reality. Quite the contrary: both it and the realist portrait are ideal types. Most

[1]Hans J. Morgenthau, *Politics Among Nations: The Struggle for Power and Peace,* 4th ed. (New York: Knopf, 1967), p. 36.

situations will fall somewhere between these two extremes. Sometimes, realist assumptions will be accurate, or largely accurate, but frequently complex interdependence will provide a better portrayal of reality. Before one decides what explanatory model to apply to a situation or problem, one will need to understand the degree to which realist or complex interdependence assumptions correspond to the situation.

THE CHARACTERISTICS OF COMPLEX INTERDEPENDENCE

Complex interdependence has three main characteristics:

1. *Multiple channels* connect societies, including: informal ties between governmental elites as well as formal foreign office arrangements; informal ties among nongovernmental elites (face-to-face and through telecommunications); and transnational organizations (such as multinational banks or corporations). These channels can be summarized as interstate, trans-governmental, and transnational relations. *Interstate* relations are the normal channels assumed by realists. *Transgovernmental* applies when we relax the realist assumption that states act coherently as units; *transnational* applies when we relax the assumption that states are the only units.

2. The agenda of interstate relationships consists of multiple issues that are not arranged in a clear or consistent hierarchy. This *absence of hierarchy among issues* means, among other things, that military security does not consistently dominate the agenda. Many issues arise from what used to be considered domestic policy, and the distinction between domestic and foreign issues becomes blurred. These issues are considered in several government departments (not just foreign offices), and at several levels. Inadequate policy coordination on these issues involves significant costs. Different issues generate different coalitions, both within governments and across them, and involve different degrees of conflict. Politics does not stop at the waters' edge.

3. Military force is not used by governments toward other governments within the region, or on the issues, when complex interdependence prevails. It may, however, be important in these governments' relations with governments outside that region, or on other issues. Military force could, for instance, be irrelevant to resolving disagreements on economic issues among members of an alliance, yet at the same time be very important for that alliance's political and military relations with a rival bloc. For the former relationships this condition of complex interdependence would be met; for the latter, it would not. . . .

Minor Role of Military Force

Political scientists have traditionally emphasized the role of military force in international politics. . . . Force dominates other means of power: *if* there are no constraints on one's choice of instruments (a hypothetical situation that has only been approximated in the two world wars), the state with superior military force will prevail. If the security dilemma for all states were extremely acute, military force, supported by economic and other resources, would clearly be the dominant source of power. Survival is the primary goal of all states, and in the worst situations, force is ultimately necessary to guarantee survival. Thus military force is always a central component of national power.

Yet particularly among industrialized, pluralist countries, the perceived margin of safety has widened: fears of attack in general have declined, and fears of attack *by one another* are virtually nonexistent. France has abandoned the *tous azimuts* (defense in all directions) strategy that President de Gaulle advocated (it was not taken entirely seriously even at the time). Canada's last war plans for fighting the United States were abandoned half a century ago. Britain and Germany no longer feel threatened by each other. Intense relationships of mutual influence exist between these countries, but in most of them force is irrelevant or unimportant as an instrument of policy.

Moreover, force is often not an appropriate way of achieving other goals (such as economic and ecological welfare) that are becoming more important. It is not impossible to imagine dramatic conflict or revolutionary change in which the use or threat of military force over an economic issue or among advanced industrial countries might become plausible. Then realist assumptions would again be a reliable guide to events. But in most situations, the effects of military force are both costly and uncertain.[2]

Even when the direct use of force is barred among a group of countries, however, military power can still be used politically. Each superpower continues to use the threat of force to deter attacks by other superpowers on itself or its allies; its deterrence ability thus serves an indirect, protective role, which it can use in bargaining on other issues with its allies. This bargaining tool is particularly important for the United States, whose allies are concerned about potential Soviet threats and which has fewer other means of influence over its allies than does the Soviet Union over its Eastern European partners. The United States has, accordingly, taken advantage of the Europeans' (particularly the Germans') desire for its protection and linked the issue of troop levels in Europe to trade and monetary negotiations. Thus, although the first-order effect of deterrent force is essentially negative—to deny effective offensive power to a superpower opponent—a state can use that force positively—to gain political influence.

Thus, even for countries whose relations approximate complex interdependence, two serious qualifications remain: (1) drastic social and political change could cause force again to become an important direct instrument of policy; and (2) even when elites' interests are complementary, a country that uses military force to protect another may have significant political influence over the other country.

In North-South relations, or relations among Third World countries, as well as in East-West relations, force is often important. Military power helps the Soviet Union to dominate Eastern Europe economically as well as politically. The threat of open or covert American military intervention has helped to limit revolutionary changes in the Caribbean, especially in Guatemala in 1954 and in the Dominican Republic in 1965. Secretary of State Kissinger, in January 1975, issued a veiled warning to members of

---

[2]For a valuable discussion, see Klaus Knorr, *The Power of Nations: The Political Economy of International Relations* (New York: Basic Books, 1975).

the Organization of Petroleum Exporting Countries (OPEC) that the United States might use force against them "where there is some actual strangulation of the industrialized world."[3]

Even in these rather conflictual situations, however, the recourse to force seems less likely now than at most times during the century before 1945. The destructiveness of nuclear weapons makes any attack against a nuclear power dangerous. Nuclear weapons are mostly used as a deterrent. Threats of nuclear action against much weaker countries may occasionally be efficacious, but they are equally or more likely to solidify relations between one's adversaries. The limited usefulness of conventional force to control socially mobilized populations has been shown by the United States failure in Vietnam as well as by the rapid decline of colonialism in Africa. Furthermore, employing force on one issue against an independent state with which one has a variety of relationships is likely to rupture mutually profitable relations on other issues. In other words, the use of force often has costly effects on non-security goals. And finally, in Western democracies, popular opposition to prolonged military conflicts is very high.[4]

It is clear that these constraints bear unequally on various countries, or on the same countries in different situations. Risks of nuclear escalation affect everyone, but domestic opinion is far less constraining for communist states, or for authoritarian regional powers, than for the United States, Europe, or Japan. Even authoritarian countries may be reluctant to use force to obtain economic objectives when such use might be ineffective and disrupt other relationships. Both the difficulty of controlling socially mobilized populations with foreign troops and the changing technology of weaponry may actually enhance the ability of certain countries, or nonstate groups, to use terrorism as a political weapon without effective fear of reprisal.

The fact that the changing role of force has uneven effects does not make the change less important, but it does make matters more complex. This complexity is compounded by differences in the usability of force among issue areas. When an issue arouses little interest or passion, force may be unthinkable. In such instances, complex interdependence may be a valuable concept for analyzing the political process. But if that issue becomes a matter of life and death—as some people thought oil might become—the use or threat of force could become decisive again. Realist assumptions would then be more relevant.

It is thus important to determine the applicability of realism or of complex interdependence to each situation. Without this determination further analysis is likely to be confused. Our purpose in developing an alternative to the realist description of world politics is to encourage a differentiated approach that distinguishes among dimensions and areas of world politics—not (as some modernist observers do) to replace one oversimplification with another.

---

[3]*Business Week,* January 13, 1975.
[4]Stanley Hoffmann, "The Acceptability of Military Force," and Laurence Martin, "The Utility of Military Force," in *Force in Modern Societies: Its Place in International Politics* (Adelphi Paper, International Institute for Strategic Studies, 1973). See also Knorr, *The Power of Nations.*

THE POLITICAL PROCESSES
OF COMPLEX INTERDEPENDENCE

Three main characteristics of complex interdependence give rise to distinctive political processes, which translate power resources into power as control of outcomes. As we argued earlier, something is usually lost or added in the translation. Under conditions of complex interdependence the translation will be different than under realist conditions, and our predictions about outcomes will need to be adjusted accordingly.

In the realist world, military security will be the dominant goal of states. It will even affect issues that are not directly involved with military power or territorial defense. Nonmilitary problems will not only be subordinated to military ones; they will be studied for their politico-military implications. Balance of payments issues, for instance, will be considered at least as much in the light of their implications for world power generally as for their purely financial ramifications. McGeorge Bundy conformed to realist expectations when he argued in 1964 that devaluation of the dollar should be seriously considered if necessary to fight the war in Vietnam.[5] To some extent, so did former Treasury Secretary Henry Fowler when he contended in 1971 that the United States needed a trade surplus of $4 billion to $6 billion in order to lead in Western defense.[6]

In a world of complex interdependence, however, one expects some officials, particularly at lower levels, to emphasize the *variety* of state goals that must be pursued. In the absence of a clear hierarchy of issues, goals will vary by issue, and may not be closely related. Each bureaucracy will pursue its own concerns; and although several agencies may reach compromises on issues that affect them all, they will find that a consistent pattern of policy is difficult to maintain. Moreover, transnational actors will introduce different goals into various groups of issues.

Linkage Strategies

Goals will therefore vary by issue area under complex interdependence, but so will the distribution of power and the typical political processes. Traditional analysis focuses on *the* international system, and leads us to anticipate similar political processes on a variety of issues. Militarily and economically strong states will dominate a variety of organizations and a variety of issues, by linking their own policies on some issues to other states' policies on other issues. By using their overall dominance to prevail on their weak issues, the strongest states will, in the traditional model, ensure a congruence between the overall structure of military and economic power and the pattern of outcomes on any one issue area. Thus world politics can be treated as a seamless web.

---

[5]Henry Brandon, *The Retreat of American Power* (New York: Doubleday, 1974), p. 218.
[6]*International Implications of the New Economic Policy,* U.S. Congress, House of Representatives, Committee on Foreign Affairs, Subcommittee on Foreign Economic Policy, Hearings, September 16, 1971.

Under complex interdependence, such congruence is less likely to occur. As military force is devalued, militarily strong states will find it more difficult to use their overall dominance to control outcomes on issues in which they are weak. And since the distribution of power resources in trade, shipping, or oil, for example, may be quite different, patterns of outcomes and distinctive political processes are likely to vary from one set of issues to another. If force were readily applicable, and military security were the highest foreign policy goal, these variations in the issue structures of power would not matter very much. The linkages drawn from them to military issues would ensure consistent dominance by the overall strongest states. But when military force is largely immobilized, strong states will find that linkage is less effective. They may still attempt such links, but in the absence of a hierarchy of issues, their success will be problematic.

Dominant states may try to secure much the same result by using overall economic power to affect results on other issues. If only economic objectives are at stake, they may succeed: money, after all, is fungible. But economic objectives have political implications, and economic linkage by the strong is limited by domestic, transnational, and transgovernmental actors who resist having their interests traded off. Furthermore, the international actors may be different on different issues, and the international organizations in which negotiations take place are often quite separate. Thus it is difficult, for example, to imagine a militarily or economically strong state linking concessions on monetary policy to reciprocal concessions in oceans policy. On the other hand, poor weak states are not similarly inhibited from linking unrelated issues, partly because their domestic interests are less complex. Linkage of unrelated issues is often a means of extracting concessions or side payments from rich and powerful states. And unlike powerful states whose instrument for linkage (military force) is often too costly to use, the linkage instrument used by poor, weak states—international organization—is available and inexpensive.

Thus as the utility of force declines, and as issues become more equal in importance, the distribution of power within each issue will become more important. If linkages become less effective on the whole, outcomes of political bargaining will increasingly vary by issue area.

The differentiation among issue areas in complex interdependence means that linkages among issues will become more problematic and will tend to reduce rather than reinforce international hierarchy. Linkage strategies, and defense against them, will pose critical strategic choices for states. Should issues be considered separately or as a package? If linkages are to be drawn, which issues should be linked, and on which of the linked issues should concessions be made? How far can one push a linkage before it becomes counterproductive? For instance, should one seek formal agreements or informal, but less politically sensitive, understandings? The fact that world politics under complex interdependence is not a seamless web leads us to expect that efforts to stitch seams together advantageously, as reflected in linkage strategies, will, very often, determine the shape of the fabric.

The negligible role of force leads us to expect states to rely more on other instruments in order to wield power. For the reasons we have already discussed, less vulnerable states will try to use asymmetrical interdependence in particular groups of issues as a source of power; they will also try to use international organizations and transnational actors and flows. States will approach economic interdependence in terms of power as well as its effects on citizens' welfare, although welfare considerations will limit their attempts to maximize power. Most economic and ecological interdependence involves the possibility of joint gains, or joint losses. Mutual awareness of potential gains and losses and the danger of worsening each actor's position through overly rigorous struggles over the distribution of the gains can limit the use of asymmetrical interdependence.

Agenda Setting

Our second assumption of complex interdependence, the lack of clear hierarchy among multiple issues, leads us to expect that the politics of agenda formation and control will become more important. Traditional analyses lead statesmen to focus on politico-military issues and to pay little attention to the broader politics of agenda formation. Statesmen assume that the agenda will be set by shifts in the balance of power, actual or anticipated, and by perceived threats to the security of states. Other issues will only be very important when they seem to affect security and military power. In these cases, agendas will be influenced strongly by considerations of the overall balance of power.

Yet, today, some nonmilitary issues are emphasized in interstate relations at one time, whereas others of seemingly equal importance are neglected or quietly handled at a technical level. International monetary politics, problems of commodity terms of trade, oil, food, and multinational corporations have all been important during the last decade; but not all have been high on interstate agendas throughout that period.

Traditional analysts of international politics have paid little attention to agenda formation: to how issues come to receive sustained attention by high officials. The traditional orientation toward military and security affairs implies that the crucial problems of foreign policy are imposed on states by the actions or threats of other states. These are high politics as opposed to the low politics of economic affairs. Yet, as the complexity of actors and issues in world politics increases, the utility of force declines and the line between domestic policy and foreign policy becomes blurred: as the conditions of complex interdependence are more closely approximated, the politics of agenda formation becomes more subtle and differentiated.

THE OBSOLESCENCE
OF MAJOR WAR

John Mueller

On May 15, 1984, the major countries of the developed world had managed to remain at peace with each other for the longest continuous stretch of time since the days of the Roman Empire. If a significant battle in a war had been fought on that day, the press would have bristled with it. As usual, however, a landmark crossing in the history of peace caused no stir: the most prominent story in the *New York Times* that day concerned the saga of a manicurist, a machinist, and a cleaning woman who had just won a big Lotto contest. . . .

For decades now, two massively armed countries, the United States and the Soviet Union, have dominated international politics, and during that time they have engaged in an intense, sometimes even desperate, rivalry over political, military, and ideological issues. Yet despite this enormous mutual hostility, they have never gone to war with each other. Furthermore, although they have occasionally engaged in confrontational crises, there have been only a few of these—and virtually none at all in the last two-thirds of the period. Rather than gradually drawing closer to armed conflict, as often happened after earlier wars, the two major countries seem to be drifting farther away from it.

Insofar as it is discussed at all, there appear to be two schools of thought to explain what John Lewis Gaddis has called the "long peace."[1]

One school concludes that we have simply been lucky. Since 1947, the *Bulletin of Atomic Scientists* has decorated its cover with a "doomsday" clock set ominously at a few minutes before midnight. From time to time the editors push the clock's big hand forward or backward a bit to demonstrate their pleasure with an arms control measure or their disapproval of what they perceive to be rising tension; but they never nudge it very far away from the fatal hour, and the message they wish to convey is clear. They believe we live perpetually on the brink, teetering on a fragile balance; if our luck turns

---

[1] Gaddis 1987b. The calculations about eras of peace are by Paul Schroeder (1985, p. 88). The previous record, he notes, was chalked up during the period from the end of the Napoleonic Wars in 1815 to the effective beginning of the Crimean War in 1854. The period between the conclusion of the Franco-Prussian War in 1871 and the outbreak of World War I in 1914—marred by a major war in Asia between Russia and Japan in 1904—was an even longer era of peace among major European countries. That record was broken on November 8, 1988. On some of these issues, see also Nye 1987; Hinsley 1963, ch. 17; Luard 1986, pp. 395–99; Russett and Starr 1981, ch. 15.

a bit sour, we are likely at any moment to topple helplessly in cataclysmic war.[2] As time goes by, however, this point of view begins to lose some of its persuasiveness. When a clock remains poised at a few minutes to midnight for decades, one may gradually come to suspect that it isn't telling us very much.

The other school stresses paradox: It is the very existence of unprecedentedly destructive weapons that has worked, so far, to our benefit—in Winston Churchill's memorable phrase, safety has been the "sturdy child of [nuclear] terror."[3] This widely held (if minimally examined) view is, to say the least, less than fully comforting, because the very weapons that have been so necessary for peace according to this argument, also possess the capability of cataclysmic destruction, should they somehow be released. For many, this perpetual threat is simply too much to bear, and to them the weapons' continued existence seals our ultimate doom even as it perpetuates our current peace. In his influential best-seller, *The Fate of the Earth*, Jonathan Schell dramatically prophesies that if we do not "rise up and cleanse the earth of nuclear weapons," we will soon "sink into the final coma and end it all."[4]

This book develops a third explanation: The long peace since World War II is less a product of recent weaponry than the culmination of a substantial historical process. For the last two or three centuries major war—war among developed countries—has gradually moved toward terminal disrepute because of its perceived repulsiveness and futility.

The book also concludes that nuclear weapons have not had an important impact on this remarkable trend—they have not crucially defined postwar stability, and they do not threaten to disturb it severely. They have affected rhetoric (we live, we are continually assured, in the atomic age, the nuclear epoch), and they certainly have influenced defense budgets and planning. However, they do not seem to have been necessary to deter major war, to cause the leaders of major countries to behave cautiously, or to determine the alliances that have been formed. Rather, it seems that things would have turned out much the same had nuclear weapons never been invented.

That something other than nuclear terror explains the long peace is suggested in part by the fact that there have been numerous nonwars since 1945 besides the nonwar

---

[2]Said Herman Kahn in 1960: "I have a firm belief that unless we have more serious and sober thought on various aspects of the strategic problem . . . we are not going to reach the year 2000—and maybe not even the year 1965—without a cataclysm" (1960, p. x). Hans J. Morgenthau stated in 1979, "In my opinion the world is moving ineluctably towards a third world war—a strategic nuclear war. I do not believe that anything can be done to prevent it. The international system is too unstable to survive for long" (quoted, Boyle 1985, p. 73). And astronomer Carl Sagan commented in 1983: "I do not think our luck can hold out forever" (quoted, Schroeder 1985, p. 87). On the history of the doomsday clock, see Feld 1978.

[3]Churchill: Bartlett 1977, p. 104. Edward Luttwak says, "We have lived since 1945 without another world war precisely because rational minds . . . extracted a durable peace from the very terror of nuclear weapons" (1983b, p. 82). Kenneth Waltz: "Nuclear weapons have banished war from the center of international politics" (1988, p. 627). See also Knorr 1985, p. 79; Mearsheimer 1984/85, pp. 25–26; Art and Waltz 1983, p. 28; Gilpin 1981, pp. 213–19; Betts 1987, pp. 1–2; Joffe 1987, p. 37; F. Lewis 1987.

[4]Schell 1982, p. 231. For a discussion of expert opinion concluding that the chances of nuclear war by the year 2000 were at least fifty-fifty, see Russett 1983, pp. 3–4.

that is currently being waged by the United States and the Soviet Union. With only one minor and fleeting exception (the Soviet invasion of Hungary in 1956), there have been no wars among the forty-four wealthiest (per capita) countries during that time.[5] Although there have been many wars since World War II, some of them enormously costly by any standard, these have taken place almost entirely within the third—or really the fourth—world. The developed countries have sometimes participated in these wars on distant turf, but not directly against each other.

Several specific nonwars are in their own way even more extraordinary than the one that has taken place between the United States and the Soviet Union. France and Germany are important countries which had previously spent decades—centuries even—either fighting each other or planning to do so. For this ages-old antagonism World War II indeed served as the war to end war: like Greece and Turkey, they have retained the creative ability to discover a motivation for war even under an overarching nuclear umbrella if they really wanted to, yet they have now lived side by side for decades, perhaps with some bitterness and recrimination, but without even a glimmer of war fever. The case of Japan is also striking: this formerly aggressive major country seems now to have fully embraced the virtues (and profits) of peace.

In fact, within the first and second worlds warfare of *all* sorts seems generally to have lost its appeal. Not only have there been virtually no international wars among the major and not-so-major countries, but the developed world has experienced virtually no civil war either. The only exception is the 1944–49 Greek civil war—more an unsettled residue of World War II than an autonomous event. The sporadic violence in Northern Ireland or the Basque region of Spain has not really been sustained enough to be considered civil war, nor have the spurts of terrorism carried out by tiny bands of self-styled revolutionaries elsewhere in Western Europe that have never coalesced into anything bigger. Except for the fleeting case of Hungary in 1956, Europeans under Soviet rule have so far accepted their fate, no matter how desperate their disaffection, rather than take arms to oppose it—though some sort of civil uprising there is certainly not out of the question.[6]

Because it is so quiet, peace often is allowed to carry on unremarked. We tend to delimit epochs by wars and denote periods of peace not for their own character, but for the wars they separate. As Geoffrey Blainey has observed, "For every thousand pages published on the causes of wars there is less than one page directly on the causes of

---

[5]Wealth is calculated using 1978 data when Iran and Iraq were at their financial peak (World Bank 1980). If later data are used, the figure of forty-four would be greater. Countries like Monaco that have no independent foreign policy are not included in the count. The Soviet invasion of Hungary was in some sense requested by ruling politicians in Hungary and for that reason is sometimes not classified as an international war. On classification issues, see Small and Singer 1982, pp. 55, 305; Luard 1986, pp. 5–7. Small and Singer consider Saudi Arabia to have been a participant in the Yom Kippur War of 1973 because it committed 1,000 troops to the anti-Israeli conflict (p. 306); if one accepts their procedure here, that war would form another example of war among the top forty-four. Some might also include the bloodless "war" between the USSR and Czechoslovakia in 1968.
[6]Even as dedicated a foe of the Soviet regime as Aleksandr Solzhenitsyn has said, "I have never advocated physical general revolution. That would entail such destruction of our people's life as would not merit the victory obtained" (quoted, S. Cohen 1985, p. 214).

peace."[7] But now, surely, with so much peace at hand in so much of the world, some effort ought to be made to explain the unprecedented cornucopia. Never before in history have so many well-armed, important countries spent so much time not using their arms against each other. . . .

THE RISING COSTS OF WAR

War is merely an idea. It is not a trick of fate, a thunderbolt from hell, a natural calamity, or a desperate plot contrivance dreamed up by some sadistic puppeteer on high. And if war begins in the minds of men, as the UNESCO charter insists, it can end there as well. Over the centuries war opponents have been trying to bring this about by discrediting war as an idea. In part, their message . . . stresses that war is unacceptably costly, and they have pointed to two kinds of costs: (1) psychic ones—war, they argue, is repulsive, immoral, and uncivilized; and (2) physical ones—war is bloody, destructive, and expensive.

It is often observed that war's physical costs have risen. World War II was the most destructive in history, and World War I was also terrible. World War III, even if nuclear weapons were not used, could easily be worse; and a thermonuclear war might, as Schell would have it, "end it all."

Rising physical costs do seem to have helped to discredit war. But there are good reasons to believe that this cannot be the whole story.

In 1889, Baroness Bertha von Suttner of Austria published a sentimental antiwar novel, *Die Waffen Nieder!,* that swiftly became an international bestseller—the *Uncle Tom's Cabin* of the nineteenth-century peace movement. In it she describes the travails of a young Austrian woman who turns against war when her husband is killed in the Franco-Austrian War of 1859. Now, in historical perspective, that brief war was one of the least memorable in modern history, and its physical costs were minor in comparison with many other wars of that, or any other, era. But Suttner's fictional young widow was repelled not by the war's size, but by its existence and by the devastating personal consequences to her. Opposition to war has been growing in the developed world because more and more people have come to find war repulsive for what it *is,* not simply for the extent of the devastation it causes.

Furthermore, it is simply not true that cataclysmic war is an invention of the 20th century.[8] To annihilate ancient Carthage in 146 B.C., the Romans used weaponry that

---

[7]Blainey, 1973, p. 3.

[8]To put things in somewhat broader perspective, it may be useful to note that war is not the century's greatest killer. Although there have been a large number of extremely destructive wars, totalitarian and extreme authoritarian governments have put more of their own people to death—three times more according to one calculation—than have died in all the century's international and civil wars combined (Rummel 1986). For example, the man-made famine in China between 1958 and 1962 apparently caused the deaths of 30 million people (see p. 165), far more than died during World War I. Governments at peace can also surpass war in their economic destruction as well; largely because of government mismanagement and corruption, the average Zairian's wages in 1988, after adjusting for inflation, were 10 percent of what they had been in 1960 (Greenhouse 1988).

was primitive by today's standard, but even nuclear weapons could not have been more thorough. And, as Thucydides recounts with shattering calm, when the Athenians invaded Melos in 416 B.C., they "put to death all the grown men whom they took and sold the women and children for slaves, and subsequently sent out five hundred colonists and inhabited the place for themselves."[9]

During the Thirty Years War of 1618–48 the wealthy city of Magdeburg, together with its 20,000 inhabitants, was annihilated. According to standard estimates accepted as late as the 1930s, Germany's population in that war declined from 21 million to under 13.5 million—absolute losses far larger than it suffered in either world war of the twentieth century. Moreover, and more importantly, most people apparently *thought* things were even worse: for centuries a legend prevailed that Germany had suffered a 75 percent decline in population, from 16 million to 4 million.[10] Yet the belief that war could cause devastation of such enormous proportions did not lead to its abandonment. After the Thirty Years War, conflict remained endemic in Europe, and in 1756 Prussia fought the Seven Years War, which, in the estimate of its king and generalissimo, Frederick the Great, cost it 500,000 lives—one-ninth of its population, a proportion higher than almost any suffered by any combatant in the wars of the nineteenth or twentieth centuries.[11]

Wars in the past have often caused revolts and economic devastation as well. Historians have been debating for a century whether the Thirty Years War destroyed a vibrant economy in Germany or whether it merely administered the final blow to an economy that was already in decline—but destruction was the consequence in either case. The Seven Years War brought Austria to virtual bankruptcy, and it so weakened France that the conditions for revolution were established. When the economic costs of war are measured as a percentage of the gross national product of the combatants, observes Alan Milward, war "has not shown any discernible long-term trend towards greater costliness."[12]

And in sheer pain and suffering wars used to be far worse than ones fought by developed countries today. In 1840 or 1640 or 1240 a wounded or diseased soldier often died slowly and in intense agony. Medical aid was inadequate, and since physicians had few remedies and were unaware of the germ theory, they often only made things worse. War, indeed, was hell. By contrast, an American soldier wounded in the Vietnam jungle could be in a sophisticated, sanitized hospital within a half hour.

Consequently, if the revulsion toward war has grown in the developed world, this development cannot be due entirely to a supposed rise in its physical costs. Also needed

---

[9]Thucydides 1934, p. 337.

[10]Wedgwood 1938, p. 516. German civilian and military deaths have been estimated at 3,160,000 in World War I and 6,221,000 in World War II (Sivard 1987, p. 29). For the latter-day argument that the losses in the Thirty Years War have been grossly overestimated, see Steinberg 1966, ch. 3. A recent estimate suggests a population decline from 20 million to 16 or 17 million (Parker 1984, p. 211).

[11]Luard 1986, p. 51. Small and Singer 1982, pp. 82–99. About 180,000 of the half-million were soldiers (Kennedy 1987, p. 115), giving a battle death rate of about 4 percent.

[12]Thirty Years War: Robb 1962. Seven Years War: Kennedy 1987, p. 114; Brodie 1973, pp. 248–49; Milward 1977, p. 3.

is an appreciation for war's increased psychic costs. Over the last century or two, war in the developed world has come widely to be regarded as repulsive, immoral, and uncivilized. There may also be something of an interactive effect between psychic and physical costs here: If for moral reasons we come to place a higher value on human life— even to have a sort of reverence for it—the physical costs of war or any other life-taking enterprise will effectively rise as cost tolerance declines.

It may not be obvious that an accepted, time-honored institution that serves an urgent social purpose can become obsolescent and then die out because a lot of people come to find it obnoxious. But this book will argue that something like that has been happening to war in the developed world. To illustrate the dynamic and to set up a framework for future discussion, it will be helpful briefly to assess two analogies: the processes through which the once-perennial institutions of dueling and slavery have been virtually expunged from the earth.

DUELING CEASES TO BE A "PECULIAR NECESSITY"

In some important respects war in the developed world may be following the example of another violent method for settling disputes, dueling, which up until a century ago was common practice in Europe and America among a certain class of young and youngish men who liked to classify themselves as gentlemen. When one man concluded that he had been insulted by another and therefore that his honor had been besmirched, he might well engage the insulter in a short, private, and potentially deadly battle. The duel was taken somehow to settle the matter, even if someone was killed in the process—or even if someone wasn't.[13]

At base, dueling was a matter of attitude more than of cosmology or technology; it was something someone might want to do, and in some respects was even expected to do, from time to time. The night before his famous fatal duel with Aaron Burr in 1804, the methodical Alexander Hamilton wrote out his evaluation of the situation. He could find many reasons to reject Burr's challenge—he really felt no ill will toward his challenger, he wrote, and dueling was against his religious and moral principles, as well as against the laws of New York (where he lived) and New Jersey (where the duel was to be held); furthermore, his death would endanger the livelihood of his wife, children, and creditors. In sum, "I shall hazard much, and can possibly gain nothing." Nevertheless, he still concluded he must fight. All these concerns were overwhelmed because he felt that "what men of the world denominate honor" imposed upon him a "peculiar necessity": his refusal to duel would reduce his political effectiveness by subjecting him to contempt and derision in the circles he considered important. Therefore, he felt that he had to conform with "public prejudice in this particular."[14] Although

---

[13]For other observations of the analogy between war and dueling, see Brodie 1973, p. 275; Angell 1914, pp. 202–3; Gooch 1911, p. 249; Cairnes 1865, p. 650n.
[14]Seitz 1929, pp. 98–101; Freeman 1884, pp. 345–48.

there were solid economic, legal, moral, and religious reasons to turn down the challenge of Vice President Burr, the prick of honor and the attendant fear of immobilizing ridicule—Hamilton's peculiar necessities—impelled him to venture out that summer morning to meet his fate, and his maker, at Weehawken, N.J.

Dueling died out as a general practice eighty years later in the United States after enjoying quite a vogue, especially in the South and in California. It finally faded, not so much because it was outlawed (like liquor—and war—in the 1920s), but because the "public prejudice" Hamilton was so fatally concerned about changed in this particular. Since dueling was an activity carried out by consenting adults in private, laws prohibiting it were difficult to enforce when the climate of opinion accepted the institution. But gradually a consensus emerged that dueling was contemptible and stupid, and it came to be duelers, not nonduelers, who suffered ridicule. As one student of the subject has concluded, "It began to be clear that pistols at ten paces did not settle anything except who was the better shot. . . . Dueling had long been condemned by both statute book and church decree. But these could make no headway against public opinion." However, when it came to pass that "solemn gentlemen went to the field of honor only to be laughed at by the younger generation, that was more than any custom, no matter how sanctified by tradition, could endure. And so the code of honor in America finally died." One of the last duels was in 1877. After the battle (at which no blood was spilled), the combatants found themselves the butt of public hilarity, causing one of them to flee to Paris, where he remained in self-exile for several years.[15]

The American experience was reflected elsewhere. Although dueling's decline in country after country was due in part to enforced legislation against it, the "most effective weapon" against it, one study concludes, "has undoubtedly been ridicule."[16] The ultimate physical cost of dueling—death—did not, and could not rise. But the psychic costs did.

Men of Hamilton's social set still exist, they still get insulted, and they still are concerned about their self respect and their standing among their peers. But they don't duel. However, they do not avoid dueling today because they evaluate the option and reject it on cost-benefit grounds—to use the jargon of a later chapter, they do not avoid it because it has become rationally unthinkable. Rather, the option never percolates into their consciousness as something that is available—that is, it has become subrationally unthinkable. Dueling under the right conditions—with boxing gloves, for example— would not violate current norms or laws. And, of course, in other social classes duel-like combat, such as the street fight or gang war, persists. But the romantic, ludicrous institution of formal dueling has faded from the scene. Insults of the sort that led to the Hamilton-Burr duel often are simply ignored or, if applicable, they are settled with peaceful methods like litigation.[17]

---

[15]Stevens 1940, pp. 280–83. See also Cochran 1963, p. 287.

[16]Baldick 1965, p. 199.

[17]It is sometimes held that dueling died out because improved access to the legal system provided a nonviolent alternative. But most duels were fought over matters of "honor," not legality. Furthermore, lawyers, hardly a group alienated or disenfranchised from the legal system, were frequent duelists—in Tennessee 90 percent of all duels were fought between attorneys (Seitz 1929, p. 30).

A dueling manual from 1847 states that "dueling, like war, is the necessary consequence of offense."[18] By now, however, dueling, a form of violence famed and fabled for centuries, is avoided not merely because it has ceased to seem "necessary," but because it has sunk from thought as a viable, conscious possibility. You can't fight a duel if the idea of doing so never occurs to you or your opponent.

The Prussian strategist Carl von Clausewitz opens his famous 1832 book, *On War,* by observing that "war is nothing but a duel on a larger scale."[19] If war, like dueling, comes to be viewed as a thoroughly undesirable, even ridiculous, policy, and if it can no longer promise gains or if potential combatants no longer value the things it can gain for them, then war could fade away first as a "peculiar necessity" and then as a coherent possibility, even if a truly viable substitute or "moral equivalent" for it were never formulated. Like dueling, it could become unfashionable and then obsolete.

SLAVERY ABRUPTLY BECOMES A "PECULIAR INSTITUTION"

From the dawn of prehistory until about 1788 it had occurred to almost no one that there was anything the least bit peculiar about the institution of slavery. Like war, it could be found just about everywhere in one form or another, and it flourished in every age.[20] Here and there, some people expressed concern about excessive cruelty, and a few found slavery an unfortunate necessity. But the abolitionist movement that broke out at the end of the eighteenth century in Britain and the United States was something new, not the culmination of a substantial historical process.

Like war opponents, the antislavery forces had come to believe that the institution that concerned them was unacceptable because of both its psychic and its physical costs. For some time a small but socially active religious sect in England and the United States, the Quakers, had been arguing that slavery, like war, was repulsive, immoral, and uncivilized, and this sentiment gradually picked up adherents.

Slavery's physical costs, opponents argued, stemmed from its inefficiency. In 1776, Adam Smith concluded that the "work done by slaves . . . is in the end the dearest of any" because "a person who can acquire no property, can have no other interest but to eat as much and to labor as little as possible." Smith's view garnered adherents, but not, as it happens, among slaveowners. That is, either Smith was wrong, or slaveholders were bad businessmen. Clearly, if the economic argument had been correct, slavery would have eventually died of its own inefficiency. Although some have argued that this process was indeed under way, Stanley Engerman observes that in "the history of slave emancipation in the Americas, it is difficult to find any cases of slavery declining economically prior to the imposition of emancipation." Rather, he says, "it took political and military action to bring it to a halt," and "political, cultural, and ideological factors"

---

[18]Stowe 1987, p. 15.
[19]Clausewitz 1976, p. 75.
[20]See Patterson 1982; Engerman 1986, pp. 318–19.

played crucial roles. In fact, at exactly the time that the antislavery movement was taking flight, the Atlantic slave economy, as Seymour Drescher notes, "was entering what was probably the most dynamic and profitable period in its existence."[21]

Thus, the abolitionists were up against an institution that was viable, profitable, and expanding, and one that had been uncritically accepted for thousands—perhaps millions—of years as a natural and inevitable part of human existence. To counter this time-honored institution, the abolitionists' principal weapon was a novel argument: it had recently occurred to them, they said, that slavery was no longer the way people ought to do things.

As it happened, it was an idea whose time had come. The abolition of slavery required legislative battles, international pressures, economic travail, and, in the United States, a cataclysmic war (but, notably, it did *not* require the fabrication of a functional equivalent or the formation of an effective supranational authority). Within a century slavery, and most similar institutions like serfdom, had been all but eradicated from the face of the globe. Slavery became controversial, then peculiar, and then obsolete.

WAR

Dueling and slavery no longer exist as effective institutions and have faded from human experience except as something one reads about in books. Although their reestablishment is not impossible, they show after a century of neglect no signs of revival. Other once-popular, even once admirable, institutions in the developed world have been, or are being, eliminated because at some point they began to seem repulsive, immoral, and uncivilized: bear-baiting, bareknuckle fighting, freak shows, casual torture, wanton cruelty to animals, the burning of heretics, Jim Crow laws, human sacrifice, family feuding, public and intentionally painful methods of execution, deforming corseting, infanticide, laughing at the insane, executions for minor crimes, eunuchism, flogging, public cigarette smoking. . . . War is not, of course, the same as dueling or slavery. Like war, dueling is an institution for settling disputes; but it usually involved only matters of "honor," not ones of physical gain. Like war, slavery was nearly universal and an apparently inevitable part of human existence, but it could be eliminated area by area: a country that abolished slavery did not have to worry about what other countries were doing. A country that would like to abolish war, however, must continue to be concerned about those that have kept it in their repertoire.

On the other hand, war has against it not only substantial psychic costs but also very obvious and widespread physical ones. Dueling brought death and injury, but only to a few people who, like Hamilton, had specifically volunteered to participate. And although slavery may have brought moral destruction, it generally was a considerable economic success in the view of those who ran the system, if not to every ivory-tower economist.

In some respects, then, the fact that war has outlived dueling and slavery is curious. But there are signs that, at least in the developed world, it has begun, like them, to suc-

---

[21]Smith 1976, p. 387 (book 3, ch. 2). Engerman 1986, pp. 322–33, 339. Drescher 1987, p. 4; see also Eltis 1987.

cumb to obsolescence. Like dueling and slavery, war does not appear to be one of life's necessities—it is not an unpleasant fact of existence that is somehow required by human nature or by the grand scheme of things. One can live without it, quite well in fact. War may be a social affliction, but in important respects it is also a social affectation that can be shrugged off.

REFERENCES

Angell, Norman. 1914. *The Great Illusion: A Study of the Relation of Military Power to National Advantage.* London: Heinemann.

————. 1933. *The Great Illusion 1933.* New York: Putnam's.

————. 1951. *After All: An Autobiography.* New York: Farrar, Straus and Young.

Art, Robert J., and Kenneth N. Waltz. 1983. Technology, Strategy, and the Uses of Force. In Robert J. Art and Kenneth N. Waltz (eds.), *The Use of Force.* Lanham, MD: University Press of America.

Baldick, Robert. 1965. *The Duel: A History of Dueling.* New York: Potter.

Bartlett, C. J. 1977. *A History of Postwar Britain, 1945–1974.* London: Longman.

Betts, Richard K. 1987. *Nuclear Blackmail and Nuclear Balance.* Washington: Brookings.

Boyle, Francis Anthony. 1985. *World Politics and International Law.* Durham, NC: Duke University Press.

Brodie, Bernard. 1946. The Weapon. In Bernard Brodie (ed.), *The Absolute Weapon.* New York: Harcourt, Brace, pp. 21–107.

————. 1959. *Strategy in the Missile Age.* Princeton, NJ: Princeton University Press.

————. 1966. *Escalation and the Nuclear Option.* Princeton, NJ: Princeton University Press.

————. 1973. *War and Politics.* New York: Macmillan.

————. 1976a. The Continuing Relevance of *On War,* and A Guide to the Reading of *On War.* In Carl von Clausewitz, *On War.* Princeton, NJ: Princeton University Press, pp. 45–58, 641–711.

————. 1976b. On the Objectives of Arms Control. *International Security,* vol. 1, no. 1 (summer), pp. 17–36.

Cairnes, J. E. 1865. International Law. *Fortnightly Review,* vol. 2 (November 1), pp. 641–50.

Clausewitz, Carl von. 1976. *On War* (edited and translated by Michael Howard and Peter Paret).

Cochran, Hamilton. 1963. *Noted American Duels and Hostile Encounters.* Philadelphia: Chilton.

Drescher, Seymour. 1987. *Capitalism and Antislavery: British Mobilization in Comparative Respective.* New York: Oxford University Press.

————. 1988. Brazilian Abolition in Comparative Perspective. *Hispanic American Historical Review,* vol. 68, no. 3 (August), pp. 429–60.

Eltis, David. 1987. *Economic Growth and the Ending of the Transatlantic Slave Trade.* New York: Oxford University Press.

Engerman, Stanley L. 1986. Slavery and Emancipation in Comparative Perspective: A Look at Some Recent Debates. *Journal of Economic History,* vol. 46, no. 2 (June), pp. 317–39.

Feld, Bernard T. 1978. To Move or Not to Move the Clock. *Bulletin of Atomic Scientists,* January, pp. 8–9.

Freeman, Major Ben C. 1884. *The Field of Honor: Being a Complete and Comprehensive History of Dueling in All Countries.* New York: Fords, Howard, and Hulbert.

Gaddis, John Lewis. 1972. *The United States and the Origins of the Cold War, 1941–1947.* New York: Columbia University Press.

————. 1974. Was the Truman Doctrine a Real Turning Point? *Foreign Affairs,* vol. 52, no. 2 (January), pp. 386–401.

————. 1982. *Strategies of Containment: A Critical Appraisal of Postwar American National Security Policy.* New York: Oxford University Press.

————. 1987a. Expanding the Data Base: Historians, Political Scientists, and the Enrichment of Security Studies. *International Security,* vol. 12, no. 1 (summer), pp. 3–21.

————. 1987b. *The Long Peace: Inquiries into the History of the Cold War.* New York: Oxford University Press.

Gilpin, Robert. 1981. *War and Change in World Politics.* Cambridge: Cambridge University Press.

Gooch, B. P. 1911. *History of Our Time, 1885–1911.* London: Williams and Norgate.

Greenhouse, Steven. 1988. Zaire, The Manager's Nightmare, So Much Potential, So Poorly Harnessed. *New York Times,* May 23, p. 48. See also correction, May 26, p. A3.

Hinsley, F. H. 1963. *Power and the Pursuit of Peace: Theory and Practice in the History of Relations between States.* London: Cambridge University Press.

Joffe, Josef. 1987. Peace and Populism: Why the European Anti-Nuclear Movement Failed. *International Security,* vol. 11, no. 4 (spring), pp. 3–40.

Kahn, Herman. 1960. *On Thermonuclear War.* Princeton, NJ: Princeton University Press.

————. 1970. Issues of Thermonuclear War Termination. *Annals of the American Academy of Political and Social Science,* vol. 390 (November), pp. 133–72.

Kennedy, Paul. 1987. *The Rise and Fall of the Great Powers.* New York: Random House.

Knorr, Klaus. 1966. *On the Uses of Military Power in the Nuclear Age.* Princeton, NJ: Princeton University Press.

————. 1985. Controlling Nuclear War. *International Security,* vol. 9, no. 4 (spring), pp. 79–98.

Lewis, Flora. 1986. Step Back from Folly. *New York Times,* November 7, p. A35.

————. 1987. Don't Be Afraid of 'Da'. *New York Times,* April 17, p. A31.

Luard, Evan. 1986. *War in International Society: A Study in International Sociology.* New Haven, CT: Yale University Press.

Luttwak, Edward N. 1983a. *The Grand Strategy of the Soviet Union.* New York: St. Martin's.

————. 1983b. Of Bombs and Men. *Commentary,* August. pp. 77–82.

————. 1988. An Emerging Postnuclear Era? *Washington Quarterly,* vol. 11, no. 1 (winter), pp. 5–15.

Mearsheimer, John J. 1983. *Conventional Deterrence.* Ithaca, NY: Cornell University Press.

————. 1984/85. Nuclear Weapons and Deterrence in Europe. *International Security,* vol. 9, no. 3 (winter), pp. 19–47.

Milward, Alan S. 1977. *War, Economy and Society, 1939–1945.* Berkeley, CA. University of California Press.

Morgenthau, Hans J. 1948. *Politics among Nations: The Struggle for Power and Peace.* New York: Knopf.

Nye, Joseph S., Jr. 1987. Nuclear Learning and U.S.–Soviet Security Regimes. *International Organization,* vol. 41, no. 3 (summer), pp. 371–402.

Parker, Geoffrey. 1984. *The Thirty Years War.* London: Routledge and Kegan Paul.

Patterson, Orlando. 1982. *Slavery and Social Death: A Comparative Study.* Cambridge, MA: Harvard University Press.

Robb, Theodore K. 1962. The Effects of the Thirty Years' War. *Journal of Modern History,* vol. 34 (March), pp. 40–51.

Rummel, Rudolph J. 1983. Libertarianism and International Violence. *Journal of Conflict Resolution,* vol. 27, no. 1 (March), pp. 27–71.

————. 1986. War Isn't This Century's Biggest Killer. *Wall Street Journal,* July 7, p. 12.

Russett, Bruce. 1963. The Calculus of Deterrence. *Journal of Conflict Resolution,* vol. 7 (June), pp. 97–109.

————. 1972. *No Clear and Present Danger: A Skeptical View of the United States' Entry into World War II.* New York: Harper and Row.

————. 1983. *The Prisoners of Insecurity: Nuclear Deterrence, the Arms Race, and Arms Control.* San Francisco: Freeman.

Russett, Bruce, and Harvey Starr. 1981. *World Politics: The Menu for Choice.* San Francisco: Freeman.

Sagan, Carl. 1983/84. Nuclear War and Climatic Catastrophe: Some Policy Implications. *Foreign Affairs,* vol. 62, no. 2 (winter), pp. 257–92.

Schell, Jonathan. 1982. *The Fate of the Earth.* New York: Knopf.

Schroeder, Paul. 1985. Does Murphy's Law Apply to History? *Wilson Quarterly,* vol. 9, no. 1 (New Year's), pp. 84–93.

Seitz, Don C. 1929. *Famous American Duels.* New York: Crowell.

Sivard, Ruth Leger. 1985. *World Military and Social Expenditures 1985.* Washington: World Priorities.

———. 1987. *World Military and Social Expenditures 1987/88.* Washington: World Priorities.

Small, Melvin, and J. David Singer. 1982. *Resort to Arms: International Civil Wars, 1816–1980.* Beverly Hills, CA: Sage.

Smith, Adam. 1976. *An Inquiry into the Nature and Causes of the Wealth of Nations.* New York: Oxford University Press.

Steinberg, S. H. 1966. *The Thirty Years War and the Conflict for European Hegemony 1600–1660.* New York: Norton.

Stevens, William Oliver. 1940. *Pistols at Ten Paces: The Story of the Code of Honor in America.* Boston: Houghton Mifflin.

Stowe, Steven M. 1987. *Intimacy and Power in the Old South: Ritual in the Lives of the Planters.* Baltimore, MD: Johns Hopkins University Press.

Thucydides. 1934. *The Peloponnesian War.* New York: Modern Library.

Waltz, Kenneth. 1959. *Man, the State, and War.* New York: Columbia University Press.

———. 1979. *Theory of International Politics.* Reading, MA: Addison-Wesley.

———. 1988. The Origins of War in Neorealist Theory. *Journal of Interdisciplinary History,* vol. 18, no. 4 (spring), pp. 615–28.

Wedgwood, C. V. 1938. *The Thirty Years War.* London: Jonathan Cape.

———. 1961. *The Thirty Years War.* Garden City, NY: Anchor.

P A R T   I V

PSYCHOLOGY AND CULTURE: UNCONSCIOUS SOURCES OF CONFLICT AND CONSCIOUS NORMS

The thinkers sampled so far view war or peace as products of political incentives and constraints. These pressures may be external or domestic, but for the most part both realist and liberal schools see politics as a rational process of adaptation to the environment or application of conscious value systems to policy. Views of human nature and social competition play a large role in the ideas of classical realists such as Machiavelli and Hobbes, and the evolution of social customs figures in Mueller's analysis, but most of the theories in the dominant approaches to international relations do not dwell on the sources of motivation or identity of the actors who make policy. The events of September 11, 2001, however, reminded us that not all strategic behavior conforms clearly to Western standards of materialistic rationality.

Observers outside political science have focused more often on unconscious roots of conflict and cooperation. Psychological and cultural explanations present political behavior, including foreign policy initiatives, as manifestations of individual impulses, social identities and customs, or institutions that are shaped by them. To deal with the problem of war requires not only explicitly political solutions—stabilization of how power is distributed among countries, or promulgation of liberal principles—but the taming and channeling of subliminal drives, or the alteration of assumptions and customs to create new ways of thinking for society.

Sigmund Freud's letter to Albert Einstein—written only months before Hitler's accession to power in Germany—presents his view of how aggressive and destructive instincts compete with erotic and constructive ones, and how cultural development works to suppress the urges conducive to war. The selection by Franco Fornari, a former president of the Italian Psychoanalytical Society, argues that subconscious fears of unreal threats lead people to seek real external enemies against whom they can fight. Fornari's extreme theory is practically a caricature of the Freudian approach. Nevertheless, it reflects views popular among many intellectuals outside of political science.[1] Anthropologist Margaret Mead asserts that war is not a universal phenomenon, but simply a custom common to many cultures, and thus not an inevitable part of human relations.[2]

The selections by Alexander Wendt and Martha Finnemore represent "constructivist" approaches to international relations. Wendt argues against the fundamental realist assumption that lack of a sovereign in the international arena inevitably makes it a "self-help" system. Conflict depends on assumptions about interests, which in turn depend on identities that are "socially constructed." Since different constructions are possible, dispositions toward peace can be as natural as the conflictual ones assumed by devotees of power politics. Finnemore provides an example of how changes in international norms and practices regarding certain types of uses of force evolve over time. The entries by Wendt and Finnemore should be considered in the context of the alternative to realist and liberal paradigms given by Samuel Huntington in Part I. Recall how Huntington poses major civilizational culture areas as the bases of international cleavage in the post-Cold War world, and sees these cleavages as a reason for both western cohesion and Western nonintervention in other civilizations' conflicts.

Huntington's particular twist on the importance and implications of identity evokes discomfort or opposition from many constructivists, who tend toward liberal constructions of their own personal identities. This is a reminder that although many who see culture as important hope that cultures will evolve in ways consistent with liberal norms and values, constructivist theory is logically one of cultural and intellectual relativism. As such, there is nothing in the causal logic of the theory that ordains that one set of norms or identities must triumph over others, or that good ones will drive out bad ones or even defend themselves successfully against them. There is nothing intrinsic in a cultural approach that makes construction of liberal-friendly identity more likely than identities consistent with racism, fascism, militarism, or religious fanaticism.[3] If anarchy is only what states make of it, war may not be inevitable, but by the same token peace may not be probable.

Paying attention to unconscious motivations does not necessarily point toward either optimism or pessimism about the future of war. If paranoid statesmen can be put in the care of psychotherapists, or groups with nasty identities can be persuaded to transform them, would-be aggressors might become reasonable cooperators. If aggression is as rooted in human nature as some psychologists believe, however, or if people exposed to liberal cultural models persist in feeling more at home with parochial rather than cosmopolitan identities, it will be difficult to eliminate conflictual impulses from foreign policies.

---

[1]See, for example Barbara Ehrenreich, *Blood Rites: Origins and History of the Passions of War* (New York: Henry Holt, 1997). For criticism of these approaches see Richard K. Betts, "Is Strategy an Illusion?" *International Security* 25, no. 2 (fall 2000), pp. 22–25.

[2]For arguments against reliance on psychological and anthropological explanations of war, see Kenneth N. Waltz, *Man, the State, and War* (New York: Columbia University Press, 1959), Chapters 2–3.

[3]See John J. Mearsheimer, "The False Promise of International Institutions," *International Security* 19, no. 3 (winter 1994/95), pp. 41–44. See rebuttals by Robert Keohane and Lisa Martin, Charles and Clifford Kupchan, John Ruggie, and Alexander Wendt, and Mearsheimer's reply, in *International Security* 20, no. 1 (summer 1995).

In academic debate, interpretations that emphasize the importance of individual, sociological, or domestic factors are usually seen as incompatible with structural realism. This is true only if Waltz's theory is used in a way that he says it should not be—to predict particular policy decisions. Waltz argues that his emphasis on the international system (anarchy and the distribution of capabilities) as the prime level of analysis is due to his mission of presenting a theory of international politics as distinct from a theory of foreign policy. The two are distinct in the same way that, in economics, a theory of the market is distinct from a theory of the firm. Theories of international politics (the market) are about typical outcomes over time; theories of foreign policy (the firm) are about particular decisions. Anarchy in the external environment is the permissive cause of war, but motives and calculations of policymakers are efficient causes. To understand particular wars, we need to look at foreign policy decisions and their sources.[4] Psychology, anthropology, sociology, and intellectual history can all illuminate the motives of those who make policy, and thus can be relevant to understanding the efficient causes of war. A structural realist in Waltz's mold will simply argue that whatever the motives behind decisions for wars made by individuals in governments, if they do not heed the imperative of self-help posed by the international system, their states will fall by the wayside.[5] In short, policymakers may sometimes act for the reasons asserted in this section, but if they do so in ways that contradict adaptation to the external distribution of power they will usually fail.

—RKB

---

[4]Many critics forget that Waltz wrote a whole book on domestic sources of policy: *Foreign Policy and Democratic Politics* (Boston: Little, Brown, 1967).

[5]Some critics deny Waltz's analogy and argue that the international system is one of oligopoly (several great powers) rather than pure market competition, and that a theory of international politics therefore cannot be separated from a theory of foreign policy. Graham Allison and Philip Zelikow, *Essence of Decision: Explaining the Cuban Missile Crisis*, 2d ed. (New York: Longman, 1999), p. 405.

WHY WAR?

Sigmund Freud

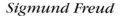

VIENNA
SEPTEMBER 1932.

DEAR PROFESSOR EINSTEIN,

When I learnt of your intention to invite me to a mutual exchange of views upon a subject which not only interested you personally but seemed deserving, too, of public interest, I cordially assented. I expected you to choose a problem lying on the borderland of the knowable, as it stands to-day, a theme which each of us, physicist and psychologist, might approach from his own angle, to meet at last on common ground, though setting out from different premises. Thus the question which you put me—what is to be done to rid mankind of the war-menace?—took me by surprise. And, next, I was dumbfounded by the thought of my (of *our*, I almost wrote) incompetence; for this struck me as being a matter of practical politics, the statesman's proper study. But then I realized that you did not raise the question in your capacity of scientist or physicist, but as a lover of his fellow-men, who responded to the call of the League of Nations much as Fridtjof Nansen, the Polar explorer, took on himself the task of succouring homeless and starving victims of the World War. And, next, I reminded myself that I was not being called on to formulate practical proposals, but, rather, to explain how this question of preventing wars strikes a psychologist.

But here, too, you have stated the gist of the matter in your letter—and taken the wind out of my sails! Still, I will gladly follow in your wake and content myself with endorsing your conclusions, which, however, I propose to amplify to the best of my knowledge or surmise.

You begin with the relations between Might and Right, and this is assuredly the proper starting-point for our inquiry. But, for the term 'might', I would substitute a tougher and more telling word: 'violence'. In right and violence we have to-day an obvious antinomy. It is easy to prove that one has evolved from the other and, when we go back to origins and examine primitive conditions, the solution of the problem follows easily enough. I must crave your indulgence if in what follows I speak of well-known, admitted facts as though they were new data; the context necessitates this method.

Conflicts of interest between man and man are resolved, in principle, by the recourse to violence. It is the same in the animal kingdom, from which man cannot claim exclusion; nevertheless men are also prone to conflicts of opinion, touching, on occasion, the loftiest peaks of abstract thought, which seem to call for settlement by quite another method. This refinement is, however, a late development. To start with, brute

"Why War?" from *The Collected Papers*, Volume 5 by Sigmund Freud. Edited by James Strachey, pp. 273–287. Published by Basic Books, Inc. by arrangement with The Hogarth Press, Ltd. and the Institute of Psycho-Analysis, London. Reprinted by permission of Basic Books, a member of Perseus Books, L.L.C. and The Random House Group Ltd.

force was the factor which, in small communities, decided points of ownership and the question which man's will was to prevail. Very soon physical force was implemented, then replaced, by the use of various adjuncts; he proved the victor whose weapon was the better, or handled the more skilfully. Now, for the first time, with the coming of weapons, superior brains began to oust brute force, but the object of the conflict remained the same: one party was to be constrained, by the injury done him or impairment of his strength, to retract a claim or a refusal. This end is most effectively gained when the opponent is definitively put out of action—in other words, is killed. This procedure has two advantages; the enemy cannot renew hostilities, and, secondly, his fate deters others from following his example. Moreover, the slaughter of a foe gratifies an instinctive craving—a point to which we shall revert hereafter. However, another consideration may be set off against this will to kill: the possibility of using an enemy for servile tasks if his spirit be broken and his life spared. Here violence finds an outlet not in slaughter but in subjugation. Hence springs the practice of giving quarter; but the victor, having from now on to reckon with the craving for revenge that rankles in his victim, forfeits to some extent his personal security.

Thus, under primitive conditions, it is superior force—brute violence, or violence backed by arms—that lords it everywhere. We know that in the course of evolution this state of things was modified, a path was traced that led away from violence to law. But what was this path? Surely it issued from a single verity; that the superiority of one strong man can be overborne by an alliance of many weaklings, that *l'union fait la force*. Brute force is overcome by union, the allied might of scattered units makes good its right against the isolated giant. Thus we may define 'right' (i.e. law) as the might of a community. Yet it, too, is nothing else than violence, quick to attack whatever individual stands in its path, and it employs the selfsame methods, follows like ends, with but one difference; it is the communal, not individual, violence that has its way. But, for the transition from crude violence to the reign of law, a certain psychological condition must first obtain. The union of the majority must be stable and enduring. If its sole *raison d'être* be the discomfiture of some overweening individual and, after his downfall, it be dissolved, it leads to nothing. Some other man, trusting to his superior power, will seek to reinstate the rule of violence and the cycle will repeat itself unendingly. Thus the union of the people must be permanent and well organised; it must enact rules to meet the risk of possible revolts; must set up machinery ensuring that its rules—the laws—are observed and that such acts of violence as the laws demand are duly carried out. This recognition of a community of interests engenders among the members of the group a sentiment of unity and fraternal solidarity which constitutes its real strength.

So far I have set out what seems to me the kernel of the matter: the suppression of brute force by the transfer of power to a larger combination, founded on the community of sentiments linking up its members. All the rest is mere tautology and glosses. Now the position is simple enough so long as the community consists of a number of equipollent individuals. The laws of such a group can determine to what extent the individual must forfeit his personal freedom, the right of using personal force as an instrument of violence, to ensure the safety of the group. But such a combination is only theoretically possible; in practice the situation is always complicated by the fact that, from the outset, the group includes elements of unequal power, men and women, elders and children, and, very soon, as a result of war and conquest, victors and the vanquished—i.e. masters and slaves—as well. From this time on the common law takes notice of these inequalities of power, laws are made by and for the rulers, giving the servile classes fewer rights. Thenceforward there exist within the state two factors making for legal instability, but legislative evolution, too: first, the attempts by members of the ruling class to set themselves above the law's restrictions and, secondly, the constant struggle of the ruled to extend their rights and see each gain embodied in the code, replacing legal disabilities by equal laws for all. The second of these tendencies will be particularly marked when there takes place a positive mutation of the balance of power within the community, the frequent outcome of certain historical conditions. In such cases the laws may gradually be adjusted to the changed conditions or (as more usually ensues) the ruling class is loath to reckon with the new developments, the result being insurrections and civil wars, a period when law is in abeyance and force once more the arbiter, followed by a new regime of law. There is another factor of constitutional change, which operates in a wholly pacific manner, namely: the cultural evolution of the mass of the community; this factor, however, is of a different order and can only be dealt with later.

Thus we see that, even within the group itself, the exercise of violence cannot be avoided when conflicting interests are at stake. But the common needs and habits of men who live in fellowship under the same sky favour a speedy issue of such conflicts and, this being so, the possibilities of peaceful solutions make steady progress. Yet the most casual glance at world-history will show an unending series of conflicts between one community and another or a group of others, between large and smaller units, between cities, countries, races, tribes and kingdoms, almost all of which were settled by the ordeal of war. Such wars end either in pillage or in conquest and its fruits, the downfall of the loser. No single all-embracing judgment can be passed on these wars of aggrandizement. Some, like the war between the Mongols and the Turks, have led to unmitigated misery; others, however, have furthered the transition from violence to law, since they brought larger units into being, within whose limits a recourse to violence was banned and a new régime determined all disputes. Thus the Roman conquests brought that boon, the *pax romana,* to the Mediterranean lands. The French kings' lust for aggrandizement created a new France, flourishing in peace and unity. Paradoxical as it sounds, we must admit that warfare well might serve to pave the way to that unbroken peace we so desire, for it is war that brings vast empires into being, within whose frontiers all warfare is proscribed by a strong central power. In practice, however, this end is not attained, for as a rule the fruits of victory are but short-lived, the new-created unit falls asunder once again, generally because there can be no true cohesion between the parts that violence has welded. Hitherto, moreover, such conquests have only led to aggregations which, for all their magnitude, had limits, and disputes between these units could be resolved only by recourse to arms. For humanity at large the sole result of all these military enterprises was that, instead of frequent not to say incessant little wars, they had now to face great wars which, for all they came less often, were so much the more destructive.

Regarding the world of to-day the same conclusion holds good, and you, too, have reached it, though by a shorter path. There is but one sure way of ending war and that is the establishment, by common consent, of a central control which shall have the last word in every conflict of interests. For this, two things are needed: first, the creation of such a supreme court of judicature; secondly, its investment with adequate executive force. Unless this second requirement be fulfilled, the first is unavailing. Obviously the League of Nations, acting as a Supreme Court, fulfils the first condition; it does not fulfil the second. It has no force at its disposal and can only get it if the members of the new body, its constituent nations, furnish it. And, as things are, this is a forlorn hope. Still we should be taking a very short-sighted view of the League of Nations were we to ignore the fact that here is an experiment the like of which has rarely—never before, perhaps, on such a scale—been attempted in the course of history. It is an attempt to acquire the authority (in other words, coercive influence), which hitherto reposed exclusively on the possession of power, by calling into play certain idealistic attitudes of mind. We have seen that there are two factors of cohesion in a community: violent compulsion and ties of sentiment ('identifications', in technical parlance) between the members of the group. If one of these factors becomes inoperative, the other may still suffice to hold the group together. Obviously such notions as these can only be significant when they are the expression of a deeply rooted sense of unity, shared by all. It is necessary, therefore, to gauge the efficacy of such sentiments. History tells us that, on occasion, they have been effective. For example, the Panhellenic conception, the Greeks' awareness of superiority over their barbarian neighbours, which found expression in the Amphictyonies, the Oracles and Games, was strong enough to humanize the methods of warfare as between Greeks, though inevitably it failed to prevent conflicts between different elements of the Hellenic race or even to deter a city or group of cities from joining forces with their racial foe, the Persians, for the discomfiture of a rival. The solidarity of Christendom in the Renaissance age was no more effective, despite its vast authority, in hindering Christian nations, large and small alike, from calling in the Sultan to their aid. And, in our times, we look in vain for some such unifying notion whose authority would be unquestioned. It is all too clear that the nationalistic ideas, paramount to-day in every country, operate in quite a contrary direction. There are some who hold that the Bolshevist conceptions may make an end of war, but, as things are, that goal lies very far away and, perhaps, could only be attained after a spell of brutal internecine warfare. Thus it would seem that any effort to replace brute force by the might of an ideal is, under present conditions, doomed to fail. Our logic is at fault if we ignore the fact that right is founded on brute force and even to-day needs violence to maintain it.

I now can comment on another of your statements. You are amazed that it is so easy to infect men with the war-fever, and you surmise that man has in him an active instinct for hatred and destruction, amenable to such stimulations. I entirely agree with you. I believe in the existence of this instinct and have been recently at pains to study its manifestations. In this connection may I set out a fragment of that knowledge of the instincts, which we psychoanalysts, after so many tentative essays and gropings in the dark, have compassed? We assume that human instincts are of two kinds: those that conserve and unify, which we call 'erotic' (in the meaning Plato gives to *Eros* in his *Symposium*), or else 'sexual' (explicitly extending the popular connotation of 'sex'), and, secondly, the instincts to destroy and kill, which we assimilate as the aggressive or destructive instincts. These are, as you perceive, the well-known opposites, Love and Hate, transformed into theoretical entities; they are, perhaps, another aspect of those eternal polarities, attraction and repulsion, which fall within your province. But we must be chary of passing over-hastily to the notions of good and evil. Each of these instincts is every whit as indispensable as its opposite and all the phenomena of life derive from their activity, whether they work in concert or in opposition. It seems that an instinct of either category can operate but rarely in isolation; it is always blended ('alloyed', as we say) with a certain dosage of its opposite, which modifies its aim or even, in certain circumstances, is a prime condition of its attainment. Thus the instinct of self-preservation is certainly of an erotic nature, but to gain its ends this very instinct necessitates aggressive action. In the same way the love-instinct, when directed to a specific object, calls for an admixture of the acquisitive instinct if it is to enter into effective possession of that object. It is the difficulty of isolating the two kinds of instinct in their manifestations that has so long prevented us from recognizing them.

If you travel with me a little further on this road, you will find that human affairs are complicated in yet another way. Only exceptionally does an action follow on the stimulus of a single instinct, which is *per se* a blend of Eros and destructiveness. As a rule several motives of similar composition concur to bring about the act. This fact was duly noted by a colleague of yours, Professor G. C. Lichtenberg, sometime Professor of Physics at Göttingen; he was perhaps even more eminent as a psychologist than as a physical scientist. He evolved the notion of a 'Compass-card of Motives' and wrote: 'The efficient motives impelling man to act can be classified like the 32 Winds, and described in the same manner; for example, *Food-Food-Fame* or *Fame-Fame-Food.*' Thus, when a nation is summoned to engage in war, a whole gamut of human motives may respond to this appeal; high and low motives, some openly avowed, others slurred over. The lust for aggression and destruction is certainly included; the innumerable cruelties of history and man's daily life confirm its prevalence and strength. The stimulation of these destructive impulses by appeals to idealism and the erotic instinct naturally facilitates their release. Musing on the atrocities recorded on history's page, we feel that the ideal motive has often served as a camouflage for the lust of destruction; sometimes, as with the cruelties of the Inquisition, it seems that, while the ideal motives occupied the foreground of consciousness, they drew their strength from the destructive instincts submerged in the unconscious. Both interpretations are feasible.

You are interested, I know, in the prevention of war, not in our theories, and I keep this fact in mind. Yet I would like to dwell a little longer on this destructive instinct which is seldom given the attention that its importance warrants. With the least of speculative efforts we are led to conclude that this instinct functions in every living being, striving to work its ruin and reduce life to its primal state of inert matter. Indeed it might well be called the 'death-instinct'; whereas the erotic instincts vouch for the struggle to live on. The death instinct becomes an impulse to destruction when, with the aid of certain organs, it directs its action outwards, against external objects. The living being, that is to say, defends its own existence by destroying foreign bodies. But, in one of its activities, the death instinct is operative *within* the living being and we have sought to trace back a number of normal and pathological phenomena to this *introversion* of the destructive instinct. We have even committed the heresy of explaining the origin of human conscience by some such 'turning inward' of the aggressive impulse. Obviously when this internal tendency operates on too large a scale, it is no trivial matter, rather a positively morbid state of things; whereas the diversion of the destructive impulse towards the external world must have beneficial effects. Here is then the bio-logical justification for all those vile, pernicious propensities which we now are com-bating. We can but own that they are really more akin to nature than this our stand against them, which, in fact, remains to be accounted for.

All this may give you the impression that our theories amount to a species of mythology and a gloomy one at that! But does not every natural science lead ultimately to this—a sort of mythology? Is it otherwise to-day with your physical science?

The upshot of these observations, as bearing on the subject in hand, is that there is no likelihood of our being able to suppress humanity's aggressive tendencies. In some happy corners of the earth, they say, where nature brings forth abundantly whatever man desires, there flourish races whose lives go gently by, unknowing of aggression or constraint. This I can hardly credit; I would like further details about these happy folk. The Bolshevists, too, aspire to do away with human aggressiveness by ensuring the sat-isfaction of material needs and enforcing equality between man and man. To me this hope seems vain. Meanwhile they busily perfect their armaments, and their hatred of outsiders is not the least of the factors of cohesion amongst themselves. In any case, as you too have observed, complete suppression of man's aggressive tendencies is not in issue; what we may try is to divert it into a channel other than that of warfare.

From our 'mythology' of the instincts we may easily deduce a formula for an indi-rect method of eliminating war. If the propensity for war be due to the destructive in-stinct, we have always its counter-agent, Eros, to our hand. All that produces ties of sen-timent between man and man must serve us as war's antidote. These ties are of two kinds. First, such relations as those towards a beloved object, void though they be of sexual intent. The psychoanalyst need feel no compunction in mentioning 'love' in this connection; religion uses the same language: Love thy neighbour as thyself. A pious in-junction easy to enounce, but hard to carry out! The other bond of sentiment is by way of identification. All that brings out the significant resemblances between men calls into play this feeling of community, identification, whereon is founded, in large measure, the whole edifice of human society.

In your strictures on the abuse of authority I find another suggestion for an indirect attack on the war-impulse. That men are divided into leaders and the led is but another manifestation of their inborn and irremediable inequality. The second class constitutes the vast majority; they need a high command to make decisions for them, to which de-cisions they usually bow without demur. In this context we would point out that men should be at greater pains than heretofore to form a superior class of independent thinkers, unamenable to intimidation and fervent in the quest of truth, whose function it would be to guide the masses dependent on their lead. There is no need to point out how little the rule of politicians and the Church's ban on liberty of thought encourage such a new creation. The ideal conditions would obviously be found in a community where every man subordinated his instinctive life to the dictates of reason. Nothing less than this could bring about so thorough and so durable a union between men, even if this in-volved the severance of mutual ties of sentiment. But surely such a hope is utterly utopian, as things are. The other indirect methods of preventing war are certainly more feasible, but entail no quick results. They conjure up an ugly picture of mills which grind so slowly that, before the flour is ready, men are dead of hunger.

As you see, little good comes of consulting a theoretician, aloof from worldly contacts, on practical and urgent problems! Better it were to tackle each successive crisis with means that we have ready to our hands. However, I would like to deal with a question which, though it is not mooted in your letter, interests me greatly. Why do we, you and I and many another, protest so vehemently against war, instead of just accepting it as another of life's odious importunities? For it seems a natural thing enough, biologically sound and practically unavoidable. I trust you will not be shocked by my raising such a question. For the better conduct of an inquiry it may be well to don a mask of feigned aloofness. The answer to my query may run as follows: Because every man has a right over his own life and war destroys lives that were full of promise; it forces the individual into situations that shame his manhood, obliging him to murder fellow-men, against his will; it ravages material amenities, the fruits of human toil, and much besides. Moreover wars, as now conducted, afford no scope for acts of heroism according to the old ideals and, given the high perfection of modern arms, war to-day would mean the sheer extermination of one of the combatants, if not of both. This is so true, so obvious, that we can but wonder why the conduct of war is not banned by general consent. Doubtless either of the points I have just made is open to debate. It may be asked if the community, in its turn, cannot claim a right over the individual lives of its members. Moreover, all forms of war cannot be indiscriminately condemned; so long as there are nations and empires, each prepared callously to exterminate its rival, all alike must be equipped for war. But we will not dwell on any of these problems; they lie outside the debate to which you have invited me. I pass on to another point, the basis, as it strikes me, of our common hatred of war. It is this: we cannot do otherwise than hate it. Pacifists we are, since our organic nature wills us thus to be. Hence it comes easy to us to find arguments that justify our standpoint.

This point, however, calls for elucidation. Here is the way in which I see it. The cultural development of mankind (some, I know, prefer to call it civilization) has been in progress since immemorial antiquity. To this processus we owe all that is best in our composition, but also much that makes for human suffering. Its origins and causes are obscure, its issue is uncertain, but some of its characteristics are easy to perceive. It well may lead to the extinction of mankind, for it impairs the sexual function in more than one respect, and even to-day the uncivilized races and the backward classes of all nations are multiplying more rapidly than the cultured elements. This process may, perhaps, be likened to the effect of domestication on certain animals—it clearly involves physical changes of structure—but the view that cultural development is an organic process of this order has not yet become generally familiar. The psychic changes which accompany this process of cultural change are striking, and not to be gainsaid. They consist in the progressive rejection of instinctive ends and a scaling down of instinctive reactions. Sensations which delighted our forefathers have become neutral or unbearable to us; and, if our ethical and æsthetic ideals have undergone a change, the causes of this are ultimately organic. On the psychological side two of the most important phenomena of culture are, firstly, a strengthening of the intellect, which tends to master our instinctive life, and, secondly, an introversion of the aggressive impulse, with all its consequent benefits and perils. Now war runs most emphatically counter to the psychic disposition imposed on us by the growth of culture; we are therefore bound to resent war, to find it utterly intolerable. With pacifists like us it is not merely an intellectual and affective repulsion, but a constitutional intolerance, an idiosyncrasy in its most drastic form. And it would seem that the æsthetic ignominies of warfare play almost as large a part in this repugnance as war's atrocities.

How long have we to wait before the rest of men turn pacifist? Impossible to say, and yet perhaps our hope that these two factors—man's cultural disposition and a well-founded dread of the form that future wars will take—may serve to put an end to war in the near future, is not chimerical. But by what ways or by-ways this will come about, we cannot guess. Meanwhile we may rest on the assurance that whatever makes for cultural development is working also against war.

With kindest regards and, should this *exposé* prove a disappointment to you, my sincere regrets,

Yours,
SIGMUND FREUD.

THE PSYCHOANALYSIS
OF WAR

Franco Fornari

. . . War was initially interpreted by psychoanalysis as a periodic discharge of repressed criminal impulses, a periodic return to barbarity. This theory of war (which does not, after all, bear a particularly psychoanalytic stamp), however, has had the merit of calling attention to the fact that in the unconscious, these repressed criminal impulses are directed against the parents (the father) and that the killing of the enemy would therefore appear to be the exportation into a foreign country of a criminal product originally intended for the father. Since this hostility against the father is in turn connected, in the child, with a conflict of rivalry for the possession of the mother, the problem of war, according to the classical psychoanalytic theory, is unconsciously connected with the dramas of impotence and fantasies of potency of infantile sexuality; this is so much the more so inasmuch as in dreams intrusive weapons are usually sexual symbols.

Subsequently war—understood as a system of security rather than a return to barbarity, that is, considered mainly in relation to the anxieties and defenses which it mobilizes and controls—was interpreted as a true paranoia, i.e., as a mental illness.

Personally I believe that war represents a social institution the aim of which is to cure the paranoid and depressive anxieties existing (in a more or less marked degree and more or less resolved in terms of integration with reality) in every man.

This organization serves two security functions and may be pictured as an iceberg, one part of which is visible and the other hidden in deep waters. The first part corresponds to the defense against external danger (i.e., the real flesh-and-blood enemy), while the other, the hidden part, corresponds to an unconscious security maneuver against terrifying fantasy entities which are not flesh and blood but represent an absolute danger (as experienced, for example, in nightmares) which we could call the "Terrifier."

If we remain on the purely politico-military level, i.e., on the external part of the iceberg, the most obvious and generally held opinion is that war protects us from enemies who threaten our security, that is to say, from *external aggressors*.

If, however, we employ the psychoanalytic instrument of investigation, the instrument invented specifically for the exploration of the unconscious, we find that the submerged part of the iceberg—the invisible part of war as a security organization—serves to defend ourselves against the "Terrifier" as an internal, absolute enemy similar to a nightmare, through *a maneuver which transforms this terrifying but ultimately unaffrontable and invulnerable entity into an external, flesh-and-blood adversary who can be faced and killed.* If we now pause to reflect on the singular relation between these two systems of security that are coinvolved in war, we arrive at the paradoxical conclusion that *war is a security organization not because it permits us to defend ourselves*

→ *from real enemies, but because it succeeds in finding, or in extreme cases, in inventing, real enemies to kill; and that if it were not for war, society would be apt to leave men defenseless before the emergence of the Terrifier as a purely internal foe.* (As we shall see later, this did happen in the case of the Kanachi tribes.)

In this manner we arrive at the incredible paradox that the most important security function is not to defend ourselves from an external enemy, but *to find a real enemy.*

Accordingly it would seem that, more profound than the anxieties caused by the external world, there exist in men deep anxieties created by the purely illusory, fantasy dangers of the internal world. We need only to fall asleep and each of us can experience, in the safe immobility of sleep (from which all external danger is eliminated), terrifying nightmares of annihilation of ourselves or of a person or thing we hold dear. Thus if we succeed in finding something bad (an enemy) to destroy in the external world, we are able to reassure ourselves both against the fear that this bad something may hurt us (reassurance against persecutory anxieties) and against the danger of our destructive attacks being directed toward what we love (reassurance against depressive anxieties).

It was precisely *outward deflection of the death instinct* that Freud called the process through which the original bad presence (the Terrifier as the emergence of the death instinct in the nightmare) is projected into the dangers of the external world, in order that it may be attacked and that the nightmare-anxiety situation, which may be regarded as the original emergence of the death instinct in our consciousness, may thus be avoided.

The fact that every man, while sleeping, may feel threatened by imminent destruction—a situation that the nightmare has in common with the attack of anxiety in waking life—may be considered the emotional nucleus of an innate paranoia. Accordingly, war could be seen as an attempt at therapy, carried out by a social institution which, precisely by institutionalizing war, increases to gigantic proportions what is initially an elementary defensive mechanism of the ego in the schizo-paranoid phase.

In clinical paranoia (understood as individual paranoia), the Terrifier is projected into a reality of the external world which is usually only imagined to be dangerous. In war, however, the Terrifier is projected into a really dangerous enemy, who may really kill and be really killed. From this point of view, war would not seem to be a mental illness, but rather an attempt to control the fear of an absolute destruction, such as that expressed by the Terrifier, through a system which, ritualizing and relativizing the destroying and the being destroyed, would appear to constitute a costly and tragic system of security, involving an intricate interplay between the inner and the outer world, between illusion and reality. The most enigmatic aspect of this system would seem to be its desire to control the uncontrollable by translating internal psychotic anxieties into real external dangers.

I have called *paranoid elaboration of mourning* that group of maneuvers through which the Internal Depressive Terrifier, emerging in the form of a sense of guilt for the death of the love object (a particularly painful part of the crucial experience of mourning), is eluded in an ambiguous manner. In other words, we imagine that the love object has died not because of our own fantasy sadistic attacks against it, but because of the evil magic of the enemy. The experience of mourning then becomes not sorrow for the death of the loved person, but the killing of the enemy who is falsely thought to be the destroyer of the loved object. . . .

I realize that this thesis may be misunderstood—as indeed it has been misunderstood—as a mystical thesis. During a public debate held before a select audience of Italian intellectuals, the thesis presented in this book elicited two opposite objections. First, it was accused of mysticism on the grounds that it did not properly show the importance of the realistic motives for war, *in primis* economic factors; second, it was charged with cynicism because my discussion was understood by some as a veritable attack on man's tendency to fight for ideal values.

I have often noted that the most common type of anxiety aroused by a psychoanalytic discussion of war is the fear of an "ideological demobilization" vaguely perceived as a betrayal of one's political beliefs, whatever they may be. The defense against such anxiety is a *true accrochement à l'objet,* a typical occurrence when profound anxieties are mobilized, but also a sign of a very strong ambivalence toward the love object one fears to betray. In my opinion, however, the thesis that each individual is responsible for war, derived from the acknowledgment of the unconscious motivations for war, represents an attempt to formulate in a new manner the dialectic between the internal and the external world, between the illusory and the real, or, if you will, an attempt to formulate in a new manner the problem of how the psychotic anxieties relative to the Internal Terrifier may be resolved.

To return to the iceberg analogy, since the psychoanalytic discussion of war concerns more the submerged, invisible part of the iceberg than its external, visible part, it may be considered by some a metahistorical, metapolitical, or even astral discourse, generic and lacking in specificity. Thus it may be affirmed that psychoanalysis can explain, at the most, some of the mechanisms of war in general but not why war breaks out at a certain historical moment; for example, why World Wars I and II broke out precisely when they did.

While a criticism of this sort is partly valid, historical facts also exist that refute it. In reference to this I should like to point out that neither the phenomenology of mourning nor its paranoid elaboration was extraneous to the beginning of World War I (the assassination at Sarajevo) or World War II (Hitler's protests to Ambassador Henderson that—and whether this was true or not is of little importance in an investigation of unconscious processes—in 1939, prior to the invasion of Poland, the Polish had castrated a number of German soldiers). In both instances we find, in actual, concrete historical situations, solid evidence which permits us to see the relation between mourning and its paranoid elaboration in war not as a generic factor but as a specific precipitating factor.

A striking example of how the paranoid elaboration of mourning affected a particular period of European history in a decisive manner may be found in Czar Alexander's role in the politics of repression of liberal movements and in the formation of the Holy Alliance after the defeat of Napoleon. Bertrand Russell, in his *History of the Ideas of the Nineteenth Century,* proposed that there is a relationship between the fact that young Prince Alexander, instigated, perhaps, by his mother, was involved in the assassination of his father, and the fact that following his accession to the throne he progressively repudiated every liberal tendency until he reached a reactionary, mystic involution which led him to promote the most merciless repression of the liberals whom he saw as the very essence of evil. In this instance the paranoid elaboration of mourning was expressed through Alexander's projection onto the liberals of the part of himself that killed his father (or participated in the conspiracy, at any rate); the liberals became the parricidal part of himself which was alienated from the self and attacked. In fact, it may be significant that Czar Alexander fantastically accused the liberal movements of wanting to *"écraser l'infâme"* (i.e., the projection of killing his own infamous father).

Another specific situation in which paranoid elaboration of mourning may be observed in a massive social phenomenon is anti-Semitism. The pre-Hitlerian anti-Semitism, as we know, accused the Jews of two basic crimes: 1) that they were the sons of Judas, who had betrayed Jesus Christ; 2) that they were the descendants of Christ's murderers.

The fact that Jews have always lived as a minority in Christian countries has constituted a most favorable condition for the paranoid elaboration of mourning. For the Christian, the entire world of guilt is based on the fact that "sins are the cause of Christ's death." Every Christian, therefore, at the moment when he feels guilty, is apt to feel that his love object has died, that it has died through his fault, through his failure to observe the precepts of his church. Depressive anxieties of this sort are rather hard to endure, and anti-Semitism offers Christians a way to avoid mourning and the sense of guilt for the death-loss of the love object by projecting into the Jews the cause of the death and betrayal of Christ.

By reversing the thesis that the psychoanalytic thesis of war is non-specific because it is metahistorical and metapolitical, we could say that the economic, political, ideological, racial, etc., factors *are specifically generators of conflicts but are not specific factors of war.*

The conflicts generated by these factors exist continuously and may express themselves in a non-warlike form. When, however, the economic, political, ideological, and racial conflicts are expressed in the form of war, it means that a new fact has come into existence. I have used the expression "paranoid elaboration of mourning" to describe the appearance of this new fact, which institutionalizes a group of processes aimed at avoiding the profound human suffering which is generated in the experience of mourning. Conflicts connected with specific historical situations reactivate the more serious conflicts which each of us has experienced in infancy, in the form of fantasies, in our affective relationship to our parents. The confusion between the real historical events and these unconscious vicissitudes lies at the basis of the transference of the problems of our internal world into the external world. The exportation of the problems of the inner world into the outer world, which is an essential part of the mechanism of paranoid elaboration of mourning, may be considered the presupposition which renders it easy for certain political operators to present war as a dramatic but definitely desirable event because it allows the externalization of both the fear of being killed by what we love and the fear of killing what we love.

From a psychological point of view, then, the *aspecific factor of war* is constituted by the unconscious depressive and persecutory anxieties. Their mobilization, in relation to the war phenomenon, requires the intervention of specific and adequate historical realities which function as elements activating the transference processes.

What distinguishes the universe of peace from the universe of war, however, would appear to be this: that while in time of peace society requires the individual to adopt realistic defenses for controlling his unconscious anxieties, in time of war it proposes as a defense the institutionalization of the expulsion of the Internal Terrifier onto the enemy. And since the enemies are now in possession of nuclear weapons, this institutionalization of the expulsion of the Internal Terrifier onto the external enemy (who has become an atomic bomb) threatens to put an end to the institutionalization of the exportation of the Internal Terrifier as a security operation.

War has always been a strange import-export agency of destruction. The new fact which comes into existence with the advent of the atomic era is the pantoclastic[1] prospect, owing to which the accumulation of aggressiveness in the state can no longer be discharged through exportation and is in danger of determining a sort of tumorous growth which would progressively absorb the energies of every nation—especially those possessing nuclear weapons. The progressive growth and inflation of military power, accompanied by the impossibility of outward discharge, is on the verge of becoming a malignant tumor which will progressively destroy the healthy tissue. The war institution, which until now could be fantasied as the powerful sorcerer who protects us, is now on the verge of becoming the sorcerer who kills us.

---

[1] *Pantoclastic:* adjective taken from psychiatric terminology. It signifies total destruction.

Warfare Is Only an Invention—Not a Biological Necessity

Margaret Mead

Is war a biological necessity, a sociological inevitability or just a bad invention? Those who argue for the first view endow man with such pugnacious instincts that some outlet in aggressive behavior is necessary if man is to reach full human stature. It was this point of view which lay back of William James's famous essay, "The Moral Equivalent of War," in which he tried to retain the warlike virtues and channel them in new directions. A similar point of view has lain back of the Soviet Union's attempt to make competition between groups rather than between individuals. A basic, competitive, aggressive, warring human nature is assumed, and those who wish to outlaw war or outlaw competitiveness merely try to find new and less socially destructive ways in which these biologically given aspects of man's nature can find expression. Then there are those who take the second view: warfare is the inevitable concomitant of the development of the state, the struggle for land and natural resources of class societies springing, not from the nature of man, but from the nature of history. War is nevertheless inevitable unless we change our social system and outlaw classes, the struggle for power, and possessions; and in the event of our success warfare would disappear, as a symptom vanishes when the disease is cured.

One may hold a sort of compromise position between these two extremes; one may claim that all aggression springs from the frustration of man's biologically determined drives and that, since all forms of culture are frustrating, it is certain each new generation will be aggressive and the aggression will find its natural and inevitable expression in race war, class war, nationalistic war and so on. All three of these positions are very popular today among those who think seriously about the problems of war and its possible prevention, but I wish to urge another point of view, less defeatist perhaps than the first and third, and more accurate than the second: that is, that warfare, by which I mean recognized conflict between two groups *as groups,* in which each group puts an army (even if the army is only fifteen pygmies) into the field to fight and kill, if possible, some of the members of the army of the other group—that warfare of this sort is an invention like any other of the inventions in terms of which we order our lives, such as writing, marriage, cooking our food instead of eating it raw, trial by jury or burial of the dead, and so on. Some of this list any one will grant are inventions: trial by jury is confined to very limited portions of the globe; we know that there are tribes that do not bury their dead but instead expose or cremate them; and we know that only part of the

Margaret Mead, "Warfare Is Only an Invention—Not a Biological Necessity," *Asia* vol. 40, no. 8 (August 1940).

human race has had the knowledge of writing as its cultural inheritance. But, whenever a way of doing things is found universally, such as the use of fire or the practice of some form of marriage, we tend to think at once that it is not an invention at all but an attribute of humanity itself. And yet even such universals as marriage and the use of fire are inventions like the rest, very basic ones, inventions which were perhaps necessary if human history was to take the turn that it has taken, but nevertheless inventions. At some point in his social development man was undoubtedly without the institution of marriage or the knowledge of the use of fire.

The case for warfare is much clearer because there are peoples even today who have no warfare. Of these the Eskimo are perhaps the most conspicuous examples, but the Lepchas of Sikkim described by Geoffrey Gorer in *Himalayan Village* are as good. Neither of these peoples understands war, not even defensive warfare. The idea of warfare is lacking, and this idea is as essential to really carrying on war as an alphabet or a syllabary is to writing. But whereas the Lepchas are a gentle, unquarrelsome people, and the advocates of other points of view might argue that they are not full human beings or that they had never been frustrated and so had no aggression to expand in warfare, the Eskimo case gives no such possibility of interpretation. The Eskimo are not a mild and meek people; many of them are turbulent and troublesome. Fights, theft of wives, murder, cannibalism, occur among them—all outbursts of passionate men goaded by desire or intolerable circumstance. Here are men faced with hunger, men faced with loss of their wives, men faced with the threat of extermination by other men, and here are orphan children, growing up miserably with no one to care for them, mocked and neglected by those about them. The personality necessary for war, the circumstances necessary to goad men to desperation are present, but there is no war. When a traveling Eskimo entered a settlement he might have to fight the strongest man in the settlement to establish his position among them, but this was a test of strength and bravery, not war. The idea of warfare, of one *group* organizing against another *group* to maim and wound and kill them was absent. And without that idea passions might rage but there was no war.

But, it may be argued, isn't this because the Eskimo have such a low and undeveloped form of social organization? They own no land, they move from place to place, camping, it is true, season after season on the same site, but this is not something to fight for as the modern nations of the world fight for land and raw materials. They have no permanent possessions that can be looted, no towns that can be burned. They have no social classes to produce stress and strains within the society which might force it to go to war outside. Doesn't the absence of war among the Eskimo, while disproving the biological necessity of war, just go to confirm the point that it is the state of development of the society which accounts for war, and nothing else?

We find the answer among the pygmy peoples of the Andaman Islands in the Bay of Bengal. The Andamans also represent an exceedingly low level of society; they are a hunting and food-gathering people; they live in tiny hordes without any class stratification; their houses are simpler than the snow houses of the Eskimo. But they knew about warfare. The army might contain only fifteen determined pygmies marching in a straight line, but it was the real thing none the less. Tiny army met tiny army in open battle, blows were exchanged, casualties suffered, and the state of warfare could only be concluded by a peace-making ceremony.

Similarly, among the Australian aborigines, who built no permanent dwellings but wandered from water hole to water hole over their almost desert country, warfare—and rules of "international law"—were highly developed. The student of social evolution will seek in vain for his obvious causes of war, struggle for lands, struggle for power of one group over another, expansion of population, need to divert the minds of a populace restive under tyranny, or even the ambition of a successful leader to enhance his own prestige. All are absent, but warfare as a practice remained, and men engaged in it and killed one another in the course of a war because killing is what is done in wars.

From instances like these it becomes apparent that an inquiry into the causes of war misses the fundamental point as completely as does an insistence upon the biological necessity of war. If a people have an idea of going to war and the idea that war is the way in which certain situations, defined within their society, are to be handled, they will sometimes go to war. If they are a mild and unaggressive people, like the Pueblo Indians, they may limit themselves to defensive warfare; but they will be forced to think in terms of war because there are peoples near them who have warfare as a pattern, and offensive, raiding, pillaging warfare at that. When the pattern of warfare is known, people like the Pueblo Indians will defend themselves, taking advantage of their natural defenses, the *mesa* village site, and people like the Lepchas, having no natural defenses and no idea of warfare, will merely submit to the invader. But the essential point remains the same. There is a way of behaving which is known to a given people and labeled as an appropriate form of behavior; a bold and warlike people like the Sioux or the Maori may label warfare as desirable as well as possible; a mild people like the Pueblo Indians may label warfare as undesirable; but to the minds of both peoples the possibility of warfare is present. Their thoughts, their hopes, their plans are oriented about this idea, that warfare may be selected as the way to meet some situation.

So simple peoples and civilized peoples, mild peoples and violent, assertive peoples, will all go to war if they have the invention, just as those peoples who have the custom of dueling will have duels and peoples who have the pattern of vendetta will indulge in vendetta. And, conversely, peoples who do not know of dueling will not fight duels, even though their wives are seduced and their daughters ravished; they may on occasion commit murder but they will not fight duels. Cultures which lack the idea of the vendetta will not meet every quarrel in this way. A people can use only the forms it has. So the Balinese have their special way of dealing with a quarrel between two individuals: if the two feel that the causes of quarrel are heavy they may go and register their quarrel in the temple before the gods, and, making offerings, they may swear never to have anything to do with each other again. Today they register such mutual "not-speaking" with the Dutch government officials. But in other societies, although individuals might feel as full of animosity and as unwilling to have any further contact as do the Balinese, they cannot register their quarrel with the gods and go on quietly about their business because registering quarrels with the gods is not an invention of which they know.

Yet, if it be granted that warfare is after all an invention, it may nevertheless be an invention that lends itself to certain types of personality, to the exigent needs of autocrats, to the expansionist desires of crowded peoples, to the desire for plunder and rape and loot which is engendered by a dull and frustrating life. What, then, can we say of this congruence between warfare and its uses? If it is a form which fits so well, is not this congruence the essential point? But even here the primitive material causes us to wonder, because there are tribes who go to war merely for glory, having no quarrel with the enemy, suffering from no tyrant within their boundaries, anxious neither for land nor loot nor women, but merely anxious to win prestige which within that tribe has been declared obtainable only by war and without which no young man can hope to win his sweetheart's smile of approval. But if, as was the case with the Bush Negroes of Dutch Guiana, it is artistic ability which is necessary to win a girl's approval, the same young man would have to be carving rather than going out on a war party.

In many parts of the world, war is a game in which the individual can win counters—counters which bring him prestige in the eyes of his own sex or of the opposite sex; he plays for these counters as he might, in our society, strive for a tennis championship. Warfare is a frame for such prestige-seeking merely because it calls for the display of certain skills and certain virtues; all of these skills—riding straight, shooting straight, dodging the missiles of the enemy and sending one's own straight to the mark—can be equally well exercised in some other framework and, equally, the virtues—endurance, bravery, loyalty, steadfastness—can be displayed in other contexts. The tie-up between proving oneself a man and proving this by a success in organized killing is due to a definition which many societies have made of manliness. And often, even in those societies which counted success in warfare a proof of human worth, strange turns were given to the idea, as when the plains Indians gave their highest awards to the man who touched a live enemy rather than to the man who brought in a scalp—from a dead enemy—because the latter was less risky. Warfare is just an invention known to the majority of human societies by which they permit their young men either to accumulate prestige or avenge their honor or acquire loot or wives or slaves or sago lands or cattle or appease the blood lust of their gods or the restless souls of the recently dead. It is just an invention, older and more widespread than the jury system, but none the less an invention.

But, once we have said this, have we said anything at all? Despite a few instances, dear to the hearts of controversialists, of the loss of the useful arts, once an invention is made which proves congruent with human needs or social forms, it tends to persist. Grant that war is an invention, that it is not a biological necessity nor the outcome of certain special types of social forms, still, once the invention is made, what are we to do about it? The Indian who had been subsisting on the buffalo for generations because with his primitive weapons he could slaughter only a limited number of buffalo did not return to his primitive weapons when he saw that the white man's more efficient weapons were exterminating the buffalo. A desire for the white man's cloth may mortgage the South Sea Islander to the white man's plantation, but he does not return to making bark cloth, which would have left him free. Once an invention is known and accepted, men do not easily relinquish it. The skilled workers may smash the first steam looms which they feel are to their undoing, but they accept them in the end, and no movement which has insisted upon the mere abandonment of usable inventions has ever had much success. Warfare is here, as part of our thought; the deeds of warriors are immortalized in the words of our poets; the toys of our children are modeled upon the weapons of the soldier; the frame of reference within which our statesmen and our diplomats work always contains war. If we know that it is not inevitable, that it is due to historical accident that warfare is one of the ways in which we think of behaving, are we given any hope by that? What hope is there of persuading nations to abandon war, nations so thoroughly imbued with the idea that resort to war is, if not actually desirable and noble, at least inevitable whenever certain defined circumstances arise?

In answer to this question I think we might turn to the history of other social inventions, and inventions which must once have seemed as firmly entrenched as warfare. Take the methods of trial which preceded the jury system: ordeal and trial by combat. Unfair, capricious, alien as they are to our feeling today, they were once the only methods open to individuals accused of some offense. The invention of trial by jury gradually replaced these methods until only witches, and finally not even witches, had to resort to the ordeal. And for a long time the jury system seemed the one best and finest method of settling legal disputes, but today new inventions, trial before judges only or before commissions, are replacing the jury system. In each case the old method was replaced by a new social invention; the ordeal did not go out because people thought it unjust or wrong, it went out because a method more congruent with the institutions and feelings of the period was invented. And, if we despair over the way in which war seems such an ingrained habit of most of the human race, we can take comfort from the fact that a poor invention will usually give place to a better invention.

For this, two conditions at least are necessary. The people must recognize the defects of the old invention, and some one must make a new one. Propaganda against warfare, documentation of its terrible cost in human suffering and social waste, these prepare the ground by teaching people to feel that warfare is a defective social institution. There is further needed a belief that social invention is possible and the invention of new methods which will render warfare as out-of-date as the tractor is making the plow, or the motor car the horse and buggy. A form of behavior becomes out-of-date only when something else takes its place, and in order to invent forms of behavior which will make war obsolete, it is a first requirement to believe that an invention is possible.

ANARCHY IS WHAT STATES MAKE OF IT

Alexander Wendt

ANARCHY AND POWER POLITICS

. . . Classical realists such as Thomas Hobbes, Reinhold Niebuhr, and Hans Morgenthau attributed egoism and power politics primarily to human nature, whereas structural realists or neorealists emphasize anarchy. The difference stems in part from different interpretations of anarchy's causal powers. Kenneth Waltz's work is important for both. In *Man, the State, and War,* he defines anarchy as a condition of possibility for or "permissive" cause of war, arguing that "wars occur because there is nothing to prevent them."[1] It is the human nature or domestic politics of predator states, however, that provide the initial impetus or "efficient" cause of conflict which forces other states to respond in kind. Waltz is not entirely consistent about this, since he slips without justification from the permissive causal claim that in anarchy war is always possible to the active causal claim that "war may at any moment occur."[2] But despite Waltz's concluding call for third-image theory, the efficient causes that initialize anarchic systems are from the first and second images. This is reversed in Waltz's *Theory of International Politics,* in which first- and second-image theories are spurned as "reductionist," and the logic of anarchy seems by itself to constitute self-help and power politics as necessary features of world politics.[3]

This is unfortunate, since whatever one may think of first- and second-image theories, they have the virtue of implying that practices determine the character of anarchy. In the permissive view, only if human or domestic factors cause A to attack B will B have to defend itself. Anarchies may contain dynamics that lead to competitive power politics, but they also may not, and we can argue about when particular structures of identity and interest will emerge. In neorealism, however, the role of practice in shaping the character of anarchy is substantially reduced, and so there is less about which to argue: self-help and competitive power politics are simply given exogenously by the structure of the state system.

I will not here contest the neorealist description of the contemporary state system as a competitive, self-help world, I will only dispute its explanation. I develop my argument in three stages. First, I disentangle the concepts of self-help and anarchy by showing that self-interested conceptions of security are not a constitutive property of

---

Alexander Wendt, "Anarchy Is What States Make of It: The Social Construction of Power Politics," *International Organization,* 46:2 (spring 1992) pp. 391–425. © by the World Peace Foundation and the Massachusetts Institute of Technology.
[1]Kenneth Waltz, *Man, the State, and War* (New York: Columbia University Press, 1959), p. 232.
[2]Ibid., p. 232.
[3]Kenneth Waltz, *Theory of International Politics* (Boston: Addison-Wesley, 1979).

anarchy. Second, I show how self-help and competitive power politics may be produced causally by processes of interaction between states in which anarchy plays only a permissive role. In both of these stages of my argument, I self-consciously bracket the first- and second-image determinants of state identity, not because they are unimportant (they are indeed important), but because like Waltz's objective, mine is to clarify the "logic" of anarchy. Third, I reintroduce first- and second-image determinants to assess their effects on identity-formation in different kinds of anarchies.

Anarchy, Self-Help, and Intersubjective Knowledge

Waltz defines political structure on three dimensions: ordering principles (in this case, anarchy), principles of differentiation (which here drop out), and the distribution of capabilities. By itself, this definition predicts little about state behavior. It does not predict whether two states will be friends or foes, will recognize each other's sovereignty, will have dynastic ties, will be revisionist or status quo powers, and so on. These factors, which are fundamentally intersubjective, affect states' security interests and thus the character of their interaction under anarchy. In an important revision of Waltz's theory, Stephen Walt implies as much when he argues that the "balance of threats," rather than the balance of power, determines state action, threats being socially constructed.[4] Put more generally, without assumptions about the structure of identities and interests in the system, Waltz's definition of structure cannot predict the content or dynamics of anarchy. Self-help is one such intersubjective structure and, as such, does the decisive explanatory work in the theory. The question is whether self-help is a logical or contingent feature of anarchy. In this section, I develop the concept of a "structure of identity and interest" and show that no particular one follows logically from anarchy.

A fundamental principle of constructivist social theory is that people act toward objects, including other actors, on the basis of the meanings that the objects have for them. States act differently toward enemies than they do toward friends because enemies are threatening and friends are not. Anarchy and the distribution of power are insufficient to tell us which is which. U.S. military power has a different significance for Canada than for Cuba, despite their similar "structural" positions, just as British missiles have a different significance for the United States than do Soviet missiles. The distribution of power may always affect states' calculations, but how it does so depends on the intersubjective understandings and expectations, on the "distribution of knowledge," that constitute their conceptions of self and other.[5] If society "forgets" what a university is, the powers and practices of professor and student cease to exist; if the United States and Soviet Union decide that they are no longer enemies, "the cold war is over." It is collective meanings that constitute the structures which organize our actions.

---

[4]Stephen Walt, *The Origins of Alliances* (Ithaca, N.Y.: Cornell University Press, 1987).
[5]The phrase "distribution of knowledge" is Barry Barnes's, as discussed in his work *The Nature of Power* (Cambridge: Polity Press, 1988); see also Peter Berger and Thomas Luckmann, *The Social Construction of Reality* (New York: Anchor Books, 1966).

Actors acquire identities—relatively stable, role-specific understandings and expectations about self—by participating in such collective meanings. Identities are inherently relational: "Identity, with its appropriate attachments of psychological reality, is always identity within a specific, socially constructed world," Peter Berger argues.[6] Each person has many identities linked to institutional roles, such as brother, son, teacher, and citizen. Similarly, a state may have multiple identities as "sovereign," "leader of the free world," "imperial power," and so on. The commitment to and the salience of particular identities vary, but each identity is an inherently social definition of the actor grounded in the theories which actors collectively hold about themselves and one another and which constitute the structure of the social world.

Identities are the basis of interests. Actors do not have a "portfolio" of interests that they carry around independent of social context; instead, they define their interests in the process of defining situations. As Nelson Foote puts it: "Motivation . . . refer[s] to the degree to which a human being, as a participant in the ongoing social process in which he necessarily finds himself, defines a problematic situation as calling for the performance of a particular act, with more or less anticipated consummations and consequences, and thereby his organism releases the energy appropriate to performing it."[7] Sometimes situations are unprecedented in our experience, and in these cases we have to construct their meaning, and thus our interests, by analogy or invent them de novo. More often they have routine qualities in which we assign meanings on the basis of institutionally defined roles. When we say that professors have an "interest" in teaching, research, or going on leave, we are saying that to function in the role identity of "professor," they have to define certain situations as calling for certain actions. This does not mean that they will necessarily do so (expectations and competence do not equal performance), but if they do not, they will not get tenure. The absence or failure of roles makes defining situations and interests more difficult, and identity confusion may result. This seems to be happening today in the United States and the former Soviet Union: without the cold war's mutual attributions of threat and hostility to define their identities, these states seem unsure of what their "interests" should be.

An institution is a relatively stable set or "structure" of identities and interests. Such structures are often codified in formal rules and norms, but these have motivational force only in virtue of actors' socialization to and participation in collective knowledge. Institutions are fundamentally cognitive entities that do not exist apart from actors' ideas about how the world works. This does not mean that institutions are not real or objective, that they are "nothing but" beliefs. As collective knowledge, they are experienced as having an existence "over and above the individuals who happen to embody them at the moment."[8] In this way, institutions come to confront individuals as more or less coercive social facts, but they are still a function of what actors collectively "know." Identities and such collective cognitions do not exist apart from each

[6]Peter Berger, "Identity as a Problem in the Sociology of Knowledge," *European Journal of Sociology,* vol. 7, no. 1, 1966, p. 111.
[7]Nelson Foote, "Identification as the Basis for a Theory of Motivation," *American Sociological Review 16* (February 1951), p. 15.
[8]Berger and Luckmann, *The Social Construction of Reality,* p. 58.

other; they are "mutually constitutive." On this view, institutionalization is a process of internalizing new identities and interests, not something occurring outside them and affecting only behavior; socialization is a cognitive process, not just a behavioral one. Conceived in this way, institutions may be cooperative or conflictual, a point sometimes lost in scholarship on international regimes, which tends to equate institutions with cooperation. There are important differences between conflictual and cooperative institutions to be sure, but all relatively stable self-other relations—even those of "enemies"—are defined intersubjectively.

Self-help is an institution, one of various structures of identity and interest that may exist under anarchy. Processes of identity-formation under anarchy are concerned first and foremost with preservation or "security" of the self. Concepts of security therefore differ in the extent to which and the manner in which the self is identified cognitively with the other, and, I want to suggest, it is upon this cognitive variation that the meaning of anarchy and the distribution of power depends. Let me illustrate with a standard continuum of security systems.

At one end is the "competitive" security system, in which states identify negatively with each other's security so that ego's gain is seen as alter's loss. Negative identification under anarchy constitutes systems of "realist" power politics: risk-averse actors that infer intentions from capabilities and worry about relative gains and losses. At the limit—in the Hobbesian war of all against all—collective action is nearly impossible in such a system because each actor must constantly fear being stabbed in the back.

In the middle is the "individualistic" security system, in which states are indifferent to the relationship between their own and others' security. This constitutes "neoliberal" systems: states are still self-regarding about their security but are concerned primarily with absolute gains rather than relative gains. One's position in the distribution of power is less important, and collective action is more possible (though still subject to free riding because states continue to be "egoists").

Competitive and individualistic systems are both "self-help" forms of anarchy in the sense that states do not positively identify the security of self with that of others but instead treat security as the individual responsibility of each. Given the lack of a positive cognitive identification on the basis of which to build security regimes, power politics within such systems will necessarily consist of efforts to manipulate others to satisfy self-regarding interests.

This contrasts with the "cooperative" security system, in which states identify positively with one another so that the security of each is perceived as the responsibility of all. This is not self-help in any interesting sense, since the "self" in terms of which interests are defined is the community; national interests are international interests. In practice, of course, the extent to which states' identification with the community varies, from the limited form found in "concerts" to the full-blown form seen in "collective security" arrangements. Depending on how well developed the collective self is, it will produce security practices that are in varying degrees altruistic or prosocial. This makes collective action less dependent on the presence of active threats and less prone to free riding. Moreover, it restructures efforts to advance one's objectives, or "power politics," in terms of shared norms rather than relative power.

On this view, the tendency in international relations scholarship to view power and institutions as two opposing explanations of foreign policy is therefore misleading, since anarchy and the distribution of power only have meaning for state action in virtue of the understandings and expectations that constitute institutional identities and interests. Self-help is one such institution, constituting one kind of anarchy but not the only kind. Waltz's three-part definition of structure therefore seems underspecified. In order to go from structure to action, we need to add a fourth: the intersubjectively constituted structure of identities and interests in the system.

This has an important implication for the way in which we conceive of states in the state of nature before their first encounter with each other. Because states do not have conceptions of self and other, and thus security interests, apart from or prior to interaction, we assume too much about the state of nature if we concur with Waltz that, in virtue of anarchy, "international political systems, like economic markets, are formed by the coaction of self-regarding units."[9] We also assume too much if we argue that, in virtue of anarchy, states in the state of nature necessarily face a "stag hunt" or "security dilemma." These claims presuppose a history of interaction in which actors have acquired "selfish" identities and interests; before interaction (and still in abstraction from first- and second-image factors) they would have no experience upon which to base such definitions of self and other. To assume otherwise is to attribute to states in the state of nature qualities that they can only possess in society. Self-help is an institution, not a constitutive feature of anarchy.

What, then, *is* a constitutive feature of the state of nature before interaction? Two things are left if we strip away those properties of the self which presuppose interaction with others. The first is the material substrate of agency, including its intrinsic capabilities. For human beings, this is the body; for states, it is an organizational apparatus of governance. In effect, I am suggesting for rhetorical purposes that the raw material out of which members of the state system are constituted is created by domestic society before states enter the constitutive process of international society, although this process implies neither stable territoriality nor sovereignty, which are internationally negotiated terms of individuality (as discussed further below). The second is a desire to preserve this material substrate, to survive. This does not entail "self-regardingness," however, since actors do not have a self prior to interaction with an other; how they view the meaning and requirements of this survival therefore depends on the processes by which conceptions of self evolve.

This may all seem very arcane, but there is an important issue at stake: are the foreign policy identities and interests of states exogenous or endogenous to the state system? The former is the answer of an individualistic or undersocialized systemic theory for which rationalism is appropriate; the latter is the answer of a fully socialized systemic theory. Waltz seems to offer the latter and proposes two mechanisms, competition and socialization, by which structure conditions state action. The content of his argument about this conditioning, however, presupposes a self-help system that is not itself a constitutive feature of anarchy. As James Morrow points out, Waltz's two mechanisms condition behavior, not identity and interest.[10] This explains how Waltz can be

---

[9]Waltz, *Theory of International Politics,* p. 91.

[10]See James Morrow, "Social Choice and System Structure in World Politics," *World Politics* 41 (October 1988), p. 89.

accused of both "individualism" and "structuralism." He is the former with respect to systemic constitutions of identity and interest, the latter with respect to systemic determinations of behavior.

Anarchy and the Social Construction of Power Politics

If self-help is not a constitutive feature of anarchy, it must emerge causally from processes in which anarchy plays only a permissive role. This reflects a second principle of constructivism: that the meanings in terms of which action is organized arise out of interaction. This being said, however, the situation facing states as they encounter one another for the first time may be such that only self-regarding conceptions of identity can survive; if so, even if these conceptions are socially constructed, neorealists may be right in holding identities and interests constant and thus in privileging one particular meaning of anarchic structure over process. In this case, rationalists would be right to argue for a weak, behavioral conception of the difference that institutions make, and realists would be right to argue that any international institutions which are created will be inherently unstable, since without the power to transform identities and interests they will be "continuing objects of choice" by exogenously constituted actors constrained only by the transaction costs of behavioral change.[11] Even in a permissive causal role, in other words, anarchy may decisively restrict interaction and therefore restrict viable forms of systemic theory. I address these causal issues first by showing how self-regarding ideas about security might develop and then by examining the conditions under which a key efficient cause—predation—may dispose states in this direction rather than others.

Conceptions of self and interest tend to "mirror" the practices of significant others over time. This principle of identity-formation is captured by the symbolic interactionist notion of the "looking-glass self," which asserts that the self is a reflection of an actor's socialization.

Consider two actors—ego and alter—encountering each other for the first time. Each wants to survive and has certain material capabilities, but neither actor has biological or domestic imperatives for power, glory, or conquest (still bracketed), and there is no history of security or insecurity between the two. What should they do? Realists would probably argue that each should act on the basis of worst-case assumptions about the other's intentions, justifying such an attitude as prudent in view of the possibility of death from making a mistake. Such a possibility always exists, even in civil society; however, society would be impossible if people made decisions purely on the basis of worst-case possibilities. Instead, most decisions are and should be made on the basis of probabilities, and these are produced by interaction, by what actors *do*.

In the beginning is ego's gesture, which may consist, for example, of an advance, a retreat, a brandishing of arms, a laying down of arms, or an attack. For ego, this gesture represents the basis on which it is prepared to respond to alter. This basis is unknown to alter, however, and so it must make an inference or "attribution" about ego's intentions

---

[11]See Robert Grafstein, "Rational Choice: Theory and Institutions," in Kristen Monroe, ed., *The Economic Approach to Politics* (New York: Harper Collins, 1991), pp. 263–64.

and, in particular, given that this is anarchy, about whether ego is a threat. The content of this inference will largely depend on two considerations. The first is the gesture's and ego's physical qualities, which are in part contrived by ego and which include the direction of movement, noise, numbers, and immediate consequences of the gesture. The second consideration concerns what alter would intend by such qualities were it to make such a gesture itself. Alter may make an attributional "error" in its inference about ego's intent, but there is also no reason for it to assume a priori—before the gesture—that ego is threatening, since it is only through a process of signaling and interpreting that the costs and probabilities of being wrong can be determined. Social threats are constructed, not natural.

Consider an example. Would we assume, a priori, that we were about to be attacked if we are ever contacted by members of an alien civilization? I think not. We would be highly alert, of course, but whether we placed our military forces on alert or launched an attack would depend on how we interpreted the import of their first gesture for our security—if only to avoid making an immediate enemy out of what may be a dangerous adversary. The possibility of error, in other words, does not force us to act on the assumption that the aliens are threatening: action depends on the probabilities we assign, and these are in key part a function of what the aliens do; prior to their gesture, we have no systemic basis for assigning probabilities. If their first gesture is to appear with a thousand spaceships and destroy New York, we will define the situation as threatening and respond accordingly. But if they appear with one spaceship, saying what seems to be "we come in peace," we will feel "reassured" and will probably respond with a gesture intended to reassure them, even if this gesture is not necessarily interpreted by them as such.

This process of signaling, interpreting, and responding completes a "social act" and begins the process of creating intersubjective meanings. It advances the same way. The first social act creates expectations on both sides about each other's future behavior: potentially mistaken and certainly tentative, but expectations nonetheless. Based on this tentative knowledge, ego makes a new gesture, again signifying the basis on which it will respond to alter, and again alter responds, adding to the pool of knowledge each has about the other, and so on over time. The mechanism here is reinforcement; interaction rewards actors for holding certain ideas about each other and discourages them from holding others. If repeated long enough, these "reciprocal typifications" will create relatively stable concepts of self and other regarding the issue at stake in the interaction.

It is through reciprocal interaction, in other words, that we create and instantiate the relatively enduring social structures in terms of which we define our identities and interests. Jeff Coulter sums up the ontological dependence of structure on process this way: "The parameters of social organization themselves are reproduced only in and through the orientations and practices of members engaged in social interactions over time. . . . Social configurations are not 'objective' like mountains or forests, but neither are they 'subjective' like dreams or flights of speculative fancy. They are, as most social scientists concede at the theoretical level, intersubjective constructions."[12]

---

[12]Jeff Coulter, "Remarks on the Conceptualization of Social Structure," *Philosophy of the Social Sciences* 12 (March 1982), pp. 42–43.

INSTITUTIONS   PROCESS

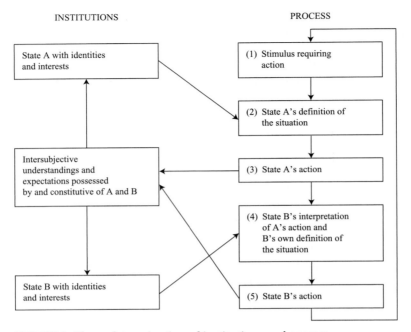

FIGURE 1. The codetermination of institutions and process

The simple overall model of identity- and interest-formation proposed in Figure 1 applies to competitive institutions no less than to cooperative ones. Self-help security systems evolve from cycles of interaction in which each party acts in ways that the other feels are threatening to the self, creating expectations that the other is not to be trusted. Competitive or egoistic identities are caused by such insecurity; if the other is threatening, the self is forced to "mirror" such behavior in its conception of the self's relationship to that other. Being treated as an object for the gratification of others precludes the positive identification with others necessary for collective security; conversely, being treated by others in ways that are empathic with respect to the security of the self permits such identification.

Competitive systems of interaction are prone to security "dilemmas," in which the efforts of actors to enhance their security unilaterally threatens the security of the others, perpetuating distrust and alienation. The forms of identity and interest that constitute such dilemmas, however, are themselves ongoing effects of, not exogenous to the interaction; identities are produced in and through "situated activity."[13] We do not *begin* our relationship with the aliens in a security dilemma; security dilemmas are not given by anarchy or nature. Of course, once institutionalized such a dilemma may be hard to

---

[13]See C. Norman Alexander and Mary Glenn Wiley, "Situated Activity and Identity Formation," in Morris Rosenberg and Ralph Turner, eds., *Social Psychology: Sociological Perspectives* (New York: Basic Books, 1981), pp. 269–89.

change (I return to this below), but the point remains: identities and interests are constituted by collective meanings that are always in process. As Sheldon Stryker emphasizes, "The social process is one of constructing and reconstructing self and social relationships."[14] If states find themselves in a self-help system, this is because their practices made it that way. Changing the practices will change the intersubjective knowledge that constitutes the system.

Predator States and Anarchy as Permissive Cause

The mirror theory of identity-formation is a crude account of how the process of creating identities and interests might work, but it does not tell us why a system of states—such as, arguably, our own—would have ended up with self-regarding and not collective identities. In this section, I examine an efficient cause, predation, which, in conjunction with anarchy as a permissive cause, may generate a self-help system. In so doing, however, I show the key role that the structure of identities and interests plays in mediating anarchy's explanatory role.

The predator argument is straightforward and compelling. For whatever reasons—biology, domestic politics, or systemic victimization—some states may become predisposed toward aggression. The aggressive behavior of these predators or "bad apples" forces other states to engage in competitive power politics, to meet fire with fire, since failure to do so may degrade or destroy them. One predator will best a hundred pacifists because anarchy provides no guarantees. This argument is powerful in part because it is so weak: rather than making the strong assumption that all states are inherently power-seeking (a purely reductionist theory of power politics), it assumes that just one is power-seeking and that the others have to follow suit because anarchy permits the one to exploit them.

In making this argument, it is important to reiterate that the possibility of predation does not in itself force states to anticipate it a priori with competitive power politics of their own. The possibility of predation does not mean that "war may at any moment occur"; it may in fact be extremely unlikely. Once a predator emerges, however, it may condition identity- and interest-formation in the following manner.

In an anarchy of two, if ego is predatory, alter must either define its security in self-help terms or pay the price. This follows directly from the above argument, in which conceptions of self mirror treatment by the other. In an anarchy of many, however, the effect of predation also depends on the level of collective identity already attained in the system. If predation occurs right after the first encounter in the state of nature, it will force others with whom it comes in contact to defend themselves, first individually and then collectively *if* they come to perceive a common threat. The emergence of such a defensive alliance will be seriously inhibited if the structure of identities and interests has already evolved into a Hobbesian world of maximum insecurity, since potential allies will strongly distrust each other and face intense collective action problems; such

---

[14]Sheldon Stryker, "The Vitalization of Symbolic Interactionism," *Social Psychology Quarterly* 50 (March 1987), p. 93.

insecure allies are also more likely to fall out amongst themselves once the predator is removed. If collective security identity is high, however, the emergence of a predator may do much less damage. If the predator attacks any member of the collective, the latter will come to the victim's defense on the principle of "all for one, one for all," even if the predator is not presently a threat to other members of the collective. If the predator is not strong enough to withstand the collective, it will be defeated and collective security will obtain. But if it is strong enough, the logic of the two-actor case (now predator and collective) will activate, and balance-of-power politics will reestablish itself.

The timing of the emergence of predation relative to the history of identity-formation in the community is therefore crucial to anarchy's explanatory role as a permissive cause. Predation will always lead victims to defend themselves, but whether defense will be collective or not depends on the history of interaction within the potential collective as much as on the ambitions of the predator. Will the disappearance of the Soviet threat renew old insecurities among the members of the North Atlantic Treaty Organization? Perhaps, but not if they have reasons independent of that threat for identifying their security with one another. Identities and interests are relationship-specific, not intrinsic attributes of a "portfolio"; states may be competitive in some relationships and solidary in others. "Mature" anarchies are less likely than "immature" ones to be reduced by predation to a Hobbesian condition, and maturity, which is a proxy for structures of identity and interest, is a function of process.

The source of predation also matters. If it stems from unit-level causes that are immune to systemic impacts (causes such as human nature or domestic politics taken in isolation), then it functions in a manner analogous to a "genetic trait" in the constructed world of the state system. Even if successful, this trait does not select for other predators in an evolutionary sense so much as it teaches other states to respond in kind, but since traits cannot be unlearned, the other states will continue competitive behavior until the predator is either destroyed or transformed from within. However, in the more likely event that predation stems at least in part from prior systemic interaction—perhaps as a result of being victimized in the past (one thinks here of Nazi Germany or the Soviet Union)—then it is more a response to a learned identity and, as such, might be transformed by future social interaction in the form of appeasement, reassurances that security needs will be met, systemic effects on domestic politics, and so on. In this case, in other words, there is more hope that process can transform a bad apple into a good one.

The role of predation in generating a self-help system, then, is consistent with a systematic focus on process. Even if the source of predation is entirely exogenous to the system, it is what states *do* that determines the quality of their interactions under anarchy. In this respect, it is not surprising that it is classical realists rather than structural realists who emphasize this sort of argument. The former's emphasis on unit-level causes of power politics leads more easily to a permissive view of anarchy's explanatory role (and therefore to a processual view of international relations) than does the latter's emphasis on anarchy as a "structural cause"; neorealists do not need predation because the system is given as self-help.

This raises anew the question of exactly how much and what kind of role human nature and domestic politics play in world politics. The greater and more destructive this role, the more significant predation will be, and the less amenable anarchy will be to formation of collective identities. Classical realists, of course, assumed that human nature was possessed by an inherent lust for power or glory. My argument suggests that assumptions such as this were made for a reason: an unchanging Hobbesian man provides the powerful efficient cause necessary for a relentless pessimism about world politics that anarchic structure alone, or even structure plus intermittent predation, cannot supply. One can be skeptical of such an essentialist assumption, as I am, but it does produce determinate results at the expense of systemic theory. A concern with systemic process over structure suggests that perhaps it is time to revisit the debate over the relative importance of first-, second-, and third-image theories of state identity-formation.[15]

Assuming for now that systemic theories of identity-formation in world politics are worth pursuing, let me conclude by suggesting that the realist-rationalist alliance "reifies" self-help in the sense of treating it as something separate from the practices by which it is produced and sustained. Peter Berger and Thomas Luckmann define reification as follows: "[It] is the apprehension of the products of human activity *as if* they were something else than human products—such as facts of nature, results of cosmic laws, or manifestations of divine will. Reification implies that man is capable of forgetting his own authorship of the human world, and further, that the dialectic between man, the producer, and his products is lost to consciousness. The reified world is . . . experienced by man as a strange facticity, an *opus alienum* over which he has no control rather than as the *opus proprium* of his own productive activity."[16] By denying or bracketing states' collective authorship of their identities and interests, in other words, the realist-rationalist alliance denies or brackets the fact that competitive power politics help create the very "problem of order" they are supposed to solve—that realism is a self-fulfilling prophecy. Far from being exogenously given, the intersubjective knowledge that constitutes competitive identities and interests is constructed every day by processes of "social will formation."[17] It is what states have made of themselves.

INSTITUTIONAL TRANSFORMATIONS OF POWER POLITICS

Let us assume that processes of identity- and interest-formation have created a world in which states do not recognize rights to territory or existence—a war of all against all. In this world, anarchy has a "realist" meaning for state action: be insecure and concerned with relative power. Anarchy has this meaning only in virtue of collective, insecurity-producing practices, but if those practices are relatively stable, they do constitute a system that may resist change. The fact that worlds of power politics are socially constructed, in other words, does not guarantee they are malleable, for at least two reasons.

---

[15]Waltz has himself helped open up such a debate with his recognition that systemic factors condition but do not determine state actions. See Kenneth Waltz, "Reflections on *Theory of International Politics:* A Response to My Critics," in Robert Keohane, ed., *Neorealism and Its Critics* (New York: Columbia University Press, 1986), pp. 322–45.

[16]See Berger and Luckmann, *The Social Construction of Reality,* p. 89.

[17]See Richard Ashley, "Social Will and International Anarchy," in Hayward Alker and Richard Ashley, eds., *After Realism,* work in progress, Massachusetts Institute of Technology, Cambridge, and Arizona State University, Tempe, 1992.

The first reason is that once constituted, any social system confronts each of its members as an objective social fact that reinforces certain behaviors and discourages others. Self-help systems, for example, tend to reward competition and punish altruism. The possibility of change depends on whether the exigencies of such competition leave room for actions that deviate from the prescribed script. If they do not, the system will be reproduced and deviant actors will not.

The second reason is that systemic change may also be inhibited by actors' interests in maintaining relatively stable role identities. Such interests are rooted not only in the desire to minimize uncertainty and anxiety, manifested in efforts to confirm existing beliefs about the social world, but also in the desire to avoid the expected costs of breaking commitments made to others—notably domestic constituencies and foreign allies in the case of states—as part of past practices. The level of resistance that these commitments induce will depend on the "salience" of particular role identities to the actor. The United States, for example, is more likely to resist threats to its identity as "leader of anticommunist crusades" than to its identity as "promoter of human rights." But for almost any role identity, practices and information that challenge it are likely to create cognitive dissonance and even perceptions of threat, and these may cause resistance to transformations of the self and thus to social change.

For both systemic and "psychological" reasons, then, intersubjective understandings and expectations may have a self-perpetuating quality, constituting path-dependencies that new ideas about self and other must transcend. This does not change the fact that through practice agents are continuously producing and reproducing identities and interests, continuously "choosing now the preferences [they] will have later."[18] But it does mean that choices may not be experienced with meaningful degrees of freedom. This could be a constructivist justification for the realist position that only simple learning is possible in self-help systems. The realist might concede that such systems are socially constructed and still argue that after the corresponding identities and interests have become institutionalized, they are almost impossible to transform.

In the remainder of this article, I examine three institutional transformations of identity and security interest through which states might escape a Hobbesian world of their own making. In so doing, I seek to clarify what it means to say that "institutions transform identities and interests," emphasizing that the key to such transformations is relatively stable practice.

Sovereignty, Recognition, and Security

In a Hobbesian state of nature, states are individuated by the domestic processes that constitute them as states and by their material capacity to deter threats from other states. In this world, even if free momentarily from the predations of others, state security does not have any basis in social recognition—in intersubjective understandings or norms that a state has a right to its existence, territory, and subjects. Security is a matter of national power, nothing more.

---

[18]James March, "Bounded Rationality, Ambiguity, and the Engineering of Choice," *Bell Journal of Economics* 9 (Autumn 1978), p. 600.

The principle of sovereignty transforms this situation by providing a social basis for the individuality and security of states. Sovereignty is an institution, and so it exists only in virtue of certain intersubjective understandings and expectations; there is no sovereignty without an other. These understandings and expectations not only constitute a particular kind of state—the "sovereign" state—but also constitute a particular form of community, since identities are relational. The essence of this community is a mutual recognition of one another's right to exercise exclusive political authority within territorial limits. These reciprocal "permissions" constitute a spatially rather than functionally differentiated world—a world in which fields of practice constitute and are organized around "domestic" and "international" spaces rather than around the performance of particular activities. The location of the boundaries between these spaces is of course sometimes contested, war being one practice through which states negotiate the terms of their individuality. But this does not change the fact that it is only in virtue of mutual recognition that states have "territorial property rights."[19] This recognition functions as a form of "social closure" that disempowers nonstate actors and empowers and helps stabilize interaction among states.

Sovereignty norms are now so taken for granted, so natural, that it is easy to overlook the extent to which they are both presupposed by and an ongoing artifact of practice. When states tax "their" "citizens" and not others, when they "protect" their markets against foreign "imports," when they kill thousands of Iraqis in one kind of war and then refuse to "intervene" to kill even one person in another kind, a "civil" war, and when they fight a global war against a regime that sought to destroy the institution of sovereignty and then give Germany back to the Germans, they are acting against the background of, and thereby reproducing, shared norms about what it means to be a sovereign state.

If states stopped acting on those norms, their identity as "sovereigns" (if not necessarily as "states") would disappear. The sovereign state is an ongoing accomplishment of practice, not a once-and-for-all creation of norms that somehow exist apart from practice. Thus, saying that "the institution of sovereignty transforms identities" is shorthand for saying that "regular practices produce mutually constituting sovereign identities (agents) and their associated institutional norms (structures)." Practice is the core of constructivist resolutions of the agent-structure problem. This ongoing process may not be politically problematic in particular historical contexts and, indeed, once a community of mutual recognition is constituted, its members—even the disadvantaged ones—may have a vested interest in reproducing it. In fact, this is part of what having an identity means. But this identity and institution remain dependent on what actors do: removing those practices will remove their intersubjective conditions of existence.

This may tell us something about how institutions of sovereign states are reproduced through social interaction, but it does not tell us why such a structure of identity and interest would arise in the first place. Two conditions would seem necessary for this to happen: (1) the density and regularity of interactions must be sufficiently high and

---

[19]See John Ruggie, "Continuity and Transformation in the World Polity: Toward a Neorealist Synthesis," *World Politics* 35 (January 1983), pp. 261–85.

(2) actors must be dissatisfied with preexisting forms of identity and interaction. Given these conditions, a norm of mutual recognition is relatively undemanding in terms of social trust, having the form of an assurance game in which a player will acknowledge the sovereignty of the others as long as they will in turn acknowledge that player's own sovereignty. Articulating international legal principles such as those embodied in the Peace of Augsburg (1555) and the Peace of Westphalia (1648) may also help by establishing explicit criteria for determining violations of the nascent social consensus. But whether such a consensus holds depends on what states do. If they treat each other as if they were sovereign, then over time they will institutionalize that mode of subjectivity; if they do not, then that mode will not become the norm.

Practices of sovereignty will transform understandings of security and power politics in at least three ways. First, states will come to define their (and our) security in terms of preserving their "property rights" over particular territories. We now see this as natural, but the preservation of territorial frontiers is not, in fact, equivalent to the survival of the state or its people. Indeed, some states would probably be more secure if they would relinquish certain territories—the "Soviet Union" of some minority republics, "Yugoslavia" of Croatia and Slovenia, Israel of the West Bank, and so on. The fact that sovereignty practices have historically been oriented toward producing distinct territorial spaces, in other words, affects states' conceptualization of what they must "secure" to function in that identity, a process that may help account for the "hardening" of territorial boundaries over the centuries.

Second, to the extent that states successfully internalize sovereignty norms, they will be more respectful toward the territorial rights of others. This restraint is *not* primarily because of the costs of violating sovereignty norms, although when violators do get punished (as in the Gulf War) it reminds everyone of what these costs can be, but because part of what it means to be a "sovereign" state is that one does not violate the territorial rights of others without "just cause." A clear example of such an institutional effect, convincingly argued by David Strang, is the markedly different treatment that weak states receive within and outside communities of mutual recognition. What keeps the United States from conquering the Bahamas, or Nigeria from seizing Togo, or Australia from occupying Vanuatu? Clearly, power is not the issue, and in these cases even the cost of sanctions would probably be negligible. One might argue that great powers simply have no "interest" in these conquests, and this might be so, but this lack of interest can only be understood in terms of their recognition of weak states' sovereignty. I have no interest in exploiting my friends, not because of the relative costs and benefits of such action but because they are my friends. The absence of recognition, in turn, helps explain the Western states' practices of territorial conquest, enslavement, and genocide against Native American and African peoples. It is in *that* world that only power matters, not the world of today.

Finally, to the extent that their ongoing socialization teaches states that their sovereignty depends on recognition by other states, they can afford to rely more on the institutional fabric of international society and less on individual national means—especially military power—to protect their security. The intersubjective understandings embodied in the institution of sovereignty, in other words, may redefine the meaning of others' power for the security of the self. In policy terms, this means that states can be less worried about short-term survival and relative power and can thus shift their resources accordingly. Ironically, it is the great powers, the states with the greatest national means, that may have the hardest time learning this lesson; small powers do not have the luxury of relying on national means and may therefore learn faster that collective recognition is a cornerstone of security.

None of this is to say that power becomes irrelevant in a community of sovereign states. Sometimes states *are* threatened by others that do not recognize their existence or particular territorial claims, that resent the externalities from their economic policies, and so on. But most of the time, these threats are played out within the terms of the sovereignty game. The fates of Napoleon and Hitler show what happens when they are not.

Cooperation Among Egoists and Transformations of Identity

We began this section with a Hobbesian state of nature. Cooperation for joint gain is extremely difficult in this context, since trust is lacking, time horizons are short, and relative power concerns are high. Life is "nasty, brutish, and short." Sovereignty transforms this system into a Lockean world of (mostly) mutually recognized property rights and (mostly) egoistic rather than competitive conceptions of security, reducing the fear that what states already have will be seized at any moment by potential collaborators, thereby enabling them to contemplate more direct forms of cooperation. A necessary condition for such cooperation is that outcomes be positively interdependent in the sense that potential gains exist which cannot be realized by unilateral action. States such as Brazil and Botswana may recognize each other's sovereignty, but they need further incentives to engage in joint action. One important source of incentives is the growing "dynamic density" of interaction among states in a world with new communications technology, nuclear weapons, externalities from industrial development, and so on.[20] Unfortunately, growing dynamic density does not ensure that states will in fact realize joint gains; interdependence also entails vulnerability and the risk of being "the sucker," which if exploited will become a source of conflict rather than cooperation.

This is the rationale for the familiar assumption that egoistic states will often find themselves facing prisoners' dilemma, a game in which the dominant strategy, if played only once, is to defect. As Michael Taylor and Robert Axelrod have shown, however, given iteration and a sufficient shadow of the future, egoists using a tit-for-tat strategy can escape this result and build cooperative institutions. The story they tell about this process on the surface seems quite similar to George Herbert Mead's constructivist analysis of interaction, part of which is also told in terms of "games." Cooperation is a

---

[20]On "dynamic density," see Ruggie, "Continuity and Transformation in the World Polity"; and Waltz, "Reflections on *Theory of International Politics.*" The role of interdependence in conditioning the speed and depth of social learning is much greater than the attention to which I have paid it. On the consequences of interdependence under anarchy, see Helen Milner, "The Assumption of Anarchy in International Relations Theory: A Critique," *Review of International Studies* 17 (January 1991), pp. 67–85.

gesture indicating ego's willingness to cooperate; if alter defects, ego does likewise, signaling its unwillingness to be exploited; over time and through reciprocal play, each learns to form relatively stable expectations about the other's behavior, and through these, habits of cooperation (or defection) form. Despite similar concerns with communication, learning, and habit-formation, however, there is an important difference between the game-theoretic and constructivist analysis of interaction that bears on how we conceptualize the causal powers of institutions.

In the traditional game-theoretic analysis of cooperation, even an iterated one, the structure of the game—of identities and interests—is exogenous to interaction and, as such, does not change. A "black box" is put around identity- and interest-formation, and analysis focuses instead on the relationship between expectations and behavior. The norms that evolve from interaction are treated as rules and behavioral regularities which are external to the actors and which resist change because of the transaction costs of creating new ones. The game-theoretic analysis of cooperation among egoists is at base behavioral.

A constructivist analysis of cooperation, in contrast, would concentrate on how the expectations produced by behavior affect identities and interests. The process of creating institutions is one of internalizing new understandings of self and other, of acquiring new role identities, not just of creating external constraints on the behavior of exogenously constituted actors. Even if not intended as such, in other words, the process by which egoists learn to cooperate is at the same time a process of reconstructing their interests in terms of shared commitments to social norms. Over time, this will tend to transform a positive interdependence of *outcomes* into a positive interdependence of *utilities* or collective interest organized around the norms in question. These norms will resist change because they are tied to actors' commitments to their identities and interests, not merely because of transaction costs. A constructivist analysis of "the cooperation problem," in other words, is at base cognitive rather than behavioral, since it treats the intersubjective knowledge that defines the structure of identities and interests, of the "game," as endogenous to and instantiated by interaction itself.

The debate over the future of collective security in Western Europe may illustrate the significance of this difference. A weak liberal or rationalist analysis would assume that the European states' "portfolio" of interests has not fundamentally changed and that the emergence of new factors, such as the collapse of the Soviet threat and the rise of Germany, would alter their cost-benefit ratios for pursuing current arrangements, thereby causing existing institutions to break down. The European states formed collaborative institutions for good, exogenously constituted egoistic reasons, and the same reasons may lead them to reject those institutions; the game of European power politics has not changed. A strong liberal or constructivist analysis of this problem would suggest that four decades of cooperation may have transformed a positive interdependence of outcomes into a collective "European identity" in terms of which states increasingly define their "self"-interests. Even if egoistic reasons were its starting point, the process of cooperating tends to redefine those reasons by reconstituting identities and interests in terms of new intersubjective understandings and commitments. Changes in the distribution of power during the late twentieth century are undoubtedly a challenge to these new understandings, but it is not as if West European states have some inherent, exogenously given interest in abandoning collective security if the price is right. Their identities and security interests are continuously in process, and if collective identities become "embedded," they will be as resistant to change as egoistic ones.[21] Through participation in new forms of social knowledge, in other words, the European states of 1990 might no longer be the states of 1950.

Critical Strategic Theory and Collective Security

The transformation of identity and interest through an "evolution of cooperation" faces two important constraints. The first is that the process is incremental and slow. Actors' objectives in such a process are typically to realize joint gains within what they take to be a relatively stable context, and they are therefore unlikely to engage in substantial reflection about how to change the parameters of that context (including the structure of identities and interests) and unlikely to pursue policies specifically designed to bring about such changes. Learning to cooperate may change those parameters, but this occurs as an unintended consequence of policies pursued for other reasons rather than as a result of intentional efforts to transcend existing institutions.

A second, more fundamental, constraint is that the evolution of cooperation story presupposes that actors do not identify negatively with one another. Actors must be concerned primarily with absolute gains; to the extent that antipathy and distrust lead them to define their security in relativistic terms, it will be hard to accept the vulnerabilities that attend cooperation. This is important because it is precisely the "central balance" in the state system that seems to be so often afflicted with such competitive thinking, and realists can therefore argue that the possibility of cooperation within one "pole" (for example, the West) is parasitic on the dominance of competition between poles (the East–West conflict). Relations between the poles may be amenable to some positive reciprocity in areas such as arms control, but the atmosphere of distrust leaves little room for such cooperation and its transformative consequences. The conditions of negative identification that make an "evolution of cooperation" most needed work precisely against such a logic.

This seemingly intractable situation may nevertheless be amenable to quite a different logic of transformation, one driven more by self-conscious efforts to change structures of identity and interest than by unintended consequences. Such voluntarism may seem to contradict the spirit of constructivism, since would-be revolutionaries are presumably themselves effects of socialization to structures of identity and interest. How can they think about changing that to which they owe their identity? The possibility lies in the distinction between the social determination of the self and the personal determination of choice, between what Mead called the "me" and the "I." The "me" is that part of subjectivity which is defined in terms of others; the character and behavioral expectations of a person's role identity as "professor," or of the United

---

[21]On "embeddedness," see John Ruggie, "International Regimes, Transactions, and Change: Embedded Liberalism in a Postwar Economic Order," in Stephen Krasner, ed., *International Regimes,* (Ithaca, N.Y.: Cornell University Press, 1983), pp. 195–232.

States as "leader of the alliance," for example, are socially constituted. Roles are not played in mechanical fashion according to precise scripts, however, but are "taken" and adapted in idiosyncratic ways by each actor. Even in the most constrained situations, role performance involves a choice by the actor. The "I" is the part of subjectivity in which this appropriation and reaction to roles and its corresponding existential freedom lie.

The fact that roles are "taken" means that, in principle, actors always have a capacity for "character planning"—for engaging in critical self-reflection and choices designed to bring about changes in their lives. But when or under what conditions can this creative capacity be exercised? Clearly, much of the time it cannot: if actors were constantly reinventing their identities, social order would be impossible, and the relative stability of identities and interests in the real world is indicative of our propensity for habitual rather than creative action. The exceptional, conscious choosing to transform or transcend roles has at least two preconditions. First, there must be a reason to think of oneself in novel terms. This would most likely stem from the presence of new social situations that cannot be managed in terms of preexisting self-conceptions. Second, the expected costs of intentional role change—the sanctions imposed by others with whom one interacted in previous roles—cannot be greater than its rewards.

When these conditions are present, actors can engage in self-reflection and practice specifically designed to transform their identities and interests and thus to "change the games" in which they are embedded. Such "critical" strategic theory and practice has not received the attention it merits from students of world politics (another legacy of exogenously given interests perhaps), particularly given that one of the most important phenomena in contemporary world politics, Mikhail Gorbachev's policy of "New Thinking," is arguably precisely that. Let me therefore use this policy as an example of how states might transform a competitive security system into a cooperative one, dividing the transformative process into four stages.

The first stage in intentional transformation is the breakdown of consensus about identity commitments. In the Soviet case, identity commitments centered on the Leninist theory of imperialism, with its belief that relations between capitalist and socialist states are inherently conflictual, and on the alliance patterns that this belief engendered. In the 1980s, the consensus within the Soviet Union over the Leninist theory broke down for a variety of reasons, principal among which seem to have been the state's inability to meet the economic-technological-military challenge from the West, the government's decline of political legitimacy at home, and the reassurance from the West that it did not intend to invade the Soviet Union, a reassurance that reduced the external costs of role change. These factors paved the way for a radical leadership transition and for a subsequent "unfreezing of conflict schemas" concerning relations with the West.

The breakdown of consensus makes possible a second stage of critical examination of old ideas about self and other and, by extension, of the structures of interaction by which the ideas have been sustained. In periods of relatively stable role identities, ideas and structures may become reified and thus treated as things that exist independently of social action. If so, the second stage is one of denaturalization, of identifying the practices that reproduce seemingly inevitable ideas about self and other; to that extent, it is a form of "critical" rather than "problem-solving" theory. The result of such a critique should be an identification of new "possible selves" and aspirations.[22] New Thinking embodies such critical theorizing. Gorbachev wants to free the Soviet Union from the coercive social logic of the cold war and engage the West in far-reaching cooperation. Toward this end, he has rejected the Leninist belief in the inherent conflict of interest between socialist and capitalist states and, perhaps more important, has recognized the crucial role that Soviet aggressive practices played in sustaining that conflict.

Such rethinking paves the way for a third stage of new practice. In most cases, it is not enough to rethink one's own ideas about self and other, since old identities have been sustained by systems of interaction with *other* actors, the practices of which remain a social fact for the transformative agent. In order to change the self, then, it is often necessary to change the identities and interests of the others that help sustain those systems of interaction. The vehicle for inducing such change is one's own practice and, in particular, the practice of "altercasting"—a technique of interactor control in which ego uses tactics of self-presentation and stage management in an attempt to frame alter's definitions of social situations in ways that create the role which ego desires alter to play. In effect, in altercasting ego tries to induce alter to take on a new identity (and thereby enlist alter in ego's effort to change itself) by treating alter *as if* it already had that identity. The logic of this follows directly from the mirror theory of identity-formation, in which alter's identity is a reflection of ego's practices; change those practices and ego begins to change alter's conception of itself.

What these practices should consist of depends on the logic by which the preexisting identities were sustained. Competitive security systems are sustained by practices that create insecurity and distrust. In this case, transformative practices should attempt to teach other states that one's own state can be trusted and should not be viewed as a threat to their security. The fastest way to do this is to make unilateral initiatives and self-binding commitments of sufficient significance that another state is faced with "an offer it cannot refuse."[23] Gorbachev has tried to do this by withdrawing from Afghanistan and Eastern Europe, implementing asymmetric cuts in nuclear and conventional forces, calling for "defensive defense," and so on. In addition, he has skillfully cast the West in the role of being morally required to give aid and comfort to the Soviet Union, has emphasized the bonds of common fate between the Soviet Union and the West, and has indicated that further progress in East–West relations is contingent upon the West assuming the identity being projected onto it. These actions are all dimensions of altercasting, the intention of which is to take away the Western "excuse"

---

[22]Hazel Markus and Paula Nurius, "Possible Selves," *American Psychologist* 41 (September 1986), pp. 954–69.

[23]See Volker Boge and Peter Wilke, "Peace Movements and Unilateral Disarmament: Old Concepts in a New Light," *Arms Control* 7 (September 1986), pp. 156–70; Zeev Maoz and Daniel Felsenthal, "Self-Binding Commitments, the Inducement of Trust, Social Choice, and the Theory of International Cooperation," *International Studies Quarterly* 31 (June 1987), pp. 177–200; and V. Sakamoto, "Unilateral Initiative as an Alternative Strategy," *World Futures,* vol. 24, nos. 1–4, 1987, pp. 107–34.

for distrusting the Soviet Union, which, in Gorbachev's view, has helped sustain competitive identities in the past.

Yet by themselves such practices cannot transform a competitive security system, since if they are not reciprocated by alter, they will expose ego to a "sucker" payoff and quickly wither on the vine. In order for critical strategic practice to transform competitive identities, it must be "rewarded" by alter, which will encourage more such practice by ego, and so on. Over time, this will institutionalize a positive rather than a negative identification between the security of self and other and will thereby provide a firm intersubjective basis for what were initially tentative commitments to new identities and interests.

Notwithstanding today's rhetoric about the end of the cold war, skeptics may still doubt whether Gorbachev (or some future leader) will succeed in building an intersubjective basis for a new Soviet (or Russian) role identity. There are important domestic, bureaucratic, and cognitive-ideological sources of resistance in both East and West to such a change, not the least of which is the shakiness of the democratic forces' domestic position. But if my argument about the role of intersubjective knowledge in creating competitive structures of identity and interest is right, then at least New Thinking shows a greater appreciation—conscious or not—for the deep structure of power politics than we are accustomed to in international relations practice.

CONCLUSION

. . . The significance of states relative to multinational corporations, new social movements, transnationals, and intergovernmental organizations is clearly declining, and "postmodern" forms of world politics merit more research attention than they have received. But I also believe, with realists, that in the medium run sovereign states will remain the dominant political actors in the international system. Any transition to new structures of global political authority and identity—to "postinternational" politics—will be mediated by and path-dependent on the particular institutional resolution of the tension between unity and diversity, or particularism and universality, that is the sovereign state. In such a world there should continue to be a place for theories of anarchic interstate politics, alongside other forms of international theory; to that extent, I am a statist and a realist. I have argued in this article, however, that statism need not be bound by realist ideas about what "state" must mean. State identities and interests can be collectively transformed within an anarchic context by many factors—individual, domestic, systemic, or transnational—and as such are an important dependent variable. Such a reconstruction of state-centric international theory is necessary if we are to theorize adequately about the emerging forms of transnational political identity that sovereign states will help bring into being. To that extent, I hope that statism, like the state, can be historically progressive.

I have argued that the proponents of strong liberalism and the constructivists can and should join forces in contributing to a process-oriented international theory. Each group has characteristic weaknesses that are complemented by the other's strengths. In part because of the decision to adopt a choice-theoretic approach to theory construction, neoliberals have been unable to translate their work on institution-building and complex learning into a systemic theory that escapes the explanatory priority of realism's concern with structure. Their weakness, in other words, is a lingering unwillingness to transcend, at the level of systemic theory, the individualist assumption that identities and interests are exogenously given. Constructivists bring to this lack of resolution a systematic communitarian ontology in which intersubjective knowledge constitutes identities and interests. For their part, however, constructivists have often devoted too much effort to questions of ontology and constitution and not enough effort to the causal and empirical questions of how identities and interests are produced by practice in anarchic conditions. As a result, they have not taken on board neoliberal insights into learning and social cognition. . . .

CONSTRUCTING NORMS
OF HUMANITARIAN
INTERVENTION

Martha Finnemore

USING NORMS TO UNDERSTAND
INTERNATIONAL POLITICS

. . . Humanitarian intervention looks odd from conventional perspectives on international political behavior because it does not conform to the conceptions of interest that they specify. Realists would expect to see some geostrategic or political advantage to be gained by intervening states. Neoliberals might emphasize economic or trade advantages for interveners.

As I discussed in the introduction, it is difficult to identify the advantage for the intervener in most post-1989 cases. The 1989 U.S. action in Somalia is a clear case of intervention without obvious interests. Economically Somalia was insignificant to the United States. Security interests are also hard to find. The U.S. had voluntarily given up its base at Berbera in Somalia because advances in communications and aircraft technology made it obsolete for the communications and refueling purposes it once served. Further, the U.S. intervention in that country was not carried out in a way that would have furthered strategic interests. If the U.S. had truly had designs on Somalia, it should have welcomed the role of disarming the clans. It did not. The U.S. resisted UN pressures to "pacify" the country as part of its mission. In fact, U.S. officials were clearly and consistently interested not in controlling any part of Somalia but in getting out of the country as soon as possible—sooner, indeed, than the UN would have liked. The fact that some administration officials opposed the Somalia intervention on precisely the grounds that no vital U.S. interest was involved underscores the realists' problem.

Intervention to reconstruct Cambodia presents similar anomalies. The country is economically insignificant to the interveners and, with the end of the Cold War, was strategically significant to none of the five on the UN Security Council except China, which bore very little of the intervention burden. Indeed, U.S. involvement appears to have been motivated by domestic opposition to the return of the Khmers Rouges on moral grounds—another anomaly for these approaches—rather than by geopolitical or economic interests.

Liberals of a more classical and Kantian type might argue that these interventions have been motivated by an interest in promoting democracy and liberal values. After all, the UN's political blueprint for reconstructing these states is a liberal one. But such arguments also run afoul of the evidence. The U.S. consistently refused to take on the state-building and democratization mission in Somalia that liberal arguments would have expected to be at the heart of U.S. efforts. Similarly, the UN stopped short of authorizing an overthrow of Saddam Hussein in Iraq even when it was militarily possible and supported by many in the U.S. armed forces. The UN, and especially the U.S., have emphasized the humanitarian rather than the democratizing nature of these interventions, both rhetorically and in their actions on the ground.

None of these realist or liberal approaches provides an answer to the question, What interests are intervening states pursuing? In part this is a problem of theoretical focus. Realism and most liberals do not investigate interests; they assume them. Interests are givens in these approaches and need to be specified before analysis can begin. In this case, however, the problem is also substantive. The geostrategic and economic interests specified by these approaches appear to be wrong.

Investigating interests requires a different kind of theoretical approach. Attention to international norms and the way they structure interests in coordinated ways across the international system provides such an approach. Further, a norms approach addresses an issue obscured by approaches that treat interests exogenously: it focuses attention on the ways in which interests change. Since norms are socially constructed, they evolve with changes in social interaction. Understanding this normative evolution and the changing interests it creates is a major focus of a constructivist research program and of this analysis.

A constructivist approach does not deny that power and interest are important. They are. Rather, it asks a different and prior set of questions: it asks what interests *are*, and it investigates the ends to which and the means by which power will be used. The answers to these questions are not simply idiosyncratic and unique to each actor. The social nature of international politics creates normative understandings among actors that, in turn, coordinate values, expectations, and behavior. Because norms make similar behavioral claims on dissimilar actors, they create coordinated patterns of behavior that we can study and about which we can theorize.

Before beginning the analysis, let me clarify the relationship postulated here among norms, interests, and actions. In this essay I understand norms to shape interests and interests to shape action. Neither connection is determinative. Factors other than norms may shape interests, and certainly no single norm or norm set is likely to shape a state's interests on any given issue. In turn, factors other than state interests, most obviously power constraints, shape behavior and outcomes. Thus, the connection assumed here between norms and action is one in which norms create permissive conditions for action but do not determine action. Changing norms may change state interests and create new interests (in this case, interests in protecting non-European non-Christians and in doing so multilaterally through an international organization). But the fact that states are now interested in these issues does not guarantee pursuit of these interests over all others on all occasions. New or changed norms enable new or different behaviors; they do not ensure such behaviors. . . .

The focus here is justification, and for the purposes of this study justification *is* important because it speaks directly to normative context. When states justify their interventions, they are drawing on and articulating shared values and expectations held by other decision makers and other publics in other states. It is literally an attempt to connect one's actions to standards of justice or, perhaps more generically, to standards of appropriate and acceptable behavior. Thus through an examination of justifications we can begin to piece together what those internationally held standards are and how they may change over time.

My aim here is to establish the plausibility and utility of norms as an explanation for international behavior. States may violate international norms and standards of right conduct that they themselves articulate. But they do not always—or even often—do so. Aggregate behavior over long periods shows patterns that correspond to notions of right conduct over time. As shared understandings about who is "human" and about how intervention to protect those people must be carried out change, behavior shifts accordingly in ways not correlated with standard conceptions of interests.

We can investigate these changes by comparing humanitarian intervention practice in the nineteenth century with that of the twentieth century. The analysis is instructive in a number of ways. First, the analysis shows that humanitarian justifications for state action and state use of force are not new.

Second, the analysis shows that while humanitarian justifications for action have been important for centuries, the content and application of those justifications have changed over time. Specifically, states' perceptions of *which* human beings merit intervention has changed. I treat this not as a change of *identity* . . . but as a change of *identification*. Nonwhite non-Christians always knew they were human. What changed was perceptions of Europeans about them. People in Western states began to identify with non-Western populations during the twentieth century, with profound political consequences, for humanitarian intervention, among other things. Perhaps one could argue that the identity of the Western states changed, but I am not sure how one would characterize or operationalize such a change. Certainly Western states have not taken on an identity of "humanitarian state." Far too many inhumane acts have been committed by these states in this century to make such a characterization credible—nor do Western states themselves proclaim any such identity. Besides, these states were "humanitarian" on their own terms in the nineteenth century. What has changed is not the fact of the humanitarian behavior but its focus. Identification emphasizes the affective relationships between actors rather than the characteristics of a single actor. Further, identification is an ordinal concept, allowing for degrees of affect as well as changes in the focus of affect. Identification—of Western Europeans with Greeks and of Russians with their fellow Slavs—existed in the nineteenth century. The task is to explain how and why this identification expanded to other groups. . . .

HUMANITARIAN INTERVENTION IN THE NINETEENTH CENTURY

Before the twentieth century virtually all instances of military intervention to protect people other than the intervener's own nationals involved protection of Christians from the Ottoman Turks. In at least four instances during the nineteenth century, European states used humanitarian claims to influence Balkan policy in ways that would have required states to use force—in the Greek War for Independence (1821–1827); in the Lebanon/Syria conflict of 1860–1861; during the Bulgarian agitation of 1876–1878; and in response to the Armenian massacres (1894–1917). Although full-scale military intervention did not result in all these instances, the claims made and their effects on policy in the other cases shed light on the evolution and influence of humanitarian claims during this period.

Greek War for Independence (1821–1827)

Russia took an immediate interest in the Greek insurrection and threatened to use force against the Turks as early as the first year of the war. Part of her motivation was geostrategic: Russia had been pursuing a general strategy of weakening the Ottomans and consolidating control in the Balkans for years. But the justifications that Russia offered were largely humanitarian. Russia had long seen herself as the defender of Orthodox Christians under Turkish rule. Atrocities such as the wholesale massacres of Christians and the sale of women into slavery, coupled with the sultan's order to seize the Venerable Patriarch of the Orthodox Church after mass on Easter morning and hang him and three archbishops, then have the bodies thrown into the Bosporus, formed the centerpiece of Russia's complaints against the Turks and the justification of her threats of force.

Other European powers, with the exception of France, opposed intervention largely because they were concerned that weakening Turkey would strengthen Russia. Although the governments of Europe seemed little affected by these atrocities, significant segments of their publics were. A philhellenic movement spread throughout Europe, especially in the more democratic societies of Britain, France, and parts of Germany. The movement drew on two popular sentiments: the European identification with the classical Hellenic tradition and the appeal of Christians oppressed by the infidel. Philhellenic aid societies in Western Europe sent large sums of money and even volunteers to Greece during the war.

Russian threats of unilateral action against the sultan eventually forced the British to become involved, and in 1827 the two powers, together with Charles X of France in his capacity as "Most Christian King," sent an armada that roundly defeated Ibrahim at Navarino in October 1827.

It would be hard to argue that humanitarian considerations were decisive in this intervention; geostrategic factors were far too important. However, the episode does bear on the evolution of humanitarian norms in several ways.

First, it illustrates the circumscribed definition of who was "human" in the nineteenth-century conception of that term. The massacre of Christians was a humanitarian disaster; the massacre of Muslims was not. This was true regardless of the fact that the initial atrocities of the war were committed by the Christian insurgents (admittedly after years of harsh Ottoman rule). The initial Christian uprising at Morea "might well have been allowed to burn itself out 'beyond the pale of civilization'"; it was only the wide-scale and very visible atrocities against Christians that put the events on the agenda of major powers.

Second, intervening states, particularly Russia and France, placed humanitarian but also religious reasons at the center of their continued calls for intervention and application of force. As will be seen in other cases from the nineteenth century, religion seems to be important in both motivating humanitarian action and defining who is human. Notions about Christian charity supported general humanitarian impulses, but specific religious identifications had the effect of privileging certain people over others. In this case Christians generally were privileged over Muslims. Elsewhere, as later in Armenia and Bulgaria, denominational differences within Christianity appear to be important both in motivating action and in restraining it.

Third, the intervention was multilateral. The reasons in this case were largely geostrategic (restraining Russia from temptation to use this intervention for other purposes), but, as subsequent discussion will show, multilateralism as a characteristic of legitimate intervention becomes increasingly important.

Fourth, mass publics were involved. It is not clear that they influenced policy making as strongly as they would in the second half of the century, but foreign civilians did become involved both financially and militarily on behalf of the Greeks. Indeed, it was a British Captain Hastings who commanded the Greek flotilla that destroyed a Turkish squadron off Salona and provoked the ultimate use of force at Navarino. . . .

The Bulgarian Agitation (1876–1878)

In May 1876 Ottoman troops massacred unarmed and poorly organized agitators in Bulgaria. A British government investigation put the number killed at twelve thousand, with fifty-nine villages destroyed and an entire church full of people set ablaze after they had already surrendered to Turkish soldiers. The investigation confirmed that Turkish soldiers and officers were promoted and decorated rather than punished for these actions.

Accounts of the atrocities, gathered by American missionaries and sent to British reporters, began appearing in British newspapers in mid-June. The reports inflamed public opinion, and protest meetings were organized around the country, particularly in the north, where W. T. Stead and his paper, the *Northern Echo,* were a focus of agitation.

The result was a split in British politics. Prime Minister Disraeli publicly refused to change British policy of support for Turkey over the matter, stating that British material interests outweighed the lives of Bulgarians. However, Lord Derby, the Conservative foreign secretary, telegraphed Constantinople that "any renewal of the outrages would be more fatal to the Porte than the loss of a battle." More important, former prime minister Gladstone came out of retirement to oppose Disraeli on the issue, making the Bulgarian atrocities the centerpiece of his anti-Disraeli campaign.

While Gladstone found a great deal of support in various public circles, he did not have similar success in government. The issue barely affected British policy. Disraeli was forced to carry out the investigation mentioned above, and he did offer proposals for internal Turkish reforms to protect minorities—proposals that were rejected by Russia as being too timid.

Russia was the only state to intervene in the wake of the Bulgarian massacres. The 1856 treaty that ended the Crimean War was supposed to protect Christians under Ottoman rule. Russia justified her threats of force on the basis of Turkey's violation of these humanitarian guarantees. In March 1877 the great powers issued a protocol reiterating demands for the protection of Christians in the Ottoman Empire that had been guaranteed in the 1856 treaty. After Constantinople rejected the protocol, Russia declared war in April 1877. She easily defeated the Ottoman troops and signed the Treaty of San Stefano, which created a large, independent Bulgarian state—an arrangement that was drastically revised by the Congress of Berlin.

As in the previous cases, saving Christians was an essential feature of this incident, and Gladstone and Russia's justifications for action were framed in that way. But military action in this case was not multilateral. Perhaps the most remarkable feature of this episode is its demonstration of the strength of public opinion and the media. While they were not able to change British policy they were able to make adherence to that policy much more difficult for Disraeli in domestic terms.

Armenia (1894–1917)

The Armenian case offers some interesting insights into the scope of Christianity requiring defense by European powers in the last century. Unlike the Orthodox Christians in Greece and Bulgaria and the Maronites in Syria, the Armenian Christians had no European champion. The Armenian Church was not in communion with the Orthodox Church, hence Armenian appeals had never resonated in Russia; the Armenians were not portrayed as "brothers" to the Russians, as were the Bulgarians and other Orthodox Slavs. Similarly, no non-Orthodox European state had ever offered protection or had historical ties as the French did with the Maronites. Thus some of the justifications that were offered for intervention in other cases were lacking in the Armenian case.

The fact that the Armenians were Christians, albeit of a different kind, does seem to have had some influence on policy. The Treaty of Berlin explicitly bound the sultan to carry out internal political reforms to protect Armenians, but the nature, timing, and monitoring of these provisions were left vague and were never enforced. The Congress of Berlin ignored an Armenian petition for an arrangement similar to that set up in Lebanon following the Maronite massacres (a Christian governor under Ottoman rule). Gladstone took up the matter in 1880 when he came back to power but dropped it when Bismarck voiced opposition. The wave of massacres against Armenians beginning in 1894 was far worse than any of the other atrocities examined here, in terms of both the number killed and the brutality of their executions. Nine hundred people were killed, and twenty-four villages burned in the Sassum massacres in August 1894. After this, the intensity increased. Between fifty thousand and seventy thousand people were killed in 1895. In 1896 the massacres moved into the capital, Constantinople, where on August 28–29, six thousand Armenians were killed.

These events were well known and highly publicized in Europe. Gladstone came out of retirement yet again to denounce the Turks and called Abd-ul-Hamid the "Great Assassin." French writers denounced him as "the Red Sultan." The European powers demanded an inquiry assisted by Europeans, which submitted to European governments and the press extensive documentation of "horrors unutterable, unspeakable, unimaginable by the mind of man." Public opinion pressed for intervention, and both Britain and France used humanitarian justifications to threaten force. But neither acted. Germany by this time was a force to be reckoned with, and the kaiser was courting Turkey. Russia was nervous about nationalist aspirations in the Balkans in general and had no special affection for the Armenians, as noted above. The combined opposition of Germany and Russia made the price of intervention higher than either the British or the French were willing to pay.

These . . . episodes are suggestive in several ways. First, humanitarian justifications for uses of force and threats of force are not new in the twentieth century.

Second, humanitarian action was rarely taken when it jeopardized other stated goals or interests of a state. Humanitarians were sometimes able to mount considerable pressure on policy makers to act contrary to stated geostrategic interests, as in the case of Disraeli and the Bulgarian agitation, but they never succeeded. Humanitarian claims did, however, provide states with new or intensified interests in an area and new reasons to act where none had existed previously. Without the massacre of Maronites in Syria, France would almost certainly not have intervened. Further, she left after her humanitarian mission was accomplished and did not stay on to pursue other geostrategic goals, as some states had feared she would. It is less clear whether there would have been intervention in the Greek war for independence without humanitarian justifications for such interventions. Russia certainly had other reasons to intervene, but she was also probably the state with the highest level of identification with the Orthodox Christian victims of these massacres. Whether the former would have been sufficient for intervention without the latter is impossible to know. Once Russia did intervene, the British certainly had an interest in restraining Russian activities in the area and joining the intervention. At the same time Britain had consistently articulated a strong doctrine of nonintervention. It may be that humanitarian claims made by important sectors of domestic opinion were necessary to override this doctrine, but it would be impossible to be certain.

Third, humanitarian action could be taken in a variety of forms. Action could be multilateral, as in the case of Greek independence. It could be unilateral, as when Russia intervened in Bulgaria. Action might also be some mixture of the two, as in Lebanon/Syria, where several states planned the intervention but execution was essentially unilateral. As will be shown below, this variety of forms for intervention shrinks over time. Specifically, the unilateral option for either planning or executing humanitarian intervention appears to have disappeared in the twentieth century.

Fourth, interveners identified with the victims of humanitarian disasters in some important *and exclusive* way. At a minimum, the victims to be protected by intervention were Christians; there were no instances of European powers' considering intervention to protect non-Christians. Pogroms against Jews did not provoke intervention. Neither did Russian massacres of Turks in Central Asia in the 1860s. Neither did mass killings in China during the Taipings rebellion against the Manchus. Neither did mass killings by colonial rulers in their colonies. Neither did massacres of Native Americans in the United States. Often there was some more specific identification or social tie between intervener and intervened, as between the Orthodox Slav Russians and Orthodox Slav Bulgarians. In fact, the Armenian case suggests, lack of such an intensified identification may contribute to inaction.

THE EXPANSION OF "HUMANITY" AND SOVEREIGNTY

This last feature of nineteenth-century intervention, the ways in which interveners identify with victims to determine who is an appropriate or compelling candidate for intervention, changed dramatically over the twentieth century as the "humanity" deserving of protection by military intervention became universalized. The seeds of this change lie in the nineteenth century, however, with efforts to end slavery and the slave trade. With the abolition of slavery in the nineteenth century and decolonization in the twentieth, a new set of norms was consolidated that universalized "humanity" and endowed it with rights, among them self-determination, which came to be equated with sovereign statehood. These processes are obviously complex and cannot be treated adequately here. What follows is a brief discussion showing how these larger normative developments contributed to the evolution of humanitarian intervention norms.[1]

Abolition of Slavery and the Slave Trade

The abolition of slavery and the slave trade in the nineteenth century was an essential part of the universalization of "humanity." European states generally accepted and legalized these practices in the seventeenth and eighteenth centuries, but by the nineteenth century the same states proclaimed them "repugnant to the principles of humanity and universal morality."[2] Human beings previously viewed as beyond the edge of humanity—as, in fact, property—came to be viewed as human, and with that status came certain, albeit minimal, privileges and protections. Further, military force was used by states, especially Britain, to suppress the slave trade. Britain succeeded in having the slave trade labeled as piracy, thus enabling her to seize and board ships sailing under non-British flags that were suspected of carrying contraband slaves.

While this is in some ways an important case of a state using force to promote humanitarian ends, the way the British framed and justified their actions also says something about the limits of humanitarian claims in the early to mid-nineteenth century. First, the British limited their military action to abolishing the trade in slaves, not slavery itself. There was no military intervention on behalf of Africans as there was on behalf of Christians. While the British public and many political figures contributed to a climate of international opinion that viewed slavery with increasing distaste, the abolition of slavery as a domestic institution of property rights was accomplished in each

---

[1]One might argue that the current plight of the Bosnian Muslims suggests that "humanity" is not as universal as we would like to think. They, after all, are Muslims being slaughtered by Christians, and the Christian West is standing by. Countering this would be the case of Somalia, where the West *did* intervene to save a largely Muslim population. I would argue that the explanation for different intervention behaviors in these cases does not lie in humanitarian norms. Strong normative claims to intervene have been made in both cases and have met with different results, for old-fashioned geostrategic reasons. As is discussed elsewhere in this essay, humanitarian norms create only permissive conditions for intervention. They create an "interest" in intervention where none existed. They do not eliminate other competing interests, such as political or strategic interests.

[2]The quotation comes from the Eight Power Declaration concerning the universal abolition of the trade in Negroes, signed February 8, 1815, by Britain, France, Spain, Sweden, Austria, Prussia, Russia, and Portugal (as quoted in Leslie Bethell, *The Abolition of the Brazilian Slave Trade* [Cambridge: Cambridge University Press, 1970], p. 14).

state where it had previously been legal without military intervention by other states.[3] Further, the British government's strategy for ending the slave trade was to have such trafficking labeled as piracy, thus making the slaves "contraband," i.e., still property. The government justified its actions on the basis of maritime rights governing commerce. Slavery and slaveholding themselves did not provoke the same reaction as Ottoman abuse of Christians did.

This may be because the perpetrators of the humanitarian violations were "civilized" Christian nations (as opposed to the infidel Turks). Another reason was probably that the targets of these humanitarian violations were black Africans, not "fellow Christians" or "brother Slavs." It thus appears that by the 1830s black Africans had become sufficiently "human" that enslaving them was illegal inside Europe, but enslaving them outside Europe was only distasteful. One could keep them enslaved if one kept them at home, within domestic borders. Abuse of Africans did not merit military intervention inside another state.

Colonization, Decolonization, and Self-determination

Justifications for both colonization and decolonization also offer interesting lenses through which to examine changing humanitarian norms and changing understandings of who is "human." Both processes—colonization and its undoing—were justified, at least in part, in humanitarian terms, but the understanding of what constituted humanity was different in the two episodes in ways that bear on the current investigation of humanitarian intervention norms.

The vast economic literature on colonization often overlooks the strong moral dimension perceived and articulated by many of the colonizers. Colonization was a crusade. It would bring the benefits of civilization to the "dark" reaches of the earth. It was a sacred trust, it was the white man's burden, it was mandated by God that these Europeans go out into unknown (to them) parts of the globe, bringing what they understood to be a better way of life to the inhabitants. Colonization for the missionaries and those driven by social conscience was a humanitarian mission of huge proportions and consequently of huge importance.

Colonialism's humanitarian mission was of a particular kind, however: it was to "civilize" the non-European parts of the world—to bring the "benefits" of European social, political, economic, and cultural arrangements to Asia, Africa, and the Americas. Until these peoples were "civilized," they were savages, barbarians, something less than

---

[3]The United States is a possible exception. One could argue that the North intervened militarily in the South to abolish slavery. Such an argument would presume that (a) there were ever two separate states such that the North's action could be understood as "intervention," rather than civil war and (b) abolishing slavery rather than maintaining the Union was the primary reason for the North's initial action. Both assumptions are open to serious question. (The Emancipation Proclamation was not signed until 1863, when the war was already half over.) Thus, while the case is suggestive of the growing power of a broader conception of "humanity," I do not treat it in this analysis.

human. Thus in an important sense the core of the colonial humanitarian mission was to *create* humanity where none had previously existed. Non-Europeans became human in European eyes by becoming Christian, by adopting European-style structures of property rights, by adopting European-style territorial political arrangements, by entering the growing European-based international economy.

Decolonization also had strong humanitarian justifications. By the mid-twentieth century, however, normative understandings about humanity had shifted. Humanity was no longer something one could create by bringing savages to civilization. Rather, humanity was inherent in individual human beings. It had become universalized and was not culturally dependent, as it has been in earlier centuries. Asians and Africans were now viewed as having human "rights," and among those rights was the right to determine their own political future—the right to self-determination. . . .

The logical expansion of these arguments fueled attacks on both slavery and colonization. Slavery, more blatantly a violation of these emerging European norms, came under attack first. Demands for decolonization came more slowly and had to contend with the counterclaims for the beneficial humanitarian effects of European rule. In both cases, former slaves and Western-educated colonial elites were instrumental in change. Having been "civilized" and Europeanized, they were able to use Europe's own norms against these institutions. These people undermined the social legitimacy of both slaveholders and colonizers not simply by being exemplars of "human" non-Europeans but also by contributing to the arguments undercutting the legitimacy of slavery and colonialism within a European framework of proclaimed human equality.

Although logic alone is not the reason that slavery and colonialism were abolished, there does appear to be some need for logical consistency in normative structures. Changes in core normative structure (in this case, changes toward recognition of human equality *within* Europe) tended to promote and facilitate associated normative changes elsewhere in society. Mutually reinforcing and logically consistent norms appear to be harder to attack and to have an advantage in the normative contestations that go on in social life. Thus, logic internal to the norms shapes their development and consequently social change.

Second, as Neta Crawford and others have noted, formal international organizations, particularly the United Nations, played a significant role in the decolonization process and the consolidation of anticolonialism norms. The self-determination norms laid out in the charter, the trusteeship system it set up, and the one-state-one-vote voting structure that gave majority power to weak, often formerly colonized states, all contributed to an international legal, organizational, and normative environment that made colonial practices increasingly illegitimate and difficult to carry out.

Third, decolonization enshrined the notion of political self-determination as a basic human right associated with a now universal humanity. Political self-determination, in turn, meant sovereign statehood. Once sovereign statehood became associated with human rights, intervention, particularly unilateral intervention, became more difficult to justify. Unilateral intervention certainly still occurs, but, as will be seen below, it cannot now be justified even by high-minded humanitarian claims.

HUMANITARIAN INTERVENTION SINCE 1945

Unlike humanitarian intervention practices in the nineteenth century, virtually all of the instances in which claims of humanitarian intervention have been made in the post-1945 period concern military action on behalf of non-Christians and/or non-Europeans. In that sense, the universalizing of the "humanity" that might be worth protecting seems to have widened in accordance with the normative changes described above.

What is interesting in these cases is that states that might legitimately have claimed humanitarian justifications for their intervention did not do so. India's intervention in East Pakistan in the wake of Muslim massacres of Hindus, Tanzania's intervention in Uganda toppling the Idi Amin regime, Vietnam's intervention in Cambodia ousting the Khmers Rouges—in every case intervening states could have justified their actions with strong humanitarian claims. None did. In fact, India initially claimed humanitarian justifications but quickly retracted them. Why?

The argument here is that this reluctance stems not from norms about what is "humanitarian" but from norms about legitimate intervention. While the scope of who qualifies as human has widened enormously and the range of humanitarian activities that states routinely undertake has expanded, norms about intervention have also changed, albeit less drastically. Humanitarian military intervention now must be *multilateral* to be legitimate.

As we saw in the nineteenth century, multilateralism is not new; it has often characterized humanitarian military action. But states in the nineteenth century still invoked humanitarian justifications, even when intervention was unilateral (for example, Russia in Bulgaria during the 1870s and, in part, France in Lebanon). That has not happened in the twentieth century. Without multilateralism, states will not and apparently cannot claim humanitarian justification.

Multilateralism had (and has) important advantages for states. It increases the transparency of each state's actions to others and so reassures states that opportunities for adventurism and expansion will not be used. Unilateral military intervention, even for humanitarian objectives, is viewed with suspicion; it is too easily subverted to serve less disinterested ends of the intervener. Further, multilateralism can be a way of sharing costs, and thus it can be cheaper for states than unilateral action.

Multilateralism carries with it significant costs of its own, however. Cooperation and coordination problems involved in such action have been examined in detail by political scientists and can make it difficult to sustain. Perhaps more important, multilateral action requires sacrifice of power and control over the intervention. Further, it may seriously compromise the military effectiveness of those operations, as recent debates over command and control in UN military operations suggest.

There are no obvious efficiency reasons for states to prefer either multilateral or unilateral intervention to achieve humanitarian ends. Each has advantages and disadvantages. The choice depends in large part on perceptions about the political acceptability and political costs of each, which, in turn, depend on normative context. As will be discussed below, multilateralism in the twentieth century has become institutionalized in ways that make unilateral intervention, particularly intervention not justified as self-defense, unacceptably costly.

The next two sections of the paper compare post-World War II interventions in situations of humanitarian disaster with nineteenth-century practice to illustrate these points. The first section provides a brief overview of unilateral intervention in the post-1945 period in which humanitarian justification could have been claimed to illustrate and elaborate these points but was not. Following that is an even briefer discussion of recent multilateral humanitarian actions that contrast with the previous unilateral cases.

Unilateral Intervention in Humanitarian Disasters

India in East Pakistan (1971)   Pakistan had been under military rule by West Pakistani officials since partition. When the first free elections were held in November 1970, the Awami League won 167 out of 169 parliamentary seats reserved for East Pakistan in the National Assembly. The Awami League had not urged political independence for the East during the elections, but it did run on a list of demands concerning one-person-one-vote political representation and increased economic autonomy for the east. The government in West Pakistan viewed the Awami electoral victory as a threat. In the wake of these electoral results, the government in Islamabad decided to postpone the convening of the new National Assembly indefinitely, and in March 1971 the West Pakistani army started indiscriminately killing unarmed civilians, raping women, burning homes, and looting or destroying property. At least one million people were killed, and millions more fled across the border into India. Following months of tension, border incidents, and increased pressure from the influx of refugees, India sent troops into East Pakistan. After twelve days the Pakistani army surrendered at Dacca, and the new state of Bangladesh was established.

As in many of the nineteenth-century cases, the intervener here had an array of geopolitical interests. Humanitarian concerns were not the only reason or even, perhaps, the most important reason to intervene. It is, however, a case in which intervention could have been *justified* in humanitarian terms, and initially the Indian representatives in both the General Assembly and the Security Council did articulate such a justification. These arguments were widely rejected by other states, including many with no particular interest in politics on the subcontinent. States as diverse as Argentina, Tunisia, China, Saudi Arabia, and the U.S. all responded to India's claims by arguing that principles of sovereignty and noninterference should take precedence and that India had no right to meddle in what they all viewed as an "internal matter." In response to this rejection of her claims, India retracted her humanitarian justifications, choosing instead to rely on self-defense to justify her actions.

Tanzania in Uganda (1979)   This episode began as a straightforward territorial dispute. In the autumn of 1978 Ugandan troops invaded and occupied the Kagera salient—territory between the Uganda-Tanzania border and the Kagera River in Tanzania. On November 1 Idi Amin announced annexation of the territory. Julius

Nyerere considered the annexation tantamount to an act of war and on November 15 launched an offensive from the south bank of the Kagera River. Amin, fearing defeat, offered to withdraw from the occupied territories if Nyerere would promise to cease support for Ugandan dissidents and not to attempt to overthrow his government. Nyerere refused and made explicit his intention to help dissidents topple the Amin regime. In January 1979 Tanzanian troops crossed into Uganda, and by April Tanzanian troops, joined by some Ugandan rebel groups, had occupied Kampala and installed a new government headed by Yusef Lule.

As in the previous case, there were nonhumanitarian reasons to intervene, but if territorial issues were the only ones that mattered, the Tanzanians could have either stopped at the border, having evicted Ugandan forces, or pushed them back into Uganda short of Kampala. The explicit statement of intent to topple the regime seems out of proportion to the low-level territorial squabble. Fernando Tesón makes a strong case that Nyerere's intense dislike of Amin's regime and its practices influenced the scale of the response. Nyerere had already publicly called Amin a murderer and refused to sit with him on the Authority of the East African Community. Tesón also presents strong evidence that the lack of support or material help for Uganda in this intervention from the UN, the OAU, or any state besides Libya suggests tacit international acceptance of what would otherwise be universally condemned as international aggression because of the human rights record of the target state.

Despite evidence of humanitarian motivations, Tanzania never claimed humanitarian justification. In fact, Tanzania went out of her way to minimize responsibility for the felicitous humanitarian outcome of her actions, saying only that she was acting in response to Amin's invasion and that her actions just happened to coincide with a revolt against Amin inside Uganda. When Sudan and Nigeria criticized Tanzania for interfering in another state's internal affairs in violation of the OAU charter, it was the new Ugandan regime that invoked humanitarian justifications for Tanzania's actions. It criticized the critics, arguing that members of the OAU should not "hide behind the formula of non-intervention when human rights are blatantly being violated."

Vietnam in Cambodia (1979)   In 1975 the Chinese-backed Khmers Rouges took power in Cambodia and launched a policy of internal "purification" entailing the atrocities and genocide now made famous by the 1984 movie *The Killing Fields*. This regime, under the leadership of Pol Pot, was also aggressively anti-Vietnamese and engaged in a number of border incursions during the late 1970s. Determined to end this border activity, the Vietnamese and an anti–Pol Pot army of exiled Cambodians invaded the country in December 1978 and by January 1979 had routed the Khmers Rouges and installed a sympathetic government under the name People's Republic of Kampuchea (PRK).

Again, humanitarian considerations may not have been central to Vietnam's decision to intervene, but humanitarian justifications would seem to have offered some political cover to the internationally unpopular Vietnamese regime. Like Tanzania, however, Vietnam made no appeal to humanitarian justifications. Instead, its leaders argued that they were only helping the Cambodian people achieve self-determination against the neocolonial regime of Pol Pot, which had been "the product of the hegemonistic and expansionist policy of the Peking authorities." Even if Vietnam *had* offered humanitarian justifications for intervention, indications are that these would have been rejected by other states. In their condemnations of Vietnam's action, a number of states mentioned Pol Pot's appalling human rights violations but said nonetheless that these violations did not entitle Vietnam to intervene. During the UN debate, no state spoke in favor of the existence of a right to unilateral humanitarian intervention, and several states— Greece, the Netherlands, Yugoslavia, and India—that had previously supported humanitarian intervention arguments in the UN voted for the resolution condemning Vietnam.

Multilateral Intervention in Humanitarian Disasters

To be legitimate, humanitarian intervention must be multilateral. The Cold War made such multilateral efforts politically difficult to orchestrate, but since 1989 several large-scale interventions have been carried out claiming humanitarian justifications as their primary raison d'être. All have been multilateral. Most visible among these have been:

- the U.S., British, and French efforts to protect Kurdish and Shiite populations inside Iraq following the Gulf War;
- the UNTAC mission to end civil war and reestablish a democratic political order in Cambodia;
- the large-scale UN effort to end starvation and construct a democratic state in Somalia; and
- current, albeit limited, efforts by UN and NATO troops to protect civilian, especially Muslim, populations from primarily Serbian forces in Bosnia.

While these efforts have attracted varying amounts of criticism concerning their effectiveness, they have received little or no criticism of their legitimacy. Further, and unlike their nineteenth-century counterparts, all have been organized through standing international organizations—most often the United Nations. Indeed, the UN charter has provided the framework in which much of the normative contestation over intervention practices has occurred since 1945. Specifically, the charter enshrines two principles that at times, and perhaps increasingly, conflict. On the one hand, article 2 enshrines states' sovereign rights as the organizing principle of the international system. The corollary for intervention is a near absolute rule of nonintervention. On the other hand, article 1 of the charter emphasizes promoting respect for human rights and justice as a fundamental mission of the organization, and subsequent UN actions (adoption of the Universal Declaration of Human Rights, among them) have strengthened these claims. Gross humanitarian abuses by states against their own citizens of the kinds discussed in this essay bring these two central principles into conflict.

The humanitarian intervention norms that have evolved within these conflicting principles appear to allow intervention in cases of humanitarian disaster and abuse, but with at least two caveats. First, they are permissive norms only. They do not require intervention, as the cases of Burundi, Sudan, and other states make clear. Second, they place strict requirements on the ways in which intervention, if employed, may be carried out: Humanitarian intervention must be multilateral if states are to accept it as legitimate and genuinely humanitarian. Further, it must be organized under UN auspices or with explicit UN consent. If at all possible, the intervention force should be composed according to UN procedures, meaning that intervening forces must include some number of troops from "disinterested" states, usually midlevel powers outside the region of conflict—another dimension of multilateralism not found in nineteenth-century practice.

Contemporary multilateralism thus differs from the multilateral action of the nineteenth century. The latter was what John Ruggie might call "quantitative" multilateralism and only thinly so. Nineteenth-century multilateralism was strategic. States intervened together to keep an eye on each other and discourage adventurism or exploitation of the situation for nonhumanitarian gains. Multilateralism was driven by shared fears and perceived threats, not by shared norms and principles. States did not even coordinate and collaborate extensively to achieve their goals. Military deployments in the nineteenth century may have been contemporaneous, but they were largely separate; there was virtually no joint planning or coordination of operations. This follows logically from the nature of multilateralism, since strategic surveillance of one's partners is not a shared goal but a private one.

Recent interventions exhibit much more of what Ruggie calls the "qualitative dimension" of multilateralism. They are organized according to and in defense of "generalized principles" of international responsibility and the use of military force, many of which are codified in the United Nations charter, declarations, and standard operating procedures. These emphasize international responsibilities for ensuring human rights and justice and dictate appropriate means of intervening, such as the necessity of obtaining Security Council authorization for action. The difference between contemporary and nineteenth-century multilateralism also appears at the operational level. The Greek intervention was multilateral only in the sense that more than one state had forces in the area at the same time. There was little joint planning and no integration of forces from different states. By contrast, contemporary multilateralism requires extensive joint planning and force integration. UN norms require that intervening forces be composed not just of troops from more than one state but of troops from disinterested states, preferably not great powers—precisely the opposite nineteenth-century multilateral practice.

Contemporary multilateralism is political and normative, not strategic. It is shaped by shared notions about when the use of force is legitimate and appropriate. Contemporary legitimacy criteria for the use of force, in turn, derive from these shared principles, articulated most often through the UN, about consultation and coordination with other states before acting and about multinational composition of forces. U.S. interventions in Somalia and Haiti were not made multilateral because the U.S. needed the involvement of other states for military or strategic reasons. The U.S. was capable of supplying the forces necessary and, in fact, did supply the lion's share of the forces. No other great power was particularly worried about U.S. opportunism in these areas, and so none joined the action for surveillance reasons. These interventions were multilateral for political and normative reasons. For these operations to be legitimate and politically acceptable, the U.S. needed UN authorization and international participation. Whereas Russia, France, and Britain tolerated each other's presence in the operation to save Christians from the infidel Turk, the U.S. had to beg other states to join it for a humanitarian operation in Haiti.

Multilateral norms create political benefits for conformance and costs for nonconforming action. They create, in part, the structure of incentives facing states. Realists or neoliberal institutionalists might argue that in the contemporary world, multilateral behavior is efficient and unproblematically self-interested because multilateralism helps to generate political support both domestically and internationally for intervention. But this argument only begs the question, *Why* is multilateralism necessary to generate political support? It was not necessary in the nineteenth century. Indeed, multilateralism as currently practiced was inconceivable in the nineteenth century. As was discussed earlier, there is nothing about the logic of multilateralism itself that makes it clearly superior to unilateral action. Each has advantages and costs to states, and the costs of multilateral intervention have become abundantly clear in recent UN operations. One testament to the power of these multilateral norms is that states adhere to them even when they know that doing so compromises the effectiveness of the mission. Criticisms of the UN's ineffectiveness for military operations are widespread. The fact that UN involvement continues to be an essential feature of these operations despite the UN's apparent lack of military competence underscores the power of multilateral norms.

Realist and neoliberal approaches cannot address changing requirements for political legitimacy like those reflected in changing multilateral practice any more than they can explain the "interest" prompting humanitarian intervention and its change over time. A century ago, protecting nonwhite non-Christians was not an "interest" of Western states, certainly not one that could prompt the deployment of troops. Similarly, a century ago states saw no interest in multilateral authorization, coordination, force integration, and use of troops from "disinterested" states. The argument of this essay is that these interests and incentives have been constituted socially through state practice and the evolution of shared norms by which states act. . . .

The foregoing account also illustrates that these changes have come about through continual contestation over norms related to humanitarian intervention. The abolition of slavery, of the slave trade, and of colonization were all highly visible, often very violent, international contests about norms. Over time some norms won, others lost. The result was that by the second half of the twentieth century norms about who was "human" had changed, expanding the population deserving of humanitarian protection. At the same time norms about multilateral action had been strengthened, making multilateralism not just attractive but imperative.

Finally, I have argued here that the international normative fabric has become increasingly institutionalized in formal international organizations, particularly the United Nations. As recent action in Iraq suggests, action in concert with others is not enough to confer legitimacy on intervention actions. States also actively seek authorization from the United Nations and restrain their actions to conform to that authorization (as the U.S. did in not going to Baghdad during the Gulf War). International organizations such as the UN play an important role in both arbitrating normative claims and structuring the normative discourse over colonialism, sovereignty, and humanitarian issues. . . .

PART V

ECONOMICS: INTERESTS AND INTERDEPENDENCE

Everyone knows that economic interests and ideas have been important influences on war and peace, but they do not agree on the direction. Does desire for wealth lead groups and governments to use force to expand their control of resources, or to avoid conflict so that profits from trade are not squandered? If in past eras greed led to beliefs that war would be profitable, does modern understanding of economic logic, and globalization of the world economy, lead to different policies today?

Liberal economic theory opposes mercantilism, imperialism, fascism, and Marxism in arguing that war should be obsolete not just because it is evil, but because it profits no one. Mercantilists and imperialists throughout history believed that nations' wealth and prosperity increased with their control of territory, and war was the main way to gain or keep territory. Thus Machiavelli opined in the excerpt from *The Discourses* below that military power was the font of wealth, not—as is now much more commonly believed—the reverse. Marxists saw violent conflict as the natural and inevitable result of opposed economic interests. In the Soviet Union, Marxism joined with nationalism and fostered the most serious attempt, apart from fascism, to develop a viable autarky—a state that is economically self-sufficient.

Unabashed mercantilism no longer exists as a serious philosophical challenge to liberal economics or as an overt political movement.[1] To varying degrees, though, it comes alive in other forms of economic nationalism.[2] Marxism—not long ago a potent challenge to international liberalism and a serious contender for wave of the future—is nearly defunct. Although four countries remain nominally Communist (China, North Korea, Vietnam, and Cuba), most of them have preserved Leninist political forms while

---

[1]See Jacob Viner, "Power and Plenty as Objectives of Foreign Policy in the Seventeenth and Eighteenth Centuries," *World Politics* 1, no. 1 (October 1948).

[2]See Robert Gilpin with the assistance of Jean M. Gilpin, *The Political Economy of International Relations* (Princeton: Princeton University Press, 1987), and James Kurth, "The Pacific Basin versus the Atlantic Alliance: Two Paradigms of International Relations," *Annals of the American Academy of Political and Social Sciences* 505 (September 1989).

moving away from Marxist-Leninist economic dogma. Excerpts from Lenin's theory of imperialism are included here, nevertheless, because it represents a major school of thought in the evolution of ideas on the subject, and makes a specific argument about why the dynamics of capitalism actually push governments toward war and conquest, to control foreign markets, instead of toward peaceful trade. Non-liberal interpretations could become more interesting again if the world economy suffers major dislocations (the Asian economic crisis of the late 1990s was a reminder that uninterrupted growth is not inevitable) or conversion of formerly Communist states falters. It is not inconceivable that bitter disillusionment with attempts to move to liberal capitalism could promote some degree of Marxist revival (it is hardly less likely than the end of the Cold War was a few years before it happened).

Still, the liberal theory of political economy is dominant among western elites. It holds that free trade in open markets yields the most efficient production and exchange of goods, and ultimately makes everyone wealthier than if governments interfere. Trade based on specialization and comparative advantage promotes efficient growth and interdependence among nations, which in turn gives them all a stake in each others' security and prosperity. Control of territory does not matter because it does not create wealth, which is only generated by production and exchange. Interdependence makes war counterproductive and wasteful for all, not only because it destroys property but because it deranges the international market and distorts global economic efficiency.

If peace is the path to profit, greed should discourage war rather than promote it. In this respect liberal theory does not see itself as an idealistic one, relying on noble motives to suppress war. Just like realism, or mercantilism, or Marxism, the theory focuses on material interest as the driving force, but sees the interest in a different way. Norman Angell summarizes this view in the selection included here, from one of the most popular tracts of the pre-World War I period.[3] If this logic is valid, the persistence of war after the arrival of industrial capitalism can only be irrational. What would account for the irrationality?

Joseph Schumpeter provides a sociological explanation, attributing militarist policies to cultural atavism, the continuing sway of feudal elites and their values in societies where capitalism was displacing them. Another source of irrationality, in terms of liberal theory, would be the nationalist ideologies of interwar fascism which promoted autarky and conquest for direct economic exploitation of subjugated populations. The rationales behind this alternative are discussed in Alan Milward's piece below. It is not surprising that liberal theories of the pacifying effect of international economic interdependence have the upper hand again today, since fascism and feudal militarism are even further gone than Marxism as a challenge.

Realism, however, is not as far gone, and it offers different explanations for the failure of capitalism to prevent wars. Some of these criticisms are noted in the pieces by

---

[3]Angell has often been pilloried by realists for having foolishly said that commercial interdependence made war impossible. He maintained that he never said that, and had argued only that war would be irrational. See Angell's post-World War I revision, *The Great Illusion, 1933* (New York: G. P. Putnam's Sons, 1933), pp. 267–270, and *After All: The Autobiography of Norman Angell* (New York: Farrar, Straus and Young, 1951), pp. 143–161.

Blainey and Waltz. Blainey argues that enthusiasts for the view that free trade, cultural exchange, and better communication foster peace mistook which was the cause and which was the effect when the phenomena coincided in the nineteenth century. Most notably, Waltz argues that interdependence actually fosters conflict rather than amity, because nations fear dependence and seek to overcome it. He cites data indicating that the level of interdependence among the great powers in the Cold War was actually lower than in the earlier part of the century, and counts it a good thing. Richard Rosecrance then argues that the specific *type* of interdependence is what matters, and the type that naturally fosters cooperation and peace (direct investment, as opposed to the portfolio investment of a century ago) has risen substantially in recent times.

—RKB

Money Is Not the Sinews of War, Although It Is Generally So Considered

Niccolò Machiavelli

Every one may begin a war at his pleasure, but cannot so finish it. A prince, therefore, before engaging in any enterprise should well measure his strength, and govern himself accordingly; and he must be very careful not to deceive himself in the estimate of his strength, which he will assuredly do if he measures it by his money, or by the situation of his country, or the good disposition of his people, unless he has at the same time an armed force of his own. For although the above things will increase his strength, yet they will not give it to him, and of themselves are nothing, and will be of no use without a devoted army. Neither abundance of money nor natural strength of the country will suffice, nor will the loyalty and good will of his subjects endure, for these cannot remain faithful to a prince who is incapable of defending them. Neither mountains nor lakes nor inaccessible places will present any difficulties to an enemy where there is a lack of brave defenders. And money alone, so far from being a means of defence, will only render a prince the more liable to being plundered. There cannot, therefore, be a more erroneous opinion than that money is the sinews of war. This was said by Quintus Curtius in the war between Antipater of Macedon and the king of Sparta, when he tells that want of money obliged the king of Sparta to come to battle, and that he was routed; whilst, if he could have delayed the battle a few days, the news of the death of Alexander would have reached Greece, and in that case he would have remained victor without fighting. But lacking money, and fearing the defection of his army, who were unpaid, he was obliged to try the fortune of battle, and was defeated; and in consequence of this, Quintus Curtius affirms money to be the sinews of war. This opinion is constantly quoted, and is acted upon by princes who are unwise enough to follow it; for relying upon it, they believe that plenty of money is all they require for their defence, never thinking that, if treasure were sufficient to insure victory, Darius would have vanquished Alexander, and the Greeks would have triumphed over the Romans; and, in our day, Duke Charles the Bold would have beaten the Swiss; and, quite recently, the Pope and the Florentines together would have had no difficulty in defeating Francesco Maria, nephew of Pope Julius II., in the war of Urbino. All that we have named were vanquished by those who regarded good troops, and not money, as the sinews of war. Amongst other objects of interest which Crœsus, king of Lydia, showed to Solon of

Niccolò Machiavelli, "Money Is Not the Sinews of War, Although It Is Generally So Considered." *Discourses on the First Ten Books of Titus Livius* (Modern Library, 1950). Christian E. Detmold, trans.

Athens, was his countless treasure; and to the question as to what he thought of his power, Solon replied, "that he did not consider him powerful on that account, because war was made with iron, and not with gold, and that some one might come who had more iron than he, and would take his gold from him." When after the death of Alexander the Great an immense swarm of Gauls descended into Greece, and thence into Asia, they sent ambassadors to the king of Macedon to treat with him for peace. The king, by way of showing his power, and to dazzle them, displayed before them great quantities of gold and silver; whereupon the ambassadors of the Gauls, who had already as good as signed the treaty, broke off all further negotiations, excited by the intense desire to possess themselves of all this gold; and thus the very treasure which the king had accumulated for his defence brought about his spoliation. The Venetians, a few years ago, having also their treasury full, lost their entire state without their money availing them in the least in their defence.

I maintain, then, contrary to the general opinion, that the sinews of war are not gold, but good soldiers; for gold alone will not procure good soldiers, but good soldiers will always procure gold. Had the Romans attempted to make their wars with gold instead of with iron, all the treasure of the world would not have sufficed them, considering the great enterprises they were engaged in, and the difficulties they had to encounter. But by making their wars with iron, they never suffered for the want of gold; for it was brought to them, even into their camp, by those who feared them. And if want of money forced the king of Sparta to try the fortune of battle, it was no more than what often happened from other causes; for we have seen that armies short of provisions, and having to starve or hazard a battle, will always prefer the latter as the more honorable course, and where fortune may yet in some way favor them. It has also often happened that a general, seeing that his opposing enemy is about to receive reinforcements, has preferred to run the risk of a battle at once, rather than wait until his enemy is reinforced and fight him then under greater disadvantage. We have seen also in the case of Asdrubal, when he was attacked upon the river Metaurus by Claudius Nero, together with another Roman Consul, that a general who has to choose between battle or flight will always prefer to fight, as then, even in the most doubtful case, there is still a chance of victory, whilst in flight his loss is certain anyhow.

There are, then, an infinity of reasons that may induce a general to give battle against his will, and the want of money may in some instances be one of them; but that is no reason why money should be deemed the sinews of war, which more than anything else will influence him to that course. I repeat it again, then, that it is not gold, but good soldiers, that insure success in war. Certainly money is a necessity, but a secondary one, which good soldiers will overcome; for it is as impossible that good soldiers should not be able to procure gold, as it is impossible for gold to procure good soldiers. History proves in a thousand cases what I maintain, notwithstanding that Pericles counselled the Athenians to make war with the entire Peloponnesus, demonstrating to them that by perseverance and the power of money they would be successful. And although it is true that the Athenians obtained some successes in that war, yet they succumbed in the end; and good counsels and the good soldiers of Sparta prevailed over the perseverance and money of the Athenians. But the testimony of Titus Livius upon this question is more direct than any other, where, in discussing whether Alexander the Great, had he come into Italy, would have vanquished the Romans, he points out that there are three things pre-eminently necessary to success in war,—plenty of good troops, sagacious commanders, and good fortune; and in examining afterwards whether the Romans or Alexander excelled most in these three points, he draws his conclusion without ever mentioning the subject of money. The Campanians, when requested by the Sidicians to take up arms in their behalf against the Samnites, may have measured their strength by their money, and not by their soldiers; for having resolved to grant the required assistance, they were constrained after two defeats to become tributary to the Romans to save themselves.

THE GREAT ILLUSION

Norman Angell

What are the fundamental motives that explain the present rivalry of armaments in Europe, notably the Anglo-German? Each nation pleads the need for defense; but this implies that someone is likely to attack, and has therefore a presumed interest in so doing. What are the motives which each State thus fears its neighbors may obey?

They are based on the universal assumption that a nation, in order to find outlets for expanding population and increasing industry, or simply to ensure the best conditions possible for its people, is necessarily pushed to territorial expansion and the exercise of political force against others (German naval competition is assumed to be the expression of the growing need of an expanding population for a larger place in the world, a need which will find a realization in the conquest of English Colonies or trade, unless these are defended); it is assumed, therefore, that a nation's relative prosperity is broadly determined by its political power; that nations being competing units, advantage, in the last resort, goes to the possessor of preponderant military force, the weaker going to the wall, as in the other forms of the struggle for life.

The author challenges this whole doctrine. He attempts to show that it belongs to a stage of development out of which we have passed; that the commerce and industry of a people no longer depend upon the expansion of its political frontiers; that a nation's political and economic frontiers do not now necessarily coincide; that military power is socially and economically futile, and can have no relation to the prosperity of the people exercising it; that it is impossible for one nation to seize by force the wealth or trade of another—to enrich itself by subjugating, or imposing its will by force on another; that, in short, war, even when victorious, can no longer achieve those aims for which peoples strive.

He establishes this apparent paradox, in so far as the economic problem is concerned, by showing that wealth in the economically civilized world is founded upon credit and commercial contract (these being the outgrowth of an economic interdependence due to the increasing division of labor and greatly developed communication). If credit and commercial contract are tampered with in an attempt at confiscation, the credit-dependent wealth is undermined, and its collapse involves that of the conqueror; so that if conquest is not to be self-injurious it must respect the enemy's property, in which case it becomes economically futile. Thus the wealth of conquered territory remains in the hands of the population of such territory. When Germany annexed Alsatia, no individual German secured a single mark's worth of Alsatian property as the spoils of war. Conquest in the modern world is a process of multiplying by x, and then obtaining the original figure by dividing by x. For a modern nation to add to its territory no

Norman Angell, *The Great Illusion: A Study of the Relation of Military Power to National Advantage,* 4th edition (New York: Putnam's, 1913), Synopsis.

more adds to the wealth of the people of such nation than it would add to the wealth of Londoners if the City of London were to annex the county of Hertford.

The author also shows that international finance has become so interdependent and so interwoven with trade and industry that the intangibility of an enemy's property extends to his trade. It results that political and military power can in reality do nothing for trade; the individual merchants and manufacturers of small nations, exercising no such power, compete successfully with those of the great. Swiss and Belgian merchants drive English from the British Colonial market; Norway has, relatively to population, a greater mercantile marine than Great Britain; the public credit (as a rough-and-ready indication, among others, of security and wealth) of small States possessing no political power often stands higher than that of the Great Powers of Europe, Belgian Three per Cents. standing at 96, and German at 82; Norwegian Three and a Half per Cents. at 102, and Russian Three and a Half per Cents. at 81.

The forces which have brought about the economic futility of military power have also rendered it futile as a means of enforcing a nation's moral ideals or imposing social institutions upon a conquered people. Germany could not turn Canada or Australia into German colonies—i. e., stamp out their language, law, literature, traditions, etc.—by "capturing" them. The necessary security in their material possessions enjoyed by the inhabitants of such conquered provinces, quick intercommunication by a cheap press, widely-read literature, enable even small communities to become articulate and effectively to defend their special social or moral possessions, even when military conquest has been complete. The fight for ideals can no longer take the form of fight between nations, because the lines of division on moral questions are within the nations themselves and intersect the political frontiers. There is no modern State which is completely Catholic or Protestant, or liberal or autocratic, or aristocratic or democratic, or socialist or individualist; the moral and spiritual struggles of the modern world go on between citizens of the same State in unconscious intellectual co-operation with corresponding groups in other States, not between the public powers of rival States.

This classification by strata involves necessarily a redirection of human pugnacity, based rather on the rivalry of classes and interests than on State divisions. War has no longer the justification that it makes for the survival of the fittest; it involves the survival of the less fit. The idea that the struggle between nations is a part of the evolutionary law of man's advance involves a profound misreading of the biological analogy.

The warlike nations do not inherit the earth; they represent the decaying human element. The diminishing role of physical force in all spheres of human activity carries with it profound psychological modifications.

These tendencies, mainly the outcome of purely modern conditions (e. g. rapidity of communication), have rendered the problems of modern international politics profoundly and essentially different from the ancient; yet our ideas are still dominated by the principles and axioms, images and terminology of the bygone days.

The author urges that these little-recognized facts may be utilized for the solution of the armament difficulty on at present untried lines—by such modification of opinion in Europe that much of the present motive to aggression will cease to be operative, and by thus diminishing the risk of attack, diminishing to the same extent the need for defense. He shows how such a political reformation is within the scope of practical politics, and the methods which should be employed to bring it about.

PARADISE IS A BAZAAR

Geoffrey Blainey

The mystery of why the nineteenth century enjoyed unusually long eras of peace did not puzzle some powerful minds. They believed that intellectual and commercial progress were soothing those human misunderstandings and grievances which had caused many earlier wars. The followers of this theory were usually democrats with an optimistic view of human nature. Though they had emerged earlier in France than in England they became most influential in the English-speaking world and their spiritual home was perhaps the industrial city of Manchester, which exported cotton goods and the philosophy of free trade to every corner of the globe.

Manchester's disciples believed that paradise was an international bazaar.[1] They favored the international flow of goods and ideas and the creation of institutions that channeled that flow and the abolition of institutions that blocked it. Nations, they argued, now grew richer through commerce than through conquest. Their welfare was now enhanced by rational discussion rather than by threats. The fortresses of peace were those institutions and inventions which promoted the exchange of ideas and commodities: parliaments, international conferences, the popular press, compulsory education, the public reading room, the penny postage stamp, railways, submarine telegraphs, three funnelled ocean liners, and the Manchester cotton exchange.

The long peace that followed the Battle of Waterloo was increasingly explained as the result of the international flow of commodities and ideas. 'It is something more than an accident which has turned the attention of mankind to international questions of every description in the same age that established freedom of commerce in the most enlightened nations.'[2] So wrote one of the early biographers of Richard Cobden, merchant of Manchester and citizen of the world. Variations of the same idea were shared by Sir Robert Peel, William Gladstone, John Stuart Mill, scores of economists and poets and men of letters, and by England's Prince Consort, Albert the Good. His sponsorship of the Great Exhibition in the new Crystal Palace in London in 1851 popularised the idea that a festival of peace and trade fair were synonymous. The Crystal Palace was perhaps the world's first peace festival.

In that palace of glass and iron the locomotives and telegraphic equipment were admired not only as mechanical wonders; they were also messengers of peace and instruments of unity. The telegraph cable laid across the English Channel in 1850 had

[1] The Manchester creed: in selecting this name my main reasons were Manchester's reputation as a symbol of free trade and the popularity of the creed among free-trade economists.

[2] 'It is something'. Apjohn, p. 234.

been welcomed as an underwater cord of friendship. The splicing of the cable that snaked beneath the Atlantic in 1858 was another celebration of brotherhood, and the first message tapped across the seabed was a proclamation of peace: 'Europe and America are united by telegraphic communication. Glory to God in the Highest, On Earth Peace, Goodwill towards Men.'[3] That cable of peace was soon snapped, and so was unable to convey the news in the following year that France and Austria were at war, or the news in 1861 that the United States was split by war.

Henry Thomas Buckle was one of many influential prophets of the idea that telegraphs and railways and steamships were powerfully promoting peace. Buckle was a wealthy young London bachelor who in the 1850s studied beneath the skylight of his great London library, writing in powerful prose a vast survey of the influences which, to his mind, were civilising Europe. A brilliant chess player who had competed with Europe's champions at the palace of peace, Buckle thought human affairs obeyed rules that were almost as clear cut as the rules of chess; and those rules permeated his writings. The first volume of the *History of Civilisation in England* appeared in 1857, the second volume in 1861, and they were devoured by thousands of English readers, published in French, Spanish, German, Hungarian and Hebrew editions, and translated four times into Russian.[4]

One of Buckle's themes was the decline of the warlike spirit in western Europe. As a freethinker he attributed that decline not to moral influences but to the progress of knowledge and intellectual activity. The invention of gunpowder had made soldiering the specialist activity of the few rather than the occasional activity of the many, thereby releasing talent for peaceful pursuits. Similarly Adam Smith's *The Wealth of Nations,* 'probably the most important book that has ever been written',[5] had perceived and popularised the idea that a nation gained most when its commercial policy enriched rather than impoverished its neighbours: free trade had replaced war and aggressive mercantilism as the road to commercial prosperity. Buckle argued that the new commercial spirit was making nations depend on one another whereas the old spirit had made them fight one another.

Just as commerce now linked nations, so the steamship and railway linked peoples: 'the greater the contact', argued Buckle, 'the greater the respect'. Frenchmen and Englishmen had curbed their national prejudices because they had done more than railways and steamships to increase their friendship. As he affirmed in his clear rolling prose: 'every new railroad which is laid down, and every fresh steamer which crosses the Channel, are additional guarantees for the preservation of that long and unbroken peace which, during forty years, has knit together the fortunes and the interests of the two most civilised nations of the earth'.[6] Buckle thought foreign travel was the greatest of all educations as well as a spur to peace; and it was while he was travelling near Damascus in 1862 that he caught the typhoid fever which ended his life.

---

[3] The Atlantic telegraph: Cruikshank, p. 72.
[4] Buckle's career: *D.N.B.,* III 208–11.
[5] Praise of Adam Smith: Buckle, I, 214.
[6] 'Every new railroad': ibid., p. 223.

Many readers must have thought that the outbreak of the Crimean War rather dinted Buckle's argument that the warlike spirit was declining in Europe. Buckle was composing that chapter of his book when war was raging in the Crimea, and he foresaw the criticism and met it head on:

> For the peculiarity of the great contest in which we are engaged is, that it was produced, not by the conflicting interests of civilised countries, but by a rupture between Russia and Turkey, the two most barbarous monarchies now remaining in Europe. This is a very significant fact. It is highly characteristic of the actual condition of society, that a peace of unexampled length should have been broken, not, as former peaces were broken, by a quarrel between two civilised nations, but by the encroachments of the uncivilised Russians on the still more uncivilised Turks.[7]

Buckle still had to explain why France and England, his heroes of civilisation, had exultantly joined in the barbarians' war. He explained that simply; the departure of their armies to the distant Crimea was a sign of their civilisation. France and England, he wrote, 'have drawn the sword, not for selfish purposes, but to protect the civilised world against the incursions of a barbarous foe'.

The shattering civil war which began in the United States in the last year of Buckle's life should have been a blow to his theory. On the contrary it seems to have heartened his supporters. They interpreted that war as another crusade against barbarism and the barbaric practice of slavery. At the end of that four-years' war Professor J. E. Cairnes, an Irish economist, wrote a powerful article reaffirming the idea that 'all the leading currents of modern civilisation' were running steadily in the direction of peace.[8] He thought that the way in which the North craved the sympathy of foreign nations during the war was a sign of the increasing force of public opinion in international affairs. He believed that the enlightened public opinion was coming mainly from the expansion of free commerce, the railways and steamships, and the study of modern languages. Henry Thomas Buckle would have sympathized with the emphasis on modern languages; he spoke nineteen.

The idea that ignorance and misunderstanding were the seeds of war inspired the hope that an international language would nourish peace—so long as the chosen language was purged of nationalism. In 1880 a south German priest, J. M. Schleyer, published a neutral language of his own manufacture and called it Volapük. It spread with the speed of rumour to almost every civilised land, claiming one million students within a decade. To Paris in 1889 came the delegates of 283 Volapük societies, and even the waiters at the dining tables of the congress could translate the following manifesto into Volapük:

> I love all my fellow-creatures of the whole world, especially those cultivated ones who believe in Volapük as one of the greatest means of nation-binding.[9]

---

[7]For the peculiarity of the great contest', ibid., p. 195.
[8]'All the leading currents'. Cairnes, p. 123.
[9]Volapük: Henry Sweet, *Encyclopaedia Britannica, 1910–11,* XXVIII 178.

The rival nation-binding language of Esperanto was then two years old. Its inventor, a Russian physician named Zamenhof, had come from a feuding region where Polish, German, Yiddish, and Russian were all spoken; and he trusted that his Esperanto would ameliorate dissensions between races. Before long, however, many supporters of Esperanto and Volapük were feuding. Even the disciples of Volapük tongue discovered that their universal language did not necessarily lead to harmony. They split after a quarrel about grammar.

In the generation before the First World War there were abundant warnings that the Manchester gospel was not infallible. The very instruments of peace—railways and international canals and steamships and bills of lading—were conspicuous in the background to some wars. The Suez Canal was a marvelous artery of international exchange, but for that reason England and France were intensely interested in controlling it; without the canal it is doubtful if there would have been an Egyptian War in 1882. The Trans-Siberian railway was a great feat of construction and a powerful link between Europe and Asia, but without that railway it is doubtful whether there could have been a Russo-Japanese war in 1904–5. This is not to argue that these new arteries of commerce *caused* those two wars; but certainly they illustrated the hazards of assuming that whatever drew nations together was an instrument of peace. The Manchester creed, to many of its adherents, was a dogma; and so contrary evidence was dismissed. . . .

A war lasting four years and involving nearly all the 'civilised' nations of the world contradicted all the assumptions of the crusaders. Admittedly most had envisaged that the movement towards international peace could meet occasional setbacks. Wars against barbarians and autocrats might have to be fought before the millennium arrived. Indeed, if the First World War had been fought by Britain, France and Germany on the one hand and Russia and Serbia on the other, the belief in the millennium might have been less shaken. Such a war could have seemed a replay of the Crimean or American Civil War and thus been interpreted as a war against the barbarians. It was, however, more difficult for learned Frenchmen, Englishmen and Russians to interpret the war against Germany as simply a war against the ignorant and uncivilised: for Germany in 1914 was the homeland of Albert Einstein, Max Planck, Max Weber and a galaxy of great contemporary intellects. On the other hand German liberals at least had the intellectual satisfaction that the Tsar of Russia was one enemy they were fighting; but another of their enemies was France which in some eyes, was the lamp of civilisation.

There was a peculiar irony in the war which divided Europe. If the length and bitterness of the war had been foreseen, the efforts to preserve the peace in 1914 would have been far more vigorous and might have even succeeded. But one of the reasons why so many national leaders and followers in 1914 could not imagine a long war was their faith in the steady flow of that civilising stream that had seemed to widen during the peaceful nineteenth century. The Great War of 1914 would be short, it was widely believed, partly because civilised opinion would rebel against the war if it began to create chaos. The willingness of hundreds of millions of Europeans to tolerate chaos, slaughter and an atmosphere of hatred was an additional surprise to those who had faith in civilisation.

Despite the shock of a world war, versions of the Manchester creed survived. Indeed that creed may have been partly responsible for the outbreak of another world war only two decades later. The military revival of Germany had complicated causes, but in many of those causes one can detect the mark of Manchester.

Germany could not have revived, militarily, without the willing or reluctant sanction of some of the victors of the First World War. In particular the United States and Britain allowed Germany to revive. As they were themselves protected by ocean they tended to be careless of threats within Europe; as they were democracies they tended to have trouble spending adequately on defense in years of peace, for other calls on revenue were more persuasive. A secure island democracy is of course the haven of the Manchester creed; its optimism about human nature and distrust of excessive force reflect the security of its home environment.

One sign of optimism in England and the United States was the widespread belief that another world war was virtually impossible. The idea of a war to end war had been one of the popular slogans in those democracies from 1914 to 1918, and the idea lived long after the slogan dissolved in the mouths of orators and faded on recruiting billboards. The prediction that the world would not again experience a war of such magnitude aided the neglect of armaments among some of the main victors of the previous war. It was probably in England too that there was the deepest faith that the League of Nations would become an efficient substitute for the use of force in international affairs; this was not surprising, for the League in a sense was a descendant of the House of Commons, the Manchester Cotton Exchange, and the old crusade for free trade. In England public opinion, more than official opinion, tended to expect more of the League of Nations than it was capable of giving. That misplaced faith indirectly helped the Germans to recover their bargaining position in Europe, for in crises the League of Nations proved to be powerless. Likewise in England the widespread mistrust of armaments in the 1920s was more than the normal reaction after a major war; it mirrored the belief that the armaments race had been a major cause of the previous war. The Great War, it was argued, had come through misunderstanding; it had been an unwanted war. This interpretation of 1914, to my mind quite invalid, matched the optimistic tenets of the Manchester creed. And since it was widely believed in England it affected future events. It also was a restraint on the English government's ability to match German rearming for part of the 1930s: to enter again into an armaments race was to endanger peace, it was believed, even more than to neglect armaments. The ways in which the Manchester creed affected Europe between the two world wars represents only one strand in the rope which raised Germany from her enforced meekness of 1919 to her might of 1939, but it was still an important strand.

In the nineteenth century the Manchester creed in all its hues was favored more by public opinion than by the reigning ministry in England. On the eve of the Second World War, however, it was powerful in Whitehall. Manchester had taken office, even if it was disguised as a former mayor of Birmingham. Neville Chamberlain, England's prime minister from 1937 to 1940, is now often seen as a naïve individualist, an eccentric out of step with British traditions, but he represented one of the most influential traditions of British thought. Though he was re-arming Britain he did not trust primarily in arms. He saw, not an evil world which reacted only to force or threats, but a world of rational men who reacted to goodwill and responded to discussion.[10] He believed that most modern wars were the result of misunderstandings or of grievances. Accordingly

---

[10]Chamberlain's faith in rational discussion: Taylor, *The Origins of the Second World War,* pp. 172, 217.

there were rational remedies for the causes of war. As he believed that Germany suffered unfairly from the Versailles Peace of 1919, he was prepared to make concessions in the belief that they would preserve the peace. He was eager to hurry to Germany—not summon Germany to England—in the belief that the conference table was the only sane field of battle. He believed Hitler would respond to rational discussion and to appeasement; so did many Englishmen in 1938.

. . . The optimistic theory of peace is still widespread. Within the United States it pervades much of the criticism of the war in Vietnam. Within the western world it is visible in the school of thought which expects quick results from the fostering of friendly contacts with Russia and China. It pervades many of the plans by which richer countries aid poorer countries. It permeates a host of movements and ventures ranging from the Olympic Games, Rotary and Telstar to international tourism and peace organizations. Irrespective of whether the creed rests on sound or false premises of human behaviour, it still influences international relations. In the short term it is a civilising influence. Whether it actually promotes peace or war, however, is open to debate. If it is based on false generalizations about the causes of war and the causes of peace its influence in promoting peace is likely to be limited and indeed haphazard. Moreover, if it is inspired by a strong desire for peace, but gnaws at the skin rather than the core of international relations, the results will be meagre.

Something is missing in that theory of peace which was shaped and popularised by so many gifted men in the nineteenth century. One may suggest that, like many other explanations of war and peace, it relied much on coincidence. Those living in the three generations after Waterloo had wondered at the long peace and sought explanations in events that were happening simultaneously.[11] They noticed that international peace coincided with industrialism, steam engines, foreign travel, freer and stronger commerce and advancing knowledge. As they saw specific ways in which these changes could further peace, they concluded that the coincidence was causal. Their explanation, however, was based on one example or one period of peace. They ignored the earlier if shorter periods of peace experience by a Europe which had no steam trains, few factories, widespread ignorance and restricted commerce. Their explanation of the cluster of European wars in the period 1848–71 was also shaky. These wars were relatively short, and to their mind the shortness of most wars in the century after Waterloo was evidence that Europe's warlike spirit was ebbing. On the contrary one can argue that most of these wars were shortened not by civilising restraints but by unusual political conditions and by new technological factors which the philosophers of peace did not closely investigate. If neglect of war led them into error their attitude was nonetheless a vital reaction to those studies of war which neglected peace.

Most of the changes which were hailed as causes of peace in the nineteenth century were probably more the effects of peace. The ease with which ideas, people and commodities flowed across international borders was very much an effect of peace though in turn the flow may have aided peace. Similarly the optimistic assessment of man's nature and the belief that civilisation was triumphing was aided by the relative peacefulness

---

[11]Likewise one explanation of the relative peace in Europe since 1945—the influence of nuclear weapons—seems to rely often on coincidence.

of the nineteenth century. That optimism would not have been so flourishing if wars had been longer and more devastating. In one sense the Manchester theory of peace was like the mountebank's diagnosis that shepherds were healthy simply because they had ruddy cheeks: therefore the cure for a sick shepherd was to inflame his cheeks.

It is difficult to find evidence that closer contacts between nations promoted peace. Swift communications which drew nations together did not necessarily promote peace: it is indisputable that during the last three centuries most wars have been fought by neighbouring countries—not countries which are far apart. The frequency of civil wars shatters the simple idea that people who have much in common will remain at peace. Even the strain of idealism which characterized most versions of the Manchester creed cannot easily be identified as an influence favoring peace, perhaps because in practice the creed is not idealistic. Thus Neville Chamberlain's concessions to Germany in 1938 were no doubt influenced partly by Germany's increasing strength: moreover his concessions were not so idealistic because they were mainly at the expense of Czechoslovakia's independence.

The conclusion seems unmistakable: the Manchester creed cannot be a vital part of a theory of war and peace. One cannot even be sure whether those influences which it emphasizes actually have promoted peace more than war.

Kenneth Boulding, an Anglo-American economist who brilliantly builds bridges across the chasms that divide regions of knowledge, made one observation which indirectly illuminates the dilemma of the Manchester brotherhood. 'Threat systems', wrote Boulding, 'are the basis of politics as exchange systems are the basis of economics.'[12] The Manchester idealists emphasized exchange and minimized the importance of threats. Believing that mankind contained much more good than evil, they thought that threats were becoming unnecessary in a world which seemed increasingly civilised. Indeed they thought that threats were the tyrannical hallmark of an old order which was crumbling. They despised the open or veiled threat as the weapon of their enemies. Thus they opposed czars and dictators who relied visibly on force and threats. For the same reason they opposed slavery, serfdom, militarism and harsh penal codes. And they mostly opposed the idea of hell, for hell was a threat.

They did not realize, nor perhaps do we, that a democratic country depends on threats and force, even if they are more veiled and more intermittent than in an autocracy. They did not realize that intellectual and commercial liberty were most assured in those two nations—Britain and the United States—which were economically strong and protected by ocean from the threat of foreign invasion. The preference of Anglo-Saxon nations for democratic forms of government had owed much to the military security which the ocean provided. On the rare occasions in the last two centuries when Britain was threatened by a powerful enemy it abandoned temporarily many of its democratic procedures; thus in the Second World War Churchill and the war cabinet probably held as much power as an autocracy of the eighteenth century. Mistakenly the Manchester creed believed that international affairs would soon repeat effortlessly the achievements visible in the internal affairs of a few favored lands. . . .

---

[12]Threat systems'. Boulding, *Beyond Economics*, p. 105.

REFERENCES

Apjohn, Lewis, *Richard Cobden and the Free Traders* (London, c. 1880).
Boulding, Kenneth, *Conflict and Defense* (New York, 1962).
————. *Beyond Economics: essays on society, religion and ethics* (Ann Arbor, 1968).
Buckle, Henry Thomas, *History of Civilization in England,* 3 vols. (London, 1885).
Cairnes, J. E., 'International Law'. *Fortnightly Review* (November 1865).
Cruikshank, R. J., *Roaring Century* (London, 1946).
Dictionary of National Biography, The, 27 vols. (Oxford, 1968).
Taylor, A. J. P., 'Otto Bismarck', *Encyclopaedia Britannica,* 1962, III 659–68.
————. *The Struggle for Mastery in Europe 1848–1918* (Oxford, 1954).
————. *The Origins of the Second World War* (London, 1964).

IMPERIALISM, THE HIGHEST STAGE OF CAPITALISM

V. I. Lenin

THE EXPORT OF CAPITAL

Under the old capitalism, when free competition prevailed, the export of goods was the most typical feature. Under modern capitalism, when monopolies prevail, the export of capital has become the typical feature.

Capitalism is commodity production at the highest stage of development, when labour power itself becomes a commodity. The growth of internal exchange, and particularly of international exchange, is the characteristic distinguishing feature of capitalism. The uneven and spasmodic character of the development of individual enterprises, of individual branches of industry and individual countries, is inevitable under the capitalist system. England became a capitalist country before any other, and in the middle of the nineteenth century, having adopted free trade, claimed to be the "workshop of the world," the great purveyor of manufactured goods to all countries, which in exchange were to keep her supplied with raw materials. But in the last quarter of the nineteenth century, *this* monopoly was already undermined. Other countries, protecting themselves by tariff walls, had developed into independent capitalist states. On the threshold of the twentieth century, we see a new type of monopoly coming into existence. Firstly, there are monopolist capitalist combines in all advanced capitalist countries; secondly, a few rich countries, in which the accumulation of capital reaches gigantic proportions, occupy a monopolist position. An enormous "superabundance of capital" has accumulated in the advanced countries.

It goes without saying that if capitalism could develop agriculture, which today lags far behind industry everywhere, if it could raise the standard of living of the masses, who are everywhere still poverty-stricken and underfed, in spite of the amazing advance in technical knowledge, there could be no talk of a superabundance of capital. This "argument" the petty-bourgeois critics of capitalism advance on every occasion. But if capitalism did these things it would not be capitalism; for uneven development and wretched conditions of the masses are fundamental and inevitable conditions and premises of this mode of production. As long as capitalism remains what it is, surplus capital will never be utilized for the purpose of raising the standard of living of the masses in a given country, for this would mean a decline in profits for the capitalists; it will be used for the purpose of increasing those profits by exporting capital abroad to the backward countries. In these backward countries profits are usually high, for capital is scarce, the price of land is relatively low, wages are low, raw materials are cheap. The possibility of exporting capital is created by the fact that numerous backward countries have been drawn into international capitalist intercourse; main railways have either been built or are being built there; the elementary conditions for industrial development have been created, etc. The necessity for exporting capital arises from the fact that in a few countries capitalism has become "over-ripe" and (owing to the backward state of agriculture and the impoverished state of the masses) capital cannot find "profitable" investment. . . .

THE DIVISION OF THE WORLD AMONG CAPITALIST COMBINES

Monopolist capitalist combines—cartels, syndicates, trusts—divide among themselves, first of all, the whole internal market of a country, and impose their control, more or less completely, upon the industry of that country. But under capitalism the home market is inevitably bound up with the foreign market. Capitalism long ago created a world market. As the export of capital increased, and as the foreign and colonial relations and the "spheres of influence" of the big monopolist combines expanded, things "naturally" gravitated towards an international agreement among these combines, and towards the formation of international cartels. . . .

International cartels show to what point capitalist monopolies have developed, and they *reveal the object* of the struggle between the various capitalist groups. This last circumstance is the most important; it alone shows us the historic-economic significance of events; for the *forms* of the struggle may and do constantly change in accordance with varying, relatively particular, and temporary causes, but the *essence* of the struggle, its class *content, cannot* change while classes exist. It is easy to understand, for example, that it is in the interests of the German bourgeoisie, whose theoretical arguments have now been adopted by Kautsky (we will deal with this later), to obscure the *content* of the present economic struggle (the division of the world) and to emphasise this or that *form* of the struggle. Kautsky makes the same mistake. Of course, we have in mind not only the German bourgeoisie, but the bourgeoisie all over the world. The capitalists divide the world, not out of any particular malice, but because the degree of concentration which has been reached forces them to adopt this method in order to get profits. And they divide it in proportion to "capital," in proportion to "strength," because there cannot be any other system of division under commodity production and capitalism. But strength varies with the degree of economic and political development. In order to understand what takes place, it is necessary to know what questions are settled by this change of forces. The question as to whether these changes are "purely" economic or *non*-economic (*e.g.,* military) is a secondary one, which does not in the least affect the fundamental view on the latest epoch of capitalism. To substitute for the question of the *content* of the struggle and agreements between capitalist combines the question of the *form* of these struggles and agreements (today peaceful, tomorrow war-like, the next day war-like again) is to sink to the role of a sophist.

The epoch of modern capitalism shows us that certain relations are established between capitalist alliances, *based* on the economic division of the world; while parallel with this fact and in connection with it, certain relations are established between political alliances, between states, on the basis of the territorial division of the world, of the struggle for colonies, of the "struggle for economic territory."

THE DIVISION OF THE WORLD AMONG THE GREAT POWERS

In his book, *The Territorial Development of the European Colonies,* A. Supan, the geographer, gives the following brief summary of this development at the end of the nineteenth century:

Percentage of Territories Belonging to the European Colonial Powers (Including United States)		
	1876	*1900*	*Increase or Decrease*
Africa	10.8	90.4	+79.6
Polynesia	56.8	98.9	+42.1
Asia	51.5	56.6	+5.1
Australia	100.0	100.0	—
America	27.5	27.2	−0.3

"The characteristic feature of this period," he concludes, "is therefore, the division of Africa and Polynesia."

As there are no unoccupied territories—that is, territories that do not belong to any state—in Asia and America, Mr. Supan's conclusion must be carried further, and we must say that the characteristic feature of this period is the final partition of the globe—not in the sense that a *new* partition is impossible—on the contrary, new partitions are possible and inevitable—but in the sense that the colonial policy of the capitalist countries has *completed* the seizure of the unoccupied territories on our planet. For the first time the world is completely divided up, so that in the future *only* redivision is possible; territories can only pass from one "owner" to another, instead of passing as unowned territory to an "owner."

Hence, we are passing through a peculiar period of world colonial policy, which is closely associated with the "latest stage in the development of capitalism," with finance capital. For this reason, it is essential first of all to deal in detail with the facts, in order to ascertain exactly what distinguishes this period from those preceding it, and what the present situation is. In the first place, two questions of fact arise here. Is an intensification of colonial policy, an intensification of the struggle for colonies, observed precisely in this period of finance capital? And how, in this respect, is the world divided at the present time?

The American writer, Morris, in his book on the history of colonization[1] has made an attempt to compile data on the colonial possessions of Great Britain, France and Germany during different periods of the nineteenth century. The following is a brief summary of the results he has obtained:

⚮ **Colonial Possessions**						
(Million square miles and million inhabitants)						
	Great Britain		*France*		*Germany*	
	Area	*Pop.*	*Area*	*Pop.*	*Area*	*Pop.*
1815–30	?	126.4	0.02	0.5	—	—
1860	2.5	145.1	0.2	3.4	—	—
1880	7.7	267.9	0.7	7.5	—	—
1899	9.3	309.0	3.7	56.4	1.0	14.7

For Great Britain, the period of the enormous expansion of colonial conquests is that between 1860 and 1880, and it was also very considerable in the last twenty years of the nineteenth century. For France and Germany this period falls precisely in these last twenty years. We saw above that the apex of premonopoly capitalist development, of capitalism in which free competition was predominant, was reached in the 'sixties and 'seventies of the last century. We now see that it is *precisely after that period* that the "boom" in colonial annexations begins, and that the struggle for the territorial division of the world becomes extraordinarily keen. It is beyond doubt, therefore, that capitalism's transition to the stage of monopoly capitalism, to finance capital, is *bound up* with the intensification of the struggle for the partition of the world.

Hobson, in his work on imperialism, marks the years 1884–1900 as the period of the intensification of the colonial "expansion" of the chief European states. According to his estimate, Great Britain during these years acquired 3,700,000 square miles of territory with a population of 57,000,000; France acquired 3,600,000 square miles with a population of 16,700,000; Belgium 900,000 square miles with 30,000,000 inhabitants; Portugal 800,000 square miles with 9,000,000 inhabitants. The quest for colonies by all the capitalist states at the end of the nineteenth century and particularly since the 1880's is a commonly known fact in the history of diplomacy and of foreign affairs.

When free competition in Great Britain was at its zenith, *i.e.,* between 1840 and 1860, the leading British bourgeois politicians were opposed to colonial policy and were of the opinion that the liberation of the colonies and their complete separation from Britain was inevitable and desirable. M. Beer, in an article, "Modern British Imperialism,"[2] published in 1898, shows that in 1852, Disraeli, a statesman generally inclined towards imperialism, declared: "The colonies are millstones round our necks." But at the end of the nineteenth century the heroes of the hour in England were Cecil

---

[1] Henry C. Morris, *The History of Colonization,* New York, 1900, II, p. 88; I, pp. 304, 419.
[2] *Die Neue Zeit,* XVI, I, 1898, p. 302.

Rhodes and Joseph Chamberlain, open advocates of imperialism, who applied the imperialist policy in the most cynical manner.

It is not without interest to observe that even at the time these leading British bourgeois politicians fully appreciated the connection between what might be called the purely economic and the politico-social roots of modern imperialism. Chamberlain advocated imperialism by calling it a "true, wise and economical policy," and he pointed particularly to the German, American and Belgian competition which Great Britain was encountering in the world market. Salvation lies in monopolies, said the capitalists as they formed cartels, syndicates and trusts. Salvation lies in monopolies, echoed the political leaders of the bourgeoisie, hastening to appropriate the parts of the world not yet shared out. The journalist, Stead, relates the following remarks uttered by his close friend Cecil Rhodes, in 1895, regarding his imperialist ideas:

> I was in the East End of London yesterday and attended a meeting of the unemployed. I listened to the wild speeches, which were just a cry for 'bread,' 'bread,' 'bread,' and on my way home I pondered over the scene and I became more than ever convinced of the importance of imperialism. . . . My cherished idea is a solution for the social problem, *i.e.,* in order to save the 40,000,000 inhabitants of the United Kingdom from a bloody civil war, we colonial statesmen must acquire new lands to settle the surplus population, to provide new markets for the goods produced by them in the factories and mines. The Empire, as I have always said, is a bread and butter question. If you want to avoid civil war, you must become imperialists. . . .[3]

IMPERIALISM AS A SPECIAL STAGE OF CAPITALISM

We must now try to sum up and put together what has been said above on the subject of imperialism. Imperialism emerged as the development and direct continuation of the fundamental attributes of capitalism in general. But capitalism only became capitalist imperialism at a definite and very high stage of its development, when certain of its fundamental attributes began to be transformed into their opposites, when the features of a period of transition from capitalism to a higher social and economic system began to take shape and reveal themselves all along the line. Economically, the main thing in this process is the substitution of capitalist monopolies for capitalist free competition. Free competition is the fundamental attribute of capitalism, and of commodity production generally. Monopoly is exactly the opposite of free competition; but we have seen the latter being transformed into monopoly before our very eyes, creating large-scale industry and eliminating small industry, replacing large-scale industry by still larger-scale industry, finally leading to such a concentration of production and capital that monopoly has been and is the result: cartels, syndicates and trusts, and merging with them, the capital of a dozen or so banks manipulating thousands of millions. At the same time monopoly, which has grown out of free competition, does not abolish the latter, but exists over it and alongside of it, and thereby gives rise to a number of very acute, intense

---

[3]*Ibid.,* p. 304.

antagonisms, friction and conflicts. Monopoly is the transition from capitalism to a higher system.

If it were necessary to give the briefest possible definition of imperialism we should have to say that imperialism is the monopoly stage of capitalism. Such a definition would include what is most important, for, on the one hand, finance capital is the bank capital of a few big monopolist banks, merged with the capital of the monopolist combines of manufacturers; and, on the other hand, the division of the world is the transition from a colonial policy which has extended without hindrance to territories unoccupied by any capitalist power, to a colonial policy of monopolistic possession of the territory of the world which has been completely divided up.

But very brief definitions, although convenient, for they sum up the main points, are nevertheless inadequate, because very important features of the phenomenon that has to be defined have to be especially deduced. And so, without forgetting the conditional and relative value of all definitions, which can never include all the concatenations of a phenomenon in its complete development, we must give a definition of imperialism that will embrace the following five essential features:

1) The concentration of production and capital developed to such a high stage that it created monopolies which play a decisive role in economic life.
2) The merging of bank capital with industrial capital, and the creation, on the basis of this "finance capital," of a "financial oligarchy."
3) The export of capital, which has become extremely important, as distinguished from the export of commodities.
4) The formation of international capitalist monopolies which share the world among themselves.
5) The territorial division of the whole world among the greatest capitalist powers is completed. . . .

Finance capital and the trusts are increasing instead of diminishing the differences in the rate of development of the various parts of world economy. When the relation of forces is changed, how else, *under capitalism,* can the solution of contradictions be found, except by resorting to *violence?* Railway statistics provide remarkably exact data on the different rates of development of capitalism and finance capital in world economy. In the last decades of imperialist development, the total length of railways has changed as follows:

Railways *(thousand kilometers)*

	1890	1913	Increase
Europe	224	346	122
U.S.A.	268	411	143
Colonies (total)	82 ⎱	210 ⎱	128 ⎱
Independent and semi-dependent states of Asia and America	43 ⎰ 125	137 ⎰ 347	94 ⎰ 222
Total	617	1,104	

Thus, the development of railways has been more rapid in the colonies and in the independent (and semi-dependent) states of Asia and America. Here, as we know, the finance capital of the four or five biggest capitalist states reigns undisputed. Two hundred thousand kilometres of new railways in the colonies and in the other countries of Asia and America represent more than 40,000,000,000 marks in capital, newly invested on particularly advantageous terms, with special guarantees of a good return and with profitable orders for steel works, etc., etc.

Capitalism is growing with the greatest rapidity in the colonies and in overseas countries. Among the latter, *new* imperialist powers are emerging (*e.g.,* Japan). The struggle of world imperialism is becoming more acute. The tribute levied by finance capital on the most profitable colonial and overseas enterprises is increasing. In sharing out this "booty," an exceptionally large part goes to countries which, as far as the development of productive forces is concerned, do not always stand at the top of the list. In the case of the biggest countries, considered with their colonies, the total length of railways was as follows (in thousands of kilometres):

	1890	*1913*	*Increase*
U.S.A.	268	413	145
British Empire	107	208	101
Russia	32	78	46
Germany	43	68	25
France	41	63	22
	——	——	——
Total	491	830	339

Thus, about 80 per cent of the total existing railways are concentrated in the hands of the five Great Powers. But the concentration of the *ownership* of these railways of finance capital, is much greater still: French and English millionaires, for example, own an enormous amount of stocks and bonds in American, Russian and other railways.

Thanks to her colonies, Great Britain has increased the length of "her" railways by 100,000 kilometres, four times as much as Germany. And yet, it is well known that the development of productive forces in Germany, and especially the development of the coal and iron industries, has been much more rapid during this period than in England—not to mention France and Russia. In 1892, Germany produced 4,900,000 tons of pig iron and Great Britain produced 6,800,000 tons; in 1912 Germany produced 17,600,000 tons and Great Britain 9,000,000 tons. Germany, therefore, had an overwhelming superiority over England in this respect. We ask, is there *under capitalism* any means of removing the disparity between the development of productive forces and the accumulation of capital on the one side, and the division of colonies and "spheres of influence" for finance capital on the other side—other than by resorting to war?

IMPERIALISM AND
CAPITALISM

Joseph Schumpeter

Our analysis of the historical evidence has shown, first, the unquestionable fact that "objectless" tendencies toward forcible expansion, without definite, utilitarian limits—that is, non-rational and irrational, purely instinctual inclinations toward war and conquest—play a very large role in the history of mankind. It may sound paradoxical, but numberless wars—perhaps the majority of all wars—have been waged without adequate "reason"—not so much from the moral viewpoint as from that of reasoned and reasonable interest. The most herculean efforts of the nations, in other words, have faded into the empty air. Our analysis, in the second place, provides an explanation for this drive to action, this will to war—a theory by no means exhausted by mere references to the "urge" or an "instinct." The explanation lies, instead, in the vital needs of situations that molded peoples and classes into warriors—if they wanted to avoid extinction—and in the fact that psychological dispositions and social structures acquired in the dim past in such situations, once firmly established, tend to maintain themselves and to continue in effect long after they have lost their meaning and their life-preserving function. Our analysis, in the third place, has shown the existence of subsidiary factors that facilitate the survival of such dispositions and structures—factors that may be divided into two groups. The orientation toward war is mainly fostered by the domestic interests of ruling classes, but also by the influence of all those who stand to gain individually from war policy, whether economically or socially. Both groups of factors are generally overgrown by elements of an altogether different character, not only in terms of political phraseology, but also of psychological motivation. Imperialisms differ greatly in detail, but they all have at least these traits in common, turning them into a single phenomenon in the field of sociology, as we noted in the introduction.

Imperialism thus is atavistic in character. It falls into that large group of surviving features from earlier ages that play such an important part in every concrete social situation. In other words, it is an element that stems from the living conditions, not of the present, but of the past—or, put in terms of the economic interpretation of history, from past rather than present relations of production. It is an atavism in the social structure, in individual, psychological habits of emotional reaction. Since the vital needs that created it have passed away for good, it too must gradually disappear, even though every warlike involvement, no matter how non-imperialist in character, tends to revive it. It tends to disappear as a structural element because the structure that brought it to the

Joseph Schumpeter, "Imperialism and Capitalism," in *Imperialism/Social Classes: Two Essays by Joseph Schumpeter,* Heinz Norden, trans. (Cleveland: World, 1968), originally published in 1919.

fore goes into a decline, giving way, in the course of social development, to other structures that have no room for it and eliminate the power factors that supported it. It tends to disappear as an element of habitual emotional reaction, because of the progressive rationalization of life and mind, a process in which old functional needs are absorbed by new tasks, in which heretofore military energies are functionally modified. If our theory is correct, cases of imperialism should decline in intensity the later they occur in the history of a people and of a culture. Our most recent examples of unmistakable, clear-cut imperialism are the absolute monarchies of the eighteenth century. They are unmistakably "more civilized" than their predecessors.

It is from absolute autocracy that the present age has taken over what imperialist tendencies it displays. And the imperialism of absolute autocracy flourished before the Industrial Revolution that created the modern world, or rather, before the consequences of that revolution began to be felt in all their aspects. These two statements are primarily meant in a historical sense, and as such they are no more than self-evident. We shall nevertheless try, within the framework of our theory, to define the significance of capitalism for our phenomenon and to examine the relationship between present-day imperialist tendencies and the autocratic imperialism of the eighteenth century.

The flood tide that burst the dams in the Industrial Revolution had its sources, of course, back in the Middle Ages. But capitalism began to shape society and impress its stamp on every page of social history only with the second half of the eighteenth century. Before that time there had been only islands of capitalist economy imbedded in an ocean of village and urban economy. True, certain political influences emanated from these islands, but they were able to assert themselves only indirectly. Not until the process we term the Industrial Revolution did the working masses, led by the entrepreneur, overcome the bonds of older life-forms—the environment of peasantry, guild, and aristocracy. The causal connection was this: a transformation in the basic economic factors (which need not detain us here) created the objective opportunity for the production of commodities, for large-scale industry, working for a market of customers whose individual identities were unknown, operating solely with a view to maximum financial profit. It was this opportunity that created an economically oriented leadership—personalities whose field of achievement was the organization of such commodity production in the form of capitalist enterprise. Successful enterprises in large numbers represented something new in the economic and social sense. They fought for and won freedom of action. They compelled state policy to adapt itself to their needs. More and more they attracted the most vigorous leaders from other spheres, as well as the manpower of those spheres, causing them and the social strata they represented to languish. Capitalist entrepreneurs fought the former ruling circles for a share in state control, for leadership in the state. The very fact of their success, their position, their resources, their power, raised them in the political and social scale. Their mode of life, their cast of mind became increasingly important elements on the social scene. . . .

A purely capitalist world therefore can offer no fertile soil to imperialist impulses. That does not mean that it cannot still maintain an interest in imperialist expansion. We shall discuss this immediately. The point is that its people are likely to be essentially of an unwarlike disposition. Hence we must expect that anti-imperialist tendencies will show themselves wherever capitalism penetrates the economy and, through the economy, the mind of modern nations—most strongly, of course, where capitalism itself is strongest, where it has advanced furthest, encountered the least resistance, and preeminently where its types and hence democracy—in the "bourgeois" sense—come closest to political dominion. We must further expect that the types formed by capitalism will actually be the carriers of these tendencies. Is such the case? The facts that follow are cited to show that this expectation, which flows from our theory, is in fact justified.

1. Throughout the world of capitalism, and specifically among the elements formed by capitalism in modern social life, there has arisen a fundamental opposition to war, expansion, cabinet diplomacy, armaments, and socially entrenched professional armies. This opposition had its origin in the country that first turned capitalist—England—and arose coincidentally with that country's capitalist development. "Philosophical radicalism" was the first politically influential intellectual movement to represent this trend successfully, linking it up, as was to be expected, with economic freedom in general and free trade in particular. Molesworth became a cabinet member, even though he had publicly declared—on the occasion of the Canadian revolution—that he prayed for the defeat of his country's arms. In step with the advance of capitalism, the movement also gained adherents elsewhere—though at first only adherents without influence. It found support in Paris—indeed, in a circle oriented toward capitalist enterprise (for example, Frédéric Passy). True, pacifism as a matter of principle had existed before, though only among a few small religious sects. But modern pacifism, in its political foundations if not its derivation, is unquestionably a phenomenon of the capitalist world.

2. Wherever capitalism penetrated, peace parties of such strength arose that virtually every war meant a political struggle on the domestic scene. The exceptions are rare—Germany in the Franco-Prussian war of 1870–1871, both belligerents in the Russo-Turkish war of 1877–1878. That is why every war is carefully justified as a defensive war by the governments involved, and by all the political parties, in their official utterances—indicating a realization that a war of a different nature would scarcely be tenable in a political sense. (Here too the Russo-Turkish war is an exception, but a significant one.) In former times this would not have been necessary. Reference to an interest or pretense at moral justification was customary as early as the eighteenth century, but only in the nineteenth century did the assertion of attack, or the threat of attack, become the only avowed occasion for war. In the distant past, imperialism had needed no disguise whatever, and in the absolute autocracies only a very transparent one; but today imperialism is carefully hidden from public view—even though there may still be unofficial appeal to warlike instincts. No people and no ruling class today can openly afford to regard war as a normal state of affairs or a normal element in the life of nations. No one doubts that today it must be characterized as an abnormality and a disaster. True, war is still glorified. But glorification in the style of King Tuglâtipalisharra is rare and unleashes such a storm of indignation that every practical politician carefully dissociates himself from such things. Everywhere there is official acknowledgment that peace is an end in itself—though not necessarily an end overshadowing all purposes that can be realized by means of war. Every expansionist urge must be carefully related to a concrete goal. All this is primarily a matter of political phraseology, to be sure. But the necessity for this phraseology is a symptom of the popular attitude. And that attitude makes a policy of imperialism more and more difficult—

indeed, the very word imperialism is applied only to the enemy, in a reproachful sense, being carefully avoided with reference to the speaker's own policies. . . .

Capitalism is by nature anti-imperialist. Hence we cannot readily derive from it such imperialist tendencies as actually exist, but must evidently see them only as alien elements, carried into the world of capitalism from the outside, supported by non-capitalist factors in modern life. The survival of interest in a policy of forcible expansion does not, by itself, alter these facts—not even, it must be steadily emphasized, from the viewpoint of the economic interpretation of history. For objective interests become effective—and, what is important, become powerful political factors—only when they correspond to attitudes of the people or of sufficiently powerful strata.

. . . The national economy as a whole, of course, is impoverished by the tremendous excess in consumption brought on by war. It is, to be sure, conceivable that either the capitalists or the workers might make certain gains as a class, namely, if the volume either of capital or of labor should decline in such a way that the remainder receives a greater share in the social product and that, even from the absolute viewpoint, the total sum of interest or wages becomes greater than it was before. But these advantages cannot be considerable. They are probably, for the most part, more than outweighed by the burdens imposed by war and by losses sustained abroad. Thus the gain of the capitalists as a class cannot be a motive for war—and it is this gain that counts, for any advantage to the working class would be contingent on a large number of workers falling in action or otherwise perishing. There remain the entrepreneurs in the war industries, in the broader sense, possibly also the large landowner—a small but powerful minority. Their war profits are always sure to be an important supporting element. But few will go so far as to assert that this element alone is sufficient to orient the people of the capitalist world along imperialist lines. At most, an interest in expansion may make the capitalist allies of those who stand for imperialist trends.

It may be stated as being beyond controversy that where free trade prevails *no* class has an interest in forcible expansion as such. For in such a case the citizens and goods of every nation can move in foreign countries as freely as though those countries were politically their own—free trade implying far more than mere freedom from tariffs. In a genuine state of free trade, foreign raw materials and foodstuffs are as accessible to each nation as though they were within its own territory. Where the cultural backwardness of a region makes normal economic intercourse dependent on colonization, it does not matter, assuming free trade, which of the "civilized" nations undertakes the task of colonization. . . .

The gain lies in the enlargement of the commodity supply by means of the division of labor among nations, rather than in the profits and wages of the export industry and the carrying trade. For these profits and wages would be reaped even if there were no export, in which case import, the necessary complement, would also vanish. Not even monopoly interests—if they existed—would be disposed toward imperialism in such a case. For under free trade only *international* cartels would be possible. Under a system of free trade there would be conflicts in economic interest neither among different nations nor among the corresponding classes of different nations. And since protectionism is not an essential characteristic of the capitalist economy—otherwise the English national economy would scarcely be capitalist—it is apparent that any economic interest in forcible expansion on the part of a people or a class is not necessarily a product of capitalism. . . .

Consider which strata of the capitalist world are actually economically benefitted by protective tariffs. They do harm to both workers and capitalists—in contrast to entrepreneurs—not only in their role as consumers, but also as producers. The damage to consumers is universal, that to producers almost so. As for entrepreneurs, they have benefitted only by the tariff that happens to be levied on their own product. But this advantage is substantially reduced by the countermeasures adopted by other countries—universally, except in the case of England—and by the effect of the tariff on the prices of other articles, especially those which they require for their own productive process. Why, then, are entrepreneurs so strongly in favor of protective tariffs? The answer is simple. Each industry hopes to score *special* gains in the struggle of political intrigue, thus enabling it to realize a net gain. Moreover, every decline in freight rates, every advance in production abroad, is likely to affect the economic balance, making it necessary for domestic enterprises to adapt themselves, indeed often to turn to other lines of endeavor. This is a difficult task to which not everyone is equal. Within the industrial organism of every nation there survive antiquated methods of doing business that would cause enterprises to succumb to foreign competition—because of poor management rather than lack of capital, for before 1914 the banks were almost forcing capital on the entrepreneurs. If, still, in most countries virtually *all* entrepreneurs are protectionists, this is owing to a reason which we shall presently discuss. Without that reason, their attitude would be different. The fact that all industries today demand tariff protection must not blind us to the fact that even the entrepreneur interest is not unequivocally protectionist. For this demand is only the consequence of a protectionism already in existence, of a protectionist spirit springing from the economic interests of relatively small entrepreneur groups and from non-capitalist elements—a spirit that ultimately carried along all groups, occasionally even the representatives of working-class interests. Today the protective tariff confers its full and immediate benefits—or comes close to conferring them—only on the large landowners. . . .

Trade and industry of the early capitalist period . . . remained strongly pervaded with precapitalist methods, bore the stamp of autocracy, and served its interests, either willingly or by force. With its traditional habits of feeling, thinking, and acting molded along such lines, the bourgeoisie entered the Industrial Revolution. It was shaped, in other words, by the needs and interests of an environment that was essentially noncapitalist, or at least precapitalist—needs stemming not from the nature of the capitalist economy as such but from the fact of the coexistence of early capitalism with another and at first overwhelmingly powerful mode of life and business. Established habits of thought and action tend to persist, and hence the spirit of guild and monopoly at first maintained itself, and was only slowly undermined, even where capitalism did not fully prevail *anywhere* on the Continent. Existing economic interests, "artificially" shaped by the autocratic state, remained dependent on the "protection" of the state. The industrial organism, such as it was, would not have been able to withstand free competition. Even where the old barriers crumbled in the autocratic state, the people did not all at once flock to the clear track. They were creatures of mercantilism and even earlier periods, and many of them huddled together and protested against the affront of being forced to depend on their own ability. They cried for paternalism, for protection, for forcible restraint of strangers, and above all for tariffs. They met with partial success, particularly because capitalism failed to take radical action in the agrarian field. Capitalism did bring about many changes on the land, springing in part from its automatic mechanisms, in part from the political trends it engendered—abolition of serfdom, freeing the soil from feudal entanglements, and so on—but initially it did not alter the basic outlines of the social structure of the countryside. Even less did it affect the spirit of the people, and least of all their political goals. This explains why the features and trends of autocracy—including imperialism—proved so resistant, why they exerted such a powerful influence on capitalist development, why the old export monopolism could live on and merge into the new.

These are facts of fundamental significance to an understanding of the soul of modern Europe. Had the ruling class of the Middle Ages—the war-oriented nobility—changed its profession and function and become the ruling class of the capitalist world; or had developing capitalism swept it away, put it out of business, instead of merely clashing head-on with it in the agrarian sphere—then much would have been different in the life of modern peoples. But as things actually were, neither eventuality occurred; or, more correctly, both are taking place, only at a very slow pace. The two groups of landowners remain social classes clearly distinguishable from the groupings of the capitalist world. The social pyramid of the present age has been formed, not by the substance and laws of capitalism alone, but by two different social substances, and by the laws of two different epochs. Whoever seeks to understand Europe must not forget this and concentrate all attention on the indubitably basic truth that one of these substances tends to be absorbed by the other and thus the sharpest of all class conflicts tends to be eliminated. Whoever seeks to understand Europe must not overlook that even today its life, its ideology, its politics are greatly under the influence of the feudal "substance," that while the bourgeoisie can assert its interests everywhere, it "rules" only in exceptional circumstances, and then only briefly. The bourgeois outside his office and the professional man of capitalism outside his profession cut a very sorry figure. Their spiritual leader is the rootless "intellectual," a slender reed open to every impulse and a prey to unrestrained emotionalism. The "feudal" elements, on the other hand, have both feet on the ground, even psychologically speaking. Their ideology is as stable as their mode of life. They believe certain things to be really true, others to be really false. This quality of possessing a definite character and cast of mind as a class, this simplicity and solidity of social and spiritual position extends their power far beyond their actual bases, gives them the ability to assimilate new elements, to make others serve their purposes—in a word, gives them *prestige,* something to which the bourgeois, as is well known, always looks up, something with which he tends to ally himself, despite all actual conflicts.

The nobility entered the modern world in the form into which it had been shaped by the autocratic state—the same state that had also molded the bourgeoisie. It was the sovereign who disciplined the nobility, instilled loyalty into it, "statized" it, and, as we have shown, imperialized it. He turned its nationalist sentiments—as in the case of the bourgeoisie—into an aggressive nationalism, and then made it a pillar of his organization, particularly his war machine. It had not been that in the immediately preceding period. Rising absolutism had at first availed itself of much more dependent organs. For that very reason in his position as leader of the feudal powers and as warlord, the sovereign survived the onset of the Industrial Revolution, and as a rule—except in France—won victory over political revolution. The bourgeoisie did not simply supplant the sovereign, nor did it make him its leader, as did the nobility. It merely wrested a portion of his power from him and for the rest submitted to him. It did not take over from the sovereign the state as an abstract form of organization. The state remained a special social power, confronting the bourgeoisie. In some countries it has continued to play that role to the present day. It is in the *state* that the bourgeoisie with its interests seeks refuge, protection against external and even domestic enemies. The bourgeoisie seeks to win over the state for itself, and in return serves the state and state interests that are different from its own. Imbued with the spirit of the old autocracy, trained by it, the bourgeoisie often takes over its ideology, even where, as in France, the sovereign is eliminated and the official power of the nobility has been broken. Because the sovereign needed soldiers, the modern bourgeois—at least in his slogans—is an even more vehement advocate of an increasing population. Because the sovereign was in a position to exploit conquests, needed them to be a victorious warlord, the bourgeoisie thirsts for national glory—even in France, worshiping a headless body, as it were. Because the sovereign found a large gold hoard useful, the bourgeoisie even today cannot be swerved from its bullionist prejudices. Because the autocratic state paid attention to the trader and manufacturer chiefly as the most important sources of taxes and credits, today even the intellectual who has not a shred of property looks on international commerce, not from the viewpoint of the consumer, but from that of the trader and exporter. Because pugnacious sovereigns stood in constant fear of attack by their equally pugnacious neighbors, the modern bourgeois attributes aggressive designs to neighboring peoples. All such modes of thought are essentially noncapitalist. Indeed, they vanish most quickly wherever capitalism fully prevails. They are survivals of the autocratic alignment of interests, and they endure wherever the autocratic state endures on the old basis and with the old orientation, even though more and more democratized and otherwise transformed. They bear witness to the extent to which essentially imperialist absolutism has patterned not only the economy of the bourgeoisie but also its mind—in the interests of autocracy and against those of the bourgeoisie itself.

This significant dichotomy in the bourgeois mind—which in part explains its wretched weakness in politics, culture and life generally; earns it the understandable contempt of the Left and the Right; and proves the accuracy of our diagnosis—is best exemplified by two phenomena that are very close to our subject: present-day nationalism and militarism. Nationalism is affirmative awareness of national character, together with an aggressive sense of superiority. It arose from the autocratic state. In conservatives, nationalism in general is understandable as an inherited orientation, as a mutation of the battle instincts of the medieval knights, and finally as a political stalking horse on the domestic scene; and conservatives are fond of reproaching the bourgeois with a lack of nationalism, which from their point of view, is evaluated in a positive sense. Socialists, on the other hand, equally understandably exclude nationalism from their general ideology, because of the essential interests of the proletariat, and by virtue of their domestic opposition to the conservative stalking horse; they, in turn, not only reproach the bourgeoisie with an excess of nationalism (which they, of course, evaluate in a negative sense) but actually identify nationalism and even the very idea of the nation with bourgeois ideology. The curious thing is that both of these groups are right in their criticism of the bourgeoisie. For, as we have seen, the mode of life that flows logically from the nature of capitalism necessarily implies an anti-nationalist orientation in politics and culture. This orientation actually prevails. We find a great many anti-nationalist members of the middle class, and even more who merely parrot the catchwords of nationalism. In the capitalist world it is actually not big business and industry at all that are the carriers of nationalist trends, but the intellectual, and the content of *his* ideology is explained not so much from definite class interests as from chance emotion and individual interest. But the submission of the bourgeoisie to the powers of autocracy, its alliance with them, its economic and psychological patterning by them—all these tend to push the bourgeois in a nationalist direction; and this too we find prevalent, especially among the chief exponents of export monopolism. The relationship between the bourgeoisie and militarism is quite similar. Militarism is not necessarily a foregone conclusion when a nation maintains a large army, but only when high military circles become a political power. The criterion is whether leading generals as such wield political influence and whether the responsible statesmen can act only with their consent. That is possible only when the officer corps is linked to a definite social class, as in Japan, and can assimilate to its position individuals who do not belong to it by birth. Militarism too is rooted in the autocratic state. And again the same reproaches are made against the bourgeois from both sides—quite properly too. According to the "pure" capitalist mode of life, the bourgeois is unwarlike. The alignment of capitalist interests should make him utterly reject military methods, put him in opposition to the professional soldier. Significantly, we see this in the example of England where, first, the struggle against a standing army generally and, next, opposition to its elaboration, furnished bourgeois politicians with their most popular slogan: "retrenchment." Even naval appropriations have encountered resistance. We find similar trends in other countries, though they are less strongly developed. The continental bourgeois, however, was used to the sight of troops. He regarded an army almost as a necessary component of the social order, ever since it had been his terrible taskmaster in the Thirty Years' War. He had no power at all to abolish the army. He might have done so if he had had the power; but not having it, he considered the fact that the army might be useful to him. In his "artificial" economic situation and because of his submission to the sovereign, he thus grew disposed toward militarism, especially where export monopolism flourished. The intellectuals, many of whom still maintained special relationships with feudal elements, were so disposed to an even greater degree.

Just as we once found a dichotomy in the social pyramid, so now we find everywhere, in every aspect of the bourgeois portion of the modern world, a dichotomy of attitudes and interests. Our examples also show in what way the two components work together. Nationalism and militarism, while not creatures of capitalism, become "capitalized" and in the end draw their best energies from capitalism. Capitalism involves them in its workings and thereby keeps them alive, politically as well as economically. And they, in turn, affect capitalism, cause it to deviate from the course it might have followed alone, support many of its interests.

Here we find that we have penetrated to the historical as well as the sociological sources of modern imperialism. It does not *coincide* with nationalism and militarism, though it *fuses* with them by supporting them as it is supported by them. It too is—not only historically, but also sociologically—a heritage of the autocratic state, of its structural elements, organizational forms, interest alignments, and human attitudes, the outcome of precapitalist forces which the autocratic state has reorganized, in part by the methods of early capitalism. It would never have been evolved by the "inner logic" of capitalism itself. This is true even of mere export monopolism. It too has its sources in absolutist policy and the action habits of an essentially precapitalist environment. That it was able to develop to its present dimensions is owing to the momentum of a situation once created, which continued to engender ever new "artificial" economic structures, that is, those which maintain themselves by political power alone. In most of the countries addicted to export monopolism it is also owing to the fact that the old autocratic state and the old attitude of the bourgeoisie toward it were so vigorously maintained. But export monopolism, to go a step further, is not yet imperialism. And even if it had been able to arise without protective tariffs, it would never have developed into imperialism in the hands of an unwarlike bourgeoisie. If this did happen, it was only because the heritage included the war machine, together with its sociopsychological aura and aggressive bent, and because a class oriented toward war maintained itself in a ruling position. This class clung to its domestic interest in war, and the pro-military interests among the bourgeoisie were able to ally themselves with it. This alliance kept alive war instincts and ideas of overlordship, male supremacy, and triumphant glory—ideas that would have otherwise long since died. It led to social conditions that, while they ultimately stem from the conditions of production, cannot be explained from capitalist production methods alone. And it often impresses its mark on present-day politics, threatening Europe with the constant danger of war. . . .

The only point at issue here was to demonstrate, by means of an important example, the ancient truth that the dead always rule the living.

WAR AS POLICY

Alan S. Milward

For Warre, consisteth not in Battell onely, or the act of fighting; but in a tract of time, wherein the will to contend by Battell is sufficiently known: and therefore the notion of Time, is to be considered in the nature of Warre; as it is in the nature of Weather. For as the nature of Foule weather, lyeth not in a shower or two of rain; but in an inclination thereto of many days together: So the nature of Warre, consisteth not in actual fighting; but in the known disposition thereto, during all the time there is no assurance to the contrary. All other time is Peace.

—*Thomas Hobbes, Leviathan, 1651*

There are two commonly accepted ideas about war which have little foundation in history. One is that war is an abnormality. The other is that with the passage of time warfare has become costlier and deadlier. The first of these ideas established itself in the eighteenth century, when the theory of natural law was used to demonstrate that peace was a logical deduction from the material laws governing the universe or, sometimes, from the psychological laws governing mankind. The second of these ideas came to reinforce the first, which might otherwise have been weakened by the weight of contrary evidence, towards the end of the nineteenth century. The historical record of that century had not been such as to substantiate the logical deductions of eighteenth-century philosophy, for it was a century of unremitting warfare. But after 1850 a large body of economic literature began to reconcile agreeable predictions with unpleasant facts by demonstrating that in spite of the prevalence of warfare it would eventually cease to be a viable economic policy because it would price itself out of the market, a process which, it was agreed, had already begun.

Neither of these ideas has ever been completely accepted by economists but their influence on economic theory has been so powerful as to focus the operation of a substantial body of that theory on to the workings of a peacetime economy only. In spite of the fact that the world has practically never been at peace since the eighteenth century peace has usually been seen as the state of affairs most conducive to the achievement of economic aims and the one which economic theory seeks to analyze and illuminate. In the early nineteenth century, indeed, it was seen as the goal to which economic theory tended.

The frequency of war is in itself the best argument against accepting the idea of its abnormality. The second idea, that war has become more costly, is based less on a refusal to consider history than on a mistaken simplification of it. It was an idea which first gained wide credence with the development of more complicated technologies. War itself was an important stimulus to technological development in many industries in the late nineteenth century such as shipbuilding, the manufacture of steel plate and the development of machine tools. The construction of complex weapons which could only be manufactured by states at a high level of economic development seemed to change the economic possibilities of war. The first heavily armed steel battleships only narrowly preceded the adaptation of the internal combustion engine to military and then to aerial use, and these new armaments coincided with a period of enormous and growing standing armies. The productive capacities which economic development had placed in the hands of developed economies raised prospects of warfare on an absolute scale of cost and deadliness never before conceived. And these prospects in themselves seemed to indicate the economic mechanism by which war would disappear after its rather disappointing persistence in the nineteenth century. These ideas were succinctly expressed by de Molinari, one of the few economists who tried to integrate the existence of war into classical economic theory.

> Can the profits of war still cover its cost? The history of all wars which have occurred between civilized peoples for a number of centuries attests that these costs have progressively grown, and, finally that any war between members of the civilized community today costs the victorious nation more than it can possibly yield it.[1]

In the half century after de Molinari so firmly expressed his opinion there were two world wars, each of a far higher absolute cost and each responsible for greater destruction than any previous war. There is, to say the least, circumstantial evidence that de Molinari's judgement was a superficial one and that nations did not continue to go to war merely because they were ignorant of what had become its real economic consequences. War not only continued to meet the social, political and economic circumstances of states but, furthermore, as an instrument of policy, it remained, in some circumstances, economically viable. War remains a policy and investment decision by the state and there seem to be numerous modern examples of its having been a correct and successful decision. The most destructive of modern technologies have not changed this state of affairs. Their deployment by those states sufficiently highly developed economically to possess them is limited by the rarity of satisfactory strategic opportunity. The strategic synthesis by which the Vietnam war was conducted on the American side, for example, is very like the rational decisions frequently taken by all combatants in the First World War against the use of poison gas. The existence of the most costly and murderous armaments does not mean that they will be appropriate or even usable in any particular war, much less that all combinations of combatants will possess them.

The question of the economic cost of war is not one of absolutes. The cost and the effectiveness of a long-range bomber at the present time must be seen in relation to that of a long-range warship in the eighteenth century and both seen in relation to the

---

[1]M. G. de Molinari, *Comment se résoudra la question sociale?*, Guillaumin, Paris, 1896, p. 126.

growth of national product since the eighteenth century. In each case we are dealing with the summation of many different technological developments, and the armament itself is in each of these cases pre-eminently the expression of an extremely high relative level of economic development. The meaningful question is whether the cost of war has absorbed an increasing proportion of the increasing Gross National Products of the combatants. As an economic choice war, measured in this way, has not shown any discernible long-term trend towards greater costliness. As for its deadliness, the loss of human life is but one element in the estimation of cost. There are no humane wars, and where the economic cost of the war can be lowered by substituting labour for capital on the battlefield such a choice would be a rational one. It has been often made. The size of the Russian armies in the First World War reflected the low cost of obtaining and maintaining a Russian soldier and was intended to remedy the Russian deficiencies in more expensive capital equipment. It may be argued that modern technology changes the analysis because it offers the possibility of near-to-total destruction of the complete human and capital stock of the enemy. But numerous societies were so destroyed in the past by sword, fire and pillage and, more appositely, by primitive guns and gunpowder. The possibility of making a deliberate choice of war as economic policy has existed since the late eighteenth century and exists still.

The origins of the Second World War lay in the deliberate choice of warfare as an instrument of policy by two of the most economically developed states. Far from having economic reservations about warfare as policy, both the German and Japanese governments were influenced in their decisions for war by the conviction that war might be an instrument of economic gain. Although economic considerations were in neither case prime reasons in the decision to fight, both governments held a firmly optimistic conviction that war could be used to solve some of their more long-term economic difficulties. Instead of shouldering the economic burden of war with the leaden and apprehensive reluctance of necessity, like their opponents, both governments kept their eyes firmly fixed on the short-term social and economic benefits which might accrue from a successful war while it was being fought, as well as on the long-term benefits of victory. In making such a choice the ruling elites in both countries were governed by the difference between their own political and economic ideas and those of their opponents. The government of Italy had already made a similar choice when it had attacked Ethiopia.

This difference in economic attitudes to warfare was partly attributable to the influence of fascist political ideas. Because these ideas were also of some importance in the formulation of Axis strategy and the economic and social policies pursued by the German occupying forces it is necessary briefly to consider some of their aspects here in so far as they relate to the themes considered in this book. Whether the National Socialist government in Germany and the Italian Fascist party are properly to be bracketed together as fascist governments and indeed whether the word fascist itself has any accurate meaning as a definition of a set of precise political and economic attitudes are complicated questions which cannot be discussed here.[2] Although the Japanese

---

[2]The reader is referred for a recent, short and relatively unbiased discussion of these issues to W. Wippermann, *Faschismustheorien. Zum Stand der gegenwärtigen Diskussion,* Wissenschaftliche Buchgesellschaft, Darmstadt, 1972.

government had few hesitations in using war as an instrument of political and economic policy there is no meaningful definition of the word fascist which can include the ruling elites in Japan. There was a small political group in that country whose political ideas resembled those of the Fascists and the National Socialists but they had practically no influence in the Home Islands although they did influence the policy of the Japanese military government in Manchuria.[3] But for the German and Italian rulers war had a deeper and more positive social purpose and this was related to certain shared ideas. Whether the word fascism is a useful description of the affinities of political outlook between the Italian and German governments is less important than the fact that this affinity existed and extended into many areas of political and economic life. The differences between National Socialism in Germany and Fascism in Italy partly consisted, in fact, of the more unhesitating acceptance of the ideas of Italian Fascism by the National Socialist party and the linking of these ideas to concepts of racial purity.

The basis of Fascist and National Socialist political and economic thought was the rejection of the ideas of the eighteenth-century Enlightenment. In the submergence of the individual will in common instinctive action, which warfare represented, rational doubts and vacillations, which were regarded as a trauma on human society produced by the Enlightenment, could be suppressed. War was seen as an instrument for the healing of this trauma and for the restoration of human society to its pristine state. Both Hitler and Mussolini, whose writings in general not only subscribed to but advanced the political ideas of fascism, referred to war constantly in this vein, seeing it as a powerful instrument for forging a new and more wholesome political society. 'Fascism', wrote Mussolini,

> the more it considers and observes the future and the development of humanity, quite apart from the political considerations of the moment, believes neither in the possibility nor the utility of perpetual peace. . . . War alone brings up to its highest tension all human energy and puts the stamp of nobility upon the peoples who have the courage to meet it.[4]

Hitler similarly wrote and spoke of war and preparation for war as an instrument of the spiritual renewal of the German people, a device for eliminating the corrupting egotistical self-seeking which he saw as the concomitant of false ideas of human liberty, progress and democracy. The basis of existence in Hitler's view was a struggle of the strong for mastery and war was thus an inescapable, necessary aspect of the human condition.[5]

What made this not uncommon viewpoint especially dangerous and what gave to the Second World War its unique characteristic of a war for the political and economic

---

[3]G. M. Wilson, 'A New Look at the Problem of "Japanese Fascism"', in *Comparative Studies in Society and History,* no. 10, 1968.

[4]Quoted in W. G. Welk, *Fascist Economic Policy. An Analysis of Italy's Economic Experiment* (Harvard Economic Studies, no. 62), Harvard University Press, Cambridge, Mass., 1938, p. 190.

[5]The connections between Hitler's political thought and his strategy are developed in an interesting way by E. Jäckel, *Hitlers Weltanschauung. Entwurf einer Herrschaft,* Rainer Wunderlich Verlag Hermann Leins, Tübingen, 1969.

destiny of the whole European continent was the way in which the ideas of fascism were developed by Hitler and the theorists of the National Socialist party. The wound that had been inflicted on European civilization could, they argued, only be healed by a process of spiritual regeneration. That process of regeneration must begin from the small surviving still uncorrupted elite. But politics was not a matter of debate and persuasion but of the instinctive recognition of social obligations, community ideas which were held to be carried not in the brain but in the blood. The elite was also a racial elite and the restoration of the lost European civilization was also a search for a lost racial purity. The nationalist conceptions of race had been derived from the rational mainstream of European politics. What now replaced them was an irrational concept of racial purity as the last hope for the salvation of European society.[6]

Within Germany, the National Socialist party from its earliest days had identified those of Jewish race as the source of corruption and racial pollution. But it was scarcely possible that the 'problem' of the German Jews could be solved as an entirely domestic issue. The spiritual regeneration of Germany and, through Germany, the continent, also required a great extension of Germany's territorial area—*Lebensraum.* This area had to be sufficiently large to enable Germany militarily to play the role of a great power and to impose her will on the rest of the continent and perhaps on an even wider front. This expansion could also take the form of the destruction of what was seen as the last and most dangerous of all the European political heresies, communism and the Soviet state. The need to achieve these goals and the messianic urgency of the political programme of National Socialism meant that war was an unavoidable part of Hitler's plans.

But it was not the intellectual antagonism to communism which determined that the ultimate target of Germany's territorial expansion should be the Ukraine. That choice was more determined by economic considerations. The task of materially and spiritually rearming the German people had meant that Germany after 1933 pursued an economic policy radically different from that of other European states. A high level of state expenditure, of which military expenditure, before 1936, was a minor part, had sharply differentiated the behaviour of the German economy from that of the other major powers. The maintenance of high levels of production and full employment in a depressed international environment had necessitated an extensive battery of economic controls which had increasingly isolated the economy. After 1936 when expenditure for military purposes was increased to still higher levels there was no longer any possibility that the German economy might come back, by means of a devaluation, into a more liberal international payments and trading system. Rather, the political decisions of 1936 made it certain that trade, exchange, price and wage controls would become more drastic and more comprehensive, and the German economy more insulated from the influence of the other major economies. This was particularly so because of the large volume of investment allocated in the Four Year Plan to the production, at prices well

---

[6]The most comprehensive discussion remains A. Kolnai's *The War against the West* (Gollancz, London, 1938), but E. Weber, in *Varieties of Fascism, Doctrines of Revolution in the Twentieth Century* (Van Nostrand, Princeton, 1964), draws out the further implications of these ideas.

above prevailing world prices, of materials of vital strategic importance, such as synthetic fuel, rubber and aluminum.[7]

The National Socialist party did not support the idea of restoring the liberal international order of the gold exchange standard. But neither did they have any clear positive alternative ideas. Economic policy was dictated by political expediency and each successive stage of controls was introduced to cope with crises as they arose. Nevertheless the political ideas of National Socialism favored an autarkic as opposed to a liberal economic order and it was not difficult to justify the apparatus of economic controls as a necessary and beneficial aspect of the National Socialist state. The international aspects of the controlled economy—exchange controls and bilateral trading treaties—could readily be assimilated to an expansionist foreign policy. Indeed Hitler himself regarded a greater degree of self-sufficiency of the German economy as a necessity if he were to have the liberty of strategic action which he desired, and also as a justification of his policy of territorial expansion. The memory of the effectiveness of the Allied naval blockade during the First World War, when Germany had controlled a much larger resource base than was left to her after the Treaty of Versailles, strengthened this line of thought.

National Socialism elaborated its own theory to justify international economic policies which were in fact only the outcome of a set of domestic economic decisions which had been accorded priority over all international aspects. This was the theory of *Grossraumwirtschaft* (the economics of large areas). Although it was only a rhetorical justification after the event of economic necessities, it also played its part in the formulation of strategy and economic policy. On the basis of these economic ideas, it was hoped that the war would bring tangible economic gain, rather than the more spiritual benefits of a transformation of civilization. At an early stage in his political career, Hitler had come to the conclusion that the Ukraine was economically indispensable to Germany if she was to be, in any worthwhile sense, independent of the international economy and thus free to function as a great power. As the insulation of the German economy from the international economy became more complete in the 1930s the economic relationship of Germany to the whole of the continent came to be reconsidered, and National Socialist writers were advocating not merely a political and racial reconstruction of Europe but an economic reconstruction as well.

National Socialist economists argued that the international depression of 1929 to 1933 had brought the 'liberal' phase of economic development, associated with diminishing tariffs and an increasing volume of international trade, to an end. On the other hand, the extent to which the developed economies of Europe still depended on access to raw materials had not diminished. They argued that the epoch of the economic unit of the national state, itself the creation of liberalism, was past, and must be replaced by the concept of large areas (*Grossräume*) which had a classifiable economic and geographical unity. Such areas provided a larger market at a time of failing demand and could also satisfy that demand from their own production and resources. Improving employment levels and increasing *per capita* incomes depended therefore, not on a

---

[7]The best account is D. Petzina's *Autarkiepolitik im Dritten Reich. Der nationalsoczialistische Vierjahresplan* (Schriftenreihe der Vj.f.Z., no. 16, Deutsche Verlags-Anstalt, Stuttgart, 1968).

recovery in international trade, which could only in any case be temporary and inadequate, but on a reordering of the map of the world into larger 'natural' economic areas. The United States and the Soviet Union each represented such an area. Germany too had its own 'larger economic area' which it must claim.[8]

The future economy of this area would be distinguished by its autarkic nature. The international division of labour would be modified into specialization of function within each *Grossraum*. Germany would be the manufacturing heartland of its own area, together with its bordering industrial areas of northeastern France, Belgium and Bohemia. The peripheral areas would supply raw materials and foodstuffs to the developed industrial core.

There were close links between these economic ideas and the political and racial ones. Such large areas were considered to have a racial unity in the sense that central Europe was developed because of the racial superiority of its inhabitants, the 'Aryans'; the periphery would always be the supplier of raw materials because its population was racially unsuitable for any more sophisticated economic activity.[9] For a time it seemed that Germany might create her *Grossraumwirtschaft* and dominate international economic exchanges in Europe through peaceful means; a series of trade agreements was signed between Germany and the underdeveloped countries of southeastern Europe after 1933. Germany was able to get better terms in bilateral trading from these lands than from more developed European economies who were able to threaten, and even, like Britain, to carry out the threat, to sequestrate German balances in order to force Germany to pay at once on her own (import) side of the clearing balance, and German trade with south-eastern Europe increased in relation to the rest of German and world trade in the thirties. But German-Russian trade after 1933 became insignificant and it was clear that a re-ordering of Europe's frontiers to correspond with Germany's economic ambitions would ultimately have to involve large areas of Russian territory. South-eastern Europe, without Russia, could make only a very limited contribution to emancipating Germany from her worldwide network of imports. A war against the Soviet Union seemed to be the necessary vehicle for political and economic gain.

Many scholars, particularly in the Soviet Union and eastern Europe, maintain that there was a further economic dimension to German policy and that the Second World War represented an even more fundamental clash over the economic and social destiny of the continent. Although the definition of fascism in Marxist analysis has varied greatly with time and place it has nevertheless been more consistent than definitions made from other standpoints. The tendency has been to represent it as the political expression of the control of 'state-monopoly capital' over the economy. It is seen as a

---

[8]Typical of this line of argument are, F. Fried, *Die Zukunft des Welthandels,* Knorr und Hirth, Munich, 1941; R. W. Krugmann, *Südosteuropa und Grossdeutschland. Entwicklung und Zukunftsmöligchkeiten der Wirtschaftsbeziehungen,* Breslauer Verlag, Breslau, 1939; H. Marschner, ed., *Deutschland in der Wirtschaft der Welt,* Deutscher Verlag für Politik und Wirtschaft, Berlin, 1937; J. Splettstoesser, *Der deutsche Wirtschaftsraum im Osten,* Limpert, Berlin, 1939; H. F. Zeck, *Die deutsche Wirtschaft und Südosteuropa,* Teubner, Leipzig, 1939.

[9]W. Daitz, *Der Weg zur völkischen Wirtschaft und zur europäischen Grossraumwirtschaft,* Meinhold, Dresden, 1938.

stage of capitalism in decline, when it can survive only by a brutal and determined imperialism and through a monopolistic control over domestic and foreign markets by the bigger capitalist firms backed by the government. The changes in the German economy after 1933 are explained as following these lines: the readiness to go to war by the bigger profits it might bring and also by the ultimate necessity for an imperialist domination of other economies. Warfare, it is argued, had become an economic necessity for Germany and its ultimate purpose was the preservation of state capitalism, for which both territorial expansion and the destruction of the communist state were essential. The argument is succinctly put by Eichholtz:

> Towards the close of the twenties Germany stood once more in the ranks of the most developed and economically advanced of the imperialist powers. The strength and aggression necessary for expansion grew with the development of her economic strength. German imperialism was an imperialism which had been deprived of colonies, and imperialism whose development was limited by financial burdens stemming from the war and by the limitations and controls, onerous to the monopolies, which the victorious powers had imposed, especially on armaments, finances, etc. On that account extreme nationalism and chauvinism were characteristic of the development of the fascist movement in Germany from the start; once in power fascism maintained from its first days an overweening purposeful imperialistic aggression—which had been obvious for a long time—towards the outside world. With fascism a ruling form of state monopoly capital had been created which aimed at overcoming the crisis of capitalism by domestic terror and, externally, by dividing the world anew.[10]

Such a theory offers not merely a serious economic explanation of the war but also implies that the most fundamental causes of the war were economic. The major German firms, it is argued, had definite plans to gain from a war of aggression and supported the National Socialist government in many of its economic aims.

> Thus the results of research on the period immediately preceding the war, although still fragmentary, already show that German monopoly capital was pursuing a large and complex programme of war aims to extend its domination over Europe and over the world. The kernel of this programme was the destruction of the Soviet Union. Two main aims of war and expansion united the Hitler clique and all important monopolies and monopoly groups from the beginning: the 'dismantling of Versailles' and the 'seizure of a new living space (*Lebensraum*) in the east'. By the 'dismantling of Versailles' the monopolies understood, as they often expressed it later, the 'recapture' of all the economic and political positions which had been lost and the 'restitution' of all the damage to the sources of profit and monopoly situations which the Versailles system had inflicted on them. As an immediate step they planned to overrun the Soviet Union, to liquidate it and appropriate its immeasurable riches to themselves, and to erect a European 'economy of large areas' (*Grossraumwirtschaft*), if possible in conjunction with a huge African colonial empire.[11]

---

[10]D. Eichholtz, *Geschichte der deutschen Kriegswirtschaft, 1939–1945,* vol. 1, 1939–1941, Akademie-Verlag, Berlin, 1969, p. 1.
[11]D. Eichholtz, *Geschichte,* p. 63.

How the *Grossraumwirtschaft* eventually functioned in practice will be examined later. But as far as pre-war plans were concerned it was a concept which attracted sympathy and support from certain business circles in Germany. Some German firms were able to benefit from the government's drive towards a greater level of autarky and hoped to expand their new interests to the limits of the future frontiers of the Reich. This was true, in spite of its extensive extra-European connections, of the large chemical cartel, I. G. Farben. Its profits increasingly came from the massive state investment in synthetic petrol and synthetic rubber production. Several of its important executives had high rank in the Four-Year Plan Organization which was entrusted with these developments, and the company had plans ready in the event of an expansion of German power over other European states.[12] These plans stemmed in part from the German trade drive into south-eastern Europe after 1933 and the consequent penetration of German capital into that region, but there were also unambiguous proposals, some part of which were later put into effect, to recapture the supremacy of the German dyestuffs industry in France, which had been lost as a result of the First World War.[13] Nor was this the only such firm with similar plans prepared.[14] Other firms regarded the expansionist foreign policy as a possible way of securing supplies of raw materials. Such was the case with the non-ferrous metal company, Mansfeld, and with the aluminum companies, who understandably were able to get a very high level of priority because of the great importance of aluminum for aircraft manufacture and the power which the Air Ministry exercised in the German government.[15]

However, the support for the National Socialist party came in large measure from a section of the population whose political sympathies were in many ways antipathetic to the world of big business. It drew its support from a protest against the apparently inexorably increasing power both of organized labour and of organized business. Its urban support came mainly from the lower income groups of the middle classes, such as clerical workers, artisans and shopkeepers, and was combined with massive rural support in Protestant areas after 1931. This support was maintained by a persistent anticapitalist rhetoric but also by a certain amount of legislation which cannot by any shift of argument be explained by a theory which assumes National Socialism to be a stage of state capitalism. Attempts to establish hereditary inalienable peasant tenures, to show favor to artisan enterprises, to restrict the size of retail firms, to restrict the movement of labour out of the agricultural sector, all of which were futile in the face of a massive state investment in reflation which produced a rapid rate of growth of Gross National

---

[12]D. Eichholtz, *Geschichte,* p. 248 ff.; H. Radandt, 'Die I G Farben-industrie und Südosteuropa 1938 bis zum Ende des zweiten Weltkriegs', in *Jahrbuch für Wirtschaftgeschichte,* no. 1, 1967.

[13]A. S. Milward, *The New Order and the French Economy,* Oxford University Press, London, 1970, p. 100 ff.

[14]W. Schumann, "Das Kriegsprogramm des Zeiss-Konzerns", in *Zeitschrift für Geschichtswissenschaft,* no. 11, 1963.

[15]H. Radandt, *Kriegsverbrecherkonzern Mansfeld. Die Rolle des Mansfeld-Konzerns bei der Vorbereitung und während des zweiten Weltkriegs* (Geschichte der Fabriken und Werke, vol. 3), Akademie-Verlag, Berlin, 1957; A. S. Milward, *The Fascist Economy in Norway,* Clarendon Press, Oxford, 1972, p. 86.

Product, show the curious ambivalence of National Socialist economic attitudes.[16] On the whole such legislation did little to affect the profits which accrued to the business world in Germany after 1933, some part of which came also from the severe controls on money wages and the destruction of the organized labour movements. But the National Socialist movement kept its inner momentum, which was driving towards a different horizon from that of the business world, a horizon both more distant and more frightening. It was in some ways a movement of protest against modern economic development and became a center of allegiance for all who were displaced and uprooted by the merciless and seemingly ungovernable swings of the German economy after 1918. National Socialism was as much a yearning for a stable utopia of the past as a close alliance between major capital interests and an authoritarian government.

These fundamental economic contradictions and tensions within the movement could only be exacerbated, not resolved, by a war of expansion. The idea—held in some conservative nationalist German business circles—that Germany must eventually dominate the exchanges of the continent if her economy was to find a lasting equilibrium, had a lineage dating from the 1890s and had found some expression in economic policy during the First World War.[17] The theory of *Grossraumwirtschaft* was only a reformulation of these ideas in terms of National Socialist foreign policy. The much more radical idea of a social and racial reconstruction of European society—accepted by some parts of the National Socialist movement—ran directly counter to it, and raised the possibility of a Europe where the 'business climate' would, to say the least, have been unpropitious.

Although, therefore, the German government in choosing war as an instrument of policy was anticipating an economic gain from that choice, it was by no means clear as to the nature of the anticipated gain. It has been argued that it was the irreconcilable contradictions in the National Socialist economy which finally made a war to acquire more resources (*ein Raubkrieg*) the only way out, and that the invasion of Poland was the last desperate attempt to sustain the Nazi economy.[18] But it is hard to make out a case that the Nazi economy was in a greater state of crisis in the autumn of 1939 than it had been on previous occasions particularly in 1936. Most of the problems which existed in 1939 had existed from the moment full employment had been reached, and some of them, on any calculation, could only be made worse by a war—as indeed they were.

In Italy there were episodes in the 1930s when foreign and economic policy seemed to be directed towards the creation of an Italian *Grossraumwirtschaft* in Europe as a solution to Italy's economic problems. But in the face of the powerful expansion of German trade in the south-east such aspirations were unattainable. In Italy, also, there

---

[16]They are well described in D. Schoenbaum's *Hitler's Social Revolution: Class and Status in Nazi Germany 1933–1939* (Weidenfeld & Nicolson, London, 1966).

[17]The history is traced by J. Freymond, *Le IIIe Reich et la réorganisation économique de l'Europe 1940–1942: origines et projets* (Institut Universitaire de Hautes Etudes, Geneva, Collection de Relations Internationales, 3), Sithoff, Leiden, 1974.

[18]T. W. Mason, 'Innere Krise und Angriffskrieg 1938/1939', in F. Forstmeier and H. E. Volkmann (eds.), *Wirtschaft und Rustung am Vorabend des zweiten Weltkrieges,* Droste, Düsseldorf, 1975.

were attempts at creating by protection and subsidy synthetic industries which might prove strategically necessary in war. But there was little resemblance between these tendencies and the full-scale politico-economic ambitions of Germany. If the Italian government viewed war as a desirable instrument of policy it did not contemplate a serious and prolonged European war and made no adequate preparations for one.

In Japan, however, the choice in favour of war was based on economic considerations which had a certain similarity to those of Germany. It lacked the radical social and racial implications but it was assumed that investment in a war which was strategically well-conceived would bring a substantial accretion to Japan's economic strength. The Japanese government hoped to establish a zone of economic domination which, under the influence of German policy, it dignified by the title 'Co-Prosperity Sphere'. As an economic bloc its trading arrangements would be like those of the *Grossraumwirtschaft*, a manufacturing core supplied by a periphery of raw material suppliers.[19] If the Co-Prosperity Sphere was to be created in the full extent that would guarantee a satisfactory level of economic self-sufficiency, war and conquest would be necessary. Germany's decision for war and early victories over the colonial powers gave Japan the opportunity to establish a zone of domination by military force while her potential opponents were preoccupied with other dangers. After the initial successes the boundaries of the Co-Prosperity Sphere were widened to include a more distant periphery, a decision which had serious strategic consequences, but the original Japanese war aims represented a positive and realistic attempt at the economic reconstruction of her own economic area in her own interests. All the peripheral areas produced raw materials and foodstuffs and semi-manufactures which were imported in large quantities into Japan; rice from Korea, iron ore, coal and foodstuffs from Manchuria, coal and cotton from Jehol, oil and bauxite from the Netherlands East Indies, tin and rubber from Malaya and sugar from Formosa. The variety of commodities and the scope for further developments in the future made the Co-Prosperity Sphere potentially more economically viable and more economically realistic than a European *Grossraumwirtschaft* still heavily dependent on certain vital imports.[20] The Japanese decision for war, like the German, was taken under the persuasion that in Japan's situation, given the correct timing and strategy, war would be economically beneficial.

Of course such plans could only have been formulated where a harshly illiberal outlook on the problems of international economic and political relationships prevailed. But in the government circles of Japan proper the ready acceptance of war had no ideological connotations beyond this generally prevailing political attitude of mind. The major influence on the Japanese decision for war was the strategic conjuncture; with German military successes in Europe, the pressure on the European empires in the Pacific became unbearable and this in turn intensified the strategic dilemma of the United States. If Japan's ambitions were to be achieved it seemed that the opportune moment had arrived.

---

[19]F. C. Jones, *Japan's New Order in East Asia: Its Rise and Fall, 1937–45,* Oxford University Press, London, 1954; M. Libal, *Japans Weg in den Krieg. Die Aussenpolitik der Kabinette Konoye 1940–41,* Droste-Verlag, Düsseldorf, 1971.

[20]J. R. Cohen, *Japan's Economy in War and Reconstruction,* University of Minnesota Press, Minneapolis, 1949, p. 7.

The probable and possible opponents of the Axis powers viewed this bellicosity with dismay. In these countries the First World War and its aftermath were seen as an economic disaster. Consequently the main problem of a future war, if it had to be fought, was thought to be that of avoiding a similar disaster. The components of that disaster were seen as a heavy loss of human beings and capital, acute and prolonged inflation, profound social unrest, and almost insuperable problems, both domestic and international, of economic readjustment once peace was restored. It was almost universally believed that the unavoidable aftermath of a major war would be a short restocking boom followed by worldwide depression and unemployment. When the *American Economic Review* devoted a special issue in 1940 to a consideration of the economic problems of war the problem of post-war readjustment was regarded by all contributors as the most serious and unavoidable. That the major economies after 1945 would experience a most remarkable period of stability and economic growth was an outcome which was quite unforeseen and unpredicted. The western European powers and the United States were as much the prisoners of their resigned pessimism about the unavoidable economic losses of war as Germany and Japan were the prisoners of their delusions about its possible economic advantages.

In fact the economic experience of the First World War had been for all combatants a chequered one. The First World War had not been a cause of unalloyed economic loss; it had on occasions brought economic and social advantages. What is more it had demonstrated to all the combatant powers that it lay in the hands of government to formulate strategic and economic policies which could to some extent determine whether or not a war would be economically a cause of gain or loss; they were not the hopeless prisoners of circumstance. The extreme importance of what governments had learned of their own potential in this way during the 1914–18 war can be observed in almost every aspect of the Second World War. Nevertheless in most countries this learning process had been thought of as an ingenious economic improvisation to meet a state of emergency, having no connection with peacetime economic activity nor with the 'normal' functioning of government. Although the First World War had left massive files of invaluable administrative experience on the shelves of government, which in 1939 had often only to be reached for and dusted, the influence of wartime events on economic attitudes in the inter-war period had been small.

Faced with a decision for war by two important powers the other major powers accepted the fact reluctantly and with much economic foreboding. The reluctance seems to have been greatest in the Soviet Union, which was in the throes of a violent economic and social transformation, and in the United States, which was less immediately threatened by German policy. The strategic initiative lay with the Axis powers; the strategies of the other powers were only responses to the initial decisions of their enemies. This fact, and the difference in economic attitudes toward warfare, operated decisively to shape each combatant power's strategic plans for fighting the war. By shaping strategy at every turn they also shaped economic policy and economic events. For the combatants the national economy had to be accommodated to a strategic plan and had to play its part in that plan. The economic dimension of the strategy was, however, only one part of the whole strategic synthesis, and the variety of the strategic and economic syntheses which were devised by the combatant powers show how complex and varied the economic experience of warfare can be.

STRUCTURAL CAUSES
AND ECONOMIC EFFECTS

Kenneth N. Waltz

In a self-help system, interdependence tends to loosen as the number of parties declines, and as it does so the system becomes more orderly and peaceful. As with other international political concepts, interdependence looks different when viewed in the light of our theory. Many seem to believe that a growing closeness of interdependence improves the chances of peace. But close interdependence means closeness of contact and raises the prospect of occasional conflict. The fiercest civil wars and the bloodiest international ones are fought within arenas populated by highly similar people whose affairs are closely knit. It is impossible to get a war going unless the potential participants are somehow linked. Interdependent states whose relations remain unregulated must experience conflict and will occasionally fall into violence. If interdependence grows at a pace that exceeds the development of central control, then interdependence hastens the occasion for war. . . .

INTERDEPENDENCE AS SENSITIVITY

. . . As now used, "interdependence" describes a condition in which anything that happens anywhere in the world may affect somebody, or everybody, elsewhere. To say that interdependence is close and rapidly growing closer is to suggest that the impact of developments anywhere on the globe are rapidly registered in a variety of far-flung places. This is essentially an economist's definition. In some ways that is not surprising. Interdependence has been discussed largely in economic terms. The discussion has been led by Americans, whose ranks include nine-tenths of the world's living economists (Strange 1971, p. 223). Economists understandably give meaning to interdependence by defining it in market terms. Producers and consumers may or may not form a market. How does one know when they do? By noticing whether changes in the cost of production, in the price of goods, and in the quality of products in some places respond to similar changes elsewhere. Parties that respond sensitively are closely interdependent. Thus Richard Cooper defines interdependence as "quick responsiveness to differential earning opportunities resulting in a sharp reduction in differences in factor rewards" (1968, p. 152). . . .

In defining interdependence as sensitivity of adjustment rather than as mutuality of dependence, Richard Cooper unwittingly reflects the lesser dependence of today's great

---

powers as compared to those of earlier times. Data excerpted from Appendix Table I graphically show this.

Exports plus Imports as a Percentage of GNP		
1909–13	U.K., France, Germany, Italy	33–52%
1975	U.S., Soviet Union	8–14%

To say that great powers then depended on one another and on the rest of the world much more than today's great powers do is not to deny that the adjustment of costs across borders is faster and finer now. Interdependence as sensitivity, however, entails little vulnerability. The more automatically, the more quickly, and the more smoothly factor costs adjust, the slighter the political consequences become. Before World War I, as Cooper says, large differences of cost meant that "trade was socially very profitable" but "less sensitive to small changes in costs, prices, and quality" (1968, p. 152). Minor variations of cost mattered little. Dependence on large quantities of imported goods and materials that could be produced at home only with difficulty, if they could be produced at all, mattered much. States that import and export 15 percent or more of their gross national products yearly, as most of the great powers did then and as most of the middle and smaller powers do now, depend heavily on having reliable access to markets outside their borders. Two or more parties involved in such relations are interdependent in the sense of being mutually vulnerable to the disruption of their exchanges. Sensitivity is a different matter.

As Cooper rightly claims, the value of a country's trade is more likely to vary with its magnitude than with its sensitivity. Sensitivity is higher if countries are able to move back and forth from reliance on foreign and on domestic production and investment "in response to relatively small margins of advantage." Under such conditions, the value of trade diminishes. If domestic substitutions for foreign imports cannot be made, or can be made only at high cost, trade becomes of higher value to a country and of first importance to those who conduct its foreign policy. The high value of Japan's trade, to use Cooper's example, "led Japan in 1941 to attack the Philippines and the United States fleet at Pearl Harbor to remove threats to its oil trade with the East Indies." His point is that high sensitivity reduces national vulnerability while creating a different set of problems. The more sensitive countries become, the more internal economic policies have to be brought into accord with external economic conditions. Sensitivity erodes the autonomy of states, but not of all states equally. Cooper's conclusion, and mine, is that even though problems posed by sensitivity are bothersome, they are easier for states to deal with than the interdependence of mutually vulnerable parties, and that the favored position of the United States enhances both its autonomy and the extent of its influence over others (1972, pp. 164, 176–80).

Defining interdependence as sensitivity leads to an economic interpretation of the world. To understand the foreign-policy implications of high or of low interdependence requires concentration on the politics of international economics, not on the economics of international politics. The common conception of interdependence omits inequalities, whether economic or political. And yet inequality is what much of politics is about. The study of politics, theories about politics, and the practice of politics have always turned upon inequalities, whether among interest groups, among religious and ethnic communities, among classes, or among nations. Internally, inequality is more nearly the whole of the political story. Differences of national strength and power and of national capability and competence are what the study and practice of international politics are almost entirely about. This is so not only because international politics lacks the effective laws and the competent institutions found within nations but also because inequalities across nations are greater than inequalities within them (Kuznets 1951). A world of nations marked by great inequalities cannot usefully be taken as the unit of one's analysis.

Most of the confusion about interdependence follows from the failure to understand two points: first, how the difference of structure affects the meaning, the development, and the effects of the interactions of units nationally and internationally; and second, how the interdependence of nations varies with their capabilities. Nations are composed of differentiated parts that become integrated as they interact. The world is composed of like units that become dependent on one another in varying degrees. The parts of a polity are drawn together by their differences; each becomes dependent on goods and services that all specialize in providing. Nations pull apart as each of them tries to take care of itself and to avoid becoming dependent on others. How independent they remain, or how dependent they become, varies with their capabilities. . . . To define interdependence as a sensitivity, then, makes two errors. First, the definition treats the world as a whole, as reflected in the clichés cited earlier. Second, the definition compounds relations and interactions that represent varying degrees of independence for some, and of dependence for others, and lumps them all under the rubric of interdependence.

INTERDEPENDENCE AS MUTUAL VULNERABILITY

A politically more pertinent definition is found in everyday usage. Interdependence suggests reciprocity among parties. Two or more parties are interdependent if they depend on one another about equally for the supply of goods and services. They are interdependent if the costs of breaking their relations or of reducing their exchanges are about equal for each of them. Interdependence means that the parties are mutually dependent. The definition enables one to identify what is politically important about relations of interdependence that are looser or tighter. Quantitatively, interdependence tightens as parties depend on one another for larger supplies of goods and services; qualitatively, interdependence tightens as countries depend on one another for more important goods and services that would be harder to get elsewhere. The definition has two components: the aggregate gains and losses states experience through their interactions and the equality with which those gains and losses are distributed. States that are interdependent at high levels of exchange experience, or are subject to, the common vulnerability that high interdependence entails.

Because states are like units, interdependence among them is low as compared to the close integration of the parts of a domestic order. States do not interact with one another as the parts of a polity do. Instead, some few people and organizations in one state interact in some part of their affairs with people and organizations abroad. Because of their similarity, states are more dangerous than useful to one another. Being functionally undifferentiated, they are distinguished primarily by their greater or lesser capabilities for performing similar tasks. This states formally what students of international politics have long noticed. The great powers of an era have always been marked off from others by both practitioners and theorists.

. . . Many believe that the mere mutualism of international exchange is becoming a true economic-social-political integration. One point can be made in support of this formulation. The common conception of interdependence is appropriate only if the inequalities of nations are fast lessening and losing their political significance. If the inequality of nations is still the dominant political fact of international life, then interdependence remains low. Economic examples in this section, and military examples in the next one, make clear that it is.

In placid times, statement and commentator employ the rich vocabulary of clichés that cluster around the notion of global interdependence. Like a flash of lightning, crises reveal the landscape's real features. What is revealed by the oil crisis following the Arab-Israeli War in October of 1973? Because that crisis is familiar to all of us and will long be remembered, we can concentrate on its lessons without rehearsing the details. Does it reveal states being squeezed by common constraints and limited to applying the remedies they can mutually contrive? Or does it show that the unequal capabilities of states continue to explain their fates and to shape international-political outcomes?

Recall how Kissinger traced the new profile of power. "Economic giants can be militarily weak," he said, "and military strength may not be able to obscure economic weakness. Countries can exert political influence even when they have neither military nor economic strength." . . . Economic, military, and political capabilities can be kept separate in gauging the ability of nations to act. Low politics, concerned with economic and such affairs, has replaced military concerns at the top of the international agenda. Within days the Arab-Israeli War proved that reasoning wrong. Such reasoning had supported references made in the early 1970s to the militarily weak and politically disunited countries of Western Europe as constituting "a great civilian power." Recall the political behavior of the great civilian power in the aftermath of the war. Not Western Europe as any kind of a power, but the separate states of Western Europe, responded to the crisis—in the metaphor of *The Economist*—by behaving at once like hens and ostriches. They ran around aimlessly, clucking loudly while keeping their heads buried deeply in the sand. How does one account for such behavior? Was it a failure of nerve? Is it that the giants of yesteryear—the Attlees and Bevins, the Adenauers and de Gaulles—have been replaced by men of lesser stature? Difference of persons explains some things; difference of situations explains more. In 1973 the countries of Western Europe depended on oil for 60 percent of their energy supply. Much of that oil came from the Middle East. . . . Countries that are highly dependent, countries that get much of what they badly need from a few possibly unreliable suppliers, must do all they can to increase the chances that they will keep getting it. The weak, lacking leverage, can plead their cause or panic. Most of the countries in question unsurprisingly did a little of each.

The behavior of nations in the energy crisis that followed the military one revealed the low political relevance of interdependence defined as sensitivity. Instead, the truth of the propositions I made earlier was clearly shown. Smooth and fine economic adjustments cause little difficulty. Political interventions that bring sharp and sudden changes in prices and supplies cause problems that are economically and politically hard to cope with. The crisis also revealed that, as usual, the political clout of nations correlates closely with their economic power and their military might. In the winter of 1973–74 the policies of West European countries had to accord with economic necessities. The more dependent a state is on others, and the less its leverage over them, the more it must focus on how its decisions affect its access to supplies and markets on which its welfare or survival may depend. This describes the condition of life for states that are no more than the equal of many others. In contrast, the United States was able to make its policy according to political and military calculations. Importing but two percent of its total energy supply from the Middle East, we did not have to appease Arab countries as we would have had to do if our economy had depended heavily on them and if we had lacked economic and other leverage. The United States could manipulate the crisis that others made in order to promote a balance of interests and forces holding some promise of peace. The unequal incidence of shortages led to the possibility of their manipulation. What does it mean then to say that the world is an increasingly interdependent one in which all nations are constrained, a world in which all nations lose control? Very little. To trace the effects that follow from inequalities, one has to unpack the word "interdependent" and identify the varying mixtures of relative dependence for some nations and of relative independence for others. As one should expect in a world of highly unequal nations, some are severely limited while others have wide ranges of choice; some have little ability to affect events outside of their borders while others have immense influence.

The energy crisis should have made this obvious, but it did not. Commentators on public affairs continue to emphasize the world's interdependence and to talk as though all nations are losing control and becoming more closely bound. Transmuting concepts into realities and endowing them with causal force is a habit easily slipped into. Public officials and students of international affairs once wrote of the balance of power causing war or preserving peace. They now attribute a comparable reality to the concept of interdependence and endow it with strong causal effect. Thus Secretary Kissinger, who can well represent both groups, wondered "whether interdependence would foster common progress or common disaster" (January 24, 1975, p. 1). He described American Middle-East policy as being to reduce Europe's and Japan's vulnerability, to engage in dialogue with the producers, and "to give effect to the principle of interdependence on a global basis" (January 16, 1975, p. 3). Interdependence has become a thing in itself: a "challenge" with its own requirements, "a physical and moral imperative" (January 24, 1975, p. 2; April 20, 1974, p. 3).

When he turned to real problems, however, Kissinger emphasized America's special position. The pattern of his many statements on such problems as energy, food, and nuclear proliferation was first to emphasize that our common plight denies all possibility of effective national action and then to place the United States in a separate category. Thus, two paragraphs after declaring our belief in interdependence, we find this query: "In what other country could a leader say, 'We are going to solve energy; we're going to solve food; we're going to solve the problem of nuclear war,' and be taken seriously?" (October 13, 1974, p. 2).

In coupling his many statements about interdependence with words about what we can do to help ourselves and others, was Kissinger not saying that we are much less dependent than most countries are? We are all constrained but, it appears, not equally. Gaining control of international forces that affect nations is a problem for all of them, but some solve the problem better than others. The costs of shortages fall on all of us, but in different proportion. Interdependence, one might think, is a euphemism used to obscure the dependence of most countries (cf. Goodwin 1976, p. 63). Not so, Kissinger says. Like others, we are caught in the web because failure to solve major resource problems would lead to recession in other countries and ruin the international economy. That would hurt all of us. Indeed it would, but again the uneven incidence of injuries inflicted on nations is ignored. Recession in some countries hurts others, but some more and some less so. An unnamed Arab oil minister's grip on economics appeared stronger than Kissinger's. If an oil shortage should drive the American economy into recession, he observed, all of the world would suffer. "Our economies, our regimes, our very survival, depend on a healthy U.S. economy" (*Newsweek,* March 25, 1974, p. 43). How much a country will suffer depends roughly on how much of its business is done abroad. As Chancellor Schmidt said in October of 1975, West Germany's economy depends much more than ours does on a strong international economic recovery because it exports 25 percent of its GNP yearly (October 7, 1975). The comparable figure for the United States was seven percent.

No matter how one turns it, the same answer comes up: We depend somewhat on the external world, and most other countries depend on the external world much more so. Countries that are dependent on others in important respects work to limit or lessen their dependence if they can reasonably hope to do so.* From late 1973 onward, in the period of oil embargo and increased prices, Presidents Nixon and Ford, Secretary Kissinger, and an endless number of American leaders proclaimed both a new era of interdependence and the goal of making the United States energy-independent by 1985. This is so much the natural behavior of major states that not only the speakers but seemingly also their audiences failed to notice the humor. Because states are in a self-help system, they try to avoid becoming dependent on others for vital goods and services. To achieve energy independence would be costly. Economists rightly point out that by their definition of interdependence the cost of achieving the goal is a measure of how much international conditions affect us. But that is to think of interdependence merely as sensitivity. Politically the important point is that only the few industrial countries of greatest capability are able to think seriously of becoming independent in energy supply. As Kissinger put it: "We have greater latitude than the others because we can do much on our own. The others can't" (January 13, 1975, p. 76). . . .

When the great powers of the world were small in geographic compass, they did a high proportion of their business abroad. The narrow concentration of power in the pre-

---

*Notice the implication of the following statement made by Leonid Brezhnev: "Those who think that we need ties and exchanges in the economic and scientific-technical fields more than elsewhere are mistaken. The entire volume of USSR imports from capitalist countries comes to less than 1.5% of our gross social product. It is clear that this does not have decisive importance for the Soviet economy's development" (October 5, 1976, p. 3).

sent and the fact that the United States and the Soviet Union are little dependent on the rest of the world produce a very different international situation. The difference between the plight of great powers in the new bipolar world and the old multipolar can be seen by contrasting America's condition with that of earlier great powers. When Britain was the world's leading state economically, the portion of her wealth invested abroad far exceeded the portion that now represents America's stake in the world. In 1910 the value of total British investment abroad was one-and-one-half times larger than her national income. In 1973 the value of total American investments abroad was one-fifth as large as her national income. In 1910 Britain's return on investment abroad amounted to eight percent of national income; in 1973 the comparable figure for the United States was 1.6 percent (British figures computed from Imlah 1958, pp. 70–75, and Woytinsky and Woytinsky 1953, p. 791, Table 335; American figures computed from CIEP, March 1976, pp. 160–62, Tables 42, 47, and *US Bureau of the Census,* 1975, p. 384, and *Survey of Current Business,* October 1975, p. 48). Britain in its heyday had a huge stake in the world, and that stake loomed large in relation to her national product. From her immense and far-flung activities, she gained a considerable leverage. Because of the extent to which she depended on the rest of the world, wise and skillful use of that leverage was called for. Great powers in the old days depended on foodstuffs and raw materials imported from abroad much more heavily than the United States and the Soviet Union do now. Their dependence pressed them to make efforts to control the sources of their vital supplies.

Today the myth of interdependence both obscures the realities of international politics and asserts a false belief about the conditions that promote peace, as World War I conclusively showed. "The statistics of the economic interdependence of Germany and her neighbors," John Maynard Keynes remarked, "are overwhelming." Germany was the best customer of six European states, including Russia and Italy; the second best customer of three, including Britain; and the third best customer of France. She was the largest source of supply for ten European states, including Russia, Austria-Hungary, and Italy; and the second largest source of supply for three, including Britain and France (Keynes 1920, p. 17). And trade then was proportionately much higher than now. Then governments were more involved internationally than they were in their national economies. Now governments are more involved in their national economies than they are internationally. This is fortunate.

Economically, the low dependence of the United States means that the costs of, and the odds on, losing our trading partners are low. Other countries depend more on us than we do on them. If links are cut, they suffer more than we do. Given this condition, sustained economic sanctions against us would amount to little more than economic self-mutilation. The United States can get along without the rest of the world better than most of its parts can get along without us. But, someone will hasten to say, if Russia, or anyone, should be able to foreclose American trade and investment in successively more parts of the world, we could be quietly strangled to death. To believe that, one has to think not in terms of politics but in terms of the apocalypse. If some countries want to deal less with us, others will move economically closer to us. More so than any other country, the United States can grant or withhold a variety of favors, in matters of trade, aid, loans, the supply of atomic energy for peaceful purposes, and military security. If peaceful means for persuading other countries to comply with preferred American policies are wanted, the American government does not have to look far to find them. The Soviet Union is even less dependent economically on the outside world than we are, but has less economic and political leverage on it. We are more dependent economically on the outside world than the Soviet Union is, but have more economic and political leverage on it.

The size of the two great powers gives them some capacity for control and at the same time insulates them with some comfort from the effect of other states' behavior. The inequality of nations produces a condition of equilibrium at a low level of interdependence. This is a picture of the world quite different from the one that today's transnationalists and interdependers paint. They cling to an economic version of the domino theory: Anything that happens anywhere in the world may damage us directly or through its repercussions, and therefore we have to react to it. This assertion holds only if the politically important nations are closely coupled. We have seen that they are not. Seldom has the discrepancy been wider between the homogeneity suggested by "interdependence" and the heterogeneity of the world we live in. A world composed of greatly unequal units is scarcely an interdependent one. A world in which a few states can take care of themselves quite well and most states cannot hope to do so is scarcely an interdependent one. A world in which the Soviet Union and China pursue exclusionary policies is scarcely an interdependent one. A world of bristling nationalism is scarcely an interdependent one. The confusion of concepts works against clarity of analysis and obscures both the possibilities and the necessities of action. Logically it is wrong, and politically it is obscurantist, to consider the world a unit and call it "interdependent."

REFERENCES

Brezhnev, L. I. (October 5, 1976). "Brezhnev gives interview on French TV." In *The Current Digest of the Soviet Press,* vol. 28. Columbus: Ohio State University, November 3, 1976.

CIEP: Council on International Economic Policy (December 1974). (March 1976). *International Economic Report of the President.* Washington, D.C.: GPO.

———. (January 1977). *International Economic Report of the President.* Washington, D.C.: GPO.

Cooper, Richard N. (1968). *The Economics of Interdependence.* New York: McGraw-Hill.

———. (January 1972). "Economic interdependence and foreign policy in the seventies." World Politics, vol. 24.

Finney, John W. (January 18, 1976). "Dreadnought or dinosaur." *New York Times Magazine.*

Goodwin, Geoffrey L. (1976). "International institutions and the limits of interdependence." In Avi Shlaim (ed.), *International Organizations in World Politics Yearbook, 1975.* London: Croom Helm.

Imlah, A. H. (1958). *Economic Elements in the Pax Britannica.* Cambridge: Harvard University Press.

Keynes, John Maynard (1920). *The Economic Consequences of the Peace.* New York: Harcourt, Brace and Howe.

———. (September 1, 1926). "The end of laissez-faire—II." *New Republic,* vol 48.

———. (n.d.) *The General Theory of Employment, Interest, and Money.* New York: Harcourt, Brace.

Kissinger, Henry A. (1957). *Nuclear Weapons and Foreign Policy.* New York: Harper.

———. (1964). *A World Restored.* New York: Grosset and Dunlap.

————. (1965). *The Troubled Partnership.* New York: McGraw-Hill.

————. (Summer 1968). "The white revolutionary: reflections on Bismarck." *Daedalus,* vol. 97.

————. (April 24, 1973). "Text of Kissinger's talk at A.P. meeting here on U.S. relations with Europe." *New York Times.*

————. (October 10, 1973). "At Pacem in Terris conference." *News Release.* Bureau of Public Affairs: Department of State.

————. (April 20, 1974). "Good partner policy for Americas described by Secretary Kissinger." *New Release.* Bureau of Public Affairs: Department of State.

————. (October 13, 1974). "Interview by James Reston of the *New York Times.*" The Secretary of State. Bureau of Public Affairs: Department of State.

————. (January 13, 1975). "Kissinger on oil, food, and trade." *Business Week.*

————. (January 16, 1975). "Interview: for Bill Moyers' Journal." *The Secretary of State.* Bureau of Public Affairs: Department of State.

————. (January 24, 1975). "A new national partnership." *The Secretary of State.* Bureau of Public Affairs: Department of State.

————. (September 13, 1975). "Secretary Henry A. Kissinger interviewed by William F. Buckley, Jr." *The Secretary of State.* Bureau of Public Affairs: Department of State.

————. (December 23, 1975). "Major topics: Angola and detente." *The Secretary of State.* Bureau of Public Affairs: Department of State.

————. (September 30, 1976). "Toward a new understanding of community." *The Secretary of State.* Bureau of Public Affairs: Department of State.

————. (January 10, 1977). "Laying the foundations of a long-term policy." *The Secretary of State.* Bureau of Public Affairs: Department of State.

Kuznets, Simon (Winter 1951). "The state as a unit in study of economic growth." *Journal of Economic History,* vol. 11.

————. (1966). *Modern Economic Growth.* New Haven: Yale University Press.

————. (January 1967). "Quantitative aspects of the economic growth of nations: Paper X." *Economic Development and Cultural Change,* vol. 15.

Marx, Karl, and Frederick Engels (1848). *Communist Manifesto.* Translator unnamed. Chicago: Charles H. Kerr, 1946.

Newsweek (March 25, 1974). "Oil embargo: the Arab's compromise."

Schmidt, Helmut (October 7, 1975). "Schmidt, Ford 'cautiously optimistic' on world's economic recovery." *The Bulletin.* Bonn: Press and Information Office, Government of the Federal Republic of Germany, vol. 23.

Snyder, Glenn H. (1966). *Stockpiling Strategic Materials.* San Francisco: Chandler.

Strange, Susan (January 1971). "The politics of international currencies." *World Politics,* vol. 22.

Survey of Current Business (various issues). U.S. Department of Commerce, Bureau of Economic Analysis. Washington, D.C.: GPO.

UN Department of Economic Affairs (1949). *International Capital Movements During the Inter-War Period.* New York.

————. Department of Economic and Social Affairs (1961). *International Flow of Long Term Capital and Official Donations.* New York.

————. Statistical Office (1957, 1961, 1970, 1974). *Yearbook of National Accounts Statistics.* New York.

————. (1966). *Demographic Yearbook,* 1965, New York.

————. (1976). *Statistical Yearbook,* 1975, vol. 27. New York.

————. (1977). *Statistical Yearbook,* 1976, vol. 28. New York.

US Agency for International Development, Statistics and Reports Divisions (various years). *US Overseas Loans and Grants: July 1, 1945–.* Washington, D.C.: GPO.

————. Bureau of the Census (1975). *Statistical Abstract,* 1974. Washington, D.C.: GPO.

————. Bureau of the Census (1976). *Historical Statistics of the United States: Colonial Times to 1970.* Washington, D.C.: GPO.

————. Department of Commerce, Bureau of Economic Analysis (1975). *Revised Data Series on US Direct Investment Abroad, 1966–1974.* Washington, D.C.: GPO.

————. Department of the Interior (June 1976). *Energy Perspectives 2.* Washington, D.C.: GPO.

————. Senate Committee on Finance (February 1973). *Implications of Multinational Firms for World Trade and Investment and for U.S. Trade and Labor.* Washington, D.C.: GPO.

————. Senate Committee on Government Operations, Permanent Subcommittee on Investigations (August 1974). *Selected Readings on Energy Self-Sufficiency and the Controlled Materials Plan.* Washington, D.C.: GPO.

Woytinsky, W. S., and E. S. Woytinsky (1953). *World Population and Production.* New York: Twentieth Century Fund.

TRADE AND POWER

Richard Rosecrance

In the age of mercantilism—an era in which power and wealth combined—statesmen and stateswomen (for who dares to slight Elizabeth I or Catherine the Great) sought not only territory but also a monopoly of markets of particular goods highly valued in Europe, gold, silver, spices, sugar, indigo, tobacco. Who controlled local production and sales also determined the market in Europe and obtained a monopoly return. Initially, Venice and Genoa vied for dominance of the spice trade from the twelfth to the fourteenth centuries, a struggle that was interrupted by Portuguese navigators, sailors, and soldiers who temporarily established control of the Indies at their source. Later Holland ousted Portugal in the East Indies, and England and France took her place in India. By the seventeenth century, Spain could no longer hold her position in the Caribbean and the New World as Holland, England, and France disputed her monopoly, first by capturing her bullion fleets, then by seizing sugar islands as well as parts of the North American mainland. In the eighteenth century Britain won victory practically everywhere, though Holland was left with the Dutch East Indies, France with her sugar islands in the Caribbean, and Spain with a reduced position in North and South America. As William Pitt the Elder pointed out, "commerce had been made to flourish by war"[1]—English monopolies of colonial produce won her great dividends in trade with the continent. Her near monopoly of overseas empire and tropical products produced a great flow of continuing revenue that supported British military and naval exploits around the world. From either standpoint—territorial or economic—military force could be used to conquer territories or commodity-producing areas that would contribute greater revenue and power in Europe. With a monopoly on goods or territories, one nation or kingdom could forge ahead of others.

Thus we have one basic means by which nations have made their way in the world—by increasing their territories and maintaining them against other states. Sometimes, less cultured or civilized nations have by this means upset ruling empires or centers of civilization. In the past the barbarian invasions disrupted Rome; Attila the Hun and his followers intruded upon Mediterranean civilization; Genghis Khan and his military nomads ranged into Eastern Europe; Islam and the Turks dynamically transformed the culture of the Mediterranean and Southern Europe. In fact, it was not until the relatively recent period that highly developed economic centers could hold their own against military and agrarian peoples. The waging of war and the seizure of territory

From *The Rise of the Trading State: Commerce and Conquest in the Modern World* by Richard Rosecrance. Copyright © 1986 by Richard Rosecrance. Reprinted by permission of Basic Books, a member of Perseus books, L.L.C. Chapters 1, 7.
[1]Quoted in Walter L. Dorn, *Competition for Empire* (New York: Harper & Row, 1940), p. 370.

have been relatively easy tasks for most of Western history. It is not surprising that when territorial states began to take shape in the aftermath of the Reformation, they were organized for the purpose both of waging and of resisting war, and the seventeenth century became the most warlike of epochs. Kings and statesmen could most rapidly enhance their positions through territorial combat.

Associated with the drive for territory is an allied system of international relations which we will here call the "military-political or territorial" system. The more nations choose to conquer territory, the more dominant the allied system of international politics will be. Because territorial expansion has been the dominant mode of national policy since 1648 and the Peace of Westphalia, it is not surprising that the military-political and territorial system has been the prevailing system of international relations since then. In this system, war and the threat of war are the omnipresent features of interstate relationships, and states fear a decisive territorial setback or even extinction. This has not been an idle concern, if one considers that 95 percent of the state-units which existed in Europe in the year 1500 have now been obliterated, subdivided, or combined into other countries.

Whatever else a nation-state does, therefore, it must be concerned with the territorial balance in international politics and no small part of its energies will be absorbed by defense. But defense and territory are not the only concerns of states, nor is territorial expansion the only means by which nations hope to improve their fortunes. If war provides one means of national advancement, peace offers another.

THE OIL CRISIS, 1973–1980

Probably more important in the long-term than the battles of the fourth Arab-Israeli war was the oil crisis and embargo of 1973–74. While the war was being fought, the Organization of Petroleum Exporting Countries (OPEC) announced on October 16, 1973, its first unilateral increase of 70 percent, bringing the cost of a barrel of oil to $5.12. At the end of the year it had been raised to $11.65 (a further 128 percent increase), and by 1980 had risen to almost $40.00 a barrel, about twenty times the price in early 1970. In addition, the Arabs announced oil production cutbacks and on October 20, embargoed all oil exports to the United States and The Netherlands, the two countries closest to Israel.

These decisions stimulated different responses in America and abroad. Most European allies and Japan quickly made it clear that they sympathized with the Arab cause and distanced themselves from the United States. Nixon in response announced "Project Independence" on November 7, which committed the United States to free itself from the need to import oil by 1980. This difficult goal was to be accomplished by conservation and the development of alternative sources of energy. The objective was not achieved, of course, for the United States imported roughly the same 36 to 37 percent of its oil needs in 1980 as it had in 1973. No evolution would allow it to return to the nearly self-sufficient 8.1 percent level of 1947.

There were four ways in which the oil crisis might have been overcome. The first was through the traditional method used by the United States in the Middle East crises of 1956 and 1967. In response to an oil embargo, the United States could simply increase its domestic production of oil, allocating stockpiles to its allies. The United States had had the leverage to do this in previous years because excess domestic capacity more than provided for national requirements, leaving a surplus to be exported abroad, if need arose. In 1956, the United States imported 11 percent of its oil but had a reserve domestic production capacity that could provide for an additional 25 percent of its needs. In 1967, while oil imports had risen to 19 percent of its oil consumption, the United States possessed a similar ability to expand its production by 25 percent, more than replacing imported oil. By 1973, however, the low price of oil and past domestic production had eroded United State reserves. It now imported 35 percent of its needs and could increase production only by an additional 10 percent.[2] When the Arabs embargoed oil shipments to the United States, there was no way for the country to increase domestic production to cover the shortfall. If a solution was to be found, it depended upon reallocating production abroad. As it turned out, the embargo caused no difficulty or shortage in America, because the oil companies simply re-routed production, sending Arab production to compliant European states and Japan, and non-Arab production to the United States and Holland. This measure solved the supply problem, but it did nothing to alleviate the high price. Extra United States production would not be sufficient to create a glut in the world marketplace and thus force a drop in the OPEC price.

A second method of coping with the crisis was to form a cartel of buyers of oil, principally the United States, Europe, and Japan, together with a few developing countries. If all could agree to buy oil at a fixed low price, OPEC would not be able to sell abroad on its terms and would have to reduce the price. Since it was the formation of the producers' cartel (OPEC) which had forced up the price of oil, many thought that only a consumers' cartel could offset its bargaining leverage and bring the price down. Despite American attempts to organize such a consumers' group in 1973 and 1974, the other nations preferred to play an independent role. France, Germany, and Japan negotiated separate oil contracts with individual Arab countries, guaranteeing access to Middle Eastern oil over the long term. They would not cooperate with the United States. When the American-sponsored International Energy Agency was finally set up in 1974, it became an information gathering agency which could allocate supplies of oil only in a crisis and had no monopoly bargaining power.

A third means of overcoming the oil crisis and reducing the real price of oil was through military intervention. This was considered at the end of 1974 and the beginning of 1975 when Secretary of State Kissinger hinted intervention if "actual strangulation of the West" was threatened. Some concluded that the Persian Gulf fields should be seized by United States marines or units of a Rapid Deployment Force. Occupation of such thinly populated areas was possible. The question, however, was whether production could be started up and maintained in the face of determined sabotage by Arab resistance groups, including the Palestine Liberation Organization. Would pipelines be cut or harbors mined? Would oil tankers have free passage through the Gulf? These uncertainties could not be resolved over the long period that would be required to break the Arab embargo and reduce the price of petroleum.

---

[2]See R. Keohane, *After Hegemony* (Princeton: Princeton University Press, 1984), p. 199.

The final and ultimately successful means of overcoming the crisis came through diplomacy and the mechanism of the world market. After the success of the Israeli-Egyptian shuttle negotiations producing a withdrawal of forces on the Sinai front, the very beginning of talks on the Golan with Syria and Israel led the Arabs to end the oil embargo on March 18, 1974.[3] This had no impact on oil prices or supply and therefore did not change the OPEC bargaining position. That awaited complex developments in the world market for oil and for industrial products. In 1973–74, it was generally believed that the market for oil was inelastic, that demand would not decline greatly with an increase in the oil price. If it did not, the Arabs would gain an incredible premium, and a huge surplus of funds. It was estimated that as much as $600 billion might flow to Arab producers over a ten-year period. They would never be able to spend that much importing goods from the industrial and oil-consuming countries; hence, huge Arab surpluses would build up—funds that could have no economic use in the Arab states themselves. The flow of funds from importing countries to OPEC was partly offset when about half the surplus was used to buy Western imports and another large portion was invested in the world financial market, largely in the form of short-term deposits in Western banks. The banks and international financial agencies could then lend funds to the consuming countries, enabling them to finance their oil purchases. At the same time consumers became unwilling or unable to pay the high price. Even in the traditionally energy-extravagant United States, the amount of energy needed to produce one dollar of the gross national product declined 25 percent from 1973 to 1983. The average gas consumption of American-made automobiles almost doubled in the same period to reach 24.6 miles per gallon. Most of the leading industrial corporations instituted energy-conservation programs. The demand for oil dropped.

Between 1973 and 1979 industrial prices in the developed world increased more than oil prices. In the wake of the oil crisis and the ensuing inflation, many governments resorted to freely fluctuating exchange rates for their currencies. No longer under the discipline of gold flows, they could experiment with domestic economic expansion, convinced that their currencies values would not get out of line or their trade balance deteriorate. The result was further inflation of wages, prices, and industrial products. This had two effects on the Arab oil countries. First, it meant that they had to pay a great deal more to buy industrial goods, using up the oil surplus that they were beginning to accumulate. Second, as inflation advanced in the West and Japan, industrial entrepreneurs hesitated to invest, uncertain of their long-run return. Western economies ground to a halt and unemployment mounted. For a decade after 1973, the industrialized world grew at only 2 percent per year, and the number of jobless workers doubled. As a result, Arab investments in the developed countries were threatened by declines in Western profits and wages. Too high oil prices temporarily forced the industrial world into economic stagnation in which it would buy little Middle Eastern oil. The oil price increase, with the exception of the sudden rise of 1979–80, halted and reversed. Even the Iran-Iraq war did not lead to a new jump in prices. Oil consumption of the advanced

---

[3]Henry A. Kissinger, *Years of Upheaval* (Boston: Little Brown, 1982), pp. 891–95, 939–45, 975–78.

industrial countries fell by seven million barrels a day between 1979 and 1982. In addition new oil production outside of OPEC increased, and OPEC production declined by twelve million barrels a day. Oil came into surplus, and the price fell back to $28 per barrel by 1983. The oil countries, which also suffered from the worldwide inflation, found they did not have sufficient export surplus to meet their needs in food and industrial imports. In 1982, eight Middle Eastern producers faced a deficit of $23 to $26 billion. Even Ayatollah Ruhollah Khomeini's Iran had to increase its oil production to finance imports and its war with Iraq.

The strange outcome was that the oil and energy crisis abated. The Arabs saw reason for increasing production while holding down the price, but the collapse in international demand for oil was so great, that the price could not be maintained. Consumers emerged in a much better position. The developing countries, which had borrowed to cover oil and industrial imports, found high interest rates imperilling their financial solvency in the first half of the 1980s. Paradoxically, there was then too little Arab money and too small an oil surplus to cover their borrowing needs.

The oil crisis underscored another means of dealing with conflict among nation-states. Instead of defending or fighting over territorial claims, nations found a way to reach a compromise through an international flow of funds, domestic economic adjustments, and world trade. The imbalance in payments threatened by the huge Arab oil surpluses in 1973–74 was reversed by the first years of the 1980s. Despite Kissinger's threats, force was not used to assure Western access to oil, and overarching cooperation was the ruling principle between industrial and oil-producing regions of the world. Each benefitted from the exchange, and consuming countries did not have to adopt policies of national self-sufficiency, reducing income and employment to the point where energy needs could be met on a national basis. Each side, instead, relied upon the other for the products it required.

Territorial gain is not the only means of advancing a nation's interest, and, in the nuclear age, wars of territorial expansion are not only dangerous, they are costly and threatening to both sides. Much more tenable is a policy of economic development and progress sustained by the medium of international trade. If national policies of economic growth depend upon an expanding world market, one country can hardly expect to rely primarily upon territorial aggression and aggrandizement. To attack one's best customers is to undermine the commercial faith and reciprocity in which exchange takes place. Thus, while the territorial and military-political means to national improvement causes inevitable conflict with other nations, the trading method is consistent with international cooperation. No other country's territory is attacked; the benefits that one nation gains from trade can also be realized by others.

If this is true, and two means of national advancement do indeed exist, why is it that Western and world history is mainly a narrative of territorial and military expansion, of unending war, to the detriment of the world's economic and trading system? Louis XIV and Napoleon would easily understand the present concern with territorial frontiers and the military balance, to the degree that one is hard put to explain what has changed in the past three hundred years.

The answer is that states have not until recently had to depend upon one another for the necessities of daily existence. In the past, trade was a tactical endeavor, a method used between wars, and one that could easily be sacrificed when military determinants so decreed. The great outpouring of trade between nations in the latter half of the nineteenth century did not prevent the First World War; it could be stanched as countries resorted to military means to acquire the territory or empire that would make them independent of others. No national leader would sacrifice territory to gain trade, unless the trade constituted a monopoly. Leaders aimed to have all needed resources in their own hands and did not wish to rely upon others.

As long as a state could get bigger and bigger, there was no incentive to regard trade with others as a strategic requirement, and for most of European history since the Renaissance, state units appeared to be growing larger. The five hundred or so units in Europe in 1500 were consolidated into about twenty-five by the year 1900.[4] If this process continued, statesmen and peoples could look forward to the creation of a few huge states like those in Orwell's *1984* which together controlled the globe. The process of imperialism in the late nineteenth century forwarded this conception: ultimately a few empires would become so enormous that they would not have to depend upon anyone else. Thus, the failure of the imperialist drive and the rapid decolonization of recent years have meant a change of direction in world politics. Since 1900, and especially after 1945, the number of nation-states has greatly increased, even more swiftly than the number belonging to the United Nations organizations. Between 170 and 180 states exist, and the number is growing. If contemporary nationalist and ethnic separatist movements succeed, some states in Europe, Africa, Asia, and Oceania may be further subdivided into new independent states or autonomous regions. These small and even weak states will scarcely be self-reliant; increasingly they will come to depend on others for economic and even military necessities, trading or sharing responsibilities with other nations. The age of the independent, self-sufficient state will be at an end. Among such states, the method of international development sustained by trade and exchange will begin to take precedence over the traditional method of territorial expansion and war. . . .

THE TRADING WORLD

. . . The role of Japan and Germany in the trading world is exceedingly interesting because it represents a reversal of past policies in both the nineteenth century and the 1930s. It is correct to say that the two countries experimented with foreign trade because they had been disabused of military expansion by World War II. For a time they were incapable of fighting war on a major scale; their endorsement of the trading system was merely an adoption of the remaining policy alternative. But that endorsement did not change even when the economic strength of the two nations might have sustained a much more nationalistic and militaristic policy. Given the choice between military expansion to achieve self-sufficiency (a choice made more difficult by modern conventional and nuclear weapons in the hands of other powers) and the procurement

---

[4]Charles Tilly, ed., *The Formation of National States in Western Europe* (Princeton: Princeton University Press, 1975), p. 24.

of necessary markets and raw materials through international commerce, Japan and Germany chose the latter.

It was not until the nineteenth century that this choice became available. During the mercantilist period (1500–1775) commerce was hobbled by restrictions, and any power that relied on it was at the mercy of the tariffs and imperial expansion of other nations. Until the late eighteenth century internal economic development was slow, and there seemed few means of adding to national wealth and power except by conquering territories which contained more peasants and grain. With the Industrial Revolution the link between territory and power was broken; it then became possible to gain economic strength without conquering new lands.[5] New sources of power could be developed within a society, simply by mobilizing them industrially. When combined with peaceful international trade, the Industrial Revolution allowed manufactured goods to find markets in faraway countries. The extra demand would lengthen production runs and increase both industrial efficiency (through economies of scale) and financial return. Such a strategy, if adhered to by all nations, could put an end to war. There was no sense in using military force to acquire power and wealth when they could be obtained more efficiently through peaceful economic development and trade.

The increasing prevalence of the trading option since 1945 raises peaceful possibilities that were neglected during the late nineteenth century and the 1930s. It seems safe to say that an international system composed of more than 160 states cannot continue to exist unless trade remains the primary vocation of most of its members. Were military and territorial orientations to dominate the scene, the trend to greater numbers of smaller states would be reversed, and larger states would conquer small and weak nations.

The possibility of such amalgamations cannot be entirely ruled out. Industrialization had two possible impacts: it allowed a nation to develop its wealth peacefully through internal economic growth, but it also knit new sinews of strength that could coerce other states. Industrialization made territorial expansion easier but also less necessary. In the mid-nineteenth century the Continental states pursued the expansion of their territories while Britain expanded her industry. The industrialization of Prussia and the development of her rail network enabled her armies to defeat Denmark, Austria, and France. Russia also used her new industrial technology to strengthen her military. In the last quarter of the century, even Britain returned to a primarily military and imperialist policy. In his book on imperialism Lenin declared that the drive for colonies was an imminent tendency of the capitalist system. Raw materials would run short and investment capital would pile up at home. The remedy was imperialism with colonies providing new sources for the former and outlets for the latter. But Lenin did not fully understand that an open international economy and intensive economic development at home obviated the need for colonies even under a capitalist, trading system.

The basic effect of World War II was to create much higher world interdependence as the average size of countries declined. The reversal of past trends toward a consolidation of states created instead a multitude of states that could not depend on themselves alone. They needed ties with other nations to prosper and remain viable as small

---

[5]It is true that the greatest imperial edifices were constructed after the start of the Industrial Revolution. It was precisely that revolution, however, which prepared the groundwork for their demise.

entities. The trading system, as a result, was visible in defense relations as well as international commerce. Nations that could not stand on their own sought alliances or assistance from other powers, and they offered special defense contributions in fighting contingents, regional experience, or particular types of defense hardware. Dutch electronics, French aircraft, German guns and tanks, and British ships all made their independent contribution to an alliance in which no single power might be able to meet its defense needs on a self-sufficient basis. Israel developed a powerful and efficient small arms industry, as well as a great fund of experience combating terrorism. Israeli intelligence added considerably to the information available from Western sources, partly because of its understanding of Soviet weapons systems accumulated in several Arab-Israeli wars.

Defense interdependencies, however, are only one means of sharing the burdens placed upon the modern state. Perhaps more important is economic interdependence among countries. One should not place too much emphasis upon the existence of interdependence per se. European nations in 1913 relied upon the trade and investment between them; that did not prevent the political crisis which led to a breakdown of the international system and to World War I. Interdependence only constrains national policy if leaders accept and agree to work within its limits. In 1914 Lloyds of London had insured the German merchant marine but that did not stop Germany attacking Belgium, a neutral nation, or England from joining the war against Berlin.[6] The United States was Japan's best customer and source of raw materials in the 1930s, but that did not deter the Japanese attack on Pearl Harbor.

At least among the developed and liberal countries, interdependent ties since 1945 have come to be accepted as a fundamental and unchangeable feature of the situation. This recognition dawned gradually, and the United States may perhaps have been the last to acknowledge it, which was not surprising. The most powerful economy is ready to make fewer adjustments, and America tried initially to pursue its domestic economic policies without taking into account the effect on others, on itself, and on the international financial system as a whole. Presidents Kennedy and Lyndon B. Johnson tried to detach American domestic growth strategies from the deteriorating United States balance of payments, but they left a legacy of needed economic change to their successors. Finally, in the 1980s two American administrations accepted lower United States growth in order to control inflation and begin to focus on the international impact of United States policies. The delay in fashioning a strategy of adjustment to international economic realities almost certainly made it more difficult. Smaller countries actively sought to find a niche in the structure of international comparative advantage and in the demand for their goods. Larger countries with large internal markets postponed that reckoning as long as they could. By the 1980s, however, such change could no longer be avoided, and the United States leaders embarked upon new industrial and tax policies designed to increase economic growth and enable America to compete more effectively abroad.

The acceptance of new approaches was a reflection of the decline in economic sovereignty. As long as governments could control all the forces impinging upon their economies, welfare states would have no difficulty in implementing domestic planning

---

[6]Paul Kennedy, *Strategy and Diplomacy 1870–1945* (London: Fontana Paperbacks 1984), pp. 95–96.

TABLE 1

Exports of Goods and Services (as a Percentage of GDP)		
Country	*1965*	*1979*
United States	5	9
Japan	11	12
Germany	18	26
United Kingdom	20	29
France	14	22

NOTE: Michael Stewart, *The Age of Interdependence* (Cambridge, Mass: MIT Press, 1981). p. 21 (derived from United Nations *Yearbook of National Accounts Statistics,* 1980, vol. 2, table 2A).

for social ends. But as trade, investment, corporations, and to some degree labor moved from one national jurisdiction to another, no government could insulate and direct its economy without instituting the extreme protectionist and "beggar thy neighbor" policies of the 1930s. Rather than do this, the flow of goods and capital was allowed to proceed, and in recent years it has become a torrent. In some cases the flow of capital has increased to compensate for barriers or rigidities to the movement of goods.

In both cases the outcome is the result of modern developments in transportation and communications. Railway and high-speed highway networks now allow previously landlocked areas to participate in the international trading network that once depended on rivers and access to the sea. Modern communications and computers allow funds to be instantaneously transferred from one market to another, so that they may earn interest twenty-four hours a day. Transportation costs for a variety of goods have reached a new low, owing to container shipping and handling. For the major industrial countries (member countries of the Organization for Economic Cooperation and Development, which include the European community, Austria, Finland, Iceland, Portugal, Norway, Spain, Sweden, Switzerland, Turkey, Australia, Canada, Japan, New Zealand, and the United States), exports have risen much faster than either industrial production or gross domestic product since 1965, with the growth of GDP (in constant prices) at 4 percent and that of exports at 7.7 percent.[7] Only Japan's domestic growth has been able to keep pace with the increase in exports (see Table 1).

Foreign trade (the sum of exports and imports) percentages were roughly twice as large as these figures in each case. The explosion of foreign trade since 1945 has, if anything, been exceeded by the enormous movement of capital.

In 1950 the value of the stock of direct foreign investment held by U.S. companies was $11.8 billions, compared with $7.2 billions in 1935, $7.6 billions in 1929 and $3.9 billions in 1914. In the following decade, these investments increased by $22.4 billions, and at the end of 1967 their total value stood at $59 billions.[8]

---

[7]Michael Stewart, *The Age of Interdependence* (Cambridge, Mass: MIT Press, 1984), p. 20.
[8]John H. Dunning, *Studies in International Investment* (London: George Allen and Unwin, 1970), p. 1.

In 1983, it had reached $226 billions.[9] And direct investment (that portion of investment which buys a significant stake in a foreign firm) was only one part of total United States investment overseas. In 1983 United States private assets abroad totaled $774 billion, or about three times as much.

The amounts, although very large, were not significant in themselves. In 1913, England's foreign investments, equaled one and one-half times her GNP as compared to present American totals of one-quarter of United States GNP. England's foreign trade was more than 40 percent of her national income as compared with contemporary American totals of 15–17 percent. England's pre-World War I involvement in international economic activities was greater than America's today.

Part of what must be explained in the evolution of interdependence is not the high level reached post-1945, but how even higher levels in 1913 could have fallen in the interim. Here the role of industrialization is paramount. As Karl Deutsch, following the work of Werner Sombart, has shown, in the early stages of industrial growth nations must import much of their needed machinery: rail and transportation networks are constructed with equipment and materials from abroad. Once new industries have been created, in a variety of fields, ranging from textiles to heavy industry, the national economy can begin to provide the goods that previously were imported.[10] The United States, the Scandinavian countries, and Japan reached this stage only after the turn of the century, and it was then that the gasoline-powered automobile industry and the manufacturing of electric motors and appliances began to develop rapidly and flourish. The further refinement of agricultural technology also rested on these innovations. Thus, even without restrictions and disruptions of trade, the 1920s would not have seen a rehabilitation of the old interdependent world economy of the 1890s. The further barriers erected in the 1930s confirmed and extended this outcome. If new industrial countries had less need for manufacturing imports, the growth and maintenance of general trade would then come to depend upon an increase in some other category of commerce than the traditional exchange of raw materials for finished goods. In the 1920s, as Albert Hirschman shows, the reciprocal exchange of industrial goods increased briefly, but fell again in the 1930s.[11] That decrease was only made up after 1945 when there was a striking and continuing growth in the trade of manufactured goods among industrial countries.[12] Some will say that this trade is distinctly expendable because countries could produce the goods they import on their own. None of the trade that the United States has today with Western Europe or Japan could really be dubbed "critical" in that the United States could not get along without it. American alternatives exist to almost all industrial products from other developed economies. Thus if interdependence means

---

[9]"International Investment Position of the United States at Year End" in *Survey of Current Business* (Washington, D.C.: Department of Commerce, June 1984).

[10]Karl W. Deutsch and Alexander Eckstein, "National Industrialism and the Declining Share of the International Economic Sector, 1890–1959" in *World Politics,* 13 (January 1961), pp. 267–99.

[11]*National Power and the Structure of Foreign Trade* (Berkeley: University of California Press, 1980), pp. 129–43.

[12]Richard Rosecrance and Arthur Stein, "Interdependence: Myth or Reality" in *World Politics* (July 1973), pp. 7–9.

a trading link which "is costly to break,"[13] there is a sense that the sheer physical dependence of one country upon another, or upon international trade as a whole, has declined since the nineteenth century.

But to measure interdependence in this way misses the essence of the concept. Individuals in a state of nature can be quite independent if they are willing to live at a low standard of living and gather herbs, nuts, and fruits. They are not forced to depend on others but decide to do so to increase their total amount of food and security. Countries in an international state of nature (anarchy) can equally decide to depend only on themselves. They can limit what they consume to what they can produce at home, but they will thereby live less well than they might with specialization and extensive trade and interchange with other nations.

There is no shortage of energy in the world, for example, and all energy needs that previously have been satisfied by imported petroleum might be met by a great increase in coal and natural gas production, fission, and hydropower. But coal-generated electric power produces acid rain, and coal liquification (to produce fuel for automobiles) is expensive. Nuclear power leaves radioactive wastes which have to be contained. Importing oil is a cheaper and cleaner alternative. Thus even though a particular country, like the United States, might become energy self-sufficient if it wanted to, there is reason for dependence on the energy supplies of other nations. Does this mean creating a "tie that is costly to break"? Yes, in the sense that we live less well if we break the tie; but that doesn't mean that the tie could not be broken. Any tie can be broken. In this respect, all ties create "vulnerability interdependence" if they are in the interest of those who form them. One could get along without Japanese cars or European fashions, but eliminating them from the market restricts consumer choice and in fact raises opportunity costs. In this manner, trade between industrial countries may be equally important as trade linking industrial and raw material producing countries.

There are other ways in which interdependence has increased since the nineteenth century. Precisely because industrial countries imported agricultural commodities and sold their manufactured goods to less developed states, their dependence upon each other was much less in the nineteenth century and the 1920s than it is today. Toward the end of the nineteenth century Britain increasingly came to depend upon her empire for markets, food, and raw materials or upon countries in the early stages of industrialization. As Continental tariffs increased, Britain turned to her colonies, the United States, and Latin America to find markets for her exports. These markets provided

> ready receptacles for British goods when other areas became too competitive or unattractive; for example, Australia, India, Brazil and Argentina took the cotton, railways, steel and machinery that could not be sold in European markets. In the same way, whilst British capital exports to the latter dropped from 52 percent in the 1860s to 25 percent in the few years before 1914, those to the empire rose from 36 percent to 46 percent, and those to Latin America from 10.5 percent to 22 percent.[14]

---

[13]Kenneth Waltz, "The Myth of National Interdependence" in Charles Kindleberger, ed., *The International Corporation* (Cambridge, Mass.: MIT Press, 1970), p. 206.
[14]Paul Kennedy, *The Rise and Fall of British Naval Mastery* (London: Allen Lane, 1976), pp. 187–88.

The British foreign trade which totalled 43.5 percent of GNP in 1913 went increasingly to the empire; thus, if one takes Britain and the colonies as a single economic unit, that unit was much less dependent upon the outside world than, say, Britain is today with a smaller (30.4 percent) ratio of trade to GNP. And Britain alone had much less stake in Germany, France, and the Continental countries' economies than she does today as a member of the European Common Market.

In the nineteenth century trade was primarily vertical in character, taking place between countries at different stages of industrial development, and involving an exchange of manufactured goods on the one hand for food and raw materials on the other. But trade was not the only element in vertical interdependence.

British investment was also vertical in that it proceeded from the developed center, London, to less developed capitals in the Western Hemisphere, Oceania, and the Far East. Such ties might contribute to community feeling in the British Empire, later the Commonwealth of Nations, but it would not restrain conflicts among the countries of Western Europe. Three-quarters of foreign investment of all European countries in 1914 was lodged outside of Europe. In 1913, in the British case 66 percent of her foreign investment went to North and South America and Australia, 28 percent to the Middle and Far East, and only 6 percent to Europe.

In addition, about 90 percent of foreign investment in 1913 was portfolio investment, that is, it represented small holdings of foreign shares that could easily be disposed of on the stock exchange. Direct investment, or investment which represented more than a 10 percent share of the total ownership of a foreign firm, was only one-tenth of the total. Today the corresponding figure for the United States is nearly 30 percent. The growth of direct foreign investment since 1945 is a reflection of the greater stake that countries have in each other's well-being in the contemporary period.

In this respect international interdependence has been fostered by a growing interpenetration of economies, in the sense that one economy owns part of another, sends part of its population to live and work in it, and becomes increasingly dependent upon the progress of the latter.[15] The multinational corporation which originates in one national jurisdiction, but operates in others as well, is the primary vehicle for such investment ownership. Stimulated by the demands and incentives of the product life cycle, the multinational corporation invests and produces abroad to make sure of retaining its market share. That market may be in the host country, or it may be in the home country, once the foreign production is imported back into the home economy. Foreign trade has grown enormously since 1945. But its necessary growth has been reduced by the operation of multinational companies in foreign jurisdictions: production abroad reduces the need for exports. In this way an interpenetrative stake has increased between developed economies even when tariffs and other restrictions might appear to have stunted

---

[15]Nothing could be more misleading than to equate these interrelations with those of nineteenth-century imperialism. Then imperial dictates went in one direction—military, economic, and social. The metropole dominated the colony. Today, does North America become a colony when Chicanos and Hispanics move to it in increasing numbers or England a tributary of the West Indies? Does Chinese or Korean investment in the United States render it a peripheral member of the system? The point is that influence goes in both directions just as does investment and trade in manufactured goods.

the growth of exports. The application of a common external tariff to the European Economic Community in the 1960s greatly stimulated American foreign investment in Europe, which became such a massive tide that Europeans reacted against the "American challenge," worrying that their prized national economic assets might be preempted by the United States.

They need not have worried. The reverse flow of European and Japanese investment in the United States is reaching such enormous proportions that America has become a net debtor nation: a country that has fewer assets overseas than foreigners have in the United States. The threatened imposition of higher American tariffs and quotas on imports led foreign companies to invest in the United States in gigantic amounts, thereby obviating the need to send exports from their home nation. Such direct investment represents a much more permanent stake in the economic welfare of the host nation than exports to that market could ever be. Foreign production is a more permanent economic commitment than foreign sales, because large shares of a foreign company or subsidiary could not be sold on a stock exchange. The attempt to market such large holdings would only have the effect of depressing the value of the stock. Direct investment is thus illiquid, as opposed to the traditional portfolio investment of the nineteenth century.

After 1945 one country slowly developed a stake in another, but the process was not initially reciprocal. Until the beginning of the 1970s, the trend was largely for Americans to invest abroad, in Europe, Latin America, and East Asia. As the American dollar cheapened after 1973, however, a reverse flow began, with Europeans and Japanese placing large blocs of capital in American firms and acquiring international companies. Third World multinationals, from Hong Kong, the OPEC countries, and East Asia also began to invest in the United States. By the end of the 1970s world investment was much more balanced, with the European stake in the American economy nearly offsetting the American investment in Europe. Japan also moved to diversify her export offensive in the American market by starting to produce in the United States. But Japan did not benefit from a reciprocal stake in her own economy. Since foreign investors have either been kept out of the Japanese market or have been forced to accept cumbersome joint ventures with Japanese firms, few multinationals have a major commitment to the Japanese market. Japan imports the smallest percentage of manufactured goods of any leading industrial nation. Thus when economic policy makers in America and Europe formulate growth strategies, they are not forced to consider the Japanese economy on a par with their own because American and Europeans have little to lose if Japan does not prosper. In her own self-interest Japan will almost certainly have to open her capital market and economy to foreign penetration if she wishes to enjoy corresponding access to economies of other nations. Greater Japanese foreign direct investment will only partly mitigate the pressures on Tokyo in this respect.

PART VI

POLITICS: IDEOLOGY AND IDENTITY

$\mathbf{A}$s the previous readings suggest, groups may conflict or cooperate for a variety of reasons having to do with incentives and constraints posed by the international political and economic environment, or psychological and cultural impulses. This section brings these two sets of concerns closer together, surveying some arguments about how what groups believe about politics, or who they think they are, influence chances for war or peace.

Ideology has played a tremendous role in international interaction, especially since the French Revolution. The twentieth century was dominated by the global clash of liberalism, communism, and fascism. Ideology has also overlapped with issues of identity, as groups conceived their interests and loyalties in terms of class, ethnicity, religion, or other attributes. At the end of the twentieth century identity concerns came to the fore again, as political violence between ethnic groups within many political units escalated in the wake of the communist collapse.

Assessment of threats even by hard-boiled realists can depend on assumptions about these questions. When E. H. Carr's *Twenty Years Crisis* was first published in 1939, its case for realism appeared to many to be an argument for accommodation with German power. Liberal idealism interfered with sensible policy, as Carr saw it, by placing principle over prudence, and by confusing the morality of international relations that coincided with the self-interest of World War I's victorious powers with a disinterested universal morality.

Western liberalism was not the only visionary philosophy interfering with realist behavior. The unfolding of World War II made clear to most that Hitler was not just another opportunistic realist statesman who could be contained or deterred by traditional balance of power politics.[1] Nazi Germany showed the awesome force that idealism can

---

[1] For the notorious yet not altogether unconvincing argument to the contrary, see A.J.P. Taylor, *The Origins of the Second World War* (New York: Atheneum, 1962).

exert in international politics. It is difficult to appreciate the unlimited nature of Nazi aims without understanding Hitler as an idealist more than a pragmatist.[2] It is also quite doubtful that realism, rather than imprudent idealism and wishful thinking, could have justified Churchill's defiant refusal to make peace, and his stirring insistence on pursuit of victory against all odds, in the dark days between the fall of France and Hitler's reckless decisions to take on the Soviet Union and United States. Whether or not realists are correct in arguing that ideology *should* not matter in relations between states, it is clear that it often does.

The triumph of liberal political principles in the postcommunist era has so far been less decisive than that of liberal economic models. Command economies have given way to the market almost everywhere, yet authoritarian polities have been slower to follow— China is the most obvious and most important example. Nevertheless, the burgeoning of democracy has been one of the major world changes since the mid-1980s. If we believe Kant, this trend must be a force for peace.

Michael Doyle supplements Kant's theory with impressive empirical evidence that democratic states do not go to war with each other. True, they have fought many wars with alacrity, but not against each other. If the authoritarian states that democracies tend to fight are disappearing, there should soon be fewer occasions for war. The "democratic peace" theory, which has burgeoned since Doyle revived it, has become in recent years the most influential idea to be adopted by U.S. foreign policy from academic political science. The Clinton administration proclaimed it as a warrant for enlarging the international community of democracies, and a reason that activism otherwise seen as humanitarian should be considered to serve the material interest of the United States.

There are several questions regarding this optimistic conclusion about the impact of the liberalization of political regimes on international conflict. First, Kant's original argument was not that democracies are pacific, but that republics are. If liberalism rather than democracy is the critical ingredient, then the theory depends on a more specific argument. Democracy has spread further than liberalism in the post-Cold War world. Democracies that are majoritarian but illiberal—postcommunist Yugoslavia, Iran, or other such states that have elections but not protections for minority rights— may not support the Democratic Peace.[3]

Second, will the postcommunist trend to democratization survive? Or will the crushing economic problems of conversion and reconstruction in some of the formerly communist states be too much for new democracies to bear, yielding disillusionment, authoritarian populism, dictatorship, a search for scapegoats, and temptations to project frustration outward? Political liberalism may subvert economic liberalism, by empowering people to resist the distribution of pain that goes with tearing down the rickety old economy before a sleek new one is constructed to take its place. The consequent disappointment with economic results may in turn subvert political liberalism. There is

---

[2]See Stanley Kober, "Idealpolitik," *Foreign Policy* No. 79 (summer 1990).
[3]Fareed Zakaria, *The Future of Freedom: Illiberal Democracy at Home and Abroad* (New York: W. W. Norton, 2003).

less anxiety in recent years than there was in the early 1990s about the danger of "Weimar Russia"—a weakly institutionalized Russian democracy vulnerable to xenophobic nationalist backlash—but full democratization in that important country still appears sluggish and incomplete.

Third, will democratization unleash violent forms of nationalism, and will national divisions compound a decline of democracy? Mansfield and Snyder's article in this section uses a careful survey of data to demonstrate that although democracy may be conducive to peace, the process of becoming a secure democracy tends toward the reverse—conflict and violence. One thing Marxism-Leninism did, in institutionalizing regimes based in principle (even if not in practice) on class solidarity, was to delegitimize divisive nationalism and suppress it by force. Now the resurgence of nationalism marks the new world just as much as the proliferation of democratic political forms. Indeed, the norm of self-determination promotes nationalism. Events in the former Yugoslavia and southern parts of the former Soviet Union dramatically highlighted the problem.

Fourth, if ethnic violence, civil war, and regional chaos result from unconstrained nationalist impulses, can such small wars be kept limited, or will they contaminate relations among great powers, creating anxieties about instability, power vacuums, or intervention by others that could catalyze a crisis and escalation to large-scale conflict in a manner similar to 1914? This has been a concern in the Balkans, as some liberals argued that outside intervention is necessary to contain local instability, while some realists argued that it is likely to bring the great power patrons of local contenders into confrontation with each other. As the twenty-first century began, the wars in Bosnia and Kosovo were stopped by NATO interventions, a result that appears consistent with the liberal rationale, but at the price of worsened diplomatic relations with Russia and China, which appears consistent with the realist fear.

Nationalism need not contradict liberalism. Indeed, in the nineteenth century the two tidal forces moved together. And if giving each nation its own state prevents civil war in multinational states, the result should favor peace. But the map does not make that solution easy. Should all nations get their own states when we are sometimes unsure what constitutes a "nation"? Or if doing so would truncate other states—for example, a Kurdistan carved from Turkey, Iran, Iraq, and Syria? Or when the intermingling of minorities would produce awkward gerrymandering for South Ossetians in Georgia, Armenians in Azerbaijan, Trans-Dniester Russians in Moldova, or Serbs in Croatia and Bosnia? Or when it could mean endless redivision into tribal ministates, as in Africa? The selection from Ernest Gellner describes some of the conceptual problems in dealing with nationalism, and differences between benign and malignant forms of it. Can visceral nationalist antipathies annealed in ethnic violence be subordinated to liberal norms, in a reintegrated state, without increasing the risk of reigniting war? Once groups have been at each others' throats, can they live together again in stable peace intermingled, or must they be separated in order to defuse the potential for renewed communal violence? Chaim Kaufmann and Radha Kumar present contrasting arguments on this question.

Neoliberal institutionalism focuses attention on movement in the other direction. Integration rather than independence, through the evolution of organizations such as the European Union, has more often seemed the wave of the future to liberal theorists in recent times. Realists too have often assumed that balance of power imperatives naturally pushed the international system toward agglomeration rather than fractionation of states.[4] Which trends will prove to be the wave of the future—integration in the West, or disintegration in the East?

—RKB

---

[4]E. H. Carr's *Nationalism and After* (New York: Macmillan, 1945) is a fascinating example of reasoning that partakes of both perspectives. It is particularly interesting considering when it was written (the closing days of World War II) and its conviction that the war had made nationalism obsolete—hardly a view that most expect from an author so associated with realism.

Liberalism and World Politics

Michael W. Doyle

Promoting freedom will produce peace, we have often been told. In a speech before the British Parliament in June of 1982, President Reagan proclaimed that governments founded on a respect for individual liberty exercise "restraint" and "peaceful intentions" in their foreign policy. He then announced a "crusade for freedom" and a "campaign for democratic development" (Reagan, June 9, 1982).

In making these claims the president joined a long list of liberal theorists (and propagandists) and echoed an old argument: the aggressive instincts of authoritarian leaders and totalitarian ruling parties make for war. Liberal states, founded on such individual rights as equality before the law, free speech and other civil liberties, private property, and elected representation, are fundamentally against war, this argument asserts. When the citizens who bear the burdens of war elect their governments, wars become impossible. Furthermore, citizens appreciate that the benefits of trade can be enjoyed only under conditions of peace. Thus the very existence of liberal states, such as the U.S., Japan, and our European allies, makes for peace.

Building on a growing literature in an international political science, I reexamine the liberal claim President Reagan reiterated for us. I look at three distinct theoretical traditions of liberalism, attributable to three theorists: Schumpeter, a brilliant explicator of the liberal pacifism the president invoked; Machiavelli, a classical republican whose glory is an imperialism we often practice; and Kant.

Despite the contradictions of liberal pacifism and liberal imperialism, I find, with Kant and other liberal republicans, that liberalism does leave a coherent legacy on foreign affairs. Liberal states are different. They are indeed peaceful, yet they are also prone to make war, as the U.S. and our "freedom fighters" are now doing, not so covertly, against Nicaragua. Liberal states have created a separate peace, as Kant argued they would, and have also discovered liberal reasons for aggression, as he feared they might. I conclude by arguing that the differences among liberal pacifism, liberal imperialism, and Kant's liberal internationalism are not arbitrary but rooted in differing conceptions of the citizen and the state.

Michael W. Doyle, "Liberalism and World Politics," *The American Political Science Review* vol. 80, no. 4 (December 1986). Reprinted with permission of Michael W. Doyle and the American Political Science Association.

LIBERAL PACIFISM

There is no canonical description of liberalism. What we tend to call liberal resembles a family portrait of principles and institutions, recognizable by certain characteristics—for example, individual freedom, political participation, private property, and equality of opportunity—that most liberal states share, although none has perfected them all. Joseph Schumpeter clearly fits within this family when he considers the international effects of capitalism and democracy. . . .

Democratic capitalism leads to peace. As evidence, Schumpeter claims that throughout the capitalist world an opposition has arisen to "war, expansion, cabinet diplomacy"; that contemporary capitalism is associated with peace parties; and that the industrial worker of capitalism is "vigorously anti-imperialist." In addition, he points out that the capitalist world has developed means of preventing war, such as the Hague Court and that the least feudal, most capitalist society—the United States—has demonstrated the least imperialistic tendencies (Schumpeter, 1955, pp. 95–96). An example of the lack of imperialistic tendencies in the U.S., Schumpeter thought, was our leaving over half of Mexico unconquered in the war of 1846–48.

Schumpeter's explanation for liberal pacifism is quite simple: Only war profiteers and military aristocrats gain from wars. No democracy would pursue a minority interest and tolerate the high costs of imperialism. When free trade prevails, "no class" gains from forcible expansion because

> foreign raw materials and food stuffs are as accessible to each nation as though they were in its own territory. Where the cultural backwardness of a region makes normal economic intercourse dependent on colonization it does not matter, assuming free trade, which of the "civilized" nations undertakes the task of colonization. (Schumpeter, 1955, pp. 75–76)

Schumpeter's arguments are difficult to evaluate. In partial tests of quasi-Schumpeterian propositions, Michael Haas (1974, pp. 464–65) discovered a cluster that associates democracy, development, and sustained modernization with peaceful conditions. However, M. Small and J. D. Singer (1976) have discovered that there is no clearly negative correlation between democracy and war in the period 1816–1965—the period that would be central to Schumpeter's argument (see also Wilkenfeld, 1968; Wright, 1942, p. 841).

Later in his career, in *Capitalism, Socialism, and Democracy,* Schumpeter (1950, pp. 127–28) acknowledged that "almost purely bourgeois commonwealths were often aggressive when it seemed to pay—like the Athenian or the Venetian commonwealths." Yet he stuck to his pacifistic guns, restating the view that capitalist democracy "steadily tells . . . against the use of military force and for peaceful arrangements, even when the balance of pecuniary advantage is clearly on the side of war which, under modern circumstances, is not in general very likely" (Schumpeter, 1950, p. 128). A recent study by R. J. Rummel (1983) of "libertarianism" and international violence is the closest test Schumpeterian pacifism has received. "Free" states (those enjoying political and economic freedom) were shown to have considerably less conflict at or above the level of economic sanctions than "nonfree" states. The free states, the partly free states (including the democratic socialist countries such as Sweden), and the nonfree states accounted for 24%, 26%, and 61%, respectively, of the international violence during the period examined.

These effects are impressive but not conclusive for the Schumpeterian thesis. The data are limited, in this test, to the period 1976 to 1980. It includes, for example, the Russo-Afghan War, the Vietnamese invasion of Cambodia, China's invasion of Vietnam, and Tanzania's invasion of Uganda but just misses the U.S., quasi-covert intervention in Angola (1975) and our not so covert war against Nicaragua (1981–). More importantly, it excludes the cold war period, with its numerous interventions, and the long history of colonial wars (the Boer War, the Spanish-American War, the Mexican Intervention, etc.) that marked the history of liberal, including democratic capitalist, states (Doyle, 1983b; Chan, 1984; Weede, 1984).

The discrepancy between the warlike history of liberal states and Schumpeter's pacifistic expectations highlights three extreme assumptions. First, his "materialistic monism" leaves little room for noneconomic objectives, whether espoused by states or individuals. Neither glory, nor prestige, nor ideological justification, nor the pure power of ruling shapes policy. These nonmaterial goals leave little room for positive-sum gains, such as the comparative advantages of trade. Second, and relatedly, the same is true for his states. The political life of individuals seems to have been homogenized at the same time as the individuals were "rationalized, individualized, and democratized." Citizens—capitalists and workers, rural and urban—seek material welfare. Schumpeter seems to presume that ruling makes no difference. He also presumes that no one is prepared to take those measures (such as stirring up foreign quarrels to preserve a domestic ruling coalition) that enhance one's political power, despite detrimental effects on mass welfare. Third, like domestic politics, world politics are homogenized. Materially monistic and democratically capitalist, all states evolve toward free trade and liberty together. Countries differently constituted seem to disappear from Schumpeter's analysis. "Civilized" nations govern "culturally backward" *regions*. These assumptions are not shared by Machiavelli's theory of liberalism.

LIBERAL IMPERIALISM

Machiavelli argues, not only that republics are not pacifistic, but that they are the best form of state for imperial expansion. Establishing a republic fit for imperial expansion is, moreover, the best way to guarantee the survival of a state.

Machiavelli's republic is a classical mixed republic. It is not a democracy—which he thought would quickly degenerate into a tyranny—but is characterized by social equality, popular liberty, and political participation (Machiavelli, 1950, bk. 1, chap. 2, p. 112; see also Huliung, 1983, chap. 2; Mansfield, 1970; Pocock, 1975, pp. 198–99; Skinner, 1981, chap. 3). The consuls serve as "kings," the senate as an aristocracy managing the state, and the people in the assembly as the source of strength.

Liberty results from "disunion"—the competition and necessity for compromise required by the division of powers among senate, consuls, and tribunes (the last representing the common people). Liberty also results from the popular veto. The powerful few threaten the rest with tyranny, Machiavelli says, because they seek to dominate. The mass demands not to be dominated, and their veto thus preserves the liberties of the state (Machiavelli, 1950, bk. 1, chap. 5, p. 122). However, since the people and the rulers have different social characters, the people need to be "managed" by the few to avoid having their recklessness overturn or their fecklessness undermine the ability of the state to expand (Machiavelli, 1950, bk. 1, chap. 53, pp. 249–50). Thus the senate and the consuls plan expansion, consult oracles, and employ religion to manage the resources that the energy of the people supplies.

Strength, and then imperial expansion, results from the way liberty encourages increased population and property, which grow when the citizens know their lives and goods are secure from arbitrary seizure. Free citizens equip large armies and provide soldiers who fight for public glory and the common good because these are, in fact, their own (Machiavelli, 1950, bk. 2, chap. 2, pp. 287–90). If you seek the honor of having your state expand, Machiavelli advises, you should organize it as a free and popular republic like Rome, rather than as an aristocratic republic like Sparta or Venice. Expansion thus calls for a free republic.

"Necessity"—political survival—calls for expansion. If a stable aristocratic republic is forced by foreign conflict "to extend her territory, in such a case we shall see her foundations give way and herself quickly brought to ruin"; if, on the other hand, domestic security prevails, "the continued tranquility would enervate her, or provoke internal dissensions, which together, or either of them separately, will apt to prove her ruin" (Machiavelli, 1950, bk. 1, chap. 6, p. 129). Machiavelli therefore believes it is necessary to take the constitution of Rome, rather than that of Sparta or Venice, as our model.

Hence, this belief leads to liberal imperialism. We are lovers of glory, Machiavelli announces. We seek to rule or, at least, to avoid being oppressed. In either case, we want more for ourselves and our states than just material welfare (materialistic monism). Because other states with similar aims thereby threaten us, we prepare ourselves for expansion. Because our fellow citizens threaten us if we do not allow them either to satisfy their ambition or to release their political energies through imperial expansion, we expand.

There is considerable historical evidence for liberal imperialism. Machiavelli's (Polybius's) Rome and Thucydides' Athens both were imperial republics in the Machiavellian sense (Thucydides, 1954, bk. 6). The historical record of numerous U.S. interventions in the postwar period supports Machiavelli's argument (Aron, 1973, chaps. 3–4; Barnet, 1968, chap. 11), but the current record of liberal pacifism, weak as it is, calls some of his insights into question. To the extent that the modern populace actually controls (and thus unbalances) the mixed republic, its diffidence may outweigh elite ("senatorial") aggressiveness.

We can conclude either that (1) liberal pacifism has at least taken over with the further development of capitalist democracy, as Schumpeter predicted it would or that (2) the mixed record of liberalism—pacifism and imperialism—indicates that some liberal states are Schumpeterian democracies while others are Machiavellian republics. Before we accept either conclusion, however, we must consider a third apparent regularity of modern world politics.

LIBERAL INTERNATIONALISM

Modern liberalism carries with it two legacies. They do not affect liberal states separately, according to whether they are pacifistic or imperialistic, but simultaneously.

The first of these legacies is the pacification of foreign relations among liberal states. During the nineteenth century, the United States and Great Britain engaged in nearly continual strife; however, after the Reform Act of 1832 defined actual representation as the formal source of the sovereignty of the British parliament, Britain and the United States negotiated their disputes. They negotiated despite, for example, British grievances during the Civil War against the North's blockade of the South, with which Britain had close economic ties. Despite several Anglo-French colonial rivalries, liberal France and liberal Britain formed an entente against illiberal Germany before World War I. And from 1914 to 1915, Italy, the liberal member of the Triple Alliance with Germany and Austria, chose not to fulfill its obligations under that treaty to support its allies. Instead, Italy joined in an alliance with Britain and France, which prevented it from having to fight other liberal states and then declared war on Germany and Austria. Despite generations of Anglo-American tension and Britain's wartime restrictions on American trade with Germany, the United States leaned toward Britain and France from 1914 to 1917 before entering World War I on their side.

Beginning in the eighteenth century and slowly growing since then, a zone of peace, which Kant called the "pacific federation" or "pacific union," has begun to be established among liberal societies. More than 40 liberal states currently make up the union. Most are in Europe and North America, but they can be found on every continent, as Appendix 1 indicates.

Here the predictions of liberal pacifists (and President Reagan) are borne out: liberal states do exercise peaceful restraint, and a separate peace exists among them. This separate peace provides a solid foundation for the United States' crucial alliances with the liberal powers, e.g., the North Atlantic Treaty Organization and our Japanese alliance. This foundation appears to be impervious to the quarrels with our allies that bedeviled the Carter and Reagan administrations. It also offers the promise of a continuing peace among liberal states, and as the number of liberal states increases, it announces the possibility of global peace this side of the grave or world conquest.

Of course, the probability of the outbreak of war in any given year between any two given states is low. The occurrence of a war between any two adjacent states, considered over a long period of time, would be more probable. The apparent absence of war between liberal states, whether adjacent or not, for almost 200 years thus may have significance. Similar claims cannot be made for feudal, fascist, communist, authoritarian, or totalitarian forms of rule (Doyle, 1983a, p. 222), nor for pluralistic or merely similar societies. More significant perhaps is that when states are forced to decide on which side of an impending world war they will fight, liberal states all wind up on the same side despite the complexity of the paths that take them there. These characteristics do not prove that the peace among liberals is statistically significant nor that liberalism is the sole valid explanation for the peace. They do suggest that we consider the possibility that liberals have indeed established a separate peace—but only among themselves.

Liberalism also carries with it a second legacy: international "imprudence" (Hume, 1963, pp. 346–47). Peaceful restraint only seems to work in liberals' relations with other liberals. Liberal states have fought numerous wars with nonliberal states. (For a list of international wars since 1816 see Appendix 2.)

Many of these wars have been defensive and thus prudent by necessity. Liberal states have been attacked and threatened by nonliberal states that do not exercise any special restraint in their dealings with the liberal states. Authoritarian rulers both stimulate and respond to an international political environment in which conflicts of prestige, interest, and pure fear of what other states might do all lead states toward war. War and conquest have thus characterized the careers of many authoritarian rulers and ruling parties, from Louis XIV and Napoleon to Mussolini's fascists, Hitler's Nazis, and Stalin's communists.

Yet we cannot simply blame warfare on the authoritarians or totalitarians, as many of our more enthusiastic politicians would have us do. Most wars arise out of calculations and miscalculations of interest, misunderstandings, and mutual suspicions, such as those that characterized the origins of World War I. However, aggression by the liberal state has also characterized a large number of wars. Both France and Britain fought expansionist colonial wars throughout the nineteenth century. The United States fought a similar war with Mexico from 1846 to 1848, waged a war of annihilation against the American Indians, and intervened militarily against sovereign states many times before and after World War II. Liberal states invade weak nonliberal states and display striking distrust in dealings with powerful nonliberal states (Doyle, 1983b).

Neither realist (statist) nor Marxist theory accounts well for these two legacies. While they can account for aspects of certain periods of international stability (Aron, 1968, pp. 151–54; Russett, 1985), neither the logic of the balance of power nor the logic of international hegemony explains the separate peace maintained for more than 150 years among states sharing one particular form of governance—liberal principles and institutions. Balance-of-power theory expects—indeed is premised upon—flexible arrangements of geostrategic rivalry that include preventive war. Hegemonies wax and wane, but the liberal peace holds. Marxist "ultra-imperialists" expect a form of peaceful rivalry among capitalists, but only liberal capitalists maintain peace. Leninists expect liberal capitalists to be aggressive toward nonliberal states, but they also (and especially) expect them to be imperialistic toward fellow liberal capitalists.

Kant's theory of liberal internationalism helps us understand these two legacies. . . .

[See the selection by Kant in Part 3. (Ed.)]

Liberal republics will progressively establish peace among themselves by means of the pacific federation, or union (foedus pacificum), described in Kant's Second Definitive Article. The pacific union will establish peace within a federation of free states and securely maintain the rights of each state. The world will not have achieved the "perpetual peace" that provides the ultimate guarantor of republican freedom until "a late stage and after many unsuccessful attempts" (Kant, *UH,* p. 47). At that time, all nations will have learned the lessons of peace through right conceptions of the appropriate constitution, great and sad experience, and good will. Only then will individuals enjoy perfect republican rights or the full guarantee of a global and just peace. In the meantime, the "pacific federation" of liberal republics—"an enduring and gradually expanding federation likely to prevent war"—brings within it more and more re-publics—despite republican collapses, backsliding, and disastrous wars—creating an ever-expanding separate peace (Kant, *PP,* p. 105). Kant emphasizes that

> it can be shown that this idea of federalism, extending gradually to encompass all states and thus leading to perpetual peace, is practicable and has objective reality. For if by good for-tune one powerful and enlightened nation can form a republic (which is by nature inclined to seek peace), this will provide a focal point for federal association among other states. These will join up with the first one, thus securing the freedom of each state in accordance with the idea of international right, and the whole will gradually spread further and further by a se-ries of alliances of this kind. (Kant, *PP,* p. 104)

The pacific union is not a single peace treaty ending one war, a world state, nor a state of nations. Kant finds the first insufficient. The second and third are impossible or potentially tyrannical. National sovereignty precludes reliable subservience to a state of nations; a world state destroys the civic freedom on which the development of human capacities rests (Kant, *UH,* p. 50). Although Kant obliquely refers to various classical interstate confederations and modern diplomatic congresses, he develops no systematic organizational embodiment of this treaty and presumably does not find institutionaliza-tion necessary (Riley, 1983, chap. 5; Schwarz, 1962, p. 77). He appears to have in mind a mutual nonaggression pact, perhaps a collective security agreement, and the cos-mopolitan law set forth in the Third Definitive Article. . . .

Perpetual peace, for Kant, is an epistemology, a condition for ethical action, and, most importantly, an explanation of how the "mechanical process of nature visibly ex-hibits the purposive plan of producing concord among men, even against their will and indeed by means of their very discord" (Kant, *PP,* p. 108; *UH,* pp. 44–45). Understand-ing history requires an epistemological foundation, for without a teleology, such as the promise of perpetual peace, the complexity of history would overwhelm human under-standing (Kant, *UH,* pp. 51–53). Perpetual peace, however, is not merely a heuristic de-vice with which to interpret history. It is guaranteed, Kant explains in the "First Addition" to *Perpetual Peace* ("On the Guarantee of Perpetual Peace"), to result from men fulfilling their ethical duty or, failing that, from a hidden plan. Peace is an ethical duty because it is only under conditions of peace that all men can treat each other as ends, rather than means to an end (Kant, *UH,* p. 50; Murphy, 1970, chap. 3). In order for this duty to be practical, Kant needs, of course, to show that peace is in fact possi-ble. The widespread sentiment of approbation that he saw aroused by the early success of the French revolutionaries showed him that we can indeed be moved by ethical senti-ments with a cosmopolitan reach (Kant, *CF,* pp. 181–82; Yovel, 1980, pp. 153–54). This does not mean, however, that perpetual peace is certain ("prophesiable"). Even the sci-entifically regular course of the planets could be changed by a wayward comet striking them out of orbit. Human freedom requires that we allow for much greater reversals in the course of history. We must, in fact, anticipate the possibility of backsliding and de-structive wars—though these will serve to educate nations to the importance of peace (Kant, *UH,* pp. 47–48).

In the end, however, our guarantee of perpetual peace does not rest on ethical con-duct. As Kant emphasizes, we now come to the essential question regarding the prospect of perpetual peace. What does nature do in relation to the end which man's own reason prescribes to him as a duty, i.e. how does nature help to promote his *moral purpose?* And how does nature guarantee that what man *ought* to do by the laws of his freedom (but does not do) will in fact be done through nature's compulsion, without prejudice to the free agency of man? . . . This does not mean that nature imposes on us a *duty* to do it, for duties can only be imposed by practical reason. On the contrary, nature does it herself, whether we are willing or not: *facta volentem ducunt, nolentem tradunt. (PP,* p. 112)

The guarantee thus rests, Kant argues, not on the probable behavior of moral angels, but on that of "devils, so long as they possess understanding" (*PP,* p. 112). In explaining the sources of each of the three definitive articles of the perpetual peace, Kant then tells us how we (as free and intelligent devils) could be motivated by fear, force, and calculated advantage to undertake a course of action whose outcome we could reasonably anticipate to be perpetual peace. Yet while it is possible to conceive of the Kantian road to peace in these terms, Kant himself recognizes and argues that social evolution also makes the conditions of moral behavior less onerous and hence more likely (*CF,* pp. 187–89; Kelly, 1969, pp. 106–13). In tracing the effects of both political and moral development, he builds an account of why liberal states do maintain peace among themselves and of how it will (by implication, has) come about that the pacific union will expand. He also explains how these republics would engage in wars with nonrepublics and therefore suffer the "sad experience" of wars that an ethical policy might have avoided. . . .

Kant shows how republics, once established, lead to peaceful relations. He argues that once the aggressive interests of absolutist monarchies are tamed and the habit of respect for individual rights engrained by republican government, wars would appear as the disaster to the people's welfare that he and the other liberals thought them to be. . . . Yet these domestic republican restraints do not end war. If they did, liberal states would not be warlike, which is far from the case. They do introduce republican caution—Kant's "hesitation"—in place of monarchical caprice. Liberal wars are only fought for popular, liberal purposes. The historical liberal legacy is laden with popular wars fought to promote freedom, to protect private property, or to support liberal allies against nonliberal enemies. Kant's position is ambiguous. He regards these wars as unjust and warns liberals of their susceptibility to them (Kant, *PP,* p. 106). At the same time, Kant argues that each nation "can and ought to" demand that its neighboring nations enter into the pacific union of liberal states (*PP,* p. 102). . . .

A further cosmopolitan source of liberal peace is the international market's removal of difficult decisions of production and distribution from the direct sphere of state policy. A foreign state thus does not appear directly responsible for these outcomes, and states can stand aside from, and to some degree above, these contentious market rivalries and be ready to step in to resolve crises. The interdependence of commerce and the international contacts of state officials help create crosscutting transnational ties that serve as lobbies for mutual accommodation. According to modern liberal scholars, international financiers and transnational and transgovernmental organizations create interests in favor of accommodation. Moreover, their variety has ensured that no single conflict sours an entire relationship by setting off a spiral of reciprocated retaliation (Brzezinski and Huntington, 1963, chap. 9; Keohane and Nye, 1977, chap. 7; Neustadt, 1970; Polanyi, 1944, chaps. 1–2). Conversely, a sense of suspicion, such as that characterizing relations between liberal and nonliberal governments, can lead to restrictions on the range of contacts between societies, and this can increase the prospect that a single conflict will determine an entire relationship.

No single constitutional, international, or cosmopolitan source is alone sufficient, but together (and only together) they plausibly connect the characteristics of liberal polities and economies with sustained liberal peace. Alliances founded on mutual strategic interest among liberal and nonliberal states have been broken; economic ties between liberal and nonliberal states have proven fragile; but the political bonds of liberal rights and interests have proven a remarkably firm foundation for mutual nonaggression. A separate peace exists among liberal states.

In their relations with nonliberal states, however, liberal states have not escaped from the insecurity caused by anarchy in the world political system considered as a whole. Moreover, the very constitutional restraint, international respect for individual rights, and shared commercial interests that establish grounds for peace among liberal states establish grounds for additional conflict in relations between liberal and nonliberal societies.

CONCLUSION

. . . Unlike Machiavelli's republics, Kant's republics are capable of achieving peace among themselves because they exercise democratic caution and are capable of appreciating the international rights of foreign republics. These international rights of republics derive from the representation of foreign individuals, who are our moral equals. Unlike Schumpeter's capitalist democracies, Kant's republics—including our own—remain in a state of war with nonrepublics. Liberal republics see themselves as threatened by aggression from nonrepublics that are not constrained by representation. Even though wars often cost more than the economic return they generate, liberal republics also are prepared to protect and promote—sometimes forcibly—democracy, private property, and the rights of individuals overseas against nonrepublics, which, because they do not authentically represent the rights of individuals, have no rights to noninterference. These wars may liberate oppressed individuals overseas; they also can generate enormous suffering.

Preserving the legacy of the liberal peace without succumbing to the legacy of liberal imprudence is both a moral and a strategic challenge. The bipolar stability of the international system, and the near certainty of mutual devastation resulting from a nuclear war between the superpowers, have created a "crystal ball effect" that has helped to constrain the tendency toward miscalculation present at the outbreak of so many wars in the past (Carnesale, Doty, Hoffmann, Huntington, Nye, and Sagan, 1983, p. 44; Waltz, 1964). However, this "nuclear peace" appears to be limited to the superpowers. It has not curbed military interventions in the Third World. Moreover, it is subject to a desperate technological race designed to overcome its constraints and to crises that have pushed even the superpowers to the brink of war. We must still reckon with the war fevers and moods of appeasement that have almost alternately swept liberal democracies.

Yet restraining liberal imprudence, whether aggressive or passive, may not be possible without threatening liberal pacification. Improving the strategic acumen of our foreign policy calls for introducing steadier strategic calculations of the national interest in the long run and more flexible responses to changes in the international political environment. Constraining the indiscriminate meddling of our foreign interventions calls for a deeper appreciation of the "particularism of history, culture, and membership" (Walzer, 1983, p. 5), but both the improvement in strategy and the constraint on intervention seem, in turn, to require an executive freed from the restraints of a representative legislature in the management of foreign policy and a political culture indifferent to the universal rights of individuals. These conditions, in their turn, could break the chain of constitutional guarantees, the respect for representative government, and the web of transnational contact that have sustained the pacific union of liberal states.

Perpetual peace, Kant says, is the end point of the hard journey his republics will take. The promise of perpetual peace, the violent lessons of war, and the experience of a partial peace are proof of the need for and the possibility of world peace. They are also the grounds for moral citizens and statesmen to assume the duty of striving for peace.

APPENDIX 1

Liberal Regimes and the Pacific Union, 1700–1982

Period	*Period*	*Period*
18th Century	**1900–1945** (cont.)	**1945** (cont.)
Swiss Cantons[a]	Netherlands, –1940	Austria, 1945–
French Republic, 1790–1795	Argentina, –1943	Brazil, 1945–1954,
United States,[a] 1776–	France, –1940	1955–1964
Total = 3	Chile, –1924, 1932–	Belgium, 1946–
	Australia, 1901	Luxemburg, 1946–
1800–1850	Norway, 1905–1940	Netherlands, 1946–
Swiss Confederation	New Zealand, 1907–	Italy, 1946–
United States	Colombia, 1910–1949	Philippines, 1946–1972
France, 1830–1849	Denmark, 1914–1940	India, 1947–1975, 1977–
Belgium, 1830–	Poland, 1917–1935	Sri Lanka, 1948–1961;
Great Britain, 1832–	Latvia, 1922–1934	1963–1971; 1978–
Netherlands, 1848–	Germany, 1918–1932	Ecuador, 1948–1963;
Piedmont, 1848–	Austria, 1918–1934	1979–
Denmark, 1849–	Estonia, 1919–1934	Israel, 1949–
Total = 8	Finland, 1919–	West Germany, 1949–
	Uruguay, 1919–	Greece, 1950–1967; 1975–
1850–1900	Costa Rica, 1919–	Peru, 1950–1962;
Switzerland	Czechoslovakia, 1920–1939	1963–1968; 1980–
United States	Ireland, 1920–	El Salvador, 1950–1961
Belgium	Mexico, 1928–	Turkey, 1950–1960;
Great Britain	Lebanon, 1944–	1966–1971
Netherlands	Total = 29	Japan, 1951–
Piedmont, –1861		Bolivia 1956–1969; 1982–
Italy, –1861	**1945–[b]**	Colombia, 1958–
Denmark, –1866	Switzerland	Venezuela, 1959–
Sweden, 1864–	United States	Nigeria, 1961–1964;
Greece, 1864–	Great Britain	1979–1984
Canada, 1867–	Sweden	Jamaica, 1962–
France, 1871–	Canada	Trinidad and Tobago,
Argentina, 1880–	Australia	1962–
Chile, 1891–	New Zealand	Senegal, 1963–
Total = 14	Finland	Malaysia, 1963–
	Ireland	Botswana, 1966–
1900–1945	Mexico	Singapore, 1965–
Switzerland	Uruguay, –1973	Portugal, 1976–
United States	Chile, –1973	Spain, 1978–
Great Britain	Lebanon, –1975	Dominican Republic,
Sweden	Costa Rica, –1948; 1953–	1978–
Canada	Iceland, 1944–	Honduras, 1981–
Greece, –1911; 1928–1936	France, 1945–	Papua New Guinea, 1982–
Italy, –1922	Denmark, 1945	Total = 50
Belgium, –1940	Norway, 1945	

NOTE: I have drawn up this approximate list of "Liberal Regimes" according to the four institutions Kant described as essential: market and private property economies; polities that are externally sovereign; citizens who possess juridical rights; and "republican" (whether republican or parliamentary monarchy), representative government. This latter includes the requirement that the legislative branch have an effective role in public policy and be formally and competitively (either inter- or intra-party) elected. Furthermore, I have taken into account whether male suffrage is wide (i.e., 30%) or, as Kant (*MM*, p. 139) would have had it, open by "achievement" to inhabitants of the national or metropolitan territory (e.g., to poll-tax payers or householders). This list of liberal regimes is thus more inclusive than a list of democratic regimes, or polyarchies (Powell, 1982, p. 5). Other conditions taken into account here are that female suffrage is granted within a generation of its being demanded by an extensive female suffrage movement and that representative government is internally sovereign (e.g., including, and especially over military and foreign affairs) as well as stable (in existence for at least three years). Sources for these data are Banks and Overstreet (1983), Gastil (1985), *The Europa Yearbook, 1985* (1985), Langer (1968), U.K. Foreign and Commonwealth Office (1980), and U.S. Department of State (1981). Finally, these lists exclude ancient and medieval "republics," since none appears to fit Kant's commitment to liberal individualism (Holmes, 1979).

[a]There are domestic variations within these liberal regimes: Switzerland was liberal only in certain cantons; the United States was liberal only north of the Mason-Dixon line until 1865, when it became liberal throughout.

[b]Selected list, excludes liberal regimes with populations less than one million. These include all states categorized as "free" by Gastil and those "partly free" (four-fifths or more free) states with a more pronounced capitalist orientation.

APPENDIX 2

International Wars Listed Chronologically

British-Maharattan (1817–1818)
Greek (1821–1828)
Franco-Spanish (1823)
First Anglo-Burmese (1823–1826)
Javanese (1825–1830)
Russo-Persian (1826–1828)
Russo-Turkish (1828–1829)
First Polish (1831)
First Syrian (1831–1832)
Texas (1835–1836)
First British-Afghan (1838–1842)
Second Syrian (1839–1940)
Franco-Algerian (1839–1847)
Peruvian-Bolivian (1841)
First British-Sikh (1845–1846)
Mexican-American (1846–1848)
Austro-Sardinian (1848–1849)
First Schleswig-Holstein (1848–1849)
Hungarian (1848–1849)
Second British-Sikh (1848–1849)
Roman Republic (1849)
La Plata (1851–1852)
First Turco-Montenegran (1852–1853)
Crimean (1853–1856)
Anglo-Persian (1856–1857)
Sepoy (1857–1859)
Second Turco-Montenegran (1858–1859)
Italian Unification (1859)
Spanish-Moroccan (1859–1860)
Italo-Roman (1860)
Italo-Sicilian (1860–1861)
Franco-Mexican (1862–1867)
Ecuadorian-Colombian (1863)
Second Polish (1863–1864)
Spanish-Santo Dominican (1863–1865)
Second Schleswig-Holstein (1864)
Lopez (1864–1870)
Spanish-Chilean (1865–1866)
Seven Weeks (1866)
Ten Years (1868–1878)
Franco-Prussian (1870–1871)
Dutch-Achinese (1873–1878)
Balkan (1875–1877)
Russo-Turkish (1877–1878)

Bosnian (1878)
Second British-Afghan (1878–1880)
Pacific (1879–1883)
British-Zulu (1879)
Franco-Indochinese (1882–1884)
Mahdist (1882–1885)
Sino-French (1884–1885)
Central American (1885)
Serbo-Bulgarian (1885)
Sino-Japanese (1894–1895)
Franco-Madagascan (1894–1895)
Cuban (1895–1898)
Italo-Ethiopian (1895–1896)
First Philippine (1896–1898)
Greco-Turkish (1897)
Spanish-American (1898)
Second Philippine (1899–1902)
Boer (1899–1902)
Boxer Rebellion (1900)
Ilinden (1903)
Russo-Japanese (1904–1905)
Central American (1906)
Central American (1907)
Spanish-Moroccan (1909–1910)
Italo-Turkish (1911–1912)
First Balkan (1912–1913)
Second Balkan (1913)
World War I (1914–1918)
Russian Nationalities (1917–1921)
Russo-Polish (1919–1920)
Hungarian-Allies (1919)
Greco-Turkish (1919–1922)
Riffian (1921–1926)
Druze (1925–1927)
Sino-Soviet (1929)
Manchurian (1931–1933)
Chaco (1932–1935)
Italo-Ethiopian (1935–1936)
Sino-Japanese (1937–1941)
Changkufeng (1938)
Nomohan (1939)
World War II (1939–1945)
Russo-Finnish (1939–1940)
Franco-Thai (1940–1941)

APPENDIX 2 (Continued)

≋ **International Wars Listed Chronologically**

Indonesian (1945–1946)	Israeli-Egyptian (1969–1970)
Indochinese (1945–1954)	Football (1969)
Madagascan (1947–1948)	Bangladesh (1971)
First Kashmir (1947–1949)	Philippine-MNLF (1972–)
Palestine (1948–1949)	Yom Kippur (1973)
Hyderabad (1948)	Turco-Cypriot (1974)
Korean (1950–1953)	Ethiopian-Eritrean (1974–)
Algerian (1954–1962)	Vietnamese-Cambodian (1975–)
Russo-Hungarian (1956)	Timor (1975–)
Sinai (1956)	Saharan (1975–)
Tibetan (1956–1959)	Ogaden (1976–)
Sino-Indian (1962)	Ugandan-Tanzanian (1978–1979)
Vietnamese (1965–1975)	Sino-Vietnamese (1979)
Second Kashmir (1965)	Russo-Afghan (1979–)
Six Day (1967)	Iran-Iraqi (1980–)

NOTE: This table is taken from Melvin Small and J. David Singer (1982, pp. 79–80). This is a partial list of international wars fought between 1816 and 1980. In Appendices A and B, Small and Singer identify a total of 575 wars during this period, but approximately 159 of them appear to be largely domestic, or civil wars.

This list excludes covert interventions, some of which have been directed by liberal regimes against other liberal regimes—for example, the United States' effort to destabilize the Chilean election and Allende's government. Nonetheless, it is significant that such interventions are not pursued publicly as acknowledged policy. The covert destabilization campaign against Chile is recounted by the Senate Select Committee to Study Governmental Operations with Respect to Intelligence Activities (1975, *Covert Action in Chile, 1963–73*).

Following the argument of this article, this list also excludes civil wars. Civil wars differ from international wars, not in the ferocity of combat, but in the issues that engender them. Two nations that could abide one another as independent neighbors separated by a border might well be the fiercest of enemies if forced to live together in one state, jointly deciding how to raise and spend taxes, choose leaders, and legislate fundamental questions of value. Notwithstanding these differences, no civil wars that I recall upset the argument of liberal pacification.

REFERENCES

Aron, Raymond. 1966. *Peace and War: A Theory of International Relations.* Richard Howard and Annette Baker Fox, trans. Garden City, NY: Doubleday.

———. 1974. *The Imperial Republic.* Frank Jellinek, trans. Englewood Cliffs, NJ: Prentice Hall.

Banks, Arthur, and William Overstreet, eds. 1983. *A Political Handbook of the World; 1982–1983.* New York: McGraw Hill.

Barnet, Richard. 1968. *Intervention and Revolution.* Cleveland: World Publishing Co.

Brzezinski, Zbigniew, and Samuel Huntington. 1963. *Political Power: USA/USSR.* New York: Viking Press.

Carnesale, Albert, Paul Doty, Stanley Hoffmann, Samuel Huntington, Joseph Nye, and Scott Sagan. 1983. *Living With Nuclear Weapons.* New York: Bantam.

Chan, Steve. 1984. Mirror, Mirror on the Wall . . . : Are Freer Countries More Pacific? *Journal of Conflict Resolution,* 28:617–48.

Doyle, Michael W. 1983a. Kant, Liberal Legacies, and Foreign Affairs: Part 1. *Philosophy and Public Affairs,* 12:205–35.

———. 1983b. Kant, Liberal Legacies, and Foreign Affairs: Part 2. *Philosophy and Public Affairs,* 12:323–53.

———. 1986. *Empires.* Ithaca: Cornell University Press.

The Europa Yearbook for 1985. 1985. 2 vols. London: Europa Publications.

Friedrich, Karl. 1948. *Inevitable Peace.* Cambridge, MA: Harvard University Press.

Gastil, Raymond. 1985. The Comparative Survey of Freedom 1985. *Freedom at Issue,* 82:3–16.

Haas, Michael. 1974. *International Conflict.* New York: Bobbs-Merrill.

Hermens, Ferdinand A. 1944. *The Tyrants' War and the People's Peace.* Chicago: University of Chicago Press.

Holmes, Stephen. 1979. Aristippus in and out of Athens. *American Political Science Review,* 73:113–28.

Huliung, Mark. 1983. *Citizen Machiavelli.* Princeton: Princeton University Press.

Hume, David. 1963. Of the Balance of Power. *Essays: Moral, Political and Literary.* Oxford: Oxford University Press.

Kant, Immanuel. 1970. *Kant's Political Writings.* Hans Reiss, ed. H. B. Nisbet, trans. Cambridge: Cambridge University Press.

Kelly, George A. 1969. *Idealism, Politics, and History.* Cambridge: Cambridge University Press.

Keohane, Robert, and Joseph Nye. 1977. *Power and Interdependence.* Boston: Little Brown.

Langer, William L., ed. 1968. *The Encyclopedia of World History.* Boston: Houghton Mifflin.

Machiavelli, Niccolo. 1950. *The Prince and the Discourses.* Max Lerner, ed. Luigi Ricci and Christian Detmold, trans. New York: Modern Library.

Mansfield, Harvey C. 1970. Machiavelli's New Regime. *Italian Quarterly.* 13:63–95.

Murphy, Jeffrie. 1970. *Kant: The Philosophy of Right.* New York: St. Martins.

Neustadt, Richard. 1970. *Alliance Politics.* New York: Columbia University Press.

Pocock, J. G. A. 1975. *The Machiavellian Moment.* Princeton: Princeton University Press.

Polanyi, Karl. 1944. *The Great Transformation.* Boston: Beacon Press.

Posen, Barry, and Stephen Van Evera. 1980. Over-arming and Underwhelming. *Foreign Policy,* 40:99–118.

Powell, G. Bingham. 1982. *Contemporary Democracies.* Cambridge, MA: Harvard University Press.

Riley, Patrick. 1983. *Kant's Political Philosophy.* Totowa, NJ: Rowman and Littlefield.

Rummel, Rudolph J. 1979. *Understanding Conflict and War,* 5 vols. Beverly Hills: Sage Publications.

Russett, Bruce. 1985. The Mysterious Case of Vanishing Hegemony. *International Organization,* 39:207–31.

Schumpeter, Joseph. 1950. *Capitalism, Socialism, and Democracy.* New York: Harper Torchbooks.

———. 1955. The Sociology of Imperialism. In *Imperialism and Social Classes.* Cleveland: World Publishing Co. (Essay originally published in 1919.)

Schwarz, Wolfgang. 1962. Kant's Philosophy of Law and International Peace. *Philosophy and Phenomenonological Research,* 23:71–80.

Shell, Susan. 1980. *The Rights of Reason.* Toronto: University of Toronto Press.

Skinner, Quentin. 1981. *Machiavelli.* New York: Hill and Wang.

Small, Melvin, and J. David Singer. 1976. The War-Proneness of Democratic Regimes. *The Jerusalem Journal of International Relations,* 1 (4):50–69.

———. 1982. *Resort to Arms.* Beverly Hills: Sage Publications.

Thucydides. 1954. *The Peloponnesian War.* Rex Warner, ed. and trans. Baltimore: Penguin.

U.K. Foreign and Commonwealth Office. 1980. *A Yearbook of the Commonwealth 1980.* London: HMSO.

U.S. Congress, Senate. Select Committee to Study Governmental Operations with Respect to Intelligence Activities. 1975. *Covert Action in Chile, 1963–74.* 94th Cong., 1st sess., Washington, D.C.: U.S. Government Printing Office.

U.S. Department of State. 1981. *Country Reports on Human Rights Practices.* Washington, D.C.: U.S. Government Printing Office.

Waltz, Kenneth. 1964. The Stability of a Bipolar World. *Daedalus,* 93:881–909.

Walzer, Michael. 1983. *Spheres of Justice.* New York: Basic Books.

Weede, Erich. 1984. Democracy and War Involvement. *Journal of Conflict Resolution,* 28:649–64.

Wilkenfield, Jonathan. 1968. Domestic and Foreign Conflict Behavior of Nations. *Journal of Peace Research,* 5:56–69.

Wright, Quincy. 1942. *A Study of History.* Chicago: Chicago University Press.

Yovel, Yirmiahu. 1980. *Kant and the Philosophy of History.* Princeton: Princeton University Press.

NATIONS AND NATIONALISM

Ernest Gellner

DEFINITIONS

Nationalism is primarily a political principle, which holds that the political and the national unit should be congruent.

Nationalism as a sentiment, or as a movement, can best be defined in terms of this principle. Nationalist *sentiment* is the feeling of anger aroused by the violation of the principle, or the feeling of satisfaction aroused by its fulfillment. A nationalist *movement* is one actuated by a sentiment of this kind.

There is a variety of ways in which the nationalist principle can be violated. The political boundary of a given state can fail to include all the members of the appropriate nation; or it can include them all but also include some foreigners; or it can fail in both these ways at once, not incorporating all the nationals and yet also including some non-nationals. Or again, a nation may live, unmixed with foreigners, in a multiplicity of states, so that no single state can claim to be *the* national one.

But there is one particular form of the violation of the nationalist principle to which nationalist sentiment is quite particularly sensitive; if the rulers of the political unit belong to a nation other than that of the majority of the ruled, this, for nationalists, constitutes a quite outstandingly intolerable breach of political propriety. This can occur either through the incorporation of the national territory in a larger empire, or by the local domination of an alien group.

In brief, nationalism is a theory of political legitimacy, which requires that ethnic boundaries should not cut across political ones, and, in particular, that ethnic boundaries within a given state—a contingency already formally excluded by the principle in its general formulation—should not separate the power holders from the rest.

The nationalist principle can be asserted in an ethical, 'universalistic' spirit. There could be, and on occasion there have been, nationalists-in-the-abstract, unbiased in favour of any special nationality of their own, and generously preaching the doctrine for all nations alike: let all nations have their own political roofs, and let all of them also refrain from including non-nationals under it. There is no formal contradiction in asserting such non-egoistic nationalism. As a doctrine it can be supported by some good arguments, such as the desirability of preserving cultural diversity, of a pluralistic international political system, and of the diminution of internal strains within states.

✓ In fact, however, nationalism has often not been so sweetly reasonable, nor so rationally symmetrical. It may be that, as Immanuel Kant believed, partiality, the tendency to make exceptions on one's own behalf or one's own case, is *the* central human weakness from which all others flow; and that it infects national sentiment as it does all else, engendering what the Italians under Mussolini called the *sacro egoismo* of nationalism. It may also be that the political effectiveness of national sentiment would be much impaired if nationalists had as fine a sensibility to the wrongs committed by their nation as they have to those committed against it.

But over and above these considerations there are others, tied to the specific nature of the world we happen to live in, which militate against any impartial, general, sweetly reasonable nationalism. To put it in the simplest possible terms: there is a very large number of potential nations on earth. Our planet also contains room for a certain number of independent or autonomous political units. On any reasonable calculation, the former number (of potential nations) is probably much, *much* larger than that of possible viable states. If this argument or calculation is correct, not all nationalisms can be satisfied, at any rate at the same time. The satisfaction of some spells the frustration of others. This argument is further and immeasurably strengthened by the fact that very many of the potential nations of this world live, or until recently have lived, not in compact territorial units but intermixed with each other in complex patterns. It follows that a territorial political unit can only become ethnically homogeneous, in such cases, if it either kills, or expels, or assimilates all non-nationals. Their unwillingness to suffer such fates may make the peaceful implementation of the nationalist principle difficult.

These definitions must, of course, like most definitions, be applied with common sense. The nationalist principle, as defined, is not violated by the presence of *small* numbers of resident foreigners, or even by the presence of the occasional foreigner in, say, a national ruling family. Just how many resident foreigners or foreign members of the ruling class there must be before the principle is effectively violated cannot be stated with precision. There is no sacred percentage figure, below which the foreigner can be benignly tolerated, and above which he becomes offensive and his safety and life are at peril. No doubt the figure will vary with circumstances. The impossibility of providing a generally applicable and precise figure, however, does not undermine the usefulness of the definition.

STATE AND NATION

Our definition of nationalism was parasitic on two as yet undefined terms: state and nation.

Discussion of the state may begin with Max Weber's celebrated definition of it, as that agency within society which possesses the monopoly of legitimate violence. The idea behind this is simple and seductive: in well-ordered societies, such as most of us live in or aspire to live in, private or sectional violence is illegitimate. Conflict as such is not illegitimate, but it cannot rightfully be resolved by private or sectional violence. Violence may be applied only by the central political authority, and those to whom it delegates this right. Among the various sanctions of the maintenance of order, the ultimate one—

force—may be applied only by one special, clearly identified, and well centralized, disciplined agency within society. That agency or group of agencies *is* the state.

The idea enshrined in this definition corresponds fairly well with the moral intuitions of many, probably most, members of modern societies. Nevertheless, it is not entirely satisfactory. There are 'states'—or, at any rate, institutions which we would normally be inclined to call by that name—which do not monopolize legitimate violence within the territory which they more or less effectively control. A feudal state does not necessarily object to private wars between its fief-holders, provided they also fulfill their obligations to their overlord; or again, a state counting tribal populations among its subjects does not necessarily object to the institution of the feud, as long as those who indulge in it refrain from endangering neutrals on the public highway or in the market. The Iraqi state, under British tutelage after the First World War, tolerated tribal raids, provided the raiders dutifully reported at the nearest police station before and after the expedition, leaving an orderly bureaucratic record of slain and booty. In brief, there are states which lack either the will or the means to enforce their monopoly of legitimate violence, and which nonetheless remain, in many respects, recognizable 'states'.

Weber's underlying principle does, however, seem valid *now,* however strangely ethnocentric it may be as a general definition, with its tacit assumption of the well-centralized Western state. The state constitutes one highly distinctive and important elaboration of the social division of labour. Where there is no division of labour, one cannot even begin to speak of the state. But not any or every specialism makes a state: the state is the specialization and concentration of order maintenance. The 'state' is that institution or set of institutions specifically concerned with the enforcement of order (whatever else they may also be concerned with). The state exists where specialized order-enforcing agencies, such as police forces and courts, have separated out from the rest of social life. They *are* the state.

Not all societies are state-endowed. It immediately follows that the problem of nationalism does not arise for stateless societies. If there is no state, one obviously cannot ask whether or not its boundaries are congruent with the limits of nations. If there are no rulers, there being no state, one cannot ask whether they are of the same nation as the ruled. When neither state nor rulers exist, one cannot resent their failure to conform to the requirements of the principle of nationalism. One may perhaps deplore statelessness, but that is another matter. Nationalists have generally fulminated against the distribution of political power and the nature of political boundaries, but they have seldom if ever had occasion to deplore the absence of power and of boundaries altogether. The circumstances in which nationalism has generally arisen have not normally been those in which the state itself, as such, was lacking, or when its reality was in any serious doubt. The state was only too conspicuously present. It was its boundaries and/or the distribution of power, and possibly of other advantages, within it which were resented.

This in itself is highly significant. Not only is our definition of nationalism parasitic on a prior and assumed definition of the state: it also seems to be the case that nationalism emerges only in milieux in which the existence of the state is already very much taken for granted. The existence of politically centralized units, and of a moral-political climate in which such centralized units are taken for granted and are treated as normative, is a necessary though by no means a sufficient condition of nationalism.

By way of anticipation, some general historical observations should be made about the state. Mankind has passed through three fundamental stages in its history: the pre-agrarian, the agrarian, and the industrial. Hunting and gathering bands were and are too small to allow the kind of political division of labour which constitutes the state; and so, for them, the question of the state, of a stable specialized order-enforcing institution, does not really arise. By contrast, most, but by no means all, agrarian societies have been state-endowed. Some of these states have been strong and some weak, some have been despotic and others law-abiding. They differ a very great deal in their form. The agrarian phase of human history is the period during which, so to speak, the very existence of the state is an option. Moreover, the form of the state is highly variable. During the hunting-gathering stage, the option was not available.

By contrast, in the post-agrarian, industrial age there is, once again, no option; but now the *presence,* not the absence of the state is inescapable. Paraphrasing Hegel, once none had the state, then some had it, and finally all have it. The form it takes, of course, still remains variable. There are some traditions of social thought—anarchism, Marxism—which hold that even, or especially, in an industrial order the state is dispensable, at least under favourable conditions or under conditions due to be realized in the fullness of time. There are obvious and powerful reasons for doubting this: industrial societies are enormously large, and depend for the standard of living to which they have become accustomed (or to which they ardently wish to become accustomed) on an unbelievably intricate general division of labour and cooperation. Some of this co-operation might under favourable conditions be spontaneous and need no central sanctions. The idea that all of it could perpetually work in this way, that it could exist without any enforcement and control, puts an intolerable strain on one's credulity.

So the problem of nationalism does not arise when there is no state. It does not follow that the problem of nationalism arises for each and every state. On the contrary, it arises only for *some* states. It remains to be seen which ones do face this problem.

THE NATION

The definition of the nation presents difficulties graver than those attendant on the definition of the state. Although modern man tends to take the centralized state (and, more specifically, the centralized national state) for granted, nevertheless he is capable, with relatively little effort, of seeing its contingency, and of imagining a social situation in which the state is absent. He is quite adept at visualizing the 'state of nature'. An anthropologist can explain to him that the tribe is not necessarily a state writ small, and that forms of tribal organization exist which can be described as stateless. By contrast, the idea of a man without a nation seems to impose a far greater strain on the modern imagination. Chamisso, an *emigré* Frenchman in Germany during the Napoleonic period, wrote a powerful proto-Kafkaesque novel about a man who lost his shadow: though no doubt part of the effectiveness of this novel hinges on the intended ambiguity of the parable, it is difficult not to suspect that, for the author, the Man without a Shadow was the Man without a Nation. When his followers and acquaintances detect his aberrant shadowlessness they shun the otherwise well-endowed Peter Schlemiehl. A man without a nation defies the recognized categories and provokes revulsion.

Chamisso's perception—if indeed this is what he intended to convey—was valid enough, but valid only for one kind of human condition, and not for the human condition as such anywhere at any time. A man must have a nationality as he must have a nose and two ears; a deficiency in any of these particulars is not inconceivable and does from time to time occur, but only as a result of some disaster, and it is itself a disaster of a kind. All this seems obvious, though, alas, it is not true. But that it should have come to *seem* so very obviously true is indeed an aspect, or perhaps the very core, of the problem of nationalism. Having a nation is not an inherent attribute of humanity, but it has now come to appear as such.

In fact, nations, like states, are a contingency, and not a universal necessity. Neither nations nor states exist at all times and in all circumstances. Moreover, nations and states are not the *same* contingency. Nationalism holds that they were destined for each other; that either without the other is incomplete, and constitutes a tragedy. But before they could become intended for each other, each of them had to emerge, and their emergence was independent and contingent. The state has certainly emerged without the help of the nation. Some nations have certainly emerged without the blessings of their own state. It is more debatable whether the normative idea of the nation, in its modern sense, did not presuppose the prior existence of the state.

What then is this contingent, but in our age seemingly universal and normative, idea of the nation? Discussion of two very makeshift, temporary definitions will help to pinpoint this elusive concept.

1. Two men are of the same nation if and only if they share the same culture, where culture in turn means a system of ideas and signs and associations and ways of behaving and communicating.
2. Two men are of the same nation if and only if they recognize each other as belonging to the same nation. In other words, *nations make the man;* nations are the artifacts of men's convictions and loyalties and solidarities. A mere category of persons (say, occupants of a given territory, or speakers of a given language, for example) becomes a nation if and when the members of the category firmly recognize certain mutual rights and duties to each other in virtue of their shared membership of it. It is their recognition of each other as fellows of this kind which turns them into a nation, and not the other shared attributes, whatever they might be, which separate that category from nonmembers.

Each of these provisional definitions, the cultural and the voluntaristic, has some merit. Each of them singles out an element which is of real importance in the understanding of nationalism. But neither is adequate. Definitions of culture, presupposed by the first definition, in the anthropological rather than the normative sense, are notoriously difficult and unsatisfactory. It is probably best to approach this problem by using this term without attempting too much in the way of formal definition, and looking at what culture does. . . .

A NOTE ON THE WEAKNESS
OF NATIONALISM

It is customary to comment on the strength of nationalism. This is an important mistake, though readily understandable since, whenever nationalism has taken root, it has tended to prevail with ease over other modern ideologies.

Nevertheless, the clue to the understanding of nationalism is its weakness at least as much as its strength. It was the dog who failed to bark who provided the vital clue for Sherlock Holmes. The numbers of potential nationalisms which failed to bark is far, far larger than those which did, though *they* have captured all our attention.

We have already insisted on the dormant nature of this allegedly powerful monster during the pre-industrial age. But even within the age of nationalism, there is a further important sense in which nationalism remains astonishingly feeble. Nationalism has been defined, in effect, as the striving to make culture and polity congruent, to endow a culture with its own political roof, and not more than one roof at that. Culture, an elusive concept, was deliberately left undefined. But an at least provisionally acceptable criterion of culture might be language, as at least a sufficient, if not a necessary touchstone of it. Allow for a moment a difference of language to entail a difference of culture (though not necessarily the reverse).

If this is granted, at least temporarily, certain consequences follow. I have heard the number of languages on earth estimated at around 8000. The figure can no doubt be increased by counting dialects separately. If we allow the 'precedent' argument, this becomes legitimate: if a kind of differential which in some places defines a nationalism is allowed to engender a 'potential nationalism' wherever else a similar difference is found, then the number of potential nationalisms increases sharply. For instance, diverse Slavonic, Teutonic and Romance languages are in fact often no further apart than are the mere dialects within what are elsewhere conventionally seen as unitary languages. Slav languages, for instance, are probably closer to each other than are the various forms of colloquial Arabic, allegedly a single language.

The 'precedent' argument can also generate potential nationalisms by analogies invoking factors other than language. For instance, Scottish nationalism indisputably exists. (It may indeed be held to contradict my model.) It ignores language (which would condemn some Scots to Irish nationalism, and the rest to English nationalism), invoking instead a shared historical experience. Yet if such additional links be allowed to count (as long as they don't contradict the requirement of my model, that they can serve as a base for an *eventually* homogeneous, internally mobile culture/polity with one educational machine servicing that culture under the surveillance of that polity), then the number of potential nationalisms goes up even higher.

However, let us be content with the figure of 8000, once given to me by a linguist as a rough number of languages based on what was no doubt rather an arbitrary estimate of language alone. The number of states in the world at present is some figure of the order of 200. To this figure one may add all the irredentist nationalisms, which have not yet attained their state (and perhaps never will), but which are struggling in that direction and thus have a legitimate claim to be counted among actual, and not merely potential, nationalisms. On the other hand, one must also subtract all those states which have come into being without the benefit of the blessing of nationalist endorsement, and which do not satisfy the nationalist criteria of political legitimacy, and indeed defy them; for instance, all the diverse mini-states dotted about the globe as survivals of a pre-nationalist age, and sometimes brought forth as concessions to geographical accident or political compromise. Once all these had been subtracted, the resulting figure would again, presumably, not be too far above 200. But let us, for the sake of charity, pretend that we have four times that number of reasonably effective nationalisms on earth, in other words, 800 of them. I believe this to be considerably larger than the facts would justify, but let it pass.

This rough calculation still gives us only *one* effective nationalism for *ten* potential ones! And this surprising ratio, depressing presumably for any enthusiastic pan-nationalist, if such a person exists, could be made much larger if the 'precedent' argument were applied to the full to determine the number of potential nationalisms, and if the criteria of entry into the class of effective nationalisms were made at all stringent.

What is one to conclude from this? That for every single nationalism which has so far raised its ugly head, nine others are still waiting in the wings? That all the bomb-throwing, martyrdoms, exchange of populations, and worse, which have so far beset humanity, are still to be repeated tenfold?

I think not. For every effective nationalism, there are *n* potential ones, groups defined either by shared culture inherited from the agrarian world or by some other link (on the 'precedent' principle) which *could* give hope of establishing a homogeneous industrial community, but which nevertheless do not bother to struggle, which fail to activate their potential nationalism, which do not even try.

So it seems that the urge to make mutual cultural substitutability the basis of the state is not so powerful after all. The members of *some* groups do indeed feel it, but members of most groups, with analogous claims, evidently do not.

To explain this, we must return to the accusation made against nationalism; that it insists on imposing homogeneity on the populations unfortunate enough to fall under the sway of authorities possessed by the nationalist ideology. The assumption underlying this accusation is that traditional, ideologically uninfected authorities, such as the Ottoman Turks, had kept the peace and extracted taxes, but otherwise tolerated, and been indeed profoundly indifferent to, the diversity of faiths and cultures which they governed. By contrast, their gunman successors seem incapable of resting in peace till they have imposed the nationalist principle of *cuius regio, eius lingua.* They do not want merely a fiscal surplus and obedience. They thirst after the cultural and linguistic souls of their subjects.

This accusation must be stood on its head. It is not the case that nationalism imposes homogeneity out of a wilful cultural *Machtbedürfniss;* it is the objective need for homogeneity which is reflected in nationalism. If it is the case that a modern industrial state can only function with a mobile, literate, culturally standardized, interchangeable population, as we have argued, then the illiterate, half-starved populations sucked from their erstwhile rural cultural ghettoes into the melting pots of shanty-towns yearn for incorporation into some one of those cultural pools which already has, or looks as if it might acquire, a state of its own, with the subsequent promise of full cultural citizenship, access to primary schools, employment, and all. Often, these alienated, uprooted, wandering populations may vacillate between diverse options, and they may often come to a provisional rest at one or another temporary and transitional cultural resting place.

But there are some options which they will refrain from trying to take up. They will hesitate about trying to enter cultural pools within which they know themselves to be spurned; or rather, within which they expect to *continue* to be spurned. Poor newcomers are, of course, almost always spurned. The question is whether they will continue to be slighted, and whether the same fate will await their children. This will depend on whether the newly arrived and hence least privileged stratum possesses traits which its members and their offspring cannot shed, and which will continue to identify them: genetically transmitted or deeply engrained religious cultural habits are impossible or difficult to drop.

The alienated victims of early industrialism are unlikely to be tempted by cultural pools that are very small—a language spoken by a couple of villages offers few prospects—or very diffused or lacking in any literary traditions or personnel capable of carrying skills, and so on. They require cultural pools which are large, and/or have a good historic base, or intellectual personnel well equipped to propagate the culture in question. It is impossible to pick out any single qualification, or set of qualifications, which will either guarantee the success as a nationalist catalyst of the culture endowed with it (or them), or which on the contrary will ensure its failure. Size, historicity, reasonably compact territory, a capable and energetic intellectual class: all these will obviously help; but no single one is necessary, and it is doubtful whether any firm predictive generalization can be established in these terms. That the principle of nationalism will be operative can be predicted; just which groupings will emerge as its carriers can be only loosely indicated, for it depends on too many historic contingencies.

Nationalism as such is fated to prevail, but not any one particular nationalism. We know that reasonably homogeneous cultures, each of them with its own political roof, its own political servicing, are becoming the norm, widely implemented but for few exceptions; but we cannot predict just which cultures, with which political roofs, will be blessed by success. On the contrary, the simple calculations made above, concerning the number of cultures or potential nationalisms and concerning the room available for proper national states, clearly show that most potential nationalisms must either fail, or, more commonly, will refrain from even trying to find political expression.

This is precisely what we do find. Most cultures or potential national groups enter the age of nationalism without even the feeblest effort to benefit from it themselves. The number of groups which in terms of the 'precedent' argument could try to become nations, which could define themselves by the kind of criterion which in some other place does in fact define some real and effective nation, is legion. Yet most of them go meekly to their doom, to see their culture (though not themselves as individuals) slowly disappear, dissolving into the wider culture of some new national state. Most cultures are led to the dust heap of history by industrial civilization without offering any resistance. The linguistic distinctiveness of the Scottish Highlands within Scotland is, of course, incomparably greater than the cultural distinctiveness of Scotland within the UK; but there is no Highland nationalism. Much the same is true of Moroccan Berbers. Dialectal and cultural differences within Germany or Italy are as great as those between recognized

Teutonic or Romance languages. Southern Russians differ culturally from Northern Russians, but, unlike Ukrainians, do not translate this into a sense of nationhood.

Does this show that nationalism is, after all, unimportant? Or even that it is an ideological artifact, an invention of febrile thinkers which has mysteriously captured some mysteriously susceptible nations? Not at all. To reach such a conclusion would, ironically, come close to a tacit, oblique acceptance of the nationalist ideologue's most misguided claim: namely, that the 'nations' are there, in the very nature of things, only waiting to be 'awakened' (a favourite nationalist expression and image) from their regrettable slumber, by the nationalist 'awakener'. One would be inferring from the failure of most potential nations ever to 'wake up', from the lack of deep stirrings waiting for reveille, that nationalism was not important after all. Such an inference concedes the social ontology of 'nations', only admitting, with some surprise perhaps, that some of them lack the vigour and vitality needed if they are to fulfill the destiny which history intended for them.

But nationalism is *not* the awakening of an old, latent, dormant force, though that is how it does indeed present itself. It is in reality the consequence of a new form of social organization, based on deeply internalized, education-dependent high cultures, each protected by its own state. It uses some of the pre-existent cultures, generally transforming them in the process, but it cannot possibly use them all. There are too many of them. A viable higher culture-sustaining modern state cannot fall below a certain minimal size (unless in effect parasitic on its neighbours); and there is only room for a limited number of such states on this earth.

The high ratio of determined slumberers, who will not rise and shine and who refuse to be woken, enables us to turn the tables on nationalism-as-seen-by-itself. Nationalism sees itself as a natural and universal ordering of the political life of mankind, only obscured by that long, persistent and mysterious somnolence. As Hegel expressed this vision: 'Nations may have had a long history before they finally reach their destination—that of forming themselves into states'.[1] Hegel immediately goes on to suggest that this pre-state period is really 'pre-historical' *(sic):* so it would seem that on this view the real history of a nation only begins when it acquires its own state. If we invoke the sleeping-beauty nations, neither possessing a state nor feeling the lack of it, against the nationalist doctrine, we tacitly accept its social metaphysic, which sees nations as the bricks of which mankind is made up. Critics of nationalism who denounce the political movement but tacitly accept the existence of nations, do not go far enough. Nations as a natural, God-given way of classifying men, as an inherent though long-delayed political destiny, are a myth; nationalism, which sometimes takes pre-existing cultures and turns them into nations, sometimes invents them, and often obliterates pre-existing cultures: *that* is a reality, for better or worse, and in general an inescapable one. Those who are its historic agents know not what they do, but that is another matter.

But we must not accept the myth. Nations are not inscribed into the nature of things, they do not constitute a political version of the doctrine of natural kinds. Nor were national states the manifest ultimate destiny of ethnic or cultural groups. What do

---

[1]G.W.F. Hegel, *Lectures on the Philosophy of World History,* tr. H.B. Nisbet, Cambridge, 1975, p. 134.

exist are cultures, often subtly grouped, shading into each other, overlapping, inter-twined; and there exist, usually but not always, political units of all shapes and sizes. In the past the two did not generally converge. There were good reasons for their failing to do so in many cases. Their rulers established their identity by differentiating themselves downwards, and the ruled micro-communities differentiated themselves laterally from their neighbors grouped in similar units.

But nationalism is not the awakening and assertion of these mythical, supposedly natural and given units. It is, on the contrary, the crystallization of new units, suitable for the conditions now prevailing, though admittedly using as their raw material the cul-tural, historical and other inheritances from the pre-nationalist world. . . .

TWO TYPES OF NATIONALISM

. . . [In nineteenth-century Europe] most Italians were ruled by foreigners, and in that sense were politically underprivileged. The Germans, most of them, lived in fragmented states, many of them small and weak, at any rate by European great power standards, and thus unable to provide German culture, as a centralized modern medium, with its political roof. (By a further paradox, multi-national great power Austria was endeavor-ing to do something of that kind, but much to the displeasure of some of its citizens.)

So the political protection of Italian and German culture was visibly and, to the Italians and Germans offensively, inferior to that which was provided for, say, French or English culture. But when it came to access to education, the facilities provided by these two high cultures, to those who were born into dialectal variants of it, were not re-ally in any way inferior. Both Italian and German were literary languages, with an ef-fective centralized standardization of their correct forms and with flourishing litera-tures, technical vocabularies and manners, educational institutions and academies. There was little if any cultural inferiority. Rates of literacy and standards of education were not significantly lower (if lower at all) among Germans than they were among the French; and they were not significantly low among the Italians, when compared with the dominant Austrians. German in comparison with French, or Italian in comparison with the German used by the Austrians, were not disadvantaged cultures, and their speakers did not need to correct unequal access to the eventual benefits of a modern world. All that needed to be corrected was that inequality of power and the absence of a political roof over a culture (and over an economy), and institutions which would be identified with it and committed to its maintenance. The Risorgimento and the unifica-tion of Germany corrected these imbalances.

There is a difference, however, between this kind of unificatory nationalism, on behalf of a fully effective high culture which only needs an improved bit of political roofing, and the classical Habsburg-and-east-and-south type of nationalism. This dif-ference is the subject of a fascinating and rather moving essay by the late Professor John Plamenatz, an essay which might well have been called 'The Sad Reflections of a Montenegrin in Oxford'.[2] Plamenatz called the two kinds of nationalism the

---

[2]John Plamenatz, 'Two types of Nationalism', in E. Kamenka (ed.), *Nationalism, The Nature and Evolution of an Idea,* London, 1973.

Western and the Eastern, the Western type being of the Risorgimento or unificatory kind, typical of the nineteenth century and with deep links to liberal ideas, while the Eastern, though he did not stress it in so many words, was exemplified by the kind of nationalism he knew to exist in his native Balkans. There can be no doubt but that he saw the Western nationalism as relatively benign and nice, and the Eastern kind as nasty, and doomed to nastiness by the conditions which gave rise to it. (It would be an interesting question to ask him whether he would have considered the markedly un-benign forms taken by these once-benign or relatively liberal and moderate Western nationalisms in the twentieth century, as accidental and avoidable aberrations or not.)

The underlying logic of Plamenatz's argument is clear. The relatively benign Western nationalisms were acting on behalf of well-developed high cultures, normatively centralized and endowed with a fairly well-defined folk clientele: all that was required was a bit of adjustment in the political situation and in the international boundaries, so as to ensure for these cultures, and their speakers and practitioners, the same sustained protection as that which was already enjoyed by their rivals. This took a few battles and a good deal of sustained diplomatic activity but, as the making of historical omelettes goes, it did not involve the breaking of a disproportionate or unusual number of eggs, perhaps no more than would have been broken anyway in the course of the normal political game within the general political framework and assumptions of the time.

By way of contrast, consider the nationalism designated as Eastern by Plamenatz. Its implementation did, of course, require battles and diplomacy, to at least the same extent as the realization of Western nationalisms. But the matter did not end there. This kind of Eastern nationalism did not operate on behalf of an already existing, well-defined and codified high culture, which had as it were marked out and linguistically pre-converted its own territory by sustained literary activities ever since the early Renaissance or since the Reformation, as the case might be. Not at all. This nationalism was active on behalf of a high culture as yet not properly crystallized, a merely aspirant or in-the-making high culture. It presided, or strove to preside, in ferocious rivalry with similar competitors, over a chaotic ethnographic map of many dialects, with ambiguous historical or linguo-genetic allegiances, and containing populations which had only just begun to identify with these emergent national high cultures. Objective conditions of the modern world were bound, in due course, to oblige them to identify with one of them. But till this occurred, they lacked the clearly defined cultural basis enjoyed by their German and Italian counterparts.

These populations of eastern Europe were still locked into the complex multiple loyalties of kinship, territory and religion. To make them conform to the nationalist imperative was bound to take more than a few battles and some diplomacy. It was bound to take a great deal of very forceful cultural engineering. In many cases it was also bound to involve population exchanges or expulsions, more or less forcible assimilation, and sometimes liquidation, in order to attain that close relation between state and culture which is the essence of nationalism. And all these consequences flowed, not from some unusual brutality of the nationalists who in the end employed these measures (they were probably no worse and no better than anyone else), but from the inescapable logic of the situation.

DEMOCRATIZATION AND WAR

Edward D. Mansfield and Jack Snyder

DANGERS OF TRANSITION

The idea that democracies never fight wars against each other has become an axiom for many scholars. It is, as one scholar puts it, "as close as anything we have to an empirical law in international relations." This "law" is invoked by American statesmen to justify a foreign policy that encourages democratization abroad. In his 1994 State of the Union address, President Clinton asserted that no two democracies had ever gone to war with each other, thus explaining why promoting democracy abroad was a pillar of his foreign policy.

It is probably true that a world in which more countries were mature, stable democracies would be safer and preferable for the United States. But countries do not become mature democracies overnight. They usually go through a rocky transition, where mass politics mixes with authoritarian elite politics in a volatile way. Statistical evidence covering the past two centuries shows that in this transitional phase of democratization, countries become more aggressive and war-prone, not less, and they do fight wars with democratic states. In fact, formerly authoritarian states where democratic participation is on the rise are more likely to fight wars than are stable democracies or autocracies. States that make the biggest leap, from total autocracy to extensive mass democracy—like contemporary Russia—are about twice as likely to fight wars in the decade after democratization as are states that remain autocracies.

This historical pattern of democratization, belligerent nationalism, and war is already emerging in some of today's new or partial democracies, especially some formerly communist states. Two pairs of states—Serbia and Croatia, and Armenia and Azerbaijan—have found themselves at war while experimenting with varying degrees of electoral democracy. The electorate of Russia's partial democracy cast nearly a quarter of its votes for the party of radical nationalist Vladimir Zhirinovsky. Even mainstream Russian politicians have adopted an imperial tone in their dealings with neighboring former Soviet republics, and military force has been used ruthlessly in Chechnya.

The following evidence should raise questions about the Clinton administration's policy of promoting peace by promoting democratization. The expectation that the spread of democracy will probably contribute to peace in the long run, once new democracies mature, provides little comfort to those who might face a heightened risk

Edward D. Mansfield and Jack Snyder, "Democratization and War." Reprinted by permission of *Foreign Affairs* Vol. 74, No. 3 (May/June 1995). Copyright © 1995 by the Council on Foreign Relations, Inc.

of war in the short run. Pushing nuclear-armed great powers like Russia or China toward democratization is like spinning a roulette wheel: many of the outcomes are undesirable. Of course, in most cases the initial steps on the road to democratization will not be produced by any conscious policy of the United States. The roulette wheel is already spinning for Russia and perhaps will be soon for China. Washington and the international community need to think not so much about encouraging or discouraging democratization as about helping to smooth the transition in ways that minimize its risks.

THE EVIDENCE

Our statistical analysis relies on the classifications of regimes and wars from 1811 to 1980 used by most scholars studying the peace among democracies. Starting with these standard data, we classify each state as a democracy, an autocracy, or a mixed regime—that is, a state with features of both democracies and autocracies. This classification is based on several criteria, including the constitutional constraints on the chief executive, the competitiveness of domestic politics, the openness of the process for selecting the chief executive, and the strength of the rules governing participation in politics. Democratizing states are those that made any regime change in a democratic direction—that is, from autocracy to democracy, from a mixed regime to democracy, or from autocracy to a mixed regime. We analyze wars between states as well as wars between a state and a non-state group, such as liberation movements in colonies, but we do not include civil wars.[1]

Because we view democratization as a gradual process, rather than a sudden change, we test whether a transition toward democracy occurring over one, five, and ten years is associated with the subsequent onset of war. To assess the strength of the relationship between democratization and war, we construct a series of contingency tables. Based on those tables,

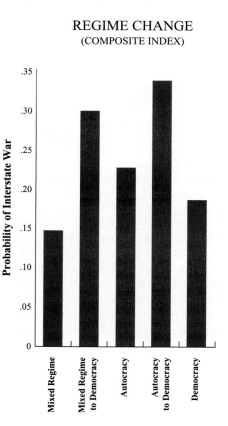

REGIME CHANGE
(COMPOSITE INDEX)

---

[1] On the definition of war and the data on war used in this analysis, see Melvin Small and J. David Singer, *Resort to Arms: International and Civil Wars, 1816–1980,* Beverly Hills: Sage, 1982.

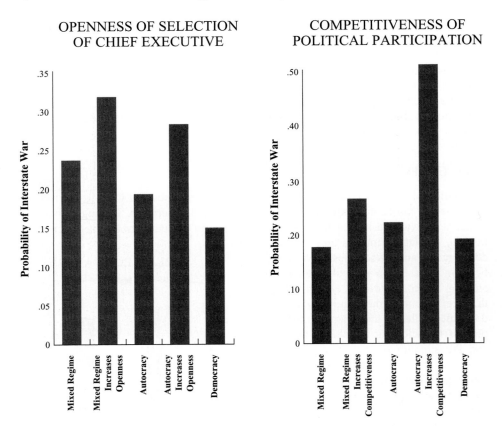

OPENNESS OF SELECTION
OF CHIEF EXECUTIVE

COMPETITIVENESS OF
POLITICAL PARTICIPATION

we compare the probability that a democratizing state subsequently goes to war with the probabilities of war for states in transition toward autocracy and for states undergoing no regime change. The results of all of these tests show that *democratizing states were more likely to fight wars than were states that had undergone no change in regime.* This relationship is weakest one year into democratization and strongest at ten years. During any given ten-year period, a state experiencing no regime change had about one chance in six of fighting a war in the following decade. In the decade following democratization, a state's chance of fighting a war was about one in four. When we analyze the components of our measure of democratization separately, the results are similar. On average, an increase in the openness of the selection process for the chief executive doubled the likelihood of war. Increasing the competitiveness of political participation or increasing the constraints on a country's chief executive (both aspects of democratization) also made war more likely. On average, these changes increased the likelihood of war by about 90 percent and 35 percent respectively.

The statistical results are even more dramatic when we analyze cases in which the process of democratization culminated in very high levels of mass participation in politics. States changing from a mixed regime to democracy were on average about

50 percent more likely to become engaged in war (and about two-thirds more
likely to go to war with another nation-
state) than states that remained mixed
regimes.

The effect was greater still for those
states making the largest leap, from full
autocracy to high levels of democracy.
Such states were on average about two-
thirds more likely to become involved in
any type of war (and about twice as likely
to become involved in an interstate war)
than states that remained autocracies.
Though this evidence shows that democratization is dangerous, its reversal offers no easy solutions. On average,
changes toward autocracy also yielded an
increase in the probability of war, though
a smaller one than changes toward
democracy, compared to states experiencing no regime change.

NATIONALISM AND DEMOCRATIZATION

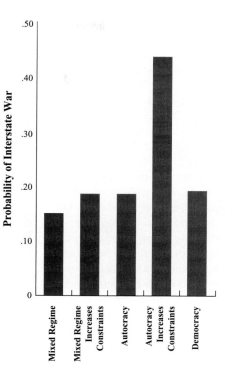

CONSTRAINTS ON THE
CHIEF EXECUTIVE

The connection between democratization
and nationalism is striking in both the his-
torical record and today's headlines. We did not measure nationalism directly in our statistical tests. Nonetheless, historical and contemporary evidence strongly suggests that
rising nationalism often goes hand in hand with rising democracy. It is no accident that
the end of the Cold War brought both a wave of democratization and a revival of nationalist sentiment in the former communist states.

In eighteenth-century Britain and France, when nationalism first emerged as an explicit political doctrine, it meant self-rule by the people. It was the rallying cry of com-
moners and rising commercial classes against rule by aristocratic elites, who were
charged with the sin of ruling in their own interests, rather than those of the nation.
Indeed, dynastic rulers and imperial courts had hardly been interested in promoting nationalism as a banner of solidarity in their realms. They typically ruled over a linguistically and culturally diverse conglomeration of subjects and claimed to govern by divine
right, not in the interest of the nation. Often, these rulers were more closely tied by kinship, language, or culture to elites in other states than to their own subjects. The position of the communist ruling class was strikingly similar: a transnational elite that ruled
over an amalgamation of peoples and claimed legitimacy from the communist party's
role as the vanguard of history, not from the consent of the governed. Popular forces

challenging either traditional dynastic rulers or communist elites naturally tended to combine demands for national self-determination and democratic rule.

This concoction of nationalism and incipient democratization has been an intoxicating brew, leading in case after case to ill-conceived wars of expansion. The earliest instance remains one of the most dramatic. In the French Revolution, the radical Brissotin parliamentary faction polarized politics by harping on the king's slow response to the threat of war with other dynastic states. In the ensuing wars of the French Revolution, citizens flocked to join the revolutionary armies to defend popular self-rule and the French nation. Even after the revolution turned profoundly anti-democratic, Napoleon was able to harness this popular nationalism to the task of conquering Europe, substituting the popularity of empire for the substance of democratic rule.

After this experience, Europe's ruling elites decided to band together in 1815 in the Concert of Europe to contain the twin evils of nationalism and democratization. In this scheme, Europe's crowned heads tried to unite in squelching demands for constitutions, electoral and social democracy, and national self-determination. For a time nationalism and democratization were both held back, and Europe enjoyed a period of relative peace.

But in the long run, the strategy failed in the face of the economic changes strengthening popular forces in Western and Central Europe. British and French politicians soon saw that they would have to rule by co-opting nationalist and democratic demands, rather than suppressing them. Once the specter of revolution returned to Europe in 1848, this reversal of political tactics was complete, and it led quickly to the Crimean War. British Foreign Secretary Palmerston and French Emperor Napoleon III both tried

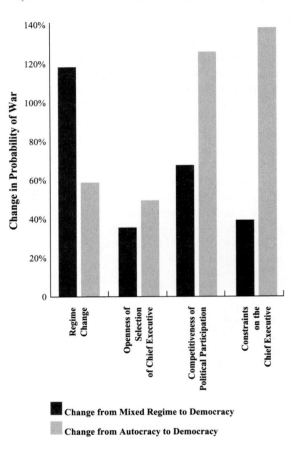

CHANGE IN THE PROBABILITY OF INTERSTATE WAR FOR A STATE UNDERGOING DEMOCRATIZATION
(BASED ON THE RESULTS IN PREVIOUS GRAPHS)

to manage the clamor for a broader political arena by giving democrats what they wanted in foreign affairs—a "liberal" war to free imprisoned nations from autocratic rule and, incidentally, to expand commerce.

But this was just the dress rehearsal for history's most potent combination of mass politics and rising nationalism, which occurred in Germany around the turn of the twentieth century. Chancellor Otto von Bismarck, counting on the conservative votes of a docile peasantry, granted universal suffrage in the newly unified Reich after 1870, but in foreign and military affairs, he kept the elected Reichstag subordinate to the cabinet appointed by the kaiser. Like the sorcerer's apprentice, however, Bismarck underestimated the forces he was unleashing. With the rise of an industrial society, Bismarck's successors could not control this truncated democracy, where over 90 percent of the population voted. Everyone was highly politicized, yet nobody could achieve their aims through the limited powers of the Reichstag. As a result, people organized direct pressure groups outside of electoral party politics. Some of these clamored for economic benefits, but many of them found it tactically useful to cloak their narrow interests in a broader vision of the nation's interests. This mass nationalist sentiment exerted constant pressure on German diplomacy in the Wilhelmine years before 1914 and pushed its vacillating elites toward war.

Democratization and nationalism also became linked in Japan on the eve of the Manchurian invasion in 1931. During the 1920s Japan expanded its suffrage and experimented with two-party electoral competition, though a council of military elder statesmen still made the ultimate decisions about who would govern. These semi-elected governments of the 1920s supported free trade, favored naval arms control, and usually tried to rein in the Japanese army's schemes to undermine the Open Door policy in China. During the 1920s, Young Turks in the army developed a populist, nationalist doctrine featuring a centrally planned economy within an autarkic, industrialized, expanded empire, while scapegoating Japan's alleged internal and external enemies, including leftist workers, rich capitalists, liberals, democrats, Americans, and Russians. After the economic crash of the late 1920s, this nationalist formula became persuasive, and the Japanese military had little trouble gaining popular support for imperial expansion and the emasculation of democracy. As in so many previous cases, nationalism proved to be a way for militarist elite groups to appear populist in a democratizing society while obstructing the advance to full democracy.

The interconnection among nationalism, democratization, and war is even clearer in new states. In today's "Weimar Russia," voters disgruntled by economic distress backed belligerent nationalists like Zhirinovsky, put ostensible liberals like President Boris Yeltsin and Foreign Minister Andrei Kozyrev on the defensive on ethnic and foreign policy issues, and contributed to the climate that led to war in Chechnya. In "Wilhelmine Serbia," the political and military elites of the old regime, facing inexorable pressure for democratization, cynically but successfully created a new basis for legitimacy through nationalist propaganda and military action, and they recently won elections that were only partially manipulated. Until its recent decree suspending the activities of the main opposition party, Armenia had moved quite far toward full democracy while at the same time supporting an invasion of its ethnic foes in Azerbaijan. The Azeris have been less successful in sustaining momentum toward democracy. However, in Azerbaijan's one relatively free and fair presidential election, the winner, Abulfaz Ali Elchibey, attacked the incumbent for being insufficiently nationalist and populist. Elchibey's platform emphasized Turkic identity and the strengthening of the Azeri nation-state to try to mount a counteroffensive against the Armenians. In other ethnically divided societies, where holding an election is like taking a census, democratization has often become an opportunity to exercise the tyranny of the majority.

THE SORCERER'S APPRENTICE

Although democratization in many cases leads to war, that does not mean that the average voter wants war. Public opinion in democratizing states often starts off highly averse to the costs and risks of war. In that sense, the public opinion polls taken in Russia in early 1994 were typical. Respondents said, for example, that Russian policy should make sure the rights of Russians in neighboring states were not infringed, but not at the cost of military intervention. Public opinion often becomes more belligerent, however, as a result of propaganda and military action presented as faits accomplis by elites. This mass opinion, once aroused, may no longer be controllable.

For example, Napoleon III successfully exploited the domestic prestige from France's share of the victory in the Crimean War to consolidate his rule, despite the popular reluctance and war-weariness that had accompanied the war. Having learned this lesson well, Napoleon tried this tactic again in 1859. On the eve of his military intervention in the Italian struggle with Austria, he admitted to his ministers that "on the domestic front, the war will at first awaken great fears; traders and speculators of every stripe will shriek, but national sentiment will [banish] this domestic fright; the nation will be put to the test once more in a struggle that will stir many a heart, recall the memory of heroic times, and bring together under the mantle of glory the parties that are steadily drifting away from one another day after day."[2] Napoleon was trying not just to follow opinion but to make public opinion bellicose, in order to stir a national feeling that would enhance the state's ability to govern a split and stalemated political arena.

Much the same has happened in contemporary Serbia. Despite the memories of Ustashe atrocities in World War II, intermarriage rates between Croats and Serbs living in Croatia were as high as one in three during the 1980s. Opinion has been bellicized by propaganda campaigns in state-controlled media that, for example, carried purely invented reports of rapes of Serbian women in Kosovo, and even more so by the fait accompli of launching the war itself.

In short, democratizing states are war-prone not because war is popular with the mass public, but because domestic pressures create incentives for elites to drum up nationalist sentiment.

---

[2]Alain Plessis, *The Rise and Fall of the Second Empire, 1852–1871,* Cambridge: Cambridge University Press, 1985, pp. 146–47.

THE CAUSES OF DEMOCRATIC WARS

Democratization typically creates a syndrome of weak central authority, unstable domestic coalitions, and high-energy mass politics. It brings new social groups and classes onto the political stage. Political leaders, finding no way to reconcile incompatible interests, resort to shortsighted bargains or reckless gambles in order to maintain their governing coalitions. Elites need to gain mass allies to defend their weakened positions. Both the newly ambitious elites and the embattled old ruling groups often use appeals to nationalism to stay astride their unmanageable political coalitions.

Needing public support, they rouse the masses with nationalist propaganda but find that their mass allies, once mobilized by passionate appeals, are difficult to control. So are the powerful remnants of the old order—the military, for example—which promote militarism because it strengthens them institutionally. This is particularly true because democratization weakens the central government's ability to keep policy coherent and consistent. Governing a society that is democratizing is like driving a car while throwing away the steering wheel, stepping on the gas, and fighting over which passenger will be in the driver's seat. The result, often, is war.

Political stalemate and imperialist coalitions. Democratization creates a wider spectrum of politically significant groups with diverse and incompatible interests. In the period when the great powers were first democratizing, kings, aristocrats, peasants, and artisans shared the historical stage with industrialists, an urban working class, and a middle-class intelligentsia. Similarly, in the post-communist world, former party apparatchiks, atavistic heavy industrialists, and downwardly mobile military officers share the stage with populist demagogues, free-market entrepreneurs, disgruntled workers, and newly mobilized ethnic groups. In principle, mature democratic institutions can integrate even the widest spectrum of interests through competition for the favor of the average voter. But where political parties and representative institutions are still in their infancy, the diversity of interests may make political coalitions difficult to maintain. Often the solution is a belligerent nationalist coalition.

In Britain during the period leading up to the Crimean War, neither the Whigs nor Tories could form a lasting governing coalition because so many groups refused to enter stable political alliances. None of the old elites would coalesce with the parliamentary bloc of radicals elected by urban middle-class and Irish voters. Moreover, protectionist Tories would not unite with free-trading Whigs and Peelite Tories. The social and political mid-Victorian equipoise between traditional and modern Britain created a temporary political stalemate. Lord Palmerston's pseudo-liberal imperialism turned out to be the only successful formula for creating a durable ruling coalition during this transitional period of democratization.

The stalemate in Wilhelmine-era electoral politics was even more serious. In principle, coalitions of the left and right might have formed a two-party system to vie for the favor of the average voter, thus moderating policy. In fact, both left and right were too internally divided to mount effective coalitions with internally consistent policies. Progressives dreamed of a bloc extending "from Bassermann to Bebel," from the liberal-democratic middle classes through the Marxist working classes, but the differences between labor and capital chronically barred this development. Conservatives had more success in forging a "marriage of iron and rye," but fundamental differences between military-feudal Junkers and Ruhr industrialists over issues ranging from the distribution of tax burdens to military strategy made their policies incoherent. Germany wound up with plans for a big army and a costly navy, and nobody willing to pay for it.

In more recent times, incipient democratization has likewise caused political impasses by widening the political spectrum to include too many irreconcilable political forces. In the final days of Yugoslavia, efforts by moderates like former Prime Minister Ante Marković to promote a federalist, democratic, economic reformist platform were hindered not only by ethnic divisions but also by the cleavage between market-oriented business interests on the one hand and party bosses and military officers on the other. Similarly, in Russia, the difficulty of reconciling liberal, neo-communist, and nationalist political platforms and the social interests behind them has led to parliamentary stalemate, attempts to break the stalemate by presidential decree, tanks in the streets, and the resort to freelancing by breakaway regions, the military, and spontaneous privatizers of state property. One interpretation of Yeltsin's decision to use force in Chechnya is that he felt it necessary to show that he could act decisively to prevent the unraveling of central authority, with respect not only to ethnic separatists but also to other ungovernable groups in a democratizing society. Chechnya, it was hoped, would allow Yeltsin to demonstrate his ability to coerce Russian society while at the same time exploiting a potentially popular nationalist issue.

Inflexible interests and short time horizons. Groups threatened by social change and democratization, including still-powerful elites, are often compelled to take an inflexible view of their interests, especially when their assets cannot be readily adapted to changing political and economic conditions. In extreme cases, there may be only one solution that will maintain the social position of the group. For Prussian landowners, it was agricultural protection in a nondemocratic state; for the Japanese military, it was organizational autonomy in an autarkic empire; for the Serbian military and party elites, it was a Serbian nationalist state. Since military bureaucracies and imperial interest groups occupied key positions in many authoritarian great powers, whether monarchal or communist, most interests threatened by democratization have been bound up with military programs and the state's international mission. Compromises that may lead down the slippery slope to social extinction or irrelevance have little appeal to such groups. This adds to the difficulty of finding an exit from the domestic political impasse and may make powerful domestic groups impervious to the international risks of their strategies.

Competing for popular support. The trouble intensifies when elites in a democratizing society try to recruit mass allies to their cause. Threatened elite groups have an overwhelming incentive to mobilize mass backers on the elites' terms, using whatever special resources they might retain. These resources have included monopolies of information (the Wilhelmine navy's unique "expertise" in making strategic assessments), propaganda assets (the Japanese army's public relations blitz justifying the invasion of Manchuria), patronage (Lord Palmerston's gifts of foreign service postings to the sons of cooperative journalists), wealth (the Krupp steel company's bankrolling of mass nationalist and militarist leagues), organizational skills and networks (the Japanese army's exploitation of rural reservist organizations to build a social base), and the ability to use the control of traditional political institutions to shape the political agenda and structure the terms of political bargains (the Wilhelmine ruling elite's agreement to eliminate anti-Catholic legislation in exchange for Catholic support in the Reichstag on the naval budget).

This elite mobilization of mass groups takes place in a highly competitive setting. Elite groups mobilize mass support to neutralize mass threats (for instance, creating patriotic leagues to counter workers' movements) and counter other elite groups' successful efforts at mass mobilization (such as the German Navy League, a political counterweight to the Junker-backed Agrarian League). The elites' resources allow them to influence the direction of mass political participation, but the imperative to compete for mass favor makes it difficult for a single elite group to control the outcome of this process. For example, mass groups that gain access to politics through elite-supported nationalist organizations often try to outbid their erstwhile sponsors. By 1911, German popular nationalist lobbies were in a position to claim that if Germany's foreign foes were really as threatening as the ruling elites had portrayed them, then the government had sold out German interests in reaching a compromise with France over the Moroccan dispute. In this way, elite mobilization of the masses adds to the ungovernability and political impasse of democratizing states.

Ideology takes on particular significance in the competition for mass support. New entrants to the political process, lacking established habits and good information, may be uncertain where their political interests lie. Ideology can yield big payoffs, particularly when there is no efficient free marketplace of ideas to counter false claims with reliable facts. Elites try out all sorts of ideological appeals depending on the social position they are defending, the nature of the mass group they want to recruit, and the kinds of appeals that seem politically plausible. A nearly universal element of these ideological appeals, however, is nationalism, which has the advantage of positing a community of interest uniting elites and masses. This distracts attention from class cleavages that divide elites from the masses they are trying to recruit.

The weakening of central authority. The political impasse and recklessness of democratizing states is deepened by the weakening of the state's authority. The autocrat can no longer dictate to elite interest groups or mass groups. Meanwhile, democratic institutions lack the strength to integrate these contending interests and views. Parties are weak and lack mass loyalty. Elections are rigged or intermittent. Institutions of public political participation are distrusted because they are subject to manipulation by elites and arbitrary constraints imposed by the state, which fears the outcome of unfettered competition.

Among the great powers, the problem was not excessive authoritarian power at the center, but the opposite. The Aberdeen coalition that brought Britain into the Crimean War was a makeshift cabinet headed by a weak leader with no substantial constituency. Likewise, on the eve of the Franco-Prussian War, Napoleon III's regime was in the process of caving in to its liberal opponents, who dominated the parliament elected in 1869. As Europe's armies prepared to hurtle from their starting gates in July 1914, Austrian leaders, perplexed by the contradictions between the German chancellor's policy and that of the German military, asked, "Who rules in Berlin?" Similarly, the 1931 Manchurian incident was a fait accompli by the local Japanese military; Tokyo was not even informed. The return to imperial thinking in Moscow today is the result of

Yeltsin's weakness, not his strength. As the well-informed Moscow analyst Sergei Karaganov recently argued, the breakdown of the Leninist state "has created an environment where elite interests influence [foreign] policy directly."[3]

In each of these cases, the weak central leadership resorts to the same strategies as do the more parochial elite interests, using nationalist ideological appeals and special-interest payoffs to maintain their short-run viability, despite the long-run risks that these strategies may unleash.

Prestige strategies. One of the simplest but riskiest strategies for a hard-pressed regime in a democratizing country is to shore up its prestige at home by seeking victories abroad. During the Chechen intervention, newspaper commentators in Moscow and the West were reminded of Russian Interior Minister Viacheslav Plehve's fateful remark in 1904, on the eve of the disastrous Russo-Japanese War, that what the tsar needed was "a short, victorious war" to boost his prestige. Though this strategy often backfires, it is a perennial temptation as a means for coping with the political strains of democratization. German Chancellor Johannes Miquel, who revitalized the imperialist-protectionist "coalition of iron and rye" at the turn of the century, told his colleagues that "successes in foreign policy would make a good impression in the Reichstag debates, and political divisions would thus be moderated."[4] The targets of such strategies often share this analysis. Richard Cobden, for example, argued that military victories abroad would confer enough prestige on the military-feudal landed elite to allow them to raise food tariffs and snuff out democracy: "Let John Bull have a great military triumph, and we shall have to take off our hats as we pass the Horse Guards for the rest of our lives."[5]

Prestige strategies make the country vulnerable to slights to its reputation. Napoleon III, for example, was easily goaded into a fateful declaration of war in 1870 by Bismarck's insulting editorial work on a leaked telegram from the kaiser. For those who want to avoid such diplomatic provocations, the lesson is to make sure that compromises forced on the leaders of democratizing states do not take away the fig leaves needed to sustain their domestic prestige.

MANAGING THE DANGERS

Though mature democratic states have virtually never fought wars against each other, promoting democracy may not promote peace because states are especially war-prone during the transition toward democracy. This does not mean, however, that democratization should be squelched in the interests of peace. Many states are now democratizing or on the verge of it, and stemming that turbulent tide, even if it were desirable, may not be possible. Our statistical tests show that movements toward

---

[3]Karaganov, "Russia's Elites," in Robert Blackwill and Sergei Karaganov, *Damage Limitation,* Washington: Brassey's, 1994, p. 42.
[4]J. C. G. Rohl, *Germany without Bismarck,* Berkeley: University of California Press, 1967, p. 250.
[5]Letter to John Bright, October 1, 1854, quoted in John Morley, *The Life of Richard Cobden,* abridged ed., London: Thomas Nelson, pp. 311–12.

autocracy, including reversals of democratization, are only somewhat less likely to result in war than democratization itself. Consequently, the task is to draw on an understanding of the process of democratization to keep its unwanted side effects to a minimum.

Of course, democratization does not always lead to extreme forms of aggressive nationalism, just as it does not always lead to war. But it makes those outcomes more likely. Cases where states democratized without triggering a nationalist mobilization are particularly interesting, since they may hold clues about how to prevent such unwanted side effects. Among the great powers, the obvious successes were the democratization of Germany and Japan after 1945, due to occupation by liberal democracies and the favorable international setting provided by the Marshall Plan, the Bretton Woods economic system, and the democratic military alliance against the Soviet threat. More recently, numerous Latin American states have democratized without nationalism or war. The recent border skirmishes between Peru and Ecuador, however, coincide with democratizing trends in both states and a nationalist turn in Ecuadorian political discourse. Moreover, all three previous wars between that pair over the past two centuries occurred in periods of partial democratization.

In such cases, however, the cure is probably more democracy, not less. In "Wilhelmine Argentina," the Falkland Islands/Malvinas War came when the military junta needed a nationalist victory to stave off pressure for the return of democracy; the arrival of full democracy has produced more pacific policies. Among the East European states, nationalist politics has been unsuccessful in the most fully democratic ones—Poland, the Czech Republic, and Hungary—as protest votes have gone to former communists. Nationalism has figured more prominently in the politics of the less democratic formerly communist states that are nonetheless partially democratizing. States like Turkmenistan that remain outright autocracies have no nationalist mobilization—indeed no political mobilization of any kind. In those recent cases, in contrast to some of our statistical results, the rule seems to be: go fully democratic, or don't go at all.

In any given case, other factors may override the relative bellicosity of democratizing states. These might include the power of the democratizing state, the strength of the potential deterrent coalition of states constraining it, the attractiveness of more peaceful options available to the democratizing state, and the nature of the groups making up its ruling coalition. What is needed is to identify the conditions that lead to relatively peaceful democratization and try to create those circumstances.

One of the major findings of scholarship on democratization in Latin America is that the process goes most smoothly when elites threatened by the transition—especially the military—are given a golden parachute. Above all, they need a guarantee that they will not wind up in jail if they relinquish power. The history of the democratizing great powers broadens this insight. Democratization was least likely to lead to war when the old elites saw a reasonably bright future for themselves in the new social order. British aristocrats, for example, had more of their wealth invested in commerce and industry than in agriculture, so they had many interests in common with the rising middle classes. They could face democratization with relative equanimity. In contrast, Prussia's capital-starved, small-scale Junker landholders had no choice but to rely on agricultural protection and military careers.

In today's context, finding benign, productive employment for the erstwhile communist nomenklatura, military officer corps, nuclear scientists, and smokestack industrialists ought to rank high on the list of priorities. Policies aimed at giving them a stake in the privatization process and subsidizing the conversion of their skills to new, peaceful tasks in a market economy seem like a step in the right direction. According to some interpretations, Russian Defense Minister Pavel Grachev was eager to use force to solve the Chechen confrontation in order to show that Russian military power was still useful and that increased investment in the Russian army would pay big dividends. Instead of pursuing this reckless path, the Russian military elite needs to be convinced that its prestige, housing, pensions, and technical competence will improve if and only if it transforms itself into a Western-style military, subordinate to civilian authority and resorting to force only in accordance with prevailing international norms. Not only do old elites need to be kept happy, they also need to be kept weak. Pacts should not prop up the remnants of the authoritarian system, but rather create a niche for them in the new system.

Another top priority must be creating a free, competitive, and responsible marketplace of ideas in the newly democratizing states. Most of the war-prone democratizing great powers had pluralistic public debates, but the debates were skewed to favor groups with money, privileged access to the media, and proprietary control over information ranging from archives to intelligence about the military balance. Pluralism is not enough. Without a level playing field, pluralism simply creates the incentive and opportunity for privileged groups to propound self-serving myths, which historically have often taken a nationalist turn. One of the rays of hope in the Chechen affair was the alacrity with which Russian journalists exposed the costs of the fighting and the lies of the government and the military. Though elites should get a golden parachute regarding their pecuniary interests, they should be given no quarter on the battlefield of ideas. Mythmaking should be held up to the utmost scrutiny by aggressive journalists who maintain their credibility by scrupulously distinguishing fact from opinion and tirelessly verifying their sources. Promoting this kind of journalistic infrastructure is probably the most highly leveraged investment the West can make in a peaceful democratic transition.

Finally, the kind of ruling coalition that emerges in the course of democratization depends a great deal on the incentives created by the international environment. Both Germany and Japan started on the path toward liberal, stable democratization in the mid-1920s, encouraged by abundant opportunities for trade with and investment by the advanced democracies and by credible security treaties that defused nationalist scaremongering in domestic politics. When the international supports for free trade and democracy were yanked out in the late 1920s, their liberal coalitions collapsed. For China, whose democratization may occur in the context of expanding economic ties with the West, a steady Western Commercial partnership and security presence is likely to play a major role in shaping the incentives of proto-democratic coalition politics.

In the long run, the enlargement of the zone of stable democracy will probably enhance prospects for peace. In the short run, much work remains to be done to minimize the dangers of the turbulent transition.

POSSIBLE AND IMPOSSIBLE SOLUTIONS TO ETHNIC CIVIL WARS

Chaim Kaufmann

Ethnic civil wars are burning in Bosnia, Croatia, Rwanda, Burundi, Angola, Sudan, Turkey, Azerbaijan, Georgia, Chechnya, Tajikistan, Kashmir, Myanmar, and Sri Lanka, and are threatening to break out in dozens of other places throughout the world. Many of these conflicts are are so violent, with so much violence directed against unarmed civilians, and are apparently intractable, that they have provoked calls for military intervention to stop them. As yet, however, the international community has done little and achieved less.

Advocates of international action seek to redress the failures of local political institutions and elites by brokering political power-sharing arrangements, by international conservatorship to rebuild a functioning state, or by reconstruction of exclusive ethnic identities into wider, inclusive civic identities. Pessimists doubt these remedies, arguing that ethnic wars express primordial hatreds which cannot be reduced by outside intervention because they have been ingrained by long histories of inter-communal conflict.

Both sides in the current debate are wrong, because solutions to ethnic wars do not depend on their causes.

This paper offers a theory of how ethnic wars end, and proposes an intervention strategy based on it. The theory rests on two insights: First, in ethnic wars both hypernationalist mobilization rhetoric and real atrocities harden ethnic identities to the point that cross-ethnic political appeals are unlikely to be made and even less likely to be heard. Second, intermingled population settlement patterns create real security dilemmas that intensify violence, motivate ethnic "cleansing," and prevent de-escalation unless the groups are separated. As a result, restoring civil politics in multi-ethnic states shattered by war is impossible because the war itself destroys the possibilities for ethnic cooperation.

Stable resolutions of ethnic civil wars are possible, but only when the opposing groups are demographically separated into defensible enclaves. Separation reduces both incentives and opportunity for further combat, and largely eliminates both reasons and chances for ethnic cleansing of civilians. While ethnic fighting can be stopped by other means, such as peace enforcement by international forces or by a conquering empire, such peaces last only as long as the enforcers remain.

Chaim Kaufmann, "Possible and Impossible Solutions to Ethnic Civil Wars," *International Security* Vol. 20, No. 4 (spring 1996), pp. 136–175. © 1996 by the President and Fellows of Harvard College and the Massachusetts Institute of Technology.

This means that to save lives threatened by genocide, the international community must abandon attempts to restore war-torn multi-ethnic states. Instead, it must facilitate and protect population movements to create true national homelands. Sovereignty is secondary: defensible ethnic enclaves reduce violence with or without independent sovereignty, while partition without separation does nothing to stop mass killing. Once massacres have taken place, ethnic cleansing will occur. The alternative is to let the *interahamwe* and the Chetniks "cleanse" their enemies in their own way. . . .

HOW ETHNIC CIVIL WARS END

Civil wars are not all alike. Ethnic conflicts are disputes between communities which see themselves as having distinct heritages, over the power relationship between the communities, while ideological civil wars are contests between factions within the same community over how that community should be governed. The key difference is the flexibility of individual loyalties, which are quite fluid in ideological conflicts, but almost completely rigid in ethnic wars.

The possible and impossible solutions to ethnic civil wars follow from this fact. War hardens ethnic identities to the point that cross-ethnic political appeals become futile, which means that victory can be assured only by physical control over the territory in dispute. Ethnic wars also generate intense security dilemmas, both because the escalation of each side's mobilization rhetoric presents a real threat to the other, and even more because intermingled population settlement patterns create defensive vulnerabilities and offensive opportunities.

Once this occurs, the war cannot end until the security dilemma is reduced by physical separation of the rival groups. Solutions that aim at restoring multi-ethnic civil politics and at avoiding population transfers—such as power-sharing, state re-building, or identity reconstruction—cannot work because they do nothing to dampen the security dilemma, and because ethnic fears and hatreds hardened by war are extremely resistant to change.

The result is that ethnic wars can end in only three ways: with complete victory of one side; by temporary suppression of the conflict by third party military occupation; or by self-governance of separate communities. The record of the ethnic wars of the last half century bears this out.

The Dynamics of Ethnic War

It is useful to compare characteristics of ethnic conflicts with those of ideological conflicts. The latter are competitions between the government and the rebels for the loyalties of the people. The critical features of these conflicts are that ideological loyalties are changeable and difficult to assess, and the same population serves as the shared mobilization base for both sides. As a result, winning the "hearts and minds" of the population is both possible and necessary for victory. The most important instruments are political, economic, and social reforms that redress popular grievances such as poverty, inequality, corruption, and physical insecurity. Control of access to population is also important, both to allow recruitment and implementation of reform promises, and to block the enemy from these tasks. Population control, however, cannot be guaranteed solely by physical control over territory, but depends on careful intelligence, persuasion, and coercion. Purely military successes are often indecisive as long as the enemy's base of political support is undamaged.

Ethnic wars, however, have nearly the opposite properties. Individual loyalties are both rigid and transparent, while each side's mobilization base is limited to members of its own group in friendly-controlled territory. The result is that ethnic conflicts are primarily military struggles in which victory depends on physical control over the disputed territory, not on appeals to members of the other group.

Identity in Ethnic Wars   Competition to sway individual loyalties does not play an important role in ethnic civil wars, because ethnic identities are fixed by birth.[1] While not everyone may be mobilized as an active fighter for his or her own group, hardly anyone ever fights for the opposing ethnic group.

Different identity categories imply their own membership rules. Ideological identity is relatively soft, as it is a matter of individual belief, or sometimes of political behavior. Religious identities are harder, because while they also depend on belief, change generally requires formal acceptance by the new faith, which may be denied. Ethnic identities are hardest, since they depend on language, culture, and religion, which are hard to change, as well as parentage, which no one can change.

Ethnic identities are hardened further by intense conflict, so that leaders cannot broaden their appeals to include members of opposing groups. As ethnic conflicts escalate, populations come increasingly to hold enemy images of the other group, either because of deliberate efforts by elites to create such images or because of increasing real threats. The intensification of the war in Southeastern Turkey, for example, has led the Turkish public more and more to identify all Kurds with the PKK guerrillas, while even assimilated Kurds increasingly see the war as a struggle for survival. Following

---

[1]Constructivist scholars of nationalism would not agree, as they argue that ethnic identities are flexible social constructions, which can be manipulated by political entrepreneurs and more or less freely adopted or ignored by individuals. Key works include Paul R. Brass, *Language, Religion, and Politics in North India* (Cambridge, England: Cambridge University Press, 1974); Benedict Anderson, *Imagined Communities: Reflections on the Origins and Spread of Nationalism* (London: Verso, 1983). Primordialists, by contrast, see ethnic identities as fixed by linguistic, racial, or religious background. Edward Shils, "Primordial, Personal, and Sacred Ties," *British Journal of Sociology,* Vol. 8 (1957), pp. 130–145; Clifford Geertz, "The Integrative Revolution: Primordial Sentiments and Civil Politics in the New States," in Geertz, ed., *Old Societies and New States* (New York: Free Press, 1963). For a recent defense, see Alexander J. Motyl, "Inventing Invention: The Limits of National Identity Formation," in Michael Kennedy and Ronald Gregor Suny, eds., *Intellectuals and the Articulation of the Nation,* book manuscript. A middle position, "perennialist," accepts that identities are social constructs but argues that their deep cultural and psychological roots make them extremely persistent, especially in literate cultures. See Walker Connor, *Ethnonationalism: The Quest for Understanding* (Princeton, N.J.: Princeton University Press, 1994). In this paper I do not take a position on the initial sources of ethnic identities or on their malleability under conditions of low conflict, but argue that massive ethnic violence creates conditions which solidify both ethnic boundaries and inter-ethnic hostility.

riots in Colombo in 1983 in which Sinhalese mobs killed 3,000 Tamils, even formerly liberal-minded Sinhalese came to view all Tamils as separatists: "They all say they are loyal to the government, but scratch a Tamil, any Tamil, and beneath the skin there is an Eelamist." Non-ethnic identity categories, such as neighborhood and friendship, cannot compete: in 1994 much of the hierarchy of the Rwandan Catholic Church split on ethnic lines.

Once the conflict reaches the level of large-scale violence, tales of atrocities—true or invented—perpetuated or planned against members of the group by the ethnic enemy provide hard-liners with an unanswerable argument. In March 1992 a Serb woman in Foča in Eastern Bosnia was convinced that "there were lists of Serbs who were marked for death. My two sons were down on the list to be slaughtered like pigs. I was listed under rape." The fact that neither she nor other townspeople had seen any such lists did not prevent them from believing such tales without question. The Croatian Ustasha in World War II went further, terrorizing Serbs in order to provoke a backlash that could then be used to mobilize Croats for defense against Serb retaliation.

In this environment, cross-ethnic appeals are not likely to attract members of the other group. The Yugoslav Partisans in World War II are often credited with transcending the ethnic conflict between the Croatian Ustasha and the Serbian Chetniks with an anti-German, pan-Yugoslav program. In fact it did not work. Tito was a Croat, but Partisan officers as well as the rank and file were virtually all Serbs and Montenegrins. Only in 1944, when German withdrawal made Partisan victory certain, did Croats begin to join the Partisans in numbers, not because they preferred a multi-ethnic Yugoslavia to a Greater Croatia, but because they preferred a multi-ethnic Yugoslavia to a Yugoslavia cleansed of Croatians.

In both Laos and Thailand in the 1960s, the hill people (Hmong) fought the lowland people (Laos and Thais). The Hmong in Laos called themselves anti-communists, while Hmong on the other side of the Mekong River turned to the Communist Party of Thailand. The ideological affiliations, however, were purely tactical; most Hmong in Laos lived in areas dominated by the communist Pathet Lao and so turned to the United States for support, while most Hmong in Thailand were fighting a U.S.-allied government. Although in both countries both communists and anti-communists offered political reform and economic development, cross-ethnic recruitment bore little fruit, and the outcomes of the rebellions were determined mainly by strictly military operations.

Ethnic war also shrinks scope for individual identity choice. Even those who put little value on their ethnic identity are pressed towards ethnic mobilization for two reasons. First, extremists within each community are likely to impose sanctions on those who do not contribute to the cause. In 1992 the leader of the Croatian Democratic Union in Bosnia was dismissed on the ground that he "was too much Bosnian, too little Croat." Conciliation is easy to denounce as dangerous to group security or as actually traitorous. Such arguments drove nationalist extremists to overthrow President Makarios of Cyprus in 1974, to assassinate Mahatma Gandhi in 1948, to massacre nearly the whole government of Rwanda in 1994, and to kill Yitzhak Rabin in 1995.

Second and more important, identity is often imposed by the opposing group, specifically by its most murderous members. Assimilation or political passivity did no good for German Jews, Rwandan Tutsis, or Azerbaijanis in Nagorno-Karabakh. A Bosnian Muslim schoolteacher recently lamented:

> We never, until the war, thought of ourselves as Muslims. We were Yugoslavs. But when we began to be murdered, because we are Muslims, things changed. The definition of who we are today has been determined by our killers. . . .

The Decisiveness of Territory   Another consequence of the hardness of ethnic identities is that population control depends wholly on territorial control. Since each side can recruit only from its own community and only in friendly-controlled territory, incentives to seize areas populated by co-ethnics are strong, as is the pressure to cleanse friendly-controlled territory of enemy ethnics by relocation to *de facto* concentration camps, expulsion, or massacre.

Because of the decisiveness of territorial control, military strategy in ethnic wars is very different than in ideological conflicts. Unlike ideological insurgents, who often evade rather than risk battle, or a counter-insurgent government, which might forbear to attack rather than risk bombarding civilians, ethnic combatants must fight for every piece of land. By contrast, combatants in ethnic wars are much less free to decline unfavorable battles because they cannot afford to abandon any settlement to an enemy who is likely to "cleanse" it by massacre, expulsion, destruction of homes, and possibly colonization. By the time a town can be retaken, its value will have been lost.

In ethnic civil wars, military operations are decisive. Attrition matters because the side's mobilization pools are separate and can be depleted. Most important, since each side's mobilization base is limited to members of its own community in friendly-controlled territory, conquering the enemy's population centers reduces its mobilization base, while loss of friendly settlements reduces one's own. Military control of the entire territory at issue is tantamount to total victory.

Security Dilemmas in Ethnic Wars

The second problem that must be overcome by any remedy for severe ethnic conflict is the security dilemma. Regardless of the origins of ethnic strife, once violence (or abuse of state power by one group that controls it) reaches the point that ethnic communities cannot rely on the state to protect them, each community must mobilize to take responsibility for its own security.

Under conditions of anarchy, each group's mobilization constitutes a real threat to the security of others for two reasons. First, the nationalist rhetoric that accompanies mobilization often seems to and often does indicate offensive intent. Under these conditions, group identity itself can be seen by other groups as a threat to their safety.[2]

---

[2]Barry R. Posen, "The Security Dilemma and Ethnic Conflict," in Michael Brown, ed., *Ethnic Conflict and International Security* (Princeton, N.J.: Princeton University Press, 1993), pp. 103–124. Posen argues that nationalism and hypernationalism are driven primarily by the need to supply recruits for mass armies, and are thus likely to be more extreme in new states which lack the capacity to field more capital-intensive and less manpower-intensive forces (pp. 106–107). See also Posen, "Nationalism, the Mass Army, and Military Power," *International Security,* Vol. 18, No. 2 (Fall 1993), pp. 80–124.

Second, military capability acquired for defense can usually also be used for offense. Further, offense often has an advantage over defense in inter-community conflict, especially when settlement patterns are inter-mingled, because isolated pockets are harder to hold than to take.

The reality of the mutual security threats means that solutions to ethnic conflicts must do more than undo the causes; until or unless the security dilemma can be reduced or eliminated, neither side can afford to demobilize.

Demography and Security Dilemmas   The severity of ethnic security dilemmas is greatest when demography is most intermixed, weakest when community settlements are most separate. The more mixed the opposing groups, the stronger the offense in relation to the defense; the more separated they are, the stronger the defense in relation to offense.[3] When settlement patterns are extremely mixed, both sides are vulnerable to attack not only by organized military forces but also by local militias or gangs from adjacent towns or neighborhoods. Since well-defined fronts are impossible, there is no effective means of defense against such raids. Accordingly, each side has a strong incentive—at both national and local levels—to kill or drive out enemy populations before the enemy does the same to it, as well as to create homogeneous enclaves more practical to defend.

Better, but still bad, are well-defined enclaves with islands of one or both sides' populations behind the other's front. Each side then has an incentive to attack to rescue its surrounded co-ethnics before they are destroyed by the enemy, as well as incentives to wipe out enemy islands behind its own lines, both to pre-empt rescue attempts and to eliminate possible bases for fifth columnists or guerrillas.

The safest pattern is a well-defined demographic front that separates nearly homogeneous regions. Such a front can be defended by organized military forces, so populations are not at risk unless defenses are breached. At the same time the strongest motive for attack disappears, since there are few or no endangered co-ethnics behind enemy lines. . . .

Ethnic Separation and Peace   Once ethnic groups are mobilized for war, the war cannot end until the populations are separated into defensible, mostly homogeneous regions. Even if an international force or an imperial conqueror were to impose peace, the conflict would resume as soon as it left. Even if a national government were somehow re-created despite mutual suspicions, neither group could safely entrust its security to it. Continuing mutual threat also ensures perpetuation of hypernationalist propaganda, both for mobilization and because the plausibility of the threat posed by

---

[3]Increased geographic intermixing of ethnic groups often intensifies conflict, particularly if the state is too weak or too biased to assure the security of all groups. Increasing numbers of Jewish settlers in the West Bank had this effect on Israeli-Palestinian relations. A major reason for the failure of the negotiations that preceded the Nigerian civil war was the inability of northern leaders to guarantee the safety of Ibo living in the northern region. Harold D. Nelson, ed., *Nigeria: A Country Study* (Washington, D.C.: U.S. GPO, 1982), p. 55.

the enemy gives radical nationalists an unanswerable advantage over moderates in intra-group debates.

Ethnic separation does not guarantee peace, but it allows it. Once populations are separated, both cleansing and rescue imperatives disappear; war is no longer mandatory. At the same time, any attempt to seize more territory requires a major conventional military offensive. Thus the conflict changes from one of mutual pre-emptive ethnic cleansing to something approaching conventional interstate war in which normal deterrence dynamics apply. Mutual deterrence does not guarantee that there will be no further violence, but it reduces the probability of outbreaks, as well as the likely aims and intensity of those that do occur.

There have been no wars among Bulgaria, Greece, and Turkey since their population exchanges of the 1920s. Ethnic violence on Cyprus, which reached crisis on several occasions between 1960 and 1974, has been zero since the partition and population exchange which followed Turkish invasion. The Armenian-Azeri ethnic conflict, sparked by independence demands of the mostly Armenian Nagorno-Karabakh Autonomous Oblast, escalated to full-scale war by 1992. Armenian conquest of all of Karabakh together with the land which formerly separated it from Armenia proper, along with displacement of nearly all members of each group from enemy-controlled territories, created a defensible separation with no minorities to fight over, leading to a cease-fire in April 1994. . . .

Alternatives to Separation

Besides demographic separation, the literature on possible solutions to ethnic conflicts contains four main alternatives: suppression, reconstruction of ethnic identities, power-sharing, and state-building.

Suppression   Many ethnic civil wars lead to the complete victory of one side and the forcible suppression of the other. This may reduce violence in some cases, but will never be an aim of outsiders considering humanitarian intervention. Further, remission of violence may be only temporary, as the defeated group usually rebels again at any opportunity. Even the fact that certain conquerors, such as the English in Scotland or the Dutch in Friesland, eventually permitted genuine political assimilation after decades of suppression, does not recommend this as a remedy for endangered peoples today.

Reconstruction of Ethnic Identities   The most ambitious program to end ethnic violence would be to reconstruct ethnic identities according to the "Constructivist Model" of nationalism. Constructivists argue that individual and group identities are fluid, continually being made and re-made in social discourse. Further, these identities are manipulable by political entrepreneurs. Violent ethnic conflicts are the result of pernicious group identities created by hypernationalist myth-making; many inter-group conflicts are quite recent, as are the ethnic identities themselves.

The key is elite rivalries within communities, in which aggressive leaders use hypernationalist propaganda to gain and hold power. History does not matter; whether past inter-community relations have in fact been peaceful or conflictual, leaders can redefine, reinterpret, and invent facts to suit their arguments, including alleged atrocities and exaggerated or imagined threats. This process can feed on itself, as nationalists use the self-fulfilling nature of their arguments both to escalate the conflict and to justify their own power, so that intra-community politics becomes a competition in hypernationalist extremism, and inter-community relations enter a descending spiral of violence.

It follows that ethnic conflicts generated by the promotion of pernicious, exclusive identities should be reversible by encouraging individuals and groups to adopt more benign, inclusive identities. Leaders can choose to mobilize support on the basis of broader identities that transcend the ethnic division, such as ideology, class, or civic loyalty to the nation-state. If members of the opposing groups can be persuaded to adopt a larger identity, ethnic antagonisms should fade away. In 1993 David Owen explained why reconciliation in Bosnia was still possible: "I think it's realistic because these people are of the same ethnic stock. . . . Many people there still see themselves as European and even now don't think of themselves as Muslim, Croat, or Serb."

However, even if ethnic hostility can be "constructed," there are strong reasons to believe that violent conflicts cannot be "reconstructed" back to ethnic harmony. Identity reconstruction under conditions of intense conflict is probably impossible because once ethnic groups are mobilized for war, they will have already produced, and will continue reproducing, social institutions and discourses that reinforce their group identity and shut out or shout down competing identities.

Replacement of ethnicity by some other basis for political identification requires that political parties have cross-ethnic appeal, but examples of this in the midst of ethnic violence are virtually impossible to find. In late 1992 Yugoslav Prime Minister Milan Panić attempted to reconstruct Serbian identity in a less nationalist direction. Running for the Serbian presidency against Milošević, Panić promised democratization, economic reform, and ends to the war in Bosnia as well as to UN sanctions. Milošević painted him as a tool of foreign interests, and Panić lost with 34 percent of the vote.

In fact, even ethnic tension far short of war often undermines not just political appeals across ethnic lines but also appeals within a single group for cooperation with other groups. In Yugoslavia in the 1920s, Malaya in the 1940s, Ceylon in the 1950s, and in Nigeria in the 1950s and 1960s, parties that advocated cooperation across ethnic lines proved unable to compete with strictly nationalist parties.

Even if constructivists are right that the ancient past does not matter, recent history does. Intense violence creates personal experiences of fear, misery, and loss which lock people into their group identity and their enemy relationship with the other group. Elite as well as mass opinions are affected; more than 5,000 deaths in the 1946 Calcutta riots convinced many previously optimistic Hindu and Muslim leaders that the groups could not live together. The Tutsi-controlled government of Burundi, which had witnessed the partial genocide against Tutsis in Rwanda in 1962–63 and survived Hutu-led coup attempts in 1965 and 1969, regarded the 1972 rebellion as another attempt at genocide, and responded by murdering between 100,000 and 200,000 Hutus. Fresh rounds of violence in 1988 and 1993–94 have reinforced the apocalyptic fears of both sides. . . .

Power-Sharing   The best-developed blueprint for civic peace in multi-ethnic states is power-sharing or "consociational democracy," proposed by Arend Lijphart. This approach assumes that ethnicity is somewhat manipulable, but not so freely as constructivists say.[4] Ethnic division, however, need not result in conflict; even if political mobilization is organized on ethnic lines, civil politics can be maintained if ethnic elites adhere to a power-sharing bargain that equitably protects all groups. The key components are: 1) joint exercise of governmental power; 2) proportional distribution of government funds and jobs; 3) autonomy on ethnic issues (which, if groups are concentrated territorially, may be achieved by regional federation); and 4) a minority veto on issues of vital importance to each group.[5] Even if power-sharing can avert potential ethnic conflicts or dampen mild ones, our concern here is whether it can bring peace under the conditions of intense violence and extreme ethnic mobilization that are likely to motivate intervention.[6]

The answer is no. The indispensable component of any power-sharing deal is a plausible minority veto, one which the strongest side will accept and which the weaker side believes that the stronger will respect. Traditions of stronger loyalties to the state than to parochial groups and histories of inter-ethnic compromise could provide reason for confidence, but in a civil war these will have been destroyed, if they were ever present, by the fighting itself and accompanying ethnic mobilization.

Only a balance of power among the competing groups can provide a "hard" veto— one which the majority must respect. Regional concentration of populations could partially substitute for balanced power if the minority group can credibly threaten to secede if its veto is overridden. In any situation where humanitarian intervention might be considered, however, these conditions too are unlikely to be met. Interventions are likely to be aimed at saving a weak group that cannot defend itself; balanced sides do not need defense. Demographic separation is also unlikely, because if the populations were already separated, the ethnic cleansing and related atrocities which are most likely to provoke intervention would not be occurring.

The core reason why power-sharing cannot resolve ethnic civil wars is that it is inherently voluntaristic; it requires conscious decisions by elites to cooperate to avoid ethnic strife. Under conditions of hypernationalist mobilization and real security threats, group leaders are unlikely to be receptive to compromise, and even if they are, they cannot act without being discredited and replaced by harder-line rivals.

---

[4]Lijphart, "Consociational Democracy," *World Politics,* Vol. 21, No. 2 (January 1969). In fact, Lijphart argues that diffuse or fluid ethnic identities are undesirable, because design of a power-sharing agreement requires clear identification of the players. Lijphart, "Power Sharing Approach," pp. 499–500.

[5]Lijphart cites Belgium as an archetypical example, as well as Malaysia, Canada, India, and Nigeria. "Power-Sharing Approach," pp. 492, 494–96.

[6]Lijphart admits that power-sharing is more difficult under conditions of high conflict but prefers it anyway, arguing that pessimism in difficult cases would be self-fulfilling; power-sharing cannot work when it is not tried. Ibid., p. 497.

Could outside intervention make power-sharing work? One approach would be to adjust the balance of power between the warring sides to a "hurting stalemate" by arming the weaker side, blockading the stronger, or partially disarming the stronger by direct military intervention. When both sides realize that further fighting will bring them costs but no profit, they will negotiate an agreement. This can balance power, although if populations are still intermingled it may actually worsen security dilemmas and increase violence—especially against civilians—as both sides eliminate the threats posed by pockets of the opposing group in their midst. . . .

Ethnic Separation

Regardless of the causes of a particular conflict, once communities are mobilized for violence, the reality of mutual security threats prevents both demobilization and de-escalation of hypernationalist discourse. Thus, lasting peace requires removal of the security dilemma. The most effective and in many cases the only way to do this is to separate the ethnic groups. The more intense the violence, the more likely it is that separation will be the only option. . . .

How Ethnic Wars Have Ended

The most comprehensive data set of recent and current violent ethnic conflicts has been compiled by Ted Robert Gurr. This data set includes 27 ethnic civil wars that have ended. Of these, twelve were ended by complete victory of one side, five by *de jure* or *de facto* partition, and two have been suppressed by military occupation by a third party. Only eight ethnic civil wars have been ended by an agreement that did not partition the country. (See Table 1.)

The data supports the argument that separation of groups is the key to ending ethnic civil wars. Every case in which the state was preserved by agreement involved a regionally concentrated minority, and in every case the solution reinforced the ethnic role in politics by allowing the regional minority group to control its own destiny through regional autonomy for the areas where it forms a majority of the population. There is not a single case where non-ethnic civil politics were created or restored by reconstruction of ethnic identities, power-sharing coalitions, or state-building. . . .

INTERVENTION TO RESOLVE ETHNIC CIVIL WARS

International interventions that seek to ensure lasting safety for populations endangered by ethnic war—whether by the United Nations, by major powers with global reach, or by regional powers—must be guided by two principles. First, settlements must aim at physically separating the warring communities and establishing a balance of relative strength that makes it unprofitable for either side to attempt to revise the territorial settlement. Second, although economic or military assistance may suffice in some cases, direct military intervention will be necessary when aid to the weaker side would create

TABLE 1

Ethnic Civil Wars Resolved 1944–94

Combatants	Dates	Deaths (000s)[1]	Outcome
Military victory (12):			
Karens vs. Myanmar	1945–	43	Defeat imminent
Kurds vs. Iran	1945–80s	40	Suppressed
Tibetans vs. China	1959–89	100	Suppressed
Papuans vs. Indonesia	1964–86	19	Suppressed
Ibo vs. Nigeria	1967–70	2000	Suppressed
Timorese vs. Indonesia	1974–80s	200	Suppressed
Aceh vs. Indonesia	1975–80s	15	Suppressed
Tigreans vs. Ethiopia	1975–91	350	Rebels victorious
Uighurs etc. vs. China	1980	2	Suppressed
Bougainville vs. Papua	1988	1	Suppressed
Tutsis vs. Rwanda	1990–94	750	Rebels victorious
Shiites vs. Iraq	1991	35	Suppressed
De facto or de jure partition (5):			
Ukrainians vs. USSR	1944–50s	150	Suppressed, independent 1991
Lithuanians vs. USSR	1945–52	40	Suppressed; independent 1991
Eritreans vs. Ethiopia	1961–91	350	Independent 1993
Armenians vs. Azerbaijan	1988–	15	De facto partition
Somali clans	1988–	350	De facto partition in N., ongoing in S.
Conflict suppressed by ongoing 3rd-party military occupation (2):			
Kurds vs. Iraq	1960–	215	De facto partition
Lebanese Civil War	1975–90	120	Nominal power sharing, de facto partition
Settled by agreements other than partition (8):			
Nagas vs. India	1952–75	13	Autonomy 1972
Basques vs. Spain	1959–80s	1	Autonomy 1980
Tripuras vs. India	1967–89	13	Autonomy 1972
Palestinians vs. Israel	1968–93	2	Autonomy 1993, partly implemented
Moros vs. Philippines	1972–87	50	Limited autonomy 1990
Chittagong hill peoples vs. Bangladesh	1975–89	24	Limited autonomy 1989
Miskitos vs. Nicaragua	1981–88	<1	Autonomy 1990
Abkhazians vs. Georgia	1992–93	10	Autonomy 1993

[1]Figures are from Ted Robert Gurr, *Minorities at Risk: A Global View of Ethnopolitical Conflicts* (Washington, D.C.: U.S. Institute of Peace, 1993), and Gurr, "Peoples Against States: Ethnopolitical Conflict and the Changing World System," *International Studies Quarterly,* Vol. 38, No. 3 (September 1994), pp. 347–377.

a window of opportunity for the stronger, or when there is an immediate need to stop ongoing genocide.

Designing Settlements

Unless outsiders are willing to provide permanent security guarantees, stable resolution of an ethnic civil war requires separation of the groups into defensible regions. The critical variable is demography, not sovereignty. Political partition without ethnic separation leaves incentives for ethnic cleansing unchanged; it actually increases them if it creates new minorities. Conversely, demographic separation dampens ethnic conflicts even without separate sovereignty, although the more intense the previous fighting, the smaller the prospects for preserving a single state, even if loosely federated.

Partition without ethnic separation increases conflict because, while boundaries of sovereign successor states may provide defensible fronts that reduce the vulnerability of the majority group in each state, stay-behind minorities are completely exposed. Significant irredenta are both a call to their ethnic homeland and a danger to their hosts. They create incentives to mount rescue or ethnic cleansing operations before the situation solidifies. Greece's 1920 invasion of Turkey was justified in this way, while the 1947 decision to partition Palestine generated a civil war in advance of implementation, and the inclusion of Muslim-majority Kashmir within India has helped cause three wars. International recognition of Croatian and Bosnian independence did more to cause than to stop Serbian invasion. The war between Armenia and Azerbaijan has the same source, as do concerns over the international security risks of the several Russian diasporas.

Inter-ethnic security dilemmas can be nearly or wholly eliminated without partition if three conditions are met: First, there must be enough demographic separation that ethnic regions do not themselves contain militarily significant minorities. Second, there must be enough regional self-defense capability that abrogating the autonomy of any region would be more costly than any possible motive for doing so. Third, local autonomy must be so complete that minority groups can protect their key interests even lacking any influence at the national level. Even after an ethnic war, a single state could offer some advantages, not least of which are the economic benefits of a common market. However, potential interveners should recognize that groups that control distinct territories can insist on the *de facto* partition, and often will.

While peace requires separation of groups into distinct regions, it does not require total ethnic purity. Rather, remaining minorities must be small enough that the host group does not fear them as either a potential military threat or a possible target for irredentist rescue operations. Before the Krajina offensive, for example, President Franjo Tudjman of Croatia is said to have thought that the 12 percent Serb minority in Croatia was too large, but that half as many would be tolerable. The 173,000 Arabs remaining in Israel by 1951 were too few and too disorganized to be seen as a serious threat.

Geographic distribution of minorities is also important; in particular, concentrations near disputed borders or astride strategic communications constitute both a military vulnerability and an irredentist opportunity, and so are likely to spark conflict. It is not surprising that India's portion of Kashmir, with its Muslim majority, has been at the center of three interstate wars and an ongoing insurgency which continues today, while there has been no international conflict over the hundred million Muslims who live dispersed throughout most of the rest of India, and relatively little violence.

Where possible, inter-group boundaries should be drawn along the best defensive terrain, such as rivers and mountain ranges. Lines should also be as short as possible, to allow the heaviest possible manning of defensive fronts. (Croatian forces were able to overrun Krajina in part because its irregular crescent shape meant that 30,000 Krajina Serb forces had to cover a frontier of more than 725 miles.) Access to the sea or to a friendly neighbor is also important, both for trade and for possible military assistance. Successor state arsenals should be encouraged, by aid to the weaker or sanctions on the stronger, to focus on defensive armaments such as towed artillery and anti-aircraft missiles and rockets, while avoiding instruments that could make blitzkrieg attacks possible, such as tanks, fighter-bombers, and mobile artillery. These conditions would make subsequent offensives exceedingly expensive and likely to fail.

Intervention Strategy

The level of international action required to resolve an ethnic war will depend on the military situation on the ground. If there is an existing stalemate along defensible lines, the international community should simply recognize and strengthen it, providing transportation, protection, and resettlement assistance for refugees. However, where one side has the capacity to go on the offensive against the other, intervention will be necessary.

Interventions should therefore almost always be on behalf of the weaker side; the stronger needs no defense. Moreover, unless the international community can agree on a clear aggressor and a clear victim, there is no moral or political case for intervention. If both sides have behaved so badly that there is little to choose between them, intervention should not and probably will not be undertaken.[7] Almost no one in the West, for instance, has advocated assisting either side in the Croatian-Serb conflict.[8] While the intervention itself could be carried out by any willing actors, UN sponsorship is highly desirable, most of all to head off possible external aid to the group identified as the aggressor.

The three available tools are sanctions, military aid, and direct military intervention. Economic sanctions have limited leverage against combatants in ethnic wars, who often see their territorial security requirements as absolute. Whereas hyperinflation and economic collapse have apparently reduced Serbian government support for the Bosnian Serb rebels and thus limited the latter's material capabilities, Armenians have already suffered five years of extreme privation rather than give up Nagorno-Karabakh. . . .

---

[7]This is why the strongest advocates of intervention in Bosnia have emphasized Serb crimes, while those opposed to intervention insist on the moral equivalence of the two sides. Anthony Lewis, "Crimes of War," *New York Times,* April 25, 1994; Charles G. Boyd, "Making Peace with the Guilty," *Foreign Affairs,* Vol. 74, No. 5 (September/October 1995), pp. 22–38.

[8]Further, attempts at even-handed intervention rarely achieve their goals, leading either to nearly complete passivity, as in the case of UNPROFOR in Bosnia, or eventually to open combat against one or all sides. At worst, peace-keeping efforts may actually prolong fighting. See Richard K. Betts, "The Delusion of Impartial Intervention," *Foreign Affairs,* Vol. 73, No. 6 (November/December 1994), pp. 20–33.

If the client is too weak to achieve a viable separation with material aid alone, or if either or both sides cannot be trusted to abide by promises of nonretribution against enemy civilians, the international community must designate a separation line and deploy an intervention force to take physical control of the territory on the client's side of the line. We might call this approach "conquer and divide."

The separation campaign is waged as a conventional military operation. The larger the forces committed the better, both to minimize intervenors' casualties and to shorten the campaign by threatening the opponent with overwhelming defeat. Although some argue that any intervention force would become mired in a Vietnam-like quagmire, the fundamentally different nature of ethnic conflict means that the main pitfalls to foreign military interventions in ideological insurgencies are either weaker or absent. Most important, the intervenors' intelligence problems are much simpler, since loyalty intelligence is both less important and easier: outsiders can safely assume that members of the allied group are friends and those of the other are enemies. Even if outsiders cannot tell the groups apart, locals can, and the loyalty of guides provided by the local ally can be counted on. As a result, the main intelligence task shifts from assessing loyalties to locating enemy forces, a task of which major power militaries are very capable. . . .

Bosnia

Early intervention in Bosnia could have saved most of the lives that have been lost, and secured the Muslims a better territorial deal than they are going to get, but only if the international community had been willing to accept that by 1992, restoration of civil politics in a multi-ethnic Bosnia had become impossible, and had been able to overcome its squeamishness about large-scale population transfers.

The Vance-Owen plan did not meet the minimum conditions for stable peace because it aimed at preservation of a multi-ethnic state, not ethnic separation. Each of the ten planned cantons would have contained large minorities, and some would have included enclaves totally surrounded by an opposing ethnic group. The 1994 Contact Group proposal to divide Bosnia 51 percent–49 percent between a Muslim-Croat federation and the Bosnian Serbs would have been better, but incorporated serious instabilities such as the isolated Muslim enclaves of Žepa, Srebrenica, and Goražde, two of which were later overrun with great loss of life.

As the progress of the war has left fewer and fewer unmoved people still to move, more realistic proposals have gradually emerged. The agreement signed at Dayton in November 1995, despite lip service to a unitary Bosnia, ratifies and seeks to strengthen existing territorial divisions. This agreement gives grounds for qualified hope for a stable, relatively peaceful Bosnia.

Future peace in Bosnia depends on resolution of three issues. First and most important, while the military fronts have gradually settled along defensible lines in most areas of the country, serious demographic security dilemmas persist in two places—Serb-held suburbs of Sarajevo which both threaten the city's supply lines and are vulnerable themselves, and the surrounded Muslim enclave of Goražde in the Drina Valley.

Accordingly, the Dayton agreement requires the withdrawal of all Bosnian Serb forces from these Sarajevo suburbs as well as from a corridor stretching from Sarajevo to Goražde, and assigns these areas to the Bosnian government. The Implementation Force (IFOR) is charged with ensuring compliance. The widespread burning of homes by Serbs and others evacuating areas which will pass to control of another group is in a sense encouraging, as it suggests they do not expect to return. More worrisome is the fact that the corridor to Goražde will be only four kilometers wide, leaving the city once again vulnerable after the IFOR departs. A wider corridor here, perhaps in exchange for territory elsewhere, would have been better, even if it meant that more civilians would have to move now.

The second issue is that the agreement, at least nominally, seeks to reconstruct some central government institutions with nationwide authority and a rotating presidency. It also requires all parties to permit the return of refugees. These provisions are undesirable and unenforceable, and should be allowed to die quietly. The procedures provided for compensating refugees for lost property should be followed instead. . . .

OBJECTIONS TO ETHNIC SEPARATION AND PARTITION

There are five important objections to ethnic separation as policy for resolving ethnic conflicts: that it encourages splintering of states, that population exchanges cause human suffering, that it simply transforms civil wars into international ones, that rump states will not be viable, and that, in the end, it does nothing to resolve ethnic antagonisms.

Among most international organizations, western leaders, and scholars, population exchanges and partition are anathema. They contradict cherished western values of social integration, trample on the international legal norm of state sovereignty, and suggest particular policies that have been condemned by most of the world (e.g., Turkey's unilateral partition of Cyprus). The integrity of states and their borders is usually seen as a paramount principle, while self-determination takes second place. In ethnic wars, however, saving lives may require ignoring state-centered legal norms. The legal costs of ethnic separation must be compared to the human consequences, both immediate and long term, if the warring groups are not separated. To paraphrase Winston Churchill: separation is the worst solution, except for all the others.

Partition Encourages Splintering of States

If international interventions for ethnic separation encourage secession attempts elsewhere, they could increase rather than decrease global ethnic violence. However, this is unlikely, because government use of force to suppress them makes almost all secession attempts extremely costly; only groups that see no viable alternative try. What intervention can do is reduce loss of life where states are breaking up anyway. An expectation that the international community will never intervene, however, encourages repression of minorities, as in Turkey or the Sudan, and wars of ethnic conquest, as by Serbia.

Population Transfers Cause Suffering

Separation of intermingled ethnic groups necessarily involves significant refugee flows, usually in both directions. Population transfers during ethnic conflicts have often led to much suffering, so an obvious question is whether foreign intervention to relocate populations would only increase suffering. In fact, however, the biggest cause of suffering

in population exchanges is spontaneous refugee movement. Planned population transfers are much safer. When ethnic conflicts turn violent, they generate spontaneous
refugee movements as people flee from intense fighting or are kicked out by neighbors,
marauding gangs, or a conquering army. Spontaneous refugees frequently suffer direct
attack by hostile civilians or armed forces. They often leave precipitately, with inadequate money, transport, or food supplies, and before relief can be organized. They make
vulnerable targets for banditry and plunder, and are often so needy as to be likely perpetrators also. Planned population exchanges can address all of these risks by preparing
refugee relief and security operations in advance.

In the 1947 India-Pakistan exchange, nearly the entire movement of between 12
and 16 million people took place in a few months. The British were surprised by the
speed with which this movement took place, and were not ready to control, support, and
protect the refugees. Estimates of deaths go as high as one million. In the first stages of
the population exchanges among Greece, Bulgaria, and Turkey in the 1920s, hundreds
of thousands of refugees moved spontaneously and many died due to banditry and exposure. When after 1925 the League of Nations deployed capable relief services, the remaining transfers—one million, over 60 percent of the total—were carried out in an organized and planned way, with virtually no losses. . . .

Separation Merely Substitutes International for Civil Wars

Post-separation wars are possible, motivated either by revanchism or by security fears if
one side suspects the other of revisionist plans. The frequency and human cost of such
wars, however, must be compared to the likely consequences of not separating. When
the alternative is intercommunal slaughter, separation is the only defensible choice.

In fact the record of twentieth-century ethnic partitions is fairly good. The partition
of Ireland has produced no interstate violence, although intercommunal violence continues in demographically mixed Northern Ireland. India and Pakistan have fought two
wars since partition, one in 1965 over ethnically mixed Kashmir, while the second in
1971 resulted not from Indo-Pakistani state rivalry or Hindu-Muslim religious conflict
but from ethnic conflict between (West) Pakistanis and Bengalis. Indian intervention resolved the conflict by enabling the independence of Bangladesh. These wars have been
much less dangerous, especially to civilians, than the political and possible physical extinction that Muslims feared if the subcontinent were not divided. The worst post-parti-
tion history is probably that of the Arab-Israeli conflict. Even here, civilian deaths
would almost certainly have been higher without partition. It is difficult even to imagine any alternative; the British could not and would not stay, and neither side would
share power or submit to rule by the other.

Rump States Will Not Be Viable

Many analysts of ethnic conflict question the economic and military viability of partitioned states. History, however, records no examples of ethnic partitions which failed
for economic reasons. In any case, intervenors have substantial influence over economic

outcomes: they can determine partition lines, guarantee trade access and, if necessary, provide significant aid in relation to the economic sizes of likely candidates. Peace itself also enhances recovery prospects.

Thus the more important issue is military viability, particularly since interventions will most often be in favor of the weaker side. If the client has economic strength comparable to the opponent, it can provide for its own defense. If it does not, the intervenors will have to provide military aid and possibly a security guarantee. . . .

Partition Does Not Resolve Ethnic Hatreds

It is not clear that it is in anyone's power to resolve ethnic hatreds once there has been large-scale violence, especially murders of civilians. In the long run, however, separation may help reduce inter-ethnic antagonism; once real security threats are reduced, the plausibility of hypernationalist appeals may eventually decline. Certainly ethnic hostility cannot be reduced without separation. As long as either side fears, even intermittently, that it will be attacked by the other, past atrocities and old hatreds can easily be aroused. If, however, it becomes and remains implausible that the other group could ever seriously endanger the nation, hypernationalist drum-beating may fall on deafer and deafer ears.

The only stronger measure would be to attempt a thorough re-engineering of the involved groups' political and social systems, comparable to the rehabilitation of Germany after World War II. The costs would be steep, since this would require conquering the country and occupying it for a long time, possibly for decades. The apparent benignification of Germany suggests that, if the international community is prepared to go this far, this approach could succeed.

CONCLUSION

Humanitarian intervention to establish lasting safety for peoples endangered by ethnic civil wars is feasible, but only if the international community is prepared to recognize that some shattered states cannot be restored, and that population transfers are sometimes necessary.

Some observers attack separation and partition as immoral, suggesting that partitioning states like Bosnia would ratify the arguments of bloody-minded extremists such as Milošević and Tudjman that ethnic cleansing is necessitated by intractable ancient hatreds, when in fact they themselves whipped up hypernationalist fears for their own political ends. This argument is mistaken. The construction of ethnic hostility might have been contained by intervention in Yugoslav political discourses in the 1980s. It is too late now, but what the international community can still do is to provide surviving Muslims with physical security and a defensible homeland. The claims of justice demand that we go further, to the capture and trial of the aggressors, but that is beyond the scope of this article, the focus of which is the minimum requirements for protection of peoples endangered by ethnic war.

Alternatively, one could argue that the Bosnia record demonstrates that the international community cannot muster the will even for much lesser enterprises, let alone the campaigns of conquest envisaged in this paper. Even if this is true, the analysis above has four values. First, it tells us what apparent cheap and easy solutions are *not* viable. Second, it identifies the types of solutions to aim at through lesser means—aid or sanctions—if those are the most that outsiders are willing to do. Third, even if we are not prepared to intervene in certain cases, it explains what we would like other, more interested, powers to do and not do. Fourth, if Western publics and elites understood that the costs of military intervention in ethnic wars are lower, the feasibility higher, and the alternatives fewer than they now believe, perhaps this option would become more politically viable.

Ultimately we have a responsibility to be honest with ourselves as well as with the victims of ethnic wars all over the world. The world's major powers must decide whether they will be willing to spend any of their own soldiers' lives to save strangers, or whether they will continue to offer false hopes to endangered peoples.

THE TROUBLED
HISTORY OF PARTITION

Radha Kumar

BOSNIA GOES THE WAY OF CYPRUS

The September [1996] elections in Bosnia highlighted what was until then an implicit aspect of the current peace: it is more likely to move Bosnia toward the ethnic states for which the war was fought than to reestablish the multiethnic Bosnia that once was. Indeed, as the Dayton process unfolds, it becomes clearer that the peace agreement signed in November 1995 after three and a half years of war was something historically familiar: a so-called peace accord that is in reality a partition agreement with an exit clause for outside powers.

At the same time, while key aspects of the document, such as the creation of two "entities" with virtually separate legislatures, administrations, and armies, tend toward partition, the pact attempts to get around some of the more hostile legacies of partition through a common economic space and arms control, and it creates structures that could reverse the partition process by returning refugees and rebuilding civil society. So far, these structures have been dormant, and the holding of national elections in a still highly uncertain peace marks the tilt toward partition. As was widely predicted, the Bosnians gave their ethnic leaders new mandates, and Bosnia took another step toward partition. However, the postponement of the municipal elections due to irregularities in voter registration means the international community is not yet in a position to accept partition as the democratically expressed will of the people.

The Bosnian war and the Dayton peace agreement have reignited a debate on whether partition is an effective solution to ethnic conflict. Although Bosnia is the starting point, the arguments in this debate have broad resonance at a time in which the rapid spread of ethnic and communal wars east and south of Bosnia is of increasing concern to the international community. Defenders of partition make an argument that runs as follows. When an ethnic war is far advanced, partition is probably the most humane form of intervention because it attempts to achieve through negotiation what would otherwise be achieved through fighting; it circumvents the conflict and saves lives. It might even save a country from disappearing altogether because an impartial intervenor will attempt to secure the rights of each contending ethnic group, whereas in war the stronger groups might oust the weaker ones. In fact, its advocates say, the ideal strategy for resolving an ethnic conflict is to intervene and take partition to its logical conclusion by dividing a country along its communal battle lines and helping make the resulting territories ethnically homogeneous through organized population transfers. This will ensure that partition is more than a temporary means of containing conflict. Less thorough partitions, however, can still be a lasting means of containment.[1]

Partition, however, has its own sordid history, not arising as a means of realizing national self-determination, but imposed as a way for outside powers to unshoulder colonies or divide up spheres of influence—a strategy of divide and quit. Although described as the lesser of two evils, the partitions in Cyprus, India, Palestine, and Ireland, rather than separating irreconcilable ethnic groups, fomented further violence and forced mass migration. Even where partition enabled outside powers to leave, as in India, it also led to a disastrous war. Often thought of as a provisional solution, it has been unable to contain the fragmentation it triggers among dispersed or overlapping ethnic groups that are not confined by neat geographic boundaries, and it gives birth to weak civil institutions demanding supervision. Similar conditions ensure that the partition of Bosnia, which from the start should have been reintegrated, will also amount only to a policy of divide and be forced to stay. The Dayton accords should not evoke memories of Munich, but rather of Cyprus.

THE ROAD TO QUITTING

The argument for ethnic partition is not new, but its terms changed considerably over this century before settling upon the current rationale of the lesser of two evils. Before World War I, most partitions were effected for the needs of empire, to strengthen rule or simplify administration. After 1918, however, colonial empires were increasingly challenged, and subsequent partitions took place as part of a devolution of authority or a Cold War policy of spheres of influence. There were two distinct rationales for the partitions resulting from the fall of colonial empires: Wilsonian national self-determination, applied to Poland and Romania, and the British colonial policy of identifying irreconcilable nationhoods, applied in Ireland, India, and, as a delayed response, Cyprus and Palestine. Though both rationales took ethnic identity as an important determinant of political rights, Wilsonian policy supported ethnic self-determination as freedom from colonial rule, while the British reluctantly espoused partition as a lesser evil than constant civil war.

After the last attempt to ratify a partition—Cyprus after the Turkish invasion in 1974—the notion that partition was an effective solution to ethnic conflict fell into disuse for a quarter-century. Paradoxically, its revival followed hard on the heels of German reunification and the potential integration of Europe that it heralded. In the first phase of the revival of partition theory, Wilsonian self-determination was invoked more

---

[1]For examples of this view, see John J. Mearsheimer, "Shrink Bosnia to Save It," *The New York Times,* March 31, 1993, p. A23; Mearsheimer and Stephen Van Evera, "When Peace Means War," *The New Republic,* December 18, 1995, pp. 16–21; and Chaim Kaufmann, "Possible and Impossible Solutions to Ethnic Civil Wars," *International Security,* Spring 1996, pp. 136–75. Kaufmann goes so far as to suggest that after an international military takeover, international forces should intern "civilians of the enemy ethnic group" and "exchange" them once peace is established.

often than the lesser-evil argument. Indeed, the prevailing feeling was that the end of the Cold War—and the relatively peaceful dissolution of the Soviet Union—meant that separations could be negotiated. In the early 1990s the most frequently cited example of a peaceful negotiated division was Czechoslovakia's "velvet divorce." When asked on *The News Hour with Jim Lehrer* in November 1995 whether the Dayton agreement was a partition, Assistant Secretary of State Richard C. Holbrooke said he preferred the example of Czechoslovakia's voluntary dissolution. But fewer people now refer to the Czech split. That the Czech Republic and Slovakia were relatively homogeneous and that dissolution of the federation did not require an alteration of internal borders or a substantial displacement of people make the comparison with Bosnia untenable. A comparison between Bosnia and the partitions of Ireland, India, and Cyprus, or the incomplete partition of Palestine, would be better, because each involved ethnically mixed and dispersed populations and each was held to be a pragmatic recognition of irreconcilable ethnic identities.

It is worth examining these partitions' relevance to Bosnia in more detail. All relied heavily on the lesser-evil argument, but in at least two of them the decision for partition was prompted not by a desire for peace and self-determination, but because the colonial power, Britain, wanted to withdraw. The recognition of irreconcilable nationhoods followed as a consequence—it would be easier to withdraw quickly if the aims of the ethnic leaders were fulfilled by territorial grants. Looking back on the 1947 partition of India in 1961, former civil servant Penderel Moon summed up as "divide and quit," in a book of the same name, the British policy of pushing partition through without establishing the boundaries of new states or planning for the wars that might ensue; it was the post-World War II imperative of quitting that drove the decision to divide, he said. It was arguably the post-World War I imperative of quitting the Irish conflict that led the British to espouse a partition of Ireland.

That both divisions were driven by considerations extraneous to the needs and desires of the people displaced does not necessarily mean that partition was not a solution to their conflicts. However, as in India and Ireland, partition has more often been a backdrop to war than its culmination in peace; although it may originate in a situation of conflict, its effect has been to stimulate further and even new conflict. Indeed, India's experience raises the question of whether a peaceful transition to partition is possible. India's political leadership agreed to partition the country before the spread of large-scale conflict; the 1947 partition agreement between the Indian National Congress and the Muslim League was intended partly to prevent the spread of communal riots from Bengal in eastern India to northwestern India, which was also to be divided. But the riots that followed in 1947–48 left more than a million people dead in six months and displaced upwards of 15 million.

Moreover, partition arises in high-level negotiations long before it becomes evident on the ground. The British partition of Ireland in 1921 was a late addition to negotiations for home rule during the 1919–21 Anglo-Irish war for independence, but partition had been on the drawing board since 1912, when it was suggested by a group of conservative and liberal members of parliament that Protestant-majority counties be excluded from the proposed Irish Home Rule Bill. Calls for partition were renewed in 1914, 1916, and 1919; the offer of a double partition of Ireland and Ulster based on religion led to the spread of conflict between English and Irish across the south, west, and north of Ireland, escalating to guerrilla warfare when Catholic rebels formed the Irish Republican Army in 1919. Nor did the war end in 1921 when Britain negotiated a treaty with Sinn Fein, the political arm of the IRA, offering dominion status to southern Ireland in return for a separate Ulster under British administration. The decision to accept partition led to a split in Sinn Fein, and internecine conflict was added to communal conflict, ending two years later with the defeat of the faction led by Eamon De Valera. It took almost four years of war to achieve the partition of Ireland, and those four years were themselves a culminating phase in a movement toward partition that had begun ten years earlier.

Significantly, the British rejected the partition option in Palestine in the same years that they espoused it in India. The two reasons they gave were infeasibility and the risk of a military conflict that would involve an expanded British presence. Although partition had been proposed in 1937 by the Peel Commission, which concluded that cooperation between Jews and Arabs in a Palestinian state was impossible, and had been the subject of debate in Britain throughout the 1930s, in 1946 the British members of the Anglo-American Committee of Inquiry argued that because ethnic groups were so dispersed, partition would entail massive forced population transfers, and that the territories created—a tiny Arab state, a Jewish state in two parts, and three blocs under continuing British administration—would be infeasible. Moreover, they said, moves toward partition could cause a war. In 1947 the British referred the dispute to the United Nations. The Security Council opted for partition, with a special U.N. regime for Jerusalem and a continuing economic union for the whole of Palestine. The plan required Britain to undertake a substantial role in its implementation, but after the Ministry of Defence forecast that Britain's military presence would have to be reinforced in the wars that would follow, Britain announced that it would withdraw in May 1948. In April the Jewish Agency, which represented the Jewish community under the British mandate, announced that it would declare a Jewish state when the British withdrew. War broke out, resulting in a kind of skewed partition by which one new state was created but not the other. Subsequently there have been three Arab-Israeli wars, and the issue of territorial feasibility continues to dog the peace process.

In many ways Cyprus offers the most striking parallels to Bosnia, and its history again raises the question of whether a peaceful transition to partition is possible. Although the British proposed the partition of the island in a divide-and-rule move in 1956, they subsequently rejected the plan on the same grounds as in Palestine—infeasibility and the risk of conflict. The British-brokered constitution of 1960 that made Cyprus independent was an attempt to avert division of the island between ethnic Turks and ethnic Greeks, but the idea that ethnic politics could be contained by providing for ethnic representation at every level proved a failure. The constitutional creation of separate municipalities and a distribution between the two ethnic groups in the presidency, legislature, civil service, police, and army added communal (that is, interreligious) conflict to internecine conflict. In 1963 the "Green Line," the first partition boundary to be drawn, divided Greek and Turkish Cypriots in Nicosia, the capital. Ethnic conflict only intensified, and a Turkish Cypriot declaration of support for partition followed in 1964. Although U.N. troops arrived that year, tensions escalated, with a counter-declaration of unification by Greece and Cyprus in 1966, a military coup in Greece, renewed conflict in Cyprus, a Turkish Cypriot announcement in 1967 of a Provisional Administration, increasing Greek support for the radical Greek underground in Cyprus, and finally a Turkish invasion in 1974 that reinforced the de facto partition of the island. Thus it took 14 years to establish what continues to be a shaky partition of Cyprus.

FOMENTING CONFLICT

How successful have these partitions been at reducing conflict and permitting outside powers to end their involvement? It is not clear that the partitions of Ireland and Cyprus can be said to have worked, even in the lesser-evil sense. Although the former was a move to divide and quit—in which all sides accepted division as the price of self-determination—the British are embroiled in a military operation in Northern Ireland that continues 70 years later. The troop presence curtailed the toll that communal conflict might otherwise have taken; indeed, it could be argued that it contained the Irish conflict and kept deaths to a minimum. But it also brought the conflict to the heart of Britain as the IRA mounted terrorist attacks in London to increase pressure for a British withdrawal, and it could just as well be argued that from the British point of view independence would have been a more effective way to contain the conflict because it would have thrown the onus of peace onto the Irish; moreover, it might have encouraged regional compromises rather than a prolonged stalemate.

The partition of Cyprus can only be described as a partition by default that the U.N. presence inadvertently aided. The conflict following independence in 1960 was compounded by the fact that Turkey, Greece, and Britain were appointed protecting powers by the constitution. The formal structure this gave to a wider engagement in the conflict drew both the Greek and Turkish armies in and permitted international acceptance of Turkey's invasion in 1974 and what was until then a de facto partition. While casualties have been restricted since then, the division of Cyprus is little more than a long standoff that remains volatile and continues to require the presence of U.N. troops. Nor can the conflict be confined to Cyprus. Over the 20 years since partition, its short fuse is evident. A violent demonstration by Cypriots in August 1996 resulted in Greece and Turkey threatening war. The costs of containment, therefore, include permanent vigilance on the part of NATO and the Atlantic allies.

In many ways, despite the violence and displacements it produced, India's was the most successful ethnic partition, both because it allowed the British to quit and because the conflicts that ensued were by and large contained. But this had less to do with the wisdom of ethnic separation than with other factors, among them the subcontinent's distance from Europe. Unlike Ireland, Cyprus, and Bosnia, the Indian subcontinent is so large that a dozen or more new states could have been created. The deployment of the ethnic two-nation theory, however, which holds that Hindus and Muslims could not live together, had a paradoxical effect—the new state created, Pakistan, was divided into two parts by roughly 2,000 miles of Indian territory. The subsequent separation of those parts points up the inadequacy of the principle of ethnic separation for effecting stable territories. In the late 1960s, resentment at West Pakistani political and economic dominance led to a regional Bengali movement for independence, a war between the two parts in which India intervened in support of the Bengalis, and the birth of Bangladesh in 1971.

In regions of multiple ethnicities—where, for example, the same individual might have loyalties to one community defined by its religion and another by its language—attempts to make one ethnic identity dominant can trigger further fragmentation and conflict. The temporary success of the Indian People's Party in whipping up Hindu nationalism during the destruction of the Babri mosque in Ayodhya and in the riots that followed in the winter of 1992–93 ultimately led to the party's isolation and failure to form a government after the 1996 elections. The case of Kashmir is more poignant. Since 1947, India and Pakistan have been embroiled in a conflict that has twice flared into war, over what has been described, in a phrase dear to politicians on both sides, as "the unfinished business of partition": Kashmir. On ethnic grounds it can be argued that the conflict has continued because India retained the Muslim-majority Kashmir Valley, which should have gone to Pakistan. But following ethnic dividing lines could well entail a further three-way partition of the state—the valley, Buddhist Ladakh, and multi-ethnic Jammu—which would not only set the stage for intensified conflict and ethnic cleansing, as much of Jammu lies between Pakistan and the valley, but would also dissolve Kashmir.

BALKAN BEDLAM

Bosnia-Herzegovina, like these other partitioned territories, has problems of dispersed populations and continuing fragmentation, which the Dayton agreement shows little promise of resolving. It is difficult to contain a conflict when partition is still in progress. Thus NATO and Implementation Force (IFOR) officials under its auspices increasingly worry that hasty implementation of civilian aspects of the agreement such as elections might renew the conflict; instead of reversing partition or facilitating its peaceful execution, the prelude to the elections brought renewed low-level conflict in August. To this extent the Bosnian elections are to the Dayton process what last year's Israeli elections were to the Palestinian peace process: they prove that partition is still incomplete on the ground. Nearly half the pre-1992 population of Bosnia is still living as refugees outside Bosnia. Ethnically homogeneous territories can be created only if the refugees are refused repatriation to the towns and villages from which they were driven, which puts pressure on their host countries not to enforce repatriation. The refugees have become a key constituency that is used both to further and to challenge the consolidation of such ethnic territories, as in the Serb efforts to force refugees to vote from towns other than their prewar residences, and the subsequent threat of Bosnian Muslims to boycott the elections.

Both IFOR and the risibly named Office of the High Representative, which oversees the civilian implementation of Dayton under former Swedish Prime Minister Carl Bildt, make no secret of a concern the elections highlighted: the third partition that always hovered in Dayton's wings, between the Herzegovinian Croats and Bosnian Muslims now living together in the Bosnian Federation. Since the 1994 agreement signed in Washington that established the federation—which was intended to limit Bosnia's partition but produced a constitution remarkably similar to the 1960 Cyprus constitution—Herzegovinian Croats have asked: If a two-way partition is acceptable, why not a three-way one? Unsurprisingly, the answer, that Croatia has already been offered a far more substantial quid pro quo than Serbia and that a tiny and probably landlocked Muslim Bosnia would perpetuate Muslims' resentment, does not satisfy Herzegovinians. But Muslim resentment should at least give partition revivalists pause. Indeed, their argument that the United States should jettison the federation in favor of a tripartite partition begs both the resentment issue and a related matter Bosnian nationalists have raised: that they be given Serbia's predominantly Muslim Sandjak province as territorial compensation. Moreover, their argument ignores the problematic relationship between Croatian and Herzegovinian Croats, whose distrust of each other rivals that between Croats and Muslims.

NATO and IFOR have also pointed out an even more crucial concern: a partition dependent on the awkward boundary line between the Bosnian Federation and Republika Srpska, the Bosnian Serb entity, can last only so long as a large international force is there to enforce it. It is not Mostar in the federation but Banja Luka in the Serb entity that may bring the simmering partition war to a head. One look at the map of the Republika Srpska shows why. Like Pakistan after the partition of India, the Serb entity is divided into two parts, connected only by the narrow Posavina corridor, in which the disputed town of Breko is key; Serb attempts to rig local elections there were a major factor in the postponement of municipal elections in Bosnia last year. Additionally, the two main parts of the Serb entity lean in opposite directions, Banja Luka toward Zagreb and the eastern strip toward Belgrade. Normalization would again pull Banja Luka toward Zagreb economically and diminish its links to the east. That might mean a further division of the Republika Srpska, rather like the division of Pakistan that created Bangladesh, in which the Serb republic would be reduced to a strip of eastern Bosnia. Banja Luka, therefore, must be forced to look eastward, and is—with tacit U.S. support, if Richard Holbrooke's recent suggestions that the Bosnian Serbs make Banja Luka their capital are anything to go by. But Banja Luka's isolation amid federation territory can be maintained only if Serb leaders keep the city in a state of anarchy and mafia rule, like Mostar. Banja Luka's location, however, makes this task much more difficult because Mostar, which remains integrated with Croatia despite being incorporated into the Bosnian Federation, is close to the Croatian border. It is debatable whether anything short of a fortified wall will keep Banja Luka isolated.

Thus, while elections may well be a step toward ratifying partition politically, efforts to consolidate a partition will not only perpetuate conflict but will eventually show that Bosnia can be successfully divided into two only if the Republika Srpska is further partitioned, with the western part reintegrated into Bosnia and the eastern part joining Serbia. Paradoxically, this may be the only way of ensuring a stable partition under the Dayton agreement, as the reintegration of Banja Luka will help keep the Croats in the federation. But if a multiethnic Bosnia can be re-created in one part, then why not in the whole, especially since a further partition will renew conflict around Goražde in eastern Bosnia?

ALL THE KING'S HORSES . . .

As pressure mounts to accept the September elections as a mandate for partition, more emphasis is being placed on the reintegration option of the Dayton agreement, which assumes that economic interests and the provisions for a common economic space will erode the partition lines by making them irrelevant. It is being argued that the partial partition the Dayton agreement partly accepts is only a means of buying time for Bosnia to undergo this process. Historically, however, the failure to inject substantial and timely aid has only hardened ethnic divisions.

Partition has rarely been seen as anything other than a temporary solution to a crisis, which can be reversed as the crisis recedes. However, ethnic partitions have never been reversed; their implementation has inexorably driven communities further apart. Sinn Fein's acquiescence to the partition of Ireland was on the condition that there be a referendum on unification; the referendum did not take place, and now that negotiations on the status of Northern Ireland have been revived, Sinn Fein faces the ironic possibility that Ireland may no longer want unification.

Ethnic partition can often hamper the development of postwar economies. Although economic cooperation could improve South Asia's economies enormously, the ongoing conflict between India and Pakistan over Kashmir has impeded attempts to build it. The Dayton agreement's hope that economic interests will militate against ethnic boundaries was also voiced in Ireland and Palestine. Irish nationalists and the U.N. mediators in Palestine both hoped that mutual dependence, geographic proximity, and the benefits of shared infrastructure would gradually dissipate the aftermath of ethnic partition. Indeed, the U.N. plan for the partition of Palestine was based explicitly on the premise that economic union would compensate for the difficulties of the proposed territories. Instead, partition's legacies thwarted economic union and kept both Ireland and what was left of Palestine in poverty.

If the lessons of these examples are noteworthy, it may be because Bosnia will constitute a turning point in partition theory. The fact that NATO is preparing for an extended presence indicates that the alliance recognizes the unlikely success of a divide and quit approach in this situation. Though divide and quit was a motive in Britain's support for partition in Ireland, Palestine, and India, it got Britain out quickly only in India, and that was because South Asia is distant from Britain. From the sequence of events in Bosnia, it is clear that European and American leaders, and the rest of the international community, were prepared to accept partition if it would curtail Western intervention in the conflict and limit Western involvement in the region. But as the partition process unfolds, it is being recognized that divide and quit might turn into divide and be forced to stay. Unlike Somalia or Rwanda, Bosnia is a high-profile intervention because the Balkans have played an important and generally unwelcome part in European security. So far, the West has not been able to walk away from this war, and each halfhearted intervention, however delusory, has led to more rather than less involvement. As the realization takes hold that a Bosnian partition may mean an indefinitely prolonged commitment to a chronically volatile region, investment in reintegration may be discovered to be an easier route to withdrawal.

PART VII

STRATEGY, I: MILITARY TECHNOLOGY, STRATEGY, AND STABILITY

Analysts of international relations are usually interested in the causes and consequences of wars, but much less in the conduct. How wars are fought is seen by many as a technical subject, something that happens between the political sources and results. The main message of the most serious philosopher of war, however, is that war is an instrument of policy and a continuation of politics.[1] As such, how it unfolds—or would be expected to unfold—affects whether, when, and how governments or groups decide to resort to force or end violent struggles.

Thus military capabilities—and political leaders' understanding or misunderstanding of them—can exert an independent influence on decisions for or against war. Depending on which side in a conflict has the edge, the military factors make it easier or harder for a government to risk resorting to force against the status quo. Military means can also become causes of conflict in their own right, by altering the balance of power and perceptions of threats, aggravating anxieties about vulnerability, and creating incentives for preemptive attack.

For all these reasons, nations engaged in political competition in peacetime also tend to compete in military preparations for the possibility of war. Arms races manifest nations' concern for preventing their adversaries from enjoying a military advantage should war break out. There has been remarkably little theorizing about arms races. One of the few serious examples, by Samuel Huntington, is excerpted in this section. Looking at historical cases in Europe and elsewhere Huntington discusses the differing implications of quantitative and qualitative competitions and other factors that affect the course and consequences of arms competition.

If military capabilities are to be reliable for protecting the nation, but not a catalyst for war in their own right, they must be distributed in some manner that is conducive to stability. What does this mean?

---

[1] Carl von Clausewitz, *On War,* Michael Howard and Peter Paret, eds. and trans. (Princeton, N.J.: Princeton University Press, 1976).

A state is not likely to start a war unless either of two conditions exists. One is if the government's leaders not only wish to overturn the status quo but believe they can win a war if they attack, and can do so at a cost more bearable than continuing to live with the existing situation. If they think their would-be victim can defend its own territory successfully, or can retaliate and inflict costly damage on them if they attack, peace should remain preferable to war. The other condition is if leaders have defensive objectives, but believe that if they do not strike first their enemy will do so, forcing war upon them on less favorable terms and increasing the chances of defeat. On the other hand, if they know the enemy would like to attack, but believe that they can fight more effectively by waiting to parry the blow when it falls, they will not have reason to initiate the war themselves.

These notions are the foundation of deterrence theory, which became so prominent in the Cold War. When the basic source and dimensions of international conflict are clear, as they were once the East-West confrontation became institutionalized in the decade after World War II, attention turns to the instrumental questions. At first, theorists wanted to design strategies that would put the revolutionary power of nuclear weapons to the purpose of deterring enemy attack. Then, when fear of relying too much on nuclear weapons came to the fore, strategists turned to applying the logic of deterrence to conventional military power. Since the Soviet collapse, deterrence seems beside the point among the great powers. If political tensions reemerge, however, so will the salience of military strategy.

How should conventional military power affect the odds of war or peace from now on? Some states will want to be able to use force actively to change situations of which they disapprove (as the United States has often done since the Cold War—in Panama, Kosovo, twice in Iraq, and elsewhere. Strategists who have that option in mind will focus on maintaining superior military capabilities, the capacity to defeat and dictate to opponents. For Americans, that should not be difficult even with big cuts in the defense budget, since no other country now has anywhere near the military capacity of the United States. If the aim is to preserve peace for its own sake, however, rather than to use force to make the world the way we think it should be, strategists will seek ways to limit the utility of military instruments.

Arms control negotiations were much more prominent in the strategic relations of the Cold War, as the two superpowers made agreements on limiting nuclear weaponry and conventional forces in Europe matters of high politics. Arms control is less prominent now in international diplomacy, although still significant in attempts to prevent the spread of weapons of mass destruction, and some other areas that would have been considered minor (for example, land mines) in periods of great power conflict. Formalized arms limitations are likely to become important in some of the smaller conflicts that typify the post-Cold War world, if those conflicts are to be ended by agreement rather than by conquest. If local political entities in the tangled conflicts of the Balkans, or Palestine, or Kashmir are to find a *modus vivendi,* and to accept it with confidence, the deals are likely to involve limitations of quantity, quality, and disposition of military capabilities.

There is one solution in principle that can unite both realists satisfied with the status quo and liberals who want to deny the legitimacy of force as a means of change: military power should be distributed, configured, and usable only in ways that maximize confidence for defenders and risks for attackers. Force structures, strategies, and arms control agreements should be crafted to minimize the role of technologies that facilitate offensive operations and boost those that aid defensive tactics. The strategic implications of such "defense dominance" should be publicized in order to make governments realize that they do not need to strike first in order to protect themselves, and cannot succeed if they strike first for aggressive reasons. In "Cooperation Under the Security Dilemma" Robert Jervis outlines the logic behind these notions.[2]

Can such norms be institutionalized to keep peace in the future? Critics question how far the principle of defense dominance can be taken in practice. Scott Sagan points out several reasons that it did not solve all the strategic problems of states in 1914, especially the challenge of supporting exposed allies (this showed up starkly in 1939 when the French and British let defense dominate on the western front while the Germans gobbled Poland). Jack Levy raises questions about how clearly the concept of defense dominance can even be defined in principle or identified in practice.

If arms control agreements are to promote stability, they must logically rest on distributions of capability that make it unappealing for leaders to decide to initiate use of those capabilities in combat. To institutionalize such a distribution, strategists and diplomats must understand what weapons are most important to limit, and how changes in the numbers and types of particular weapons will affect an overall balance of military power. Charles Fairbanks and Abram Shulsky offer cautionary arguments, drawn from historical cases, about ways in which formal arms limitation can have unexpectedly destabilizing effects.

Nuclear weapons remain a particularly sticky issue. The fewer of them in the world the better, according to conventional wisdom. In the Introduction to this volume, on the other hand, John Mearsheimer claimed that "managed" nuclear proliferation could be the least dangerous way to save Europe from the instability that will otherwise follow the end of the Cold War. The reasoning behind this argument was first elaborated by Kenneth Waltz in the essay included in this section. Many skeptics will remain unconvinced, but they should ask themselves whether it is consistent to reject the idea that nuclear deterrence may be stabilizing for Third World countries if they believe, as so many do, that mutual nuclear deterrence between the United States and Soviet Union during the Cold War was quite stable. By the same token, we should ask how much of what we learned from the Cold War lore of deterrence is applicable to a very different set of conflicts and contenders in the twenty-first century.[3]

—RKB

---

[2]Other examples of literature that find bases of stability in configurations that advantage the defense include George Quester, *Offense and Defense in the International System,* 2d ed. (New Brunswick, N.J.: Transaction Books, 1988); Stephen Van Evera, *Causes of War: Power and the Roots of Conflict* (Ithaca, N.Y.: Cornell University Press, 1999), Chapters 6–8; Jack L. Snyder, *The Ideology of the Offensive: Military Decision Making and the Disasters of 1914* (Ithaca, N.Y.: Cornell University Press, 1984); and Sean Lynn-Jones, "Offense-Defense Theory and Its Critics," *Security Studies* 4, no. 4 (summer 1995). For a skeptical view see Richard K. Betts, "Must War Find a Way?" *International Security* 24, no. 2 (fall 1999).

[3]See Richard K. Betts, "The New Threat of Mass Destruction," *Foreign Affairs* 77, no. 1 (January/ February 1998).

ARMS RACES: PREREQUISITES AND RESULTS

Samuel P. Huntington

. . . Capacity for Qualitative and Quantitative Increases in Military Power

An arms race requires the progressive increase from domestic sources of the absolute military power of a state. This may be done quantitatively, by expanding the numerical strength of its existing forms of military force, or qualitatively, by replacing its existing forms of military force (usually weapons systems) with new and more effective forms of force. The latter requires a dynamic technology, and the former the social, political and economic capacity to reallocate resources from civilian to military purposes. Before the nineteenth century the European states possessed only a limited capacity for either quantitative or qualitative increases in military strength. Naval technology, for instance, had been virtually static for almost three centuries: the sailing ship of 1850 was not fundamentally different from that of 1650, the naval gun of 1860 not very much removed from that of 1560. As a result, the ratio of construction time to use time was extremely low: a ship built in a few months could be used for the better part of a century. Similarly, with land armaments, progress was slow, and only rarely could a power hope to achieve a decisive edge by a "technological breakthrough." Beginning with the Industrial Revolution, however, the pace of innovation in military technology constantly quickened, and the new weapons systems inevitably stimulated arms races. The introduction, first, of the steam warship and then of the ironclad, for instance, directly intensified the naval competition between England and France in the 1850s and 1860s. Throughout the nineteenth century, the importance of the weapons technician constantly increased relative to the importance of the strategist.

Broad changes in economic and political structure were at the same time making quantitative arms races feasible. The social system of the *ancien regime* did not permit a full mobilization of the economic and manpower resources of a nation. So long as participation in war was limited to a small class, competitive increases in the size of armies could not proceed very far. The destruction of the old system, the spread of democracy and liberalism, the increasing popularity among all groups of the "nation in arms" concept, all permitted a much more complete mobilization of resources for military purposes than had been possible previously. In particular, the introduction of universal military service raised the ceiling on the size of the army to the point where the limiting factor was the civilian manpower necessary to support the army. In addition, the development of industry permitted the mass production and mass accumulation of the new weapons which the new technology had invented. The countries which lagged behind in the twin processes of democratization and industrialization were severely handicapped in the race for armaments.

In the age of limited wars little difference existed between a nation's military strength in peace and its military strength in war. During the nineteenth century, however, the impact of democracy and industrialism made wars more total, victory or defeat in them became more significant (and final), military superiority became more critically important, and consequently a government had to be more fully assured of the prospect of victory before embarking upon war. In addition, the professional officer corps which developed during the nineteenth century felt a direct responsibility for the military security of the state and emphasized the desirability of obtaining a safe superiority in armaments. As a result, unless one of the participants possessed extensive staying power due to geography or resources, the outcome of a war depended almost as much upon what happened before the declarations of war as after. By achieving superiority in armaments it might be possible for a state to achieve the fruits of war without suffering the risks and liabilities of war. Governments piled up armaments in peacetime with the hope either of averting war or of insuring success in it should it come.

Absolute and Relative Armaments Goals

A state may define its armaments goals in one of two ways. It can specify a certain *absolute* level or type of armaments which it believes necessary for it to possess irrespective of the level or type possessed by other states. Or, it can define its goal in *relative* terms as a function of the armaments of other states. Undoubtedly, in any specific case, a state's armaments reflect a combination of both absolute and relative considerations. Normally, however, one or the other will be dominant and embodied in official statements of the state's armaments goals in the form of an "absolute need" or a ratio-goal. Thus, historically Great Britain followed a relative policy with respect to the capital ships in its navy but an absolute policy with respect to its cruisers, the need for which, it was held, stemmed from the unique nature of the British Empire.

If every state had absolute goals, arms races would be impossible: each state would go its separate way uninfluenced by the actions of its neighbors. Nor would a full scale arms race develop if an absolute goal were pursued consistently by only one power in an antagonistic relationship: whatever relative advantage the second power demanded would be simply a function of the constant absolute figure demanded by the first power. An arms race only arises when two or more powers consciously determine the quantitative or qualitative aspects of their armaments as functions of the armaments of the other power. Absolute goals, however, are only really feasible when a state is not a member of or only on the periphery of a balance of power system. Except in these rare cases, the formulation by a state of its armaments goal in absolute terms is more likely to reflect the desire to obscure from its rivals the true relative superiority which it wishes to achieve or to obscure from itself the need to participate actively in the balancing process. Thus, its Army Law of 1893 was thought to give Germany a force which in quantity and quality would be unsurpassable by any other power. Hence Germany

> was, in the eyes of her rulers, too powerful to be affected by a balancing movement restricted only to the continent. . . . From this time on Germany considered herself militarily invulnerable, as if in a state of splendid isolation, owing to the excellence of her amalgam army.[1]

As a result, Germany let her army rest, turned her energies to the construction of a navy, and then suddenly in 1911 became aware of her landpower inferiority to the Dual Alliance and had to make strenuous last minute efforts to increase the size of her forces. Somewhat similarly, states may define absolute qualitative goals, such as the erection of an impenetrable system of defenses (Maginot Line) or the possession of an "ultimate" or "absolute" weapon, which will render superfluous further military effort regardless of what other states may do. In 1956 American airpower policy was consciously shaped not to the achievement of any particular level of air strength relative to that of the Soviet Union, but rather to obtaining an absolute "sufficiency of airpower" which would permit the United States to wreak havoc in the Soviet Union in the event of an all-out war. The danger involved in an absolute policy is that, if carried to an extreme, it may lead to a complacent isolationism blind to the relative nature of power.

The armaments of two states can be functionally interrelated only if they are also similar or complementary. An arms race is impossible between a power which possesses only a navy and one which possesses only an army: no one can match divisions against battleships. A functional relationship between armaments is complementary when two military forces possessing different weapons systems are designed for combat with each other. In this sense, an air defense fighter command complements an opposing strategic bombing force or one side's submarine force complements the other's antisubmarine destroyers and hunter-killer groups. A functional relationship is similar when two military forces are not only designed for combat with each other but also possess similar weapons systems, as has been very largely the case with land armies and with battle fleets of capital ships. In most instances in history, arms races have involved similar forces rather than complementary forces, but no reason exists why there should not be an arms race in the latter. The only special problem posed by a complementary arms race is that of measuring the relative strengths of the opposing forces. In a race involving similar forces, a purely quantitative measurement usually suffices; in one of complementary forces, qualitative judgments are necessary as to the effectiveness of one type of weapons system against another.

Even if both parties to an arms race possess similar land, sea and air forces, normally the race itself is focused on only one of these components or even on only one weapons system within one component, usually that type of military force with which

---

[1]Arpad Kovacs, "Nation in Arms and Balance of Power: The Interaction of German Military Legislation and European Politics, 1866–1914" (Ph.D. Thesis, University of Chicago, 1934), p. 159.

they are best able to harm each other.[2] This component or weapons system is viewed by the states as the decisive form of military force in their mutual relationship, and competition in other forces or components is subordinated to the race in this decisive force. The simple principles of concentration and economy of force require states to put their major efforts where they will count most. The arms race between Germany and England before World War I was in capital ships. The arms race between the same two countries before World War II was in bombers and fighters. The current race between the Soviet Union and the United States has largely focused upon nuclear weapons and their means of delivery, and has not extended to the massing of conventional weapons and manpower. In general, economic considerations also preclude a state from becoming involved at the same time in two separate arms races with two different powers in two different forms of military force. When her race in land forces with France slackened in the middle 1890s, Germany embarked upon her naval race with Great Britain, and for the first decade of the twentieth century the requirements of this enterprise prevented any substantial increase in the size of the army. When the naval race in turn slackened in 1912, Germany returned to the rebuilding of her ground forces and to her military manpower race with France.

Two governments can consciously follow relative arms policies only if they are well informed of their respective military capabilities. The general availability of information concerning armaments is thus a precondition for an arms race. Prior to the nineteenth century when communication and transportation were slow and haphazard, a state would frequently have only the vaguest notions of the military programs of its potential rivals. Often it was possible for one state to make extensive secret preparations for war. In the modern world, information with respect to military capabilities has become much more widespread and has been one of the factors increasing the likelihood of arms races. Even now, however, many difficulties exist in getting information concerning the arms of a rival which is sufficiently accurate to serve as the basis for one's own policy. At times misconceptions as to the military strengths and policies of other states become deeply ingrained, and at other times governments simply choose to be blind to significant changes in armaments. Any modern government involved in an arms race, moreover, is confronted with conflicting estimates of its opponent's strength. Politicians, governmental agencies and private groups all tend to give primary credit to intelligence estimates which confirm military policies which they have already espoused for other reasons. The armed services inevitably overstate the military capabilities of the opponent: in 1914, for instance, the Germans estimated the French army to have 121,000 more men than the German army, the French estimated the German army to have 134,000 more men than the French army, but both countries agreed in their estimates of the military forces of third powers. Governments anxious to reduce expenditures and taxes pooh-pooh warnings as to enemy strength: the reluctance of the Baldwin government to credit reports of the German air build-up seriously delayed British rearmament in the 1930s. At other times, exaggerated reports as to enemy forces

---

[2]Other things being equal, this will probably be the "dominant weapon" in Fuller's sense, that is, the weapon with the longest effective range. See J. F. C. Fuller, *Armament and History* (New York, 1945), pp. 7–8.

may lead a government to take extraordinary measures which are subsequently revealed to have been unnecessary. Suspicions that the Germans were exceeding their announced program of naval construction led the English government in 1909 to authorize and construct four "contingency" Dreadnoughts. Subsequently revelations proved British fears to be groundless. Similarly, in 1956 reports of Soviet aircraft production, later asserted to be considerably exaggerated, influenced Congress to appropriate an extra $900 million for the Air Force. At times, the sudden revelation of a considerable increase in an enemy's capabilities may produce a panic, such as the invasion panics of England in 1847–48, 1851–53, and 1859–61. The tense atmosphere of an arms race also tends to encourage reports of mysterious forces possessed by the opponent and of his development of secret new weapons of unprecedented power. Nonetheless, fragmentary and uncertain though information may be, its availability in one form or another is what makes the arms race possible.

ABORTIVE AND SUSTAINED ARMS RACES

An arms race may end in war, formal or informal agreement between the two states to call off the race, or victory for one state which achieves and maintains the distribution of power which it desires and ultimately causes its rival to give up the struggle. The likelihood of war arising from an arms race depends in the first instance upon the relation between the power and grievances of one state to the power and grievances of the other. . . .

For the purposes of analysis it is necessary to specify a particular increase in armaments by one state as marking the formal beginning of the arms race. This is done not to pass judgment on the desirability or wisdom of the increase, but simply to identify the start of the action and reaction which constitute the race. In most instances, this initial challenge is not hard to locate. It normally involves a major change in the policy of the challenging state, and more likely than not it is formally announced to the world. The reasons for the challenging state's discontent with the status quo may stem from a variety of causes. It may feel that the growth of its economy, commerce, and population should be reflected in changes in the military balance of power (Germany, 1898; United States, 1916; Soviet Union, 1946). Nationalistic, bellicose, or militaristic individuals or parties may come to power who are unwilling to accept an equilibrium which other groups in their society had been willing to live with or negotiate about (Germany and Japan, 1934). New political issues may arise which cause a deterioration in the relationships of the state with another power and which consequently lead it to change its estimate of the arms balance necessary for its security (France, 1841, 1875; England, 1884).

Normally the challenging state sets a goal for itself which derives from the relation between the military strengths of the two countries prior to the race. If the relation was one of disparity, the initial challenge usually comes from the weaker power which aspires to parity or better. Conceivably a stronger power could initiate an arms race by deciding that it required an even higher ratio of superiority over the weaker power. But in actual practice this is seldom the case: the gain in security achieved in upping a 2:1 ratio to 3:1, for instance, rarely is worth the increased economic costs and political tensions.

If parity of military power existed between the two countries, the arms race begins when one state determines that it requires military force superior to that of the other country.

In nine out of ten races the slogan of the challenging state is either "parity" or "superiority." Only in rare cases does the challenger aim for less than this, for unless equality or superiority is achieved, the arms race is hardly likely to be worthwhile. The most prominent exception to the "parity or superiority" rule is the Anglo-German naval race of 1898–1912. In its initial phase, German policy was directed not to the construction of a navy equal to England's but rather to something between that and the very minor navy which she possessed prior to the race. The rationale for building such a force was provided by Tirpitz's "risk theory": Germany should have a navy large enough so that Britain could not fight her without risking damage to the British navy to such an extent that it would fall prey to the naval forces of third powers (i.e., France and Russia). The fallacies in this policy became obvious in the following decade. On the one hand, for technical reasons it was unlikely that an inferior German navy could do serious damage to a superior British fleet, and, on the other hand, instead of making Britain wary of France and Russia the expansion of the German navy tended to drive her into their arms and consequently to remove the hostile third powers who were supposed to pounce upon a Britain weakened by Germany. One can only conclude that it is seldom worthwhile either for a superior power to attempt significantly to increase its superiority or for a weaker power to attempt only to reduce its degree of inferiority. The rational goals in an arms race are parity or superiority.

In many respects the most critical aspect of a race is the initial response which the challenged state makes to the new goals posited by the challenger. In general, these responses can be divided into four categories, two of which preserve the possibility of peace, two of which make war virtually inevitable. The challenged state may, first, attempt to counterbalance the increased armaments of its rival through diplomatic means or it may, secondly, immediately increase its own armaments in an effort to maintain or directly to restore the previously existing balance of military power. While neither of these responses guarantees the maintenance of peace, they at least do not precipitate war. The diplomatic avenue of action, if it exists, is generally the preferred one. It may be necessary, however, for the state to enhance its own armaments as well as attempting to secure reliable allies. Or, if alliances are impossible or undesirable for reasons of state policy, the challenged state must rely upon its own increases in armaments as the way of achieving its goal. In this case a sustained arms race is likely to result. During her period of splendid isolation, for instance, England met the French naval challenge of the 1840s by increasing the size and effectiveness of her own navy. At the end of the century when confronted by the Russo-French challenge, she both increased her navy and made tentative unsuccessful efforts to form an alliance with Germany. In response to the German challenge a decade later, she again increased her navy and also arrived at a rapprochement with France and Russia.

If new alliances or increased armaments appear impossible or undesirable, a state which sees its superiority or equality in military power menaced by the actions of another state may initiate preventive action while still strong enough to forestall the change in the balance of power. The factors which enter into the decision to wage preventive war are complex and intangible, but, conceivably, if the state had no diplomatic opportunities and if it was dubious of its ability to hold its own in an arms race, this might well be a rational course of behavior. Tirpitz explicitly recognized this in his concept of a "danger zone" through which the German navy would pass and during which a strong likelihood would exist that the British would take preventive action to destroy the German fleet. Such an attack might be avoided, he felt, by a German diplomatic "peace offensive" designed to calm British fears and to assure them of the harmless character of German intentions. Throughout the decade after 1898 the Germans suffered periodic scares of an imminent British attack. Although preventive action was never seriously considered by the British government, enough talk went on in high British circles of "Copenhagening" the German fleet to give the Germans some cause for alarm. In the "war in sight" crisis of 1875, the initial success of French rearmament efforts aimed at restoring an equality of military power with Germany stimulated German statesmen and military leaders carefully to consider the desirability of preventive war. Similarly, the actions of the Nazis in overthrowing the restrictions of the Treaty of Versailles in the early 1930s and starting the European arms build-up produced arguments in Poland and France favoring preventive war. After World War II at the beginning of the arms race between the United States and the Soviet Union a small but articulate segment of opinion urged the United States to take preventive action before the Soviet Union developed nuclear weapons. To a certain extent, the Japanese attack on the United States in 1941 can be considered a preventive action designed to forestall the inevitable loss of Japanese naval superiority in the western Pacific which would have resulted from the two-ocean navy program begun by the United States in 1939. In 1956 the Egyptians began to rebuild their armaments from Soviet sources and thus to disturb the equilibrium which had existed with Israel since 1949. This development was undoubtedly one factor leading Israel to attack Egypt and thereby attempt to resolve at least some of the outstanding issues between them before the increase in Egyptian military power.

At the other extreme from preventive action, a challenged state simply may not make any immediate response to the upset of the existing balance of power. The challenger may then actually achieve or come close to achieving the new balance of military force which it considers necessary. In this event, roles are reversed, the challenged suddenly awakens to its weakened position and becomes the challenger, engaging in frantic and strenuous last-ditch efforts to restore the previously existing military ratio. In general, the likelihood of war increases just prior to a change in military superiority from one side to the other. If the challenged state averts this change by alliances or increased armaments, war is avoidable. On the other hand, the challenged state may precipitate war in order to prevent the change, or it may provoke war by allowing the change to take place and then attempting to undo it. In the latter case, the original challenger, having achieved parity or superiority, is in no mood or position to back down; the anxious efforts of its opponent to regain its military strength appear to be obvious war preparation; and consequently the original challenger normally will not hesitate to risk or provoke a war while it may still benefit from its recent gains.

Belated responses resulting in last-gasp arms races are most clearly seen in the French and British reactions to German rearmament in the 1930s. The coming-to-power of the Nazis and their subsequent rearmament efforts initially provoked little military response in France. In part, this reflected confidence in the qualitative superiority of the French army and the defensive strength of the Maginot Line. In part, too, it reflected the French political situation in which those groups most fearful of Nazi Germany were generally those most opposed to large armies and militarism, while the usual right-wing supporters of the French army were those to whom Hitler appeared least dangerous. As a result, the French army and the War Ministry budget remained fairly constant between 1933 and 1936. Significant increases in French armaments were not made until 1937 and 1938, and the real French rearmament effort got under way in 1939. France proposed to spend more on armaments in that single year than the total of her expenditures during the preceding five years. By then, however, the five-to-one superiority in military effectives which she had possessed over Germany in 1933 had turned into a four-to-three inferiority.

Roughly the same process was going on with respect to the ratio between the British and German air forces. At the beginning of the 1930s the Royal Air Force, although a relatively small force, was undoubtedly much stronger than anything which the Germans had managed to create surreptitiously. During the period from 1934 to 1938, however, the strength of the RAF in comparison to the Luftwaffe steadily declined. In July 1934, Churchill warned Parliament that the German air force had then reached two-thirds the strength of the British Home Defense Air Force, and that if present and proposed programs were continued, the Germans would achieve parity by December 1935. Baldwin assured the Commons that Britain would maintain a fifty per cent superiority over Germany. Subsequently, however, Churchill's estimates proved to be more correct than those of the Government, and the air program had to be drastically increased in 1936 and 1937. By then, however, two years had been lost. In 1936 Germany achieved parity with Britain. In the spring of 1937 the Luftwaffe exceeded the RAF in first-line strength and reserves. By September 1938 it was almost twice as large as the RAF, and the production of aircraft in Germany was double that in England. The British vigorously pushed their efforts to make up for lost time: British aviation expenditures which had amounted to 16.8 million pounds in 1934–35 rose to 131.4 millions in 1937–38, and were budgeted at 242.7 millions for 1939–40. The Germans were now on top and the British the challengers moving to close the gap. The readiness of the Germans to go to war consequently was not unnatural. As far back as 1936, the British Joint Planning Staff had picked September 1939 as the most likely date for the beginning of a war because in the fall of 1939 Germany's armed strength would reach its peak in comparison with that of the allies. This forecast proved true on both points, and it was not until after the start of the war that the British began seriously to catch up with the head start of the Luftwaffe. British aircraft production first equalled that of the Germans in the spring of 1940. . . .

The danger of war is highest in the opening phases of an arms race, at which time the greatest elements of instability and uncertainty are present. If the challenged state neither resorts to preventive war nor fails to make an immediate response to the challenger's activities, a sustained arms race is likely to result with the probability of war decreasing as the initial action and counteraction fade into the past. Once the initial disturbances to the pre-arms race static equilibrium are surmounted, the reciprocal increases of the two states tend to produce a new, dynamic equilibrium reflecting their relative strength and participation in the race. In all probability, the relative military power of the two states in this dynamic equilibrium will fall somewhere between the previous status quo and the ratio-goal of the challenger. The sustained regularity of the increases in itself becomes an accepted and anticipated stabilizing factor in the relations between the two countries. A sustained quantitative race still may produce a war, but a greater likelihood exists that either the two states will arrive at a mutual accommodation reducing the political tensions which started the race or that one state over the long haul will gradually but substantially achieve its objective while the other will accept defeat in the race if this does not damage its vital interests. Thus, a twenty-five year sporadic naval race between France and England ended in the middle 1860s when France gave up any serious effort to challenge the 3 : 2 ratio which England had demonstrated the will and the capacity to maintain. Similarly, the Anglo-German naval race slackened after 1912 when, despite failure to reach formal agreement, relations improved between the two countries and even Tirpitz acquiesced in the British 16 : 10 ratio in capital ships. Britain also successfully maintained her two-power standard against France and Russia for twenty years until changes in the international scene ended her arms competition with those two powers. Germany and France successively increased their armies from the middle 1870s to the middle 1890s when tensions eased and the arms build-up in each country slackened. The incipient naval races among the United States, Britain, and Japan growing out of World War I were restricted by the Washington naval agreement; the ten-year cruiser competition between the United States and England ended in the London Treaty of 1930; and eventually the rise of more dangerous threats in the mid-1930s removed any remaining vestiges of Anglo-American naval rivalry. The twelve-year arms race between Chile and Argentina ended in 1902 with a comprehensive agreement between the two countries settling their boundary disputes and restricting their armaments. While generalizations are both difficult and dangerous, it would appear that a sustained arms race is much more likely to have a peaceful ending than a bloody one.

QUANTITATIVE AND QUALITATIVE ARMS RACES

A state may increase its military power quantitatively, by expanding the numerical strength of its existing military forces, or qualitatively, by replacing its existing forms of military force (normally weapons systems) with new and more effective forms of force. Expansion and innovation are thus possible characteristics of any arms race, and to some extent both are present in most races. Initially and fundamentally every arms race is quantitative in nature. The race begins when two states develop conflicting goals as to what should be the distribution of military power between them and give these goals explicit statement in quantitative ratios of the relative strengths which each hopes to achieve in the decisive form of military force. The formal start of the race is the decision of the challenger to upset the existing balance and to expand its forces quantitatively. If at some point in the race a qualitative change produces a new decisive form of military force, the quantitative goals of the two states still remain roughly the same. The relative balance of power which each state desires to achieve is independent of the specific weapons and forces which enter into the balance. Despite the underlying adherence of both states to their original ratio-goals, however, a complex qualitative race produced by rapid technological innovation is a very different phenomenon from a race which remains simply quantitative.

Probably the best examples of races which were primarily quantitative in nature are those between Germany and France between 1871 and 1914. The decisive element was the number of effectives each power maintained in its peacetime army and the number of reserves it could call to the colors in an emergency. Quantitative increases by one state invariably produced comparable increases by the other. The German army bill of 1880, for instance, added 25,000 men to the army and declared in its preamble that "far-reaching military reforms had been carried out outside of Germany which cannot remain without influence upon the military power of the neighboring countries." These increases it was alleged would produce "too considerable a numerical superiority of the enemy's forces."[3] Again in 1887 Bismarck used Boulanger's agitation for an increase in the French army as a means of putting through an expansion of the German one. After the French reorganized their army in 1889 and drastically increased the proportion of young men liable to military service, the Germans added 20,000 men to their force in 1890. Three years later a still larger increase was made in the German army and justified by reference to recent French and Russian expansions. Similarly, the naval race of 1884–1905 between England, on the one hand, and France and Russia, on the other, was primarily quantitative in nature. Naval budgets and numerical strengths of the two sides tended to fluctuate in direct relation with each other.

A qualitative arms race is more complex than a quantitative one because at some point it involves the decision by one side to introduce a new weapons system or form of military force. Where the capacity for technological innovation exists, the natural tendency is for the arms race to become qualitative. The introduction of a new weapons system obviously is normally desirable from the viewpoint of the state which is behind in the quantitative race. The English-French naval rivalry of 1841–1865 grew out of the deteriorating relations between the two countries over Syria, Tahiti and Spain. Its first manifestation was quantitative: in 1841 the number of seamen in the French navy which for nearly a century had been about two-thirds the number in the British navy was suddenly increased so as to almost equal the British strength. Subsequently the large expansions which the French proposed to make in their dockyards, especially at Toulon, caused even Cobden to observe that "a serious effort seemed really to be made to rival us at sea."[4] The Anglo-French quantitative rivalry subsided with the departure of Louis Philippe in 1848, but shortly thereafter it resumed on a new qualitative level with the determination of Napoleon III to push the construction of steam warships. The *Napoléon,* a screw propelled ship of the line of 92 guns, launched by the French in 1850 was significantly superior to anything the British could bring against it, until the *Agamemnon* was launched two years later. The alliance of the two countries in the Crimean War only temporarily suspended the naval

---

[3]Kovacs, "Nation in Arms," p. 36.
[4]Richard Cobden, "Three Panics: An Historical Episode," *Political Writings* (London, 2 vols., 1867), II, p. 224.

race, and by 1858 the French had achieved parity with the British in fast screw ships of the line. In that year the French had 114 fewer sailing vessels in their navy than they had in 1852, while the number of British sailing ships had declined only from 299 to 296. On the other hand, the British in 1852 had a superiority of 73 sailing ships of the line to 45 for the French. By 1858, however, both England and France had 29 steam ships of the line while England had an enhanced superiority of 35 to 10 in sailing ships. A head start in steam construction and conversion plus the concentration of effort on this program had enabled the French, who had been hopelessly outnumbered in the previously decisive form of naval power, to establish a rough parity in the new form. In view of the British determination to restore their quantitative superiority and the superior industrial resources at their disposal, however, parity could only be temporary. In 1861 the British had 53 screw battleships afloat and 14 building while the French had only 35 afloat and two building.

By the time that the British had reëstablished their superiority in steam warships, their opponents had brought forward another innovation which again threatened British control of the seas. The French laid down four ironclads in 1858 and two in 1859. The first was launched in November 1859 and the next in March 1860. The British launched their first ironclad in December 1860. The British program, however, was hampered by the Admiralty's insistence upon continuing to build wooden warships. The French stopped laying down wooden line of battle ships in 1856, yet the British, despite warnings that wooden walls were obsolete, continued building wooden ships down through 1860, and in 1861 the Admiralty brought in the largest request in its history for the purchase of timber. Meanwhile, in the fall of 1860 the French started a new construction program for ten more ironclads to supplement the six they already had underway. The British learned of these projects in February 1861 and responded with a program to add nine new ironclads to their fleet. In May 1861, the French had a total of fifteen ironclads built or building, the British only seven. From 1860 until 1865 the French possessed superiority or parity with the British in ironclad warships. In February 1863, for instance, the French had four ironclads mounting 146 guns ready for action, the British four ironclads mounting 116 guns. Thanks to the genius and initiative of the director of French naval construction, Dupuy de Lôme, and the support of Napoleon III, there had occurred, as one British military historian put it,

> an astonishing change in the balance of power which might have been epoch-making had it not been so brief, or if France and Britain had gone to war, a reversal which finds no place in any but technical histories and which is almost entirely unknown in either country to-day. In a word, supremacy at sea passed from Britain to France.[5]

This was not a supremacy, however, which France could long maintain. By 1866, Britannia had retrieved the trident. In that year England possessed nineteen ironclads, France thirteen, and the English superiority was enhanced by heavier guns. Thereafter the naval strengths of the two powers resumed the 3:2 ratio which had existed prior to 1841.

---

[5]Cyril Falls, *A Hundred Years of War* (London, 1953), p. 102.

In general, as this sequence of events indicates, technological innovation favors, at least temporarily, the numerically weaker power. Its long-run effects, however, depend upon factors other than the currently prevailing balance of military strength. It was indeed paradoxical that France should make the innovations which she did make in her naval race with England. In the 1850s and 1860s France normally had twice as much timber on hand in her dockyards as had the British, and she was, of course, inferior to England in her coal and iron resources. Nonetheless she led the way in the introduction of steam and iron, while the Royal Navy, which was acutely hampered by a timber shortage, clung to the wooden ships. In this instance, on both sides, immediate needs and the prospects of immediate success prevailed over a careful consideration of long-term benefits.

The problem which technological innovation presents to the quantitatively superior power is somewhat more complex. The natural tendencies for such a state are toward conservatism: any significant innovation will undermine the usefulness of the current type of weapons system in which it possesses a superiority. What, however, should be the policy of a superior power with respect to making a technological change which its inferior rivals are likely to make in the near future? The British navy had a traditional answer to this problem: never introduce any development which will render existing ships obsolete but be prepared if any other state does make an innovation to push ahead an emergency construction program which will restore the previously existing ratio. While this policy resulted, as we have seen above, in some close shaves, by the beginning of the twentieth century it had become a fundamental maxim of British naval doctrine. Consequently, Sir John Fisher's proposal in 1904 to revolutionize naval construction by introducing the "all big gun ship" which would render existing capital ships obsolete was also a revolution in British policy. In terms of its impact upon the Anglo-German naval balance, Fisher's decision was welcomed by many Germans and condemned by many British. Although the construction of Dreadnoughts would force Germany to enlarge the Kiel Canal, the Germans seized the opportunity to start the naval race afresh in a class of vessels in which the British did not have an overwhelming numerical superiority. For the first few years the British by virtue of their headstart would have a larger number of Dreadnoughts, but then the German yards would start producing and the gap which had to be closed would be much smaller in the Dreadnoughts than in the pre-Dreadnought battle ships. The introduction of the Dreadnought permitted the Germans to raise their sights from a "risk" navy (which had become meaningless since the Anglo-French entente in any event) to the possibility of parity with Britain. To many Britishers, on the other hand, construction of the Dreadnought seemed to be tantamount to sinking voluntarily a large portion of the British navy. The tremendous number of pre-Dreadnought capital ships which the Royal Navy possessed suddenly decreased in value. Great Britain, one British naval expert subsequently argued, had to write off seventy-five warships, the Germans only twenty-eight. British naval superiority fell by 40 or 50 per cent: in 1908 England had authorized twelve Dreadnoughts and the Germans nine; in pre-Dreadnought battleships the British had 63 and the Germans 26.

Fisher's policy, however, was undoubtedly the correct one. Plans for an all-big-gun ship had been under consideration by various navies since 1903. The Russo-Japanese War underwrote the desirability of heavy armaments. The United States authorized the construction of two comparable vessels in March, 1905, and the Germans themselves were moving in that direction. The all-big-gun ship was inevitable, and this consideration led Fisher to insist that Britain must take the lead. While the superiority of the Royal Navy over the German fleet was significantly reduced, nonetheless at no time in the eight years after 1905 did the Germans approach the British in terms of numerical equality. Their highest point was in 1911 when their Dreadnought battle-ship and battlecruiser strength amounted to 64 per cent of the British strength. Thus, by reversing the nineteenth century policy of the British navy, Fisher avoided the British experience of the 1850s and 1860s when technological innovations by an inferior power temporarily suspended Britain's supremacy on the seas. . . .

Qualitative and Quantitative Races and the Balance of Power

In a simple quantitative race one state is very likely to develop a definite superiority in the long run. The issue is simply who has the greater determination and the greater resources. Once a state falls significantly behind, it is most unlikely that it will ever be able to overcome the lead of its rival. A qualitative race, on the other hand, in which there is a series of major technological innovations in reality consists of a number of distinct races. Each time a new weapons system is introduced a new race takes place in the development and accumulation of that weapon. As the rate of technological innovation increases each separate component race decreases in time and extent. The simple quantitative race is like a marathon of undetermined distance which can only end with the exhaustion of one state or both, or with the state which is about to fall behind in the race pulling out its firearms and attempting to despatch its rival. The qualitative race, on the other hand, resembles a series of hundred yard dashes, each beginning from a fresh starting line. Consequently, in a qualitative race hope springs anew with each phase. Quantitative superiority is the product of effort, energy, resources, and time. Once achieved it is rarely lost. Qualitative superiority is the product of discovery, luck, and circumstance. Once achieved it is always lost. Safety exists only in numbers. While a quantitative race tends to produce inequality between the two competing powers, a qualitative race tends toward equality irrespective of what may be the ratio-goals of the two rival states. Each new weapon instead of increasing the distance between the two states reduces it. The more rapid the rate of innovation the more pronounced is the tendency toward equality. Prior to 1905, for instance, Great Britain possessed a superiority in pre-Dreadnought battleships. By 1912 she had also established a clear and unassailable superiority in Dreadnoughts over Germany. But if Germany had introduced a super-Dreadnought in 1909, Great Britain could never have established its clear superiority in Dreadnoughts. She would have had to start over again in the new race. A rapid rate of innovation means that arms races are always beginning, never ending. In so far as the likelihood of war is decreased by the existence of an equality of power between rival states, a qualitative arms race tends to have this result. A quantitative arms race, on the other hand, tends to have the opposite effect. If in a qualitative race one power stopped technological innovation and instead shifted its resources to the multiplication of existing weapons systems, this would be a fairly clear sign that it was intending to go to war in the immediate future.

Undoubtedly many will question the proposition that rapid technological innovation tends to produce an equality of power. In an arms race each state lives in constant fear that its opponent will score a "technological breakthrough" and achieve a decisive qualitative superiority. This anxiety is a continuing feature of arms races but it is one which has virtually no basis in recent experience. The tendency toward simultaneity of innovation is overwhelming. Prior to World War I simultaneity was primarily the result of the common pool of knowledge among the advanced nations with respect to weapons technology. The development of weapons was largely the province of private firms who made their wares available to any state which was interested. As a result at any given time the armaments of the major powers all strikingly resembled one another.[6] During and after World War I military research and development became more and more a governmental activity, and, as a result, more and more enshrouded in secrecy. Nonetheless relative equality in technological innovation continued among the major powers. The reason for this was now not so much access to common knowledge as an equal ability and opportunity to develop that knowledge. The logic of scientific development is such that separate groups of men working in separate laboratories on the same problem are likely to arrive at the same answer to the problem at about the same time. Even if this were not the case, the greatly increased ratio of production time to use time in recent years has tended to diminish the opportunity of the power which has pioneered an innovation to produce it in sufficient quantity in sufficient time to be militarily decisive. When it takes several years to move a weapons system from original design to quantity operation, knowledge of it is bound to leak out, and the second power in the arms race will be able to get its own program under way before the first state can capitalize on its lead. The *Merrimac* reigned supreme for a day, but it was only for a day and it could be only for a day.

The fact that for four years from 1945 to 1949 the United States possessed a marked qualitative superiority over the Soviet Union has tended to obscure how rare this event normally is. American superiority, however, was fundamentally the result of carrying over into a new competitive rivalry a weapons system which had been developed in a previous conflict. In the latter rivalry the tendency toward simultaneity of development soon manifested itself. The Soviet Union developed an atomic bomb four years after the United States had done so. Soviet explosion of a hydrogen weapon lagged only ten months behind that of the United States. At a still later date in the arms race, both powers in 1957 were neck and neck in their efforts to develop long-range ballistic missiles.

The ending of an arms race in a distinct quantitative victory for one side is perhaps best exemplified in the success of the British in maintaining their supremacy on the

---

[6]See Victor Lefebure, "The Decisive Aggressive Value of the New Agencies of War," in The Inter-Parliamentary Union, *What Would Be the Character of a New War?* (New York, 1933), pp. 97–101. See also Marion W. Boggs, *Attempts to Define and Limit 'Aggressive' Armament in Diplomacy and Strategy* (Columbia, Mo., 1941), p. 76: ". . . the history of war inventions tends to emphasize the slowness and distinctively international character of peacetime improvements; no weapon has been perfected with secrecy and rapidity as the exclusive national property of any one state. At an early stage all nations secure access to the information, and develop not only the armament, but measures against it."

seas. Three times within the course of a hundred years the British were challenged by continental rivals, and three times the British outbuilt their competitors. In each case, also, implicitly or explicitly, the bested rivals recognized their defeat and abandoned their efforts to challenge the resources, skill and determination of the British. At this point in a quantitative race when it appears that one power is establishing its superiority over the other, proposals are frequently brought forward for some sort of "disarmament" agreement. These are as likely to come from the superior side as from the inferior one. The stronger power desires to clothe its *de facto* supremacy in *de jure* acceptance and legitimacy so that it may slacken its own arms efforts. From 1905 to 1912, for instance, virtually all the initiatives for Anglo-German naval agreement came from the British. Quite properly, the Germans regarded those advances as British efforts to compel "naval competition to cease at the moment of its own greatest preponderance." Such proposals only heightened German suspicion and bitterness. Similarly, after World War II the Soviet Union naturally described the American nuclear disarmament proposal as a device to prevent the Soviet Union from developing its own nuclear capability. A decade later a greater common interest existed between the Soviet Union and the United States in reaching an arms agreement which would permanently exclude "fourth powers" from the exclusive nuclear club. In disarmament discussions the superior power commonly attempts to persuade the inferior one to accept as permanent the existing ratio of strength, or, failing in this effort, the superior power proposes a temporary suspension of the race, a "holiday" during which period neither power will increase its armaments. In 1899 the Russians, with the largest army in Europe, proposed that for five years no increases be made in military budgets. In 1912–14 Churchill repeatedly suggested the desirability of a naval building holiday to the Germans who were quite unable to perceive its advantages. In 1936 the United States could easily agree to a six year holiday in 10,000 ton cruisers since it had already underway all the cruisers it was permitted by the London Treaty of 1930. Similarly, in its 1957 negotiations with the Soviet Union the United States could also safely propose an end to the production of nuclear weapons. The inferior participant in disarmament negotiations, on the other hand, inevitably supports measures based not upon the existing situation but either upon the abstract principle of "parity" or upon the inherent evil of large armaments as such and the desirability of reducing all arms down to a common low level. Thus, in most instances, a disarmament proposal is simply a maneuver in the arms race: the attempt by a state to achieve the ratio-goal it desires by means other than an increase in its armaments.

The Domestic Burden of Quantitative and Qualitative Races

Quantitative and qualitative arms races have markedly different effects upon the countries participating in them. In a quantitative race the decisive ratio is between the resources which a nation devotes to military purposes and those which it devotes to civilian ones. A quantitative race of any intensity requires a steady shift of resources from the latter to the former. As the forms of military force are multiplied a larger and larger proportion of the national product is devoted to the purposes of the race, and, if it is a race in military manpower, an increasing proportion of the population serves a longer and longer time in the armed forces. A quantitative race of any duration thus imposes ever increasing burdens upon the countries involved in it. As a result, it becomes necessary for governments to resort to various means of stimulating popular support and eliciting a willingness to sacrifice other goods and values. Enthusiasm is mobilized, hostility aroused and directed against the potential enemy. Suspicion and fear multiply with the armaments. Such was the result of the quantitative races between the Triple Alliance and the Triple Entente between 1907 and 1914:

> In both groups of powers there was a rapid increase of military and naval armaments. This caused increasing suspicions, fears, and newspaper recriminations in the opposite camp. This in turn led to more armaments; and so to the vicious circle of ever growing war preparations and mutual fears and suspicions.[7]

Eventually a time is reached when the increasing costs and tensions of a continued arms race seem worse than the costs and the risks of war. Public opinion once aroused cannot be quieted. The economic, military and psychological pressures previously generated permit only further expansion or conflict. The extent to which an arms race is likely to lead to war thus varies with the burdens it imposes on the peoples and the extent to which it involves them psychologically and emotionally in the race. Prolonged sufficiently, a quantitative race must necessarily reach a point where opinion in one country or the other will demand that it be ended, if not by negotiation, then by war. The logical result of a quantitative arms race is a "nation in arms," and a nation in arms for any length of time must be a nation at war.

A qualitative arms race, however, does not have this effect. In such a race the essential relationship is not between the military and the civilian, but rather between the old and the new forms of military force. In a quantitative race the principal policy issue is the extent to which resources and manpower should be diverted from civilian to military use. In a qualitative race, the principal issue is the extent to which the new weapons systems should replace the old "conventional" ones. In a quantitative race the key question is "How much?" In a qualitative race, it is "How soon?" A quantitative race requires continuous expansion of military resources, a qualitative race continuous redeployment of them. A qualitative race does not normally increase arms budgets, even when, as usually happens, the new forms of military force are more expensive than the old ones. The costs of a qualitative race only increase significantly when an effort is made to maintain both old and new forms of military force: steam and sail; ironclads and wooden walls; nuclear and nonnuclear weapons. Transitions from old to new weapons systems have not normally been accompanied by marked increases in military expenditures. During the decade in which the ironclad replaced the wooden ship of the line British naval expenditures declined from £12,779,000 in 1859 to less than eleven million pounds in 1867. Similarly, the five years after the introduction of the Dreadnought saw British naval expenditures drop from £35,476,000 in 1903–04 to £32,188,000 in 1908–09. During the same period estimates for shipbuilding and repairs

---

[7]Fay, *Origins of the World War,* I, p. 226.

dropped from £17,350,000 to £14,313,900. The years 1953–1956 saw the progressive adoption of nuclear weapons in the American armed forces, yet military budgets during this period at first dropped considerably and then recovered only slightly, as the increased expenditures for the new weapons were more than compensated for by reductions in expenditures for nonnuclear forces.

Quantitative and qualitative arms races differ also in the interests they mobilize and the leadership they stimulate. In the long run, a quantitative race makes extensive demands on a broad segment of the population. A qualitative race, however, tends to be a competition of elites rather than masses. No need exists for the bulk of the population to become directly involved. In a quantitative arms race, the users of the weapons—the military leaders—assume the key role. In a qualitative race, the creators of the weapons—the scientists—rival them for preëminence. Similarly, the most important private interests in a quantitative race are the large mass production industrial corporations, while in a qualitative race they tend to be the smaller firms specializing in the innovation and development of weapons systems rather than in their mass output.

While the rising costs of a quantitative race may increase the likelihood of war, they may also enhance efforts to end the race by means of an arms agreement. Undoubtedly the most powerful motive (prior to the feasibility of utter annihilation) leading states to arms limitations has been the economic one. The desire for economy was an important factor leading Louis Philippe to propose a general reduction in European armaments in 1831. In the 1860s similar motives stimulated Napoleon III to push disarmament plans. They also prompted various British governments to be receptive to arms limitation proposals, provided, of course, that they did not endanger Britain's supremacy on the seas: the advent of the Liberal government in 1905, for instance, resulted in renewed efforts to reach accommodation with the Germans. In 1898 the troubled state of Russian finances was largely responsible for the Tsar's surprise move in sponsoring the first Hague Conference. Eight years later it was the British who, for economic reasons, wished to include the question of arms limitation on the agenda of the second Hague Conference.

The success of rising economic costs in bringing about the negotiated end of an arms race depends upon their incidence being relatively equal on each participant. A state which is well able to bear the economic burden normally spurns the efforts of weaker powers to call off the race. Thus, the Kaiser was scornful of the Russian economic debility which led to the proposal for the first Hague Conference, and a German delegate to that conference, in explaining German opposition to limitation, took pains to assure the participants that:

> The German people are not crushed beneath the weight of expenditures and taxes; they are not hanging on the edge of the precipice; they are not hastening towards exhaustion and ruin. Quite the contrary; public and private wealth is increasing, the general welfare, and standard of life, are rising from year to year.[8]

On the other hand, the relatively equal burdens of their arms race in the last decade of the nineteenth century eventually forced Argentina and Chile to call the race off in

---

[8]Quoted in Merze Tate, *The Disarmament Illusion* (New York, 1942), p. 281.

1902. The victory of Chile in the War of the Pacific had brought her into conflict with an "expanding and prosperous Argentina" in the 1880s, and a whole series of boundary disputes exacerbated the rivalry which developed between the two powers for hegemony on the South American continent. As a result, after 1892 both countries consistently expanded their military and naval forces, and relations between them staggered from one war crisis to another. Despite efforts made to arbitrate the boundary disputes,

> an uneasy feeling still prevailed that hostilities might break out, and neither State made any pretence of stopping military and naval preparations. Orders for arms, ammunition, and warships were not countermanded, and men on both sides of the Andes began to declaim strongly against the heavy expenditure thus entailed. The reply to such remonstrances invariably was that until the question of the boundary was settled, it was necessary to maintain both powers on a war footing. Thus the resources of Argentina and Chile were strained to the utmost, and public works neglected in order that funds might be forthcoming to pay for guns and ships bought in Europe.[9]

These economic burdens led the presidents of the two countries to arrive at an agreement in 1899 restricting additional expenditures on armaments. Two years later, however, the boundary issue again flared up, and both sides recommended preparations for war. But again the resources of the countries were taxed beyond their limit. In August 1901 the Chilean president declared to the United States minister "that the burden which Chile is carrying . . . is abnormal and beyond her capacity and that the hour has come to either make use of her armaments or reduce them to the lowest level compatible with the dignity and safety of the country."[10] Argentina was also suffering from severe economic strain, and as a result, the two countries concluded their famous *Pactos de Mayo* in 1902 which limited their naval armaments and provided for the arbitration of the remaining boundary issues.

In summary, two general conclusions emerge as to the relations between arms races and war:

1. War is more likely to develop in the early phases of an arms race than in its later phases.
2. A quantitative race is more likely than a qualitative one to come to a definite end in war, arms agreement, or victory for one side.

ARMS RACES, DISARMAMENT, AND PEACE

In discussions of disarmament, a distinction has frequently been drawn between the presumably technical problem of arms limitation, on the one hand, and political problems, on the other. Considerable energy has been devoted to arguments as to whether it is necessary to settle political issues before disarming or whether disarmament is a

---

[9]Charles E. Akers, *A History of South America* (New York, new ed., 1930), p. 112.
[10]Quoted in Robert N. Burr, "The Balance of Power in Nineteenth-Century South America: An Exploratory Essay," *Hispanic American Historical Review*, XXXV (February, 1955), 58n.

prerequisite to the settlement of political issues. The distinction between arms limitation and politics, however, is a fallacious one. The achievement of an arms agreement cannot be made an end in itself. Arms limitation is the essence of politics and inseparable from other political issues. What, indeed, is more political than the relative balance of power between two distinct entities? Whether they be political parties competing for votes, lobbyists lining up legislative blocs, or states piling up armaments, the power ratio between the units is a decisive factor in their relationship. Virtually every effort (such as the Hague Conferences and the League of Nations) to reach agreement on arms apart from the resolution of other diplomatic and political issues has failed. Inevitably attempts to arrive at arms agreements have tended to broaden into discussions of all the significant political issues between the competing powers. On the other hand, it cannot be assumed that arms negotiations are hopeless, and that they only add another issue to those already disrupting the relations between the two countries and stimulating passion and suspicion. Just as the problem of armaments cannot be settled without reference to other political issues, so is it also impossible to resolve these issues without facing up to the relative balance of military power. The most notable successes in arms limitation agreements have been combined, implicitly or explicitly, with a resolution of other controversies. The Rush-Bagot Agreement, for instance, simply confirmed the settlement which had been reached in the Treaty of Paris. The *Pactos de Mayos* dealt with both armaments and boundaries and implicitly recognized that Argentina would not intervene in west coast politics and that Chile would not become involved in the disputes of the Plata region. The Washington naval agreements necessarily were part and parcel of a general Far Eastern settlement involving the end of the Anglo-Japanese alliance and at least a temporary resolution of the diplomatic issues concerning China. As has been suggested previously, in one sense armaments are to the twentieth century what territory was to the eighteenth. Just as divisions of territory were then the essence of general diplomatic agreements, so today are arrangements on armaments. If both sides are to give up their conflicting ratio-goals and compromise the difference, this arrangement must coincide with a settlement of the other issues which stimulated them to develop the conflicting ratio-goals in the first place. If one state is to retreat further from its ratio-goal than the other, it will have to receive compensations with respect to other points in dispute.

While arms limitation is seldom possible except as part of a broader political settlement, it is also seldom possible if the scope of the arms limitation is itself too broad. One of the corollaries of the belief that arms races produce wars is the assumption that disarmament agreements are necessary to peace. Too frequently it has been made to appear that failure to reach a disarmament agreement leaves war as the only recourse between the powers. In particular, it is false and dangerous to assume that any disarmament to be effective must be total disarmament. The latter is an impossible goal. Military force is inherent in national power and national power is inherent in the existence of independent states. In one way or another all the resources of a state contribute to its military strength. The discussions in the 1920s under the auspices of the League conclusively demonstrated that what are armaments for one state are the pacific instruments of domestic well-being and tranquility for another. The history of general disarmament conferences persuasively suggests the difficulties involved in deciding what elements of power should be weighed in the balance even before the issue is faced as to what the relative weight of the two sides should be. At the first Hague Conference, for instance, the Germans were quick to point out that the Russian proposal for a five year holiday in military budget increases was fine for Russia who had all the men in her army that she needed, but that such a restriction would not prevent Russia from building strategic railways to her western border which would constitute a greater menace to Germany than additional Russian soldiers. The demand for total disarmament frequently reflects an unwillingness to live with the problems of power. A feasible arms limitation must be part of the process of politics not of the abolition of politics.

The narrower the scope of a proposed arms limitation agreement, the more likely it is to be successful. Disarmament agreements seldom actually disarm states. What they do is to exclude certain specified areas from the competition and thereby direct that competition into other channels. The likelihood of reaching such an agreement is greater if the states can have a clear vision of the impact of the agreement on the balance of power. The more restricted the range of armaments covered by the agreement, the easier it is for them to foresee its likely effects. In general, also, the less important the area in the balance of power between the two states, the easier it is to secure agreement on that area. Part of the success of the Washington agreements was that they were limited to capital ships, and, at that time, particularly in the United States the feeling existed that existing battleships were obsolete and that in any event the battleship had passed its peak as the supreme weapon of naval power. Similarly, in 1935 Germany and England were able to arrive at an agreement (which lasted until April 1939) fixing the relative size of their navies—something which had been beyond the capability of sincere and well-meaning diplomats of both powers before World War I—because air power had replaced sea power as the decisive factor in the arms balance between Germany and England. Restrictions on land armaments have generally been harder to arrive at than naval agreements because the continental European nations usually felt that their large armies were directly essential to their national existence and might have to be used at a moment's notice.

Successful disarmament agreements (and a disarmament agreement is successful if it remains in force for a half decade or more) generally establish quantitative restrictions on armaments. The quantitative ratio is the crucial one between the powers, and the quantitative element is much more subject to the control of governments than is the course of scientific development. Furthermore, a quantitative agreement tends to channel competition into qualitative areas, while an agreement on innovation tends to do just the reverse. Consequently, quantitative agreement tends to reduce the likelihood of war, qualitative agreement to enhance it. In the current arms race, for instance, some sort of quantitative agreement might be both feasible, since the race is primarily qualitative in nature, and desirable, since such an agreement would formally prohibit the more dangerous type of arms race. On the other hand, a qualitative agreement between the two countries prohibiting, say, the construction and testing of intercontinental ballistic missiles, might well be disastrous if it should stimulate a quantitative race in aircraft production, the construction of bases, and the multiplication of other forms of military force. In addition, the next phase in the arms race, for instance, may well be the development of defenses against ballistic missiles. A qualitative answer to this problem, such as an effective anti-missile missile, would, in the long run, be much less expensive and much less disturbing to peace than a quantitative answer, such as a mammoth shelter construction program, which would tax public resources, infringe on many established interests, and arouse popular concern and fear. Continued technological innovation could well be essential to the avoidance of war. Peace, in short, may depend less upon the ingenuity of the rival statesmen than upon the ingenuity of the rival scientists.

The balancing of power in any bipolar situation is inherently difficult due to the absence of a "balancer." In such a situation, however, a qualitative arms race may be the most effective means of achieving and maintaining parity of power over a long period of time. The inherent tendency toward parity of such a race may to some extent provide a substitute for the missing balancer. In particular, a qualitative race tends to equalize the differences which might otherwise exist between the ability and willingness of a democracy to compete with a totalitarian dictatorship. The great problem of international politics now is to develop forms of international competition to replace the total wars of the first half of the twentieth century. One such alternative is limited war. Another is the qualitative arms race. The emerging pattern of rivalry between the West and the Soviet bloc suggests that these may well be the primary forms of military activity which the two coalitions will employ. As wars become more frightening and less frequent, arms races may become longer and less disastrous. The substitution of the one for the other is certainly no mean step forward in the restriction of violence. In this respect the arms race may serve the same function which war served: "the intensely sharp competitive *preparation* for war by the nations," could become, as William James suggested, "*the real war,* permanent, unceasing. . . ."[11] A qualitative race regularizes this preparation and introduces an element of stability into the relations between the two powers. Even if it were true, as Sir Edward Grey argued, that arms races inevitably foster suspicion and insecurity, these would be small prices to pay for the avoidance of destruction. Until fundamental changes take place in the structure of world politics, a qualitative arms race may well be a most desirable form of competition between the Soviet Union and the United States. . . .

---

[11]*Memories and Studies* (New York, 1912), p. 273.

COOPERATION UNDER
THE SECURITY DILEMMA

Robert Jervis

. . . The security dilemma: many of the means by which a state tries to increase its se-curity decrease the security of others. In domestic society, there are several ways to in-crease the safety of one's person and property without endangering others. One can move to a safer neighborhood, put bars on the windows, avoid dark streets, and keep a distance from suspicious-looking characters. Of course these measures are not conve-nient, cheap, or certain of success. But no one save criminals need be alarmed if a per-son takes them. In international politics, however, one state's gain in security often in-advertently threatens others. In explaining British policy on naval disarmament in the inter-war period to the Japanese, Ramsey MacDonald said that "Nobody wanted Japan to be insecure."[1] But the problem was not with British desires, but with the conse-quences of her policy. In earlier periods, too, Britain had needed a navy large enough to keep the shipping lanes open. But such a navy could not avoid being a menace to any other state with a coast that could be raided, trade that could be interdicted, or colonies that could be isolated. When Germany started building a powerful navy before World War I, Britain objected that it could only be an offensive weapon aimed at her. As Sir Edward Grey, the Foreign Secretary, put it to King Edward VII: "If the German Fleet ever becomes superior to ours, the German Army can conquer this country. There is no corresponding risk of this kind to Germany; for however superior our Fleet was, no naval victory could bring us any nearer to Berlin." The English position was half cor-rect: Germany's navy was an anti-British instrument. But the British often overlooked what the Germans knew full well: "in every quarrel with England, German colonies and trade were . . . hostages for England to take." Thus, whether she intended it or not, the British Navy constituted an important instrument of coercion. . . .[2]

How a statesman interprets the other's past behavior and how he projects it into the future is influenced by his understanding of the security dilemma and his ability to

"Cooperation Under Security Dilemma" by Robert Jervis from *World Politics,* January 1978, Vol. 30, No. 2, pp. 167–214. Copyright © 1978 by Center of International Studies, Princeton University. Reprinted by permission of the Johns Hopkins University Press.

[1] From *Prelude to Pearl Harbor* by Gerald Wheeler. Copyright © 1963 by the Curators of the University of Missouri. Reprinted by permission of the University of Missouri Press.

[2] Quoted in Leonard Wainstein, "The Dreadnought Gap," in Robert Art and Kenneth Waltz, eds., *The Use of Force* (Boston: Little, Brown 1971), 155; Raymond Sontag, *European Diplomatic History, 1871–1932* (New York: Appleton-Century-Crofts 1933), 147. The French had made a similar argument 50 years earlier; see James Phinney Baxter III, *The Introduction of the Ironclad Warship* (Cambridge: Harvard University Press 1933), 149. For a more detailed discussion of the security dilemma, see Jervis, *Perception and Misperception in International Politics* (Princeton: Princeton University Press 1976), 62–76.

place himself in the other's shoes. The dilemma will operate much more strongly if statesmen do not understand it, and do not see that their arms—sought only to secure the status quo—may alarm others and that others may arm, not because they are contemplating aggression, but because they fear attack from the first state. These two failures of empathy are linked. A state which thinks that the other knows that it wants only to preserve the status quo and that its arms are meant only for self-preservation will conclude that the other side will react to its arms by increasing its own capability only if it is aggressive itself. Since the other side is not menaced, there is no legitimate reason for it to object to the first state's arms; therefore, objection proves that the other is aggressive. Thus, the following exchange between Senator Tom Connally and Secretary of State Acheson concerning the ratification of the NATO treaty:

Secretary Acheson: [The treaty] is aimed solely at armed aggression.

Senator Connally: In other words, unless a nation . . . contemplates, meditates, or makes plans looking toward aggression or armed attack on another nation, it has no cause to fear this treaty.

Secretary Acheson: That is correct, Senator Connally, and it seems to me that any nation which claims that this treaty is directed against it should be reminded of the Biblical admonition that 'The guilty flee when no man pursueth.'

Senator Connally: That is a very apt illustration. What I had in mind was, when a State or Nation passes a criminal act, for instance, against burglary, nobody but those who are burglars or getting ready to be burglars need have any fear of the Burglary Act. Is that not true?

Secretary Acheson: The only effect [the law] would have [on an innocent person] would be for his protection, perhaps, by deterring someone else. He wouldn't worry about the imposition of the penalties on himself.[3]

The other side of this coin is that part of the explanation for détente is that most American decision makers now realize that it is at least possible that Russia may fear American aggression; many think that this fear accounts for a range of Soviet actions previously seen as indicating Russian aggressiveness. Indeed, even 36 percent of military officers consider the Soviet Union's motivations to be primarily defensive. Less than twenty years earlier, officers had been divided over whether Russia sought world conquest or only expansion.[4]

Statesmen who do not understand the security dilemma will think that the money spent is the only cost of building up their arms. This belief removes one important restraint on arms spending. Furthermore, it is also likely to lead states to set their security

---

[3]U.S. Congress, Senate, Committee on Foreign Relations, *Hearings, North Atlantic Treaty,* 81st Cong., 1st sess. (1949), 17.

[4]Bruce Russett and Elizabeth Hanson, *Interest and Ideology* (San Francisco: Freeman 1975), 260; Morris Janowitz, *The Professional Soldier* (New York: Free Press 1960), chap. 13.

requirements too high. Since they do not understand that trying to increase one's security can actually decrease it, they will overestimate the amount of security that is attainable; they will think that when in doubt they can "play it safe" by increasing their arms. Thus it is very likely that two states which support the status quo but do not understand the security dilemma will end up, if not in a war, then at least in a relationship of higher conflict than is required by the objective situation.

The belief that an increase in military strength always leads to an increase in security is often linked to the belief that the only route to security is through military strength. As a consequence, a whole range of meliorative policies will be downgraded. Decision makers who do not believe that adopting a more conciliatory posture, meeting the other's legitimate grievances, or developing mutual gains from cooperation can increase their state's security, will not devote much attention or effort to these possibilities.

On the other hand, a heightened sensitivity to the security dilemma makes it more likely that the state will treat an aggressor as though it were an insecure defender of the status quo. Partly because of their views about the causes of World War I, the British were predisposed to believe that Hitler sought only the rectification of legitimate and limited grievances and that security could best be gained by constructing an equitable international system. As a result they pursued a policy which, although well designed to avoid the danger of creating unnecessary conflict with a status-quo Germany, helped destroy Europe.

GEOGRAPHY, COMMITMENTS, BELIEFS, AND SECURITY THROUGH EXPANSION

. . . Situations vary in the ease or difficulty with which all states can simultaneously achieve a high degree of security. The influence of military technology on this variable is the subject of the next section. Here we want to treat the impact of beliefs, geography, and commitments (many of which can be considered to be modifications of geography, since they bind states to defend areas outside their homelands). In the crowded continent of Europe, security requirements were hard to mesh. Being surrounded by powerful states, Germany's problem—or the problem created by Germany—was always great and was even worse when her relations with both France and Russia were bad, such as before World War I. In that case, even a status-quo Germany, if she could not change the political situation, would almost have been forced to adopt something like the Schlieffen Plan. Because she could not hold off both of her enemies, she had to be prepared to defeat one quickly and then deal with the other in a more leisurely fashion. If France or Russia stayed out of a war between the other state and Germany, they would allow Germany to dominate the Continent (even if that was not Germany's aim). They therefore had to deny Germany this ability, thus making Germany less secure. Although Germany's arrogant and erratic behavior, coupled with the desire for an unreasonably high level of security (which amounted to the desire to escape from her geographic plight), compounded the problem, even wise German statesmen would have been hard put to gain a high degree of security without alarming their neighbors. . . .

OFFENSE, DEFENSE, AND THE SECURITY DILEMMA

Another approach starts with the central point of the security dilemma—that an increase in one state's security decreases the security of others—and examines the conditions under which this proposition holds. Two crucial variables are involved: whether defensive weapons and policies can be distinguished from offensive ones, and whether the defense or the offense has the advantage. The definitions are not always clear, and many cases are difficult to judge, but these two variables shed a great deal of light on the question of whether status-quo powers will adopt compatible security policies. All the variables discussed so far leave the heart of the problem untouched. But when defensive weapons differ from offensive ones, it is possible for a state to make itself more secure without making others less secure. And when the defense has the advantage over the offense, a large increase in one state's security only slightly decreases the security of the others, and status-quo powers can all enjoy a high level of security and largely escape from the state of nature.

Offense-Defense Balance

When we say that the offense has the advantage, we simply mean that it is easier to destroy the other's army and take its territory than it is to defend one's own. When the defense has the advantage, it is easier to protect and to hold than it is to move forward, destroy, and take. If effective defenses can be erected quickly, an attacker may be able to keep territory he has taken in an initial victory. Thus, the dominance of the defense made it very hard for Britain and France to push Germany out of France in World War I. But when superior defenses are difficult for an aggressor to improvise on the battlefield and must be constructed during peacetime, they provide no direct assistance to him.

The security dilemma is at its most vicious when commitments, strategy, or technology dictate that the only route to security lies through expansion. Status-quo powers must then act like aggressors; the fact that they would gladly agree to forego the opportunity for expansion in return for guarantees for their security has no implications for their behavior. Even if expansion is not sought as a goal in itself, there will be quick and drastic changes in the distribution of territory and influence. Conversely, when the defense has the advantage, status-quo states can make themselves more secure without gravely endangering others. Indeed, if the defense has enough of an advantage and if the states are of roughly equal size, not only will the security dilemma cease to inhibit status-quo states from cooperating, but aggression will be next to impossible, thus rendering international anarchy relatively unimportant. If states cannot conquer each other, then the lack of sovereignty, although it presents problems of collective goods in a number of areas, no longer forces states to devote their primary attention to self-preservation. Although, if force were not usable, there would be fewer restraints on the use of nonmilitary instruments, these are rarely powerful enough to threaten the vital interests of a major state.

Two questions of the offense-defense balance can be separated. First, does the state have to spend more or less than one dollar on defensive forces to offset each dollar spent by the other side on forces that could be used to attack? If the state has one dollar to spend on increasing its security, should it put it into offensive or defensive forces? Second, with a given inventory of forces, is it better to attack or to defend? Is there an incentive to strike first or to absorb the other's blow? These two aspects are often linked: if each dollar spent on offense can overcome each dollar spent on defense, and if both sides have the same defense budgets, then both are likely to build offensive forces and find it attractive to attack rather than to wait for the adversary to strike.

These aspects affect the security dilemma in different ways. The first has its greatest impact on arms races. If the defense has the advantage, and if the status-quo powers have reasonable subjective security requirements, they can probably avoid an arms race. Although an increase in one side's arms and security will still decrease the other's security, the former's increase will be larger than the latter's decrease. So if one side increases its arms, the other can bring its security back up to its previous level by adding a smaller amount to its forces. And if the first side reacts to this change, its increase will also be smaller than the stimulus that produced it. Thus a stable equilibrium will be reached. Shifting from dynamics to statics, each side can be quite secure with forces roughly equal to those of the other. Indeed, if the defense is much more potent than the offense, each side can be willing to have forces much smaller than the other's, and can be indifferent to a wide range of the other's defense policies.

The second aspect—whether it is better to attack or to defend—influences short-run stability. When the offense has the advantage, a state's reaction to international tension will increase the chances of war. The incentives for pre-emption and the "reciprocal fear of surprise attack" in this situation have been made clear by analyses of the dangers that exist when two countries have first-strike capabilities.[5] There is no way for the state to increase its security without menacing, or even attacking, the other. Even Bismarck, who once called preventive war "committing suicide from fear of death," said that "no government, if it regards war as inevitable even if it does not want it, would be so foolish as to leave to the enemy the choice of time and occasion and to wait for the moment which is most convenient for the enemy."[6] In another arena, the same dilemma applies to the policeman in a dark alley confronting a suspected criminal who appears to be holding a weapon. Though racism may indeed be present, the security dilemma can account for many of the tragic shootings of innocent people in the ghettos.

Beliefs about the course of a war in which the offense has the advantage further deepen the security dilemma. When there are incentives to strike first, a successful attack will usually so weaken the other side that victory will be relatively quick, bloodless, and decisive. It is in these periods when conquest is possible and attractive that states consolidate power internally—for instance, by destroying the feudal barons—and expand externally. There are several consequences that decrease the chance of cooperation among status-quo states. First, war will be profitable for the winner. The costs will be low and the benefits high. Of course, losers will suffer; the fear of losing could induce states to try to form stable cooperative arrangements, but the temptation of victory

---

[5]Thomas Schelling, *The Strategy of Conflict* (New York: Oxford University Press 1963), chap. 9.
[6]Quoted in Fritz Fischer, *War of Illusions* (New York: Norton 1975), 377, 461.

will make this particularly difficult. Second, because wars are expected to be both frequent and short, there will be incentives for high levels of arms, and quick and strong
reaction to the other's increases in arms. The state cannot afford to wait until there is
unambiguous evidence that the other is building new weapons. Even large states that
have faith in their economic strength cannot wait, because the war will be over before
their products can reach the army. Third, when wars are quick, states will have to recruit
allies in advance.[7] Without the opportunity for bargaining and re-alignments during the
opening stages of hostilities, peacetime diplomacy loses a degree of the fluidity that facilitates balance-of-power policies. Because alliances must be secured during peacetime, the international system is more likely to become bipolar. It is hard to say whether
war therefore becomes more or less likely, but this bipolarity increases tension between
the two camps and makes it harder for status-quo states to gain the benefits of cooperation. Fourth, if wars are frequent, statesmen's perceptual thresholds will be adjusted accordingly and they will be quick to perceive ambiguous evidence as indicating that others are aggressive. Thus, there will be more cases of status-quo powers arming against
each other in the incorrect belief that the other is hostile.

When the defense has the advantage, all the foregoing is reversed. The state that
fears attack does not pre-empt—since that would be a wasteful use of its military resources—but rather prepares to receive an attack. Doing so does not decrease the security of others, and several states can do it simultaneously; the situation will therefore be
stable, and status-quo powers will be able to cooperate. When Herman Kahn argues
that ultimatums "are vastly too dangerous to give because . . . they are quite likely to
touch off a preemptive strike,"[8] he incorrectly assumes that it is always advantageous to
strike first.

More is involved than short-run dynamics. When the defense is dominant, wars are
likely to become stalemates and can be won only at enormous cost. Relatively small
and weak states can hold off larger and stronger ones, or can deter attack by raising the
costs of conquest to an unacceptable level. States then approach equality in what they
can do to each other. Like the .45-caliber pistol in the American West, fortifications
were the "great equalizer" in some periods. Changes in the status quo are less frequent
and cooperation is more common wherever the security dilemma is thereby reduced.

Many of these arguments can be illustrated by the major powers' policies in the periods preceding the two world wars. Bismarck's wars surprised statesmen by showing
that the offense had the advantage, and by being quick, relatively cheap, and quite decisive. Falling into a common error, observers projected this pattern into the future.[9] The

---

[7]George Quester, *Offense and Defense in the International System* (New York: John Wiley 1977),
105–06; Sontag (fn. 5), 4–5.
[8]Herman Kahn, *On Thermonuclear War* (Princeton: Princeton University Press 1960), 211.
[9]For a general discussion of such mistaken learning from the past, see Jervis (fn. 5), chap. 6. The important and still not completely understood question of why this belief formed and was maintained
throughout the war is examined in Bernard Brodie, *War and Politics* (New York: Macmillan 1973),
262–70; Brodie, "Technological Change, Strategic Doctrine, and Political Outcomes," in Klaus Knorr,
ed., *Historical Dimensions of National Security Problems* (Lawrence: University Press of Kansas
1976), 290–92; and Douglas Porch, "The French Army and the Spirit of the Offensive, 1900–14," in
Brian Bond and Ian Roy, eds., *War and Society* (New York: Holmes & Meier 1975), 117–43.

resulting expectations had several effects. First, states sought semi-permanent allies. In the early stages of the Franco-Prussian War, Napoleon III had thought that there would be plenty of time to recruit Austria to his side. Now, others were not going to repeat this mistake. Second, defense budgets were high and reacted quite sharply to increases on the other side. It is not surprising that Richardson's theory of arms races fits this period well. Third, most decision makers thought that the next European war would not cost much blood and treasure.[10] That is one reason why war was generally seen as inevitable and why mass opinion was so bellicose. Fourth, once war seemed likely, there were strong pressures to pre-empt. Both sides believed that whoever moved first could penetrate the other deep enough to disrupt mobilization and thus gain an insurmountable advantage. (There was no such belief about the use of naval forces. Although Churchill made an ill-advised speech saying that if German ships "do not come out and fight in time of war they will be dug out like rats in a hole,"[11] everyone knew that submarines, mines, and coastal fortifications made this impossible. So at the start of the war each navy prepared to defend itself rather than attack, and the short-run destabilizing forces that launched the armies toward each other did not operate.)[12] Furthermore, each side knew that the other saw the situation the same way, thus increasing the perceived danger that the other would attack, and giving each added reasons to precipitate a war if conditions seemed favorable. In the long and the short run, there were thus both offensive and defensive incentives to strike. This situation casts light on the common question about German motives in 1914: "Did Germany unleash the war deliberately to become a world power or did she support Austria merely to defend a weakening ally," thereby protecting her own position?[13] To some extent, this question is misleading. Because of the perceived advantage of the offense, war was seen as the best route both to gaining expansion and to avoiding drastic loss of influence. There seemed to be no way for Germany merely to retain and safeguard her existing position.

Of course the war showed these beliefs to have been wrong on all points. Trenches and machine guns gave the defense an overwhelming advantage. The fighting became deadlocked and produced horrendous casualties. It made no sense for the combatants to bleed themselves to death. If they had known the power of the defense beforehand, they would have rushed for their own trenches rather than for the enemy's territory. Each side could have done this without increasing the other's incentives to strike. . . .

Technology and Geography   Technology and geography are the two main factors that determine whether the offense or the defense has the advantage. As Brodie notes, "On the tactical level, as a rule, few physical factors favor the attacker but many

---

[10]Some were not so optimistic. Gray's remark is well-known: "The lamps are going out all over Europe; we shall not see them lit again in our life-time." The German Prime Minister, Bethmann Hollweg, also feared the consequences of the war. But the controlling view was that it would certainly pay for the winner.

[11]Quoted in Martin Gilbert, *Winston S. Churchill, III, The Challenge of War, 1914–1916* (Boston: Houghton Mifflin 1971), 84.

[12]Quester (fn. 7), 98–99. Robert Art, *The Influence of Foreign Policy on Seapower,* II (Beverly Hills: Sage Professional Papers in International Studies Series, 1973), 14–18, 26–28.

[13]Konrad Jarausch, "The Illusion of Limited War: Chancellor Bethmann Hollweg's Calculated Risk, July 1914," *Central European History,* II (March 1969), 50.

favor the defender. The defender usually has the advantage of cover. He characteristically fires from behind some form of shelter while his opponent crosses open ground."[14] Anything that increases the amount of ground the attacker has to cross, or impedes his progress across it, or makes him more vulnerable while crossing, increases the advantage accruing to the defense. When states are separated by barriers that produce these effects, the security dilemma is eased, since both can have forces adequate for defense without being able to attack. Impenetrable barriers would actually prevent war; in reality, decision makers have to settle for a good deal less. Buffer zones slow the attacker's progress; they thereby give the defender time to prepare, increase problems of logistics, and reduce the number of soldiers available for the final assault. At the end of the 19th century, Arthur Balfour noted Afghanistan's "non-conducting" qualities. "So long as it possesses few roads, and no railroads, it will be impossible for Russia to make effective use of her great numerical superiority at any point immediately vital to the Empire." The Russians valued buffers for the same reasons; it is not surprising that when Persia was being divided into Russian and British spheres of influence some years later, the Russians sought assurances that the British would refrain from building potentially menacing railroads in their sphere. Indeed, since railroad construction radically altered the abilities of countries to defend themselves and to attack others, many diplomatic notes and much intelligence activity in the late 19th century centered on this subject.[15]

Oceans, large rivers, and mountain ranges serve the same function as buffer zones. Being hard to cross, they allow defense against superior numbers. The defender has merely to stay on his side of the barrier and so can utilize all the men he can bring up to it. The attacker's men, however, can cross only a few at a time, and they are very vulnerable when doing so. If all states were self-sufficient islands, anarchy would be much less of a problem. A small investment in short defenses and a small army would be sufficient to repel invasion. Only very weak states would be vulnerable, and only very large ones could menace others. As noted above, the United States, and to a lesser extent Great Britain, have partly been able to escape from the state of nature because their geographical positions approximated this ideal.

Although geography cannot be changed to conform to borders, borders can and do change to conform to geography. Borders across which an attack is easy tend to be unstable. States living within them are likely to expand or be absorbed. Frequent wars are almost inevitable since attacking will often seem the best way to protect what one has. This process will stop, or at least slow down, when the state's borders reach—by expansion or contraction—a line of natural obstacles. Security without attack will then be possible. Furthermore, these lines constitute salient solutions to bargaining problems and, to the extent that they are barriers to migration, are likely to divide ethnic groups, thereby raising the costs and lowering the incentives for conquest.

---

[14]Bernard Brodie, *Strategy in the Missile Age* (Princeton: Princeton University Press 1959), 179.

[15]Arthur Balfour, "Memorandum," Committee on Imperial Defence, April 30, 1903, pp. 2–3; see the telegrams by Sir Arthur Nicolson, in G. P. Gooch and Harold Temperley, eds., *British Documents on the Origins of the War*, Vol. 4 (London: H.M.S.O. 1929), 429, 524. These barriers do not prevent the passage of long-range aircraft; but even in the air, distance usually aids the defender.

Attachment to one's state and its land reinforce one quasi-geographical aid to the defense. Conquest usually becomes more difficult the deeper the attacker pushes into the other's territory. Nationalism spurs the defenders to fight harder; advancing not only lengthens the attacker's supply lines, but takes him through unfamiliar and often devastated lands that require troops for garrison duty. These stabilizing dynamics will not operate, however, if the defender's war materiel is situated near its borders, or if the people do not care about their state, but only about being on the winning side. In such cases, positive feedback will be at work and initial defeats will be insurmountable.[16]

Imitating geography, men have tried to create barriers. Treaties may provide for demilitarized zones on both sides of the border, although such zones will rarely be deep enough to provide more than warning. Even this was not possible in Europe, but the Russians adopted a gauge for their railroads that was broader than that of the neighboring states, thereby complicating the logistics problems of any attacker—including Russia.

Perhaps the most ambitious and at least temporarily successful attempts to construct a system that would aid the defenses of both sides were the interwar naval treaties, as they affected Japanese-American relations. As mentioned earlier, the problem was that the United States could not defend the Philippines without denying Japan the ability to protect her home islands.[17] (In 1941 this dilemma became insoluble when Japan sought to extend her control to Malaya and the Dutch East Indies. If the Philippines had been invulnerable, they could have provided a secure base from which the U.S. could interdict Japanese shipping between the homeland and the areas she was trying to conquer.) In the 1920's and early 1930's each side would have been willing to grant the other security for its possessions in return for a reciprocal grant, and the Washington Naval Conference agreements were designed to approach this goal. As a Japanese diplomat later put it, their country's "fundamental principle" was to have "a strength insufficient for attack and adequate for defense."[18] Thus, Japan agreed in 1922 to accept a navy only three-fifths as large as that of the United States, and the U.S. agreed not to fortify its Pacific islands.[19] (Japan had earlier been forced to agree not to fortify the islands she had taken from Germany in World War I.) Japan's navy would not be large enough to defeat America's anywhere other than close to the home islands. Although the Japanese could still take the Philippines, not only would they be unable to move farther, but they might be weakened enough by their efforts to be vulnerable to counterattack. Japan, however, gained security. An American attack was rendered more difficult because the American bases were unprotected and because, until 1930, Japan

---

[16]See, for example, the discussion of warfare among Chinese warlords in Hsi-Sheng Chi, "The Chinese Warlord System as an International System," in Morton Kaplan, ed., *New Approaches to International Relations* (New York: St. Martin's 1968), 405–25.

[17]Some American decision makers, including military officers, thought that the best way out of the dilemma was to abandon the Philippines.

[18]Quoted in Elting Morrison, *Turmoil and Tradition: A Study of the Life and Times of Henry L. Stimson* (Boston: Houghton Mifflin 1960), 326.

[19]The U.S. "refused to consider limitations on Hawaiian defenses, since these works posed no threat to Japan." William Braisted, *The United States Navy in the Pacific, 1909–1922* (Austin: University of Texas Press 1971), 612.

was allowed unlimited numbers of cruisers, destroyers, and submarines that could weaken the American fleet as it made its way across the ocean.[20]

The other major determinant of the offense-defense balance is technology. When weapons are highly vulnerable, they must be employed before they are attacked. Others can remain quite invulnerable in their bases. The former characteristics are embodied in unprotected missiles and many kinds of bombers. (It should be noted that it is not vulnerability *per se* that is crucial, but the location of the vulnerability. Bombers and missiles that are easy to destroy only after having been launched toward their targets do not create destabilizing dynamics.) Incentives to strike first are usually absent for naval forces that are threatened by a naval attack. Like missiles in hardened silos, they are usually well protected when in their bases. Both sides can then simultaneously be prepared to defend themselves successfully.

In ground warfare under some conditions, forts, trenches, and small groups of men in prepared positions can hold off large numbers of attackers. Less frequently, a few attackers can storm the defenses. By and large, it is a contest between fortifications and supporting light weapons on the one hand, and mobility and heavier weapons that clear the way for the attack on the other. As the erroneous views held before the two world wars show, there is no simple way to determine which is dominant. "[T]hese oscillations are not smooth and predictable like those of a swinging pendulum. They are uneven in both extent and time. Some occur in the course of a single battle or campaign, others in the course of a war, still others during a series of wars." Longer-term oscillations can also be detected:

> The early Gothic age, from the twelfth to the late thirteenth century, with its wonderful cathedrals and fortified places, was a period during which the attackers in Europe generally met serious and increasing difficulties, because the improvement in the strength of fortresses outran the advance in the power of destruction. Later, with the spread of firearms at the end of the fifteenth century, old fortresses lost their power to resist. An age ensued during which the offense possessed, apart from short-term setbacks, new advantages. Then, during the seventeenth century, especially after about 1660, and until at least the outbreak of the War of the Austrian Succession in 1740, the defense regained much of the ground it had lost since the great medieval fortresses had proved unable to meet the bombardment of the new and more numerous artillery.[21]

Another scholar has continued the argument: "The offensive gained an advantage with new forms of heavy mobile artillery in the nineteenth century, but the stalemate of

---

[20]That is part of the reason why the Japanese admirals strongly objected when the civilian leaders decided to accept a seven-to-ten ratio in lighter craft in 1930. Stephen Pelz, *Race to Pearl Harbor* (Cambridge: Harvard University Press 1974), 3.

[21]John Nef, *War and Human Progress* (New York: Norton 1963), 185. Also see *ibid.,* 237, 242–43, and 323; C. W. Oman, *The Art of War in the Middle Ages* (Ithaca, N.Y.: Cornell University Press 1953), 70–72; John Beeler, *Warfare in Feudal Europe, 730–1200* (Ithaca, N.Y.: Cornell University Press 1971), 212–14; Michael Howard, *War in European History* (London: Oxford University Press 1976), 33–37.

World War I created the impression that the defense again had an advantage; the German invasion in World War II, however, indicated the offensive superiority of highly mechanized armies in the field."[22]

The situation today with respect to conventional weapons is unclear. Until recently it was believed that tanks and tactical air power gave the attacker an advantage. The initial analyses of the 1973 Arab-Israeli war indicated that new anti-tank and anti-aircraft weapons have restored the primacy of the defense. These weapons are cheap, easy to use, and can destroy a high proportion of the attacking vehicles and planes that are sighted. It then would make sense for a status-quo power to buy lots of $20,000 missiles rather than buy a few half-million dollar tanks and multi-million dollar fighter-bombers. Defense would be possible even against a large and well-equipped force; states that care primarily about self-protection would not need to engage in arms races. But further examinations of the new technologies and the history of the October War cast doubt on these optimistic conclusions and leave us unable to render any firm judgment. . . .[23]

Offense-Defense Differentiation

The other major variable that affects how strongly the security dilemma operates is whether weapons and policies that protect the state also provide the capability for attack. If they do not, the basic postulate of the security dilemma no longer applies. A state can increase its own security without decreasing that of others. The advantage of the defense can only ameliorate the security dilemma. A differentiation between offensive and defensive stances comes close to abolishing it. Such differentiation does not mean, however, that all security problems will be abolished. If the offense has the advantage, conquest and aggression will still be possible. And if the offense's advantage is great enough, status-quo powers may find it too expensive to protect themselves by defensive forces and decide to procure offensive weapons even though this will menace others. Furthermore, states will still have to worry that even if the other's military posture shows that it is peaceful now, it may develop aggressive intentions in the future.

Assuming that the defense is at least as potent as the offense, the differentiation between them allows status-quo states to behave in ways that are clearly different from those of aggressors. Three beneficial consequences follow. First, status-quo powers can identify each other, thus laying the foundations for cooperation. Conflicts growing out of the mistaken belief that the other side is expansionist will be less frequent. Second, status-quo states will obtain advance warning when others plan aggression. Before a state can attack, it has to develop and deploy offensive weapons. If procurement of these weapons cannot be disguised and takes a fair amount of time, as it almost always does, a status-quo state will have the time to take countermeasures. It need not maintain

---

[22]Quincy Wright, *A Study of War* (abridged ed.; Chicago: University of Chicago Press 1964), 142. Also see 63–70, 74–75. There are important exceptions to these generalizations—the American Civil War, for instance, falls in the middle of the period Wright says is dominated by the offense.

[23]Geoffrey Kemp, Robert Pfaltzgraff, and Uri Ra'anan, eds., *The Other Arms Race* (Lexington, Mass.: D. C. Heath 1975); James Foster, "The Future of Conventional Arms Control," *Policy Sciences*, No. 8 (Spring 1977), 1–19.

a high level of defensive arms as long as its potential adversaries are adopting a peaceful posture. . . .

The third beneficial consequence of a difference between offensive and defensive weapons is that if all states support the status quo, an obvious arms control agreement is a ban on weapons that are useful for attacking. As President Roosevelt put it in his message to the Geneva Disarmament Conference in 1933: "If all nations will agree wholly to eliminate from possession and use the weapons which make possible a successful attack, defenses automatically will become impregnable, and the frontiers and independence of every national will become secure."[24] The fact that such treaties have been rare—the Washington naval agreements discussed above and the anti-ABM treaty can be cited as examples—shows either that states are not always willing to guarantee the security of others, or that it is hard to distinguish offensive from defensive weapons.

Is such a distinction possible? Salvador de Madariaga, the Spanish statesman active in the disarmament negotiations of the interwar years, thought not: "A weapon is either offensive or defensive according to which end of it you are looking at." The French Foreign Minister agreed (although French policy did not always follow this view): "Every arm can be employed offensively or defensively in turn. . . . The only way to discover whether arms are intended for purely defensive purposes or are held in a spirit of aggression is in all cases to enquire into the intentions of the country concerned." Some evidence for the validity of this argument is provided by the fact that much time in these unsuccessful negotiations was devoted to separating offensive from defensive weapons. Indeed, no simple and unambiguous definition is possible and in many cases no judgment can be reached. Before the American entry into World War I, Woodrow Wilson wanted to arm merchantmen only with guns in the back of the ship so they could not initiate a fight, but this expedient cannot be applied to more common forms of armaments.[25]

There are several problems. Even when a differentiation is possible, a status-quo power will want offensive arms under any of three conditions. (1) If the offense has a great advantage over the defense, protection through defensive forces will be too expensive. (2) Status-quo states may need offensive weapons to regain territory lost in the opening stages of a war. It might be possible, however, for a state to wait to procure these weapons until war seems likely, and they might be needed only in relatively small numbers, unless the aggressor was able to construct strong defenses quickly in the occupied areas. (3) The state may feel that it must be prepared to take the offensive either because the other side will make peace only if it loses territory or because the state has commitments to attack if the other makes war on a third party. As noted above, status-quo states with extensive commitments are often forced to behave like aggressors. Even when they lack such commitments, status-quo states must worry about the possibility that if they are able to hold off an attack, they will still not be able to end the war unless they move into the other's territory to damage its military forces and inflict pain. Many

---

[24]Quoted in Merze Tate, *The United States and Armaments* (Cambridge: Harvard University Press 1948), 108.

[25]Marion Boggs, *Attempts to Define and Limit "Aggressive" Armament in Diplomacy and Strategy* (Columbia: University of Missouri Studies, XVI, No. 1, 1941), 15, 40.

American naval officers after the Civil War, for example, believed that "only by destroying the commerce of the opponent could the United States bring him to terms."[26]

A further complication is introduced by the fact that aggressors as well as status-quo powers require defensive forces as a prelude to acquiring offensive ones, to protect one frontier while attacking another, or for insurance in case the war goes badly. Criminals as well as policemen can use bulletproof vests. Hitler as well as Maginot built a line of forts. Indeed, Churchill reports that in 1936 the German Foreign Minister said: "As soon as our fortifications are constructed [on our western borders] and the countries in Central Europe realize that France cannot enter German territory, all these countries will begin to feel very differently about their foreign policies, and a new constellation will develop."[27] So a state may not necessarily be reassured if its neighbor constructs strong defenses.

More central difficulties are created by the fact that whether a weapon is offensive or defensive often depends on the particular situation—for instance, the geographical setting and the way in which the weapon is used. "Tanks . . . spearheaded the fateful German thrust through the Ardennes in 1940, but if the French had disposed of a properly concentrated armored reserve, it would have provided the best means for their cutting off the penetration and turning into a disaster for the Germans what became instead an overwhelming victory."[28] Anti-aircraft weapons seem obviously defensive—to be used, they must wait for the other side to come to them. But the Egyptian attack on Israel in 1973 would have been impossible without effective air defenses that covered the battlefield. Nevertheless, some distinctions are possible. Sir John Simon, then the British Foreign Secretary, in response to the views cited earlier, stated that just because a fine line could not be drawn, "that was no reason for saying that there were not stretches of territory on either side which all practical men and women knew to be well on this or that side of the line." Although there are almost no weapons and strategies that are useful only for attacking, there are some that are almost exclusively defensive. Aggressors could want them for protection, but a state that relied mostly on them could not menace others. More frequently, we cannot "determine the absolute character of a weapon, but [we can] make a comparison . . . [and] discover whether or not the offensive potentialities predominate, whether a weapon is more useful in attack or in defense."[29]

The essence of defense is keeping the other side out of your territory. A purely defensive weapon is one that can do this without being able to penetrate the enemy's land. Thus a committee of military experts in an interwar disarmament conference declared that armaments "incapable of mobility by means of self-contained power," or movable only after long delay, were "only capable of being used for the defense of a State's territory."[30] The most obvious examples are fortifications. They can shelter attacking forces,

---

[26]Kenneth Hagan, *American Gunboat Diplomacy and the Old Navy, 1877–1889* (Westport, Conn.: Greenwood Press 1973), 20.

[27]Winston Churchill, *The Gathering Storm* (Boston: Houghton 1948), 206.

[28]Bernard Brodie, *War and Politics* (New York: Macmillan 1973), 325.

[29]Boggs (fn. 25), 42, 83. For a good argument about the possible differentiation between offensive and defensive weapons in the 1930's, see Basil Liddell Hart, "Aggression and the Problem of Weapons," *English Review,* Vol. 55 (July 1932), 71–78.

[30]Quoted in Boggs (fn. 25), 39.

especially when they are built right along the frontier,[31] but they cannot occupy enemy territory. A state with only a strong line of forts, fixed guns, and a small army to man them would not be much of a menace. Anything else that can serve only as a barrier against attacking troops is similarly defensive. In this category are systems that provide warning of an attack, the Russian's adoption of a different railroad gauge, and nuclear land mines that can seal off invasion routes.

If total immobility clearly defines a system that is defensive only, limited mobility is unfortunately ambiguous. As noted above, short-range fighter aircraft and anti-aircraft missiles can be used to cover an attack. And, unlike forts, they can advance with the troops. Still, their inability to reach deep into enemy territory does make them more useful for the defense than for the offense. Thus, the United States and Israel would have been more alarmed in the early 1970's had the Russians provided the Egyptians with long-range instead of short-range aircraft. Naval forces are particularly difficult to classify in these terms, but those that are very short-legged can be used only for coastal defense. . . .

FOUR WORLDS

The two variables we have been discussing—whether the offense or the defense has the advantage, and whether offensive postures can be distinguished from defensive ones—can be combined to yield four possible worlds.

The first world is the worst for status-quo states. There is no way to get security without menacing others, and security through defense is terribly difficult to obtain. Because offensive and defensive postures are the same, status-quo states acquire the same kind of arms that are sought by aggressors. And because the offense has the advantage over the defense, attacking is the best route to protecting what you have; status-quo states will therefore behave like aggressors. The situation will be unstable. Arms races are likely. Incentives to strike first will turn crises into wars. Decisive victories and conquests will be common. States will grow and shrink rapidly, and it will be hard for any state to maintain its size and influence without trying to increase them. Cooperation among status-quo powers will be extremely hard to achieve.

There are no cases that totally fit this picture, but it bears more than a passing resemblance to Europe before World War I. Britain and Germany, although in many respects natural allies, ended up as enemies. Of course much of the explanation lies in Germany's ill-chosen policy. And from the perspective of our theory, the powers' ability to avoid war in a series of earlier crises cannot be easily explained. Nevertheless, much of the behavior in this period was the product of technology and beliefs that magnified the security dilemma. Decision makers thought that the offense had a big advantage and saw little difference between offensive and defensive military postures. The era was

---

[31]On these grounds, the Germans claimed in 1932 that the French forts were offensive (*ibid.,* 49). Similarly, fortified forward naval bases can be necessary for launching an attack; see Braisted (fn. 19), 643.

	OFFENSE HAS THE ADVANTAGE	DEFENSE HAS THE ADVANTAGE
	1	*2*
OFFENSIVE POSTURE NOT DISTINGUISHABLE FROM DEFENSIVE ONE	Doubly dangerous	Security dilemma, but security requirements may be compatible.
	3	*4*
OFFENSIVE POSTURE DISTINGUISHABLE FROM DEFENSIVE ONE	No security dilemma, but aggression possible. Status-quo states can follow different policy than aggressors. Warning given.	Doubly stable

characterized by arms races. And once war seemed likely, mobilization races created powerful incentives to strike first. . . .

In the second world, the security dilemma operates because offensive and defensive postures cannot be distinguished; but it does not operate as strongly as in the first world because the defense has the advantage, and so an increment in one side's strength increases its security more than it decreases the other's. So, if both sides have reasonable subjective security requirements, are of roughly equal power, and the variables discussed earlier are favorable, it is quite likely that status-quo states can adopt compatible security policies. Although a state will not be able to judge the other's intentions from the kinds of weapons it procures, the level of arms spending will give important evidence. Of course a state that seeks a high level of arms might be not an aggressor but merely an insecure state, which if conciliated will reduce its arms, and if confronted will reply in kind. To assume that the apparently excessive level of arms indicates aggressiveness could therefore lead to a response that would deepen the dilemma and create needless conflict. But empathy and skillful statesmanship can reduce this danger. Furthermore, the advantageous position of the defense means that a status-quo state can often maintain a high degree of security with a level of arms lower than that of its expected adversary. Such a state demonstrates that it lacks the ability or desire to alter the status quo, at least at the present time. The strength of the defense also allows states to react slowly and with restraint when they fear that others are menacing them. So, although status-quo powers will to some extent be threatening to others, that extent will be limited.

This world is the one that comes closest to matching most periods in history. Attacking is usually harder than defending because of the strength of fortifications and obstacles. But purely defensive postures are rarely possible because fortifications are usually supplemented by armies and mobile guns which can support an attack.

. . . In the third world there may be no security dilemma, but there are security problems. Because states can procure defensive systems that do not threaten others, the dilemma need not operate. But because the offense has the advantage, aggression is possible, and perhaps easy. If the offense has enough of an advantage, even a status-quo state may take the initiative rather than risk being attacked and defeated. If the offense has less of an advantage, stability and cooperation are likely because the status-quo states will procure defensive forces. They need not react to others who are similarly armed, but can wait for the warning they would receive if others started to deploy offensive weapons. But each state will have to watch the others carefully, and there is room for false suspicions. The costliness of the defense and the allure of the offense can lead to unnecessary mistrust, hostility, and war, unless some of the variables discussed earlier are operating to restrain defection. . . .

The fourth world is doubly safe. The differentiation between offensive and defensive systems permits a way out of the security dilemma; the advantage of the defense disposes of the problems discussed in the previous paragraphs. There is no reason for a status-quo power to be tempted to procure offensive forces, and aggressors give notice of their intention by the posture they adopt. Indeed, if the advantage of the defense is great enough, there are no security problems. The loss of the ultimate form of the power to alter the status quo would allow greater scope for the exercise of nonmilitary means and probably would tend to freeze the distribution of values.

This world would have existed in the first decade of the 20th century if the decision makers had understood the available technology. In that case, the European powers would have followed different policies both in the long run and in the summer of 1914. Even Germany, facing powerful enemies on both sides, could have made herself secure by developing strong defenses. France could also have made her frontier almost impregnable. Furthermore, when crises arose, no one would have had incentives to strike first. There would have been no competitive mobilization races reducing the time available for negotiations.

1914 REVISITED

Scott D. Sagan

The origins of the First World War continue to be of great interest today because there are a number of striking similarities between the events of 1914 and contemporary fears about paths by which a nuclear war could begin. July 1914 was a brinksmanship crisis, resulting in a war that everyone was willing to risk but that no one truly wanted. During the crisis, the political leaderships' understanding of military operations and control over critical war preparations were often tenuous at best. In 1914, the perceived incentives to strike first, once war was considered likely, were great, and the rapidity and inflexibility of offensive war plans limited the time available to diplomats searching for an acceptable political solution to the crisis. In a world in which the possibility of massive nuclear retaliation has made the deliberate, premeditated initiation of nuclear war unlikely, there is widespread concern that a repetition of the Sarajevo Scenario may occur: an apparently insignificant incident sparking—through a dangerous mixture of miscalculations, inadvertent escalation, and loss of control over events—a tragic and unintended war.[1] Indeed, for a student of the July crisis, even specific phrases in the current nuclear debate can be haunting: what former Secretary of Defense Harold Brown meant to be a comforting metaphor, that the Soviet Union would never risk its society on "a cosmic throw of the dice," is less reassuring to those who recall German Chancellor Theobald von Bethmann-Hollweg's statement, "If the iron dice are now to be rolled, may God help us," made just hours before Germany declared war against Russia on August 1, 1914.[2]

Prior to 1914, the general staffs of each of the European great powers had designed elaborate and inflexible offensive war plans, which were implemented in a series of mobilizations and counter mobilizations at the end of the July crisis. In August, all the continental powers took the offensive: the Germans attacked across Belgium and Luxembourg into France; the French army launched a massive assault against German

Scott D. Sagan, "1914 Revisited: Allies, Offense, and Instability," *International Security,* Vol. 11, No. 2 (fall 1986) pp. 151–175. Copyright © 1986 by the President and Fellows of Harvard College and of the Massachusetts Institute of Technology.

[1] Recent discussions of nuclear strategy that utilize the 1914 analogy include Graham T. Allison, Albert Carnesale, and Joseph S. Nye, Jr., eds., *Hawks, Doves, and Owls* (New York: Norton, 1985), especially pp. 210–217; Paul J. Bracken, *The Command and Control of Nuclear Forces* (New Haven: Yale University Press, 1983), pp. 222–223, 239–240; and Miles Kahler, "Rumors of War: The 1914 Analogy," *Foreign Affairs,* Vol. 58, No. 2 (Winter 1979–80).

[2] Harold Brown, *Department of Defense Annual Report for Fiscal Year 1979* (Washington, D.C.: U.S. Government Printing Office, 1978), p. 63; and Karl Kautsky, ed., *Outbreak of the World War: German Documents* (New York: Oxford University Press, 1924), No. 553, p. 441. (Hereinafter, *German Documents.*)

positions in Alsace-Lorraine; and the Russian army, although not yet fully mobilized, immediately began simultaneous offenses against Germany and Austria-Hungary. In retrospect, the war plans of the great powers had disastrous political and military consequences. The negative political consequences were seen at the cabinet meetings during the July crisis, for the pressures to begin mobilization and launch offensives promptly, according to the military timetables, contributed greatly to the dynamic of escalation and the political leaderships' loss of freedom of action. In Berlin, for example, as Bethmann-Hollweg frankly admitted to the Prussian Ministry of State, once the Russians began to mobilize, "control had been lost and the stone had started rolling."[3] The military consequences were seen on the battlefield. Each of the major offensive campaigns was checked or repulsed with enormous costs: some 900,000 men were missing, taken prisoner, wounded, or dead by the end of 1914.[4]

Historians and political scientists have long sought to understand why the great powers all had offensive military doctrines when the military technology of 1914— barbed wire, machine guns, and railroads—appears to have favored the defense. The popular explanation is that European soldiers and statesmen blithely ignored the demonstrations of defensive firepower in the American Civil War and the Russo-Japanese War and simply believed that the next European war would be like the last (an offensive victory as in the Franco-Prussian war), but that has never been satisfactory. For, in fact, numerous European military observers were in the United States from 1861–65 and in Manchuria during the 1904–5 conflict. Observer reports were widely distributed, the German, French, and British armies sponsored multivolume official histories of the Russo-Japanese War, and throughout the period prior to 1914 prolonged and heated debates raged in European military journals about the relative effectiveness of offensive and defensive tactics and strategies.[5]

Recent scholarship has suggested a new explanation which, using organization theory, emphasizes the degree to which the organizational interests of the professional military are advanced by offensive military doctrines, regardless of whether offensives are recommended by perceived national interests or prevailing technology.[6] Jack Snyder and Stephen Van Evera have found, in the 1914 case, an extreme example of this

---

[3]*German Documents,* No. 456, p. 382.

[4]The estimate is from Michael Howard, "Men Against Fire: The Doctrine of the Offensive in 1914," in Peter Paret, ed., *The Makers of Modern Strategy from Machiavelli to the Nuclear Age* (Princeton: Princeton University Press, 1986), p. 510.

[5]These writings are reviewed in ibid.; and Michael Howard, "Men Against Fire: Expectations of War in 1914," in Steven E. Miller, ed., *Military Strategy and the Origins of the First World War: An International Security Reader* (Princeton: Princeton University Press, 1985), pp. 41–57. Also see T.H.E. Travers, "The Offensive and the Problem of Innovation in British Military Thought 1870–1915," *Journal of Contemporary History,* Vol. 13 (1978), pp. 531–553; Travers, "Technology, Tactics, and Morale: Jean de Bloch, The Boer War, and British Military Theory, 1900–1914," *Journal of Modern History,* Vol. 51, No. 2 (June 1979), pp. 264–286; and Jay Luvaas, *The Military Legacy of the Civil War: The European Inheritance* (Chicago: University of Chicago Press, 1959).

[6]See Barry R. Posen, *The Sources of Military Doctrine: France, Britain and Germany Between the World Wars* (Ithaca: Cornell University Press, 1984); and Stephen Van Evera, "Causes of War" (Ph.D. dissertation, University of California, Berkeley, 1984), especially chapter 7.

phenomenon: the "cult of the offensive."[7] This new explanation for the origins of the First World War is becoming widely accepted, and no one has challenged its validity.[8]

This essay reviews the organizational theory arguments and their "cult of the offensive" application to the events of 1914. It concludes that this approach seriously misrepresents the *causes* of the offensive doctrines of 1914 and, therefore, the underlying causes of the war. By focusing on the organizational interests of the professional military, the "cult of the offensive" theory has overlooked the more fundamental causes of the World War I offensive doctrines: the political objective and alliance commitments of the great powers.

This essay also argues that the "cult of the offensive" theory misrepresents the *consequences* of the 1914 offensive military doctrines. Although offensive military doctrines were necessary, they were not sufficient to cause the strategic instability witnessed in the July crisis; the critical preemptive incentives and pressures to move quickly felt by the German General Staff would not have been so strong without specific military vulnerabilities of the Entente powers and Belgium. In addition, even given the German offensive doctrine and war plans, it appears likely that Berlin would have been deterred in 1914 if the British government had issued a clear and credible threat to intervene in a continental war early in the July crisis. Furthermore, while the "cult of the offensive" theory correctly identifies the problem of offensive instability during the July crisis, it ignores the critical strategic dangers that would have resulted if European statesmen had adopted purely defensive strategies in 1914. These conclusions are, finally, of more than historical interest, for they suggest that the explicit lessons that the "cult of the offensive" theorists offer for contemporary American deterrent strategy are quite misleading.

OFFENSES, MILITARY BIASES, AND THE SECURITY DILEMMA

International relations theory posits the existence of a common security dilemma between sovereign states and has stressed the pernicious impact of offensive military forces and doctrines in exacerbating the problem.[9] The security dilemma exists when

---

[7]Jack Snyder, "Civil-Military Relations and the Cult of the Offensive, 1914 and 1984" and Stephen Van Evera, "The Cult of the Offensive and the Origins of the First World War," both in Miller, *Military Strategy and the Origins of the First World War.* Also see Snyder, *The Ideology of the Offensive: Military Decision Making and the Disasters of 1914* (Ithaca: Cornell University Press, 1984); and Van Evera, "Why Cooperation Failed in 1914," *World Politics,* Vol. 38, No. 1 (October 1985), pp. 97–98.

[8]See Allison et al., *Hawks, Doves, and Owls,* p. 212; Robert Axelrod and Robert O. Keohane, "Achieving Cooperation under Anarchy: Strategies and Institutions," *World Politics,* Vol. 38, No. 1 (October 1985), pp. 230–231; Richard Ned Lebow, "The Soviet Offensive in Europe: The Schlieffen Plan Revisited?," *International Security,* Vol. 9, No. 4 (Spring 1985), pp. 52–53, 68–69; Jack S. Levy, "Organizational Routines and the Causes of War," *International Studies Quarterly,* Vol. 30, No. 2 (June 1986); and Steven E. Miller, "Introduction: The Great War and the Nuclear Age," in Miller, *Military Strategy and the Origins of the First World War,* p. 3.

[9]Robert Jervis, "Cooperation Under the Security Dilemma," *World Politics,* Vol. 30, No. 2 (January 1978), pp. 167–214. Also see George H. Quester, *Offense and Defense in the International System* (New York: John Wiley and Sons, 1977); Van Evera, "Causes of War," chapter 3; and Jack S. Levy, "The Offensive/Defensive Balance of Military Technology: A Theoretical and Historical Analysis," *International Studies Quarterly,* Vol. 28 (1984), pp. 219–238.

actions taken by one state solely for the purposes of increasing its own security simultaneously threaten another state, decreasing its security. This dilemma can be vicious "even in the extreme case in which all states would like to freeze the status quo," when two conditions exist: first, when defensive weapons and strategies cannot be distinguished from offensive ones and, second, when offensive military operations are considered easier than defensive operations.[10] Such conditions are said to produce a number of dangers. When offense is easier, or when one cannot differentiate between offenses and defenses, "unnecessary" arms races are made more likely. Under such conditions, the incentives to launch preventive wars are increased whenever the balance of power is shifting in favor of an adversary. Likewise, when war is considered likely, preemptive incentives are increased to the degree that striking the first offensive blow is considered advantageous compared to waiting to be attacked.

Earlier work on the subject focused largely on the effect of military technology on the offensive/defensive balance, and many arms control negotiations have sought to promote "stability" by identifying and limiting offensive weapons and promoting defensive ones.[11] This approach's assumption, that status quo powers will pursue defensive, "stabilizing" military capabilities if possible, is challenged by the new "cult of the offensive" literature which emphasizes that military organizations display a strong preference for offensive forces and doctrines, even if the predominant military technology favors defense.

Five related and reinforcing explanations are offered for the military's bias in favor of the offense. First, offensive doctrines enhance the power and size of military organizations.[12] Offenses are usually technologically more complex and quantitatively more demanding than defenses. They often require larger forces, longer range weapons, and more extensive logistic capabilities. Since military organizations, like other organizations, seek to enhance their own size and wealth, as a rule, they will prefer offenses. Second, offensive doctrines tend to promote military autonomy. As Jack Snyder explains, "The operational autonomy of the military is most likely to be allowed when the operational goal is to disarm the adversary quickly and decisively by offensive means."[13] Not only are defensive operations, because they tend to be less complex, easier for civilian leaders to understand, but defenses also can lead to prolonged conflict on one's own soil, increasing the likelihood of civilian interference. In addition, offensive doctrines may require professional armies, rather than more "civilianized" conscripted armies. Third, offenses enhance the prestige and self-image of military officers. Defensive operations are often seen as passive, less challenging, and less glorious. As Barry Posen puts it, offenses can

---

[10]Jervis, "Cooperation Under the Security Dilemma," pp. 167, 186–187.

[11]Ibid., pp. 186–214. For related works see Quester, *Offense and Defense in the International System;* Marion W. Boggs, *Attempts to Define and Limit "Aggressive" Armament in Diplomacy and Strategy* (Columbia, Mo.: University of Missouri, 1941); and B.H. Liddell Hart, "Aggression and the Problem of Weapons," *The English Review,* July 1932, pp. 71–78.

[12]Posen, *Sources of Military Doctrine,* p. 49.

[13]Snyder, "Civil-Military Relations and the Cult of the Offensive," p. 121; see also Posen, *Sources of Military Doctrine,* pp. 49–50.

make soldiers "specialists in victory," while defenses merely turn them into "specialists in attrition."[14]

The fourth explanation offered for the military's offensive bias is that offenses structure military campaigns in favorable ways. Taking the initiative helps ensure that your standard scenario and operations plans, instead of the enemy's, dominate at least in the initial battles of a war.[15] This advantage of offensive operations has been repeated in statements of the "principle of the initiative" in military manuals at least since Jomini's maxim of 1807: The general who takes the initiative knows what he is going to do; he conceals his movements, surprises and crushes an extremity or weak point. The general who waits is beaten at one point before he learns of the attack.[16]

The fifth explanation emphasizes the effect that military officers' training and duties have on their beliefs about the need for decisive military operations that tend to be offensive in nature. Officers, it is argued, are necessarily preoccupied with the possibility of war; they tend to see the adversary as extremely hostile and war as a natural, indeed often an inevitable, part of international politics. Such beliefs lead them to favor preventive wars or preemptive strikes when necessary and decisive operations when possible. "Seeing war more likely than it really is," Snyder concludes, "[military professionals] increase its likelihood by adopting offensive plans and buying offensive forces."[17]

THE 1914 CULT OF THE OFFENSIVE

Jack Snyder and Stephen Van Evera have found, in the origins of the First World War, the most extreme example of what can go wrong if the endemic military bias in favor of offensive doctrines is allowed to determine a state's strategy. Why did all the continental powers immediately launch offensives at the outburst of war? Snyder argues, "The offensive strategies of 1914 were largely domestic in origin, rooted in bureaucratic, sociopolitical, and psychological causes."[18] In France, the offensive nature of Plan XVII is seen as the result of the professional military's use of offensive doctrine as a defense of its institutional interests. After the Dreyfus affair, political leaders sought to "republicanize" the French military, hoping to create an army based largely on reservists and capable of conducting only defensive operations. The French military countered this threat to its institutional "essence," Snyder explains, by adopting the *offensive à outrance* doctrine which required the discipline and élan that only a professional standing

---

[14]Posen, *Sources of Military Doctrine,* p. 49. A recent examination of the causes of the persistence of offensive tactics on the part of the Confederacy emphasizes the influence of Southern culture's romantic notions of soldierly honor. See Grady McWhiney and Perry D. Jamieson, *Attack and Die: Civil War Military Tactics and Southern Heritage* (Tuscaloosa, Ala.: University of Alabama Press, 1982).

[15]Posen, *Sources of Military Doctrine,* pp. 47–48. It should be noted, however, that this advantage need not be a military bias, as the civilian leadership as well as the military would favor it.

[16]Antoine-Henri Jomini, "L'art de la guerre," *Pallas: Eine Zeitschrift für Staats und Kreigs Kunst,* Vol. 1 (1808), pp. 32–40, as quoted in John I. Alger, *The Quest for Victory: The History of the Principles of War* (Westport, Conn.: Greenwood Press, 1982), p. 22.

[17]Snyder, "Civil-Miliary Relations and the Cult of the Offensive," p. 119.

[18]Ibid., p. 137.

army's long training and service together could provide.[19] The offensive strategy of the Schlieffen Plan, according to Snyder, was adopted in Germany because of the Prussian General Staff's bias in favor of decisive operations and because an offensive strategy promoted their power, prestige, and autonomy. In Russia, the ambitious war plans calling for offensive operations against both Germany and Austria-Hungary were adopted because the absence of a strong central political authority enabled each of the conflicting military factions, one favoring an offense against Germany and the other supporting an offense against Austria-Hungary, to pursue its own preferred campaign. Because a realistic assessment of the chances of success would have threatened their fundamental beliefs, Russian military leaders resorted to what Snyder calls "needful thinking," believing that both "necessary" offensives could succeed when objective assessment would have shown that they would fail.[20] The conclusion is clear:

> Strategic instability in 1914 was caused not by military technology, which favored the defender and provided no first-strike advantage, but by offensive war plans that defied technological constraints. The lesson here is that doctrines can be destabilizing even when weapons are not, since doctrine may be more responsive to the organizational needs of the military than to the implications of the prevailing weapon technology.[21]

While Snyder has focused on the causes of the "cult of the offensive," Van Evera's work concentrates on its consequences; his detailed analysis of the July crisis goes considerably further than earlier work on this subject in identifying precisely how the military plans of the European powers contributed to strategic instability in 1914.[22] He finds the "cult of the offensive" to be the "mainspring" driving the numerous mechanisms that led the great powers to war and illustrates his argument by imagining what 1914 would have looked like had military and civilian leaders not had such strong beliefs about the efficacy of offenses. The expansionist aims of Germany, the perceived incentives for preventive war and preemptive strikes, and the dynamics of rapid escalation in the crisis could have all been avoided, Van Evera argues, had European leaders "recognized the actual power of the defense":

> German expansionists then would have met stronger arguments that empire was needless and impossible, and Germany could have more easily let the Russian military buildup run

---

[19]Ibid., pp. 129–133; and Snyder, *Ideology of the Offensive,* chapters 2 and 3. For a different argument, stressing that offensive doctrine was adopted so that the morale of patriotic French recruits could compensate for superior German materiel strength, see Douglas Porch, *The March to the Marne: The French Army, 1871–1914* (Cambridge: Cambridge University Press, 1981), chapter 11.

[20]Snyder, "Civil-Military Relations and the Cult of the Offensive," pp. 125–129, 133–137; and Snyder, *Ideology of the Offensive,* chapters 4–7.

[21]Snyder, *Ideology of the Offensive,* pp. 10–11.

[22]Van Evera, "The Cult of the Offensive and the Origins of the First World War." Also see Levy, "Organizational Routines and the Causes of War." For earlier interpretations, see Herman Kahn, *On Thermonuclear War* (Princeton: Princeton University Press, 1960), pp. 357–375; and Thomas Schelling's discussion of "the dynamics of mutual alarm" in Schelling, *Arms and Influence* (New Haven: Yale University Press, 1966), pp. 221–244.

its course, knowing that German defenses could still withstand Russian attack. All European states would have been less tempted to mobilize first, and each could have tolerated more preparations by adversaries before mobilizing themselves, so the spiral of mobilization and counter-mobilization would have operated more slowly, if at all.[23]

Van Evera even concludes that the First World War might not have broken out at all if leaders had understood the strength of defenses: "If armies [had] mobilized, they might have rushed to defend their own trenches and fortifications, instead of crossing frontiers. . . ." Indeed, "In all likelihood, the Austro-Serbian conflict would have been a minor and soon-forgotten disturbance on the periphery of European politics."[24]

AN ALTERNATIVE EXPLANATION: STRATEGIC INTERESTS AND ALLIANCE COMMITMENTS

Snyder's work has identified a number of ways in which the organizational interests of the military can affect strategic doctrine, and Van Evera's writings have persuasively demonstrated the alarming consequences that specific aspects of the offensive war plans of 1914 had on the political leadership's ability to control events during the July crisis. But their "cult of the offensive" analysis greatly exaggerates the degree to which the offensive doctrines in 1914 were caused by military-motivated biases or misperceptions of the offense/defense balance. Moreover, by focusing exclusively on the problems of the 1914 offensive military doctrines, they have overlooked the negative consequences that would have resulted if the great powers had adopted purely defensive military doctrines.

Three related problems exist with the "cult of the offensive" theory explanation. First, the theory exaggerates the probability that critical offensive military operations would fail. This theory is perhaps the strongest in explaining the French military's *offensive à outrance* doctrine, which even Field Marshall Joffre admitted was influenced by "le culte de l'offensive."[25] But it was *not* this *French* offensive doctrine that produced the dynamic of rapid escalation during the July crisis. For the French, a decision to mobilize was *not* a decision to attack Germany, and the Paris government specifically ordered its army not to move within 10 kilometers of the German border upon general mobilization.[26] Instead, the most critical offensive war plan in 1914 was that of

---

[23]Van Evera, "The Cult of the Offensive and the Origins of the First World War," p. 105.

[24]Ibid. For a similar argument, that the European armies should have been "rushing to their own trenches rather than the enemy's territory" in 1914, see Jervis, "Cooperation Under the Security Dilemma," p. 191.

[25]As quoted by Van Evera, "The Cult of the Offensive and the Origins of the First World War," p. 61, fn. 14.

[26]See Luigi Albertini, *The Origins of the War of 1914* (London: Oxford University Press, 1957), Vol. 3, pp. 66–111.

Germany, for it was the German military's perceived need to mobilize quickly to imple-ment the Schlieffen Plan's preemptive attack on Liège and attack in the West before Russian mobilization was complete that caused the crisis to move beyond control.

With 20–20 hindsight, however, it is too easy to argue that the German offensive plan for conquest was doomed to fail. Thus, when Snyder writes of the *"vain attempt* to knock France out of the war" and complains that the German General Staff "could not accept that a future war *would inevitably take the form of an inglorious, unproductive stalemate,"* he assumes that the historical outcome, the defeat of the Schlieffen Plan, was the only one possible.[27] Similarly, when Van Evera writes, "Had statesmen under-stood that in reality the defense had the advantage, they also would have known that *the possession of the initiative could not be decisive"* or that "German expansionists then would have met stronger arguments that empire was *needless and impossible,"* he as-sumes that the outcome of the war was a forgone conclusion.[28]

In fact, the Schlieffen Plan came very close to succeeding and the Germans almost did win the short war they had expected to fight. The French, who call the decisive bat-tle outside Paris "the Miracle of the Marne," have a better sense of the probability of German victory than do those who assume that the German attack was bound to fail. It would be beyond the scope of this article to reexamine the long-standing debate among military analysts and historians on whether Moltke's timidity and poor judgment ruined what could have been a major German victory in September 1914. A number of major participants and historians have maintained that the German offense would have suc-ceeded if Moltke had moved more vigorously and had not weakened the strength of the attacking right wing by moving forces to defend Alsace-Lorraine; others have coun-tered that, even if the Germans had won an overwhelming victory at the Marne, the French would not have capitulated and a stalemate would still have developed. Defense-advocates have maintained that the Germans came close to an offensive vic-tory only because the French launched their offensive Plan XVII.[29] Others have stressed, however, that knowledge that the French would attack in Alsace-Lorraine was the underlying premise of the Schlieffen Plan. The subtlety of the German offense was that, as Liddell Hart put it, "it would operate like a revolving door—the harder the French pushed on one side, the more sharply would the other swing around and strike their back."[30]

The key point for this critique of "cult of the offensive" theory is not how this counterfactual debate is resolved, but rather that it exists at all. For it demonstrates that the theory's assumption, that only gross misperceptions of the offensive/defensive bal-ance can explain why offensive strategies were chosen in 1914, is questionable. In addi-tion, it should be remembered that Schlieffen was acutely aware of the danger of frontal

---

[27]Snyder, "Civil-Military Relations and the Cult of the Offensive," p. 128; and Snyder, *Ideology of the Offensive,* p. 17. Emphasis added.

[28]Van Evera, "The Cult of the Offensive and the Origins of the First World War," pp. 75, 105. Emphasis added.

[29]Snyder, *Ideology of the Offensive,* p. 9.

[30]B.H. Liddell Hart, "Foreward" to Gerhard Ritter, *The Schlieffen Plan: Critique of a Myth* (London: Oswald Wolff, 1958), p. 6; see also Turner, "The Significance of the Schlieffen Plan," p. 204.

attacks against fortified positions, which was precisely why the German plan emphasized an enveloping attack on the French flanks.[31] Thus, although the professional military's excessive faith in "the offensive spirit" is likely to have played a role in the fruitless British and French frontal assaults along the Western Front during the war,[32] the "cult" explanation is far less persuasive in the case of the offensive Schlieffen Plan, which is what caused the dynamic of escalation in the July crisis.

The second major problem with the "cult of the offensive" explanation is that it ignores the fundamental issue of the military balances. After all, what do the terms used in this literature, "offense-dominance" and "defense-dominance," really mean? Robert Jervis's definition, that offense has the advantage when "it is easier to destroy the other's army and take its territory than it is to defend one's own" is problematic, because it has been generally recognized since Clausewitz that defense is almost always "easier" in land warfare because of advantages of cover and the capability to choose and prepare terrain and fortify positions.[33] This is why military analysts usually think in terms of the force ratios—the required superiority of the offensive forces ($2:1$, $3:1$, etc.) in order to achieve victory—rather than in all-or-nothing terms such as "offense-dominance" or "defense-dominance."

By focusing on the effects of military technology on the "offense/defense balance," the "cult of the offensive" theory fails to consider adequately the quantity or quality of military forces opposed to one another in a particular territorial campaign. How "defense-dominant" was the world of 1914? Certainly the range and rate of fire of small-caliber magazine rifles, machine guns, and field artillery strongly favored the defensive. And yet, even if one assumes that the historical outcome of 1914–1918 was the likely one, it is doubtful that defenses were so dominant or advantageous as to make all states simultaneously secure if they had maintained defensive military doctrines.

The point is best made by imagining what would have happened if individual armies had rejected offensive doctrines and had, as Stephen Van Evera and Robert Jervis recommend, "rushed to their trenches" instead of others' territory. Serbia did, after all, adopt what was essentially a defensive strategy and was eventually conquered by the overwhelming forces of the Central Powers.[34] What if the French had no offensive plans but had "rushed to their trenches," staying completely on the defensive in 1914? The outcome of the war in the East suggests that the Central Powers could have defeated the Russians even more soundly if there had been no Western Front. If the

---

[31]Ritter, *The Schlieffen Plan,* pp. 50–51.

[32]Michael Howard argues, however, that "the worst losses were those due not to faulty doctrine but to inefficiency, inexperience, and the sheer organizational problems of combining fire and movement on the requisite scale." Howard, "Men Against Fire: The Doctrine of the Offensive in 1914," p. 526.

[33]Jervis, "Cooperation Under the Security Dilemma," p. 187. For an excellent review of literature on the offense-defense balance, see Levy, "The Offensive/Defensive Balance of Military Technology." Also see Jack Snyder, "Perceptions of the Security Dilemma in 1914," in Robert Jervis, Richard Ned Lebow, and Janice Gross Stein (with contributions from Patrick M. Morgan and Jack L. Snyder), *Psychology and Deterrence* (Baltimore: Johns Hopkins University Press, 1985), pp. 157–160.

[34]For a brief review of the campaigns in Serbia, see Trevor N. Dupuy and Molly R. Mayo, *Campaigns in Southern Europe* (New York: Franklin Watts, 1967), pp. 9–20, 38–46.

Germans, after defeating the Russians, had turned and quickly attacked the French, would the technology of 1914 have proven the "dominance" of the defense? One can, of course, only speculate on such a question, but the near victory of the German offensive in 1918 against the French, a fully mobilized and deployed British army, and the arriving Americans suggests that a massive German offensive against the French alone (or the French and the small British Expeditionary Force) would have stood a strong chance of success.

This leads to the third problem. The "cult of the offensive" argument, by focusing primarily upon narrow issues of military planning, ignores the critical role of the states' political objectives in determining their military doctrines. Here I am not referring to the expansionist war aims of Germany and the other great powers, for, as Jack Snyder correctly notes, the desire to annex territory had its most important influence on decision-making *after* the war began, and the doctrinal decisions of the military officers who prepared the prewar offensive war plans in France, Germany, and Russia were not strongly influenced by such territorial ambitions.[35] Yet, the "cult of the offensive" argument overlooks a key point: offensive military doctrines are needed not only by states with expansionist war aims, but also by states that have a strong interest in protecting an exposed ally. Unless sufficient capability to protect an ally at the point of attack exists, "protector" powers require offensive strategies even if their goals are defensive in nature. This consideration is often recognized with respect to extended deterrence today; it also, however, lay at the heart of the offensive doctrines of 1914.

Thus, the Russians needed an offensive capability against Austria-Hungary, in order to be able to prevent the Austrians from attacking Serbia with overwhelming offensive superiority. The French required offensive capabilities against Germany in order to support Russia. Germany needed an offense to protect Austria-Hungary if Russia launched an attack against Germany's ally. Particular conditions of the military balance in 1914—the slowness of the Russian mobilization and what General von Falkenhayn called "the almost unlimited power of the Russians to evade a final decision by arms"[36] due to its vast territory—resulted in the German plan to attempt to knock France out of the war first. This further complicated the issue, for the German offensive plans against France resulted in both a Russian need for an offensive against Germany and even Austrian plans to attack Russia as a "relief offensive" to give Moltke more time to defeat the French.

This need for offensive capabilities to provide support for allies can be seen as the root cause of the offensive war plans of the great powers. This argument does not mean that motivated biases, due to organizational or psychological factors, had no influence whatsoever on military doctrine prior to 1914. It does suggest that the states' strategic

---

[35] Snyder, *Ideology of the Offensive,* pp. 19–20. Snyder does make an exception for Russia: the Russian offensive plans against Austria-Hungary were influenced by ambitions in the Balkans as well as military operational considerations. It should also be noted that Austria-Hungary, because of its punitive policy toward Serbia, required an offensive doctrine.

[36] General Erich von Falkenhayn, *The German General Staff and Its Decisions, 1914–1916* (Freeport, N.Y.: Books for Libraries Press, 1971 reprint), p. 16.

interests were dominant. For example, minor powers, such as Belgium and Serbia, may have had military cults of the offensive, but they did *not* have offensive military doctrines or war plans when war broke out in 1914.[37] In contrast, the great powers required offensive military doctrines because of their alliance commitments. This connection between alliance commitments and offensive doctrine was well understood in the years preceding the First World War. The Franco-Russian military convention, written in 1892, specified:

> If France is attacked by Germany or by Italy with Germany's support, Russia will bring all her available forces to bear against Germany. If Russia is attacked by Germany or by Austria with Germany's support, France will bring all her available forces to bear against Germany. . . . These troops will proceed to launch a vigorous and determined offensive, so that Germany will be forced to give battle in the East and West simultaneously.[38]

The spectre of Germany being able to defeat the French or the Russians in a piecemeal fashion haunted the allies before 1914: Joffre states that he replaced the more defensive-oriented Plan XVI with the offensive Plan XVII when he took office in part because the former failed to take into account "an eventuality which was altogether likely, namely, that the Germans might return to the old Von Moltke plan of an immediate offensive directed against the Russians." Foreign Minister Poincaré promised the Russians in 1912 that France would launch an immediate offensive against Germany if war broke out and demanded that the Russians give similar assurances in writing. Furthermore, the French and Russian General Staffs specifically rejected the possibility of war being "conducted defensively" and confirmed the need for immediate offenses in their joint meetings in 1911, 1912, and 1913.[39]

Similarly, the Russian initial offensive against the Germans in 1914 demonstrates "wishful thinking" due to faith in the offensive less than the critical need to stop Germany from amassing its forces against France alone. According to Joffre, in 1912 Grand Duke Nicholas "fully understood the necessity of the Russian Army taking the offensive rapidly, whatever the risks such an attitude might seem to involve; for it was essential to bring some relief to our front at any price. . . ."[40] Thus, in the summer of

---

[37]As Van Evera notes, some Belgian officers proposed that Belgium attack Germany at the outbreak of war. Van Evera, "The Cult of the Offensive and the Origins of the First world War," p. 61; and Van Evera, "Why Cooperation Failed in 1914," p. 84. It is important to note, however, that the "temerity of such an operation" was immediately pointed out by the Belgian Chief of Staff, and Belgium pursued a defensive strategy despite such "cult of the offensive" influences. The best discussion is Albertini, *The Origins of the War of 1914*, vol. 3, pp. 455–463, quoting Antonin Selliers de Moranville, *Contribution à l'histoire de la guerre mondiale 1914–19* (Paris, 1933), pp. 163–164.

[38]George Michon, *The Franco-Russian Alliance* (New York: Macmillan, 1929), p. 54.

[39]*The Personal Memoirs of Joffre* (New York: Harper and Brothers, 1932), Vol. 1, p. 20; Jan Karl Tannenbaum, "French Estimates of Germany's Operational War Plans," in Ernest R. May, ed., *Knowing One's Enemies: Intelligence Assessment Before the Two World Wars* (Princeton: Princeton University Press, 1984), pp. 167–168; Michon, *The Franco-Russian Alliance*, p. 54; and L.C.F. Turner, "The Russian Mobilization in 1914," in Paul M. Kennedy, ed., *The War Plans of the Great Powers, 1880–1914* (Boston: Allen & Unwin, 1979), pp. 256–258.

[40]*The Personal Memoirs of Joffre*, Vol. 1, p. 59.

1914 Russian Foreign Minister Sazonov and the military commanders of the East Prussian front believed that a hasty offensive against Germany might indeed fail, but that, as Sazonov reportedly argued, "we have no right to leave our Ally in danger, and it is our duty to attack at once, notwithstanding the indubitable risk of the operation as planned."[41] The Chief of Staff of the Russian field army also stressed this point, telling his troops to attack Germany "by virtue of the same inter-allied obligations" that were demonstrated by the French offensive.[42]

The logic of the strategic situation was similarly understood in Germany. Offenses were required to support Austria-Hungary, albeit an offensive against France first, to be followed by the combined attack on Russia. When confronted with Austrian complaints that German offense in the West would leave them unprotected, Schlieffen responded that "the fate of Austria will be decided not on the Bug but on the Seine," a line that Moltke repeated to Conrad in February 1913.[43] The need for offensive action to protect Germany's ally was also the central argument of Moltke's urgent memorandum to Bethmann-Hollweg on July 29, 1914, written after Moltke learned that Russia had instituted only *partial* mobilization against Austria-Hungary:

> If Germany is not to be false to her word and permit her ally to suffer annihilation at the hands of Russian superiority, she, too, must mobilize. And that would bring about the mobilization of the rest of Russia's military districts as a result.[44]

The German threat to Russia—that it would soon be forced to mobilize, which meant war, which meant the Schlieffen Plan's offensive, if Russia did not stop the *partial* mobilization against Austria-Hungary—underscores the importance of the alliance commitment in Berlin's calculations.[45] Moreover, it was the long-standing belief of the Russian military, which these threats reinforced in 1914, that the Germans would not passively tolerate Russian preparations for war against Austria-Hungary, which had led them to plan for and then in 1914 to insist upon, not a partial mobilization on the Austrian front, but rather a full mobilization against both Central Powers.[46] This decision was critical, for once the full mobilization of the Russian army began, Bethmann-Hollweg called off the attempt to avert war by having Austro-Hungarian forces "Halt in

---

[41]As quoted in Nicolas N. Golovine, *The Russian Army in the World War* (New Haven: Yale University Press, 1931), p. 213.

[42]Norman Stone, *The Eastern Front, 1914–1917* (New York: Scribner, 1975), p. 48.

[43]See Stone, "Moltke and Conrad: Relations between the Austro-Hungarian and German General Staffs, 1909–1914," pp. 224, 232.

[44]The Grand General Staff to the Imperial Chancellor, July 29, 1914, *German Documents,* No. 349, p. 307.

[45]See ibid., Nos. 342, 343, 401, and 490. It should be added, however, that both Bethmann-Hollweg and Jagow originally misled the Russians on this issue. See ibid., No. 219; and Albertini, *The Origins of the War of 1914,* Vol. 2, pp. 481–485 and Vol. 3, pp. 220–221.

[46]As General Kokovtzov put it, arguing against *partial* mobilization in 1912: "no matter what we chose to call the projected measures, a mobilization remained a mobilization, to be countered by our adversaries with actual war." Quoted in Turner, "The Russian Mobilization in 1914," p. 255. For detailed examinations of the interaction of mobilization plans, see Van Evera, "The Cult of the Offensive and the Origins of the First World War," pp. 85–94; and Ulrich Trumpener, "War Premeditated? German Intelligence Operations in July 1914." *Central European History,* Vol. 9, No. 1 (March 1976).

Belgrade." Thus, the alliance system—or more properly, the strategic interests the great powers had in maintaining their alliance partners—led not only to the offensive doctrines of 1914 but even to one of the specific conditions that contributed to the dynamic of rapid mobilization and counter-mobilization that constrained last minute efforts to prevent the outbreak of war.

The failure of the "cult of the offensive" theory to examine the influence of alliances on military doctrines is significant. While the theory has done a service by highlighting a number of the risks and instabilities that can result from offensive doctrines, it has ignored the risks and instabilities that result from purely defensive military strategies. For states with a security interest in preserving an exposed ally, offensive forces and strategies are necessary. Defensive military doctrines may not produce the same degree of preventive war or preemptive war incentives, but they can undercut extended deterrence by denying a government sufficient capability to protect its allies. As France discovered in 1938 and 1939, when the lack of offensive capabilities against Germany enabled Hitler to conquer France's East European allies in a piecemeal manner, a purely defensive military doctrine can also prove strategically disastrous.

THE OFFENSIVE/ DEFENSIVE BALANCE OF MILITARY TECHNOLOGY

Jack S. Levy

While many of the hypotheses regarding the consequences of the offensive/defensive balance are inherently plausible, there are critical analytical problems which must be resolved before they can be accepted as meaningful or valid. These problems have to do with the theoretical logic of the hypotheses, the definition of the offensive/defensive balance, and the empirical validity of the hypotheses.

The hypothesis that the likelihood of war is increased when the military technology favors the offense is theoretically plausible only on the basis of the rather strong assumption that decision makers correctly perceive the offensive/defensive balance. However, it is perceptions of one's psychological environment that determine decisions, not the 'objective' operational environment (Sprout and Sprout, 1965). The assumption of accurate perceptions is therefore open to question. The inherent difficulty of determining the offensive/defensive balance and the alleged tendency of the military to prepare for the last war rather than the next one may result in some profound misperceptions. It is widely agreed, for example, that in 1914 military technology favored the defense (Hart, 1932:75; Fuller, 1961: ch. 8–9; Montgomery, 1983:472) but that most decision makers perceived that it favored the offense. It was not the offensive/defensive balance that intensified worst-case analysis and increased the incentives for preemption, but decision makers' perceptions of that balance. If the offensive/defensive balance is not defined in terms of the perceptions of decision makers (and in most conceptualizations it is not so defined), then the hypothesis is technically misspecified. Hypotheses regarding the consequences of war, on the other hand, are properly defined in terms of the 'objective' balance.

The second problem relates to the definition of the offensive/defensive balance. What does it mean to say that the offense is superior to the defense, or *vice versa?* This will be treated at length in the following section, but one point should be made here. An hypothesis regarding the offensive/defensive balance has no explanatory power unless that concept can be nominally and operationally defined independently of its hypothesized effects. For example, Wright (1965:796–97) states that

> . . . it is difficult to judge the relative power of the offensive and defensive except by a historical audit to determine whether on the whole, in a given state of military technology, military violence had or had not proved a useful instrument of political change. . . . During

"The Offensive/Defensive Balance of Military Technology: A Theoretical and Historical Analysis," by Jack S. Levy from *International Studies Quarterly,* Vol. 28, No. 2, June 1984. Copyright © 1984 by International Studies Association. Reprinted by permission of Blackwell Publishers.

periods when dissatisfied powers have, on the whole, gained their aims by a resort to arms, it may be assumed, on the level of grand strategy, that the power of the offensive has been greater. During the periods when they have not been able to do so, it may be assumed that the power of the grand strategic defensive has been greater.

It would be tautological to use this conception of the offensive/defensive balance to predict to the military success of the aggressor, though it would be legitimate to predict to the frequency of war. Similarly, it is meaningless to hypothesize that offensive superiority increases the incentive to strike first if the offensive/defensive balance is defined by the incentive to strike first. The separation of hypothesis construction from concept definition and the absence of rigorous definition has increased the dangers of tautological propositions.

The failure to subject these hypotheses to systematic empirical testing is another major problem. Most attempts to identify the offensive/defensive advantage in various historical eras are not guided by an explicit definition of the concept, and rarely is there a demonstration that a given balance had an effect on the frequency of wars occurring or on the decisions for a particular war. The apparent *a priori* plausibility of a particular hypothesis may derive more from its tautological construction than from its correspondence with reality. In the absence of a more thorough analytic treatment and a more systematic empirical analysis the validity of any of these hypotheses cannot be accepted.

DEFINITIONS OF THE OFFENSIVE/ DEFENSIVE BALANCE

Use of the concept of offensive/defensive balance to refer to a variety of different things has led to a great deal of confusion. Theoretical propositions which are meaningful or interesting for one use of the term may not be very meaningful for another, and for this reason the various usages of the concept must be identified and examined.

Concern here is with the offensive/defensive distinction with respect to military technology and perhaps tactics but not with respect to policy. The question of whether national policy is offensive (aggressive) or defensive is not unimportant, but is analytically distinct and not directly relevant to the hypotheses surveyed earlier. These propositions all suggest that there is something about military technology itself that affects the likelihood or nature of war, and that what is important is whether technology gives an advantage to the offense or defense. This relative advantage may be one of several variables affecting the likelihood of war by affecting policy, but itself is analytically distinct from policy.

The offensive/defensive balance of military technology has been defined primarily in terms of the ease of territorial conquest, the characteristics of armaments, the resources needed by the offense in order to overcome the defense, and the incentive to strike first.

Territorial Conquest

The most common use of the concept of the offensive/defensive balance is based on territorial conquest and the defeat of enemy forces. Quester (1977:15) states that 'the territorial fixation then logically establishes our distinction between offense and defense.' Jervis (1978:187) argues that an offensive advantage means that 'it is easier to destroy the other's army and take its territory than it is to defend one's own.' 'The essence of defense,' on the other hand, 'is keeping the other side out of your territory. A purely defensive weapon is one that can do this without being able to penetrate the enemy's land' (1978:203). A defensive advantage means that 'it is easier to protect and hold than it is to move forward, destroy, and take' (Jervis, 1978:187). Wright (1965:793) includes these notions of defeat of enemy forces and territorial seizure in his rather complex definition:

> On a tactical level the offensive or defensive quality of a unit may be estimated by considering its utility in an attack upon an enemy unit like itself or in an attack upon some other concrete enemy objective, such as territory, commerce, or morale.

A primary purpose of protecting territory, of course, is the protection of people and property. What is perhaps implicit in the above definitions is made explicit by Tarr (1983): 'Defense refers to techniques and action, both active and passive, to repel attack, to protect people and property, to hold territory, and to minimize damage by the attacker.' This linkage of territorial conquest to population defense creates a problem, however. While territorial defense was sufficient for the protection of people and property in the pre-nuclear era (or at least in the era before strategic bombardment), that is no longer true. As Schelling (1966:ch. 1) and others have noted, the uniqueness of the nuclear age lies in the fact that the defeat of the adversary's military forces and territorial penetration are no longer necessary for the destruction of his population centers. The destruction of population and the coercive power that it makes possible are no longer contingent upon military victory. For this reason the protection of territory (from invasion) is analytically distinct from the protection of population. The inclusion of both in a definition of the offensive/defensive distinction only creates confusion (unless the use of that concept is explicitly restricted to the pre-nuclear era), for the hypothesized effects of an 'offensive' advantage are precisely the opposite for the two concepts. The likelihood of war presumably increases as territorial conquest becomes easier, because the probability of victory increases while its expected costs decrease. But the ability to destroy enemy population and industrial centers contributes to deterrence in the nuclear age, and therefore it decreases the likelihood of war (or at least nuclear war).

It is because of the distinction between deterrence and defense (Snyder, 1961:14–16) that the meaning of the offensive/defensive balance may differ in the nuclear and pre-nuclear eras. Whereas in the pre-nuclear era both deterrence and defense were based on the capacity to defeat the armed forces of the enemy, that is only true for defense in the nuclear age, for deterrence is ultimately based on countervalue punishment. The use of military force for the purpose of defeating enemy armed forces is analytically distinct from the use of force for coercion (Schelling, 1966:ch. 2). Consequently, traditional hypotheses (Wright and others) regarding the effects of the offensive/defensive balance of military technology are not necessarily applicable for nuclear powers at the strategic level. Neither the concepts nor the hypotheses are interchangeable.

Now let us return to the territorial conception of the offensive/defensive balance. Our earlier discussion leads to the question of what, besides the numbers of troops or weapons, contributes to the defeat of enemy forces and conquest of territory. One answer is provided at the tactical level, based on movement towards the armed forces, possessions, or territory of the enemy. A condition of relative passivity and immobility in waiting for the enemy to attack defines the strategic and tactical defensive (Wright, 1965:807). Clausewitz (as quoted in Boggs, 1941:68) states:

> What is defense in conception? The warding off a blow. What is then its characteristic sign? The state of expectancy (or of waiting for this blow) . . . by this sign alone can the defensive be distinguished from the offensive in war. . . .

Clausewitz also writes: 'In tactics every combat, great or small, is defensive if we leave the initiative to the enemy, and wait for his appearance on our front' (as quoted in Boggs, 1941:68).

Both offensive and defensive modes of war on the tactical level are necessary, of course, for the achievement of either offensive or defensive objectives. The pursuit of any offensive goal requires a supporting defense, and the defense alone can never bring victory but only stalemate. Mahan refers to 'the fundamental principle of naval war, that defense is insured only by offence' (Boggs, 1941:70). Clausewitz writes that an absolute defense is an 'absurdity' which 'completely contradicts the idea of war' (Boggs, 1941:71). At some point it is necessary to seize the tactical offensive in order to avoid defeat. Thus the familiar maxim: the best defense is a good offense. It is necessary, however, to distinguish between the strategic and tactical levels. A general fighting offensively in strategic terms needs only to invade and then hold territory to enable him to adopt the tactical defensive (Strachan, 1983). It may be strategically advantageous to maneuver the enemy into a position in which he is forced to take the tactical offensive under unfavorable conditions. As the elder Moltke stated in 1865, 'our strategy must be offensive, our tactics defensive' (Dupuy, 1980:200). In addition, military tactics may be offensive in one theater and defensive in another. The Schlieffen Plan, for example, required a holding action against Russia in the east in order to move against France in the west. Nevertheless, with certain types of weapons systems more movement and tactical mobility is possible than with others. It is difficult to measure movement historically while controlling for non-technological factors, however. This leads us to the question of whether the offensive/defensive balance can be defined by the characteristics of weapons systems themselves.

The Characteristics of Armaments

While nearly all weapons can be used for either the strategic or tactical offensive or the strategic or tactical defensive, the question is whether there are some weapons systems which contribute disproportionately more to one than to the other. As stated by the Naval Commission of the League of Nations Conference for the Reduction and Limitation of Armaments (1932–1936) (Boggs, 1941:82):

> Supposing one state either a) adopts a policy of armed aggression or b) undertakes offensive operations against another state, what are the weapons which, by reason of their specific character, and without prejudice to their defensive purposes, are most likely to enable that policy or those operations to be brought rapidly to a successful conclusion?

Hart (1932:73) argues that certain weapons 'alone make it possible under modern conditions to make a decisive offensive against a neighboring country.' What are the characteristics of such weapons?

Both Fuller and Hart identify mobility, striking power, and protection as the essential characteristics of an offensive weapon (Wright, 1965:808). Striking power (the impact of the blow) is not alone sufficient. A mobile gun contributes more to the tactical offensive than an immobile one, and its penetrating power is further enhanced if it is protected. But protection is even more important for the defense. Mobility and protection are inversely related, for it is easier to protect immobile weapons and wait passively for the enemy to attack. The offensive value of the medieval knight ultimately was negated by the heavy armor which protected him but restricted his mobility. Thus Dupuy and Eliot (1937:103) give particular emphasis to the offensive advantages of mobility and striking power, noting that they too may be in conflict. Boggs (1941:84–85) argues that 'the defense disposes especially of striking power and protection, to a lesser degree of mobility, while the offense possesses mobility and striking power, and protection to a lesser degree.' He concludes that mobility is the central characteristic of an offensive weapon and argues that 'armament which greatly facilitates the forward movement of the attacker might be said tentatively to possess relatively greater offensive power than weapons which contribute primarily to the stability of the defender' (Boggs, 1941:85). Our later survey of attempts by military historians to identify the offensive/defensive balance in various historical eras will show that tactical mobility is the primary criterion used to identify an advantage to the offense.

In terms of the characteristics of armaments, then, tactical mobility and movement toward enemy forces and territory are the primary determinants of the offense, at least in land warfare; protection and holding power contribute more to the defense. Other weapon characteristics such as striking power, rapidity of fire, and the range of a weapons system do not contribute disproportionately to either the offense or the defense. Much more work needs to be done here, however, because of the lack of precision of some of these concepts.

The classification of weapons systems by their contribution to mobility and tactical movement toward enemy forces and territory is much less useful for naval warfare. This was evident from the proceedings of the League of Nations Conference for the Reduction and Limitation of Armaments, where the problems and disagreements confronting the Naval Commission were even more serious than those confronting the Land Commission and where technical arguments were even more likely to follow the flag (Boggs, 1941:50–60). The United States, among others, declared that the qualitative distinction could not be applied to navies. Hart, a proponent of the qualitative principle in general, restricted it to the materials of land warfare (Boggs, 1941:50, 81). The main problem with attempts to apply these principles of mobility and tactical movement to naval warfare is the absence of anything comparable to the territorial standard occurring in land warfare. The command of the seas, the ultimate objective of naval warfare (Mahan, 1957), can be served by passive as well as aggressive action, for the neutralization of the enemy fleet by a blockade may serve the same function as its defeat. Moreover, aggressive action toward the enemy fleet does not always result in battle, for an inferior navy can often avoid battle without sacrificing major territorial objectives, unlike land warfare.

Application of the territorially-based criterion of tactical mobility to aerial weapons systems raises the question of whether the offensive or defensive character of these weapons is determined independently of land warfare or by their contribution to the defeat of enemy ground forces and territorial conquest. Many aerial weapons systems do contribute to the tactical offensive on the ground because of their striking power, mobility, and surprise (for example, in the Nazi *blitzkrieg*). Yet air power also has an independent capability to destroy the enemy's war making industrial capabilities, and hence contributes to deterrence in the nuclear age. This deterrent effect of air power takes place independently of its effect on the tactical offensive on the ground but cannot easily be incorporated into a conception of the offensive/defensive balance based on tactical mobility.

Some armaments that traditionally have been considered as defensive and therefore assumed to be 'stabilizing' (in the sense that they discourage aggression and reduce the likelihood of war) are often considered to be destabilizing in the nuclear age. Air defenses, anti-ballistic missile defenses, and even civil defenses are considered under the prevailing strategic doctrine to be destabilizing because by protecting populations they threaten to undermine deterrence. This reinforces our earlier point that the hypothesized consequences of a military technology favoring the offense (or the defense) may not be interchangeable between the nuclear and pre-nuclear eras.

The definition of the offensive/defensive balance, in terms of the characteristics of armaments, raises other questions as well. One is whether it is possible to define the offensive/defensive character of a weapon by its intrinsic performance characteristics alone, apart from the prevailing doctrine that determines it use. For example, essentially the same tank that was used in much of World War I as protected fire support was used in World War II as the organizing element of mobile offensive warfare (Fuller, 1945:ch. VI). The offensive character of Napoleonic warfare was due far more to the innovative tactics of Napoleon than to weapons systems themselves (Howard, 1976:75–76; Preston and Wise, 1979:189–191). It must be concluded that the offensive or defensive character of a weapons system must be defined by both its intrinsic characteristics and the tactical doctrine which determines its use.

What is important, of course, is not the characteristics of an individual weapon, but rather the aggregate impact of all weapons systems in a given arsenal. How is a given mixture of armaments, designed for different purposes and deployed for use in different theaters on land, sea, and air, to be aggregated so that their net effect on the offense and defense can be classified? This overall impact cannot be determined apart from the composition of an enemy's weapons systems and the terrain where the combat takes place. The offensive value of the tank, for example, was reduced by the development of new anti-tank technologies in the early 1970s. To complicate matters further, most hypotheses relating to the offensive/defensive balance treat that concept as a systemic-level attribute (the hypotheses that offensive superiority contributes to an increased frequency of war and to empire-building, for example). They suggest that at a given time the offensive/defensive balance can be characterized by a single value throughout the system. The balance must be aggregated not only over all weapons, functional roles, and theaters for a given state, but also over all states in the system. This is difficult given differential levels of industrialization and military power, uneven rates of technological diffusion, and doctrinal differences among various states in the system. Some of these problems are minimized, however, if the focus is restricted to the leading powers in the system, because they are often comparable in terms of power and technology.

Relative Resources Expended

Gilpin distinguishes between the offense and the defense in terms of an economic cost-benefit framework. 'To speak of a shift in favor of the offense means that fewer resources than before must be expended on the offense in order to overcome the defense' (Gilpin, 1981:62–63). Gilpin goes on to say that 'the defense is said to be superior if the resources required to capture territory are greater than the value of the territory itself; the offense is superior if the cost of conquest is less than the value of the territory' (p. 63).

Clearly the second definition does not follow from the first. Whereas the first uses the relative costs of overcoming the defense at two different times and independently of the resulting benefits, the second definition introduces an entirely new concept—the actual value of the territorial conquest itself. The value of territorial conquest is undoubtedly an important variable leading to war but it is analytically distinct from military technology and ought to be treated separately. Under Gilpin's second definition the hypothesis becomes equivalent to the statement that a positive (expected) utility of territorial conquest increases the likelihood of war. This may be true (Bueno de Mesquita, 1981), but it is not the hypothesis under consideration here. Moreover, the definition of the offensive/defensive balance by the utility of territorial conquest reduces to a tautology the hypothesis that offensive superiority increases the utility of territorial conquest.

One of the two conceptualizations of the offensive/defensive balance suggested by Jervis is more consistent with Gilpin's first formulation. Jervis (1978:188) poses the question as follows: 'Does the state have to spend more or less than one dollar on defensive forces to offset each dollar spent by the other side on forces that could be used to attack?' That is, what is the relative marginal utility of devoting military spending to the offense rather than to the defense? This approach is potentially valuable, but it is incomplete. It defines what it means to say that the offense (or the defense) has an advantage, but fails to provide any criteria for specifying what constitutes the offense or the defense in the first place. The marginal utilities cannot be compared until the offense and defense are first defined, and until this is done the concept is not particularly useful.

The definition of the offensive/defensive balance by the relative resources that must be expended on the offense in order to overcome the defense can be conceptualized in another way and related to the conception based on territorial conquest. This refers to attack/defense ratios rather than military spending. What ratio of troops does an attacker need in order to overcome an enemy defending fixed positions? This notion is mentioned but not developed by Quester (1977:212): 'The significant impact of defensive or offensive technology shows up in the minimum ratios of numerical superiority required for such an offensive.' It follows the same logic as Foch's comment regarding the power of the offensive prior to World War I: 'Formerly many guns were necessary to produce an effect. Today a few suffice' (Montross, 1960:686). The conventional wisdom is that the offense needs at least a three-to-one advantage, but the point here is that this ratio varies as a function of existing military technology and the tactical doctrine guiding its use. The offensive/defensive balance is then defined as being inversely proportional to the minimum ratio of forces needed by the attacker in order to overcome an adversary defending fixed positions. The greater the minimum ratio, the greater the advantage of the defense.

It is important to note here that the minimum *ratio* of forces needed by the attacker in a particular era is analytically distinct from the relative *numbers* of forces actually possessed by two adversaries in a particular situation. The probability of victory is a function of both. To say that the balance of military technology (as a function of attack/defense ratios) favors the offense does *not* mean the attacker is likely to win. That would be true only if the attacker actually possessed the requisite number of troops in a particular situation.

The problem arises as to what ratio should be used as a baseline, the zero-point indicating the transition from a defensive advantage to an offensive advantage. The most obvious ratio is one to one, but that is widely regarded as favoring the defense. While it would not be technically incorrect to say that the balance always favors the defense because the attacker always requires numerical superiority, this is neither interesting nor useful. If the offensive/defensive balance is defined as attack/defense ratios, it is preferable to conceive of this in relative rather than absolute terms. It is useful to speak of shifts in the balance and to compare the balance at different times, but not to speak about the absolute state of the balance. Thus the hypothesis should technically state that 'the higher the minimum ratio of forces needed by the attacker in order to overcome an adversary defending fixed positions, the lower the likelihood of war.'

This conception of the offensive/defensive balance is more useful than the others surveyed above, at least for land warfare. The attack/defense ratio could be measured in one of two ways. It could be determined empirically from an analysis of a variety of battles in a given era, with the force ratios and results determined for each and some kind of average computed. The problem, of course, would be the need to control for asymmetries in geography, troop quality, and doctrine. Alternatively, the ratio could be conceived in perceptual terms and measured by the perceptions of military and political elites of what ratio of forces is necessary for either attack or defense. While this information is not readily available it might be inferred from an examination of the war plans of the leading states. The methodological problems involved in either of these approaches are quite serious, however.

The Incentive to Strike First

One of the questions asked by Jervis (1978:188) of the offensive/defensive balance is the following: 'With a given inventory of forces, is it better to attack or to defend? Is there an incentive to strike first or to absorb the other's blow?' This conceptualization is more flexible than earlier criteria based on tactical mobility and characteristics of armaments because it can incorporate considerations of deterrence and be applied to the nuclear age. It creates some problems, however, which Jervis may recognize but does not fully develop. For one thing, the hypothesis that a military technology favoring the offense increases the incentive to strike first is reduced to a tautology and hence carries no explanatory power. In focusing attention on the linkage between the incentive to strike first and war, it ignores the more basic question of what conditions create an incentive to strike first. These antecedent conditions possess the greatest explanatory power and operate through the intervening variable of the incentive to strike first. This leads to a related problem: there are numerous factors besides technology and doctrine affecting the incentive to strike first, including geographic constraints and diplomatic and domestic political considerations, factors which also have an independent effect on war. If the offensive/defensive balance is *defined* as the incentive to strike first, then it becomes confounded with these other variables and it becomes impossible to distinguish their independent effects. The incentive to strike first is best conceptualized as an intervening variable leading to war and as the product of several distinct variables, one of which is military technology and doctrine. One key issue is to elaborate the aspects of military technology or doctrine which affect the incentives to strike first, but this cannot be fully analyzed here.

It is important to distinguish the incentive to strike first from other concepts that have also been used to define the offensive/defensive balance. The incentive to strike first should not be confused with aggressive policy, which is influenced by a wide range of variables. A state may have revisionist ambitions but be constrained by a military technology favoring the tactical defense, as well as by other variables. Or, a state with purely defensive ambitions may rationally initiate war if it perceives that through a preemptive strike it can minimize its losses against an assumed aggressor. The distinction between the incentive to strike first and seizing territory is particularly likely to be confused. These are clearly distinct for naval and air warfare (particularly in the nuclear age) but the difference is more profound. One may simultaneously have a policy of not striking first *and* a strategy of active defense and territorial penetration in the event that war does break out. This was Bismarck's policy in the 1870s and 1880s (Langer, 1964) and perhaps Israel's in 1973. Germany's Schlieffen Plan called for passive defense (holding ground) in the East and rapid territorial penetration in northern France regardless of who initiated the war.

The failure to recognize these distinctions only creates confusion and may result in the incorrect use of hypotheses designed for other purposes. Hypotheses appropriate for a territorially-based definition of the offensive/defensive balance of military technology may not be valid for a definition based on the incentive to strike first. While the ease of territorial seizure may shorten wars and lower their costs (Wright, 1965:673), this may not necessarily be true for the incentive to strike first. Nor is an incentive to strike first in the nuclear age likely to have the same consequences as an attack/defense ratio which favors the offense. Further, it is not clear that the incentive to strike first itself has the same causes or consequences in the pre-nuclear period as it does in the nuclear age, though this might be an interesting area for future research.

The same types of problems arise with respect to the various other conceptualizations of the offensive/defensive balance examined above. The concept has been defined in terms of the defeat of enemy armed forces, territorial conquest, protection of population, tactical mobility, the characteristics of armaments, attack/defense ratios, the relative resources expended on the offense and the defense, and the incentive to strike first. These separate definitions are often not interchangeable, and hypotheses based on one definition are often either implausible or tautological for another definition. This is particularly true for applications of the offensive/defensive balance to the nuclear age. Because the most advanced weapons of this era are used primarily for coercive purposes and the weapons of earlier eras were used primarily to engage enemy armed forces, the concept of the offensive/defensive balance of military technology may mean entirely different things in the two different situations. Certainly one reason for the confusion and ambiguity among these hypotheses is the fact that they are based on common concepts such as 'offense', 'aggressor', and 'initiator' which have ordinary language meanings apart from more precise technical meanings. This is all the more reason why any attempt to use such a concept must first define it explicitly and be very clear regarding precisely which hypotheses are relevant.

CLASSIFICATION OF THE OFFENSIVE/ DEFENSIVE BALANCE IN HISTORY

The third section of this article surveys a variety of efforts to classify the offensive/defensive balance of military technology in the Western international system over the last eight centuries. This survey will be useful because of the absence of any previous review of this body of literature and because of the general failure of earlier studies to acknowledge or build upon each other. More importantly, it may reveal whether or not the concept has acquired an informal definition in its empirical application, in spite of the conceptual ambiguity demonstrated above. While the concept of the offensive/defensive balance of military technology has taken on a variety of meanings, the question arises as to how the concept has been used in attempts to classify the offensive/defensive balance in past historical eras. If different authorities have generally used the offensive/defensive balance to mean the same thing (even in the absence of any formal nominal or operational definition), and if they have generally agreed on the state of the balance in various historical eras, then it can be concluded that the ambiguity of the concept has not precluded its effective use in empirical analysis. Consistent usage and agreement by various authorities on the state of the balance in different historical eras would permit 'intercoder agreement' to be used as the basis for accurate historical measurement (provided these measurements are independent). Lack of agreement on classification, however, would suggest that the collective judgment of authorities cannot be used as the basis for measurement. It would also support the earlier conclusion that the offensive/defensive concept needs to be defined much more explicitly and rigorously before it can be used in historical analysis. . . .

   [*At this point in the original article Levy includes a survey of several pages on varying interpretations of the offense/defense balance in several historical epochs.* (Ed.)]

   There is unanimous agreement among the references cited that the period from 1200 to 1450 was characterized by defensive superiority and that the period from 1450 to 1525 was characterized by offensive superiority. The authorities are split on the 1525 to 1650 period. There is complete agreement that the defense was superior from 1650 to 1740. Some argue that this defensive superiority continues until 1789, though Frederick's emphasis on the tactical offensive leads some to assert the opposite and others to make no specific evaluation. The 1789 to 1815 period is generally regarded to favor the offense but because of innovations in tactics rather than armaments. Little attention is given to the 1815–1850 period. The next hundred years pose a problem because of the gap between the objective and perceived balance and the uncertain conceptual status of the latter. These authorities generally agree that from 1850 to 1925 or so the balance favored the defense but that nearly all statesmen perceived that it favored the offense from 1870 to 1914. Similarly, from 1930 to 1945 the balance favored the offense but that the actors themselves perceived that it favored the defense.

A rough calculation shows the following degree of consensus among our authorities. Of the 450 years from 1495–1945, only two periods totaling 55 years claim a definite consensus of offensive superiority. Two periods totaling at most 130 years claim a consensus of defensive superiority. Four periods constituting a minimum of 265 years are uncertain, either because of diverging views, or because of the diametric opposition of the evaluations of actors and analysts and the ambiguous conceptual status of perceptions in definitions of the balance. The inescapable conclusion is that there exists considerable divergence of opinion among leading authorities regarding the offensive/defensive balance during the last five centuries of the modern era, and that a method of 'intercoder agreement' cannot be used to provide a basis for classification during this period. . . .

To conclude, the concept of the offensive/defensive balance is too vague and encompassing to be useful in theoretical analysis. Many of the individual variables that have been incorporated into the more general idea may themselves be useful, however. Few would doubt the utility for deterrence theory of the concept of the incentive to strike first, for example, and the concept of attack/defense ratios suggested here deserves further exploration. Much more conceptualization is necessary before these individual variables can be effectively used in empirical analysis, however. There is already a body of theory regarding the consequences of an incentive to strike first. What is needed are comparable theories regarding the consequences of military technologies which contribute to tactical mobility or to the ease of territorial conquest, or which reduce the ratio of forces needed by the attacker to overcome an adversary defending fixed positions. Interaction effects between these separate variables also need to be explored. Further theoretical development of this kind is necessary, because in its absence there is little reason to believe that these individual concepts have an important impact on war, and therefore little reason to use these concepts in empirical analysis.

REFERENCES

Boggs, M. W. (1941) 'Attempts to Define and Limit "Aggressive" Armament in Diplomacy and Strategy.' *University of Missouri Studies,* XVI, No. 1. Columbia, Missouri.

Bueno de Mesquita, B. (1981) *The War Trap.* New Haven: Yale University Press.

Dupuy, R. E. and G. F. Eliot (1937) *If War Comes.* New York: Macmillan.

Dupuy, T. N. (1980) *The Evolution of Weapons and Warfare.* Bloomington: Indiana University Press.

Fuller, J. F. C. (1945) *Armament and History.* New York: Charles Scribner's Sons.

———. (1961) *The Conduct of War, 1789–1961.* New Brunswick: Rutgers University Press.

Gilpin, R. (1981) *War and Change in World Politics.* Cambridge: Cambridge University Press.

Hart, B. H. L. (1964) *Strategy.* New York: Praeger.

Howard, M. (1976) *War in European History.* New York: Oxford University Press.

———. (1983) *Clausewitz.* Oxford: Oxford University Press.

Jervis, R. (1978) 'Cooperation Under the Security Dilemma.' *World Politics* 30: 167–214.

Langer, W. L. (1964) *European Alliances and Alignments, 1871–1890,* 2nd ed. New York: Vintage Books.

Mahan, A. T. (1957) *The Influences of Sea Power Upon History, 1660–1783.* New York: Hill and Wang.

Montgomery of Alamein, V. (1983) *A History of Warfare.* New York: William Morrow.

Montross, L. (1960) *War Through the Ages,* 3rd ed., rev. New York: Harper & Row.

Preston, R. A. and S. F. Wise (1979) *Men in Arms.* New York: Holt, Rinehart and Winston.

Quester, G. H. (1977) *Offense and Defense in the International System.* New York: Wiley.

Schelling, T. C. (1966) *Arms and Influence.* New Haven: Yale University Press.

Snyder, G. H. (1961) *Deterrence and Defense.* Princeton: Princeton University Press.

Sprout, H. and M. Sprout (1965) *The Ecological Perspective on Human Affairs.* Princeton: Princeton University Press.

Strachan, H. (1983) *European Armies and the Conduct of War.* London: George Allen & Unwin.

Tarr, D. (1984) 'Defense as Strategy: A Conceptual Analysis,' in S. J. Cimbala (ed.) *National Security Strategy.* New York: Praeger.

Wright, Q. (1949) 'Modern Technology and the World Order,' in W. F. Ogburn (ed.) *Technology and International Relations.* Chicago: University of Chicago Press.

——. (1965) *A Study of War,* rev. ed. Chicago: Chicago University Press.

ARMS CONTROL: THE HISTORICAL EXPERIENCE

Charles H. Fairbanks, Jr.
and Abram N. Shulsky

. . . Faced with proposals for radical reductions in arms levels, it is surprising how little public discussion there has been of their wisdom and desirability. A major reason appears to be the prevalence of the notion that the danger of international tension or war comes not so much, or at all, from any given level (quantitative or qualitative) of arms, but from their uncontrolled growth—that is, from the "arms race." Thus, for example, the apparent views of the nuclear freeze movement, which seemed oblivious to the significance or consequences of any given level of armaments, but was concerned solely with stopping any increase in that level.

Our focus on arms races, and on arms control as a means of "stopping" them, has resulted in a lack of attention to the question of what role given levels of armaments play in maintaining a given international system, and what the consequences of radically reducing those levels are likely to be. Proposals for deep reductions, or for the elimination of classes of armaments, force us to look more carefully at these questions.

As a way of beginning to think about this problem—not so much a new issue as a new way of looking at a perennial one—we will look at several instances of deep reductions in, or steady and low levels of, armaments to see what kinds of issues they raise and what kinds of (mainly unintended) consequences they may have.

If we are entering an age of deep cuts, or even an age in which the arms control agenda centers on deep cuts, we must become more aware of the historical experience of deep reductions in all its diversity: not only of deep reductions that come through bilateral arms control agreements, but also deep reductions imposed on one side (as in the Versailles Treaty), of demobilizations (bilateral but not by agreement), and cases where countries have simply decided to make deep reductions in their own forces.

DEMOBILIZATION: THE USSR, 1945–1948

We can begin with demobilizations—probably the deepest cuts in our experience that are based on a nation's own choice. In the case of the Soviet Union after World War II, the ability to choose force levels freely was particularly great because the other great military powers, with the exception of the United States and Britain, had been shattered

Charles H. Fairbanks, Jr., and Abram N. Shulsky, "From 'Arms Control' to Arms Reductions: The Historical Experience," *The Washington Quarterly* Vol. 10, No. 3 (summer 1987) pp. 59–73. © 1997 by the Center for Strategic and International Studies (CSIS) and the Massachusetts Institute of Technology.

by the war. A far-reaching Soviet demobilization did take place, with army divisions of all types being cut down from 455 to 175, many of which would have needed to be brought back up to strength by remobilization before they could fight. Military aircraft decreased from 20,000 to 13,000.[1] The navy, reduced during the war to a marginal supplement to the ground forces, may have actually grown in mobilizable strength. Scrappings were offset by the transfer of many German and Japanese ships.

There was thus a transformation of Soviet force posture, due to the fact that the air force and navy were not demobilized to the same extent as the ground forces. (One can compare this to the United States, where the Army Air Corps was reduced by three quarters, from 79,000 to 20,000.) Another way of expressing the same fact would be to say that, as a result of demobilization, Soviet forces suddenly became much more technology-intensive; elements of the armed forces reliant on high-technology weapons became much more important relative to the other elements. This shift took place on a much broader and deeper scale within many of the services. In the ground forces, for example, the ratio in 1945 of infantry division to tank and mechanized divisions had been ten to one. By 1947 it became two to one, a vast change in the character of the force.[2] The changes within the division were also great, as a recent book by Marshal Pavlovskii makes clear:

> In the table of organization of the [rifle] division was included a tank/self-propelled regiment, and in the rifle regiment a battery of SU76's. As a result of the change in establishments and the exchange of old weapons for new models the weight of the volley of a division's artillery and mortars grew *already by the end of 1946,* in comparison with 1944, from 1589 to 3500 kilograms, and the [small arms] shots per minute from 491,000 to 652,000. . . . The division as organized in 1948 already had 1,488 trucks, tank transporters and tractors, while in 1944 there were only 419 trucks and tractors.[3]

Such was the consequence of a deep reduction, Soviet demobilization. Of course, it is likely that a force in which the balance of elements was so different would require a different organization (that the air force and navy would obtain greater autonomy, for example). More tanks and trucks would tend to create more mobile tactics, and so forth; many ripples spread outward from the basic cut.

Why did Soviet demobilization bring such wide transformations in Soviet forces? One possibility is, of course, that Stalin decided to create a stronger rather than weaker military establishment. But there are reasons inherent in the situation, and seen in other countries, why demobilization tends to create such transformations to a greater or lesser degree. First, the demands of economic recovery drew more on the manpower in the army than any other part of the military structure. Second, the very nature of the forces is likely to create disproportionate shrinkage in the infantry. Tanks and planes do not want to go home at the end of the war, but men do. Finally, organizational interests (as well as desire for military strength) tend to go in the direction of retaining the best

[1] Alexander Boyd, *The Soviet Air Force Since 1918* (New York: Stein and Day, 1977), pp. 180, 216.
[2] Cristann Gibson, "Patterns of Demobilization: the US and USSR after World War II," unpublished Ph.D. dissertation, University of Denver, 1983, p. 210.
[3] I.G. Pavlovskii, *Sukhoputniye voiska USSR* (Moscow: Voenizdat, 1985), p. 210.

equipment within the shrunken structure of the active forces, thus raising their relative technological level.

In demobilizations, a cut is not just a cut. It is a massive disruption of an interconnected system made up of soldiers, organizations, weapons, reserves, supplies, and the tactics and strategy by which all these elements are employed. Thus demobilizations inevitably force deep cuts in some units, lesser cuts in other units, and increases in still others, leading to a general transformation of the military forces. If, for example, there are tanks in wartime armored formations that were not needed there in peacetime, but are reassigned to infantry divisions, the infantry divisions will need new logistics and maintenance units. This transformation is strongly shaped by the outside environment, by the needs of the economy, the desires of men who want to go home, or (certainly in Stalin's case) the opportunities and exigencies of the international situation.

Perhaps it is also true that the deeper the cut—and the cuts in demobilization are very deep—the greater the disruption of the system, and the greater the transformation finally produced.

THE EFFECTS OF LOW ARMAMENT LEVELS: THE 1920S AND 1930S

The last great period of history in which most nations' armaments levels were low was the 1920s: in Germany because of the arms limitations imposed on it in the Versailles Treaty, and in British (and to a lesser extent, French and Soviet) ground forces and air forces, because, given German weakness, there did not seem to be a threat. The case of the British, U.S., and Japanese navies, limited by the Washington Naval Arms Agreements, is discussed below. This period is thus important for understanding what reductions to low (or, in the case of Germany with respect to certain weapon systems, zero) levels of arms might mean.

Following World War I, Britain disarmed "explosively," with the exception of the brief naval arms race with the United States and Japan, which was ended by the Washington Naval Conference. At the end of demobilization, in October 1921, Britain had three air squadrons at home (other than those equipped solely for support of ground forces). The army, intended strictly for colonial wars, was far weaker in strength that could be mobilized for European service than it was before 1914.

It is easy to see why Britain acted as it did. There was great hope that the post–World War I peace settlement, including the creation of the League of Nations, would in fact achieve the war aim—an end to war—proclaimed by the victors during the fighting. This hope was encapsulated in the well-known "Ten Years' Rule," adopted by the cabinet in 1919 and confirmed, in this more definitive form, in 1928: "It should be assumed, in framing the Estimates of the Fighting Services, that at any given date there will be no major war for ten years."[4] Britain thus assumed that the favorable conditions it enjoyed (ultimately due to Germany's willingness to respect, more or less, the

---

[4]N.H. Gibbs, *Rearmament Policy,* vol. I of *Grand Strategy, History of the Second World War,* United Kingdom Military History Series, Her Majesty's Stationery Office, London, 1977, p. 58.

arms limitation provisions of the Versailles Treaty) would change only gradually. Britain further seemed to assume that its own disarmament would not tend to weaken this German willingness.

Britain was confronted in 1933 with German "breakout." The German aircraft production plan, adopted in June 1933, four months after Hitler came to power, envisaged moving from no air force to parity with Britain (51 squadrons) in a little over two years (by fall 1935). By November 1934 British intelligence had estimated the goal of this plan correctly, and unofficial British estimates were far higher. But by this time there was a new German plan, adopted in March 1934, which was aiming at a strength of 243 squadrons in four years, on the basis of a production of 17,015 aircraft (including 2,887 bombers and 2,225 fighters).[5]

German rearmament differed from any of the arms races before World War I or after World War II in that it violated an arms control treaty that had been imposed on Germany. One might have thought that its illicit character would have made France and Britain more reactive. This does not seem to have been the case. The buildup of the German armed forces was not officially proclaimed until 1935, though known to everyone. Although it was in violation of Germany's treaty obligations, Britain and France were at a loss as to what to do about it.

This is an important case for understanding the full problem involved in the violation of arms control agreements. U.S. writing on this question has tended to identify the problem posed by violation of arms control agreements with the problem of verification or detection of infringements. The case of German rearmament points out that there is at least as great a problem in what to do about arms control violations once detected.[6] As A.J.P. Taylor has pointed out, the disarmament of Germany "could only work with the cooperation of the German government":

> German disarmament worked if the Germans chose to make it work. And if not? Once more the Allies were faced with the problem of enforcement. The Germans had this measureless advantage that they could undermine the system of security against them merely by doing nothing; by not paying reparations and by not disarming. They could behave as an independent country normally behaves.[7]

Any British or French effort at enforcing German disarmament demanded an effort vaguely comparable to that of a war, and ran up against the problem that it offended contemporary customs of international good behavior. In this situation, the common British reaction was to try to trade legitimization of the German rearmament already

---

[5]Edward L. Homze, *Arming the Luftwaffe: The Reich Air Ministry and the German Aircraft Industry, 1919–1939* (Lincoln, Nebraska: University of Nebraska Press, 1976), p. 75; Gibbs, *Rearmament Policy,* p. 136; R.J. Overy, "The German Pre-War Aircraft Production Plans: November 1936–April 1939," *The English Historical Review,* Vol. XC, no. 357 (October 1975), pp. 778–780.

[6]For a full discussion of this issue, see Fred C. Iklé, "After Detection—What?" in *Foreign Affairs,* vol. 39, no. 2 (January 1961), pp. 208–220.

[7]A.J.P. Taylor, *Origins of the Second World War,* pp. 28, 31.

accomplished for a halt to future rearmament.[8] As British Foreign Secretary Sir John Simon remarked in 1934 in a cabinet paper:

> If the alternative to legalizing German rearmament was to prevent it, there would be everything to be said for not legalizing it. But the alternative to legalizing it is for German rearmament to continue just the same. . . . The party that is bound [by disarmament agreements] has already burst his chains and nobody is going to put the shackles on him again.[9]

Although unwilling to enforce the Versailles Treaty provisions limiting German armaments, the Western allies did react by looking to their own rearmament. Successive British air armament programs called for rapid increases in air strength in response to what seemed to be the most worrying and most "strategic" threat from Germany, the establishment and rapid growth of the Luftwaffe.

The responsiveness of British air programs to estimates of German programs is sufficient to show that German aerial rearmament created enormous fear. The 1930s is obviously a case in which an arms race helped create tension. Upon examination, however, it appears that the instability created was not unrelated to the prior situation of low levels of armaments.

The intense fear of German air power was conditioned by the antagonistic political aims expressed by the German government and by the fact that German rearmament was emphasizing the quintessentially high-technology area of air power. In part, this fear was conditioned by the particular exaggeration of the effectiveness of bombing current in the 1930s. It also probably stemmed from the tendency to view air power as the single variable which best embodied the measure of a nation's overall military might.

But a very important precondition of the fear produced by German aerial rearmament was that this was not only illegal but unusually rapid rearmament. The building up of the Luftwaffe, completely forbidden (unlike the army) to Germany under the Versailles Treaty, produced what Tom Brown has called an "arms panic," as opposed to an arms race—an explosive mutual increase of weapons.[10] The rapidity of the German rearmament in the air was connected with its technological character. Viewed from outside, equipment rather than personnel determines the strength of an air force or a navy. Therefore mere production—the normal activity of industrial society—can, when shifted to aircraft, create a very quick impression of increased strength. The tremendous fear and tension generated by the revival of the Luftwaffe was grounded in this characteristic of industrial society. In the 1930s there was very little discussion, except to some degree in military circles, of the necessarily inadequate training and readiness of the new German air force; people were dazzled by the sudden appearance of equipment where there was none before.

Thus the rapidity of German aerial rearmament created the greatest fear. In other highly technological areas where the change of balance could not be rapid—as in the

---

[8]Gibbs, *Rearmament Policy,* pp. 141–142, 160.
[9]Ibid.
[10]Thomas Brown, *What Is an Arms Race,* California Arms Control and Foreign Policy Seminar paper (unpublished, October 1975), pp. 16–17.

naval rearmament of the various powers—much less fear was created. These facts suggest an important point about arms control. The arms race in the air frightened people precisely because it moved so rapidly, and it moved so rapidly because it began from a very low level. In the case of Britain and France, a minute proportion of industrial effort was devoted to the air force. World War II showed that the major industrial states had the potential to produce military aircraft in the range of 25,000–100,000 a year, but their production in the early 1930s was a few dozen a year. Germany had similar production capacity, but was restricted to having no military aircraft under the Versailles Treaty. Thus on both sides there were perfect conditions for a sudden—and in the eyes of observers, enormous—increase when political conditions changed.

Germany's abandonment of the Versailles restrictions is the most important historical case of breakout from an arms control agreement. The effects of breakout, or of an arms panic more generally, in creating international tension are exacerbated by having low levels of armament to start with. In this sense, our world is safer than that of the 1920s and early 1930s, since most major states now maintain relatively larger forces and expend a larger proportion of their economic resources on defense than they did then. These forces provide a cushion against sudden disturbances of the military balance. One has to ask whether in this sense a continuous world arms competition, as opposed to an arms panic, may not actually be "stabilizing." This line of reasoning suggests that reduction of armaments to low levels can, in certain circumstances, risk endangering international harmony rather than aiding it.

REDUCTIONS THROUGH ARMS CONTROL: THE WASHINGTON NAVAL AGREEMENTS

The arms limitation provisions of the Versailles Treaty are an unrepresentative example of arms control in that they were not the result of agreement between potential adversaries, but rather were imposed by the allies on a Germany that had been rendered defenseless by defeat in the war. Thus they sought to embody a temporary relationship that did not reflect the real power of the countries involved.

The Washington Naval Treaty of 1922, on the other hand, represented a voluntary agreement which, unlike the SALT I and II agreements on strategic offensive arms, involved serious arms reduction: indeed, it is the only historical example of reductions of this magnitude. Each of the three main naval powers scrapped roughly half of their existing battleships and almost all of the enormous tonnage under construction. It was agreed that for a decade no new battleships would be built. The core of the treaty was a ratio freezing the parties' existing approximate relative strength in battleships and extending it to aircraft carriers. The ratio among the United States, Britain and Japan was 5:5:3.

Qualitative limits were imposed as well, limiting battleships to 35,000 tons and cruisers to 10,000 tons (with 8-inch guns). In the London Treaty of 1930, numerical limits were placed on other types of ships as well.

The Washington Treaty had real accomplishments. It saved all the countries involved a vast amount of money and stopped for nearly 20 years the increase in battleship size, just then swelling monstrously. The treaty also showed that in circumstances like these, where there was no deep opposition of political interests, stopping an arms race could indeed decrease international tension. Finally, the treaty provided a universal and principled covering which psychologically eased acceptance of shifts in power relationships—Britain's loss of naval superiority for the first time in 200 years and the abandonment of the Anglo-Japanese alliance—that could have been far more disturbing if boldly presented.

However, the treaty turned out not to be, as Lord Balfour, the head of the British delegation, proclaimed, an "absolute unmixed benefit to mankind, which carried no seeds of future misfortune." To begin with, it soon became apparent that the treaty had actually spurred the arms race in important ways. Stephen Roskill, the naval historian, writes that "all in all, the first effect of the limitation treaty on Britain . . . was to produce greater activity in naval building than at any time since the armistice [of 1918]."[11] No one foresaw this outcome, but it is hardly surprising. To negotiate, a nation needs to carefully compare its forces with those of other countries, highlighting areas of relative weakness. In the new situation created by the agreement, it may be felt to be necessary, or actually may be necessary, to remedy these weaknesses. Thus, the prospect of removing INF missiles from Europe has focused attention on the imbalance, favoring the Soviets, in shorter-range nuclear missiles. It is thus all too easy for the arms limitation process to wind up in incessant arms accumulation to remedy security weaknesses created or brought to light by the original negotiations—the equivalent of pouring water into a perforated bucket.

As soon as the battleship race was halted in the early 1920s, another race began in cruisers, which had been relatively neglected. The United States had only three modern cruisers, the British Empire 60. The cruisers constructed after the treaty displaced 10,000 tons and were armed with 8-inch guns (the treaty limits), while almost all existing cruisers were half this size and armed with 6- or 4-inch guns. The arms limitation treaty had quickly brought into existence a new and much more powerful weapon, the "treaty cruiser," the naval historians' ironic name for the new 10,000 ton, 8-inch gun warships.

It is easy to see why this was likely to take place. The pace of technological innovation in weapons is normally limited by the fact that military staffs, like all bureaucracies, are embedded in a mass of routine administrative duties. From these ordinary duties there are most likely to emerge conservative, incremental decisions on weapons: adding a few, or improving the type slightly, with each budget cycle.

A treaty negotiation, on the other hand, forces far-reaching reassessment of weapons policy. To develop their negotiating positions, the U.S., British, and Japanese governments needed to know from their naval staffs what was the most useful type of cruiser. It is scarcely surprising that the answer turned out to be that the optimum cruiser was one twice as big as existing cruisers.

By a somewhat similar process the Washington Treaty encouraged the emergence of the aircraft carrier. One of the mysterious events of modern military history is the rapid emergence of air power, and particularly carrier air power, so soon

---

[11]*Naval Policy Between the Wars* (London: Collins, 1968), p. 332.

after the weapon was invented. The first ship originally designed as an aircraft carrier was completed in 1922, the year the Washington Naval Treaty was signed. Nevertheless, the treaty defined the aircraft carrier as a "capital ship," thus putting it in the same category as the battleship, a weapon some 300 years older. Only 19 years later, carrier air power was the weapon Japan chose—rather than battleships—to attempt a decisive victory. It is remarkable that a weapon so new, so far from the dominant strategy and tactics of the period, and so untested in combat was taken as seriously as it was.

The more one studies this transformation, the more it appears that it had something to do with arms control. In ordinary circumstances the battleship admirals then dominating every major navy would never have chosen to invest in aircraft carriers rather than battleships. Once their cherished battleship force had been cut to the bone in negotiations, however, they developed a sudden but natural awareness of the need for aircraft carriers, and discovered that the unfinished hulls of four battleships just stricken under the treaty terms could be converted quite nicely into giant aircraft carriers for the United States and Japan.

In this way, the treaty regime facilitated the emergence of air power at its very beginning. Subsequently, the environment created by the treaty continued to affect the role of air power in ways that were less visible and dramatic but perhaps even more important.

The treaty largely froze technological change in the battleship (and, shortly, in the cruiser as well), changing the particular relationship between technology, tactics, and strategy that had existed from the advent of the new *Dreadnought*-class battleship in 1904 up to World War I, and again from 1918 to 1922. The war itself had shown that although Britain and Germany had developed powerful battleships, they had only vague ideas about how to fight with them. An important reason seems to be the very pace of technological advance, which concentrated the energy of the naval bureaucracies on the development of more powerful battleships and the solution of immediate problems posed by them (e.g., fire control at long ranges).

The Washington Naval Treaty created an environment that was in many ways the opposite: technological development was frozen, and the naval officers were left free to concentrate on how to fight a real war with the existing technology. This was expressed in the United States and Japan in annual, detailed war games and in increasingly voluminous and concrete war plans. At first, the ideas were relatively crude, similar to those of 1914: a naval Armageddon fought between main battleship fleets in the Central Pacific. Increasingly, however, the planners were compelled to confront the many unanswered questions underlying this scenario, one of which was whether the battleships would suffer substantial attrition on their way to the battle area. Attention was thus gradually turned to the auxiliary weapons that could inflict or counter this attrition, and among them, to air power.

This logic particularly affected the inferior power, Japan, and attracted the Japanese to carrier air power as one means of righting the unfavorable balance (itself highlighted by the 5:5:3 ratio) with the United States. Thus the treaty created not only new weapons in a narrow sense, but new tactics and strategy for the employment of all naval weapons and a new seriousness about how to fight a war.

From the standpoint of defense policy and arms control, these results were of mixed value. The treaty probably encouraged serious planning for war within the U.S.

Navy, while discouraging it within the wider public. Public opinion in the United States and Britain tended to be lulled by the treaty into ignoring defense. In 10 of the 18 years between the treaty and World War II, the U.S. Congress did not authorize the building of a single warship, while Japan laid down several ships every year. The result was that by the late 1930s Japan, entitled by the 1922 and 1930 treaties to 60 percent of U.S. strength, had actually been allowed to build to 80 percent of parity. It proved impossible to restore the treaty ratio by December 7, 1941.

In any case, the treaty undoubtedly hurried an evolution away from a weapon whose era was waning, the battleship, and toward the air power weapon of the future. But from the standpoint of arms control, this was a step backwards.

As Pearl Harbor made clear, the aircraft carrier was a weapon that, as compared with the battleship, encouraged striking first in a crisis, and therefore somewhat increased the chances of war. The aircraft carrier was far better adapted to carry out swift attack from a distance than the lumbering battleship, yet at the same time its thin, gasoline-laden hull could not withstand attack like the battleship's thick carapace.

At Midway and other carrier battles there was a strong tendency for the side that struck first to win. If one wanted to do everything that would make war less likely—the primary object of all arms limitation agreements—one did not want to encourage shifting the weapons mix toward weapons, like the aircraft carrier, that might have encouraged striking first. But the Washington treaty had precisely this effect.

Fortifications—a "weapon" that impedes successful offensive war—were actually prohibited by the treaty in the Western Pacific. This destabilizing concession had to be made to get Japan to accept the politically disagreeable 5 : 5 : 3 ratio. The general spirit that dominated arms limitation efforts in the 1920s as in SALT—the opposition to greater quantities of weapons in the abstract—tended to blind negotiators and planners to the particular effects of specific weapons on the preservation of peace.

When freed of the treaty limits by Japanese abrogation (as of 1936), the United States and Britain continued to build 35,000-ton battleships with 14-inch or 16-inch guns, while Japan went immediately to 64,000 tons and 18-inch guns.

As this suggests, the signatories had different conceptions of what the treaty meant. The United States and Britain tended to see their commitment to the treaty as a commitment to the spirit of the treaty, which might call for more than its formal provisions. Japan quite honorably interpreted the treaty to mean the letter of the treaty. To get around treaty limits, Japan laid down submarine tenders that could be quickly converted into aircraft carriers and cruisers whose 6-inch guns could be quickly exchanged for the 8-inch guns of heavy cruisers.

The United States also exploited the treaty provisions in less startling ways. By a somewhat sophistic interpretation of an apparently unrelated clause in the Washington treaty, U.S. officials squeezed out another 3,000-ton displacement for their new aircraft carriers, but then nervously did not list it in official tables.

These cases bring us to a further unintended consequence which the Washington and London Treaties share with other arms limitation agreements: they encourage attempts to extract from the treaty unforeseen advantage for one side, and, at the extreme, cheating. Deception is always an attractive possibility in arms races, but the need to work within the definite limits imposed by a formal agreement vastly increases the incentives for deception or for testing the limits of the treaty. This sort of behavior creates in turn new uncertainty, which is precisely one of the greatest aims of arms limitation agreements to avoid.

The end of the Washington–London Treaty system was clear in 1934 when Japan gave the required two years' warning to abrogate the treaty. It is little reproach to an arms limitation treaty that it could not dam up the volcanic forces that had begun to stir and crackle in Japan in the 1930s.

But this case does point out a final problem that all arms limitation agreements must face. Arms limitation agreements, which by their very nature involve precise ratios and numbers of arms permitted to each side, are far more specific and detailed than most treaties. They thus lack the flexibility that enables most international agreements to bend with change and be infused with a new political content—as the meaning of NATO, for example, has shifted substantially over the years. When the rigid structure of an arms limitation agreement can no longer contain changed political forces, it will snap apart. The cost may be heavy: after an arms limitation treaty not renewed, as after a divorce, one cannot return to the starting point. . . .

CONCLUSION

. . . Experience suggests that the power of arms control itself to stabilize political relationships is limited. The Washington Naval Treaty did stabilize the Anglo-American relationship, but the underlying tensions in that relationship were superficial. It could stabilize the Japanese-American relationship only temporarily.

Finally, the examples discussed suggest that the question of the appropriate level of armaments—for example, the levels at which arms control agreements ought to be aiming—is much more complicated than is suggested by the view which sees the primary purpose of arms control as that of breaking the "mad momentum" of the arms race. Such a view implies that once increases in arms levels have been stopped, there is no theoretical obstacle to reductions as deep as possible. The reason for this conclusion is that the role of arms in the international system is seen as totally negative: not only do they not resolve the political tensions in the system but, by causing mutual fear, they can easily exacerbate them.

The above examples suggest, on the other hand, that, given political tensions, armaments can, depending on the circumstances, be stabilizing for the international system as well. Large military forces may add to the sense of tension in some circumstances, such as those before World War I, but they can also provide a cushion that absorbs sudden fluctuations in the international political environment. Arms control treaties, because of their unusually specific and rigid character, are more likely to be broken by major political fluctuations than to absorb them.

Critics of a specific weapon system often complain that its proponents fail to take into consideration how the adversary will react to it, negating many of the benefits it is supposed to provide. Proponents of an arms control agreement must meet the same test of trying to foresee the inevitable adjustments both sides will make to this agreement and how they will alter a complicated web of political and military realities.

THE SPREAD OF
NUCLEAR WEAPONS:
MORE MAY BE BETTER

Kenneth N. Waltz

Most people believe that the world will become a more dangerous one as nuclear weapons spread. The chances that nuclear weapons will be fired in anger or accidentally exploded in a way that prompts a nuclear exchange are finite, though unknown. Those chances increase as the number of nuclear states increases. More is therefore worse. Most people also believe that the chances that nuclear weapons will be used vary with the character of the new nuclear states—their sense of responsibility, inclination toward peace, devotion to the *status quo,* political stability, and administrative competence. If the supply of states of good character is limited, as is widely thought, then the larger the number of nuclear states, the greater the chances of nuclear war become. If nuclear weapons are acquired by countries whose governments totter and frequently fall, should we not worry more about the world's destruction than we do now? And if nuclear weapons are acquired by two states that are traditional and bitter rivals, should that not also foster our concern? . . .

THE EFFECTS OF NUCLEAR WEAPONS

Nuclear weapons have been the second force [in addition to bipolarity] working for peace in the post-war world. They make the cost of war seem frighteningly high and thus discourage states from starting any wars that might lead to the use of such weapons. Nuclear weapons have helped maintain peace between the great powers and have not led their few other possessors into military adventures.[1] Their further spread, however, causes widespread fear. Much of the writing about the spread of nuclear weapons has this unusual trait: It tells us that what did *not* happen in the past is likely to happen in the future, that tomorrow's nuclear states are likely to do to one another what today's nuclear states have not done. A happy nuclear past leads many to expect an unhappy nuclear future. This is odd, and the oddity leads me to believe that we should reconsider how weapons affect the situation of their possessors. . . .

From "The Spread of Nuclear Weapons: More May Be Better" by Kenneth N. Waltz from *Adelphi Papers,* 1981. Volume 17, pp. 1–7, 10–13, 16, 17, 19–23, 26, 28, & 29. Reprinted by permission of Oxford University Press, UK.

[1]Cf. John J. Weltman, 'Nuclear Devolution and World Order', *World Politics,* vol. 32, January 1980, pp. 172–4.

How can one state dissuade another state from attacking? In either or in some combination of two ways. One way to counter an intended attack is to build fortifications and to muster forces that look forbiddingly strong. To build defences so patently strong that no one will try to destroy or overcome them would make international life perfectly tranquil. I call this the defensive ideal. The other way to inhibit a country's intended aggressive moves is to scare that country out of making them by threatening to visit unacceptable punishment upon it. 'To deter' literally means to stop someone from doing something by frightening him. In contrast to dissuasion by defence, dissuasion by deterrence operates by frightening a state out of attacking, not because of the difficulty of launching an attack and carrying it home, but because the expected reaction of the attacked will result in one's own severe punishment. Defence and deterrence are often confused. One frequently hears statements like this: 'A strong defence in Europe will deter a Russian attack'. What is meant is that a strong defence will dissuade Russia from attacking. Deterrence is achieved not through the ability to defend but through the ability to punish. Purely deterrent forces provide no defence. The message of a deterrent strategy is this: 'Although we are defenceless, if you attack we will punish you to an extent that more than cancels your gains'. Second-strike nuclear forces serve that kind of strategy. Purely defensive forces provide no deterrence. They offer no means of punishment. The message of a defensive strategy is this: 'Although we cannot strike back, you will find our defences so difficult to overcome that you will dash yourself to pieces against them'. The Maginot line was to serve that kind of strategy.[2]

States may also use force for coercion. One state may threaten to harm another state not to deter it from taking a certain action but to compel one. Napoleon III threatened to bombard Tripoli if the Turks did not comply with his demands for Roman Catholic control of the Palestinian Holy Places. This is blackmail, which can now be backed by conventional and by nuclear threats.

Do nuclear weapons increase or decrease the chances of war? The answer depends on whether nuclear weapons permit and encourage states to deploy forces in ways that make the active use of force more or less likely and in ways that promise to be more or less destructive. If nuclear weapons make the offence more effective and the blackmailer's threat more compelling, then nuclear weapons increase the chances of war—the more so the more widely they spread. If defence and deterrence are made easier and more reliable by the spread of nuclear weapons, we may expect the opposite result. . . .

Wars can be fought in the face of deterrent threats, but the higher the stakes and the closer a country moves toward winning them, the more surely that country invites retaliation and risks its own destruction. States are not likely to run major risks for minor gains. Wars between nuclear states may escalate as the loser uses larger and larger warheads. Fearing that, states will want to draw back. Not escalation but de-escalation becomes likely. War remains possible, but victory in war is too dangerous to fight for. If states can score only small gains, because large ones risk retaliation, they have little incentive to fight.

---

[2]Cf. Robert J. Art and Kenneth N. Waltz, "Technology, Strategy, and the Uses of Force," *The Use of Force* (Boston: Little, Brown, 1971). For the different implications of defence and deterrence, see Glenn H. Snyder, *Deterrence and Defence* (Princeton: Princeton University Press, 1961).

Second, states act with less care if the expected costs of war are low and with more care if they are high. In 1853 and 1854, Britain and France expected to win an easy victory if they went to war against Russia. Prestige abroad and political popularity at home would be gained, if not much else. The vagueness of their plans was matched by the carelessness of their acts. In blundering into the Crimean War they acted hastily on scant information, pandered to their people's frenzy for war, showed more concern for an ally's whim than for the adversary's situation, failed to specify the changes in behaviour that threats were supposed to bring, and inclined towards testing strength first and bargaining second.[3] In sharp contrast, the presence of nuclear weapons makes states exceedingly cautious. Think of Kennedy and Kruschev in the Cuban missile crisis. Why fight if you can't win much and might lose everything? . . .

Certainty about the relative strength of adversaries also improves the prospects for peace. From the late nineteenth century onwards the speed of technological innovation increased the difficulty of estimating relative strengths and predicting the course of campaigns. Since World War II, technology has advanced even faster, but short of an anti-ballistic missile (ABM) breakthrough, this does not matter very much. It does not disturb the American-Russian equilibrium because one side's missiles are not made obsolete by improvements in the other side's missiles. In 1906 the British *Dreadnought,* with the greater range and fire power of its guns, made older battleships obsolete. This does not happen to missiles. As Bernard Brodie put it: 'Weapons that do not have to fight their like do not become useless because of the advent of newer and superior types. . . .'[4]

Countries more readily run the risks of war when defeat, if it comes, is distant and is expected to bring only limited damage. Given such expectations, leaders do not have to be insane to sound the trumpet and urge their people to be bold and courageous in the pursuit of victory. The outcome of battles and the course of campaigns are hard to foresee because so many things affect them, including the shifting allegiance and determination of alliance members. Predicting the result of conventional wars has proved difficult.

Uncertainty about outcomes does not work decisively against the fighting of wars in conventional worlds. Countries armed with conventional weapons go to war knowing that even in defeat their suffering will be limited. Calculations about nuclear war are differently made. Nuclear worlds call for and encourage a different kind of reasoning. If countries armed with nuclear weapons go to war, they do so knowing that their suffering may be unlimited. Of course, it also may not be. But that is not the kind of uncertainty that encourages anyone to use force. In a conventional world, one is uncertain about winning or losing. In a nuclear world, one is uncertain about surviving or being annihilated. If force is used and not kept within limits, catastrophe will result. That prediction is easy to make because it does not require close estimates of opposing forces. The number of one's cities that can be severely damaged is at least equal to the number

---

[3]See Richard Smoke, *War: Controlling Escalation* (Cambridge, Mass.: Harvard University Press, 1977), pp. 175–88.

[4]Bernard Brodie, *War and Politics* (New York: Macmillan, 1973), p. 321.

of strategic warheads an adversary can deliver. Variations of number mean little within wide ranges. The expected effect of the deterrent achieves an easy clarity because wide margins of error in estimates of probable damage do not matter. Do we expect to lose one city or two, two cities or ten? When these are the pertinent questions, we stop thinking about running risks and start worrying about how to avoid them. In a conventional world, deterrent threats are ineffective because the damage threatened is distant, limited, and problematic. Nuclear weapons make military miscalculations difficult and politically pertinent prediction easy. . . .

NUCLEAR WEAPONS AND REGIONAL STABILITY

. . . Many Westerners who write fearfully about a future in which third-world countries have nuclear weapons seem to view their people in the once familiar imperial manner as 'lesser breeds without the law'. As is usual with ethnocentric views, speculation takes the place of evidence. How do we know, someone has asked, that a nuclear-armed and newly hostile Egypt or a nuclear-armed and still hostile Syria would not strike to destroy Israel at the risk of Israeli bombs falling on some of their cities? More than a quarter of Egypt's people live in four cities: Cairo, Alexandria, Giza, and Aswan. More than a quarter of Syria's live in three: Damascus, Aleppo, and Homs.[5] What government would risk sudden losses of such proportion or indeed of much lesser proportion? Rulers want to have a country that they can continue to rule. Some Arab country might wish that some other Arab country would risk its own destruction for the sake of destroying Israel, but there is no reason to think that any Arab country would do so. One may be impressed that, despite ample bitterness, Israelis and Arabs have limited their wars and accepted constraints placed on them by others. Arabs did not marshal their resources and make an all-out effort to destroy Israel in the years before Israel could strike back with nuclear warheads. We cannot expect countries to risk more in the presence of nuclear weapons than they have in their absence.

Third, many fear that states that are radical at home will recklessly use their nuclear weapons in pursuit of revolutionary ends abroad. States that are radical at home, however, may not be radical abroad. Few states have been radical in the conduct of their foreign policy, and fewer have remained so for long. Think of the Soviet Union and the People's Republic of China. States coexist in a competitive arena. The pressures of competition cause them to behave in ways that make the threats they face manageable, in ways that enable them to get along. States can remain radical in foreign policy only if they are overwhelmingly strong—as none of the new nuclear states will be—or if their radical acts fall short of damaging vital interests of nuclear powers. States that acquire

---

[5]Shai Feldman, *Israeli Nuclear Deterrence: A Strategy for the 1980s?* (Berkeley, CA: Ph.D. Dissertation, 1980), Table 1.

nuclear weapons will not be regarded with indifference. States that want to be free-wheelers have to stay out of the nuclear business. A nuclear Libya, for example, would have to show caution, even in rhetoric, lest she suffer retaliation in response to someone else's anonymous attack on a third state. That state, ignorant of who attacked, might claim that its intelligence agents had identified Libya as the culprit and take the opportunity to silence her by striking a conventional or nuclear blow. Nuclear weapons induce caution, especially in weak states.

Fourth, while some worry about nuclear states coming in hostile pairs, others worry that the bipolar pattern will not be reproduced regionally in a world populated by larger numbers of nuclear states. The simplicity of relations that obtains when one party has to concentrate its worry on only one other, and the ease of calculating forces and estimating the dangers they pose, may be lost. The structure of international politics, however, will remain bipolar so long as no third state is able to compete militarily with the great powers. Whatever the structure, the relations of states run in various directions. This applied to relations of deterrence as soon as Britain gained nuclear capabilities. It has not weakened deterrence at the centre and need not do so regionally. The Soviet Union now has to worry lest a move made in Europe cause France and Britain to retaliate, thus possibly setting off American forces. She also has to worry about China's forces. Such worries at once complicate calculations and strengthen deterrence.

Fifth, in some of the new nuclear states civil control of the military may be shaky. Nuclear weapons may fall into the hands of military officers more inclined than civilians to put them to offensive use. This again is an old worry. I can see no reason to think that civil control of the military is secure in the Soviet Union, given the occasional presence of serving officers in the Politburo and some known and some surmised instances of military intervention in civil affairs at critical times.[6] And in the People's Republic of China military and civil branches of government have been not separated but fused. Although one may prefer civil control, preventing a highly destructive war does not require it. What is required is that decisions be made that keep destruction within bounds, whether decisions are made by civilians or soldiers. Soldiers may be more cautious than civilians.[7] Generals and admirals do not like uncertainty, and they do not lack patriotism. They do not like to fight conventional wars under unfamiliar conditions. The offensive use of nuclear weapons multiplies uncertainties. Nobody knows what a nuclear battlefield would look like, and nobody knows what happens after the first city is hit. *Uncertainty* about the course that a nuclear war might follow, along with the *certainty* that destruction can be immense, strongly inhibits the first use of nuclear weapons. . . .

---

[6]For brief accounts, see S. E. Finer, *The Man on Horseback* (London: Pall Mall Press, 1962), pp. 106–8; and Roy Medvedev, 'Soviet Policy Reported Reversed by SALT II', *Washington Star,* 7 July 1979, p. 1.

[7]Kenneth N. Waltz, 'America's European Policy Viewed in Global Perspectives', in Wolfram F. Hanrieder (ed.), *The United States and Western Europe* (Cambridge, Mass.: Winthrop, 1974), p. 31; Richard K. Betts, *Soldiers, Statesmen, and Cold War Crises* (Cambridge, Mass.: Harvard University Press, 1977), App. A.

DETERRENCE WITH SMALL NUCLEAR FORCES

A number of problems are thought to attend the efforts of minor powers to use nuclear weapons for deterrence. In this section, I ask how hard these problems are for new nuclear states to solve.

The Forces Required for Deterrence

In considering the physical requirements of deterrent forces, we should recall the difference between prevention and pre-emption. A preventive war is launched by a stronger state against a weaker one that is thought to be gaining strength. A pre-emptive strike is launched by one state to blunt an attack that another state is presumably preparing to launch.

The first danger posed by the spread of nuclear weapons would seem to be that each new nuclear state may tempt an old one to strike preventively in order to destroy an embryonic nuclear capability before it can become militarily effective. Because of America's nuclear arsenal, the Soviet Union could hardly have destroyed the budding forces of Britain and France; but the United States could have struck the Soviet Union's early nuclear facilities, and the United States and the Soviet Union could have struck China's. Such preventive strikes have been treated as more than abstract possibilities. When Francis P. Matthews was President Truman's Secretary of the Navy, he made a speech that seemed to favour our waging a preventive war. The United States, he urged, should be willing to pay 'even the price of instituting a war to compel cooperation for peace'.[8]

The United States and the Soviet Union considered making preventive strikes against China early in her nuclear career. Preventive strikes against nuclear installations can also be made by non-nuclear states and have sometimes been threatened. Thus President Nasser warned Israel in 1960 that Egypt would attack if she were sure that Israel was building a bomb. 'It is inevitable', he said, 'that we should attack the base of aggression, even if we have to mobilize four million to destroy it'.[9]

The uneven development of the forces of potential and of new nuclear states creates occasions that seem to permit preventive strikes and may seem to invite them. Two stages of nuclear development should be distinguished. First, a country may be in an early stage of nuclear development and be obviously unable to make nuclear weapons. Second, a country may be in an advanced stage of nuclear development, and whether or not it has some nuclear weapons may not be surely known. All of the present nuclear countries went through both stages, yet until Israel struck Iraq's nuclear facility in June of 1981 no one had launched a preventive strike. A number of reasons combined may account for the reluctance of states to strike in order to prevent adversaries from developing nuclear forces. A preventive strike would seem to be most promising during the

---

[8]Quoted in Walter H. Waggoner, 'U.S. Disowns Matthews Talk of Waging War to Get Peace', *New York Times,* 27 August 1950, p. 1.

[9]Quoted in William B. Bader, *The United States and the Spread of Nuclear Weapons* (New York: Pegasus, 1968), p. 96.

first stage of nuclear development. A state could strike without fearing that the country it attacked would return a nuclear blow. But would one strike so hard as to destroy the very potential for future nuclear development? If not, the country struck could simply resume its nuclear career. If the blow struck is less than devastating, one must be prepared to repeat it or to occupy and control the country. To do either would be difficult and costly.

In striking Iraq, Israel showed that a preventive strike can be made, something that was not in doubt. Israel's act and its consequences, however, make clear that the likelihood of useful accomplishment is low. Israel's strike increased the determination of Arabs to produce nuclear weapons. Arab states that may attempt to do so will now be all the more secretive and circumspect. Israel's strike, far from foreclosing Iraq's nuclear future, gained her the support of some other Arab states in pursuing it. And despite Prime Minister Begin's vow to strike as often as need be, the risks in doing so would rise with each occasion.

A preventive strike during the second stage of nuclear development is even less promising than a preventive strike during the first stage. As more countries acquire nuclear weapons, and as more countries gain nuclear competence through power projects, the difficulties and dangers of making preventive strikes increase. To know for sure that the country attacked has not already produced or otherwise acquired some deliverable warheads becomes increasingly difficult. If the country attacked has even a rudimentary nuclear capability, one's own severe punishment becomes possible. Fission bombs may work even though they have not been tested, as was the case with the bomb dropped on Hiroshima. Israel has apparently not tested weapons, yet Egypt cannot know whether Israel has zero, ten, or twenty warheads. And if the number is zero and Egypt can be sure of that, she would still not know how many days are required for assembling components that may be on hand.

Preventive strikes against states that have, or may have, nuclear weapons are hard to imagine, but what about pre-emptive ones? The new worry in a world in which nuclear weapons have spread is that states of limited and roughly similar capabilities will use them against one another. They do not want to risk nuclear devastation anymore than we do. Pre-emptive strikes nevertheless seem likely because we assume that their forces will be 'delicate'. With delicate forces, states are tempted to launch disarming strikes before their own forces can be struck and destroyed.

To be effective a deterrent force must meet three requirements. First, a part of the force must appear to be able to survive an attack and launch one of its own. Second, survival of the force must not require early firing in response to what may be false alarms. Third, weapons must not be susceptible to accidental and unauthorized use. Nobody wants vulnerable, hair-trigger, accident-prone forces. Will new nuclear states find ways to hide their weapons, to deliver them, and to control them? Will they be able to deploy and manage nuclear weapons in ways that meet the physical requirements of deterrent forces? . . .

Deterrent forces are seldom delicate because no state wants delicate forces and nuclear forces can easily be made sturdy. Nuclear weapons are fairly small and light. They are easy to hide and to move. Early in the nuclear age, people worried about atomic bombs being concealed in packing boxes and placed in the holds of ships to be exploded when a signal was given. Now more than ever people worry about terrorists stealing nuclear warheads because various states have so many of them. Everybody seems to believe that terrorists are capable of hiding bombs.[10] Why should states be unable to do what terrorist gangs are thought to be capable of?

It is sometimes claimed that the few bombs of a new nuclear state create a greater danger of nuclear war than additional thousands for the United States and the Soviet Union. Such statements assume that pre-emption of a small force is easy. It is so only if the would-be attacker knows that the intended victim's warheads are few in number, knows their exact number and locations, and knows that they will not be moved or fired before they are struck. To know all of these things, and to know that you know them for sure, is exceedingly difficult. How can military advisers promise the full success of a disarming first strike when the penalty for slight error may be so heavy? In 1962, Tactical Air Command promised that an American strike against Soviet missiles in Cuba would certainly destroy 90% of them but would not guarantee 100%.[11] In the best case a first strike destroys all of a country's deliverable weapons. In the worst case, some survive and can still be delivered.

If the survival of nuclear weapons requires their dispersal and concealment, do not problems of command and control become harder to solve? Americans think so because we think in terms of large nuclear arsenals. Small nuclear powers will neither have them nor need them. Lesser nuclear states might deploy, say, ten real weapons and ten dummies, while permitting other countries to infer that the numbers are larger. The adversary need only believe that some warheads may survive his attack and be visited on him. That belief should not be hard to create without making command and control unreliable. All nuclear countries must live through a time when their forces are crudely designed. All countries have so far been able to control them. Relations between the United States and the Soviet Union, and later among the United States, the Soviet Union, and China, were at their bitterest just when their nuclear forces were in early stages of development, were unbalanced, were crude and presumably hard to control. Why should we expect new nuclear states to experience greater difficulties than the old ones were able to cope with? Moreover, although some of the new nuclear states may be economically and technically backward, they will either have an expert and highly trained group of scientists and engineers or they will not produce nuclear weapons. Even if they buy the weapons, they will have to hire technicians to maintain and control them. We do not have to wonder whether they will take good care of their weapons. They have every incentive to do so. They will not want to risk retaliation because one or more of their warheads accidentally strikes another country.

Hiding nuclear weapons and keeping them under control are tasks for which the ingenuity of numerous states is adequate. Nor are means of delivery difficult to devise or procure. Bombs can be driven in by trucks from neighbouring countries. Ports can be torpedoed by small boats lying off shore. Moreover, a thriving arms trade in ever more sophisticated military equipment provides ready access to what may be wanted, including planes and missiles suited [to] nuclear warhead delivery.

---

[10]For example, David M. Rosenbaum, 'Nuclear Terror', *International Security*, vol. 1, Winter 1977.

[11]Graham T. Allison, *Essence of Decision* (Boston: Little, Brown, 1971), p. 126.

Lesser nuclear states can pursue deterrent strategies effectively. Deterrence requires the ability to inflict unacceptable damage on another country. 'Unacceptable damage' to the Soviet Union was variously defined by Robert McNamara as requiring the ability to destroy a fifth to a fourth of her population and a half to two-thirds of her industrial capacity. American estimates of what is required for deterrence have been absurdly high. To deter, a country need not appear to be able to destroy a fourth or a half of another country, although in some cases that might be easily done. Would Libya try to destroy Israel's nuclear weapons at the risk of two bombs surviving to fall on Tripoli and Bengazi? And what would be left of Israel if Tel Aviv and Haifa were destroyed? . . .

Prevention and pre-emption are difficult games because the costs are so high if the games are not perfectly played. Inhibitions against using nuclear forces for such attacks are strong, although one cannot say they are absolute. Some of the inhibitions are simply human. Can country *A* find justification for a preventive or pre-emptive strike against *B* if *B*, in acquiring nuclear weapons, is imitating *A?* The leader of a country that launches a preventive or pre-emptive strike courts condemnation by his own people, by the world's people, and by history. Awesome acts are hard to perform. Some of the inhibitions are political. As Bernard Brodie tirelessly and wisely said, war has to find a political objective that is commensurate with its cost. Clausewitz's central tenet remains valid in the nuclear age.[12] Ultimately, the inhibitions lie in the impossibility of knowing for sure that a disarming strike will totally destroy an opposing force and in the immense destruction even a few warheads can wreak. . . .

In a nuclear world, conservative would-be attackers will be prudent, but will all would-be attackers be conservative? A new Hitler is not unimaginable. Would the presence of nuclear weapons have moderated Hitler's behaviour? Hitler did not start World War II in order to destroy the Third Reich. Indeed, he was surprised and dismayed by the British and French declaration of war on Poland's behalf. After all, the western democracies had not come to the aid of a geographically defensible and militarily strong Czechoslovakia. Why then should they have declared war on behalf of a less defensible Poland and against a Germany made stronger by the incorporation of Czechoslovakia's armour? From the occupation of the Rhineland in 1936 to the invasion of Poland in 1939, Hitler's calculations were realistically made. In those years, Hitler would almost surely have been deterred from acting in ways that immediately threatened massive death and widespread destruction in Germany. And, if Hitler had not been deterred, would his generals have obeyed his commands? In a nuclear world, to act in blatantly offensive ways is madness. Under the circumstances, how many generals would obey the commands of a madman? One man alone does not make war.

To believe that nuclear deterrence would have worked against Germany in 1939 is easy. It is also easy to believe that in 1945, given the ability to do so, Hitler and some few around him would have fired nuclear warheads at the United States, Great Britain, and the Soviet Union as their armies advanced, whatever the consequences for Germany.

---

[12]See, for example, Bernard Brodie, 'The Development of Nuclear Strategy', *International Security,* vol. 2, Spring 1978, p. 12.

Two considerations, however, work against this possibility. When defeat is seen to be inevitable, a ruler's authority may vanish. Early in 1945 Hitler apparently ordered the initiation of gas warfare, but no one responded.[13] The first consideration applies in a conventional world; the second in a nuclear world. In the latter, no country will press another to the point of decisive defeat. In the desperation of defeat desperate measures may be taken, but the last thing anyone wants to do is to make a nuclear nation feel desperate. The unconditional surrender of a nuclear nation cannot be demanded. . . .

Arms Races among New Nuclear States

. . . Deterrent balances are . . . inherently stable. If one can say how much is enough, then within wide limits a country can be insensitive to changes in its adversaries' forces. This is the way French leaders have thought. France, as former President Giscard d'Estaing said, 'fixes its security at the level required to maintain, regardless of the way the strategic situation develops in the world, the credibility—in other words, the effectiveness—of its deterrent force'.[14] With deterrent forces securely established, no military need presses one side to try to surpass the other. Human error and folly may lead some parties involved in deterrent balance to spend more on armaments than is needed, but other parties need not increase their armaments in response, because such excess spending does not threaten them. The logic of deterrence eliminates incentives for strategic arms racing. This should be easier for lesser nuclear states to understand than it has been for the US and the USSR. Because most of them are economically hard pressed, they will not want to have more than enough.

Allowing for their particular circumstances, lesser nuclear states confirm these statements in their policies. Britain and France are relatively rich countries, and they tend to over-spend. Their strategic forces are nevertheless modest enough when one considers that their purpose is to deter the Soviet Union rather than states with capabilities comparable to their own. China of course faces the same task. These three countries show no inclination to engage in nuclear arms races with anyone. India appears content to have a nuclear military capability that may or may not have produced deliverable warheads, and Israel maintains her ambiguous status. New nuclear states are likely to conform to these patterns and aim for a modest sufficiency rather than vie with each [other] for a meaningless superiority.

Second, because strategic nuclear arms races among lesser powers are unlikely, the interesting question is not whether they will be run but whether countries having strategic nuclear weapons can avoid running conventional races. No more than the United States and the Soviet Union will lesser nuclear states want to rely on the deterrent threat that risks all. And will not their vulnerability to conventional attack induce them to continue their conventional efforts? . . .

---

[13]Frederic J. Brown, *Chemical Warfare: A Study in Restraints,* excerpted in Art and Waltz, *op. cit.* in n. 2, p. 183.

[14]Valéry Giscard d'Estaing, 'Part II of the press conference by Valéry Giscard d'Estaing, President of the French Republic' (New York: French Embassy, Press and Information Division, 15 February 1979), p. 6.

The expense of mounting conventional defences, and the difficulties and dangers of fighting conventional wars, will keep most new nuclear states from trying to combine large war-fighting forces with deterrent forces. Disjunction within their forces will enhance the value of deterrence.

Israeli policy seems to contradict these propositions. From 1971 through 1978, both Israel and Egypt spent from 20% to 40% of their GNPs on arms. Israel's spending on conventional arms remains high, although it has decreased since 1978. The decrease followed from the making of peace with Egypt and not from increased reliance on nuclear weapons. The seeming contradiction in fact bears out deterrent logic. So long as Israel holds the West Bank and the Gaza Strip she has to be prepared to fight for them. Since they are by no means unambiguously hers, deterrent threats, whether implicit or explicit, will not cover them. Moreover, while America's large subsidies continue, economic constraints will not drive Israel to the territorial settlement that would shrink her borders sufficiently to make a deterrent policy credible.

From previous points it follows that nuclear weapons are likely to decrease arms racing and reduce military costs for lesser nuclear states in two ways. Conventional arms races will wither if countries shift emphasis from conventional defence to nuclear deterrence. For Pakistan, for example, acquiring nuclear weapons is an alternative to running a ruinous conventional race with India.[15] And deterrent strategies make nuclear arms races pointless.

Finally, arms races in their ultimate form—the fighting of offensive wars designed to increase national security—also become pointless. The success of a deterrent strategy does not depend on the extent of territory a state holds. . . .

---

[15]Richard K. Betts, 'Paranoids, Pygmies, Pariahs, and Nonproliferation', *Foreign Policy* no. 26, Spring 1977, pp. 161–2.

PART VIII

STRATEGY, II: TERRORISM AND UNCONVENTIONAL WARFARE

W hen Al Qaeda hijackers flew airliners into the World Trade Center and Pentagon on September 11, 2001, many people were stunned by an action that seemed entirely unprecedented. Many believed that everything in the realm of security policy had changed, that we had entered a new era for which the conflicts of history offered few lessons. For the most part this common perception was untrue.

The specific tactic that the hijackers of September 11 chose—using captured aircraft as bombers on a kamikaze mission—was indeed novel and unexpected. Nearly all the rest of what happened on that day, however, was anticipated by professional observers of terrorism. For several years experts had warned of the danger of catastrophic attack (although they tended to focus on the threat of terrorist use of biological or chemical weapons); such warnings simply did not register forcefully on ordinary people when they heard them.

Nor were the motives and logic of the Al Qaeda attackers as unusual or irrational as many assumed.[1] In many respects they reflected the strategic outlook of terrorists at other times and places in history, which in turn overlap the logic of unconventional or "asymmetric" warfare in general. Although some terrorists are clearly more fanatical than most political movements and make demands that seem impossible to their targets,

---

[1]Trends in terrorism did change somewhat after the Cold War, as groups with leftist ideological agendas faded and those with religious, millenarian, or diffuse anti-Western motives grew in prominence. By some accountings the number of terrorist incidents declined while their average lethality increased. See Audrey Kurth Cronin, "Behind the Curve: Globalization and International Terrorism," *International Security* 27, no. 3 (winter 2002/03); Steven Simon and Daniel Benjamin, *The Age of Sacred Terror: Radical Islam's War Against America* (New York: Random House, 2003); Michael Mousseau, "Market Civilization and Its Clash with Terror," *International Security* 27, no. 3 (winter 2002/03); Martha Crenshaw, *Terrorism in Context* (University Park: Pennsylvania State University Press, 1995); Rohan Gunaratna, *Inside Al Qaeda: Global Network of Terror* (New York: Columbia University Press, 2002); James F. Hoge, Jr. and Gideon Rose, eds., *How Did This Happen: Terrorism and the New War* (New York: Public Affairs, 2001). While it is reasonable to speak of "the new terrorism" in regard to specific movements and tactics, the general political and coercive purpose of the new terrorists has been less nihilistic than many in the public have assumed.

few aim at mass murder for its own sake. As Martha Crenshaw argues in the essay that follows, terrorists use the tactics they do for instrumental reasons. They see terror as a means to an end, the achievement of a better political and social order on Earth.[2] The prominence of religious motives, especially radical Islamist terrorists but also among a wide variety of other groups, is highlighted in the selection by Mark Juergensmeyer. This prominence too seems new in the context of twentieth-century ideological conflict, but not in a wider historical context.[3]

Guerrilla warfare is a form of unconventional war that has seemed, to many in the West, more sensible and legitimate than terrorism. This was not true before the twentieth century, however, when antifascist resistance movements cast a more positive light on the practice of irregular combat to sympathetic Western liberals. For much of history, however, guerrilla warfare was lumped with terrorism as an illegal and unacceptable means of waging war.[4] Terrorist tactics such as assassination, coercive threats against civilians, and combat out of uniform have often merged into guerrilla war. Counterinsurgency forces in many different cases often refer to insurgents as terrorists.

In fact, in terms of a neutral analysis of tactics, shorn of moral context, unconventional warfare forms a rough continuum from terrorism at the low end, when antigovernment forces (or those resisting a victorious foreign invader) lack any military capability, through small-scale episodic ambushes and other quasiconventional forms of partisan warfare in the middle range, to increasingly large-scale conventional attacks at the high end, as the antiregime movement gathers steam and becomes an effective challenger. Mao Tse-tung (Mao Ze-dong) emphasizes this transitional nature of guerrilla war, and the interdependence of political and military success in moving from one stage to another, in the selections from his work included here.[5]

The hallmark of both terrorism and guerrilla warfare is the effective wielding of force by a weak contender against an opponent that is far superior in conventional military power. In the essay that follows, T. E. Lawrence ("Lawrence of Arabia") explores the ways in which guerrilla forces differ in character and operation from regular military forces, and how they can exploit geography and demography to hamstring an occupying power. Although their political purposes may differ profoundly, the strategic incentive to find ways to use force despite relative weakness is the same for either revolutionary or resistance movements within a given state or for transnational or subnational terrorist groups. Neither sort of group can compete with the resources of a

---

[2]There is a widely shared alternative view, however, that emphasizes the unconscious psychic imperatives driving terrorists, and which harks back to the reasoning of Franco Fornari in Part IV of this volume. See Jerrold M. Post, "Terrorist Psycho-Logic: Terrorist Behavior as a Product of Psychological Forces," in Walter Reich, ed., *Origins of Terrorism: Psychologies, Ideologies, Theologies, States of Mind* (Washington, D.C.: Woodrow Wilson Center Press, 1998). See also the discussion of "solipsistic" terrorism in Ian S. Lustick, "Terrorism in the Arab-Israeli Conflict," in Crenshaw, ed., *Terrorism in Context.*

[3]David C. Rapoport, "Fear and Trembling: Terrorism in Three Religious Traditions," *American Political Science Review* 78, no. 3 (september 1984).

[4]J. B. Firth, "The Guerrilla in History," *Fortnightly Review* (W. L. Courtney, ed.) 70, New Series (July–December 1901).

[5]See the more detailed argument in Mao Tse-tung, *On the Protracted War* (Peking: Foreign Languages Press, 1954).

government within a state, or of a more powerful invader who has defeated the home government, until the accelerating success of initial attacks mobilizes enough support to reach a higher level of power.

Lawrence and Mao's insights came from their experience in promoting irregular resistance to invaders—Turks and Japanese. In the second half of the twentieth century, however, guerrilla warfare was most often undertaken by ideological movements aiming to overthrow their own governments. This is the context that highlights the relevance of Huntington's discussion of the differences between dualistic intergovernmental war and tripartite antigovernmental war. His emphasis on the importance of the "target group" in unconventional warfare—the uncommitted mass whose loyalty will tilt the balance in the political contest—carries over to today's global war on terror. As the Muslim world becomes more polarized, forcing choices between extremists such as Al Qaeda and that group's conservative Islamic and liberal Western opponents, which way will Muslims in the middle tilt?

As the rest of this volume indicates, the vast bulk of thinking on war and peace has been about force and its alternatives in relations among states, and whether norms and institutions or specific distributions of power may hold impulses to war in check. Realists focus on material power, liberals on the moral power of particular ideological values, and culturalists or constructivists on the role of identity. All these factors interact in important ways in the contests within states, or between Western societies and transnational opponents of globalization, that today fuel terrorism and irregular warfare. The Betts essay at the end of this section connects the structure of the current international system (American primacy without omnipotence) with these questions and applies some of the lessons of earlier insights on unconventional conflict to the conflict with international terrorist movements. If any phenomenon reflects the inadequacy of any monocausal explanation of conflict, it is unconventional warfare in the forms discussed in this section.

—RKB

Science of Guerrilla Warfare

T. E. Lawrence

This study of the science of guerrilla, or irregular, warfare is based on the concrete experience of the Arab Revolt against the Turks 1916–1918. But the historical example in turn gains value from the fact that its course was guided by the practical application of the theories here set forth.

The Arab Revolt began in June, 1916, with an attack by the half-armed and inexperienced tribesmen upon the Turkish garrisons in Medina and about Mecca. They met with no success, and after a few days' effort withdrew out of range and began a blockade. This method forced the early surrender of Mecca, the more remote of the two centres. Medina, however, was linked by railway to the Turkish main army in Syria, and the Turks were able to reinforce the garrison there. The Arab forces which had attacked it then fell back gradually and took up a position across the main road to Mecca.

At this point the campaign stood still for many weeks. The Turks prepared to send an expeditionary force to Mecca, to crush the revolt at its source, and accordingly moved an army corps to Medina by rail. Thence they began to advance down the main western road from Medina to Mecca, a distance of about 250 miles. The first 50 miles were easy, then came a belt of hills 20 miles wide, in which were Feisal's Arab tribesmen standing on the defensive: next a level stretch, for 70 miles along the coastal plain to Rabegh, rather more than half-way. Rabegh is a little port on the Red Sea, with good anchorage for ships, and because of its situation was regarded as the key to Mecca. Here lay Sherif Ali, Feisal's eldest brother, with more tribal forces, and the beginning of an Arab regular army, formed from officers and men of Arab blood who had served in the Turkish Army. As was almost inevitable in view of the general course of military thinking since Napoleon, the soldiers of all countries looked only to the regulars to win the war. Military opinion was obsessed by the dictum of Foch that the ethic of modern war is to seek for the enemy's army, his centre of power, and destroy it in battle. Irregulars would not attack positions and so they were regarded as incapable of forcing a decision.

While these Arab regulars were still being trained, the Turks suddenly began their advance on Mecca. They broke through the hills in 24 hours, and so proved the second theorem of irregular war—namely, that irregular troops are as unable to defend a point or line as they are to attack it. This lesson was received without gratitude, for the Turkish success put the Rabegh force in a critical position, and it was not capable of repelling the attack of a single battalion, much less of a corps.

In the emergency it occurred to the author that perhaps the virtue of irregulars lay in depth, not in face, and that it had been the threat of attack by them upon the Turkish

T. E. Lawrence, "Science of Guerrilla Warfare," Vol. 10. Reprinted with permission from *Encyclopedia Britannica,* 14th ed., © 1929 by Encyclopedia Britannica, Inc.

northern flank which had made the enemy hesitate for so long. The actual Turkish flank ran from their front line to Medina, a distance of some 50 miles: but, if the Arab force moved towards the Hejaz railway behind Medina, it might stretch its threat (and, accordingly, the enemy's flank) as far, potentially, as Damascus, 800 miles away to the north. Such a move would force the Turks to the defensive, and the Arab force might regain the initiative. Anyhow, it seemed the only chance, and so, in Jan. 1917, Feisal's tribesmen turned their backs on Mecca, Rabegh and the Turks, and marched away north 200 miles to Wejh.

This eccentric movement acted like a charm. The Arabs did nothing concrete, but their march recalled the Turks (who were almost into Rabegh) all the way back to Medina. There, one half of the Turkish force took up the entrenched position about the city, which it held until after the Armistice. The other half was distributed along the railway to defend it against the Arab threat. For the rest of the war the Turks stood on the defensive and the Arab tribesmen won advantage over advantage till, when peace came, they had taken 35,000 prisoners, killed and wounded and worn out about as many, and occupied 100,000 square miles of the enemy's territory, at little loss to themselves. However, although Wejh was the turning point its significance was not yet realized. For the moment the move thither was regarded merely as a preliminary to cutting the railway in order to take Medina, the Turkish headquarters and main garrison.

Strategy and Tactics   However, the author was unfortunately as much in charge of the campaign as he pleased, and lacking a training in command sought to find an immediate equation between past study of military theory and the present movements—as a guide to, and an intellectual basis for, future action. The text books gave the aim in war as "the destruction of the organized forces of the enemy" by "the one process battle." Victory could only be purchased by blood. This was a hard saying, as the Arabs had no organized forces, and so a Turkish Foch would have no aim: and the Arabs would not endure casualties, so that an Arab Clausewitz could not buy his victory. These wise men must be talking metaphors, for the Arabs were indubitably winning their war . . . and further reflection pointed to the deduction that they had actually won it. They were in occupation of 99% of the Hejaz. The Turks were welcome to the other fraction till peace or doomsday showed them the futility of clinging to the window pane. This part of the war was over, so why bother about Medina? The Turks sat in it on the defensive, immobile, eating for food the transport animals which were to have moved them to Mecca, but for which there was no pasture in their now restricted lines. They were harmless sitting there; if taken prisoner, they would entail the cost of food and guards in Egypt: if driven out northward into Syria, they would join the main army blocking the British in Sinai. On all counts they were best where they were, and they valued Medina and wanted to keep it. Let them!

This seemed unlike the ritual of war of which Foch had been priest, and so it seemed that there was a difference of kind. Foch called his modern war "absolute." In it two nations professing incompatible philosophies set out to try them in the light of force. A struggle of two immaterial principles could only end when the supporters of one had no more means of resistance. An opinion can be argued with: a conviction is best shot. The logical end of a war of creeds is the final destruction of one, and Salammbo the classical textbook-instance. These were the lines of the struggle between

France and Germany, but not, perhaps, between Germany and England, for all efforts to make the British soldier hate the enemy simply made him hate war. Thus the "absolute war" seemed only a variety of war; and beside it other sorts could be discerned, as Clausewitz had numbered them, personal wars for dynastic reasons, expulsive wars for party reasons, commercial wars for trading reasons.

Now the Arab aim was unmistakably geographical, to occupy all Arabic-speaking lands in Asia. In the doing of it Turks might be killed, yet "killing Turks" would never be an excuse or aim. If they would go quietly, the war would end. If not, they must be driven out: but at the cheapest possible price, since the Arabs were fighting for freedom, a pleasure only to be tasted by a man alive. The next task was to analyse the process, both from the point of view of strategy, the aim in war, the synoptic regard which sees everything by the standard of the whole, and from the point of view called tactics, the means towards the strategic end, the steps of its staircase. In each were found the same elements, one algebraical, one biological, a third psychological. The first seemed a pure science, subject to the laws of mathematics, without humanity. It dealt with known invariables, fixed conditions, space and time, inorganic things like hills and climates and railways, with mankind in type-masses too great for individual variety, with all artificial aids, and the extensions given our faculties by mechanical invention. It was essentially formulable.

In the Arab case the algebraic factor would take first account of the area to be conquered. A casual calculation indicated perhaps 140,000 square miles. How would the Turks defend all that—no doubt by a trench line across the bottom, if the Arabs were an army attacking with banners displayed . . . but suppose they were an influence, a thing invulnerable, intangible, without front or back, drifting about like a gas? Armies were like plants, immobile as a whole, firm-rooted, nourished through long stems to the head. The Arabs might be a vapour, blowing where they listed. It seemed that a regular soldier might be helpless without a target. He would own the ground he sat on, and what he could poke his rifle at. The next step was to estimate how many posts they would need to contain this attack in depth, sedition putting up her head in every unoccupied one of these 100,000 square miles. They would have need of a fortified post every four square miles, and a post could not be less than 20 men. The Turks would need 600,000 men to meet the combined ill wills of all the local Arab people. They had 100,000 men available. It seemed that the assets in this sphere were with the Arabs, and climate, railways, deserts, technical weapons could also be attached to their interests. The Turk was stupid and would believe that rebellion was absolute, like war, and deal with it on the analogy of absolute warfare.

Humanity in Battle   So much for the mathematical element; the second factor was biological, the breaking-point, life and death, or better, wear and tear. Bionomics seemed a good name for it. The war-philosophers had properly made it an art, and had elevated one item in it, "effusion of blood," to the height of a principle. It became humanity in battle, an art touching every side of our corporal being. There was a line of variability (man) running through all its estimates. Its components were sensitive and illogical, and generals guarded themselves by the device of a reserve, the significant medium of their art. Goltz had said that when you know the enemy's strength, and he is fully deployed, then you know enough to dispense with a reserve. But this is never.

There is always the possibility of accident, of some flaw in materials, present in the general's mind: and the reserve is unconsciously held to meet it. There is a "felt" element in troops, not expressible in figures, and the greatest commander is he whose intuitions most nearly happen. Nine-tenths of tactics are certain, and taught in books: but the irrational tenth is like the kingfisher flashing across the pool and that is the test of generals. It can only be ensued by instinct, sharpened by thought practising the stroke so often that at the crisis it is as natural as a reflex.

Yet to limit the art to humanity seemed an undue narrowing down. It must apply to materials as much as to organisms: In the Turkish Army materials were scarce and precious, men more plentiful than equipment. Consequently the cue should be to destroy not the army but the materials. The death of a Turkish bridge or rail, machine or gun, or high explosive was more profitable than the death of a Turk. The Arab army just then was equally chary of men and materials: of men because they being irregulars were not units, but individuals, and an individual casualty is like a pebble dropped in water: each may make only a brief hole, but rings of sorrow widen out from them. The Arab army could not afford casualties. Materials were easier to deal with. Hence its obvious duty to make itself superior in some one branch, guncotton or machine guns, or whatever could be most decisive. Foch had laid down the maxim, applying it to men, of being superior at the critical point and moment of attack. The Arab army might apply it to materials, and be superior in equipment in one dominant moment or respect.

For both men and things it might try to give Foch's doctrine a negative twisted side, for cheapness' sake, and be weaker than the enemy everywhere except in one point or matter. Most wars are wars of contact, both forces striving to keep in touch to avoid tactical surprise. The Arab war should be a war of detachment: to contain the enemy by the silent threat of a vast unknown desert, not disclosing themselves till the moment of attack. This attack need be only nominal, directed not against his men, but against his materials: so it should not seek for his main strength or his weaknesses, but for his most accessible material. In railway cutting this would be usually an empty stretch of rail. This was a tactical success. From this theory came to be developed ultimately an unconscious habit of never engaging the enemy at all. This chimed with the numerical plea of never giving the enemy's soldier a target. Many Turks on the Arab front had no chance all the war to fire a shot, and correspondingly the Arabs were never on the defensive, except by rare accident. The corollary of such a rule was perfect "intelligence," so that plans could be made in complete certainty. The chief agent had to be the general's head (de Feuquière said this first), and his knowledge had to be faultless, leaving no room for chance. The headquarters of the Arab army probably took more pains in this service than any other staff.

The Crowd in Action   The third factor in command seemed to be the psychological, that science (Xenophon called it diathetic) of which our propaganda is a stained and ignoble part. It concerns the crowd, the adjustment of spirit to the point where it becomes fit to exploit in action. It considers the capacity for mood of the men, their complexities and mutability, and the cultivation of what in them profits the intention. The command of the Arab army had to arrange their men's minds in order of battle, just as carefully and as formally as other officers arranged their bodies: and not only their own men's minds, though them first: the minds of the enemy, so far as it could reach them:

and thirdly, the mind of the nation supporting it behind the firing-line, and the mind of the hostile nation waiting the verdict, and the neutrals looking on.

It was the ethical in war, and the process on which the command mainly depended for victory on the Arab front. The printing press is the greatest weapon in the armoury of the modern commander, and the commanders of the Arab army being amateurs in the art, began their war in the atmosphere of the 20th century, and thought of their weapons without prejudice, not distinguishing one from another socially. The regular officer has the tradition of 40 generations of serving soldiers behind him, and to him the old weapons are the most honoured. The Arab command had seldom to concern itself with what its men did, but much with what they thought, and to it the diathetic was more than half command. In Europe it was set a little aside and entrusted to men outside the General Staff. But the Arab army was so weak physically that it could not let the metaphysical weapon rust unused. It had won a province when the civilians in it had been taught to die for the ideal of freedom: the presence or absence of the enemy was a secondary matter.

These reasonings showed that the idea of assaulting Medina, or even of starving it quickly into surrender, was not in accord with the best strategy. Rather, let the enemy stay in Medina, and in every other harmless place, in the largest numbers. If he showed a disposition to evacuate too soon, as a step to concentrating in the small area which his numbers could dominate effectively, then the Arab army would have to try and restore his confidence, not harshly, but by reducing its enterprises against him. The ideal was to keep his railway just working, but only just, with the maximum of loss and discomfort to him.

The Turkish army was an accident, not a target. Our true strategic aim was to seek its weakest link, and bear only on that till time made the mass of it fall. The Arab army must impose the longest possible passive defence on the Turks (this being the most materially expensive form of war) by extending its own front to the maximum. Tactically it must develop a highly mobile, highly equipped type of force, of the smallest size, and use it successively at distributed points of the Turkish line, to make the Turks reinforce their occupying posts beyond the economic minimum of 20 men. The power of this striking force would not be reckoned merely by its strength. The ratio between number and area determined the character of the war, and by having five times the mobility of the Turks the Arabs could be on terms with them with one-fifth their number.

Range over Force Success was certain, to be proved by paper and pencil as soon as the proportion of space and number had been learned. The contest was not physical, but moral, and so battles were a mistake. All that could be won in a battle was the ammunition the enemy fired off. Napoleon had said it was rare to find generals willing to fight battles. The curse of this war was that so few could do anything else. Napoleon had spoken in angry reaction against the excessive finesse of the 18th century, when men almost forgot that war gave licence to murder. Military thought had been swinging out on his dictum for 100 years, and it was time to go back a bit again. Battles are impositions on the side which believes itself weaker, made unavoidable either by lack of land-room, or by the need to defend a material property dearer than the lives of soldiers. The Arabs had nothing material to lose, so they were to defend nothing and to shoot nothing. Their cards were speed and time, not hitting power, and these gave them strategical rather than tactical strength. Range is more to strategy than force. The invention of bully-beef had modified land-war more profoundly than the invention of gunpowder.

The British military authorities did not follow all these arguments, but gave leave for their practical application to be tried. Accordingly the Arab forces went off first to Akaba and took it easily. Then they took Tafileh and the Dead Sea; then Azrak and Deraa, and finally Damascus, all in successive stages worked out consciously on these theories. The process was to set up ladders of tribes, which should provide a safe and comfortable route from the sea-bases (Yenbo, Wejh or Akaba) to the advanced bases of operation. These were sometimes 300 miles away, a long distance in lands without railways or roads, but made short for the Arab Army by an assiduous cultivation of desert-power, control by camel parties of the desolate and unmapped wilderness which fills up all the centre of Arabia, from Mecca to Aleppo and Baghdad.

The Desert and the Sea   In character these operations were like naval warfare, in their mobility, their ubiquity, their independence of bases and communications, in their ignoring of ground features, of strategic areas, of fixed directions, of fixed points. "He who commands the sea is at great liberty, and may take as much or as little of the war as he will": he who commands the desert is equally fortunate. Camel raiding-parties, self-contained like ships, could cruise securely along the enemy's land-frontier, just out of sight of his posts along the edge of cultivation, and tap or raid into his lines where it seemed fittest or easiest or most profitable, with a sure retreat always behind them into an element which the Turks could not enter.

Discrimination of what point of the enemy organism to arrange came with practice. The tactics were always tip and run; not pushes, but strokes. The Arab army never tried to maintain or improve an advantage, but to move off and strike again somewhere else. It used the smallest force in the quickest time at the farthest place. To continue the action till the enemy had changed his dispositions to resist it would have been to break the spirit of the fundamental rule of denying him targets.

The necessary speed and range were attained by the frugality of the desert men, and their efficiency on camels. In the heat of summer Arabian camels will do about 250 miles comfortably between drinks: and this represented three days' vigorous marching. This radius was always more than was needed, for wells are seldom more than 100 miles apart. The equipment of the raiding parties aimed at simplicity, with nevertheless a technical superiority over the Turks in the critical department. Quantities of light machine guns were obtained from Egypt for use not as machine guns, but as automatic rifles, snipers' tools, by men kept deliberately in ignorance of their mechanism, so that the speed of action would not be hampered by attempts at repair. Another special feature was high explosives, and nearly every one in the revolt was qualified by rule of thumb experience in demolition work.

Armoured Cars   On some occasions tribal raids were strengthened by armoured cars, manned by Englishmen. Armoured cars, once they have found a possible track, can keep up with a camel party. On the march to Damascus, when nearly 400 miles off their base, they were first maintained by a baggage train of petrol-laden camels, and afterwards from the air. Cars are magnificent fighting machines, and decisive whenever they can come into action on their own conditions. But though each has for main principle that of "fire in movement," yet the tactical employments of cars and camel-corps are so different that their use in joint operations is difficult. It was found demoralizing to both to use armoured and unarmoured cavalry together.

The distribution of the raiding parties was unorthodox. It was impossible to mix or combine tribes, since they disliked or distrusted one another. Likewise the men of one tribe could not be used in the territory of another. In consequence, another canon of orthodox strategy was broken by following the principle of the widest distribution of force, in order to have the greatest number of raids on hand at once, and fluidity was added to speed by using one district on Monday, another on Tuesday, a third on Wednesday. This much reinforced the natural mobility of the Arab army, giving it priceless advantages in pursuit, for the force renewed itself with fresh men in every new tribal area, and so maintained its pristine energy. Maximum disorder was, in a real sense its equilibrium.

An Undisciplined Army The internal economy of the raiding parties was equally curious. Maximum irregularity and articulation were the aims. Diversity threw the enemy intelligence off the track. By the regular organization in identical battalions and divisions information builds itself up, until the presence of a corps can be inferred on corpses from three companies. The Arabs, again, were serving a common ideal, without tribal emulation, and so could not hope for any *esprit de corps.* Soldiers are made a caste either by being given great pay and rewards in money, uniform or political privileges; or, as in England, by being made outcasts, cut off from the mass of their fellow-citizens. There have been many armies enlisted voluntarily: there have been few armies serving voluntarily under such trying conditions, for so long a war as the Arab revolt. Any of the Arabs could go home whenever the conviction failed him. Their only contract was honour.

Consequently the Arab army had no discipline, in the sense in which it is restrictive, submergent of individuality, the Lowest Common Denominator of men. In regular armies in peace it means the limit of energy attainable by everybody present: it is the hunt not of an average, but of an absolute, a 100-per-cent standard, in which the 99 stronger men are played down to the level of the worst. The aim is to render the unit a unit, and the man a type, in order that their effort shall be calculable, their collective output even in grain and in bulk. The deeper the discipline, the lower the individual efficiency, and the more sure the performance. It is a deliberate sacrifice of capacity in order to reduce the uncertain element, the bionomic factor, in enlisted humanity, and its accompaniment is *compound* or social war, that form in which the fighting man has to be the product of the multiplied exertions of long hierarchy, from workshop to supply unit, which maintains him in the field.

The Arab war, reacting against this, was *simple* and individual. Every enrolled man served in the line of battle, and was self-contained. There were no lines of communication or labour troops. It seemed that in this articulated warfare, the sum yielded by single men would be at least equal to the product of a compound system of the same strength, and it was certainly easier to adjust to tribal life and manners, given elasticity and understanding on the part of the commanding officers. Fortunately for its chances nearly every young Englishman has the roots of eccentricity in him. Only a sprinkling were employed, not more than one per 1,000 of the Arab troops. A larger proportion would have created friction, just because they were foreign bodies (pearls if you please) in the oyster: and those who were present controlled by influence and advice, by their superior knowledge, not by an extraneous authority.

The practice was, however, not to employ in the firing line the greater numbers which the adoption of a "simple" system made available theoretically. Instead, they were used in relay: otherwise the attack would have become too extended. Guerrillas must be allowed liberal work-room. In irregular war if two men are together one is being wasted. The moral strain of isolated action makes this simple form of war very hard on the individual soldier, and exacts from him special initiative, endurance and enthusiasm. Here the ideal was to make action a series of single combats to make the ranks a happy alliance of commanders-in-chief. The value of the Arab army depended entirely on quality, not on quantity. The members had to keep always cool, for the excitement of a blood-lust would impair their science, and their victory depended on a just use of speed, concealment, accuracy of fire. Guerrilla war is far more intellectual than a bayonet charge.

The Exact Science of Guerrilla Warfare   By careful persistence, kept strictly within its strength and following the spirit of these theories, the Arab army was able eventually to reduce the Turks to helplessness, and complete victory seemed to be almost within sight when General Allenby by his immense stroke in Palestine threw the enemy's main forces into hopeless confusion and put an immediate end to the Turkish war. His too-greatness deprived the Arab revolt of the opportunity of following to the end the dictum of Saxe that a war might be won without fighting battles. But it can at least be said that its leaders worked by his light for two years, and the work stood. This is a pragmatic argument that cannot be wholly derided. The experiment, although not complete, strengthened the belief that irregular war or rebellion could be proved to be an exact science, and an inevitable success, granted certain factors and if pursued along certain lines.

Here is the thesis: Rebellion must have an unassailable base, something guarded not merely from attack, but from the fear of it: such a base as the Arab revolt had in the Red Sea ports, the desert, or in the minds of men converted to its creed. It must have a sophisticated alien enemy, in the form of a disciplined army of occupation too small to fulfil the doctrine of acreage: too few to adjust number to space, in order to dominate the whole area effectively from fortified posts. It must have a friendly population, not actively friendly, but sympathetic to the point of not betraying rebel movements to the enemy. Rebellions can be made by 2% active in a striking force, and 98% passively sympathetic. The few active rebels must have the qualities of speed and endurance, ubiquity and independence of arteries of supply. They must have the technical equipment to destroy or paralyze the enemy's organized communications, for irregular war is fairly Willisen's definition of strategy, "the study of communication," in its extreme degree, of attack where the enemy is not. In 50 words: Granted mobility, security (in the form of denying targets to the enemy), time, and doctrine (the idea to convert every subject to friendliness), victory will rest with the insurgents, for the algebraical factors are in the end decisive, and against them perfections of means and spirit struggle quite in vain.

ON GUERRILLA WARFARE

Mao Tse-tung

WHAT IS GUERRILLA WARFARE?

In a war of revolutionary character, guerrilla operations are a necessary part. This is particularly true in a war waged for the emancipation of a people who inhabit a vast nation. China is such a nation, a nation whose techniques are undeveloped and whose communications are poor. She finds herself confronted with a strong and victorious Japanese imperialism. Under these circumstances, the development of the type of guerrilla warfare characterized by the quality of mass is both necessary and natural. This warfare must be developed to an unprecedented degree and it must coordinate with the operations of our regular armies. If we fail to do this, we will find it difficult to defeat the enemy.

These guerrilla operations must not be considered as an independent form of warfare. They are but one step in the total war, one aspect of the revolutionary struggle. They are the inevitable result of the clash between oppressor and oppressed when the latter reach the limits of their endurance. In our case, these hostilities began at a time when the people were unable to endure any more from the Japanese imperialists. Lenin, in *People and Revolution,* said: "A people's insurrection and a people's revolution are not only natural but inevitable." We consider guerrilla operations as but one aspect of our total or mass war because they, lacking the quality of independence, are of themselves incapable of providing a solution to the struggle.

Guerrilla warfare has qualities and objectives peculiar to itself. It is a weapon that a nation inferior in arms and military equipment may employ against a more powerful aggressor nation. When the invader pierces deep into the heart of the weaker country and occupies her territory in a cruel and oppressive manner, there is no doubt that conditions of terrain, climate, and society in general offer obstacles to his progress and may be used to advantage by those who oppose him. In guerrilla warfare, we turn these advantages to the purpose of resisting and defeating the enemy.

During the progress of hostilities, guerrillas gradually develop into orthodox forces that operate in conjunction with other units of the regular army. Thus the regularly organized troops, those guerrillas who have attained that status, and those who have not reached that level of development combine to form the military power of a national revolutionary war. There can be no doubt that the ultimate result of this will be victory.

Both in its development and in its method of application, guerrilla warfare has certain distinctive characteristics. We first discuss the relationship of guerrilla warfare to national policy. Because ours is the resistance of a semicolonial country against an imperialism, our hostilities must have a clearly defined political goal and firmly

Mao Tse-tung, *On Guerrilla Warfare,* translated by Brig. Gen. Samuel B. Griffith, USMC (Ret.) (New York: Praeger, 1961), Chapters 1, 2, and 6.

established political responsibilities. Our basic policy is the creation of a national united anti-Japanese front. This policy we pursue in order to gain our political goal, which is the complete emancipation of the Chinese people. There are certain fundamental steps necessary in the realization of this policy, to wit:

1. Arousing and organizing the people.
2. Achieving internal unification politically.
3. Establishing bases.
4. Equipping forces.
5. Recovering national strength.
6. Destroying enemy's national strength.
7. Regaining lost territories.

There is no reason to consider guerrilla warfare separately from national policy. On the contrary, it must be organized and conducted in complete accord with national anti-Japanese policy. It is only those who misinterpret guerrilla action who say, as does Jen Ch'i Shan, "The question of guerrilla hostilities is purely a military matter and not a political one." Those who maintain this simple point of view have lost sight of the political goal and the political effects of guerrilla action. Such a simple point of view will cause the people to lose confidence and will result in our defeat.

What is the relationship of guerrilla warfare to the people? Without a political goal, guerrilla warfare must fail, as it must if its political objectives do not coincide with the aspirations of the people and their sympathy, cooperation, and assistance cannot be gained. The essence of guerrilla warfare is thus revolutionary in character. On the other hand, in a war of counterrevolutionary nature, there is no place for guerrilla hostilities. Because guerrilla warfare basically derives from the masses and is supported by them, it can neither exist nor flourish if it separates itself from their sympathies and cooperation. There are those who do not comprehend guerrilla action, and who therefore do not understand the distinguishing qualities of a people's guerrilla war, who say: "Only regular troops can carry on guerrilla operations." There are others who, because they do not believe in the ultimate success of guerrilla action, mistakenly say: "Guerrilla warfare is an insignificant and highly specialized type of operation in which there is no place for the masses of the people" (Jen Ch'i Shan). Then there are those who ridicule the masses and undermine resistance by wildly asserting that the people have no understanding of the war of resistance (Yeh Ch'ing, for one). The moment that this war of resistance dissociates itself from the masses of the people is the precise moment that it dissociates itself from hope of ultimate victory over the Japanese.

What is the organization for guerrilla warfare? Though all guerrilla bands that spring from the masses of the people suffer from lack of organization at the time of their formation, they all have in common a basic quality that makes organization possible. All guerrilla units must have political and military leadership. This is true regardless of the source or size of such units. Such units may originate locally, in the masses of the people; they may be formed from an admixture of regular troops with groups of the people, or they may consist of regular army units intact. And mere quantity does not affect this matter. Such units may consist of a squad of a few men, a battalion of several hundred men, or a regiment of several thousand men.

All these must have leaders who are unyielding in their policies—resolute, loyal, sincere, and robust. These men must be well educated in revolutionary technique, self-confident, able to establish severe discipline, and able to cope with counterpropaganda. In short, these leaders must be models for the people. As the war progresses, such leaders will gradually overcome the lack of discipline, which at first prevails; they will establish discipline in their forces, strengthening them and increasing their combat efficiency. Thus eventual victory will be attained.

Unorganized guerrilla warfare cannot contribute to victory and those who attack the movement as a combination of banditry and anarchism do not understand the nature of guerrilla action. They say: "This movement is a haven for disappointed militarists, vagabonds and bandits" (Jen Ch'i Shan), hoping thus to bring the movement into disrepute. We do not deny that there are corrupt guerrillas, nor that there are people who under the guise of guerrillas indulge in unlawful activities. Neither do we deny that the movement has at the present time symptoms of a lack of organization, symptoms that might indeed be serious were we to judge guerrilla warfare solely by the corrupt and temporary phenomena we have mentioned. We should study the corrupt phenomena and attempt to eradicate them in order to encourage guerrilla warfare, and to increase its military efficiency. "This is hard work, there is no help for it, and the problem cannot be solved immediately. The whole people must try to reform themselves during the course of the war. We must educate them and reform them in the light of past experience. Evil does not exist in guerrilla warfare but only in the unorganized and undisciplined activities that are anarchism," said Lenin, in *On Guerrilla Warfare.*

What is basic guerrilla strategy? Guerrilla strategy must be based primarily on alertness, mobility, and attack. It must be adjusted to the enemy situation, the terrain, the existing lines of communication, the relative strengths, the weather, and the situation of the people.

In guerrilla warfare, select the tactic of seeming to come from the east and attacking from the west; avoid the solid, attack the hollow; attack; withdraw; deliver a lightning blow, seek a lightning decision. When guerrillas engage a stronger enemy, they withdraw when he advances; harass him when he stops; strike him when he is weary; pursue him when he withdraws. In guerrilla strategy, the enemy's rear, flanks, and other vulnerable spots are his vital points, and there he must be harassed, attacked, dispersed, exhausted and annihilated. Only in this way can guerrillas carry out their mission of independent guerrilla action and coordination with the effort of the regular armies. But, in spite of the most complete preparation, there can be no victory if mistakes are made in the matter of command. Guerrilla warfare based on the principles we have mentioned and carried on over a vast extent of territory in which communications are inconvenient will contribute tremendously towards ultimate defeat of the Japanese and consequent emancipation of the Chinese people.

A careful distinction must be made between two types of guerrilla warfare. The fact that revolutionary guerrilla warfare is based on the masses of the people does not in itself mean that the organization of guerrilla units is impossible in a war of counterrevolutionary character. As examples of the former type we may cite Red guerrilla hostilities during the Russian Revolution; those of the Reds in China; of the Abyssinians against the Italians for the past three years; those of the last seven years in Manchuria, and the vast anti-Japanese guerrilla war that is carried on in China today. All these struggles have been carried on in the interests of the whole people or the greater part of them; all had a broad basis in the national manpower, and all have been in accord with the laws of historical development. They have existed and will continue to exist, flourish, and develop as long as they are not contrary to national policy.

The second type of guerrilla warfare directly contradicts the law of historical development. Of this type, we may cite the examples furnished by the White Russian guerrilla units organized by Denikin and Kolchak; those organized by the Japanese; those organized by the Italians in Abyssinia; those supported by the puppet governments in Manchuria and Mongolia, and those that will be organized here by Chinese traitors. All such have oppressed the masses and have been contrary to the true interests of the people. They must be firmly opposed. They are easy to destroy because they lack a broad foundation in the people.

If we fail to differentiate between the two types of guerrilla hostilities mentioned, it is likely that we will exaggerate their effect when applied by an invader. We might arrive at the conclusion that "the invader can organize guerrilla units from among the people." Such a conclusion might well diminish our confidence in guerrilla warfare. As far as this matter is concerned, we have but to remember the historical experience of revolutionary struggles.

Further, we must distinguish general revolutionary wars from those of a purely "class" type. In the former case, the whole people of a nation, without regard to class or party, carry on a guerrilla struggle that is an instrument of the national policy. Its basis is, therefore, much broader than is the basis of a struggle of class type. Of a general guerrilla war, it has been said: "When a nation is invaded, the people become sympathetic to one another and all aid in organizing guerrilla units. In civil war, no matter to what extent guerrillas are developed, they do not produce the same results as when they are formed to resist an invasion by foreigners" (*Civil War in Russia*). The one strong feature of guerrilla warfare in a civil struggle is its quality of internal purity. One class may be easily united and perhaps fight with great effect, whereas in a national revolutionary war, guerrilla units are faced with the problem of internal unification of different class groups. This necessitates the use of propaganda. Both types of guerrilla war are, however, similar in that they both employ the same military methods.

National guerrilla warfare, though historically of the same consistency, has employed varying implements as times, peoples, and conditions differ. The guerrilla aspects of the Opium War, those of the fighting in Manchuria since the Mukden incident, and those employed in China today are all slightly different. The guerrilla warfare conducted by the Moroccans against the French and the Spanish was not exactly similar to that which we conduct today in China. These differences express the characteristics of different peoples in different periods. Although there is a general similarity in the quality of all these struggles, there are dissimilarities in form. This fact we must recognize. Clausewitz wrote, in *On War:* "Wars in every period have independent forms and independent conditions, and, therefore, every period must have its independent theory of war." Lenin, in *On Guerrilla Warfare,* said: "As regards the form of fighting, it is unconditionally requisite that history be investigated in order to discover the conditions of environment, the state of economic progress, and the political ideas that obtained, the national characteristics, customs, and degree of civilization." Again: "It is necessary to be completely unsympathetic to abstract formulas and rules and to study with sympathy the conditions of the actual fighting, for these will change in accordance with the political and economic situations and the realization of the people's aspirations. These progressive changes in conditions create new methods."

If, in today's struggle, we fail to apply the historical truths of revolutionary guerrilla war, we will fall into the error of believing with T'ou Hsi Sheng that under the impact of Japan's mechanized army, "the guerrilla unit has lost its historical function." Jen Ch'i Shan writes: "In olden days, guerrilla warfare was part of regular strategy but there is almost no chance that it can be applied today." These opinions are harmful. If we do not make an estimate of the characteristics peculiar to our anti-Japanese guerrilla war, but insist on applying to it mechanical formulas derived from past history, we are making the mistake of placing our hostilities in the same category as all other national guerrilla struggles. If we hold this view, we will simply be beating our heads against a stone wall and we will be unable to profit from guerrilla hostilities.

To summarize: What is the guerrilla war of resistance against Japan? It is one aspect of the entire war, which, although alone incapable of producing the decision, attacks the enemy in every quarter, diminishes the extent of area under his control, increases our national strength, and assists our regular armies. It is one of the strategic instruments used to inflict defeat on our enemy. It is the one pure expression of anti-Japanese policy, that is to say, it is military strength organized by the active people and inseparable from them. It is a powerful special weapon with which we resist the Japanese and without which we cannot defeat them. . . .

THE RELATION OF GUERRILLA HOSTILITIES TO REGULAR OPERATIONS

The general features of orthodox hostilities, that is, the war of position and the war of movement, differ fundamentally from guerrilla warfare. There are other readily apparent differences such as those in organization, armament, equipment, supply, tactics, command; in conception of the terms "front" and "rear"; in the matter of military responsibilities.

When considered from the point of view of total numbers, guerrilla units are many; as individual combat units, they may vary in size from the smallest, of several score or several hundred men, to the battalion or the regiment, of several thousand. This is not the case in regularly organized units. A primary feature of guerrilla operations is their dependence upon the people themselves to organize battalions and other units. As a result of this, organization depends largely upon local circumstances. In the case of guerrilla groups, the standard of equipment is of a low order, and they must depend for their sustenance primarily upon what the locality affords.

The strategy of guerrilla warfare is manifestly unlike that employed in orthodox operations, as the basic tactic of the former is constant activity and movement. There is in guerrilla warfare no such thing as a decisive battle; there is nothing comparable to the fixed, passive defense that characterizes orthodox war. In guerrilla warfare, the transformation of a moving situation into a positional defensive situation never arises. The general features of reconnaissance, partial deployment, general deployment, and development of the attack that are usual in mobile warfare are not common in guerrilla war.

There are differences also in the matter of leadership and command. In guerrilla warfare, small units acting independently play the principal role, and there must be no excessive interference with their activities. In orthodox warfare, particularly in a moving situation, a certain degree of initiative is accorded subordinates, but in principle, command is centralized. This is done because all units and all supporting arms in all districts must coordinate to the highest degree. In the case of guerrilla warfare, this is not only undesirable but impossible. Only adjacent guerrilla units can coordinate their activities to any degree. Strategically, their activities can be roughly correlated with those of the regular forces, and tactically, they must cooperate with adjacent units of the regular army. But there are no strictures on the extent of guerrilla activity nor is it primarily characterized by the quality of cooperation of many units.

When we discuss the terms "front" and "rear," it must be remembered, that while guerrillas do have bases, their primary field of activity is in the enemy's rear areas. They themselves have no rear. Because an orthodox army has rear installations (except in some special cases as during the 10,000-mile march of the Red Army or as in the case of certain units operating in Shansi Province), it cannot operate as guerrillas can.

As to the matter of military responsibilities, those of the guerrillas are to exterminate small forces of the enemy; to harass and weaken large forces; to attack enemy lines of communication; to establish bases capable of supporting independent operations in the enemy's rear; to force the enemy to disperse his strength; and to coordinate all these activities with those of the regular armies on distant battle fronts.

From the foregoing summary of differences that exist between guerrilla warfare and orthodox warfare, it can be seen that it is improper to compare the two. Further distinction must be made in order to clarify this matter. While the Eighth Route Army is a regular army, its North China campaign is essentially guerrilla in nature, for it operates in the enemy's rear. On occasion, however, Eighth Route Army commanders have concentrated powerful forces to strike an enemy in motion, and the characteristics of orthodox mobile warfare were evident in the battle at P'ing Hsing Kuan and in other engagements.

On the other hand, after the fall of Feng Ling Tu, the operations of Central Shansi, and Suiyuan, troops were more guerrilla than orthodox in nature. In this connection, the precise character of Generalissimo Chiang's instructions to the effect that independent brigades would carry out guerrilla operations should be recalled. In spite of such temporary activities, these orthodox units retained their identity and after the fall of Feng Ling Tu, they not only were able to fight along orthodox lines but often found it necessary to do so. This is an example of the fact that orthodox armies may, due to changes in the situation, temporarily function as guerrillas.

Likewise, guerrilla units formed from the people may gradually develop into regular units and, when operating as such, employ the tactics of orthodox mobile war. While these units function as guerrillas, they may be compared to innumerable gnats, which, by biting a giant both in front and in rear, ultimately exhaust him. They make themselves as unendurable as a group of cruel and hateful devils, and as they grow and attain gigantic proportions, they will find that their victim is not only exhausted but practically perishing. It is for this very reason that our guerrilla activities are a source of constant mental worry to Imperial Japan.

While it is improper to confuse orthodox with guerrilla operations, it is equally improper to consider that there is a chasm between the two. While differences do exist, similarities appear under certain conditions, and this fact must be appreciated if we wish to establish clearly the relationship between the two. If we consider both types of warfare as a single subject, or if we confuse guerrilla warfare with the mobile operations of orthodox war, we fall into this error: We exaggerate the function of guerrillas and minimize that of the regular armies. If we agree with Chang Tso Hua, who says, "Guerrilla warfare is the primary war strategy of a people seeking to emancipate itself," or with Kao Kang, who believes that "Guerrilla strategy is the only strategy possible for an oppressed people," we are exaggerating the importance of guerrilla hostilities. What these zealous friends I have just quoted do not realize is this: If we do not fit guerrilla operations into their proper niche, we cannot promote them realistically. Then, not only would those who oppose us take advantage of our varying opinions to turn them to their own uses to undermine us, but guerrillas would be led to assume responsibilities they could not successfully discharge and that should properly be carried out by orthodox forces. In the meantime, the important guerrilla function of coordinating activities with the regular forces would be neglected.

Furthermore, if the theory that guerrilla warfare is our only strategy were actually applied, the regular forces would be weakened, we would be divided in purpose, and guerrilla hostilities would decline. If we say, "Let us transform the regular forces into guerrillas," and do not place our first reliance on a victory to be gained by the regular armies over the enemy, we may certainly expect to see as a result the failure of the anti-Japanese war of resistance. The concept that guerrilla warfare is an end in itself and that guerrilla activities can be divorced from those of the regular forces is incorrect. If we assume that guerrilla warfare does not progress from beginning to end beyond its elementary forms, we have failed to recognize the fact that guerrilla hostilities can, under specific conditions, develop and assume orthodox characteristics. An opinion that admits the existence of guerrilla war, but isolates it, is one that does not properly estimate the potentialities of such war.

Equally dangerous is the concept that condemns guerrilla war on the ground that war has no other aspects than the purely orthodox. This opinion is often expressed by those who have seen the corrupt phenomena of some guerrilla regimes, observed their lack of discipline, and have seen them used as a screen behind which certain persons have indulged in bribery and other corrupt practices. These people will not admit the fundamental necessity for guerrilla bands that spring from the armed people. They say, "Only the regular forces are capable of conducting guerrilla operations." This theory is a mistaken one and would lead to the abolition of the people's guerrilla war.

A proper conception of the relationship that exists between guerrilla effort and that of the regular forces is essential. We believe it can be stated this way: "Guerrilla operations during the anti-Japanese war may for a certain time and temporarily become its paramount feature, particularly insofar as the enemy's rear is concerned. However, if we view the war as a whole, there can be no doubt that our regular forces are of primary importance, because it is they who are alone capable of producing the decision. Guerrilla warfare assists them in producing this favorable decision. Orthodox forces may under certain conditions operate as guerrillas, and the latter may, under certain conditions, develop to the status of the former. However, both guerrilla forces and regular forces have their own respective development and their proper combinations."

To clarify the relationship between the mobile aspect of orthodox war and guerrilla war, we may say that general agreement exists that the principal element of our strategy must be mobility. With the war of movement, we may at times combine the war of position. Both of these are assisted by general guerrilla hostilities. It is true that on the battlefield mobile war often becomes positional; it is true that this situation may be reversed; it is equally true that each form may combine with the other. The possibility of such combination will become more evident after the prevailing standards of equipment have been raised. For example, in a general strategical counterattack to recapture key cities and lines of communication, it would be normal to use both mobile and positional methods. However, the point must again be made that our fundamental strategical form must be the war of movement. If we deny this, we cannot arrive at the victorious solution of the war. In sum, while we must promote guerrilla warfare as a necessary strategical auxiliary to orthodox operations, we must neither assign it the primary position in our war strategy nor substitute it for mobile and positional warfare as conducted by orthodox forces. . . .

THE POLITICAL PROBLEMS OF GUERRILLA WARFARE

. . . I mentioned the fact that guerrilla troops should have a precise conception of the political goal of the struggle and the political organization to be used in attaining that goal. This means that both organization and discipline of guerrilla troops must be at a high level so that they can carry out the political activities that are the life of both the guerrilla armies and of revolutionary warfare.

First of all, political activities depend upon the indoctrination of both military and political leaders with the idea of anti-Japanism. Through them, the idea is transmitted to the troops. One must not feel that he is anti-Japanese merely because he is a member of a guerrilla unit. The anti-Japanese idea must be an ever-present conviction, and if it is forgotten, we may succumb to the temptations of the enemy or be overcome with discouragements. In a war of long duration, those whose conviction that the people must be emancipated is not deep rooted are likely to become shaken in their faith or actually revolt. Without the general education that enables everyone to understand our goal of driving out Japanese imperialism and establishing a free and happy China, the soldiers fight without conviction and lose their determination.

The political goal must be clearly and precisely indicated to inhabitants of guerrilla zones and their national consciousness awakened. Hence, a concrete explanation of the political systems used is important not only to guerrilla troops but to all those who are concerned with the realization of our political goal. The Kuomintang has issued a pamphlet entitled *System of National Organization for War,* which should be widely distributed throughout guerrilla zones. If we lack national organization, we will lack the essential unity that should exist between the soldiers and the people.

A study and comprehension of the political objectives of this war and of the anti-Japanese front is particularly important for officers of guerrilla troops. There are some militarists who say: "We are not interested in politics but only in the profession of arms." It is vital that these simpleminded militarists be made to realize the relationship that exists between politics and military affairs. Military action is a method used to attain a political goal. While military affairs and political affairs are not identical, it is impossible to isolate one from the other.

It is to be hoped that the world is in the last era of strife. The vast majority of human beings have already prepared or are preparing to fight a war that will bring justice to the oppressed peoples of the world. No matter how long this war may last, there is no doubt that it will be followed by an unprecedented epoch of peace. The war that we are fighting today for the emancipation of the Chinese is a part of the war for the freedom of all human beings, and the independent, happy, and liberal China that we are fighting to establish will be a part of that new world order. A conception like this is difficult for the simple-minded militarist to grasp and it must therefore be carefully explained to him.

There are three additional matters that must be considered under the broad question of political activities. These are political activities, first, as applied to the troops; second, as applied to the people; and, third, as applied to the enemy. The fundamental problems are: first, spiritual unification of officers and men within the army; second, spiritual unification of the army and the people; and, last, destruction of the unity of the enemy. The concrete methods for achieving these unities are discussed in detail in pamphlet Number 4 of this series, entitled *Political Activities in Anti-Japanese Guerrilla Warfare.*

A revolutionary army must have discipline that is established on a limited democratic basis. In all armies, obedience of the subordinates to their superiors must be exacted. This is true in the case of guerrilla discipline, but the basis for guerrilla discipline must be the individual conscience. With guerrillas, a discipline of compulsion is ineffective. In any revolutionary army, there is unity of purpose as far as both officers and men are concerned, and, therefore, within such an army, discipline is self-imposed. Although discipline in guerrilla ranks is not as severe as in the ranks of orthodox forces, the necessity for discipline exists. This must be self-imposed, because only when it is, is the soldier able to understand completely why he fights and why he must obey. This type of discipline becomes a tower of strength within the army, and it is the only type that can truly harmonize the relationship that exists between officers and soldiers.

In any system where discipline is externally imposed, the relationship that exists between officer and man is characterized by indifference of the one to the other. The idea that officers can physically beat or severely tongue-lash their men is a feudal one and is not in accord with the conception of a self-imposed discipline. Discipline of the feudal type will destroy internal unity and fighting strength. A discipline self-imposed is the primary characteristic of a democratic system in the army.

A secondary characteristic is found in the degree of liberties accorded officers and soldiers. In a revolutionary army, all individuals enjoy political liberty and the question, for example, of the emancipation of the people must not only be tolerated but discussed, and propaganda must be encouraged. Further, in such an army, the mode of living of the officers and the soldiers must not differ too much, and this is particularly true in the case of guerrilla troops. Officers should live under the same conditions as their men, for that is the only way in which they can gain from their men the admiration and confidence so vital in war. It is incorrect to hold to a theory of equality in all things, but there must be equality of existence in accepting the hardships and dangers of war. Thus we may attain to the unification of the officer and soldier groups, a unity both horizontal within the group itself, and vertical, that is, from lower to higher echelons. It is only when such unity is present that units can be said to be powerful combat factors.

There is also a unity of spirit that should exist between troops and local inhabitants. The Eighth Route Army put into practice a code known as "The Three Rules and the Eight Remarks," which we list here:

Rules:
1. All actions are subject to command.
2. Do not steal from the people.
3. Be neither selfish nor unjust.

Remarks:
1. Replace the door when you leave the house.
2. Roll up the bedding on which you have slept.
3. Be courteous.
4. Be honest in your transactions.
5. Return what you borrow.
6. Replace what you break.
7. Do not bathe in the presence of women.
8. Do not without authority search the pocketbooks of those you arrest.

The Red Army adhered to this code for ten years and the Eighth Route Army and other units have since adopted it.

Many people think it impossible for guerrillas to exist for long in the enemy's rear. Such a belief reveals lack of comprehension of the relationship that should exist between the people and the troops. The former may be likened to water and the latter to the fish who inhabit it. How may it be said that these two cannot exist together? It is only undisciplined troops who make the people their enemies and who, like the fish out of its native element, cannot live.

We further our mission of destroying the enemy by propagandizing his troops, by treating his captured soldiers with consideration, and by caring for those of his wounded who fall into our hands. If we fail in these respects, we strengthen the solidarity of our enemy.

PATTERNS OF VIOLENCE
IN WORLD POLITICS

Samuel P. Huntington

THE CHANGING LOCUS OF VIOLENCE

"An arena is *military,*" say Lasswell and Kaplan, "when the expectation of violence is high; *civic,* when the expectation of violence is low."[1] For three centuries in the West international politics has been viewed as a military arena, and the domestic politics of nation-states have been thought to be civic arenas. Continuing this pattern, after World War II the expectations and apprehensions of international war, particularly war between Communist and Western states, were high. In practice, however, international violence was relatively infrequent. The Korean War was the only major prolonged interstate war between 1945 and 1960. Previously, of course, much longer periods of time had passed with even fewer interstate wars. These, however, were also periods of relative harmony with few significant clashes of interest between states. The fifteen years after World War II were marked by intense international conflicts, not only between the Soviet bloc and the West, but also between many other states over local issues. Nonetheless, with a few exceptions, governments did not resort to war. Never before in human history, one might say, were such high expectations of interstate violence accompanied by so little interstate violence in actuality.

The willingness of governments to resort to interstate violence presumably is affected by considerations of domestic politics and calculations of international gains. The decision to go to war or to take action that seriously risks war is seldom made casually.[2] In the past, when governments "blundered" into wars they did not want or could not win, the result was usually caused not by a refusal to act in a rational manner but by deficiencies in knowledge concerning the intentions and capabilities of other states. As long as governments choose war or peace in terms of their own interests and sometimes miscalculate those interests, interstate war is never impossible.

After 1945, however, the evolution of international politics produced new inhibitions reinforcing the reluctance of governments to resort to violence. In the past interstate wars were almost always associated with changes in control or influence over

---

Samuel P. Huntington, "Patterns of Violence in World Politics," in Samuel P. Huntington, ed., *Changing Patterns of Military Politics* (New York: Free Press of Glencoe, 1962).
[1]Harold D. Lasswell and Abraham Kaplan, *Power and Society* (New Haven, 1950), p. 252.
[2]See, e.g., T. Abel, "The Element of Decision in the Pattern of War," *American Sociological Review,* Vol. 6 (December, 1941), 853–859. The assumption that decisions to risk or to provoke war are carefully calculated was, of course, basic to the entire strategy of deterrence pursued by the United States after World War II.

territory. They were the natural concomitant of the "territoriality" of the nation-state.[3] In the mid-twentieth century, however, prospective gains in territorial control began to decrease in value compared to the risks and the costs involved in procuring them. Governments became more willing to live with disputed boundaries, unsettled claims, and irredentist hopes. In part this was due to the existence of nuclear weapons, and in part also it was the result of improvements in international communication and organization, which made more visible any resort to violence and provided mechanisms for avoiding violence or bringing it quickly to an end. Increasingly, in effect, the territorial status quo became stabilized and even sanctified beyond the ability of any one state, however powerful, unilaterally to change it. The destruction of Hiroshima and the humiliation of Suez were strong deterrents to the resort to force.

The decline in the likelihood of intergovernmental violence was marked by a change in the nature of the Cold War. In the early years of the struggle between the Soviet Union and the United States bipolarity prevailed, and the conflict between the two powers and their allies was largely over territory. A gain in territory (e.g., China) for one side was a direct loss for the other. In the mid–1950's, however, bipolarity began to decline, and the struggle between the two great powers shifted from territory to the "peaceful competition" of economic development, military build-ups, scientific achievements, and diplomatic successes. The relevant model for world politics was less a two-person zero-sum game than a multiperson nonzero-sum game. A gain for one country did not necessarily mean an equivalent loss for another. A finite limit existed on territory, but there were no limits on the goals which a government might set for itself in expanding its production, developing its military strength, and exploring outer space. All these activities served as substitutes for the actual recourse to violence.[4] In the international competition for prestige resort to violence was often a sign of weakness or failure.

As a result, the conflict between the major powers tended to become regularized or stabilized. The periodic threats made by one government or the other to destroy this stability were in themselves an index of its pervasiveness and value. The relative military power of the major states still remained decisively important. It was important, however, more for its contribution to Cold War diplomacy than for its potential contribution to hot war victory. In the early years of the Cold War statesmen on both sides seemed primarily concerned with ending the international deadlock. Increasingly, in the 1950's, they seemed more concerned with preserving it lest a worse fate befall them.

The inhibition of direct intergovernmental violence contrasted with the frequency and variety of violence in the domestic politics of the colonial territories and independent states of Latin America, Africa, the Middle East, and southern Asia. These were the principal military arenas in world politics. The Korean War was rivaled in either duration or intensity by the Chinese civil war, the Indonesian war for independence, the struggle between the French and the Viet Minh in Indochina. Insurrection, terrorism, or

---

[3]See John H. Herz, *International Politics in the Atomic Age* (New York, 1959), Part One.
[4]On the conditions under which arms races may substitute for war, see my "Arms Races: Prerequisites and Results," *Public Policy* (Yearbook of the Graduate School of Public Administration, Harvard University), 8 (1958), 41–86.

civil war occurred in Greece, Malaya, the Philippines, Kenya, Cyprus, Algeria, Cuba, the Congo, and Laos. In the Republic of Colombia 100,000 persons were killed in civil strife between 1948 and 1953.[5] In other Latin American countries, and in many Middle Eastern ones, coups d'état were a recurring phenomenon. The year 1960 could well be labeled the "year of revolt":[6] Korea, Turkey, the Congo, Cuba, the Dominican Republic, Ethiopia, Vietnam, Laos all shared in the pattern in one way or another. In Moscow and Washington strategists plotted and replotted the probable course of hypothetical wars between the Soviet Union and the United States. In the underdeveloped areas of the world, however, violence was an immediate actuality. The dominant pattern was not interstate war in the sense of sustained violence between the forces of two or more governments roughly comparable in structure and function, if not in power. Instead, it was insurrectionary violence, in which a nongovernmental body—a clique, a party, a movement—attempted to overthrow and to supersede the existing government. Territorial boundaries served not as the focus of conflict but as its parameters.

The frequency of violence in the domestic politics of the underdeveloped areas reflected the prevalence of rapid social and political change. "Social revolution," to quote Lasswell and Kaplan again, "occurs within a short time span only by the exercise of violence."[7] In the late 1950's the international situation was commonly described by such words as "stalemate," "deadlock," "equilibrium," and "balance." Within the principal countries of the West and even within the Soviet Union domestic politics was often spoken of in terms of "the absence of issues," "the end of ideology," "the apathy of the masses," "the prevalence of pragmatism," "other-directedness," and "organization men." In the underdeveloped areas, however, the key words were "development," "growth," "modernization," "westernization," "transition," and "independence." Here were the principal causes of insurrectionary violence.

DIFFERENCES BETWEEN INTERGOVERNMENTAL AND ANTIGOVERNMENTAL VIOLENCE

The classic theory of intergovernmental war was formulated by Clausewitz. When he said that war was a continuation of policy by other means, he meant that it was a continuation of foreign policy. He was concerned with the "war of a community—of whole nations and particularly of civilized nations. . . ."[8] For Clausewitz war was an instrument of governments and an interaction between governments. "War," he said, "is thus

---

[5]See Vernon Lee Fluharty, *Dance of the Millions: Military Rule and the Social Revolution in Colombia, 1930–1956* (Pittsburgh, 1957), pp. 2, 234, 250.

[6]*New York Herald Tribune,* Dec. 6, 1960, p. 24.

[7]Lasswell and Kaplan, *op. cit.,* p. 274. See also Quincy Wright, *A Study of War* (Chicago, 1942), I, 256–257.

[8]Karl von Clausewitz, *On War,* trans. O. J. Matthijs Jolles (Washington, 1950), pp. 15–16. Cf. Herz, *op. cit.,* p. 60.

an act of force to compel our adversary to do our will. . . . Each of the adversaries forces the hand of the other, and a reciprocal action results which in theory can have no limit." Clausewitz's theory of war was dualistic, concerned solely with the interaction of two contestants. His analysis of the relation of military force to politics postulated a system of objective civilian control. His was the military theory of the nation-state, reflecting eighteenth-century practice and anticipating nineteenth-century developments. It is only partially relevant to intrastate war. Intrastate war is also the continuation of policy by other means, but it is the continuation of the policies of antigovernment and government within a common territory and society, each endeavoring to win support from at least some of the same groups. The patterns of intergovernmental war reflect the processes and structure of international politics; those of antigovernmental war reflect the processes and structure of domestic politics.

Intergovernmental war is initially symmetrical. The war begins between two independent governments, and it ends when one government succeeds in imposing its will on the other or when both governments conclude that their interests will no longer be served by continuing the struggle. The abstract pattern of insurrectionary war, on the other hand, is asymmetrical. It begins with a government confronting a nongovernment (institution, clique, movement, or party), and it ends with a similar relationship, although perhaps with the positions of the participants reversed. In the interval a symmetrical phase may occur, but prolonged symmetry means civil war in which two governments contend for authority within a single state. This closely resembles intergovernmental war. The American Civil War, for example, was a struggle between two governments each exercising effective authority over well-defined populations and territories. It differed little from the normal international war. A successful coup d'état, on the other hand, moves directly from one asymmetrical phase to another. The frequency of antigovernmental violence reflects the extent to which antigovernments monopolize the initiative in resorting to violence. They exist in greater numbers and variety than governments; possessing fewer responsibilities, they are restrained by fewer inhibitions. The distinctive characteristics of antigovernmental war stem from the fact that it is waged between qualitatively different types of organizations, each of which has its own liabilities and advantages.

In intergovernmental war the initiative is normally presumed to rest with the stronger of the two contestants: a three-to-one superiority, according to the traditional military maxim, was necessary to pass from the defensive to the offensive. In this sense, as Clausewitz maintained, defense was the stronger form of warfare because it could be sustained with weaker forces. In intrastate war, however, this relationship is reversed. As in nonviolent domestic politics, the offensive is the strategy of the weaker and the defensive that of the stronger. The strategic initiative always rests with the antigovernment, and larger forces are required by the defensive government than by the offensive clique or party. The offensive is the stronger form of warfare. In international warfare the offensive is the result of material superiority, while in domestic warfare the offensive is a means to material superiority. Inferiority can be converted to superiority, however, only because of the fundamentally tripartite nature of antigovernmental war as contrasted with the duality of intergovernmental war.

Abstractly, two general types of competitive situations can be distinguished: those in which the two parties interact directly and attempt to secure their aims by strengthening themselves and reducing the strength of their opponents and those in which the two contestants compete indirectly by attempting to win for themselves the support of third parties. The former situation, to adapt Spykman's terminology, involves "direct action," the latter "political action."[9] In actuality, of course, any competitive situation contains elements of both. To the extent, however, that only two parties exist, politics becomes impossible. Two men on a desert island can bargain or fight, but they cannot politick; when the waves wash up a third, however, politics begins. In competition between any two of the three, inherent differences in strength and cunning will still be important, but the extent to which one or the other can secure the support of the third will also be important. The classic recurring situations of politics always involve this tripartite relationship: two parties appealing for the vote of an electorate, two lobbyists attempting to influence legislators, two lawyers contesting before a judge, two states attempting to make an ally out of a neutral. In most interstate wars each participant has an interest in encouraging neutrality or belligerence in other powers. If, however, the support of a third party is essential to the victory of either of two participants in an interstate controversy, neither side is likely to risk war until it is assured of that support. In domestic violence, on the other hand, the essence of the conflict is the appeal to third parties. The direct action of the opponents upon each other, particularly in coups d'état, remains important, but the decisive characteristic of the struggle is the effort to gain the support of those who initially are neither friend nor foe. Apart from a prolonged intergovernmental civil war, the dichotomization of population and social institutions is seldom complete. All the distinctive methods of revolutionary war are devoted to the appeal for third-party support, and even in a coup d'état the great advantage of the quick seizure of the government is the opportunity it gives the insurrectionists to appeal to the uncommitted: the first act of the leaders of any successful coup invariably is the issuance of a manifesto demanding the support of the populace for "their" new government against the sinister forces of the counterrevolution.

The contestants in interstate wars are governments, and their goals may be limited to the acquisition of a particular piece of territory or some other specific value, or they may be total, requiring the elimination or complete subordination, of the opposing government. Insurrectionary war, on the other hand, is almost always total. The government aims at the elimination of the challenge to its authority; the insurrectionists aim at the capture or destruction of the government. Thus, the political character of domestic war, in the competing appeals of the contestants to third parties, tends to be stronger than that of interstate war. On the other hand, negotiation and compromise between the contestants, which often characterize intergovernmental war, are normally lacking in domestic wars. Neither side wants to recognize the legitimacy of the other, and negotiations, much less agreements, imply such recognition. Armistices and peace treaties are possible between governments, but rarely between governments and antigovernments. When they do exist, they are generally recognized as temporary in nature, similar to the "political truces" which in national emergencies momentarily suspend partisan competition

---

[9]Nicholas Spykman, *America's Strategy in World Politics* (New York, 1942), p. 13. See also Simmel's comments on the dyad and the triad, *The Sociology of Georg Simmel* trans. and ed. Kurt H. Wolff (Glencoe, Ill., 1950), pp. 135–169.

in constitutional democracies. When discussion does take place between domestic contestants, it usually results in the surrender of one or the other.

Antigovernmental war encourages civil-military relations different from those
stimulated by interstate conflict. Other things being equal, the more a state achieves a
system of objective civilian control the more effective it is in providing for its external
security and in conducting foreign wars. Domestic war, on the other hand, demands
subjective civilian control. In particular, in the post-World War II period the strategies
of deterrence and of limited war not only required types of military forces that were of
little use in internal wars, but they also tended to demand a relationship between military institutions and the government opposite to that required by internal war. In terms
of type of military force, deterrence and limited war demanded reasonably small, ready,
professional "constabulary forces," in Morris Janowitz's happy phrase.[10] In terms of
military relations to the government, both the deterrent force and the limited war force
had clearly defined missions and had to be highly responsive to the political leaders of
the government in the performance of these missions. In domestic war, on the other
hand, the political and military roles of the principal actors are merged on both sides,
and political and military means become indistinguishable. In a coup d'état generals
play political roles and governmental leaders, if they are able, exercise military command.
In domestic war, moreover, the targets of both contestants are political institutions,
social groups, and the general population. Both insurrectionaries and the government
attempt to arouse these groups on their behalf. The employment of arms, like the exercise of the franchise, becomes a concomitant of citizenship. Thus the military forces
which are employed and the nature of their leadership, on both sides, tend to be directly
opposed to that required for interstate wars. Traditionally, the European powers made a
relatively sharp distinction between the colonial army and the metropolitan army.[11]
Certainly, it is an open question whether a government can maintain simultaneously
within the same territory the systems required for both international war and domestic
war. As Raoul Girardet has demonstrated, the change in function from interstate to domestic conflict may have drastic effect upon the attitudes of military officers toward
their government and upon their amenability to the traditional forms of objective civilian control.[12]

VARIETIES OF DOMESTIC VIOLENCE

Different forms of government are associated with different forms of war. The decline
of limited war and the rise of total war normally has been linked, for example, with the
shift from absolute monarchy to democracy. Even monarchies, democracies, and totalitarian dictatorships, however, share much in common as governments, and the variations in the forms of war that they wage are neither numerous nor extensive.
Insurrections, on the other hand, may be launched by the most varied groups, from a

---

[10]Morris Janowitz, *The Professional Soldier: A Social and Political Portrait* (Glencoe, Ill., 1960),
ch. 20.
[11]See Maury Feld, "A Typology of Military Organization," *Public Policy,* 8 (1958), 3–40.
[12]See his essay, *infra,* pp. 123–129.

small junta of top military officers to a fanatic revolutionary party. Insurrectionary wars, consequently, seem to exist in an almost endless variety of forms. Perhaps for this reason the temptation to catalog them is virtually irresistible. Lasswell and Kaplan speak of palace revolutions, political revolutions, and social revolutions.[13] Bonnet distinguishes among *guerres civiles, guerres de libération,* and *guerres révolutionnaires. Guerres civiles* are subdivided into riots, insurrections, pronunciamentos, and revolutions. *La guerre révolutionnaire,* in turn, is a compound of *la guerre de partisans* plus *la guerre psychologique.*[14] Stokes, in his analysis of violence in Latin America, identifies *machetismo, cuartelazo, golpe de estado,* and *revolución* as means of direct action, and *imposición, candidato único, continuismo,* and election as outwardly peaceful means of obtaining power which "rest upon a foundation of force."[15] In his volume on Latin American violence Lieuwen discusses *caudillismo,* "predatory militarism," coups d'état, and social revolutions.[16] Other writers speak of subversion, *émeutes,* general strikes, and assassination, and almost everyone attempts to draw a line between national revolutions and social revolutions. The variety of forms reflects differences in the nature of the participants, their relations with each other, and the political culture of the society in which they exist.

Historically the classic form of domestic violence in Europe was the urban revolt or revolution in which the principal focus was the seizure or attempted seizure of power by one class or social group through violence directed primarily against the established government in the capital city. For this Gallic tradition, epitomized by Halévy's "Insurgent," 1789 was the model.

> There were [in the words of D. W. Brogan] the June Days of 1848; the resistance to the Coup d'Etat of 1851; the Commune of 1871. There were the less dramatic or less dramatized days of 1848 in Berlin and Vienna; there were riots and risings in the Romagna, in Valencia; there were the great strikes—and their bloody consequences, Fetherstonhaugh and the battle between the steel workers and the Pinkerton gunmen hired by Carnegie and Frick. There were Moscow and Petersburg in 1905; Paterson and Lowell; the 'Wobblies' and the mutineers of the 17th Infantry at Montpellier; all the tradition of insurrection and defiance that runs continuously from the first Fourteenth of July. . . .[17]

At the end of the line, there is Petersburg again in 1917. This type of insurrection reflected the politics of bourgeoisie, proletariat, and industrialism. A distinctive mark of the nineteenth century, it is out of date in the middle of the twentieth century.

After World War II politics in the underdeveloped areas centered about the struggle for independence and the processes of modernization and development. These were the principal causes of the two dominant forms of insurrectionary violence in these areas— the revolutionary war and the reform coup d'état. The struggle for independence often

---

[13]Lasswell and Kaplan, *op. cit.,* pp. 274–275.

[14]Gabriel Bonnet, *Les Guerres insurrectionelles et révolutionnaires* (Paris, 1958), pp. 34ff.

[15]W. S. Stokes, "Violence as a Power Factor in Latin American Politics," *Western Political Quarterly,* 5 (Summer, 1952), 445–468.

[16]Edwin Lieuwen, *Arms and Politics in Latin America* (New York, 1960), *passim.*

[17]D. W. Brogan, *The Price of Revolution* (New York, 1951), pp. 19–20.

took the form of revolutionary war. The processes of modernization and westernization often required either revolutionary war or a succession of coups d'état.

REVOLUTIONARY WAR AND GROUP ALIENATION

Revolutionary wars of the post-World War II period included the later phases of the Chinese civil war, the struggle between the Viet Minh and the French in Indochina, the guerrilla war of the Communist rebels in Greece, the Hukbalahap rebellion in the Philippines, the jungle fighting in Malaya, the Algerian insurrection, and the Castro revolt against Batista.[18] Revolutionary war is linked with the end of colonialism, agrarian movements, and the process of community definition and state creation. The difference between it and the old European urban revolution is the difference between the Chinese revolution and the Russian revolution.

Revolutionary wars occur when the government is distant—politically, socially, and even geographically—from a significant counterelite. Recourse to revolutionary war is a sign that the counterelite has failed to penetrate the existing political structure. Colonial revolts, consequently, often take the form of revolutionary wars. The base of the colonial government in its home territory is out of reach of the nationalist counterelite, and this distance is normally reinforced by ethnic differences between the colonial rulers and the native population. Where revolutionary wars occur in noncolonial areas, similar obstacles usually prevent the permeation of the government by the counterelite. In the Philippines, for instance, the Hukbalahaps first attempted to achieve their goals through peaceful means, electing seven members of the Philippine legislature. When the legislature refused to seat them, the Huk leaders returned to the countryside to precipitate revolt.

Divorced from the existing political system, the counterelite attempts to develop a parallel structure independent of the government. Its goal is usually the overthrow of the entire existing political and social system. A long, arduous route to power, revolutionary war can only be pursued by dedicated parties or movements sustained by a coherent ideology or sense of mission. The war usually begins in an area distant from the capital and the main centers of governmental power. If successful, the instigating group gradually expands the locus of its authority, acquires more and more of the attributes of a government, and eventually exhausts and overwhelms the previously existing government. Lenin, it is reported, once said that "no revolution of the masses can triumph without the help of a portion of the armed forces that sustained the old regime."[19] The successful revolutionary wars in Asia and Africa and the Castro revolution in Cuba are exceptions to this rule. Revolutionary war proceeds on the premise that the government

---

[18]This discussion deals with the *phenomenon* of revolutionary war. For analysis of the French *doctrine* of *la guerre révolutionnaire,* see *infra,* pp. 40–44, and the two excellent discussions of Raoul Girardet, *infra,* pp. 127–134, and Peter Paret, "The French Army and La Guerre Révolutionnaire," *Journal of the Royal United Service Institution,* 104 (February, 1959), 59–69.

[19]Quoted in Lieuwen, *op. cit.,* p. 134. See also Katherine Chorley, *Armies and the Art of Revolution* (London, 1943), p. 23.

controls the armed forces of the state and that it is necessary to develop distinct revolutionary armed forces to employ against the state. In a successful revolutionary war a party creates an army, which, in turn, brings into existence a government.

The decisive aspect of the revolutionary war is the contest between the counterelite and the government for the support of a communal or socioeconomic group that is imperfectly integrated into the existing political system. The causes of the alienation of the group may stem either from the refusal of the government to recognize its distinctive characteristics and problems or the relegation of the group to a secondary position in society. As Lucien Pye has suggested, alienation often has its roots in the rationalism of modern government.[20] The doctrines of equality and individualism undermine the ties of the community to the government. The abolition of the Arab bureaus in Algeria was justified on the grounds that no distinction should be drawn between Frenchmen of different faiths. The Chinese secretariat in Malaya was emasculated because there "were no separate corps of officials to deal with Malay or Indian problems, and it bordered on the invidious to treat the Chinese as a special case."[21] In each case these actions symbolized an apparent indifference by the governing authorities to communal differences and hence encouraged feelings of alienation in the affected groups at the same time that they reduced the ability of the government to counteract them. Just as the educated Chinese in Malaya resented their "restricted citizenship," the Indochinese resented their "second class citizenship." Similarly, in the Philippines, "For too many years the government had been set apart from the common people in the farm lands of Central Luzon. . . . At the end of the war the peasants felt no obligation to support the government nor to be loyal to it in the struggle with the Huks."[22] The decline in identification and communication between communal group and the governmental authorities opens the group as a target for the counterelite.

The counterelite attempts to win the target group through terrorism and persuasion. In the "normal" intergovernmental war violence is directed primarily against the enemy; it is a means of reducing his numbers and of undermining his will to resist. In the initial phases of a revolutionary war, however, the counterelite directs its terrorism and violence primarily against the members of the target group. The aim of the violence is not to eliminate the forces of the government but to win the members of the target group. In Algeria between November, 1954, and April, 1957, the rebels killed 891 European civilians and 3,438 members of the French security forces but 5,576 Moslem civilians. In Malaya through June, 1957, the insurrectionists killed 106 Europeans, 226 Indians, 318 Malayans, and 1,700 Chinese civilians. In the first year of the Kenya emergency the Mau Mau killed eleven Asians, twenty-one Europeans, and at least 704 Africans. In Cyprus the EOKA killed three Greeks for every two non-Greeks.[23] In the Philippines the Huks killed farmers, burned homes, and raided villages in efforts to build up their

---

[20]Lucien Pye, *Guerrilla Communism in Malaya* (Princeton, 1956), ch. 15.
[21]Lennox A. Mills, *Malaya: A Political and Economic Appraisal* (Minneapolis, 1958), pp. 48–49; Michael K. Clark, *Algeria in Turmoil* (New York, 1959), pp. 8, 131.
[22]Alvin H. Scaff, *The Philippine Answer to Communism* (Stanford, 1955), p. 135; Mills, *op. cit.,* pp. 54–55; Ellen J. Hammer, *The Struggle for Indochina* (Stanford, 1954), pp. 71–75.
[23]Clark, *op. cit.,* p. 453; Mills, *op. cit.,* p. 51; D. H. Rawcliffe, *The Struggle for Kenya* (London, 1954), p. 93; Brian Crozier, *The Rebels: A Study of Post-War Insurrections* (Boston, 1960), p. 53.

support among the peasants. Similarly, the Viet Minh penetrated the Tonkin delta and established a codominion with the French, the one ruling by day and the other by night, through "its two most useful weapons, nationalism and terror."[24] Since the terrorism of the counterelite is useful only in the effects it has *pour encourager les autres,* it frequently includes blatant brutalities and atrocities. The elimination of prominent members of the target group who refuse to cooperate with the rebels convinces other members of the group that the only prudent course is to buy safety by contributing money to the rebels, furnishing them with information, or cooperating with them in other ways.

Simultaneously with their use of terror the counterelite and its military forces also employ persuasion. Propaganda and psychological war are the partners of terrorism. In Malaya, for example, Lucien Pye found that virtually all the surrendered Communist prisoners interviewed emphasized the importance of propaganda, identifying it with politics.[25] While the motivations of the counterelite may be ideological in character, the appeal to the target group is normally couched in the nationalistic or economic terms which are most meaningful to the target group. The revolutionaries particularly attempt to create and to maintain in the target group a sense of the ineptitude and weakness of the established government and a belief in the ultimate victory of the revolutionary group. The appearance of strength must be cultivated at the sacrifice of all else; a "bandwagon" psychology is essential in winning the target group.[26] In reply, the government attempts to convince the target group that it has the will and the strength to stamp out the insurrection. To win supporters in the target group, the government must guarantee not to abandon them at a later date. If it once breaks its word, it creates a doubt which will haunt it continuously. In a dualistic intergovernmental war the sense of inferiority, of fighting against great odds, may inspire great effort. In a tripartite revolutionary war, however, the decisive factor is the support of the target group. The members of the target group, in turn, want to be on the winning side. Whichever side can convince the target group that it is winning is in fact winning.

Terrorism, Brian Crozier argues, is the weapon of the weak.[27] It is a weapon, however, which is effective not against the strong but against the vulnerable. Though sporadic murders and bombings would never suffice to destroy the forces of the government, they may suffice to win the active or passive support of the target group. The protection of the target group against the terrorism may well strain the government's resources or impose upon it a burden that it does not wish to bear. The peculiar strength of the counterelite derives precisely from the fact that it is *not* a government and that it *is* pursuing an offensive strategy. Dramatic differences in strength usually exist between the antigovernmental and governmental forces. In Malaya, at their top strength, the Communists had 5,500 fighters in the jungle, while the British mobilized against them over 40,000 regular troops plus 100,000 men in auxiliary and constabulary forces. In Indochina the Viet Minh came out of World War II with slightly over 10,000 men. By

---

[24]Hammer, *op. cit.,* p. 292.

[25]Pye, *op. cit.,* pp. 182ff.

[26]*Ibid.,* pp. 8, 67–69; Clark, *op. cit.,* pp. 6, 133; Robert A. Smith, *Philippine Freedom 1946–1958* (New York, 1958), p. 142.

[27]See Crozier, *op. cit.,* pp. 159–191, for an enlightening analysis of the successes and limitations of terrorism as a weapon.

the last year of the war their forces numbered 300,000 to 400,000 troops, including local militia, but the French Union forces were still more numerous. In March, 1956, FLN military strength in Algeria totalled 29,050 men, more than ever before, while French forces included about 200,000 men at that time and more than twice that number five months later.[28]

To carry out its efforts to conquer the target group, the counterelite and its military forces require a reasonably secure base of operations. One great weakness of the Hukbalahap movement was the inadequacy of the relatively restricted and heavily populated farm areas of central Luzon as a base for revolutionary operations. In Malaya the jungle furnished a base for the Communist guerrillas so long as they could procure food and supplies from villages and other settled areas. In Cuba the rugged terrain of the Sierra Maestrae furnished Castro with a base for operations against the peasants. In all three of these cases the rebel bases were within the territory of the government the rebels were attempting to overthrow. If a base can be established upon external territory, secure from governmental attack, the revolutionary movement has a much greater chance of success. Furnishing such a base for supplies and training purposes is the greatest assistance a foreign government can give a revolutionary movement. If the territory of the foreign government is contiguous with that of the target government, this assistance may be of decisive importance in the outcome of the revolutionary war. The withdrawal of Tito from the Comintern helped end the Greek war at the same time that the Communist victory in China insured the continuation of the Indochinese war. The Algerian Nationalists originally received extensive assistance from Egypt and then, after its independence, from Tunisia. Since a revolutionary war is a war of attrition, a relatively secure base is essential for its successful prosecution. A colonial power has an inherent advantage in fighting against a revolutionary movement that lacks a contiguous external base. On the other hand, a revolutionary movement with such a base has an inherent advantage in fighting an independent government without a home territory to draw upon. In the latter case, substantial support from allies, as in Greece, may be essential for the government to maintain itself. If the colonial government is secure in its home base and the revolutionary forces also possess a secure contiguous external base, it is possible that the war may, as in Indochina, drag on indefinitely with neither side able to force a decision.

Eventually, of course, if it is to achieve its ultimate goal, the revolutionary counterelite has to establish "liberated" base areas within the contested territory. As it gradually expands its locus of control, the revolutionary movement takes on more and more of the functions and characteristics of a government. Along with the collection of taxes and supplies from a liberated area, it also organizes the population into local militia units. The establishment of such units for the revolutionary forces, as for their opponents, is essential to free the mobile, "regular" forces for offensive operations in other areas. Terrorism gives way to guerrilla war and then to full-scale war.[29]

[28]Pye, *op. cit.,* pp. 91, 96*n.*; Mills, *op. cit.,* p. 53; Hammer, *op. cit.,* p. 287; E. L. Katzenbach, Jr., "Indo-China: A Military-Political Appreciation," *World Politics,* 4 (January, 1952), 205–206; Clark, *op. cit.,* pp. 299, 307.
[29]See Girardet, *infra,* pp. 130–137; Crozier, *op. cit.,* pp. 127ff.

The reaction of the government in a revolutionary war normally goes through two phases. At first the government tends to treat the insurrection as a traditional problem for the police and the military. It minimizes the threat of the revolutionary forces and confidently proclaims that the "brigands" will be quickly eliminated and order restored. In 1946 the Philippine government declared that it would exterminate the Huks within sixty days. General Boucher confidently announced in the summer of 1948 that he would quickly clean up the Malayan guerrillas.[30] The government retains confidence in its superior conventional military forces, and it attempts to use those forces in the conventional fashion. The continued success of the revolutionary forces, however, precipitates a crisis within the government. It now recognizes that the revolution requires not only a much larger and different military effort to suppress it but also an integrated political-economic effort to counter the appeals of the revolutionaries to the target group. It also recognizes the need to overhaul its organizational structure dealing with the rebellion and to merge political and military responsibilities in a single individual. In November, 1952, for example, Oliver Lyttleton emphasized that the three great needs in Malaya were to unify civil-military authority, to secure Chinese cooperation in the antiguerrilla campaigns, and to organize Chinese militia units for the self-protection of the loyal Chinese population. Similarly, in the fall of 1950, the French were forced to the realization that "an effective end must be put to the antipathy between French civil and military authorities" in Indochina and that new efforts must be made to win the support of the Vietnamese in the struggle against the Viet Minh.[31]

As the government's response moves into its second phase, the new supreme political-military director of the effort plays a critical role. He not only concentrates in himself the direction of the war on all fronts, but he also dramatizes the determination and ability of the government to carry through the struggle and to maintain the safety of its supporters. In varying degrees this critically important role was played by Magsaysay in the Philippines, Templer in Malaya, Papagos in Greece, and de Lattre de Tassigny in Indochina. Above all, the leader plays the role of the politician in campaigning for the support and the confidence of the target group. Templer and Magsaysay devoted large portions of their time to touring the disturbed areas, restoring direct communications with the target group, and demonstrating personally the interests of the government in the well-being and safety of the target-group members.

The director of the counterrevolutionary effort may be a civilian cabinet officer (Magsaysay), a military theater commander (de Lattre), or military commander and civilian governor (Templer). Irrespective of his formal position, however, to be successful he must effectively exercise complete control of the counterrevolutionary effort. Magsaysay, for instance, insisted upon the unification of the Philippine Constabulary and the military forces, previously in separate departments, under a single chief of staff. Like Hoche in the pacification of the Vendée, he must be a "skilled politician as well as soldier." Magsaysay, for instance, although a civilian, personally commanded units in the field. The essential element is the vigor, determination, and ability of the individual, not his previous background or experience. Like the great colonial soldiers Bugeaud,

---

[30]Scaff, *op. cit.,* p. 28; Harry Miller, *The Communist Menace in Malaya* (New York, 1954), pp. 92–93.
[31]Katzenbach, *loc. cit.,* 192–193; Mills, *op. cit.,* p. 61.

Galliéni, and Lyautey, he must play both political and military roles; and, as Lyautey said, it is not the label but the man that matters, "the right man in the right place."[32]

The crucial step in the change in the approach of the government toward the revolutionary war is the recognition that the decisive aspect of the struggle is not the defeat of the enemy forces but the reconquest of the confidence of the contested population. To win the population, it is necessary to know the population, to win an audience with it, to detach it from the revolutionary forces, and eventually to control it.[33] The first necessity is for the government to convince the target group that it can provide for its security. This is the military job. Then, however, it must reintegrate the target group into the existing community. New organizational units devoted to this end provide help. In Algeria in 1955, for example, the government established the Special Administrative Sections to work with the Algerian Moslems and to carry on the activities which before 1945 had been performed by the Arab Bureaus. A nongovernmental group, the Malayan Chinese Association, founded in February, 1949, played an important role in combatting the appeal of the Communists to the Malayan Chinese and in bringing about their reintegration into the Malayan community. In the Philippines civil-affairs officers were appointed to undertake the "important tasks of interpreting the army to the people and of winning civilian support for the army activities against the Huks." The basic goal is to stimulate favorable attitudes toward the government on the part of the target group. In Malaya Templer taught the police that "in the long run their most important task was not to catch the terrorists but to persuade the public to look upon them as friends." In the Philippines Magsaysay ruthlessly suppressed police terrorism against the peasants and instituted a campaign of "attraction and fellowship."[34]

The reintegration of portions of the target group into the community may require extensive physical movement and resettlement. In Malaya, for instance, thousands of "squatters" making a meager living on government land close to the jungle became a major source of support and supplies for the guerrillas. One decisive action of the government in its struggles against the guerrillas was the movement and resettlement of these "squatters" in new villages, where they were provided with adequate work, land, and protection. According to one French officer the three most effective methods of pacification were the "tache d'huile" of Lyautey, the establishment of forbidden zones in which all nongovernment personnel were presumed to be enemies, and the regrouping of the population. In Cambodia, in 1952–1953, thousands of peasants were regrouped to provide for their own security and welfare.[35] In the Philippines Magsaysay created the EDCOR farms in Mindanao for the resettlement and rehabilitation of the

[32]Jean Gottmann, "Bugeaud, Galliéni, Lyautey: The Development of French Colonial Warfare," in Edward Mead Earle (ed.), *Makers of Modern Strategy* (Princeton, 1943), pp. 240–241; G. J. Younghusband, *Indian Frontier Warfare* (London, 1898), pp. 54–55; Scaff, *op. cit.,* p. 36; Smith, *op. cit.,* pp. 154–157.

[33]Ximenes, "La guerre révolutionnaire et ses données fondamentales," *Revue militaire d'information* (February-March, 1957), 19–20.

[34]Girardet, *infra,* pp. 135–137; Clark, *op. cit.,* pp. 8–9; Mills, *op. cit.,* pp. 63–72ff.; Scaff, *op. cit.,* p. 36; Lt. Col. T. C. Tirona, "The Philippine Anti-Communist Campaign," *Air University Quarterly Review,* 7 (Summer, 1954), 50.

[35]J. Hogard, "Guerre révolutionnaire et pacification," *Revue militaire d'information* (January, 1957), 19.

Hukbalahaps. Significantly, one of the principal attractions of EDCOR to the rebels was the promise of peace and security which they offered.

The conduct of an effective counterrevolutionary action by a government thus requires a major change in the leadership, attitude, and functions of the military forces. The armed forces of the state become an instrument of persuasion as well as an instrument of coercion. The military become the chain which binds a potentially disaffected social group to the broader community. As one student of the Philippine anti-Huk campaign observed:

> The EDCOR farms created a radically new role for the army. No longer were the armed forces limited to defending the nation and destroying the enemy. The army was to serve the people in a new way—constructively and creatively. It would rehabilitate the Huks and restore them to the nation as loyal productive citizens.
>
> A foreign news correspondent [observing the EDCOR villages] . . . said, "I have seen many armies, but this one beats them all. This is an army with a social conscience."[36]

As Girardet makes clear in his essay in this volume, the French Army in Algeria not only developed nonmilitary functions and organizations but also a political program based on the continuing French presence in Algeria and social, economic, and political equality for the Moslem population. This "social conscience" of the French Army contrasted with the indecisiveness of the French government and the self-interested devotion to the status quo of the French colons.

As a result of the weakness of the defense in revolutionary war, the security of the target group can be protected only by the mobilization of the group itself. Militarily speaking, the formation of local militia units for this purpose is absolutely essential, as the regular military forces of the government would never suffice to guarantee security. One French officer has estimated that at least a ten-to-one superiority is necessary for effective internal defense, and in some areas of Malaya it was necessary to have a ratio of sixty-five armed men to every known terrorist.[37] Local militia units not only serve to re-establish confidence and security within the target group but also tend to cement its commitment to the side of the government. By 1952 the British in Malaya had organized over 244,000 home guards for the protection of the villages. In the Philippines and Indochina similar units were found to be indispensable.[38]

The goals of the conflicting parties and the importance of maintaining confidence in victory generally render nugatory any efforts to arrive at truces or agreements between the government and antigovernment forces. Between 1946 and 1948 the Roxas and Quirino Administrations in the Philippines attempted to reach a peaceful settlement with the Huks. One three-month truce ended "in bitter fighting," and a subsequent suspension of hostilities came to naught when the Huks refused to surrender their arms. Efforts to work out a basis for cooperation between the Communists and the

---

[36]Scaff, *op. cit.,* p. 38.
[37]Col. Nemo, "Suggestions pour l'étâblissement d'une doctrine," *Revue militaire générale* (April, 1958), 490; Mills, *op. cit.,* p. 54.
[38]Mills, *op. cit.,* p. 54; Tirona, *loc. cit.,* 54.

Nationalists in China inevitably failed. Repeated negotiations between the French and the Viet Minh in Indochina did not produce any basis for agreement. In 1955 efforts to arrange a peaceful settlement in Malaya also broke down. In most of these instances the government was willing to offer a general amnesty to rebels who would surrender their arms, abandon their revolutionary activities, and resume normal peacetime employment. The rebels, on the other hand, normally were willing to abandon temporarily the military struggle, but not to surrender their arms or to give up their organization and its revolutionary aims. For them the truce or armistice was a shift in tactics but not in goal. On the other hand, any compromise by the government or agreement with the revolutionaries inevitably would raise questions in the minds of members of the target group about the determination of the government to maintain itself and to maintain order. As Jacques Soustelle remarked about Algeria:

> If the conviction that France will remain in Algeria is not inculcated in everyone, no Moslem, no matter how closely he may be bound to us by heart or by interest, will remain at our side. . . . Any political movement, any statement, any article in the press giving the impression that we will come to terms with terrorism—in other words, that the terrorists will some day be in a position to settle outstanding scores—drives the Algerian Moslems further from us.[39]

The decisive aspect of revolutionary war thus is the struggle for the loyalty of the vulnerable sector. In a sense, the war is conducted like an agonizing and bloody electoral campaign. If the counterelite can establish and maintain itself as the leader of the alienated sector, it has won its battle. If that sector is insufficient to maintain a state, continued strife is inevitable. If a territorially defined and viable state is feasible, succession from the old political community is the only solution. Victory for the government, in turn, can only be achieved by the reintegration of the alienated group into the over-all community and its participation in the political system.

The ability of a government to react successfully to a revolutionary war depends upon the perception and political strength of its leaders. The operations required in the second phase of the war often run counter to traditional ideas and established interests. The more detached a government is from the society disrupted by revolutionary war, the more able it will be to surmount these obstacles. An imperial government, for instance, may develop a broad view of the relations among the various groups in the colonial society and possess the ability to impose upon that society the social, economic, and political reforms necessary to reintegrate the target group into the community. A non-imperial government faced with revolutionary war may be unable to deal effectively with the war because it depends upon the very groups which the counterelite is challenging. In such circumstances the guidance and discipline of an allied government may be necessary to institute the measures required to win the revolutionary war. The British government was able to handle the Chinese insurrection in Malaya much easier than a Malayan government could have. On the other hand, divisions of opinion in the home country of the imperial government may hamper the ability of that government to

---

[39] Quoted in Clark, *op. cit.*, p. 6; Scaff, *op. cit.*, pp. 28–30; Crozier, *op. cit.*, p. 16.

fight the war. If these divisions make the government unable to devise at the political level a strategy for the conduct of the war, subordinate groups, such as the French Army in Algeria, may well attempt to assume that responsibility.

Many French writers have called revolutionary war the most probable form of future conflict. It is, however, the product of peculiar conditions. The decline of colonialism removes its best breeding ground. The revolutionary wars of the late 1940's, moreover, were in many respects an outgrowth of World War II: the insurrectionary counterelites usually began as anti-Axis guerrillas and accumulated weapons and experience which they used in the postwar period.[40] In southeast Asia the tactics of the Communist parties were shaped by the Chinese Communist victory; the revolutionary wars in the Philippines, Malaya, Indochina, and the attempted insurrections in Indonesia, Burma, and India, all reflected the Communist line of the moment. That line may again, of course, endorse these tactics. In the independent states of Asia and Africa, however, this hardly seems necessary. Their governments are often too weak to require it, and easier routes to power exist through propaganda, infiltration, and coup d'état. The Cold War competition of the major powers, however, could lead them to intervene to strengthen incipient revolutionary movements or tottering counter-revolutionary governments. Such interventions would then increase the ability of both sides to wage a prolonged revolutionary war.

Revolutionary war is most likely in a society occupying an extensive territory and divided between different communities and races in which one group predominates in the government. Potentialities for revolutionary war exist in many Latin American countries: the "Prestes column" of the 1920's in Brazil could well be the embryonic prototype of more elaborate movements to come. Conceivably the struggles between settler governments and African natives could also take this form. In South Africa, and possibly elsewhere, however, the lines may become so tightly drawn that the violence will take the form of direct intercommunal warfare rather than political competition between government and counterelite for support from the same group. . . .

INTERNATIONAL TENSION AND DOMESTIC VIOLENCE—THE DOCTRINES OF *LA GUERRE RÉVOLUTIONNAIRE* AND INDIRECT AGGRESSION

Various attempts have been made in the West to interpret and explain the violence in the politics of the underdeveloped areas. One common interpretation sees the rise of the new forms of domestic violence as directly related to the decline of the old forms of intergovernmental violence. In its most general form, the argument that a decrease in the frequency of intergovernmental conflict is likely to increase the frequency of domestic violence usually assumes that mankind's propensity to fight remains roughly constant. War is inevitable, and if it becomes unprofitable in one locale, it reappears in

---

[40]See Crozier, *op. cit.,* pp. 106–107.

another. As a general truth, however, this proposition is not valid. To be sure, some relationship exists between the internal and external conflicts of a state, and external conflict does tend to increase internal unity and cohesion.[41] It does not, however, follow that external peace stimulates internal conflict, and the students of conflict have produced no significant evidence to show that such a relationship exists. Sweden and Switzerland have enjoyed both internal and external peace for decades. Governments, on the other hand, may attempt to stave off internal war with a nongovernment at home by instigating external war with a foreign government abroad. To the extent that the new inhibitory factors on interstate wars tend to close off this course of action, they also tend to make it more difficult to avoid domestic violence. Governments, however, are fairly ingenious. As alternatives to foreign wars as unifiers, they may resort to more intensive domestic action to suppress the embryonic conflict, in which case "police state" measures are the result of the absence rather than the presence of external conflict. In addition, governments may engage in nonviolent, peaceful adventurism, in which an external enemy is identified and castigated and serves as a target for group hostility, although the government carefully refrains from resorting to violence. The government may instead go to some lengths to provoke the opposing government to use violence first. Also, the reduction in interstate wars moderates one of the causes of domestic strife. "Civil war," as Sir George Clark observed of the seventeenth century, "was often a sequel to external victory . . . [and] a consequence of external defeat."[42]

While there may be no necessary general relationship between the inhibition of interstate violence and the prevalence of intrastate violence, this does not exclude the possibility of a relationship existing between the two in the special circumstances of the mid-twentieth century. That such a relationship does exist is a key assumption of the French doctrine of *la guerre révolutionnaire* and the American concept of indirect aggression. For both theories the new forms of domestic violence are primarily methods of intergovernmental conflict.

The French doctrine of *la guerre révolutionnaire* was in many respects the counterpart to the American doctrine of limited war.[43] The American doctrine was a reaction to a traumatic military experience in Korea, the French doctrine to similar experiences in Indochina and Algeria. To American thinkers the logical result of the balance of terror was limited war; to French military men it was insurrectionary war. While American

---

[41]See Georg Simmel, *Conflict,* trans. Kurt H. Wolff (Glencoe, Ill., 1955), pp. 87ff.; Lewis A. Coser, *The Functions of Social Conflict* (Glencoe, Ill., 1956), pp. 87ff.; Wright, *op. cit.,* I, 253ff.; R. F. Murphy, "Intergroup Hostility and Social Cohesion," *American Anthropologist,* 59 (December, 1957), 1018ff. Cf. David Rapoport, "Praetorianism" (Ph.D. Thesis, Univ. of California at Berkeley, 1960), pp. 85–86, 155ff., 230.

[42]Sir George Clark, *War and Society in the Seventeenth Century* (Cambridge, 1958), p. 20.

[43]For analyses of the French doctrine, see Girardet, *infra,* and Paret, *loc. cit.* The literature on *la guerre révolutionnaire* is immense. Between 1956 and 1960, almost every issue of the *Revue de défense nationale,* the *Revue militaire d'information* and the *Revue militaire générale* contained something on the subject. Among leading expositions are: Claude Delmas, *La guerre révolutionnaire* (Paris, 1959); Gabriel Bonnet, *op. cit.; Revue militaire d'information* (February-March, 1957); *Contre Révolution: stratégie et tactique* (Paris, 1958); J. Hogard, "Guerre révolutionnaire et pacification," *Revue militaire d'information* (January, 1957), 7–24. The first three items include helpful bibliographies.

theory distinguished between general war involving thermonuclear weapons, on the one hand, and limited war with conventional or tactical nuclear weapons, on the other, French theory drew a threefold distinction. "La guerre classique," the traditional form of general war, was now highly improbable. The two relevant types of military action were "la guerre nucléaire" and "la guerre révolutionnaire."[44] The former, the French emphasized, was likely to include all forms of interstate war; it was expensive, destructive, and relatively unlikely. While American theorists saw limited war as the most probable form of future Soviet military action, French writers assigned a similar role to *la guerre révolutionnaire.* In both countries it was argued that this new phenomenon required a major reorientation of military thought and new military doctrines. Yet, while the novel features of the new form of warfare were emphasized, in both countries extensive efforts were also made to develop its historical precedents. In both countries also it was emphasized that the new form of warfare was peculiarly suited to Marxist-Leninist theory and practice.

The parallels in the development of the doctrines of limited war and *la guerre révolutionnaire* should not obscure significant differences in the substances of these doctrines. The doctrine of limited war was a pure theory of intergovernmental war. The model for it was derived from the eighteenth-century world of territorial nation-states in which absolute governments exercised strict control over their military forces and used them as instruments in their diplomacy, and in which the struggles among the states were normally over specific pieces of territory and did not involve either the existence of the state or the overthrow of its political and social system. The basic model for the French doctrine, on the other hand, was not eighteenth-century Europe but twentieth-century China. While the limited-war theorists harked back to Clausewitz, those of *la guerre révolutionnaire* invoked Mao Tse-tung. *La guerre révolutionnaire,* they emphasized, was total war within a society. In it, to be sure, war was the instrument of politics, but its distinguishing characteristic was the intermingling of economic, political, and military means. The theory of limited war, in many respects so classically military, was in large part articulated in the United States by civilian social scientists. The theory of *la guerre révolutionnaire,* on the other hand, involving the intimate mixture of political and military roles, techniques, and forces, was to a much larger extent the product of professional military officers.

The theorists of *la guerre révolutionnaire* recognized that it was a form of domestic war. It was, however, they insisted, a product of interstate conflict. They argued that it was primarily an instrument of one government, the Soviet Union, against another government, France, waged through satellites and political instruments. "The Algerian rebellion," one official French document stated, "is incontestably a movement inspired and actively supported by foreign countries which interfere impudently in the internal affairs of France."[45] *La guerre révolutionnaire,* Claude Delmas said, is the means whereby one state can make war against another without provoking general conflict and

---

[44]See, e.g., Général d'Armée Jean Valluy, "Le corps des officiers devant la Nation," *Revue militaire générale* (December, 1958), 591–611; Delmas, *op. cit.,* pp. 9, 17; Gen. Paul Gerardot, "La renaissance militaire et le problème militaire français," *Revue militaire générale* (February, 1958), 173–195.

[45]1956 Supplement to dossier on Algeria prepared for French UN delegation, quoted in Crozier, *op. cit.,* pp. 130–31.

without even appearing to be resorting to war. The peculiar nature of *la guerre révolutionnaire* (guerrilla warfare plus psychological warfare) bore the imprint of the doctrine and tactics of international Communism. As Delmas declared, "la guerre révolutionnaire n'existerait pas (ou en resterait au stade de la guerila) si les parties communistes n'etaient pas des instruments de la politique soviétique."[46] In some cases the French thinkers suggested that *la guerre révolutionnaire* was always the instrument of Communists; in others they argued that even where it was not the product of Communism the Communists always benefitted from its use; always, however, they maintained that the methods of *la guerre révolutionnaire* were inspired by Communist theory and practice, and that the Communists were the instruments of the Soviet Union.[47] Having linked the origins of *la guerre révolutionnaire* with the deterrence of intergovernmental wars and the nature of it with Communist theory and practice, the French thinkers inevitably were drawn to argue that every manifestation of *la guerre révolutionnaire* was the product of Communist action on behalf of the Soviet Union. The French military thus arrived at the conclusion shared by many civilian leaders of the government that in Algeria as in Indochina the real enemy was international Communism.[48]

Like the doctrine of *la guerre révolutionnaire,* the concept of indirect aggression was stimulated initially by the struggle with the Communist movements of southeast Asia. The Manila pact of September, 1954, provided that the parties would cooperate not only "to resist armed aggression" but also "to prevent and counter subversive activities directed from without against their territorial integrity and political stability." Although the operative terms of the pact in Article II were directed primarily at what Professor W. Macmahon Ball has called "subversion from without," the actual antisubversive activities jointly undertaken by members of the pact have been largely directed at "subversion from within." Committees and a staff established under the pact help to coordinate the antisubversive efforts of the members and to provide for the exchange of information.[49] The invocation of indirect aggression as a justification for direct American counteraction did not come until the 1958 coup d'état in Baghdad and the American intervention in Lebanon. Here the evidence of subversion from without was much more definite. American action was justified, the President argued, because the "Cairo, Damascus and Soviet radios" had encouraged an insurrection against the established government of Lebanon and the insurrectionists were being supplied with "sizeable amounts of arms, ammunition, and money and by personnel infiltrated from Syria to fight against the lawful authorities." The aim of these actions was to "overthrow the legally constituted Government of Lebanon and to install by violence a government

---

[46]Delmas, *op. cit.,* p. 44.
[47]See e.g., Gen. Coche, "Armée et guerre subversive," *Revue militaire générale* (March, 1959), 367–399; Contre-Amiral Peltier, "La pensée militaire soviétique," *Revue militaire générale* (December, 1957), 649–679; Chef d'escadrons Louis Pichon, "Caractères généraux de la guerre insurrectionnelle," *Revue militaire générale* (July, 1957), 158–186; *Revue militaire d'information* (February-March, 1957), 25; Delmas, *op. cit.,* p. 50.
[48]Paret, *loc. cit.,* 67.
[49]M. Margaret Ball, "Seato and Subversion," *Political Science,* 11 (March, 1959), 25ff.; W. Macmahon Ball, "Political Re-examination of SEATO," *International Organization,* 12 (Winter, 1958), 21–23.

which would subordinate the independence of Lebanon to the policies of the United Arab Republic."[50]

The doctrine of *la guerre révolutionnaire* began with the result—the struggles in Indochina, Algeria, and elsewhere—and argued that the Soviet Union and its subservient international Communist movement were in large part causes of this result. The doctrine of indirect aggression, on the other hand, began with the causes—the means by which one government can encourage violence against another government—and then argued that these causes could produce calamitous results. "Through use of inflammatory radio broadcasts; through infiltration of weapons, agents, and of bribe money," Mr. Dulles said, "through incitement to murder and assassination; and through threats of personal violence it becomes possible for one nation to destroy the genuine independence of another." Toleration of indirect aggression, he warned, would lead to a third world war.[51] Thus, while the doctrine of *la guerre révolutionnaire* stressed the extent to which Communist influence was responsible for actual revolutionary wars, the doctrine of indirect aggression stressed the extent to which one government, without resort to force, can produce revolution in another. The existence of an external base of support beyond the territory of the target government is, of course, a major aid to revolutionary forces. The basis for the revolution, however, must exist within the society in which it takes place. The techniques mentioned by President Eisenhower and Mr. Dulles can only serve to encourage and to support already existing antigovernmental forces in the target country.

The doctrine of indirect aggression tends to underestimate its pervasiveness and to overestimate its effectiveness. If "indirect aggression were to be admitted as a legitimate means of promoting international policy," Mr. Dulles declared, "small nations would be doomed and the world would become one of constant chaos, if not of war." Any change of government in any country, however, whether by violence or otherwise, presumably affects the interests of the major world powers. Governments attempt to encourage favorable changes in foreign governments and to prevent unfavorable ones. The pervasiveness of indirect aggression in this broad sense is, however, no testimony to its effectiveness. Because all domestic violence has implications for interstate conflict, it cannot be concluded that all domestic violence is caused by interstate conflict.

The tendency to overestimate the ease with which the Soviet Union can subvert or overthrow foreign governments leads to the conclusion that the United States can also profitably employ such tactics. "In the perfection of the instrument of subversion," one writer has said, for example, "the Soviets may have fashioned a form of unconventional military action capable of achieving victories as great as any expected from the more conventional forms of war." From this he concluded that "Subversion is not a form of action reserved for use by the Soviets alone; it can be fully as powerful if turned against them."[52] The Administration which Mr. Dulles served, however, came into power com-

---

[50]Dwight D. Eisenhower, Message to Congress, July 15, 1958, *Department of State Bulletin,* 39 (August 4, 1958), 182.
[51]John Foster Dulles, "Foundations of Peace," Address, Veterans of Foreign Wars, New York, N. Y., *Department of State Bulletin,* 39 (September 8, 1958), 375f.
[52]Theodore Wyckoff, "War by Subversion," *South Atlantic Quarterly,* 59 (Winter, 1960), 35, 45.

mitted to a program of indirect aggression—liberation and political warfare—against the Soviet satellites. Its protestations were sufficient to make the Soviet Union until 1957 a leading advocate of UN condemnation of indirect aggression.[53] Its accomplishments, however, are a significant index of the effectiveness of the tactic.

Insurrection and subversion are primarily the weapons of indigenous antigovernments. Foreign governments, of course, may encourage antigovernments. Intervention by one government against another, however, has the potentialities and the limitations of intervention by outside personnel and money in a local election campaign. Though it can influence the result, it cannot create support where the basis for that support does not already exist, and it cannot reverse a drastically unfavorable balance of forces within the contested area. Intervention on behalf of an established government, moreover, is usually easier than intervention against it. Traditional liberal thinking has often been criticized for analyzing war and international relations in terms of the ideas and categories of domestic politics. The doctrines of *la guerre révolutionnaire* and indirect aggression, on the other hand, tend to apply to domestic political struggles the assumptions and concepts of international politics. Domestic violence, obviously, is influenced by the intensity and nature of international conflict, but it cannot be explained *simply* as the result of that conflict.

Foreign governmental intervention more often is the result of domestic violence than is domestic violence the product of foreign intervention. The longer the domestic violence continues, moreover, the more likely are foreign governments to become involved on one side or another. The Soviet Union initiated neither the Indochinese and Algerian insurrections nor the Castro revolution, but once these became established facts of political life, it could hardly be expected not to capitalize upon them. Thus, a quick coup d'état is more likely to minimize the involvement of external powers and maximize international stability than a prolonged revolutionary war. From the Western viewpoint, even a coup that topples a friendly government, such as the Kassim coup of 1958, but that installs a government with whom one can negotiate, might be preferable to an unsuccessful coup degenerating into extensive civil strife, which inevitably would involve the Soviet Union and the Western powers.

VIOLENCE AND TRANSNATIONAL COMMUNITY

While the principal manifestations of domestic violence cannot be explained only by reference to *international* politics, neither can they be explained on an individual basis without reference to the general patterns of *world* politics. Outbreaks of domestic violence tend to occur in waves. In his study of Latin American politics Lieuwen identifies one wave of radical reform coups beginning with Peron's conquest of power in Argentina in 1943 and including coups or revolts in Bolivia in 1943, Ecuador and

---

[53]See Geoffrey Barraclough, "What Is Indirect Aggression?" *The Listener,* 60 (September 18, 1958), 403–405. For a stimulating analysis of the relations between internal and external conflict, see George Modelski, *The International Relations of Internal War* (Princeton University, Center of International Studies, Research Monograph No. 11, May 24, 1961).

Guatemala in 1944, Brazil in 1945, El Salvador and Costa Rica in 1948, Panama and Bolivia in 1952, and Colombia in 1953. In addition, reformers came to power peacefully in Venezuela and Peru in 1945. Overlapping the reform wave was a progression of conservative coups: Venezuela and Peru in 1948, Haiti in 1950, Cuba in 1952, Guatemala and Brazil in 1954, Panama and Argentina in 1955, and Colombia in 1957.[54] In other waves of domestic violence the individual manifestations were much more closely grouped in time. In 1948, as the Communist line in Asia shifted, revolutionary wars or insurrections began in the Philippines, Burma, Indonesia, India, and Malaya. In 1956 anti-Soviet disorders shook the eastern European satellites, particularly Hungary and Poland. In 1958 military coups d'état took place in Iraq, the Sudan, Thailand, Burma, and Pakistan. In 1960 student demonstrations and riots helped to overturn the existing regimes in South Korea and Turkey, to cancel President Eisenhower's visit to Japan, and to stimulate the abortive insurrection of the Algerian colons.[55]

The reasons for these waves of violence undoubtedly vary. All of them, however, reflect the shrinking of world politics, the similarity of political conditions and forces in different countries, and the extent to which events in one country may affect those in another. At least three possible explanations exist for the waves of violence. First, they may be the result of common direction. This was certainly the case with the Communist-inspired revolutionary wars and insurrections of 1948 and 1949. Presumably it could be the case again if the Kremlin should decide that insurrection on a broad scale was a desirable way of achieving its objectives in the underdeveloped areas. Common direction, however, will not explain most of the waves of violence in domestic politics. Nor will the alternative extreme explanation of isolated parallelism, that is, the emergence in different countries of similar but unrelated situations that lead to similar and almost simultaneous coups or domestic wars. Undoubtedly, the processes of evolution in newly independent countries do follow certain broad common channels. But even if the paths of development were much more closely parallel than they are, this would still not completely explain the waves of violence. Parallelism does not necessarily imply simultaneity.

In addition to similarity of political condition, emulation is also necessary to create a wave. The power of example, the influence exercised by the "pace-setter," is a critically important result of the improvement in worldwide communications. A successful coup or insurrection by one party or group in one country inspires similar parties or groups in other countries to similar action. The conditions breeding insurrection or coup d'état must be present in these other countries, while the action of the "pace-setting" country indicates that the time may well be ripe. The success of Peron in Argentina stimulated radical military reformers in other Latin American states. The revolt in Bolivia a few months later was "obviously an echo of the events in Buenos Aires."[56] Similarly, the fall of Peron in 1955 stimulated the efforts to remove Rojas

---

[54]Lieuwen, *op. cit.,* pp. 63–65.
[55]See the fears expressed in London of the tendency toward "government by students," *New York Times,* June 17, 1960, p. 11.
[56]Lieuwen, *op. cit.,* p. 65.

Pinilla in Colombia. The defeat of the French in one revolutionary war in Indochina directly encouraged the launching of another in Algeria. The successful toppling of Syngmann Rhee's government by student, civilian, and military action in 1960 demonstrated that the United States would not intervene to uphold an unpopular ally against a popular uprising and directly encouraged students, liberals, and soldiers to undertake similar successful action in Turkey.

A wave of violence presupposes a degree of transnational political community, involving some similarity of political conditions in the different countries and some influence by the political events in one country on the political events of another. A successful coup by conservative groups in Venezuela may stimulate action by conservative groups in Peru, but it is not likely to produce any comparable response in the United States, France, or Pakistan. In this sense, Peru and Venezuela are part of a political community from which the other three countries are excluded. On the other hand, a swing to the right in the United States may be the product of conditions that also produce a shift to the right in Canada, and the change in the United States may hasten the change in Canada. Or a military coup in Pakistan may serve as a model for comparable coups in other southern Asian states, but it is not likely to be relevant to political developments in Italy, Japan, or the Congo. Revolutions (and other forms of domestic violence reflecting changing political tides) are seldom exported, but they are often imitated. They can only be imitated, however, in countries where the necessary raw materials already exist.

The dominant forms of violence of each age reflect the politics of the age. The violence of the seventeenth century reflected the decline of the Hapsburg Empire and the conflicts over religion. The limited wars and colonial wars of the eighteenth century were the natural products of the national monarchies of the old regime. The nineteenth century encompassed insurrections devoted to liberalism, democracy, and social change, on the one hand, and renewed colonial wars on the other. The first half of the twentieth century saw nationalistic rivalries and expansion produce two world wars. The rapid political and economic change in Latin America, Africa, and southern Asia has produced and will continue to produce its own distinctive patterns of violence. This violence may take the form of revolutionary wars or reform coups, and it may assume still different forms. In the new states traditionalist elements are likely to reassert themselves and to challenge the nationalist leaders who led the fight against the colonial power. Wars of secession and integration are likely between the regions of artificially defined "nation-states." In Africa intertribal wars are still possible, and intercommunal wars between white settlers and natives seem unavoidable. Governments which have achieved their independence through revolutionary war or other forms of violence have their own distinctive problems in breaking the patterns of violence established in the pre-independence era.[57] All of these forms of violence are likely to involve military forces and civil-military relations very different from those usually associated with interstate wars along European lines. Most violence will be civil violence in that it

---

[57]D. E. Ashford, "Politics and Violence in Morocco," *Middle East Journal,* 13 (Winter, 1959), 11–25. See also R. A. LeVine, "Anti-European Violence in Africa: A Comparative Analysis," *Conflict Resolution,* 3 (December, 1959), 420–429.

occurs within the accepted boundaries of particular political units. All violence will be civil violence in that it occurs within the great society of world politics in which almost all nations and governments recognize a common interest in minimizing intergovernmental war and in which domestic violence in one country resembles and is influenced by the patterns of violence in other countries belonging to the same transnational political community.

For the future, the "general mêlée" of the seventeenth century may be a more applicable model than the calculated wars of the eighteenth. The distinction between intergovernmental and domestic wars may fade, with violence becoming more pervasive, more dispersed, and less within the control of governments. In a sense, vast areas of the world may evolve in the direction of Europe at the beginning of the seventeenth century when

> wars were not continuations of religious or dynastic or any other policy by the use of organized force, but collisions of communities. Some of these communities were the imperfect and improvised assemblages of civil war, others were the comparatively complete societies called monarchies or republics. They sometimes blundered into their struggles and sometimes went into them methodically, with their eyes open, through the regular procedure of negotiation, ultimatum, and declaration of war; sometimes they managed hostilities equally methodically, but sometimes their forces, even if they did not become mutinous or barbarous, were not servants at all but were moved by a will of their own. Peace sometimes came by rational stages, but sometimes by exhaustion and anarchy. Any component part of society might break loose and smash or obstruct any other in its movements.[58]

As in the seventeenth century, however, the proliferation of new forms of violence may herald the emergence of new and more stable political institutions.

---

[58]Sir George Clark, *op. cit.,* pp. 73–74.

THE STRATEGIC LOGIC
OF TERRORISM

Martha Crenshaw

This chapter examines the ways in which terrorism can be understood as an expression of political strategy. It attempts to show that terrorism may follow logical processes that can be discovered and explained. For the purpose of presenting this source of terrorist behavior, rather than the psychological one, it interprets the resort to violence as a willful choice made by an organization for political and strategic reasons, rather than as the unintended outcome of psychological or social factors.[1]

In the terms of this analytical approach, terrorism is assumed to display a collective rationality. A radical political organization is seen as the central actor in the terrorist drama. The group possesses collective preferences or values and selects terrorism as a course of action from a range of perceived alternatives. Efficacy is the primary standard by which terrorism is compared with other methods of achieving political goals. Reasonably regularized decision-making procedures are employed to make an intentional choice, in conscious anticipation of the consequences of various courses of action or inaction. Organizations arrive at collective judgments about the relative effectiveness of different strategies of opposition on the basis of observation and experience, as much as on the basis of abstract strategic conceptions derived from ideological assumptions. This approach thus allows for the incorporation of theories of social learning.

Conventional rational-choice theories of individual participation in rebellion, extended to include terrorist activities, have usually been considered inappropriate because of the "free rider" problem. That is, the benefits of a successful terrorist campaign would presumably be shared by all individual supporters of the group's goals, regardless of the extent of their active participation. In this case, why should a rational person become a terrorist, given the high costs associated with violent resistance and the expectation that everyone who supports the cause will benefit, whether he or she participates or not? One answer is that the benefits of participation are psychological.

Martha Crenshaw, "The Logic of Terrorism: Terrorist Behavior as a Product of Strategic Choice," in Walter Reich, ed., *Origins of Terrorism: Psychologies, Ideologies, Theologies, States of Mind*, pp. 7–24 © 1998 Woodrow Wilson Center Press, Washington, D. C. Reprinted with the permission of The Johns Hopkins University Press.
[1]For a similar perspective (based on a different methodology) see James DeNardo, *Power in Numbers: The Political Strategy of Protest and Rebellion* (Princeton, N.J.: Princeton University Press, 1985). See also Harvey Waterman, "Insecure 'Ins' and Opportune 'Outs': Sources of Collective Political Activity," *Journal of Political and Military Sociology* Vol. 8 (1980): 107–12, and "Reasons and Reason: Collective Political Activity in Comparative and Historical Perspective," *World Politics* Vol. 33 (1981): 554–89. A useful review of rational choice theories is found in James G. March, "Theories of Choice and Making Decisions," *Society* Vol. 20 (1982): 29–39.

A different answer, however, supports a strategic analysis. On the basis of surveys conducted in New York and West Germany, political scientists suggest that individuals can be *collectively* rational.[2] People realize that their participation is important because group size and cohesion matter. They are sensitive to the implications of free-riding and perceive their personal influence on the provision of public goods to be high. The authors argue that "average citizens may adopt a collectivist conception of rationality because they recognize that what is individually rational is collectively irrational."[3] Selective incentives are deemed largely irrelevant.

One of the advantages of approaching terrorism as a collectively rational strategic choice is that it permits the construction of a standard from which deviations can be measured. For example, the central question about the rationality of some terrorist organizations, such as the West German groups of the 1970s or the Weather Underground in the United States, is whether or not they had a sufficient grasp of reality—some approximation, to whatever degree imperfect—to calculate the likely consequences of the courses of action they chose. Perfect knowledge of available alternatives and the consequences of each is not possible, and miscalculations are inevitable. The Popular Front for the Liberation of Palestine (PFLP), for example, planned the hijacking of a TWA flight from Rome in August 1969 to coincide with a scheduled address by President Nixon to a meeting of the Zionist Organization of America, but he sent a letter instead.[4]

Yet not all errors of decision are miscalculations. There are varied degrees of limited rationality. Are some organizations so low on the scale of rationality as to be in a different category from more strategically minded groups? To what degree is strategic reasoning modified by psychological and other constraints? The strategic choice framework provides criteria on which to base these distinctions. It also leads one to ask what conditions promote or discourage rationality in violent underground organizations.

The use of this theoretical approach is also advantageous in that it suggests important questions about the preferences or goals of terrorist organizations. For example, is the decision to seize hostages in order to bargain with governments dictated by strategic considerations or by other, less instrumental motives?

The strategic choice approach is also a useful interpretation of reality. Since the French Revolution, a strategy of terrorism has gradually evolved as a means of bringing about political change opposed by established governments. Analysis of the historical development of terrorism reveals similarities in calculation of ends and means. The strategy has changed over time to adapt to new circumstances that offer different possibilities for dissident action—for example, hostage taking. Yet terrorist activity consid-

---

[2]Edward N. Muller and Karl-Dieter Opp, "Rational Choice and Rebellious Collective Action," *American Political Science Review* 80 (1986): 471–87.

[3]Ibid., 484. The authors also present another puzzling question that may be answered in terms of either psychology or collective rationality. People who expected their rebellious behavior to be punished were more likely to be potential rebels. This propensity could be explained either by a martyr syndrome (or an expectation of hostility from authority figures) or intensity of preference—the calculation that the regime was highly repressive and thus deserved all the more to be destroyed. See pp. 482 and 485.

[4]Leila Khaled, *My People Shall Live: The Autobiography of a Revolutionary* (London: Hodder and Stoughton, 1973), 128–31.

ered in its entirety shows a fundamental unity of purpose and conception. Although this analysis remains largely on an abstract level, the historical evolution of the strategy of terrorism can be sketched in its terms.[5]

A last argument in support of this approach takes the form of a warning. The wide range of terrorist activity cannot be dismissed as "irrational" and thus pathological, unreasonable, or inexplicable. The resort to terrorism need not be an aberration. It may be a reasonable and calculated response to circumstances. To say that the reasoning that leads to the choice of terrorism may be logical is not an argument about moral justifiability. It does suggest, however, that the belief that terrorism is expedient is one means by which moral inhibitions are overcome. . . .

THE CONDITIONS FOR TERRORISM

The central problem is to determine when extremist organizations find terrorism useful. Extremists seek either a radical change in the status quo, which would confer a new advantage, or the defense of privileges they perceive to be threatened. Their dissatisfaction with the policies of the government is extreme, and their demands usually involve the displacement of existing political elites.[6] Terrorism is not the only method of working toward radical goals, and thus it must be compared to the alternative strategies available to dissidents. Why is terrorism attractive to some opponents of the state, but unattractive to others?

The practitioners of terrorism often claim that they had no choice but terrorism, and it is indeed true that terrorism often follows the failure of other methods. In nineteenth-century Russia, for example, the failure of nonviolent movements contributed to the rise of terrorism. In Ireland, terrorism followed the failure of Parnell's constitutionalism. In the Palestinian-Israeli struggle, terrorism followed the failure of Arab efforts at conventional warfare against Israel. In general, the "nonstate" or "substate" users of terrorism—that is, groups in opposition to the government, as opposed to government itself—are constrained in their options by the lack of active mass support and by the superior power arrayed against them (an imbalance that has grown with the development of the modern centralized and bureaucratic nation-state). But these constraints have not prevented oppositions from considering and rejecting methods other than terrorism. Perhaps because groups are slow to recognize the extent of the limits to action, terrorism is often the last in a sequence of choices. It represents the outcome of a learning process. Experience in opposition provides radicals with information about the potential consequences of their choices. Terrorism is likely to be a reasonably informed choice among available alternatives, some tried unsuccessfully. Terrorists also learn from the experiences of others, usually communicated to them via the news media. Hence the existence of patterns of contagion in terrorist incidents.[7]

---

[5]See Martha Crenshaw, "The Strategic Development of Terrorism," paper presented to the 1985 Annual Meeting of the American Political Science Association, New Orleans.
[6]William A. Gamson, *The Strategy of Social Protest* (Homewood, Illinois: Dorsey Press, 1975).
[7]Manus I. Midlarsky, Martha Crenshaw, and Fumihiko Yoshida, "Why Violence Spreads: The Contagion of International Terrorism," *International Studies Quarterly* 24 (1980): 262–98.

Thus the existence of extremism or rebellious potential is necessary to the resort to terrorism but does not in itself explain it, because many revolutionary and nationalist organizations have explicitly disavowed terrorism. The Russian Marxists argued for years against the use of terrorism.[8] Generally, small organizations resort to violence to compensate for what they lack in numbers.[9] The imbalance between the resources terrorists are able to mobilize and the power of the incumbent regime is a decisive consideration in their decision making.

More important than the observation that terrorism is the weapon of the weak, who lack numbers or conventional military power, is the explanation for weakness. Particularly, why does an organization lack the potential to attract enough followers to change government policy or overthrow it?

One possibility is that the majority of the population does not share the ideological views of the resisters, who occupy a political position so extreme that their appeal is inherently limited. This incompatibility of preferences may be purely political, concerning, for example, whether or not one prefers socialism to capitalism. The majority of West Germans found the Red Army Faction's promises for the future not only excessively vague but distasteful. Nor did most Italians support aims of the neofascist groups that initiated the "strategy of tension" in 1969. Other extremist groups, such as the *Euzkadi ta Akatasuna* (ETA) in Spain or the Provisional Irish Republican Army (PIRA) in Northern Ireland, may appeal exclusively to ethnic, religious, or other minorities. In such cases, a potential constituency of like-minded and dedicated individuals exists, but its boundaries are fixed and limited. Despite the intensity of the preferences of a minority, its numbers will never be sufficient for success.

A second explanation for the weakness of the type of organization likely to turn to terrorism lies in a failure to mobilize support. Its members may be unwilling or unable to expend the time and effort required for mass organizational work. Activists may not possess the requisite skills or patience, or may not expect returns commensurate with their endeavors. No matter how acute or widespread popular dissatisfaction may be, the masses do not rise spontaneously; mobilization is required.[10] The organization's leaders, recognizing the advantages of numbers, may combine mass organization with conspiratorial activities. But resources are limited and organizational work is difficult and slow even under favorable circumstances. Moreover, rewards are not immediate. These difficulties are compounded in an authoritarian state, where the organization of independent opposition is sure to incur high costs. Combining violent provocation with nonviolent organizing efforts may only work to the detriment of the latter.

For example, the debate over whether to use an exclusively violent underground strategy that is isolated from the masses (as terrorism inevitably is) or to work with the

---

[8]See the study by David A. Newell, *The Russian Marxist Response to Terrorism: 1878–1917* (Ph.D. dissertation, Stanford University, University Microfilms, 1981).

[9]The tension between violence and numbers is a fundamental proposition in DeNardo's analysis; see *Power in Numbers,* chapters 9–11.

[10]The work of Charles Tilly emphasizes the political basis of collective violence. See Charles Tilly, Louise Tilly, and Richard Tilly, *The Rebellious Century 1830–1930* (Cambridge: Harvard University Press, 1975), and Charles Tilly, *From Mobilization to Revolution* (Reading, Mass.: Addison-Wesley, 1978).

people in propaganda and organizational efforts divided the Italian left-wing groups, with the Red Brigades choosing the clandestine path and Prima Linea preferring to maintain contact with the wider protest movement. In prerevolutionary Russia the Socialist-Revolutionary party combined the activities of a legal political party with the terrorist campaign of the secret Combat Organization. The IRA has a legal counterpart in Sinn Fein.

A third reason for the weakness of dissident organizations is specific to repressive states. It is important to remember that terrorism is by no means restricted to liberal democracies, although some authors refuse to define resistance to authoritarianism as terrorism.[11] People may not support a resistance organization because they are afraid of negative sanctions from the regime or because censorship of the press prevents them from learning of the possibility of rebellion. In this situation a radical organization may believe that supporters exist but cannot reveal themselves. The depth of this latent support cannot be measured or activists mobilized until the state is overthrown.

Such conditions are frustrating, because the likelihood of popular dissatisfaction grows as the likelihood of its active expression is diminished. Frustration may also encourage unrealistic expectations among the regime's challengers, who are not able to test their popularity. Rational expectations may be undermined by fantastic assumptions about the role of the masses. Yet such fantasies can also prevail among radical undergrounds in Western democracies. The misperception of conditions can lead to unrealistic expectations.

In addition to small numbers, time constraints contribute to the decision to use terrorism. Terrorists are impatient for action. This impatience may, of course, be due to external factors, such as psychological or organizational pressures. The personalities of leaders, demands from followers, or competition from rivals often constitute impediments to strategic thinking. But it is not necessary to explain the felt urgency of some radical organizations by citing reasons external to an instrumental framework. Impatience and eagerness for action can be rooted in calculations of ends and means. For example, the organization may perceive an immediate opportunity to compensate for its inferiority vis-à-vis the government. A change in the structure of the situation may temporarily alter the balance of resources available to the two sides, thus changing the ratio of strength between government and challenger.

Such a change in the radical organization's outlook—the combination of optimism and urgency—may occur when the regime suddenly appears vulnerable to challenge. This vulnerability may be of two sorts. First, the regime's ability to respond effectively, its capacity for efficient repression of dissent, or its ability to protect its citizens and property may weaken. Its armed forces may be committed elsewhere, for example, as British forces were during World War I when the IRA first rose to challenge British rule, or its coercive resources may be otherwise overextended. Inadequate security at embassies, airports, or military installations may become obvious. The poorly protected

---

[11]See Conor Cruise O'Brien, "Terrorism under Democratic Conditions: The Case of the IRA," in *Terrorism, Legitimacy, and Power: The Consequences of Political Violence,* edited by Martha Crenshaw (Middletown, Conn.: Wesleyan University Press, 1983).

U.S. Marine barracks in Beirut were, for example, a tempting target. Government strategy may be ill-adapted to responding to terrorism.

Second, the regime may make itself morally or politically vulnerable by increasing the likelihood that the terrorists will attract popular support. Government repressiveness is thought to have contradictory effects: it both deters dissent and provokes a moral backlash.[12] Perceptions of the regime as unjust motivate opposition. If government actions make average citizens willing to suffer punishment for supporting antigovernment causes, or lend credence to the claims of radical opponents, the extremist organization may be tempted to exploit this temporary upsurge of popular indignation. A groundswell of popular disapproval may make liberal governments less willing (as opposed to less able) to use coercion against violent dissent.

Political discomfort may also be internationally generated. If the climate of international opinion changes so as to reduce the legitimacy of a targeted regime, rebels may feel encouraged to risk a repression that they hope will be limited by outside disapproval. In such circumstances the regime's brutality may be expected to win supporters to the cause of its challengers. The current situation in South Africa furnishes an example. Thus a heightened sensitivity to injustice may be produced either by government actions or by changing public attitudes.

The other fundamental way in which the situation changes to the advantage of challengers is through acquiring new resources. New means of financial support are an obvious asset, which may accrue through a foreign alliance with a sympathetic government or another, richer revolutionary group, or through criminal means such as bank robberies or kidnapping for ransom. Although terrorism is an extremely economical method of violence, funds are essential for the support of full-time activists, weapons purchases, transportation, and logistics.

Technological advances in weapons, explosives, transportation, and communications also may enhance the disruptive potential of terrorism. The invention of dynamite was thought by nineteenth-century revolutionaries and anarchists to equalize the relationship between government and challenger, for example. In 1885, Johann Most published a pamphlet titled *Revolutionary War Science,* which explicitly advocated terrorism. According to Paul Avrich, the anarchists saw dynamite "as a great equalizing force, enabling ordinary workmen to stand up against armies, militias, and police, to say nothing of the hired gunmen of the employers."[13] In providing such a powerful but easily concealed weapon, science was thought to have given a decisive advantage to revolutionary forces.

Strategic innovation is another important way in which a challenging organization acquires new resources. The organization may borrow or adapt a technique in order to exploit a vulnerability ignored by the government. In August 1972, for example, the Provisional IRA introduced the effective tactic of the one-shot sniper. IRA Chief of Staff Sean MacStiofain claims to have originated the idea: "It seemed to me that prolonged sniping from a static position had no more in common with guerrilla theory

---

[12]For example, DeNardo, in *Power in Numbers,* argues that "the movement derives moral sympathy from the government's excesses" (p. 207).

[13]Paul Avrich, *The Haymarket Tragedy* (Princeton: Princeton University Press, 1984), 166.

than mass confrontations."[14] The best marksmen were trained to fire a single shot and escape before their position could be located. The creation of surprise is naturally one of the key advantages of an offensive strategy. So, too, is the willingness to violate social norms pertaining to restraints on violence. The history of terrorism reveals a series of innovations, as terrorists deliberately selected targets considered taboo and locales where violence was unexpected. These innovations were then rapidly diffused, especially in the modern era of instantaneous and global communications.

It is especially interesting that, in 1968, two of the most important terrorist tactics of the modern era appeared—diplomatic kidnappings in Latin America and hijackings in the Middle East. Both were significant innovations because they involved the use of extortion or blackmail. Although the nineteenth-century Fenians had talked about kidnapping the prince of Wales, the People's Will (Narodnaya Volya) in nineteenth-century Russia had offered to halt its terrorist campaign if a constitution were granted, and American marines were kidnapped by Castro forces in 1959, hostage taking as a systematic and lethal form of coercive bargaining was essentially new. This chapter later takes up the issue in more detail as an illustration of strategic analysis.

Terrorism has so far been presented as the response by an opposition movement to an opportunity. This approach is compatible with the findings of Harvey Waterman, who sees collective political action as determined by the calculations of resources and opportunities.[15] Yet other theorists—James Q. Wilson, for example—argue that political organizations originate in response to a threat to a group's values.[16] Terrorism can certainly be defensive as well as opportunistic. It may be a response to a sudden downturn in a dissident organization's fortunes. The fear of appearing weak may provoke an underground organization into acting in order to show its strength. The PIRA used terrorism to offset an impression of weakness, even at the cost of alienating public opinion: in the 1970s periods of negotiations with the British were punctuated by outbursts of terrorism because the PIRA did want people to think that they were negotiating from strength.[17] Right-wing organizations frequently resort to violence in response to what they see as a threat to the status quo from the left. Beginning in 1969, for example, the right in Italy promoted a "strategy of tension," which involved urban bombings with high numbers of civilian casualties, in order to keep the Italian government and electorate from moving to the left.

CALCULATION OF COST AND BENEFIT

An organization or a faction of an organization may choose terrorism because other methods are not expected to work or are considered too time-consuming, given the urgency of the situation and the government's superior resources. Why would an extremist organization expect that terrorism will be effective? What are the costs and benefits

---

[14]Sean MacStiofain, *Memoirs of a Revolutionary* (N.p.: Gordon Cremonisi, 1975), 301.
[15]Waterman, "Insecure 'Ins' and Opportune 'Outs'" and "Reasons and Reason."
[16]*Political Organizations* (New York: Basic Books, 1973).
[17]Maria McGuire, *To Take Arms: My Year with the IRA Provisionals* (New York: Viking, 1973), 110–11, 118, 129–31, 115, and 161–62.

of such a choice, compared with other alternatives? What is the nature of the debate over terrorism? Whether or not to use terrorism is one of the most divisive issues resistance groups confront, and numerous revolutionary movements have split on the question of means even after agreeing on common political ends.[18]

The Costs of Terrorism   The costs of terrorism are high. As a domestic strategy, it invariably invites a punitive government reaction, although the organization may believe that the government reaction will not be efficient enough to pose a serious threat. This cost can be offset by the advance preparation of building a secure underground. *Sendero Luminoso* (Shining Path) in Peru, for example, spent ten years creating a clandestine organizational structure before launching a campaign of violence in 1980. Furthermore, radicals may look to the future and calculate that present sacrifice will not be in vain if it inspires future resistance. Conceptions of interest are thus long term.

Another potential cost of terrorism is loss of popular support. Unless terrorism is carefully controlled and discriminate, it claims innocent victims. In a liberal state, indiscriminate violence may appear excessive and unjustified and alienate a citizenry predisposed to loyalty to the government. If it provokes generalized government repression, fear may diminish enthusiasm for resistance. This potential cost of popular alienation is probably least in ethnically divided societies, where victims can be clearly identified as the enemy and where the government of the majority appears illegal to the minority. Terrorists try to compensate by justifying their actions as the result of the absence of choice or the need to respond to government violence. In addition, they may make their strategy highly discriminate, attacking only unpopular targets.

Terrorism may be unattractive because it is elitist. Although relying only on terrorism may spare the general population from costly involvement in the struggle for freedom, such isolation may violate the ideological beliefs of revolutionaries who insist that the people must participate in their liberation. The few who choose terrorism are willing to forgo or postpone the participation of the many, but revolutionaries who oppose terrorism insist that it prevents the people from taking responsibility for their own destiny. The possibility of vicarious popular identification with symbolic acts of terrorism may satisfy some revolutionaries, but others will find terrorism a harmful substitute for mass participation.

The Advantages of Terrorism   Terrorism has an extremely useful agenda-setting function. If the reasons behind violence are skillfully articulated, terrorism can put the issue of political change on the public agenda. By attracting attention it makes the claims of the resistance a salient issue in the public mind. The government can reject but not ignore an opposition's demands. In 1974 the Palestinian Black September organization, for example, was willing to sacrifice a base in Khartoum, alienate the Sudanese government, and create ambivalence in the Arab world by seizing the Saudi Arabian embassy and killing American and Belgian diplomats. These costs were appar-

---

[18]DeNardo concurs; see *Power in Numbers,* chapter 11.

ently weighed against the message to the world "to take us seriously." Mainstream Fatah leader Salah Khalef (Abu Iyad) explained: "We are planting the seed. Others will harvest it. . . . It is enough for us now to learn, for example, in reading the Jerusalem Post, that Mrs. Meir had to make her will before visiting Paris, or that Mr. Abba Eban had to travel with a false passport."[19] George Habash of the PFLP noted in 1970 that "we force people to ask what is going on."[20] In these statements, contemporary extremists echo the nineteenth-century anarchists, who coined the idea of propaganda of the deed, a term used as early as 1877 to refer to an act of insurrection as "a powerful means of arousing popular conscience" and the materialization of an idea through actions.[21]

Terrorism may be intended to create revolutionary conditions. It can prepare the ground for active mass revolt by undermining the government's authority and demoralizing its administrative cadres—its courts, police, and military. By spreading insecurity—at the extreme, making the country ungovernable—the organization hopes to pressure the regime into concessions or relaxation of coercive controls. With the rule of law disrupted, the people will be free to join the opposition. Spectacular humiliation of the government demonstrates strength and will and maintains the morale and enthusiasm of adherents and sympathizers. The first wave of Russian revolutionaries claimed that the aims of terrorism were to exhaust the enemy, render the government's position untenable, and wound the government's prestige by delivering a moral, not a physical, blow. Terrorists hoped to paralyze the government by their presence merely by showing signs of life from time to time. The hesitation, irresolution, and tension they would produce would undermine the processes of government and make the Czar a prisoner in his own palace.[22] As Brazilian revolutionary Carlos Marighela explained: "Revolutionary terrorism's great weapon is initiative, which guarantees its survival and continued activity. The more committed terrorists and revolutionaries devoted to anti-dictatorship terrorism and sabotage there are, the more military power will be worn down, the more time it will lose following false trails, and the more fear and tension it will suffer through not knowing where the next attack will be launched and what the next target will be."[23]

These statements illustrate a corollary advantage to terrorism in what might be called its excitational function: it inspires resistance by example. As propaganda of the deed, terrorism demonstrates that the regime can be challenged and that illegal opposition is possible. It acts as a catalyst, not a substitute, for mass revolt. All the tedious and time-consuming organizational work of mobilizing the people can be avoided.

---

[19]See Jim Hoagland, "A Community of Terror," *Washington Post,* 15 March 1973, pp. 1 and 13; also *New York Times,* 4 March 1973, p. 28. Black September is widely regarded as a subsidiary of Fatah, the major Palestinian organization headed by Yasir Arafat.

[20]John Amos, *Palestinian Resistance: Organization of a Nationalist Movement* (New York: Pergamon, 1980), 193; quoting George Habash, interviewed in *Life Magazine,* 12 June 1970, 33.

[21]Jean Maitron, *Histoire du mouvement anarchiste en France (1880–1914),* 2d ed. (Paris: Société universitaire d'éditions et de librairie, 1955), 74–5.

[22]"Stepniak" (pseud. for Sergei Kravshinsky), *Underground Russia: Revolutionary Profiles and Sketches from Life* (London: Smith, Elder, 1883), 278–80.

[23]Carlos Marighela, *For the Liberation of Brazil* (Harmondsworth: Penguin, 1971), 113.

Terrorism is a shortcut to revolution. As the Russian revolutionary Vera Figner described its purpose, terrorism was "a means of agitation to draw people from their torpor," not a sign of loss of belief in the people.[24]

A more problematic benefit lies in provoking government repression. Terrorists often think that by provoking indiscriminate repression against the population, terrorism will heighten popular disaffection, demonstrate the justice of terrorist claims, and enhance the attractiveness of the political alternative the terrorists represent. Thus, the West German Red Army Faction sought (in vain) to make fascism "visible" in West Germany.[25] In Brazil, Marighela unsuccessfully aimed to "transform the country's political situation into a military one. Then discontent will spread to all social groups and the military will be held exclusively responsible for failures."[26]

But profiting from government repression depends on the lengths to which the government is willing to go in order to contain disorder, and on the population's tolerance for both insecurity and repression. A liberal state may be limited in its capacity for quelling violence, but at the same time it may be difficult to provoke to excess. However, the government's reaction to terrorism may reinforce the symbolic value of violence even if it avoids repression. Extensive security precautions, for example, may only make the terrorists appear powerful.

Summary　To summarize, the choice of terrorism involves considerations of timing and of the popular contribution to revolt, as well as of the relationship between government and opponents. Radicals choose terrorism when they want immediate action, think that only violence can build organizations and mobilize supporters, and accept the risks of challenging the government in a particularly provocative way. Challengers who think that organizational infrastructure must precede action, that rebellion without the masses is misguided, and that premature conflict with the regime can only lead to disaster favor gradualist strategies. They prefer methods such as rural guerrilla warfare, because terrorism can jeopardize painfully achieved gains or preclude eventual compromise with the government.

The resistance organization has before it a set of alternatives defined by the situation and by the objectives and resources of the group. The reasoning behind terrorism takes into account the balance of power between challengers and authorities, a balance that depends on the amount of popular support the resistance can mobilize. The proponents of terrorism understand this constraint and possess reasonable expectations about the likely results of action or inaction. They may be wrong about the alternatives that are open to them, or miscalculate the consequences of their actions, but their decisions are based on logical processes. Furthermore, organizations learn from their mistakes and from those of others, resulting in strategic continuity and progress toward the development of more efficient and sophisticated tactics. Future choices are modified by the consequences of present actions.

---

[24]Vera Figner, *Mémoires d'une révolutionnaire* (Paris: Gallimard, 1930), 206.
[25]*Textes des prisonniers de la "fraction armée rouge" et dernières lettres d'Ulrike Meinhof* (Paris: Maspéro, 1977), 64.
[26]Marighela, *For the Liberation of Brazil,* 46.

HOSTAGE TAKING AS BARGAINING

Hostage taking can be analyzed as a form of coercive bargaining. More than twenty years ago, Thomas Schelling wrote that "hostages represent the power to hurt in its purest form."[27] From this perspective, terrorists choose to take hostages because in bargaining situations the government's greater strength and resources are not an advantage. The extensive resort to this form of terrorism after 1968, a year that marks the major advent of diplomatic kidnappings and airline hijackings, was a predictable response to the growth of state power. Kidnappings, hijackings, and barricade-type seizures of embassies or public buildings are attempts to manipulate a government's political decisions.

Strategic analysis of bargaining terrorism is based on the assumption that hostage takers genuinely seek the concessions they demand. It assumes that they prefer government compliance to resistance. This analysis does not allow for deception or for the possibility that seizing hostages may be an end in itself because it yields the benefit of publicity. Because these limiting assumptions may reduce the utility of the theory, it is important to recognize them.

Terrorist bargaining is essentially a form of blackmail or extortion.[28] Terrorists seize hostages in order to affect a government's choices, which are controlled both by expectations of outcome (what the terrorists are likely to do, given the government reaction) and preferences (such as humanitarian values). The outcome threatened by the terrorist—the death of the hostages—must be worse for the government than compliance with terrorist demands. The terrorist has two options, neither of which necessarily excludes the other: to make the threat both more horrible and more credible or to reward compliance, a factor that strategic theorists often ignore.[29] That is, the cost to the government of complying with the terrorists' demands may be lowered or the cost of resisting raised.

The threat to kill the hostages must be believable and painful to the government. Here hostage takers are faced with a paradox. How can the credibility of this threat be assured when hostage takers recognize that governments know that the terrorists' control over the situation depends on live hostages? One way of establishing credibility is to divide the threat, making it sequential by killing one hostage at a time. Such tactics also aid terrorists in the process of incurring and demonstrating a commitment to carrying out their threat. Once the terrorists have murdered, though, their incentive to surrender voluntarily is substantially reduced. The terrorists have increased their own costs of yielding in order to persuade the government that their intention to kill all the hostages is real.

Another important way of binding oneself in a terrorist strategy is to undertake a barricade rather than a kidnapping operation. Terrorists who are trapped with the

---

[27]Schelling, *Arms and Influence* (New Haven, Conn.: Yale University Press, 1966), 6.

[28]Daniel Ellsberg, *The Theory and Practice of Blackmail* (Santa Monica: Rand Corporation, 1968).

[29]David A. Baldwin, "Bargaining with Airline Hijackers," in *The 50% Solution,* edited by William I. Zartman, 404–29 (Garden City, N.Y.: Doubleday, 1976), argues that promises have not been sufficiently stressed. Analysts tend to emphasize threats instead, surely because of the latent violence implicit in hostage taking regardless of outcome.

hostages find it more difficult to back down (because the government controls the escape routes) and, by virtue of this commitment, influence the government's choices. When terrorists join the hostages in a barricade situation, they create the visible and irrevocable commitment that Schelling sees as a necessary bond in bargaining. The government must expect desperate behavior, because the terrorists have increased their potential loss in order to demonstrate the firmness of their intentions. Furthermore, barricades are technically easier than kidnappings.

The terrorists also attempt to force the "last clear chance" of avoiding disaster onto the government, which must accept the responsibility for noncompliance that leads to the deaths of hostages. The seizure of hostages is the first move in the game, leaving the next move—which determines the fate of the hostages—completely up to the government. Uncertain communications may facilitate this strategy.[30] The terrorists can pretend not to receive government messages that might affect their demonstrated commitment. Hostage takers can also bind themselves by insisting that they are merely agents, empowered to ask only for the most extreme demands. Terrorists may deliberately appear irrational, either through inconsistent and erratic behavior or unrealistic expectations and preferences, in order to convince the government that they will carry out a threat that entails self-destruction.

Hostage seizures are a type of iterated game, which explains some aspects of terrorist behavior that otherwise seem to violate strategic principles. In terms of a single episode, terrorists can be expected to find killing hostages painful, because they will not achieve their demands and the government's desire to punish will be intensified. However, from a long-range perspective, killing hostages reinforces the credibility of the threat in the next terrorist incident, even if the killers then cannot escape. Each terrorist episode is actually a round in a series of games between government and terrorists.

Hostage takers may influence the government's decision by promising rewards for compliance. Recalling that terrorism represents an iterative game, the release of hostages unharmed when ransom is paid underwrites a promise in the future. Sequential release of selected hostages makes promises credible. Maintaining secrecy about a government's concessions is an additional reward for compliance. France, for example, can if necessary deny making concessions to Lebanese kidnappers because the details of arrangements have not been publicized.

Terrorists may try to make their demands appear legitimate so that governments may seem to satisfy popular grievances rather than the whims of terrorists. Thus, terrorists may ask that food be distributed to the poor. Such demands were a favored tactic of the *Ejercito Revolucionario del Pueblo* (ERP) in Argentina in the 1970s.

A problem for hostage takers is that rewarding compliance is not easy to reconcile with making threats credible. For example, if terrorists use publicity to emphasize their threat to kill hostages (which they frequently do), they may also increase the costs of compliance for the government because of the attention drawn to the incident.

---

[30]See Roberta Wohlstetter's case study of Castro's seizure of American marines in Cuba: "Kidnapping to Win Friends and Influence People," *Survey* 20 (1974): 1–40.

In any calculation of the payoffs for each side, the costs associated with the bargaining process must be taken into account.[31] Prolonging the hostage crisis increases the costs to both sides. The question is who loses most and thus is more likely to concede. Each party presumably wishes to make the delay more costly to the other. Seizing multiple hostages appears to be advantageous to terrorists, who are thus in a position to make threats credible by killing hostages individually. Conversely, the greater the number of hostages, the greater the cost of holding them. In hijacking or barricade situations, stress and fatigue for the captors increase waiting costs for them as well. Kidnapping poses fewer such costs. Yet the terrorists can reasonably expect that the costs to governments in terms of public or international pressures may be higher when developments are visible. Furthermore, kidnappers can maintain suspense and interest by publishing communications from their victims.

Identifying the obstacles to effective bargaining in hostage seizures is critical. Most important, bargaining depends on the existence of a common interest between two parties. It is unclear whether the lives of hostages are a sufficient common interest to ensure a compromise outcome that is preferable to no agreement for both sides. Furthermore, most theories of bargaining assume that the preferences of each side remain stable during negotiations. In reality, the nature and intensity of preferences may change during a hostage-taking episode. For example, embarrassment over the Iran-*contra* scandal may have reduced the American interest in securing the release of hostages in Lebanon.

Bargaining theory is also predicated on the assumption that the game is two-party. When terrorists seize the nationals of one government in order to influence the choices of a third, the situation is seriously complicated. The hostages themselves may sometimes become intermediaries and participants. In Lebanon, Terry Waite, formerly an intermediary and negotiator, became a hostage. Such developments are not anticipated by bargaining theories based on normal political relationships. Furthermore, bargaining is not possible if a government is willing to accept the maximum cost the terrorists can bring to bear rather than concede. And the government's options are not restricted to resistance or compliance; armed rescue attempts represent an attempt to break the bargaining stalemate. In attempting to make their threats credible—for example, by sequential killing of hostages—terrorists may provoke military intervention. There may be limits, then, to the pain terrorists can inflict and still remain in the game.

CONCLUSIONS

This essay has attempted to demonstrate that even the most extreme and unusual forms of political behavior can follow an internal, strategic logic. If there are consistent patterns in terrorist behavior, rather than random idiosyncrasies, a strategic analysis may

---

[31]Scott E. Atkinson, Todd Sandler, and John Tschirhart, "Terrorism in a Bargaining Framework," *Journal of Law and Economics* 30 (1987): 1–21.

reveal them. Prediction of future terrorism can only be based on theories that explain past patterns.

Terrorism can be considered a reasonable way of pursuing extreme interests in the political arena. It is one among the many alternatives that radical organizations can choose. Strategic conceptions, based on ideas of how best to take advantage of the possibilities of a given situation, are an important determinant of oppositional terrorism, as they are of the government response. However, no single explanation for terrorist behavior is satisfactory. Strategic calculation is only one factor in the decision-making process leading to terrorism. But it is critical to include strategic reasoning as a possible motivation, at a minimum as an antidote to stereotypes of "terrorists" as irrational fanatics. Such stereotypes are a dangerous underestimation of the capabilities of extremist groups. Nor does stereotyping serve to educate the public—or, indeed, specialists—about the complexities of terrorist motivations and behaviors.

RELIGIOUS RA
AND POLITICAL ⅂

Mark Juergensmeyer

. . . What is striking about religious terrorism is that it is almost exclusively symbolic, performed in remarkably dramatic ways. Moreover, these disturbing displays of violence have been accompanied by strong claims of moral justification and an enduring absolutism, characterized by the intensity of the religious activists' commitment and the transhistorical scope of their goals.

The absolutism of religion has been revealed especially in the notion of cosmic war. Although left-wing movements subscribe to what may seem a similar idea—the concept of class conflict—ordinarily this contest is thought to take place only on a social plane and within the temporal limitations of history. In fact, in the more humane versions of Marxist conflict theory, persons can be separated from their class roles: capitalists, for instance, can be reeducated, as the leaders in Mao Zedong's Chinese communist regime attempted to do with former landlords and businessmen. Religious concepts of cosmic war, however, are ultimately beyond historical control, even though they are identified with this-worldly struggles. A satanic enemy cannot be transformed; it can only be destroyed.

The vast time lines of religious struggles also set them apart from secular conflicts. Most social and political struggles have sought conclusion within the lifetimes of their participants. But religious struggles have taken generations to succeed. As we have seen, the leaders of Hamas have claimed that they can preserve even in the face of Israel's overwhelming military superiority. "Palestine was occupied before," Dr. Rantisi reminded me, "for two hundred years." He assured me that he and his Palestinian comrades "can wait again—at least that long."[1] In some cases religious activists have been prepared to wait for eons—and some struggles have not been expected to be completed within human history; they must await their fulfillment in some transtemporal realm. There is no need, therefore, to compromise one's goals in a struggle that has been waged in divine time and with the promise of heaven's rewards. There is no need, also, to contend with society's laws and limitations when one is obeying a higher authority. In spiritualizing violence, therefore, religion has given terrorism a remarkable power.

Ironically, the reverse is also true: terrorism has given religion power as well. Although, as I have noted, sporadic acts of terrorism do not lead to the establishment of

---

Mark Juergensmeyer, *Terror in the Mind of God: The Global Rise of Religious Violence* (Berkeley, CA: University of California Press, 2000), Chapter 11.

[1]Interview with Abdul Aziz Rantisi, cofounder and political leader of Hamas, Khan Yunis, Gaza, March 1, 1998.

ᵣew religious states, they make the political potency of religious ideology impossible to ignore. Along with empowering individuals and movements, therefore, violence has empowered religion: it has given religious organizations and ideas a public importance that they have not enjoyed for many years. When Mike Bray told me he hoped that the bombing of abortion clinics would make people reflect "not on what they think, but what God thinks," he was asserting a claim for the primacy of religion in public life.[2] . . .

All of the groups that have sanctioned violence in the form of terrorism have been marginal—in varying degrees—to their own religious societies. Their violence has been in part a counterbalance to their marginality, a way of empowering them within their own religious communities. This marginality often preceded their acts of violence, and became more extreme afterward. In some cases the movements were proudly peripheral, and the disdain that the wider religious community displayed toward them was reciprocated.

The Aum Shinrikyo movement, for instance, regarded itself as a perfect synthesis of all forms of Buddhism, and indeed all religions. But in the public outcry after the nerve gas incident, many religious leaders denied that Aum was even a religion, much less a form of Buddhism. Even the movement to which it was most closely related—a new religion called Agonshu, in which Shoko Asahara had once participated—questioned Aum's legitimacy as a religious organization.[3] Asahara, for his part, questioned the legitimacy of Agonshu and other forms of Japanese Buddhism.

In America, members of Christian militia groups have disdained liberal Protestantism and even mocked Christian conservatives. Richard Butler left the Presbyterian ministry to form his own Church. William Pierce, writing in *The Turner Diaries,* observed that "the Jewish takeover of the Christian churches and corruption of the ministry is now virtually complete."[4] Pierce went on to say that the liberal clergy was less interested in the teachings of Christianity than in "government 'study' grants, 'brotherhood' awards, fees for speaking engagements, and a good press." He was even more vituperative about conservative Christians, whom he called "the world's greatest cowards." Adding insult to injury, Pierce claimed that the cowardice of most Christian conservatives was "excelled only by their stupidity."[5] It was the rare Christian who saw, as Pierce's characters did, that the governmental system played a key role in "undermining and perverting Christendom" and that its destruction was essential for the emergence of true Christianity.[6] Matthew Hale took this position one step further and rejected Christian churches entirely, claiming them to be a Jewish conspiracy. His World Church of the Creator was intended, therefore, to be not just a branch of Christianity but an antidote to it.

---

[2]Interview with Rev. Michael Bray, pastor, Reformation Lutheran Church, Bowie, Maryland, March 20, 1998.
[3]Interview with Setsufumi Kamuro, secretary general, Tokyo office, and Chieko Haniu, public affairs officer, Kanto Main Tokyo office, Agonshu religious movement, Tokyo, January 10, 1996.
[4]Andrew Macdonald [William L. Pierce], *The Turner Diaries* (Arlington, VA: National Alliance Vanguard Books, 1978), 64.
[5]Macdonald [Pierce], *Turner Diaries,* 63.
[6]Macdonald [Pierce], *Turner Diaries,* 64.

The tension between militant and mainstream religion has existed within virtually every tradition. In Judaism, for example, at the time of the assassination of Yitzhak Rabin, the orthodox Jewish leadership in Israel was dubious that rabbis could be found who would give religious sanction to such an act, and their doubt turned to astonishment when several rabbis were located who indeed gave authorization for killing another Jew under the moral precedents of traditional law. Yoel Lerner told me that he regarded the rabbinic establishment in Israel as "comfortable" and "cowardly"—"unwilling to rock the boat" over political issues that he thought their beliefs should command them to champion.[7]

Among Muslim groups, Hamas has also been marginal. Though the movement has had its clerical supporters—sheiks and mullahs who have provided religious legitimization for its ventures and been widely revered throughout Palestinian society, Hamas has not been authorized by all members of the Islamic hierarchy in Palestine, nor has it ever sought such authorization. Only in Gaza has it enjoyed much support from traditional Muslim clerics. Elsewhere in Palestine it has prided itself on its prophetic role, somewhere on the margins of social respectability.

Much the same can be said of other militant Islamic movements. The men who were members of the al Gamaa-i Islamiya (Islamic Party) led by Sheik Omar Abdul Rahman and were sentenced to life in prison for their part in the bombing of New York City's World Trade Center in 1993 were participants in a semisecret male society that had an uneasy relationship with the immigrant Muslim community to which they were connected. In fact, one of the first signs of the movement's violence in the United States was the takeover of the Abu Bakr mosque in Brooklyn. In 1992 Mahmud Abouhalima is said to have engineered a leadership coup over the protests of its more moderate members.[8]

Perhaps the most successful of the recent radical male Islamic movements, Afganistan's Taliban, also has had an uneasy relationship with the more moderate clergy of its country. Shoving aside many of the traditional leaders, these former students of Islamic schools seized power through military means, capturing the capital, Kabul, in 1995. In August 1998 the last outposts of opposition in northern Afghanistan crumbled to their control. Still the young leaders displayed the trappings and organization of their brigand past. They wore the traditional clothing of their rural homelands and treated the modern city of Kabul as if it were a village. Adopting an even stricter interpretation of Islamic law than most of the Kabul clergy, the Taliban leaders refuse to let women work, even as nurses and doctors in the hospitals or as teachers in women's schools.

In India, the radical Sikh leader Jarnail Singh Bhindranwale emerged from the pastorate of a relatively obscure religious shrine—marginal to the traditional bases of Sikh political power—and was elevated to the leadership of a large and potent movement. Although after his death many Sikhs revered Bhindranwale as a martyr, and some Sikh

---

[7]Interview with Yoel Lerner, director of the Sannhedrin Institute, Jerusalem, March 2, 1998.
[8]For an account of the Abu Bakr takeover, see Jim Dwyer, David Kocieniewski, Deidre Murphy, and Peg Tyre, *Two Seconds under the World: Terror Comes to America—The Conspiracy behind the World Trade Center Bombing* (New York: Crown Publishers, 1994), 140–56.

congregations (*gurdwaras*) were dedicated to his memory, many Sikhs have expressed uncertainty about his legitimacy in their tradition and questioned the role that history would ultimately accord him.

In many recent cases of religious terrorism, therefore, the function of violence has been not only to empower individuals and their ideological causes, but also to vault marginal religious movements into positions of power vis-à-vis their moderate, mainstream rivals. Aum Shinrikyo, for example, in a moment when its leadership seemed trapped and the movement was dying off, chose to demolish itself in a dramatic way, thus ensuring its place in history.

Yet violence alone does not allow marginal religious groups to enjoy positions of prominence, at least not for very long. The groups that have made a long-term impact, such as Hamas, the Khalistan movement, Christian Identity, and the Jewish right wing, have used violence not only to draw attention to themselves but also to articulate the concerns of those within their wider cultures. Within these circles they have not been marginal at all. Radical though they may be, they have represented widely held feelings of alienation and oppression, and for this reason their strident language and violent acts have been considered by their cohorts as perhaps intemperant but understandable.

This point was brought home to me in Gaza when a young man who worked as a waiter at a seaside cafe and attended business school told me that although he was not a member of Hamas, he was glad it existed. He supported the movement, he told me, because he thought that it kept Yasir Arafat "more Islamic and more aggressive towards Israel."[9] Even Aum Shinrikyo had a kind of tacit support within Japan. Though few Japanese outside the movement would publicly support it, the members of Aum were not unlike those of Japan's many other new religious movements. They shared the same dedication to a cause, the same disaffection toward society, and the same sense of alienation that many young Japanese felt toward the bureaucracy and competition of modern urban life.

The radical religious movements that emerged from these cultures of violence throughout the world are remarkably similar, be they Christian, Jewish, Muslim, Buddhist, or Sikh. What they have in common are three things. First, they have rejected the compromises with liberal values and secular institutions that were made by most mainstream religious leaders and organizations. Second, they refuse to observe the boundaries that secular society has imposed around religion—keeping it private rather than allowing it to intrude into public spaces. And third, they have replaced what they regard as weak modern substitutes with the more vibrant and demanding forms of religion that they imagine to be a part of their tradition's beginnings.

The fact that these movements are marginal, however, does not mean that they are intrinsically different from mainstream religion. As strident as some of them appear, I hesitate to label them "cultic" or "fundamentalist," as some observers have described these politically active religious movements that have emerged in the late twentieth century. In my view, it is not their spirituality that is unusual, but their religious ideas, cultural contexts, and world views—perspectives shaped by the sociopolitical forces of their times. These movements are not simply aberrations but religious responses to social situations

---

[9]Interview with Ashraf Yaghi, Gaza, August 19, 1995.

and expressions of deeply held convictions. In talking with many of the supporters of these cultures of violence, I was struck with the intensity of their quests for a deeper level of spirituality than that offered by the superficial values of the modern world.

Mahmud Abouhalima told me that the critical moment in his religious life came when he realized that he could not compromise his Islamic integrity with the easy vices offered by modern society. Abouhalima claimed that he had spent the early part of his life running away from himself. Although involved in radical Egyptian Islamic movements since his college years in Alexandria, he felt there was no place where he could settle down. He told me that the low point came when he was in Germany, trying to live the way that he imagined Europeans and Americans carried on: a life in which the superficial comforts of sex and inebriants masked an internal emptiness and despair.[10] Abouhalima said his return to Islam as the center of his life carried with it a renewed sense of obligation to make Islamic society truly Islamic—to "struggle against oppression and injustice" wherever it existed.[11] What was constant, Abouhalima said, was his family and his faith. Islam was both "a rock and a pillar of mercy."[12] But it was not the Islam of liberal, modern Muslims: they, he felt, had compromised the tough and disciplined life the faith demanded.

Abouhalima wanted his religion to be hard, unlike the humiliating, mind-numbing comforts of secular modernity. His newfound religion was what he perceived to be traditional Islam. This was also the case with born-again Sikhs in the separatist movement in India: theirs, they claimed, was real Sikhism. . . .

Activists such as McVeigh and Abouhalima—and for that matter, Abdul Rahman, Rantisi, Bhindranwale, Asahara, Kahane, Lerner, Bray, and Hill—have imagined themselves as defenders of ancient faiths. But in fact they have created new religious forms: like many present-day spiritual leaders, they have used the language of traditional religion to build bulwarks around aspects of modernity that have threatened them and to suggest ways out of the mindless humiliation of modern life. It was vital to their image of religion, however, that it be perceived as ancient.

The need for religion—a "hard" religion as Abouhalima called it, an "ancient" one as Pierce imagined it—was a response to the soft treachery they observed in the new societies around them. The modern secular world that Abouhalima, Pierce, and the others inhabited was a dangerous, chaotic, and violent sea for which religion was an anchor in a harbor of calm. At some deep and almost transcendent level of consciousness, they sensed their lives slipping out of control, and they felt both responsible for the disarray and a victim of it. To be abandoned by religion in such a world would mean a loss of their own individual identities. In fashioning a "traditional religion" of their own, they exposed their concerns not so much with their religious, ethnic, or national communities as with their own personal, imperiled selves.

These intimate concerns of Abouhalima, McVeigh, and other activists were prompted by the perceived failures of public institutions. As Pierre Bourdieu has

[10]Interview with Mahmud Abouhalima, convicted codefendant in the bombing of the World Trade Center, federal penitentiary, Lompoc, California, August 19, 1997.
[11]Interview with Abouhalima, August 19, 1997.
[12]Interview with Abouhalima, September 30, 1997.

observed, social structures never have a disembodied reality; they are always negotiated by individuals in their own strategies for maintaining personal identity and success in life. Such institutions are legitimized by the "symbolic capital" they accrue
through the collective trust of many individuals.[13] When that symbolic capital is devalued, when political and religious institutions undergo what Jürgen Habermas has
called a "crisis of legitimacy," this devaluation of authority is experienced not only as
a political problem but as an intensely personal one, as a loss of agency.[14] . . .

POSTMODERN TERROR

One of the reasons government is easily labeled the enemy of religion is that to some
degree it is. By its nature, the secular state is opposed to the idea that religion should
have a role in public life. From the time that modern secular nationalism emerged in the
eighteenth century as a product of the European Enlightenment's political values, it has
assumed a distinctly antireligious, or at least anticlerical, posture. The ideas of John
Locke about the origins of a civil community and the "social contract" theories of Jean
Jacques Rousseau required very little commitment to religious belief. Although they
allowed for a divine order that made the rights of humans possible, their ideas had the
effect of taking religion—at least Church religion—out of public life. At the time, religious "enemies of the Enlightenment"—as the historian Darrin McMahon described
them—protested religion's public demise.[15] But their views were submerged in a wave
of approval for a new view of social order in which secular nationalism was thought to
be virtually a natural law, universally applicable and morally right.

Enlightenment modernity proclaimed the death of religion. Modernity signaled not
only the demise of the Church's institutional authority and clerical control, but also the
loosening of religion's ideological and intellectual grip on society. Scientific reasoning
and the moral claims of the secular social contract replaced theology and the Church as
the bases for truth and social identity. The result of religion's devaluation has been "a
general crisis of religious belief," as Bourdieu has put it.[16] This has been a problem not
just for believers but for society as a whole, for it has undercut the public's ability to
rely on public symbols. According to Bourdieu, "The crisis of religious language and
its performative efficacy" is part of the collapse of an old world view: "the disintegration of an entire universe of social relations."[17]

In countering this disintegration, resurgent religious activists have proclaimed the
death of secularism. They have dismissed the efforts of secular culture and its forms of
nationalism to replace religion. They have challenged the notion that secular society
and the modern nation-state can provide the moral fiber that unites national communi-

[13]Pierre Bourdieu, *Language and Symbolic Power,* Gino Raymond and Matthew Adamson, trans.
(Cambridge, MA: Harvard University Press, 1991), 72–76. See also Pierre Bourdieu, *Outline of a
Theory of Practice,* Richard Nice, trans. (Cambridge: Cambridge University Press, 1977) 171–83.
[14]Jürgen Habermas, *Legitimation Crisis,* Thomas McCarthy, trans. (Boston: Beacon Press, 1975).
[15]Darrin McMahon, *Enemies of the Enlightenment: The French Counter-Enlightenment and the
Making of Modernity* (New York: Oxford, 2001).
[16]Bourdieu, *Language and Symbolic Power,* 116.
[17]Bourdieu, *Language and Symbolic Power,* 116.

ties or the ideological strength to sustain states buffeted by ethical, economic, and military failures. Their message has been easy to believe and has been widely received because the failures of the secular state have been so apparent.

The moral leadership of the secular state has become increasingly challenged in the last decade of the twentieth century following the end of the Cold War and the rise of a global economy. The Cold War provided contesting models of moral politics—communism and democracy—that have been replaced by a global market that has weakened national sovereignty and is conspicuously devoid of political ideals. The global economy became characterized by transnational businesses accountable to no single governmental authority and with no clear ideological or moral standards of behavior. But while both Christian and Enlightenment values were left behind, transnational commerce transported aspects of Westernized popular culture to the rest of the world. American and European music, videos, and films were beamed across national boundaries, where they threatened to obliterate local and traditional forms of artistic expression. Added to this social confusion were convulsive shifts in political power that followed the breakup of the Soviet Union and the faltering of Asian economies. . . .

Is the rise of religious terrorism related to these global changes? We know that some groups associated with violence in industrialized societies have an antimodernist political agenda. At the extreme end of this religious rejection of modernism in the United States are members of the American anti-abortion group Defensive Action, the Christian militia and Christian Identity movement, and isolated groups such as the Branch Davidian sect in Waco, Texas. When Michael Bray and other members of the religious right cast aspersions at "the new world order" allegedly promoted by President Bill Clinton and the United Nations, what he and his colleagues feared was the imposition of a reign of order that was not just tyrannical but atheist. They saw evidence of an anti-religious governmental pogrom in what they regarded as a pandering to pluralist cultural values in a society with no single set of religious moorings.

Similar attitudes toward secular government have emerged in Israel—the religious nationalist ideology of the Kach party is an extreme example—and, as the Aum Shinrikyo movement demonstrated, in Japan. Like the United States, contentious groups within these countries became disillusioned about the ability of secular leaders to guide their countries' destinies. They identified government as the enemy. In Israel, for instance, Hamas and the Jewish right have been in opposition not so much to each other as to their own secular leaders. This fact was demonstrated by the reaction of Jewish settlers in Gaza to a Hamas suicide bombing attempt in 1998, soon after the Wye River accords, in which an activist attempted to ram a car loaded with explosives into a school bus filled with forty of the settlers' children. One of the parents immediately lashed out in hatred—not against the Arabs who tried to kill her child, but against her own secular leader, Netanyahu, whom she blamed for precipitating the action by entering into peace agreements with Arafat.[18] Her comments demonstrated that the religious war in Israel and Palestine has not been a war between religions, but a double set of religious wars—Jewish and Muslim—against secularism.

---

[18]Margot Dudkevitch, "Settlers: Netanyahu No Longer Our Leader," *Jerusalem Post* (Internet edition), October 26, 1998.

The global shifts that have given rise to antimodernist movements, have also affected less-developed nations. India's Jawaharlal Nehru, Egypt's Gamal Abdel Nasser,
and Iran's Riza Shah Pahlavi were once committed to creating versions of America—or
a kind of cross between America and the Soviet Union—in their own countries. But
new generations of leaders no longer believed in the Westernized visions of Nehru,
Nasser, or the shah. Rather, they were eager to complete the process of decolonialization and build new, indigenous nationalisms.

When activists in Algeria demonstrating against the crackdown on the Islamic
Salvation Front in 1991 proclaimed that they were continuing the war of liberation
against French colonialism, they had the ideological rather than political reach of
European influence in mind. Religious activists such as the Algerian leaders, Ayatollah
Khomeini in Iran, Sheik Ahmed Yassin in Palestine, Sayyid Qutb and his disciple Sheik
Omar Abdul Rahman in Egypt, L. K. Advani in India, and Sant Jarnail Singh
Bhindranwale in India's Punjab have asserted the legitimacy of a postcolonial national
identity based on traditional culture.[19]

The result of this disaffection with the values of the modern West has been what I
have called a "loss of faith" in the ideological form of that culture, secular nationalism.[20] Although a few years ago it would have been a startling notion, the idea has now
become virtually commonplace that secular nationalism—the principle that the nation
is rooted in a secular compact rather than a religious or ethnic identity—is in crisis. In
many parts of the world it is seen as an alien cultural construction, one closely linked
with what has been called "the project of modernity."[21] In such cases, religious alternatives to secular ideologies have had extraordinary appeal. . . .

The postmodern religious rebels that we have examined . . . have therefore been
neither anomalies nor anachronisms. From Algeria to Idaho, these small but potent
groups of violent activists have represented growing masses of supporters, and they
have exemplified currents of thinking and cultures of commitment that have risen to
counter the prevailing modernism—the ideology of individualism and skepticism—
that has emerged in the past three centuries from the European Enlightenment and
spread throughout the world. They have come to hate secular governments with an almost transcendent passion. These guerrilla nationalists have dreamed of revolutionary
changes that would establish a godly social order in the rubble of what the citizens of
most secular societies have regarded as modern, egalitarian democracies. Their enemies
have seemed to most people to be both benign and banal: modern, secular leaders such
as Yitzhak Rabin and Anwar Sadat, and such symbols of prosperity and authority as the
World Trade Center and the Japanese subway system. The logic of this kind of militant
religiosity has therefore been difficult for many people to comprehend. Yet its challenge

---

[19]Some scholars have also called for the creation of a postcolonial culture. See Partha Chatterjee, *The
Nation and Its Fragments: Colonial and Postcolonial Histories* (Princeton, NJ: Princeton University
Press, 1993).

[20]Mark Juergensmeyer, *The New Cold War? Religious Nationalism Confronts the Secular State*
(Berkeley: University of California Press, 1993), 11–25.

[21]Jürgen Habermas, "Modernity—An Incomplete Project," in Paul Rabinow and William M. Sullivan,
eds., *Interpretive Social Science: A Second Look* (Berkeley: University of California Press, 1987), 148.

has been profound, for it has contained a fundamental critique of the world's post-Enlightenment secular culture and politics.

For this reason these acts of guerrilla religious warfare have been not only attempts at "delegitimization," as Ehud Sprinzak has put it, but also relegitimization: attempts to purchase public recognition of the legitimacy of religious world views with the currency of violence.[22] . . .

In such a war, one that seems so absolute and unyielding on both sides, what can be the possible outcomes? Extrapolating from current trends and recent examples, I see the following five possibilities.

Destroying Violence

The first scenario is one of a solution forged by force. It encompasses instances in which terrorists have literally been killed off or have been forcibly controlled. If Osama bin Laden had been in residence in his camp in Afghanistan on August 20, 1998, along with a large number of leaders of other militant groups when the United States launched one hundred Tomahawk cruise missiles into his quarters, for instance, this air strike might have removed some of the persons involved in planning future terrorist acts in various parts of the world.

It would not have removed all of them, however, and the attempt may well have elevated the possibility of more terrorist acts in reprisal. The war-against-terrorism strategy can be dangerous, in that it can play into the scenario that religious terrorists themselves have fostered: the image of a world at war between secular and religious forces. A belligerent secular enemy has often been just what religious activists have hoped for. In some cases it makes recruitment to their causes easier, for it demonstrates that the secular side can be as brutal as it has been portrayed by their own religious ideologues.

The 1998 U.S. attack on Osama bin Laden's camp neither destroyed the militant Muslim's operations nor deterred his aggression. Immediately after the attack several other American embassies were targeted, and several months later, in February 1999, George Tenet, head of the U.S. Central Intelligence Agency, announced to the press that he had "no doubt" that "Osama bin Laden and his world-wide allies and sympathizers" were plotting "further attacks" against U.S. installations and symbols of American power.[23] In Algeria, attempts to eliminate Muslim militants also had violent repercussions. When the military junta in Algeria halted the elections and began running the country with an iron hand, popular support for the Islamic party and violent resistance against the junta escalated.

In order for the destructive strategy to work, a secular government must be willing to declare total war against religious terrorism and wage it over many years, as the

---

[22]Ehud Sprinzak, "The Process of Delegitimization: Towards a Linkage Theory of Political Terrorism," *Terrorism and Political Violence* 3:1, Spring 1991, 50–68; Ehud Sprinzak, "Right-Wing Terrorism in a Comparative Perspective: The Case of Split Delegitimization," in Tore Bjørgo, ed., *Terror from the Extreme Right* (London: Frank Cass, 1995), 17–43.
[23]George Tenet, ABC News, February 2, 1999.

Israeli government attempted to do against its terrorist opponents. Even under these conditions the prognosis for victory has been good only when the opponents were easily identified and—perhaps more important—contained within a specific region. Because Israel's enemies have been mobile, its attempts to squash them have had a limited degree of success. The government of India, on the other hand, was able to virtually obliterate the most militant Sikhs in 1992, in part because it embarked on a ruthless search-and-destroy mission against the activists within the confines of the state of Punjab. . . .

Terrifying Terrorists (2)

A second scenario is one in which the threat of violent reprisals or imprisonment so frightens religious activists that they hesitate to act. This is the strategy adopted by many law enforcement agencies to "crack down" on terrorists: even if the authorities cannot eliminate the terrorists completely, they can at least frighten them by raising the stakes associated with involvement in terrorist activity.

Though some fringe members of activist groups may have been sobered by such threats, it is doubtful that the "get tough with terrorists" strategy has had much of an effect on the more dedicated members. In the view of most of them, the world is already at war, and they have always expected the enemy to act harshly. In fact, they would be puzzled if it did not. So the threat of an additional increment of penalty to be meted out for their actions has had little if any deterrent effect.

The case that is sometimes offered as a successful instance of terrorist intimidation is the one involving Libya. In the mid-1980s Libya was thought to harbor Muslim activists responsible for a series of acts of international terrorism against the United States. In 1986 the United States undertook an air strike against the leader of the country, Muammar el-Qaddafi, in reprisal. The missiles were aimed at one of his residences, and in fact a member of his family was killed in the attack, but el-Qaddafi himself survived. Over ten years later there were very few terrorist acts aimed at the United States attributed to Libya. Were the air strikes effective?

It is doubtful. Although it is possible that Libya was eventually intimidated by the strikes, the immediate response was quite different. According to the RAND–St. Andrews Chronology of International Terrorism, the number of terrorist incidents linked to Libya and directed against the United States rose in the two years following the U.S. air strikes: fifteen in 1987 and eight in 1988. The most devastating terrorist attack against the United States in which Libya has been implicated—the tragic explosion of Pan Am flight 103 over Lockerbie, Scotland, killing all 259 on board—occurred in December 1988.

It is not clear why the number of terrorist attacks from Libya has decreased in the years since then. Comments made by el-Qaddafi in 1998 indicated that the economic sanctions leveled against Libya were much on his mind. He broke off relations with Arab states in a pique of anger after they failed to support the abandonment of the boycott. Perhaps he was eager to normalize relations with other governments for trade reasons as much as any other. In any event, there is no clear evidence that he or any other supporter of international terrorism has been intimidated by America's show of military might. . . .

Violence Wins   ③

The third scenario is the reverse of those cases in which terrorism is defeated or diffused: it is when terrorism, in some way, wins. This is the outcome for which every religious activist, understandably, has yearned. When I asked the Hamas leader Dr. Abdul Aziz Rantisi whether Jews and Muslims could live in harmony in the area he described as Palestine, he affirmed that they could—but not under the present arrangement. He could not accept "Israel's sovereignty over Palestinian land," he said. But the two groups could live in peace if the situation were reversed and the land were controlled by Palestinian Arabs.[24] "Jews would be welcomed in our nation," Rantisi explained, adding that he did not hate Jews as such. He pledged not to mistreat them "when we become strong."[25] He hoped for a South Africa–type solution, where the whole of the area would be united—Israel, Gaza, and the West Bank—and the Palestinians who had left the region would be allowed to return. With Arabs then a majority, Rantisi would accept democratic rule over the united region, which would be called something other than Israel.

It is a solution that would delight Palestinians both inside and outside the Hamas movement. Needless to say, it has not been a solution enthusiastically embraced by Israel. Given that fact, and considering that Israel holds a preponderance of military power in the region, could any part of the radical Islamic Palestinian objective be achieved? As I suggested earlier, acts of terrorism tend to be strategically unproductive and do not usually lead to transformations of power. If one is not willing to wait, as Dr. Rantisi claimed he was willing to do, beyond his own generation and perhaps the next, symbolic action will have to be replaced by the kind of strategic planning aimed at achieving goals either totally or incrementally. Revolutionary changes can occur through a well-organized mass movement, as in Iran, or an effective military force, as in Afghanistan. They might also come about through political pressures, as in Sudan and Pakistan, where regimes have capitulated to religious nationalist ideologies in what have been incremental but virtually bloodless coups. But as noted earlier, none of these cases has involved terrorist acts as the primary means of achieving power.

There have been instances, however, where the power accrued through terrorist acts was converted into bargaining chips for negotiated settlements, and where formerly terrorist organizations were forged into effective political parties. An example of this process, which might be called the domesticization of violence, was the negotiated peace settlement in Northern Ireland and the emergence of Sinn Féin as an effective force in local elections. Yet, as the bombing in the village of Omagh in August 1998 revealed, such compromises are not always accepted gracefully by renegade members of activist movements, who insist on continuing their violent paramilitary campaigns. After all, the ideology of cosmic war does not easily submit to accommodation. Yet, as the Omagh incident also indicated, public support for a compromise solution may isolate perpetrators of acts of violence, and their continued terrorism may undercut their public support.

---

[24]Interview with Abdul Aziz Rantisi, March 1, 1998.
[25]Interview with Rantisi, March 1, 1998.

The approach taken by the opponent—the old enemy of a terrorist struggle—has sometimes made all the difference in a successful transition from violence to the politics of compromise. The attempted resolutions of the Northern Ireland and Palestine conflicts are interesting cases in point. In Northern Ireland, the British did not blame Sinn Féin for the Omagh violence, and both British and Sinn Féin leaders formed a united front against it. Hence the public perception of Omagh was that of a senseless act, one that was peripheral and counterproductive to the political purposes of the Northern Irish Catholic community. In Israel, however, when Hamas terrorist activities were renewed after the peace accords, Benjamin Netanyahu and other Israeli leaders publicly blamed the Palestinian peacemaker, Yasir Arafat, for the terrorism. Thus, perhaps inadvertently, the Hamas activists were given credibility by Netanyahu through his equating them with Arafat, and the legitimacy of the secular Palestinian leader was undercut by his being blamed for the acts of renegade activists whom he could hardly control. With Arafat weakened and Hamas emboldened by the effect of their incidents of terrorism, the spiral of violence continued.

Thus a negotiated compromise with activists involved in terrorism is fraught with difficulties. It is a solution that does not always work. A few activists may be appeased, but others may be angered by what they regard as a sellout of their principles. The case of Arafat and Hamas was complicated not only by the lack of cooperation from the Israeli side following the elections that brought Netanyahu into power, but also by the intractability of Hamas and its own fears of losing whatever leverage it had gained through its previous tactics. In 1996 some members of the movement advocated a shift of strategy and participation in Palestinian elections as a political party. It was a shift that the leadership of Hamas rejected. One of their concerns was political: they knew that although they might have won in Gaza, their level of support in the West Bank was not sufficient to rout Fateh and the other parties that supported Arafat's Palestinian Authority. Another concern of the Hamas leadership was ideological: once one has entered into the rhetoric of cosmic war, the struggle cannot easily be abandoned without forsaking the will of God.

Separating Religion from Politics

The fourth scenario for peace is one in which religion is taken out of politics and retired to the moral and metaphysical planes. As long as images of spiritual warfare remain strong in the minds of religious activists and are linked with struggles in the social world around them, the scenarios we have just discussed—achieving an easy victory over religious activists, intimidating them into submission, or forging a compromise with them—are problematic at best. In some cases where religious politics had previously been strong, however, the image of cosmic war itself has been transformed. A more moderate view of the image of religious warfare has been conceived, one that is deflected away from political and social confrontation.

The extreme form of this solution—one in which religion returns to what Casanova described as its privatization in the post-Enlightenment world—is unlikely, however.[26] Few religious activists are willing to retreat to the time when secular au-

---

[26]Casanova, *Public Religions in the Modern World,* 40ff.

thorities ran the public arena and religion remained safely within the confines of churches, mosques, temples, and synagogues. Most religious activists regard the social manifestation of cosmic struggle to be at the very heart of their faith and dream of restoring religion to what they regard as its rightful position at the center of public consciousness.

Yet, in the 1990s, many Islamic countries witnessed a certain reaction against politicized religion. In 1999, Iranian students demonstrated in support of such leaders as the moderate theologian Abdol Karim Soroush, who argued that interpretations of religion are relative and change over time.[27] He made a distinction between ideology and religion, and claimed that Muslim clergy had no business being in politics.[28] Similar statements have been made by such moderate Islamic thinkers as Hassan Hanafi in Egypt, Rashid Ghannouchi in Tunisia, and Algeria's Mohammed Arkoun. For them, the image of struggle consists largely of a spiritual battle or a contest between moral positions rather than between armed enemies.

To some degree these thinkers advocated what René Girard recommended in his analysis of how religion can cure violence. He regarded the rite of sacrifice as deflected violence—a token of what I call ritualized cosmic war. According to Girard, when religion conducts its business adequately, it provides for society a symbolic way of acting out violent impulses so that they need not be expressed in the real world.[29] One of Girard's colleagues, Mark Anspach, observed that Islam lacks the developed sacrificial ritual structure of many other religious traditions, and hence it has always skirted the danger of "the confusion of ritual and history," resulting in ritualized—albeit real—violence against its sacred enemies.[30] What Soroush and his fellow Islamic thinkers proposed was not necessarily a moderate Islam but a revitalized one, a Muslim religiosity sufficiently vital and symbolically rich to do what Girard and Anspach argued all religion should be able to do: deflect violence through its ritual enactment.

Moreover, Soroush's vision of Islam allows religion to play a significant albeit a noncontrolling public role. Like the Protestant Reformation's Martin Luther, Soroush advocates an unmediated form of religion that is both personal and public. He places little stock in the clerical hierarchy and its privileges—a position that has gotten him into a fair amount of difficulty in Iran—but at the same time his reformed Islam is not privatistic. Like socially responsible Protestants, he sees a prophetic role for religion in the public arena. This is a form of social activism that eschews political power in favor of moral suasion, and it has transformed the idea of struggle into a contestation of ideas rather than opposing political sides.

---

[27]Robin Wright, "Islamist's Theory of Relativity," *Los Angeles Times,* January 27, 1995, A1.

[28]Behrooz Ghamari-Tabrizi, "From Liberation Theology to State Ideology—Modern Conceptions of Islam in Revolutionary Iran: Ali Shari'ati and Abdolkarim Soroush," unpublished article, 1997. See also a book on Soroush by Prof. Ghamari-Tabrizi to be published jointly by I. B. Tauris and St. Martin's Press, and an article by Robin Wright, "Iran Moves to Stifle Exchange of Reformist Views," *Los Angeles Times,* December 30, 1995, A6.

[29]René Girard, *Violence and the Sacred,* Patrick Gregory, trans. (Baltimore: Johns Hopkins University Press, 1977) (originally published in French as *La Violence et le sacré,* 1972).

[30]Mark Anspach, "Violence against Violence: Islam in Comparative Context," in Mark Juergensmeyer, ed., *Religion and the Sacred in the Modern World* (London: Frank Cass, 1991), 25.

Solutions such as the one Soroush formulated in Iran do not require the image of cosmic war to be removed from public life or abandoned altogether. Rather, it is redirected to the battlefield of ideas. For such a transformation to come about, however, two conditions must be met: members of the activists' religious community have to embrace this moderate form of social struggle as a legitimate representation of cosmic war, and the opponents have to accept it without being threatened by it. Secular authorities can do little about the first criterion, since it requires a transformation of thinking and leadership within the religion itself. But they can effect the second criterion by resisting the temptation to act like an enemy in a cosmic war and being open to a social role for religion on a less violently confrontational level.

When one is treated like an enemy, however, the temptation to respond like an enemy is considerable. This has been especially so when the provocations have been savage. After American embassies in Africa were bombed in August 1998, for instance, the U.S. government found itself in a position similar to that of the Israeli government in being motivated to retaliate swiftly and strongly in order to appease their constituencies. Yet such retaliations have seldom been effective. As we have seen, retaliatory strikes usually have not destroyed their targets completely, they have invited more terrorist acts in return, and they have played into the terrorists' scenarios of war in which there can be no easy compromise.

Understandably, governments cannot afford to let acts of terrorism go unaddressed. Governments must be vigilant in their surveillance of potential terrorist groups, diligent in their attempts to apprehend those suspected of committing terrorist acts, and swift in bringing them to courts of law. But the tit-for-tat approach to terrorism has usually failed if for no other reason than that few governments have been willing to sink to the savage levels and adopt the same means of gutter combat as the groups involved in terrorist acts. Moreover, government authorities are usually aware that those within cultures of violence from which acts of terrorism have emerged are watching to see how the authorities respond to the violence. Any response to the perpetration of violent acts, even in the form of retaliatory strikes, will enhance the credibility of the terrorists within their own community. Supporting moderate leadership within the communities, however, would diminish support for the extremists. . . .

Healing Politics with Religion

These moderate solutions have required the opponents in the conflict to summon at least a minimal level of mutual trust and respect. This respect has been enhanced and the possibilities of a compromise solution strengthened when religious activists have perceived governmental authorities as having a moral integrity in keeping with, or accommodating of, religious values. This, then, is the fifth solution: when secular authorities embrace moral values, including those associated with religion.

In some cases where religious violence has been quelled, religion has literally been subsumed under the aegis of governmental authorities. In Sri Lanka, for instance, the efforts of the government to destroy the Janatha Vimukthi Peramuna (JVP)—the People's Liberation Front—a movement supported by many radical Buddhist monks, were double-pronged. The harsh measures involved tracking down and killing the most dedicated members of the movement. The more accommodating measures included efforts to win the support of militant religious leaders. In 1990 President Ranasinghe Premadasa provided a fund for the financial support of Buddhist schools and social services, and created a Ministry of Buddhist Affairs, naming himself the first minister. Premadasa created a council of Buddhist advisers, including Buddhist monks who had been quite critical of the secular government previously. One of these told me in 1991 that after Premadasa's proreligious measures, the government was finally beginning to "reflect Buddhist values."[31]

In other cases, such as the British response to Irish terrorism, the government's stance in following the rule of law and not overreacting to terrorist provocations demonstrated its subscription to moral values. This made it difficult for religious activists—with the exception of Rev. Ian Paisley—to portray the government as a satanic enemy. It also increased the possibility of some sort of accommodation with religious activists on both sides of the Northern Ireland dispute—leading to the signing of a peace accord in 1998.

Governments that chose the other route—abandoning their own democratic principles in response to terrorism—have embarked on perilous journeys. A case in point is the Algerian military junta that seized control and annulled the elections that appeared to be leading to a victory for the Islamic Salvation Front in 1992. The result was years of increased terrorism, in part due to the perception that the government had discredited itself and demonstrated that it could not meet the mundane moral standards of secular democracies, much less the presumably higher standards suggested by religion.

It is poignant that the governments of modern nations have so often been perceived as being morally corrupt and spiritually vacuous since the Enlightenment concepts that launched the modern nation-state were characterized by a fair amount of moralistic fervor. Jean-Jacques Rousseau coined the term civil religion to describe what he regarded as the moral and spiritual foundation essential for any modern society that wanted to sustain an enduring political order. Such a "religion," Rousseau claimed, was to be based not on the "dogmas of religion" but on what he called the "the sanctity of the social contract."[32]

Despite the noble rhetoric of these Enlightenment thinkers, their opponents at the time belittled the secularists' morality just as their modern critics have done; and just as they have done today, they accused them of hypocrisy. As McMahon has pointed out, religious critics of thinkers such as Rousseau accused them, perhaps unfairly, of cloaking self-interest in the garb of high-minded abstractions.[33] It is this apparent hypocrisy—and what they regard as the inherent vacuousness of secular life—that has continued to disturb religious activists from the time of the Enlightenment to the present day. . . .

---

[31]Interview with the Venerable Palipana Chandananda, Mahanayake, Asigiriya chapter, Sinhalese Buddhist Sangha, Kandy, Sri Lanka, January 4, 1991.
[32]Jean-Jacques Rousseau, "On Civil Religion," Chapter 8, Book IV of *On the Social Contract* [see *Basic Political Writings,* Donald A. Cress, ed., trans., (Indianapolis: Hackett, 1987), 226].
[33]McMahon, *Enemies of Enlightenment,* Chapter 1.

THE SOFT UNDERBELLY
OF PRIMACY

Richard K. Betts

In given conditions, action and reaction can be ridiculously out of proportion. . . .
One can obtain results monstrously in excess of the effort. . . . Let's consider this
auto smash-up. . . . The driver lost control at high speed while swiping at a wasp
which had flown in through a window and was buzzing around his face. . . . The
weight of a wasp is under half an ounce. Compared with a human being, the
wasp's size is minute, its strength negligible. Its sole armament is a tiny syringe
holding a drop of irritant, formic acid. . . . Nevertheless, that wasp killed four big
men and converted a large, powerful car into a heap of scrap.

—Eric Frank Russell[1]

To grasp some implications of the new first priority in U.S. foreign policy, it is necessary to understand the connections among three things: the imbalance of power between terrorist groups and counterterrorist governments; the reasons that groups choose terror tactics; and the operational advantage of attack over defense in the interactions of terrorists and their opponents. On September 11, 2001, Americans were reminded that the overweening power that they had taken for granted over the past dozen years is not the same as omnipotence. What is less obvious but equally important is that the power is itself part of the cause of terrorist enmity and even a source of U.S. vulnerability.

There is no consensus on a definition of "terrorism," mainly because the term is so intensely pejorative.[2] When defined in terms of tactics, consistency falters, because most people can think of some "good" political cause that has used the tactics and whose purposes excuse them or at least warrant the group's designation as freedom fighters rather than terrorists. Israelis who call the Khobar Towers bombers of 1996 terrorists might reject that characterization for the Irgun, which did the same thing to the King David Hotel in 1946, or some Irish Americans would bridle at equating IRA bombings in Britain with Tamil Tiger bombings in Sri Lanka. Anticommunists labeled

---

Richard K. Betts, "The Soft Underbelly of American Primacy: Tactical Advantages of Terror," *Political Science Quarterly* Vol. 117, No. 1 (Spring 2002).
[1]William Wolf in Eric Frank Russell, *Wasp* (London: Victor Gollancz, 2000, originally published 1957), 7.
[2]"The word has become a political label rather than an analytical concept." Martha Crenshaw, *Terrorism and International Cooperation* (New York: Institute for East-West Security Studies, 1989), 5.

520

the Vietcong terrorists (because they engaged in combat out of uniform and assassinated local officials), but opponents of the Saigon government did not. Nevertheless, a functional definition is more sensible than one conditioned on the identity of the perpetrators. For this article, terrorism refers to the illegitimate, deliberate killing of civilians for purposes of punishment or coercion. This holds in abeyance the questions of whether deliberate killing of civilians can ever be legitimate or killing soldiers can be terrorism.

In any case, for all but the rare nihilistic psychopath, terror is a means, not an end in itself. Terror tactics are usually meant to serve a strategy of coercion.[3] They are a use of force designed to further some substantive aim. This is not always evident in the heat of rage felt by the victims of terror. Normal people find it hard to see instrumental reasoning behind an atrocity, especially when recognizing the political motives behind terrorism might seem to make its illegitimacy less extreme. Stripped of rhetoric, however, a war against terrorism must mean a war against political groups who choose terror as a tactic.

American global primacy is one of the causes of this war. It animates both the terrorists' purposes and their choice of tactics. To groups like al Qaeda, the United States is the enemy because American military power dominates their world, supports corrupt governments in their countries, and backs Israelis against Muslims; American cultural power insults their religion and pollutes their societies; and American economic power makes all these intrusions and desecrations possible. Japan, in contrast, is not high on al Qaeda's list of targets, because Japan's economic power does not make it a political, military, and cultural behemoth that penetrates their societies.

Political and cultural power makes the United States a target for those who blame it for their problems. At the same time, American economic and military power prevents them from resisting or retaliating against the United States on its own terms. To smite the only superpower requires unconventional modes of force and tactics that make the combat cost exchange ratio favorable to the attacker. This offers hope to the weak that they can work their will despite their overall deficit in power.

PRIMACY ON THE CHEAP

The United States has enjoyed military and political primacy (or hegemony, unipolarity, or whatever term best connotes international dominance) for barely a dozen years. Those who focus on the economic dimension of international relations spoke of American hegemony much earlier, but observers of the strategic landscape never did. For those who focus on national security, the world before 1945 was multipolar, and the world of the Cold War was bipolar. After 1945 the United States had exerted hegemony within the First World and for a while over the international economy. The strategic competition against the Second World, however, was seen as a titanic struggle between equal politicomilitary coalitions and a close-run thing until very near

---

[3] For a survey of types, see Christopher C. Harmon, "Five Strategies of Terrorism," *Small Wars and Insurgencies* 12 (Autumn 2001).

the end. Only the collapse of the Soviet pole, which coincided fortuitously with renewed relative strength of the American economy, marked the real arrival of U.S. global dominance.

The novelty of complete primacy may account for the thoughtless, indeed innocently arrogant way in which many Americans took its benefits for granted. Most who gave any thought to foreign policy came implicitly to regard the entire world after 1989 as they had regarded Western Europe and Japan during the past half-century: partners in principle but vassals in practice. The United States would lead the civilized community of nations in the expansion and consolidation of a liberal world order. Overwhelming military dominance was assumed to be secure and important across most of the domestic political spectrum.

Liberal multilateralists conflated U.S. primacy with political globalization, indeed, conflated ideological American nationalism with internationalist altruism.[4] They assumed that U.S. military power should be used to stabilize benighted countries and police international violence, albeit preferably camouflaged under the banner of institutions such as the United Nations, or at least NATO. They rejected the idea that illiberal impulses or movements represented more than a retreating challenge to the West's mission and its capacity to extend its values worldwide.

Conservative unilateralists assumed that unrivaled power relieved the United States of the need to cater to the demands of others. When America acted strategically abroad, others would have to join on its terms or be left out of the action. The United States should choose battles, avoid entanglements in incompetent polities, and let unfortunates stew in their own juice. For both multilateralists and nationalists, the issue was whether the United States would decide to make an effort for world welfare, not whether a strategic challenge could threaten its truly vital interests. (Colloquial depreciation of the adjective notwithstanding, literally vital U.S. interests are those necessary to life.)

For many, primacy was confused with invulnerability. American experts warned regularly of the danger of catastrophic terrorism—and Osama bin Laden explicitly declared war on the United States in his *fatwa* of February 1998. But the warnings did not register seriously in the consciousness of most people. Even some national security experts felt stunned when the attacks occurred on September 11. Before then, the American military wanted nothing to do with the mission of "homeland defense," cited the Posse Comitatus act to suggest that military operations within U.S. borders would

---

[4]Rationalization of national power as altruism resembles the thinking about benign Pax Britannica in the Crowe Memorandum: " . . . the national policy of the insular and naval State is so directed as to harmonize with the general desires and ideals common to all mankind, and more particularly . . . is closely identified with the primary and vital interests of a majority, or as many as possible, of the other nations. . . . England, more than any other non-insular Power, has a direct and positive interest in the maintenance of the independence of nations, and therefore must be the natural enemy of any country threatening the independence of others, and the natural protector of the weaker communities." Eyre Crowe, "Memorandum on the Present State of British Relations with France and Germany," 1 January 1907, in G. P. Gooch and Harold Temperley, eds., *British Documents on the Origins of the War, 1898–1914*, vol. 3: *The Testing of the Entente, 1904–6* (London: His Majesty's Stationery Office, 1928), 402–403.

be improper, and argued that homeland defense should be the responsibility of civilian agencies or the National Guard. The services preferred to define the active forces' mission as fighting and winning the nation's wars—as if wars were naturally something that happened abroad—and homeland defense involved no more than law enforcement, managing relief operations in natural disasters, or intercepting ballistic missiles outside U.S. airspace. Only in America could the nation's armed forces think of direct defense of national territory as a distraction.

Being Number One seemed cheap. The United States could cut the military burden on the economy by half after the Cold War (from 6 percent to 3 percent of GNP) yet still spend almost five times more than the combined military budgets of all potential enemy states. And this did not count the contributions of rich U.S. allies.[5] Of course the margin in dollar terms does not translate into a comparable quantitative margin in manpower or equipment, but that does not mean that a purchasing power parity estimate would reduce the implied gap in combat capability. The overwhelming qualitative superiority of U.S. conventional forces cuts in the other direction. Washington was also able to plan, organize, and fight a major war in 1991 at negligible cost in blood or treasure. Financially, nearly 90 percent of the bills for the war against Iraq were paid by allies. With fewer than 200 American battle deaths, the cost in blood was far lower than almost anyone had imagined it could be. Less than a decade later, Washington waged another war, over Kosovo, that cost no U.S. combat casualties at all.

In the one case where costs in casualties exceeded the apparent interests at stake—Somalia in 1993—Washington quickly stood down from the fight. This became the reference point for vulnerability: the failure of an operation that was small, far from home, and elective. Where material interests required strategic engagement, as in the oil-rich Persian Gulf, U.S. strategy could avoid costs by exploiting its huge advantage in conventional capability. Where conventional dominance proved less exploitable, as in Somalia, material interests did not require strategic engagement. Where the United States could not operate militarily with impunity, it could choose not to operate.

Finally, power made it possible to let moral interests override material interests where some Americans felt an intense moral concern, even if in doing so they claimed, dubiously, that the moral and material stakes coincided. To some extent this happened in Kosovo, although the decision to launch that war apparently flowed from overoptimism about how quickly a little bombing would lead Belgrade to capitulate. Most notably, it happened in the Arab-Israeli conflict. For more than three decades after the 1967 Six Day War, the United States supported Israel diplomatically, economically, and militarily against the Arabs, despite the fact that doing so put it on the side of a tiny

---

[5]At the end of the twentieth century, the combined military budgets of China, Russia, Iraq, Yugoslavia (Serbia), North Korea, Iran, Libya, Cuba, Afghanistan, and Sudan added up to no more than $60 billion. *The Military Balance, 1999–2000* (London: International Institute for Strategic Studies, 1999), 102, 112, 132, 133, 159, 186, 275.

country of a few million people with no oil, against more than ten times as many Arabs who controlled over a third of the world's oil reserves.

This policy was not just an effect of primacy, since the U.S.–Israel alignment began in the Cold War. The salience of the moral motive was indicated by the fact that U.S. policy proceeded despite the fact that it helped give Moscow a purchase in major Arab capitals such as Cairo, Damascus, and Baghdad. Luckily for the United States, however, the largest amounts of oil remained under the control of the conservative Arab states of the Gulf. In this sense the hegemony of the United States within the anticommunist world helped account for the policy. That margin of power also relieved Washington of the need to make hard choices about disciplining its client. For decades the United States opposed Israeli settlement of the West Bank, terming the settlements illegal; yet in all that time the United States never demanded that Israel refrain from colonizing the West Bank as a condition for receiving U.S. economic and military aid.[6] Washington continued to bankroll Israel at a higher per capita rate than any other country in the world, a level that has been indispensable to Israel, providing aid over the years that now totals well over $100 billion in today's dollars.[7] Although this policy enraged some Arabs and irritated the rest, U.S. power was great enough that such international political costs did not outweigh the domestic political costs of insisting on Israeli compliance with U.S. policy.

Of course, far more than subsidizing Israeli occupation of Palestinian land was involved in the enmity of Islamist terrorists toward the United States. Many of the other explanations, however, presuppose U.S. global primacy. When American power becomes the arbiter of conflicts around the world, it makes itself the target for groups who come out on the short end of those conflicts.

PRIMACY AND ASYMMETRIC WARFARE

The irrational evil of terrorism seems most obvious to the powerful. They are accustomed to getting their way with conventional applications of force and are not as accustomed as the powerless to thinking of terror as the only form of force that might make their enemies do their will. This is why terrorism is the premier form of "asymmetric warfare," the Pentagon buzzword for the type of threats likely to confront the United

---

[6]Washington certainly did exert pressure on Israel at some times. The administration of Bush the Elder, for example, threatened to withhold loans for housing construction, but this was a marginal portion of total U.S. aid. There was never a threat to cut off the basic annual maintenance payment of several billion dollars to which Israel became accustomed decades ago.

[7]The United States has also given aid to friendly Arab governments—huge amounts to Egypt and some to Jordan. This does not counterbalance the aid to Israel, however, in terms of effects on opinions of strongly anti-Israeli Arabs. Islamists see the regimes in Cairo and Amman as American toadies, complicit in betrayal of the Palestinians.

States in the post-Cold War world.[8] Murderous tactics may become instrumentally appealing by default—when one party in a conflict lacks other military options.

Resort to terror is not necessarily limited to those facing far more powerful enemies. It can happen in a conventional war between great powers that becomes a total war, when the process of escalation pits whole societies against each other and shears away civilized restraints. That is something seldom seen, and last seen over a half-century ago. One does not need to accept the tendentious position that allied strategic bombing in World War II constituted terrorism to recognize that the British and Americans did systematically assault the urban population centers of Germany and Japan. They did so in large part because precision bombing of industrial facilities proved ineffective.[9] During the early phase of the Cold War, in turn, U.S. nuclear strategy relied on plans to counter Soviet conventional attack on Western Europe with a comprehensive nuclear attack on communist countries that would have killed hundreds of millions. In the 1950s, Strategic Air Command targeteers even went out of their way to plan "bonus" damage by moving aim points for military targets so that blasts would destroy adjacent towns as well.[10] In both World War II and planning for World War III, the rationale was less to kill civilians per se than to wreck the enemy economies—although that was also one of Osama bin Laden's rationales for the attacks on the World Trade Center.[11] In short, the instrumental appeal of strategic attacks on noncombatants

---

[8]Theoretically, this was anticipated by Samuel P. Huntington in his 1962 analysis of the differences between symmetrical intergovernmental war and asymmetrical antigovernmental war. "Patterns of Violence in World Politics" in Huntington, ed., *Changing Patterns of Military Politics* (New York: Free Press of Glencoe, 1962), 19–21. Some of Huntington's analysis of insurrectionary warfare within states applies as well to transnational terrorism.

[9]The Royal Air Force gave up on precision bombing early and focused deliberately on night bombing of German cities, while the Americans continued to try precision daylight bombing. Firestorms in Hamburg, Darmstadt, and Dresden, and less incendiary attacks on other cities, killed several hundred-thousand German civilians. Over Japan, the United States quickly gave up attempts at precision bombing when weather made it impractical and deliberately resorted to an incendiary campaign that burned most Japanese cities to the ground and killed at least 300,000 civilians (and perhaps more than half a million) well before the nuclear attacks on Hiroshima and Nagasaki, which killed another 200,000. Michael S. Sherry, *The Rise of American Air Power: The Creation of Armageddon* (New Haven: Yale University Press, 1987), 260, 413–43.

[10]The threat of deliberate nuclear escalation remained the bedrock of NATO doctrine throughout the Cold War, but after the Kennedy administration, the flexible response doctrine made it conditional and included options for nuclear first-use that did not involve deliberate targeting of population centers. In the Eisenhower administration, however, all-out attack on the Soviet bloc's cities was integral to plans for defense of Western Europe against Soviet armored divisions.

[11]In a videotape months after the attacks, bin Laden said, "These blessed strikes showed clearly that this arrogant power, America, rests on a powerful but precarious economy, which rapidly crumbled . . . the global economy based on usury, which America uses along with its military might to impose infidelity and humiliation on oppressed people, can easily crumble. . . . Hit the economy, which is the basis of military might. If their economy is finished, they will become too busy to enslave oppressed people. . . . America is in decline; the economic drain is continuing but more strikes are required and the youths must strike the key sectors of the American economy." Videotape excerpts quoted in "Bin Laden's Words: 'America Is in Decline,' the Leader of Al Qaeda Says," *New York Times,* 28 December 2001.

may be easier to understand when one considers that states with legitimate purposes have sometimes resorted to such a strategy. Such a double standard, relaxing prohibitions against targeting noncombatants for the side with legitimate purposes (one's own side), occurs most readily when the enemy is at least a peer competitor threatening vital interests. When one's own primacy is taken for granted, it is easier to revert to a single standard that puts all deliberate attacks against civilians beyond the pale.

In contrast to World War II, most wars are limited—or at least limited for the stronger side when power is grossly imbalanced. In such cases, using terror to coerce is likely to seem the only potentially effective use of force for the weaker side, which faces a choice between surrender or savagery. Radical Muslim zealots cannot expel American power with conventional military means, so they substitute clandestine means of delivery against military targets (such as the Khobar Towers barracks in Saudi Arabia) or high-profile political targets (embassies in Kenya and Tanzania). More than once the line has been attributed to terrorists, "If you will let us lease one of your B-52s, we will use that instead of a truck bomb." The hijacking and conversion of U.S. airliners into kamikazes was the most dramatic means of asymmetric attack.

Kamikaze hijacking also reflects an impressive capacity for strategic judo, the turning of the West's strength against itself.[12] The flip-side of a primacy that diffuses its power throughout the world is that advanced elements of that power become more accessible to its enemies. Nineteen men from technologically backward societies did not have to rely on home-grown instruments to devastate the Pentagon and World Trade Center. They used computers and modern financial procedures with facility, and they forcibly appropriated the aviation technology of the West and used it as a weapon. They not only rebelled against the "soft power" of the United States, they trumped it by hijacking the country's hard power.[13] They also exploited the characteristics of U.S. society associated with soft power—the liberalism, openness, and respect for privacy that allowed them to go freely about the business of preparing the attacks without observation by the state security apparatus. When soft power met the clash of civilizations, it proved too soft.

Strategic judo is also apparent in the way in which U.S. retaliation may compromise its own purpose. The counter offensive after September 11 was necessary, if only to demonstrate to marginally motivated terrorists that they could not hope to strike the United States for free. The war in Afghanistan, however, does contribute to polarization in the Muslim world and to mobilization of potential terrorist recruits. U.S. leaders can say that they are not waging a war against Islam until they are blue in the face, but this

---

[12]This is similar to the concept of political judo discussed in Samuel L. Popkin, "Pacification: Politics and the Village," *Asian Survey* 10 (August 1970); and Popkin, "Internal Conflicts—South Vietnam" in Kenneth N. Waltz and Steven Spiegel, eds., *Conflict in World Politics* (Cambridge, MA: Winthrop, 1971).

[13]Soft power is "indirect or cooptive" and "can rest on the attraction of one's ideas or on the ability to set the political agenda in a way that shapes the preferences that others express." It "tends to be associated with intangible power resources such as culture, ideology, and institutions." Joseph S. Nye, Jr., "The Changing Nature of World Power," *Political Science Quarterly* 105 (Summer 1990): 181. See also Nye, *Bound to Lead: The Changing Nature of American Power* (New York: Basic Books, 1990).

will not convince Muslims who already distrust the United States. Success in deposing the Taliban may help U.S. policy by encouraging a bandwagon effect that rallies governments and moderates among the Muslim populace, but there will probably be as many who see the U.S. retaliation as confirming al Qaeda's diagnosis of American evil. Victory in Afghanistan and follow-up operations to prevent al Qaeda from relocating bases of operation to other countries will hurt that organization's capacity to act. The number of young zealots willing to emulate the "martyrdom operation" of the nineteen on September 11, however, is not likely to decline.

ADVANTAGE OF ATTACK

The academic field of security studies has some reason to be embarrassed after September 11. Having focused primarily on great powers and interstate conflict, literature on terrorism was comparatively sparse; most of the good books were by policy analysts rather than theorists.[14] Indeed, science fiction has etched out the operational logic of terrorism as well as political science. Eric Frank Russell's 1957 novel, from which the epigraph to this article comes, vividly illustrates both the strategic aspirations of terrorists and the offense-dominant character of their tactics. It describes the dispatch of a single agent to one of many planets in the Sirian enemy's empire to stir up fear, confusion, and panic through a series of small covert activities with tremendous ripple effects. Matched with deceptions to make the disruptions appear to be part of a campaign by a big phantom rebel organization, the agent's modest actions divert large numbers of enemy policy and military personnel, cause economic dislocations and social unrest, and soften the planet up for invasion. Wasp agents are infiltrated into numerous planets, multiplying the effects. As the agents' handlers tell him, "The pot is coming slowly but surely to the boil. Their fleets are being widely dispersed, there are vast troop movements from their overcrowded home-system to the outer planets of their empire. They're gradually being chivvied into a fix. They can't hold what they've got without spreading all over it. The wider they spread the thinner they get. The thinner they get, the easier it is to bite lumps out of them."[15]

Fortunately al Qaeda and its ilk are not as wildly effective as Russell's wasp. By degree, however, the phenomenon is quite similar. Comparatively limited initiatives prompt tremendous and costly defensive reactions. On September 11 a small number of men killed 3,000 people and destroyed a huge portion of prime commercial real estate,

---

[14]For example, Bruce Hoffman, *Inside Terrorism* (New York: Columbia University Press, 1998); Paul R. Pillar, *Terrorism and American Foreign Policy* (Washington, DC: Brookings Institution Press, 2001); Richard A. Falkenrath, Robert D. Newman, and Bradley S. Thayer, *America's Achilles' Heel: Nuclear, Biological, and Chemical Terrorism and Covert Attack* (Cambridge: MIT Press, 1998).

[15]Russell, *Wasp,* 64. The ripple effects include aspects of strategic judo. Creating a phony rebel organization leads the enemy security apparatus to turn on its own people. "If some Sirians could be given the full-time job of hunting down and garroting other Sirians, and if other Sirians could be given the full-time job of dodging or shooting down the garroters, then a distant and different life form would be saved a few unpleasant chores. . . . Doubtless the military would provide a personal bodyguard for every big wheel on Jaimec; that alone would pin down a regiment." Ibid., 26, 103.

part of the military's national nerve center, and four expensive aircraft. The ripple effects, however, multiplied those costs. A major part of the U.S. economy—air travel—shut down completely for days after September 11. Increased security measures dramatically increased the overall costs of the air travel system thereafter. Normal law enforcement activities of the Federal Bureau of Investigation were radically curtailed as legions of agents were transferred to counterterror tasks. Anxiety about the vulnerability of nuclear power plants, major bridges and tunnels, embassies abroad, and other high-value targets prompted plans for big investments in fortification of a wide array of facilities. A retaliatory war in Afghanistan ran at a cost of a couple billion dollars a month beyond the regular defense budget for months. In one study, the attacks on the World Trade Center and the Pentagon were estimated to cost the U.S. economy 1.8 million jobs.[16]

Or consider the results of a handful of 34-cent letters containing anthrax, probably sent by a single person. Besides killing several people, they contaminated a large portion of the postal system, paralyzed some mail delivery for long periods, provoked plans for huge expenditures on prophylactic irradiation equipment, shut down much of Capitol Hill for weeks, put thousands of people on a sixty-day regimen of strong antibiotics (potentially eroding the medical effectiveness of such antibiotics in future emergencies), and overloaded police and public health inspectors with false alarms. The September 11 attacks and the October anthrax attacks together probably cost the perpetrators less than a million dollars. If the cost of rebuilding and of defensive investments in reaction came to no more than $100 billion, the cost exchange ratio would still be astronomically in favor of the attack over the defense.

Analysts in strategic studies did not fall down on the job completely before September 11. At least two old bodies of work help to illuminate the problem. One is the literature on guerrilla warfare and counterinsurgency, particularly prominent in the 1960s, and the other is the offense-defense theory that burgeoned in the 1980s. Both apply well to understanding patterns of engagement between terrorists and counterterrorists. Some of the axioms derived from the empirical cases in the counterinsurgency literature apply directly, and offense-defense theory applies indirectly.

Apart from the victims of guerrillas, few still identify irregular paramilitary warfare with terrorism (because the latter is illegitimate), but the two activities do overlap a great deal in their operational characteristics. Revolutionary or resistance movements in the preconventional phase of operations usually mix small-unit raids on isolated outposts of the government or occupying force with detonations and assassinations in urban areas to instill fear and discredit government power. The tactical logic of guerrilla operations resembles that in terrorist attacks: the weaker rebels use stealth and the cover of civilian society to concentrate their striking power against one among many of the stronger enemy's dispersed assets; they strike quickly and eliminate the target before the defender can move forces from other areas to respond; they melt back into civilian society to avoid detection and reconcentrate against another target. The government or occupier has far superior strength in terms of conventional military power, but cannot

---

[16]Study by the Milken Institute discussed in "The Economics: Attacks May Cost 1.8 Million Jobs," *New York Times,* 13 January 2002.

counterconcentrate in time because it has to defend all points, while the insurgent attacker can pick its targets at will.[17] The contest between insurgents and counterinsurgents is "tripartite," polarizing political alignments and gaining the support of *attentistes* or those in the middle. In today's principal counterterror campaign, one might say that the yet-unmobilized Muslim elites and masses of the Third World—those who were not already actively committed either to supporting Islamist radicalism or to combating it—are the target group in the middle. As Samuel Huntington noted, "a revolutionary war is a war of attrition."[18] As I believe Stanley Hoffman once said, in rebellions the insurgents win as long as they do not lose, and the government loses as long as it does not win. If al Qaeda-like groups can stay in the field indefinitely, they win.

Offense-defense theory applied nuclear deterrence concepts to assessing the stability of conventional military confrontations and focused on what conditions tended to give the attack or the defense the advantage in war.[19] There were many problems in the specification and application of the theory having to do with unsettled conceptualization of the offense-defense balance, problematic standards for measuring it, and inconsistent applications to different levels of warfare and diplomacy.[20] Offense-defense theory, which flourished when driven by the urge to find ways to stabilize the

---

[17]Mao Tse-Tung's classic tracts are canonical background. For example, "Problems of Strategy in China's Revolutionary War" (especially chap. 5) in *Selected Works of Mao Tse-Tung* (Beijing: Foreign Languages Press, 1967), vol. i, and "Problems of Strategy in Guerrilla War Against Japan," in *Selected Works,* vol. ii (1967). Much of the Western analytical literature grew out of British experience in the Malayan Emergency and France's role in Indochina and Algeria. For example, Franklin Mark Osanka, ed., *Modern Guerrilla Warfare* (New York: Free Press, 1962); Gerard Chaliand, ed., *Guerrilla Strategies: An Historical Anthology from the Long March to Afghanistan* (Berkeley: University of California Press, 1982); Roger Triniquier, *Modern Warfare: A French View of Counterinsurgency,* Daniel Lee, trans. (New York: Praeger, 1964); David Galula, *Counterinsurgency Warfare: Theory and Practice* (New York: Praeger, 1964); Sir Robert Thompson, *Defeating Communist Insurgency* (New York: Praeger, 1966); Richard L. Clutterbuck, *The Long Long War: Counterinsurgency in Malaya and Vietnam* (New York: Praeger, 1966); George Armstrong Kelly, *Lost Soldiers: The French Army and Empire in Crisis, 1947–1962* (Cambridge: MIT Press, 1965), chaps. 5–7, 9–10; W. P. Davison, *Some Observations on Viet Cong Operations in the Villages* (Santa Monica, CA: RAND Corporation, 1968). See also Douglas S. Blaufarb, *The Counter-Insurgency Era: U.S. Doctrine and Performance, 1950 to the Present* (New York: Free Press, 1977); D. Michael Shafer, *Deadly Paradigms: The Failure of U.S. Counterinsurgency Policy* (Princeton: Princeton University Press, 1988); Timothy J. Lomperis, *From People's War to People's Rule: Insurgency, Intervention, and the Lessons of Vietnam* (Chapel Hill: University of North Carolina Press, 1996).
[18]Huntington, "Patterns of Violence in World Politics," 20–27.
[19]George Quester, *Offense and Defense in the International System,* 2nd ed. (New Brunswick, NJ: Transaction Books, 1988); Robert Jervis, "Cooperation Under the Security Dilemma," *World Politics* 30 (January 1978); Jack L. Snyder, *The Ideology of the Offensive: Military Decision Making and the Disasters of 1914* (Ithaca, NY: Cornell University Press, 1984); Stephen Van Evera, *Causes of War: Power and the Roots of Conflict* (Ithaca, NY: Cornell University Press, 1999), chaps. 6–8; Charles L. Glaser and Chaim Kaufmann, "What Is the Offense-Defense Balance and Can We Measure It?" *International Security* 22 (Spring 1998).
[20]For critiques, see Jack S. Levy, "The Offensive/Defensive Balance of Military Technology," *International Studies Quarterly* 28 (June 1984); Scott D. Sagan, "1914 Revisited," *International Security* 11 (Fall 1986); Jonathan Shimshoni, "Technology, Military Advantage, and World War I: A Case for Military Entrepreneurship," *International Security* 15 (Winter 1990/91); Richard K. Betts, "Must War Find a Way?" *International Security* 24 (Fall 1999); Betts, "Conventional Deterrence: Predictive Uncertainty and Policy Confidence," *World Politics* 37 (January 1985).

NATO-Warsaw Pact balance in Europe, has had little to say directly about unconventional war or terrorism. It actually applies more clearly, however, to this lower level of strategic competition (as well as to the higher level of nuclear war) than to the middle level of conventional military power. This is because the exchange ratio between opposing conventional forces of roughly similar size is very difficult to estimate, given the complex composition of modern military forces and uncertainty about their qualitative comparisons; but the exchange ratio in both nuclear and guerrilla combat is quite lopsided in favor of the attacker. Counterinsurgency folklore held that the government defenders need something on the order of a ten-to-one advantage over the guerrillas if they were to drive them from the field.

There has been much confusion about exactly how to define the offense-defense balance, but the essential idea is that some combinations of military technology, organization, and doctrine are proportionally more advantageous to the attack or to the defense when the two clash. "Proportionally" means that available instruments and circumstances of engagement give either the attack or the defense more bang for the buck, more efficient power out of the same level of resources. The notion of an offense-defense balance as something conceptually distinct from the balance of power means, however, that it cannot be identified with which side wins a battle or a war. Indeed, the offense-defense balance can favor the defense, while the attacker still wins, because its overall margin of superiority in power was too great, despite the defense's more efficient use of power. (I am told that the Finns had a saying in the Winter War of 1939–40: "One Finn is worth ten Russians, but what happens when the eleventh Russian comes?") Thus, to say that the offense-defense balance favors the offensive terrorists today against the defensive counterterrorists does not mean that the terrorists will prevail. It does mean that terrorists can fight far above their weight, that in most instances each competent terrorist will have much greater individual impact than each good counterterrorist, that each dollar invested in a terrorist plot will have a bigger payoff than each dollar expended on counterterrorism, and that only small numbers of competent terrorists need survive and operate to keep the threat to American society uncomfortably high.

In the competition between terrorists on the attack and Americans on the defense, the disadvantage of the defense is evident in the number of high-value potential targets that need protection. The United States has "almost 600,000 bridges, 170,000 water systems, more than 2,800 power plants (104 of them nuclear), 190,000 miles of interstate pipelines for natural gas, 463 skyscrapers . . . nearly 20,000 miles of border, airports, stadiums, train tracks."[21] All these usually represented American strength; after September 11 they also represent vulnerability:

> Suddenly guards were being posted at water reservoirs, outside power plants, and at bridges and tunnels. Maps of oil and gas lines were removed from the Internet. In Boston, a ship carrying liquefied natural gas, an important source of fuel for heating New England homes,

---

[21]Jerry Schwartz, Associated Press dispatch, 6 October 2001, quoted in Brian Reich, "Strength in the Face of Terror: A Comparison of United States and International Efforts to Provide Homeland Security" (unpublished paper, Columbia University, December 2001), 5.

was forbidden from entering the harbor because local fire officials feared that if it were targeted by a terrorist the resulting explosion could lay low much of the city's densely populated waterfront. An attack by a knife-wielding lunatic on the driver of a Florida-bound Greyhound bus led to the immediate cessation of that national bus service. . . . Agricultural crop-dusting planes were grounded out of a concern that they could be used to spread chemical or biological agents.[22]

Truly energetic defense measures do not only cost money in personnel and equipment for fortification, inspection, and enforcement; they may require repealing some of the very underpinnings of civilian economic efficiency associated with globalization. "The competitiveness of the U.S. economy and the quality of life of the American people rest on critical infrastructure that has become increasingly more concentrated, more inter-connected, and more sophisticated. Almost entirely privately owned and operated, there is very little redundancy in this system."[23] This concentration increases the potential price of vulnerability to single attacks. Tighter inspection of cargoes coming across the Canadian border, for example, wrecks the "just-in-time" parts supply system of Michigan auto manufacturers. Companies that have invested in technology and infra-structure premised on unimpeded movement "may see their expected savings and effi-ciencies go up in smoke. Outsourcing contracts will have to be revisited and inventories will have to be rebuilt."[24] How many safety measures will suffice in improving airline security without making flying so inconvenient that the air travel industry never recov-ers as a profit-making enterprise? A few more shoe-bomb incidents, and Thomas Friedman's proposal to start an airline called "Naked Air—where the only thing you wear is a seat belt" becomes almost as plausible as it is ridiculous.[25]

The offense-dominant character of terrorism is implicit in mass detentions of Arab young men after September 11, and proposals for military tribunals that would compro-mise normal due process and weaken standard criminal justice presumptions in favor of the accused. The traditional liberal axiom that it is better to let a hundred guilty people go free than to convict one innocent reflects confidence in the strength of society's defenses—confidence that whatever additional crimes may be committed by the guilty who go free will not grossly outweigh the injustice done to innocents convicted, that one criminal who slips through the net will not go on to kill hundreds or thousands of innocents. Fear of terrorists plotting mass murder reversed that presumption and makes unjust incarceration of some innocents appear like unintended but expected collateral damage in wartime combat.

Offense-defense theory helps to visualize the problem. It does not help to provide attractive solutions, as its proponents believed it did during the Cold War. Then offense-defense theory was popular because it seemed to offer a way to stabilize the East-West military confrontation. Mutual deterrence from the superpowers' confidence in their

---

[22]Stephen E. Flynn, "The Unguarded Homeland" in James F. Hoge, Jr. and Gideon Rose, eds., *How Did This Happen? Terrorism and the New War* (New York: Public Affairs, 2001), 185.
[23]Ibid., 185–186.
[24]Ibid., 193–194.
[25]Thomas L. Friedman, "Naked Air," *New York Times,* 26 December 2001.

counteroffensive capability could substitute for defense at the nuclear level, and both sides' confidence in their conventional defenses could dampen either one's incentives to attack at that level. Little of this applies to counterterrorism. Both deterrence and defense are weaker strategies against terrorists than they were against communists.

Deterrence is still relevant for dealing with state terrorism; Saddam Hussein or Kim Jong-Il may hold back from striking the United States for fear of retaliation. Deterrence offers less confidence for preventing state sponsorship of terrorism; it did not stop the Taliban from hosting Osama bin Laden. It offers even less for holding at bay transnational groups like al Qaeda, which may lack a return address against which retaliation can be visited, or whose millenialist aims and religious convictions make them unafraid of retaliation. Defense, in turn, is better than a losing game only because the inadequacy of deterrence leaves no alternative.[26] Large investments in defense will produce appreciable reductions in vulnerability, but will not minimize vulnerability.

Deterrence and defense overlap in practice. The U.S. counteroffensive in Afghanistan constitutes retaliation, punishing the Taliban for shielding al Qaeda and sending a warning to other potential state sponsors. It is also active defense, whittling down the ranks of potential perpetrators by killing and capturing members of the Islamist international brigades committed to jihad against the United States. At this writing, the retaliatory function has been performed more effectively than the defensive, as the Taliban regime has been destroyed, but significant numbers of Arab Afghans and al Qaeda members appear to have escaped, perhaps to plot another day.

Given the limited efficacy of deterrence for modern counterterrorism, it remains an open question how much of a strategic success we should judge the impressive victory in Afghanistan to be. Major investments in passive defenses (airline security, border inspections, surveillance and searches for better intelligence, fortification of embassies, and so forth) are necessary, but will reduce vulnerability at a cost substantially greater than the costs that competent terrorist organizations will have to bear to probe and occasionally circumvent them. The cost-exchange ratio for direct defense is probably worse than the legendary 10:1 ratio for successful counterinsurgency, and certainly worse than the more than 3:1 ratio that Robert McNamara's analysts calculated for the advantage of offensive missile investments over antiballistic missile systems—an advantage that many then and since have thought warranted accepting a situation of mutual vulnerability to assured destruction.[27]

The less prepared we are to undertake appropriate programs and the more false starts and confusions that are likely, the worse the cost-exchange ratio will be in the short term. The public health system, law enforcement organizations, and state and local bureaucrats are still feeling their way on what, how, and in which sequence to boost

---

[26]See Steven Simon and Daniel Benjamin, "America and the New Terrorism," *Survival* 42 (Spring 2000): 59, 66–69, 74.

[27]Estimates in the 1960s indicated that even combining ABM systems with counterforce strikes and fallout shelters, the United States would have to counter each Soviet dollar spent on ICBMs with three U.S. dollars to protect 70 percent of the industry, assuming highly effective ABMs (.8 kill probability). To protect up to 80 percent of the population, far higher ratios would be necessary. Fred Kaplan, *The Wizards of Armageddon* (New York: Simon and Schuster, 1983), 321–324.

efforts. The U.S. military will also have to overcome the natural and powerful effects of inertia and attachments to old self-conceptions and preferred programs and modes of operation. Impulses to repackage old priorities in the rhetoric of new needs will further dilute effectiveness of countermeasures.

Nevertheless, given low confidence that deterrence can prevent terrorist attacks, major improvements in defenses make sense.[28] This is especially true because the resource base from which the United States can draw is vastly larger than that available to transnational terrorists. Al Qaeda may be rich, but it does not have the treasury of a great power. Primacy has a soft underbelly, but it is far better to have primacy than to face it. Even at an unfavorable cost exchange ratio, a number of defensive measures are a sensible investment, but only because our overwhelming advantage in resources means that we are not constrained to focus solely on the most efficient countermeasures.

At the same time, as long as terrorist groups remain potent and active, a serious war plan must exploit efficient strategies as well. Given the offense-dominant nature of terrorist operations, this means emphasis on counteroffensive operations. When terrorists or their support structures can be found and fixed, preemptive and preventive attacks will accomplish more against them, dollar for dollar, than the investment in passive defenses. Which is the more efficient use of resources: to kill or capture a cell of terrorists who might otherwise choose at any time to strike whichever set of targets on our side is unguarded, or to try to guard all potential targets? Here the dangers are that counteroffensive operations could prove counterproductive. This could easily happen if they degenerate into brutalities and breaches of laws of war that make counterterrorism begin to appear morally equivalent to its target, sapping political support and driving the uncommitted to the other side in the process of polarization that war makes inevitable. Whether counteroffensive operations gain more in eliminating perpetrators than they lose in alienating and mobilizing "swing voters" in the world of Muslim opinion depends on how successful the operations are in neutralizing significant numbers of the organizers of terrorist groups, as opposed to foot soldiers, and in doing so with minimal collateral damage.

PRIMACY AND POLICY

September 11 reminded those Americans with a rosy view that not all the world sees U.S. primacy as benign, that primacy does not guarantee security, and that security may now entail some retreats from the economic globalization that some had identified with American leadership. Primacy has two edges—dominance and provocation. Americans can enjoy the dominance but must recognize the risks it evokes. For terrorists who want to bring the United States down, U.S. strategic primacy is a formidable challenge, but one that can be overcome. On balance, Americans have overestimated the benefits of primacy, and terrorists have underestimated them.

---

[28]For an appropriate list of recommendations see *Countering the Changing Threat of International Terrorism,* Report of the National Commission on Terrorism, Pursuant to Public Law 277, 105th Congress (Washington, DC, June 2000). This report holds up very well in light of September 11.

For those who see a connection between American interventionism, cultural expansiveness, and support of Israel on one hand, and the rage of groups that turn to terrorism on the other, primacy may seem more trouble than it's worth, and the need to revise policies may seem more pressing. But most Americans have so far preferred the complacent and gluttonous form of primacy to the ascetic, blithely accepting steadily growing dependence on Persian Gulf oil that could be limited by compromises in lifestyle and unconventional energy policies. There have been no groundswells to get rid of SUVs, support the Palestinians, or refrain from promoting Western standards of democracy and human rights in societies where some elements see them as aggression.

There is little evidence that any appreciable number of Americans, elite or mass, see our primacy as provoking terrorism. Rather, most see it as a condition we can choose at will to exploit or not. So U.S. foreign policy has exercised primacy in a muscular way in byways of the post-Cold War world when intervention seemed cheap, but not when doing good deeds threatened to be costly. Power has allowed Washington to play simultaneously the roles of mediator and partisan supporter in the Arab-Israeli conflict. For a dozen years nothing, with the near exception of the Kosovo War, suggested that primacy could not get us out of whatever problems it generated.

How far the United States goes to adapt to the second edge of primacy probably depends on whether stunning damage is inflicted by terrorists again, or September 11 gradually fades into history. If al Qaeda and its ilk are crippled, and some years pass without more catastrophic attacks on U.S. home territory, scar tissue will harden on the soft underbelly, and the positive view of primacy will be reinforced. If the war against terrorism falters, however, and the exercise of power fails to prevent more big incidents, the consensus will crack. Then more extreme policy options will get more attention. Retrenchment and retreat will look more appealing to some, who may believe the words of Sheik Salman al-Awdah, a dissident Saudi religious scholar, who said, "If America just let well enough alone, and got out of their obligations overseas . . . no one would bother them."[29]

More likely, however, would be a more violent reaction. There is no reason to assume that terrorist enemies would let America off the hook if it retreated and would not remain as implacable as ever. Facing inability to suppress the threat through normal combat, covert action, and diplomatic pressure, many Americans would consider escalation to more ferocious strategies. In recent decades, the march of liberal legalism has delegitimized tactics and brutalities that once were accepted, but this delegitimation has occurred only in the context of fundamental security and dominance of the Western powers, not in a situation where they felt under supreme threat. In a situation of that sort, it is foolhardy to assume that American strategy would never turn to tactics like those used against Japanese and German civilians, or by the civilized French in the *sale guerre* in Algeria, or by the Russians in Chechnya in hopes of effectively eradicating terrorists despite astronomical damage to the civilian societies within which they lurk.

---

[29]Quoted in Douglas Jehl, "After Prison, a Saudi Sheik Tempers His Words," *New York Times,* 27 December 2001.

This possibility would highlight how terrorists have underestimated American primacy. There is much evidence that even in the age of unipolarity, opponents have mistakenly seen the United States as a paper tiger. For some reason—perhaps wishfully selective perception—they tend to see retreats from Vietnam, Beirut, and Somalia as typical weakness of American will, instead of considering decisive exercises of power in Panama, Kuwait, Kosovo, and now, Afghanistan.[30] As Osama bin Laden said in 1997, the United States left Somalia "after claiming that they were the largest power on earth. They left after some resistance from powerless, poor, unarmed people whose only weapon is the belief in Allah. . . . The Americans ran away."[31]

This apparently common view among those with an interest in pinning America's ears back ignores the difference between elective uses of force and desperate ones. The United States retreated where it ran into trouble helping others, not where it was saving itself. Unlike interventions of the 1990s in Africa, the Balkans, or Haiti, counterterrorism is not charity. With vital material interests involved, primacy unleashed may prove fearsomely potent.

Most likely America will see neither absolute victory nor abject failure in the war against terror. Then how long will a campaign of attrition last and stay popular? If the United States wants a strategy to cut the roots of terrorism, rather than just the branches, will American power be used effectively against the roots? Perhaps, but probably not. This depends of course on which of many possible root causes are at issue. Ironically, one problem is that American primacy itself is one of those roots.

A common assertion is that Third World poverty generates terrorism. While this must certainly be a contributing cause in many cases, there is little evidence that it is either a necessary or sufficient condition. Fundamentalist madrassas might not be full to overflowing if young Muslims had ample opportunities to make money, but the fifteen Saudis who hijacked the flights on September 11 were from one of the most affluent of Muslim countries. No U.S. policy could ever hope to make most incubators of terrorism less poor than Saudi Arabia. Iran, the biggest state sponsor of anti-American terrorism, is also better off than most Muslim countries. Poverty is endemic in the Third World, but terrorism is not.

Even if endemic poverty were the cause, the solution would not be obvious. Globalization generates stratification, creating winners and losers, as efficient societies with capitalist cultures move ahead and others fall behind, or as elite enclaves in some societies prosper while the masses stagnate. Moreover, even vastly increased U.S. development assistance would be spread thin if all poor countries are assumed to be incubators of terrorism. And what are the odds that U.S. intervention with economic aid would significantly reduce poverty? Successes in prompting dramatic economic development by outside assistance in the Third World have occurred, but they are the exception more than the rule.

---

[30]See data in the study by Barry M. Blechman and Tamara Cofman Wittes, "Defining Moment: The Threat and Use of Force in American Foreign Policy," *Political Science Quarterly* 114 (Spring 1999).
[31]Quoted in Simon and Benjamin, "America and the New Terrorism," 69.

The most virulent anti-American terrorist threats, however, do not emerge randomly in poor societies. They grow out of a few regions and are concentrated overwhelmingly in a few religiously motivated groups. These reflect political causes— ideological, nationalist, or transnational cultural impulses to militant mobilization— more than economic causes. Economic development in an area where the political and religious impulses remain unresolved could serve to improve the resource base for terrorism rather than undercut it.

A strategy of terrorism is most likely to flow from the coincidence of two conditions: intense political grievance and gross imbalance of power. Either one without the other is likely to produce either peace or conventional war. Peace is probable if power is imbalanced but grievance is modest; the weaker party is likely to live with the grievance. In that situation, conventional use of force appears to offer no hope of victory, while the righteous indignation is not great enough to overcome normal inhibitions against murderous tactics. Conventional war is probable if grievance is intense but power is more evenly balanced, since successful use of respectable forms of force appears possible.[32] Under American primacy, candidates for terrorism suffer from grossly inferior power by definition. This should focus attention on the political causes of their grievance.

How are political root causes addressed? At other times in history we have succeeded in fostering congenial revolutions—especially in the end of the Cold War, as the collapse of the Second World heralded an End of History of sorts.[33] The problem now, however, is the rebellion of anti-Western zealots against the secularist end of history. Remaking the world in the Western image is what Americans assume to be just, natural, and desirable, indeed only a matter of time. But that presumption is precisely what energizes many terrorists' hatred. Secular Western liberalism is not their salvation, but their scourge. Primacy could, paradoxically, remain both the solution and the problem for a long time.*

---

[32] On why power imbalance is conducive to peace and parity to war, see Geoffrey Blainey, *The Causes of War*, 3rd. ed. (New York: Free Press, 1988), chap. 8.

[33] Francis Fukuyama's thesis was widely misunderstood and caricatured. He noted that the Third World remained mired in history and that some developments could lead to restarting history. For the First World, the defeated Second World, and even some parts of the Third World, however, the triumph of Western liberalism could reasonably be seen by those who believe in its worth (as should Americans) as the final stage of evolution through fundamentally different forms of political and economic organization of societies. See Fukuyama, "The End of History?" *National Interest* no. 16 (Summer 1989); and Fukuyama, *The End of History and the Last Man* (New York: Free Press, 1992).

*The author thanks Robert Jervis for comments on the first draft.

PART IX

TRANSNATIONAL TENSIONS: MIGRATION, RESOURCES, AND ENVIRONMENT

Some potential sources of conflict transcend borders and may not be caused or controlled by specific governments. Such problems were not well-recognized during the Cold War era, or seemed less important then because the East-West struggle absorbed concern. With superpower threats like that of the Cold War no longer preoccupying us, these other challenges to international stability may become a higher priority. How far such matters will become real issues of national security, however, is an open question. It would be a traditionalist conceit to ignore the emergence of novel grounds of conflict, yet not all new international problems turn into security problems.

Some transnational sources of conflict are old and well-recognized—most notably, religion and revolutionary ideology. After a century in which international relations were more ideologically charged than at any other time in the modern era, there is no longer any ideology that is globally or even regionally competitive with Western liberalism. After a few centuries in which religion had receded as a source of severe international strife, however, its profile has risen in conflicts both between and within countries—conflicts among Orthodox and Roman Catholic Christians in the Balkans, Catholics and Protestants in Northern Ireland, Hindus and Muslims in South Asia, Muslims and Jews in the Middle East, and radical Islamists in the Persian Gulf and elsewhere and the secular societies of the West. In the past two decades much attention focused on the notion of a threat to the West from radical Islam because of the Iranian revolution, the victory of the Taliban in Afghanistan, the emergence of terrorist organizations such as Osama Bin Ladin's, and the popular association of Islamic "fundamentalism" with fanaticism and terrorism. Since the crackup of Marxism-Leninism as a secular religion, moreover, Islam appears to some to be the only major transnational belief system that poses an alternative to Western liberalism as a model for social organization (Islam prevails in countries as disparate as Indonesia, Egypt, Nigeria, and Pakistan). Radical Islamists, however, are not a large proportion of the world's

Muslims, and there is scant evidence yet of globally or even regionally coordinated action on the basis of religious motivation.[1]

Other sources of conflict that may loom larger in coming years are those that involve competition for resources, damage to the natural environment, or the effects of population displacements. Myron Weiner points out the many ways in which unprecedented transfers of population in the contemporary world put new pressure on governments and prompt international friction. Large populations of political refugees contribute to violent conflict in many regions. Illegal immigration by economic refugees reflects one of the most enduring obstacles to the notion that market economics and free trade will be the font of peace. A world economy based on fully free markets and production according to comparative advantage would be one that allowed mobility of *both* major factors of production, labor as well as capital, yet scarcely anyone dreams that rich countries will open their doors without restriction.

Another set of global problems that has risen in salience involves international collective goods, access to resources, and preservation of the balance of nature that all countries need but that none can control individually. The idea that security should be redefined to cover environmental and other nonmilitary dangers has been popular in recent years. Sometimes that argument is a cover for diverting attention earmarked for security studies from military matters that the redefiners consider narrow and *passé* to problems of real importance. Depletion of the ozone layer, coral reefs, or rain forests may indeed prove to be a greater threat to our survival than the Russians ever were. If it is counted a matter of security, however, that term becomes so inclusive as to be meaningless. If "security" is synonymous with national interests in general, or with human safety, we might as well include educational policy and medicine in security studies.

Some environmental disasters, nevertheless, may affect security in the sense in which the term is traditionally used. The point at which the line should be drawn is where issues not traditionally addressed in security studies may cause social conflict and political violence. If some country were to contemplate using force against another to prevent it from releasing ozone-destroying chemicals into the atmosphere, for example, the ozone issue would qualify as a matter of security policy. Similarly, as John Cooley's discussion of control of water in the Middle East suggests, disputes over natural resources might easily become a source of armed conflict between states. Cooley traces the evolution of the issue in earlier decades, but its importance can only increase in a region that has growing population and unresolved questions of sovereignty over territory.

---

[1]Limitations of alarmist views about Islam are noted in Graham Fuller, *Islamic Fundamentalism in Pakistan,* R—3964-USDP (Santa Monica, CA: Rand Corporation, 1991) and Fuller, *Islamic Fundamentalism in Afghanistan,* R—3970-USDP (Santa Monica, CA: Rand Corporation, 1991). See also Abdulaziz A. Sachedina, "The Development of *Jihad* in Islamic Revelation and History," in James Turner Johnson and John Kelsay, eds., *Cross, Crescent, and Sword* (Westport, CT: Greenwood Press, 1990); and the series of monographs published by the Council on Foreign Relations (New York) in 1999: William Maley, *The Foreign Policy of the Taliban;* Vali Nasr, *International Relations of an Islamist Movement: The Case of the Jama'at-i Islami of Pakistan;* Robert Satloff, *U.S. Policy Toward Islamism: A Theoretical and Operational Overview;* Muhammad Muslih, *The Foreign Policy of Hamas;* Augustus Richard Norton, *Hizballah of Lebanon: Extremist Ideals vs. Mundane Politics;* and Olivier Roy, *The Foreign Policy of the Central Asian Islamic Renaissance Party.*

Thomas Homer-Dixon shows how a wide range of developments that degrade the environment and thereby put pressure on economies and societies (especially in Third World countries that live closer to the margin of subsistence) could also lead to significant political violence.[2]

The ultimate consequences of damage to the balance of nature are unknown, and potentially of significance beyond political and economic disputes. In the near term, however, environmental decline is likely to cause conflict mainly through its economic effects. The combination of these issues also aggravates the old North-South clash over the international distribution of wealth. The developed countries got their development in earlier eras by exploiting nature's collective goods without a thought. Now they expect poorer countries to exercise restraint and leave some of their natural resources intact, to preserve the collective goods.

Who should pay for that preservation? What compensation should go to those who do not despoil their forests, plunder the oceans, or run their industries on polluting fuels, and how should the prices for such transactions be determined? Who will make the rules? Could environmental regulation come to justify forcible intervention against those who refuse it? (For example, if China comes to burn as much fossil fuel per capita as the Western nations in the process of its economic development, the resulting pollution and atmospheric warming will be a global, not local problem. In the context of growing tension between China and the United States over other issues, this development could spill over into the economic, diplomatic, and strategic competition between the two.) These are the questions that could make all this the stuff of international conflict.

—RKB

---

[2]See also Norman Myers, "Environment and Security," *Foreign Policy* no. 74 (spring 1989); Roy L. Thompson, "Water as a Source of Conflict," *Strategic Review* 6, no. 2 (spring 1978); Richard Ullman, "Redefining Security," *International Security* 8, no. 1 (summer 1983); Jessica Tuchman Mathews, "Redefining Security," *Foreign Affairs* 68, no. 2 (spring 1989); and Robert L. Paarlberg, "Ecodiplomacy," in Kenneth Oye, Robert Lieber, and Donald Rothchild, eds., *Eagle in a New World* (New York: HarperCollins, 1992).

SECURITY, STABILITY, AND MIGRATION

Myron Weiner

CONCEPTUAL APPROACHES

. . . Consider the following:

- As a result of an international embargo following its invasion of Kuwait the government of Iraq seized western immigrants, placed them at strategic locations in order to prevent air strikes, and offered to exchange Asian immigrants for shiploads of food.
- Palestinian immigrants in Kuwait collaborated with the Iraqi invaders, thereby strengthening Iraq's hold on Kuwait but at the same time threatening the position of Palestinian immigrants in other countries in the Gulf.
- Iraq recruited 1.5 million Egyptian farm laborers as replacements for the nearly one million men conscripted into the military to serve in the war with Iran. Many remained in the country even as relations between Iraq and Egypt deteriorated.
- As a result of an exodus of East Germans to Austria through Czechoslovakia and Hungary in July and August 1989, the East German government opened its western borders. The result was a massive flight to West Germany, clashes between refugees and the police, the fall of the East German government, and the absorption of East Germany by the Federal Republic of Germany.
- Following an announcement by Palestinian radicals that they would launch terrorist attacks against airlines that carried Soviet Jews to Israel, several governments instructed their state-owned airlines not to carry the immigrants.
- A band of armed refugees in Uganda from the Tutsi tribe launched an invasion of Rwanda in an effort to overthrow the Hutu dominated government and restore Tutsi domination.
- Fearful that a large scale influx of Vietnamese refugees might jeopardize the security of Hong Kong, the British government ordered the return of the Vietnamese in spite of considerable international protest.

These developments suggest the need for a security/stability framework for the study of international migration which focuses on state policies toward emigration and immigration as shaped by concerns over internal stability and international security.

Myron Weiner, *Security, Stability, and Migration,* Defense and Arms Control Studies Program Working Paper (Cambridge: MIT Center for International Studies, December 1990). Reprinted with permission of Myron Weiner.

Such a framework would consider political changes within states as a major determinant of international population flows, and migration—including refugee flows—both as a cause and a consequence of international conflict.

A security/stability framework can be contrasted with an international political economy framework which explains international migration primarily by focusing on global inequalities, the economic linkages between sending and receiving states, including the movement of capital, technology, and the role played by transnational institutions, and structural changes in labor markets linked to changes in the international division of labor. . . .

While at times complementary, the frameworks often yield different outcomes. A political economy perspective, for example, may lead the analyst to regard the movement of people from a poor to a rich country as mutually advantageous (the one benefitting from remittances, the other from needed additions to its labor force) whereas a security/stability perspective of the same migration flow may lead one to point to the political risks associated with changes in the ethnic composition of the receiving country and of the attending international strains that result if there are clashes between natives and migrants. A reverse assessment may also be rendered: a political economy perspective may lead the analyst to conclude that migration results in a brain drain from the sending country while worsening unemployment and creating housing shortages in the receiving country, while a security/stability framework may lead the analyst looking at the same migration flow to argue that internal security and international peace can be enhanced because the migrants are an ethnic minority unwelcomed in their home country but welcomed or at least readily accepted by another country. The movement of people may be acceptable to both countries even though each incurs an economic loss. Thus, a cost/benefit analysis may yield different assessments and policies depending upon which framework is chosen.

Much of the contemporary literature on international migration focuses on global economic conditions as the key determinants of population movements. Differentials in wages and employment opportunities—a high demand for labor in one country and a surplus in another—stimulate the movement of labor. According to economic theories of migration, individuals will emigrate if the expected benefits exceed the costs, with the result that the propensity to migrate from one region or country to another is viewed as being determined by average wages, the cost of travel, and labor market conditions. Accordingly, it is argued, changes in the global economy, such as a rise in the world price of oil or shifts in terms of trade and international flows of capital, will increase the demand for labor in some countries and decrease it in others. Moreover, the development strategies pursued by individual countries may lead to high growth rates in some and low growth rates and stagnation in others. Uneven economic development among states and a severe maldistribution of income within states may induce individuals and families to move across international boundaries to take advantage of greater opportunities.

These economic explanations go a long way toward explaining a great deal of international population movements but they neglect two critical political elements. The first is that international population movements are often impelled, encouraged, or prevented by governments or political forces for reasons that may have little to do with economic conditions. Indeed, much of the international population flows, especially within Africa and South Asia, are only marginally determined, if at all, by changes in the global or regional political economy. And secondly, even when economic conditions create inducements for people to leave one country for another it is governments that decide whether their citizens should be allowed to leave and governments that decide whether immigrants should be allowed to enter and their decisions are frequently based on non-economic considerations. Any effort, therefore, to develop a framework for the analysis of transnational flows of people must also take into account the political determinants and constraints upon these flows. . . .

FORCED AND INDUCED EMIGRATIONS: A GLOBAL PERSPECTIVE

. . . First, governments may force emigration as a means of achieving cultural homogeneity or for asserting the dominance of one ethnic community over another. Such flows have a long and sordid world-wide history. The rise of nationalism in Europe was accompanied by state actions to eject religious communities that did not subscribe to the established religion, and ethnic minorities that did not belong to the dominant ethnic community. In the fifteenth century, the Spanish crown expelled the Jews. In the sixteenth century the French expelled the Huguenots. In the seventeenth and eighteenth centuries the British crown induced Protestant dissenters to settle in the American colonies. And in the nineteenth century minorities throughout Eastern Europe—Bulgarians, Greeks, Jews, Turks, Hungarians, Serbs, Macedonians—were put to flight.

Many of the population movements in post-independence Africa, the Middle East, South and Southeast Asia are similarly linked to the rise of nationalism and the emergence of new states. The boundaries of many of new post-colonial regimes divided linguistic, religious and tribal communities, with the result that minorities, fearful of their future and often faced with discrimination and violence, migrated to join their ethnic brethren in a neighboring country. Many third world countries also expelled their ethnic minorities, especially when the minorities constituted an industrious class of migrant origin in competition with a middle class ethnic majority. Governments faced with unemployment within the majority community and conflicts among ethnic groups over language and educational opportunities often regarded the expulsion of a prosperous, well placed minority as a politically popular policy. Minorities were often threatened by the state's antagonistic policies toward their religion, their language and their culture, as the state sought to impose a hegemonic ethnic or religious identity upon its citizens. Economically successful minorities were often told that others would be given preferences in employment, a policy of reverse discrimination which effectively made it difficult for minorities to compete on the basis of merit. Many governments expelled their minorities or created conditions which induced them to leave, and thereby forced other countries, on humanitarian grounds, out of cultural affinity, to accept them as refugees. The list is long: Chinese in Vietnam, Indians and Pakistanis in East Africa, Tamils in Sri Lanka, Bahais in Iran, Kurds in Turkey, Iran and Iraq, Ahmediyas in Pakistan, Chakmas in Bangladesh, and in Africa communities in Rwanda, Ethiopia and Sudan, to name a few.

Secondly, governments have forced emigration as a means of dealing with political dissidents and class enemies. The ancient Greeks were among the earliest to strip dissidents of citizenship and cast them to exile. Socrates himself was offered the option of going into exile rather than being executed. Contemporary authoritarian governments have expelled dissidents or allowed them to go into exile as an alternative to imprisonment. In the United States exiles from the third world—from Ethiopia, Iran, Cuba, South Korea, Nicaragua, Vietnam, Chile—have largely replaced exiles from Europe.

Governments may expel not only a handful of dissidents, but a substantial portion of the population hostile to the regime. Revolutionary regimes often see large scale emigration of a social class as a way of transforming the country's social structure. The exodus of more than a half million members of the Cuban middle class was regarded by the Castro regime as a way of disposing of a social class hostile to socialism. In 1971 the Pakistan government sought to weaken the insurgency in East Pakistan by forcing large numbers of Bengali Hindus out of the country. The Vietnamese government justified expulsions as a way of eliminating a bourgeois social class opposed to the regime. The Kampuchean government killed or forced into exile citizens tainted with French and other western cultural influences in an effort to reduce its cultural and economic ties with the west. And in Afghanistan, the Soviet and Afghan military forced populations hostile to the regime to flee to Pakistan and Iran.

A third type of forced emigration can be described as part of a strategy to achieve a foreign policy objective. Governments, for example, may force emigration as a way of putting pressure on neighboring states, though they may deny any such intent. The refugee receiving country, however, often understands that a halt to unwanted migration is not likely to take place unless it yields on a demand made by the country from which the refugees come. In the late 1970s, for example, the United States government believed that the government of Haiti was encouraging its citizens to flee by boat to Florida to press the United States to substantially increase its economic aid. (It did.) In the 1980s Pakistan officials believed that Soviet pressure on Afghans to flee was in part intended to force Pakistan to seek a settlement with the Afghan regime and to withdraw military aid to the insurgents. The Malaysian government feared that the government of Vietnam sought to destabilize them by forcing them to accept Chinese refugees. The Federal Republic of Germany believed that the German Democratic Republic was permitting Tamil refugees to enter through the Berlin border to force the FRG to establish new rules of entry that would tacitly recognize the East German state, or alternatively, as a bargaining ploy for additional financial credits (which it subsequently granted in return for halting the flow). . . .

WHEN IS MIGRATION A THREAT TO SECURITY AND STABILITY?

. . . Before turning to an analysis of how, why and when states regard immigrants and refugees as potential threats, it is first necessary to note that some obvious explanations are of limited utility. Plausibly a country with little unemployment, a high demand for labor, and the financial resources to provide the housing and social services required by immigrants would regard migration as beneficial while a country low on each of these dimensions would regard migration as economically and socially destabilizing. Using these criteria, therefore, one might expect Japan to welcome migrants and Israel to reject them!

A second plausible explanation is the volume of immigration. It is self-evident that a country faced with a large-scale influx would feel threatened, compared with a country experiencing a small influx of migrants. From this perspective one might have expected the Federal Republic of Germany to regard the influx of a trickle of Sri Lankans with equanimity, but to move swiftly to halt an influx of 2,000 East Germans daily, or for the countries of Africa to feel more threatened by the onrush of refugees and hence less receptive than the countries of Western Europe confronted with a trickle from the third world.

Economics does, of course, matter. A country willing to accept immigrants when its economy is booming is likely to close its doors in a recession. But economics does not explain many of the differences between countries nor does it explain the criteria countries employ to decide whether a particular group of migrants or refugees is acceptable or is regarded as threatening. Similarly, volume can matter, but again it depends upon who is at the door.

Ethnic affinity would appear to be the most likely explanation for accepting or rejecting migrants. Presumably a country is receptive to those who share the same language, religion or race, but may regard as threatening those with whom such an identity is not shared. While generally true, there are striking exceptions. For more than half a century Americans rejected "Oriental" immigrants while today most Americans regard Asians as a model minority whose educational and economic successes and patriotism make them more desirable immigrants than others who are in language, religion and race closer to most Americans but are less successful. Moreover, what constitutes cultural affinity for one group in a multi-ethnic society may represent a cultural, social and economic threat to another: note, for example, the response of Afro-Americans in Florida to Cuban migrants, Indian Assamese response to Bangladeshis, and Pakistan Sindhi response to Biharis. . . .

Refugees and Immigrants as a Source of International Conflict

Since refugees are legally defined by most countries as individuals with a well founded fear of persecution the decision to grant asylum or refugee status implies a severe criticism of another state. Thus, the bitter debate in Congress in January 1990 over whether Chinese students should be permitted to remain because of the persecutions in China was regarded by the People's Republic of China as "interference" in its internal affairs, a judgment which many members of Congress (but not the President) were prepared to make. Moreover, to classify individuals as refugees with a well founded fear of persecution is also to grant them the moral (as distinct from political) right to oppose a regime engaged in persecution so judged by the country that has granted them asylum. The view of the United Nations High Commissioner for Refugees is that the granting of refugee status does not imply criticism of the sending by the receiving country, but such a view clearly contradicts the conception of the refugee as one with a fear of *persecution*. Moreover, democratic regimes generally allow their refugees to speak out against the regime of their country of origin, grant them access to the media, and permit them (to the extent the law permits) to send information and money back home in support of the opposition. The decision to grant refugee status thus often creates an adversary relationship with the country that produces refugees.

The receiving country may have no such intent, but even where its motives are humanitarian the mere granting of asylum can be sufficient to create an antagonistic relationship. In the most famous asylee related episode in this century, Iranian revolutionaries took violent exception to the U.S. decision to permit the Shah of Iran to enter the U.S. for medical reasons (which many Iranians regarded as a form of asylum) and used it as an occasion for taking American hostages.

A refugee-receiving country may actively support the refugees in their quest to change the regime of their country of origin. Refugees are potentially a tool in interstate conflict. Numerous examples abound: the United States armed Cubans in an effort to overthrow the Castro regime at the Bay of Pigs; the United States armed Contra exiles from Nicaragua; the Indian government armed Bengali "freedom fighters" against the Pakistan military; the Indian government provided military support for Tamil refugees from Sri Lanka to give the Indian government leverage in the Tamil-Sinhalese dispute; Pakistan, Saudi Arabia, China and the U.S. armed Afghan refugees in order to force Soviet troops to withdraw from Afghanistan; the Chinese provided arms to Khmer Rouge refugees to help overthrow the Vietnamese-backed regime in Cambodia; the Palestinian refugees received Arab support against Israelis. Refugee-producing countries may thus have good reason for fearing an alliance between the refugees and their national adversaries. . . .

There are numerous examples of diasporas seeking to undermine the regime of their home country: South Koreans and Taiwanese in the United States (who supported democratic movements at home), Iranians in France (Khomeini himself during the reign of the Shah, and opponents of Khomeini's Islamic regime thereafter), Asian Indians in North America and the U.K. (after Mrs. Gandhi declared an emergency), Indian Sikhs (supporting secession), and dissident Sri Lankan Tamils and Northern Ireland Catholics among others.

The home country may take a dim view of the activities of its citizens abroad, and hold the host country responsible for their activities. Host countries, especially if they are democratic, are loath to restrict migrants engaged in lawful activities, especially since some of the migrants have already become citizens. The home country may even plant intelligence operators abroad to monitor the activities of its migrants and take steps to prevent further emigration. The embassy of the home country may also provide encouragement to its supporters within the diaspora. The diaspora itself may become a focal point of controversy: between the home and host countries, among contending groups within the diaspora, as well as between sections of the diaspora and the home government. Thus, struggles that might overwise only take place within a country become internationalized if the country has a significant overseas population.

Refugees and Immigrants as a Political Risk to the Host Country

Governments are often concerned that refugees to whom they give protection may turn against them if they are unwilling to assist them in their opposition to the government of their country of origin. Paradoxically, the risk may be particularly high if the host country arms the refugees against their country of origin. Guns can be pointed in both directions and the receiving country takes the risk that refugees will dictate the host country's policies toward the sending country. Two examples come to mind. The decision by Arab countries to provide political support and arms to Palestinian refugees from Israel created within the Arab states a population capable of influencing their own foreign policies and internal politics. Palestinians, for example, became a political force within Lebanon in ways that subsequently made them political and security problems for Lebanon, Syria, Jordan, Israel, France and the United States. The support of Iraqi invaders by Palestinians in Kuwait was an asset to Iraq since Palestinians (who number 400,000 in Kuwait) hold important positions in the Kuwaiti administration. Throughout the Middle East governments must consider the capacity of the Palestinians to undermine their regimes should they adopt policies that are unacceptable. Similarly, the arming of Afghan refugees in Pakistan limited the options available to the government of Pakistan in its dealings with the governments of Afghanistan and the Soviet Union. The Pakistan government armed the Afghans in order to pressure the Soviets to withdraw their forces and to agree to a political settlement, but the Pakistan government is also constrained by the knowledge that it cannot sign an agreement with the Soviet or Afghan governments that is unacceptable to the armed Afghan.

Refugees have launched terrorist attacks within their host country, illegally smuggled arms, allied with the opposition against host government policies, participated in drug traffic, and in other ways eroded a government's willingness to admit refugees. Palestinians, Sikhs, Croatians, Kurds, Armenians, Sri Lankan Tamils, and northern Irish, among others, are regarded with suspicion by intelligence and police authorities and their request for asylum is scrutinized not only for whether they have a well-founded fear of persecution; but for whether their presence constitutes a threat to the host country. . . .

Migrants Perceived as a Threat to Cultural Identity

Cultures differ with respect to how they define who belongs to or can be admitted into their community. These norms govern whom one admits, what rights and privileges are given to those who are permitted to enter, and whether the host culture regards a migrant community as potential citizens. A violation of these norms (by unwanted immigrants, for example) is often regarded as a threat to basic values and in that sense is perceived as a threat to national security.

These norms are often embedded in the law of citizenship, that is who by virtue of birth is entitled as a matter of right to be a citizen and who is permitted to become a naturalized citizen. The familiar distinction is between the concept of *jus sanguinis,* whereby a person wherever born is a citizen of the state of his parents, and *jus soli,* the rule that a child receives its nationality from the soil or place of birth. The ties of blood descent are broader than merely parentage for they suggest a broader "volk" or people to whom one belongs in a kind of fictive relationship. The Federal Republic of Germany has such a legal norm. Under a law passed in 1913—and still valid—German citizenship at birth is based exclusively on descent; thus the children of migrants born in Germany are not thereby entitled to citizenship. The Basic Law, as it is called, also accords citizenship to those Germans who no longer live in Germany and may no longer speak German but came (or their ancestors came) from the territories from which Germans were expelled after the war. Thus, thousands of immigrants who entered the Federal Republic from East Germany or from Poland were regarded as German citizens returning "home." Other countries share a similar conception. Israel, for example, has a Law of Return, under which all Jews, irrespective of where they presently live, are entitled to "return" home to reclaim, as it were, their citizenship. Nepal also has a law which entitles those who are of Nepali "origin," though they have lived in India, Singapore, Hong Kong or elsewhere for several generations, to reclaim their citizenship by returning home. . . .

A norm of indigenousness may also be widely shared by a section of a country's population and even incorporated into its legal system. This norm prescribes differential rights between those who are classified as indigenous and those who, irrespective of the length of time they or their ancestors resided in the country, are not so classified. An indigenous people assert a superior claim to land, employment, education, political power, and to the central national symbols not accorded to others who live within the country. The indigenous—called *bhoomiputras* in Malaysia, sons of the soil in India, and native peoples in some societies—may assert an exclusiveness denied to others, often resting on the notion that they as a people exist only within one country, while others have other homes to which they can return. Thus, the Sinhalese in Sri Lanka, the Malays in Malaysia, the Assamese in Assam, and the Melanesians in Fiji, among others, subscribe to an ideology of indigenousness which has, in various guises, been enshrined in the legal system and which shapes the response of these societies to immigrants. The *bhoomiputras* in Malaysia regarded the influx of Chinese and others from Vietnam as a fundamental threat, indeed so threatening as to lead the government to sink Vietnamese boats carrying refugees. Similarly, the Assamese rejected the influx of Bengalis, Nepalis and Marwaris from the other parts of India (as well as immigrants from Bangladesh), fearing that any demographic change would threaten their capacity to maintain the existing legal arrangement under which native Assamese are provided opportunities in education and employment not accorded other residents of the state who are also citizens of India.

Nativism, a variant of the norm of indigenousness, played an important role in shaping the U.S. Immigration Act of 1924 with its national origins clause providing for national quotas. This legislation, and the political sentiment that underlay it, resulted in a restrictive policy toward refugees throughout the 1930s and early 1940s. After the war, however, the older American tradition of civic pluralism was politically triumphant. It shaped the 1965 Immigration Act which eliminated national quotas and gave preferences to individuals with skills and to family unification. The numbers and composition of migrants then significantly changed. From the mid 1960s to the later 1980s between five hundred thousand and one million migrants and refugees entered each year, with nearly half the immigrants coming from Asia.

Citizenship in the United States is acquired by birth or by naturalization. Originally, American law permitted naturalization only to "free white persons," but subsequent acts permitted naturalization to all irrespective of race. Apart from the usual residence requirements, U.S. naturalization law requires applicants to demonstrate their knowledge of the American Constitution and form of government and to swear allegiance to the principles of the U.S. Constitution. Political knowledge and loyalty are thus the norms for membership, not consanguinity. It is in part because the United States has political rather than ethnic criteria for naturalization that the United States has been more supportive of immigration and in the main has felt less threatened by immigration than most other countries.

For much of its history a low level of threat perception has also characterized the French response to immigration. While a concern for cultural unity is a central element in the French conception of nationhood, the French have also had a political conception of citizenship derived from the revolutionary origins of the notion of citizenship. The French, as Rogers Brubaker has written,[1] are universalist and assimilationist in contrast with the Volk-centered Germans. The result is that the French have been more willing to naturalize immigrants than have the Germans and more open to political refugees than most other West European countries. . . .

Legal definitions of citizenship aside, most societies react with alarm when there is an unregulated large-scale illegal migration of people who do not share the same culture and national identity. Examples abound. The people of India's northeastern state of Assam are fearful that the influx of Bangladeshis will reduce them to a minority, a realistic fear given the precarious hold of the Assamese on the state. Illegal migration into Sabah from the Philippines and Indonesia—an estimated 700,000 or half of Sabah's 1.4 million indigenous population—has created anxieties in that state of Malaysia. The government of Malaysia is particularly uneasy since the Philippines lays claim to Sabah and some of its leaders insist that so long as the dispute continues Malaysia has no right to consider Filipinos as illegal aliens. Should the Filipinos acquire citizenship, it has been noted, they might win a third or more of Sabah's parliamentary seats and pursue a merger with the Philippines. The Philippines might thereby acquire through colonization what it is unable to win through diplomatic or military means.

Concern over colonization, it should be noted, can also be an internal affair in multi-ethnic societies. A central government may regard internal migration as a right of all citizens, but territorially based ethnic groups may regard an influx of people from other parts of the country as a cultural and political threat. Hence, the Moros in Mindanao revolted at the in-migration of people from other parts of the Philippines, Sri Lanka's Tamils oppose settlement by Sinhalese in "their" region, and a variety of India's linguistic communities regard in-migration as a form of colonization.

Colonization as a means of international conquest and annexation can in fact be the deliberate intent of a state. The government of Morocco, for example, moved 350,000 civilians into Western Sahara in an effort to claim and occupy disputed territory. The Israeli government provides housing subsidies to its citizens to settle on the West Bank. Since the annexation of the Turkic regions of central Asia in the 19th century the Czarist and Soviet regimes have encouraged Russian settlement while a similar policy of settling Han people has been pursued by the Chinese government in Sinkiang province.

---

[1]Brubaker, William Rogers, editor, *Immigration and the Politics of Citizenship in Europe and North America,* Lanham, MD: University Press of America, 1989.

Migrants Perceived as a Social or Economic Burden

Ethnicity aside, societies may react to immigrants because of their social behavior—criminality, welfare dependency, delinquency, etc.—or simply because their numbers are so large (or so poor) that they place a substantial economic burden on society even if the migrants are of the same ethnic community as that of the host society. This sense of threat can be particularly acute if the government of the sending country appears to be engaged in a policy of population "dumping" by exporting its criminals, unwanted ethnic minorities, and "surplus" population at the cost of the receiving country. The United States, for example, distinguished between those Cubans who fled the Communist regime and Cuban convicts removed from prisons and placed on boats for the United States. India accepted Hindus from Pakistan in the late 1940s and early 1950s who preferred to live in India, but regarded as destabilizing and threatening the forced exodus of East Pakistanis in the early 1970s, which India saw as a Pakistan effort to change the demographic balance between East and West Pakistan at India's expense. Governments also distinguished between situations in which ethnic minorities are permitted to leave (e.g., Jews from the Soviet Union) and situations in which minorities are forced to flee (e.g., Bulgarian Turks and Sri Lankan Tamils).

In the eighteenth and nineteenth centuries several European governments promoted emigration as a way of easing the social and political burdens that might result from poverty and crime. In the latter part of the eighteenth century the British exported prisoners to Australia. It has been estimated[2] that between 1788 and 1868 England exiled 160,000 of its criminals to Australia as a convenient way to get rid of prisoners and reduce the costs of maintaining prisons. In the middle of the nineteenth century the British regarded emigration as a form of famine relief for Ireland. In seven famine years, from 1849 to 1856, one and a half million Irish emigrated, mostly across the Atlantic.[3] In Germany, where 1,500,000 emigrated between 1871 and 1881, local officials believed that "a large body of indigent subjects constitute a social danger and a serious burden on meager public funds; better let them go."[4] Reacting to these policies one American scholar wrote in 1890 that "there is something almost revolting in the anxiety of certain countries to get rid of their surplus population and to escape the burden of supporting the poor, the helpless and the depraved."[5]

The fears of western countries notwithstanding, population dumping has not been a significant element in the flow of migrants from the third world to advanced industrial countries. To the extent that population dumping has occurred, it has largely been of ethnic minorities and the flight has been primarily to neighboring developing countries rather than to advanced industrial countries.

---

[2]Hughes, Robert, *The Fatal Shore,* 1987.

[3]Jonston, H.J.M., *British Emigration Policy 1815–1830, Shovelling out Paupers.* Oxford: Clarendon Press, 1972.

[4]Walker, Mack, *Germany and the Emigration 1860–1885.* Cambridge: Harvard University Press, 1964.

[5]Mayo-Smith, Richard, *Emigration and Immigration: A Study in Social Science.* New York: Charles Scribner and Sons, 1890. Reprinted 1968, pp. 197–198.

Forced population movements of ethnic minorities took place in eastern Europe during the interwar period, placing enormous economic and social strains upon the receiving countries, taking a heavy toll upon the migrants themselves, and worsening relations among states. But because there was an element of exchange, and minorities moved to states in which their ethnic community was a majority, settlement was possible and violent international conflict was avoided. In 1922–23 Greeks fled Turkey and Turks fled Greece. An estimated 1.5 million people from both nations were involved. In a different though related population exchange, the Greek government in 1923, in an effort to Hellenize its Macedonian region, forced the exodus of its Bulgarian population. As the Bulgarian refugees moved into Greek-speaking areas of Bulgaria, the local Greek population fled southward to Greece.[6] The world's largest population exchange was in South Asia where fourteen million people moved between India and Pakistan between 1947 and 1950. But since both countries respected the wishes of ethnic minorities in each country to settle in the country in which they constituted a majority, the exchange took place without a conflict between the two countries. Similarly, the forced exit of Jews from North Africa to Israel in the 1950s was not a source of international conflict since the refugees were welcomed by Israel. In contrast, however, the flight of Arabs from Israel in 1948 led to an interminable conflict between Israel and its Arab neighbors since the Arab states did not recognize the legitimacy of the new state.

Where one state promotes or compels emigration to a state that limits or prohibits entry, the situation is fraught with a high potential for armed conflict.[7] The flow of refugees from East Pakistan to northeastern India, from Vietnam, Cambodia, and Laos to Thailand, from Burma to Bangladesh, and from Bangladesh to India has been the basis for regional conflicts that have often become violent. The magnitude of the flows, the element of forced emigration, the social and economic burden on the receiving country, a history of enmity between sending and receiving countries, the absence of a population exchange that might ease the land problem are all elements making these movements major inter-state crises. . . .

Migrants as Hostages: Risks for the Sending Country

Following the invasion of Kuwait on August 2, 1990, the government of Iraq announced a series of measures in which migrants were used as instruments for the achievement of political objectives. The first measure was to declare that westerners living in Iraq and Kuwait would be forcibly held as a shield against armed attack in an effort to deter the United States and its allies from launching airstrikes against military facilities where hostages might be located. The Iraqi government then made distinctions among Asian

---

[6]Marrus, Michael R., *The Unwanted: European Refugees in the Twentieth Century.* New York: Oxford University Press, 1985.

[7]For an analysis of how conflicting rules of exit and entry affect interstate relations, see Weiner, Myron, "International Migration and International Relations," *Population and Development Review,* II (3), 1985, 441–456.

migrants, indicating its willingness to treat more favorably those countries (such as India) which did not send troops to Saudi Arabia than those countries (Pakistan and Bangladesh) that did. The Iraqi government subsequently declared that food would not be provided for Asian migrants (including Indians) unless their countries sent food supplies and medicines, thereby weakening the United Nations embargo.

While the Iraqi strategy of using their control over migrants for international bargaining is unique, it should be noted that the mere presence of migrants in a country from which they could be expelled has been for some time an element in the behavior of the migrants' home country. The countries of South Asia have long been aware of their dependence upon migration to the Gulf and have recognized that any sudden influx of returning migrants would create a major problem for domestic security as remittances came to an end, balance of payments problems were created, families dependent upon migrant income were threatened with destitution, and large numbers of people were thrown into labor markets where there already existed substantial unemployment. All these fears have now materialized. In the past, sending governments aware of these potential consequences have hesitated to criticize host governments for the treatment of migrant workers. When workers have been expelled for strikes and other agitational activities, the home governments have sought to pacify their migrants—and the host government—in an effort to avoid further expulsions. Governments have often remained silent even when workers' contracts have been violated. Thus, the instinctive and understandable reaction of some governments with migrants in Kuwait and Iraq was to see first whether it was possible for their migrants to remain, and to assure the security of their citizens rather than to support international efforts against Iraqi aggression. . . .

IMPLICATIONS FOR IMMIGRATION AND REFUGEE POLICIES

For the foreseeable future the numbers of people who wish to leave or are forced to leave their countries will continue to substantially exceed the numbers other countries are willing to accept. Indeed, for many reasons, the gap is likely to increase.

Democratization, or at least political liberalization of authoritarian regimes, is enabling some people to leave who previously were denied the right of exit. The removal of the Berlin wall resulted in an East German exodus although the government of the German Democratic Republic had hoped that by removing the wall they might thereby induce their citizens to remain at home. Under glasnost the Soviet Union has permitted a substantial number of Jews to obtain exit permits. And given the economic and political difficulties the new regimes in Eastern Europe are likely to encounter, we should anticipate a steady and perhaps rising demand for exit.

The political liberalization of multi-ethnic communist regimes has been accompanied by a reappearance of older conflicts among ethnic groups. There have been conflicts between Turks and Bulgarians in Turkey, Romanians and Hungarians in Transylvania, Armenians and Azerbaijanis in the Caucasus, Albanians and Serbians in Kosovo, and a variety of ethnic conflicts in Central Asia. There is thus a high potential for emigration from the multiethnic regions of Eastern Europe and from the Soviet Union, especially from the Baltic states, the Caucasus, and Central Asia.

Africa's authoritarian regimes have had little success in preventing conflicts among tribal and ethnic groups, although they have often justified one party states and military rule as necessary for avoiding violent conflict. But even if democratization begins to take root in Africa as it has in Eastern Europe, it is uncertain that ethnic conflicts, and the refugee movements that often result, will thereby decline. Indeed, the political transformations now under way in South Africa could result in increased conflicts as each of the various groups contends for control of the political system. Thus, struggles are already under way between Zulu supporters of Inkatha and Zulu supporters of the United Democratic Front in Natal, and among a variety of ethnic groups throughout the country.

A long-term decline in the birth rate in advanced industrial countries combined with continued economic growth is likely to lead employers to seek low-wage laborers from abroad. Transnational investment in manufacturing industries may reduce some of the manpower needs, but the demand for more workers in the service sector seems likely to grow, barring technological breakthroughs that will replace waiters, bus conductors, nurses, and household help. Employers in Japan, Singapore, and portions of the United States and Western Europe are prepared to hire illegal migrants, notwithstanding the objections of their governments and much of the citizenry. So long as employer demand remains high, borders are porous, and government enforcement of employer sanctions is limited, illegal migration seems likely to continue and in some countries increase. . . .

However many immigrants are admitted the numbers who want to enter will far exceed how many migrants countries are prepared to admit. Sealing borders is one response, but rarely wholly effective even in the case of islands. Control is difficult for any country with large coastlines or land borders. State regulation of employers (including penalties for employing illegals) and the use of identity cards has made a difference in the countries of Western Europe but is not an option readily usable for a country with large numbers of small firms, a poorly developed administrative structure, and officials who are easily corrupted. Moreover, however opposed the government and a majority of the population are to illegal migration, there are often elements within the society who welcome refugees and migrant workers: employers, ethnic kinfolk, political sympathizers, and officials willing to accept bribes.

Faced with unwanted flows whose entrance they cannot control, governments have increasingly turned to strategies for halting *emigration*. We can identify three such strategies.

The first is to pay for what one does not want. It has been suggested that an infusion of aid and investment, an improvement in trade, the resolution of the debt crisis and other measures that would improve income and unemployment in low income countries would reduce the rate of emigration. Meritorious as these proposals are there is no evidence that they can reduce emigration, at least not in the short run. Indeed, high rates of emigration have often been associated with high economic growth rates. It was so for Great Britain in the 19th century, and in recent years for South Korea, Taiwan, Turkey, Algeria and Greece. Moreover, economic aid is unlikely to affect the political factors which induce people to leave. Nonetheless, under some circumstances, economic assistance can reduce unwanted migrations, but primarily when the sending country has the means to prevent people from leaving. As noted earlier, U.S. economic assistance to Haiti halted a growing refugee flow; similarly, the flow of Sri Lankan refugees to West Germany from East Germany was reduced when the Federal Republic of Germany agreed to provide credits to the German Democratic Republic. In the Haitian case, government-to-government aid was intended by the donor country to persuade the recipient country to halt the exodus; in the German case, the aid was intended to persuade the recipient country to cease providing transit to unwanted refugees.

Assistance can also be used by governments to persuade other governments to retain their refugees. Thus, the United States and France have been willing to provide economic assistance to Thailand if the Thais would hold Vietnamese refugees rather than permit these refugees to seek entrance into the U.S. and France. The UNHCR [United Nations High Commission on Refugees] and other largely western-financed international agencies provide resources to refuge-receiving countries—especially in Africa—not only as an expression of Western humanitarian concerns, but also as a means of enabling refugees to remain in the country of first asylum rather than attempting to move elsewhere, especially to advanced industrial countries.

Secondly, where generosity does not work or is not financially feasible, receiving countries may employ a variety of threats to halt emigration. Diplomatic pressures may be exerted. The Indian government, for example, put the pressure on the government of Bangladesh to halt Bangladeshi land settlement in the Chittagong Hill tracts after land settlement led the local Chakma tribals to flee into India. The Indian government is in a position to damage Bangladesh trade and to affect the flow of river waters if the government is not accommodating. Where diplomatic means are not sufficient, the threat of force can be employed. When Muslim refugees moved from Burma into Bangladesh as a result of a similar policy of colonization, this time by the Burmese, the Bangladesh government threatened to arm the Burmese Muslim refugees if the colonization did not end. In both cases the threats worked to reduce or halt the flow. In another example, Palestinian supporters threatened international carriers who agreed to carry Jews emigrating from the Soviet Union to Israel, an instance of intervention by a third party which did not want an unimpeded flow between a sending and receiving country. The Arab League representative to the United Nations said that the influx of Soviet Jews into Israel could constitute a threat to international peace and security under the UN charter.[8]

Thirdly, there is the ultimate sanction of armed intervention to change the political conditions within the sending country. In 1971 an estimated ten million refugees fled from East Pakistan to India following the outbreak of a civil war between the eastern and western provinces of Pakistan. This refugee flow was regarded by India as the result of a deliberate policy by the Pakistan military to resolve Pakistan's own internal political problems by forcing upon India East Pakistan's Hindu population. Many Indian officials also believed that the Pakistan government was seeking to change the demographic balance between East and West Pakistan by shifting millions of East Pakistanis to India. The Indian government responded by sending its armed forces into Pakistan, occupied East Pakistan and thereby forced the partition of the country. Within months India moved the refugees home.

---

[8]*New York Times,* February 8, 1990.

There were two other instances in South Asia where armed support for refugees was an instrument of policy by the receiving country. The Pakistan government armed a portion of the 3.7 million Afghan refugees who entered Pakistan following a communist coup in April 1978 and the subsequent Soviet invasion in December 1979. The aim of the Pakistan government was to arm the Afghans to force a Soviet withdrawal, to bring down the Soviet-supported Communist regime, and to repatriate the refugees. . . . The other instance of intervention was the initial Indian support for the Tamil Tigers, a militant group fighting against the Sri Lankan government. The Indian government supported Tamil Tiger refugees in India and enabled arms to flow into Sri Lanka in an effort to force a political settlement between the Tamils and the Sri Lankan government, but the result was that the ethnic conflict worsened and the refugee exodus continued, a factor which led to subsequent direct intervention by the Indian military. . . .

While the notion of sovereignty is still rhetorically recognized, a variety of internal actions by states are increasingly regarded as threats to others. Thus, the spewing of nuclear waste and other hazardous materials into the atmosphere and the contamination of waterways which then flow into other countries is no longer regarded as an internal matter. In the same spirit a country which forces its citizens to leave or creates conditions which induce them to leave has internationalized its internal actions.

A conundrum for liberal democratic regimes, however, is that they are reluctant to insist that governments restrain the exit of citizens simply because they or others are unwilling to accept them. Liberal democracies believe in the right of emigration by individuals but they simultaneously believe that governments retain the right to determine who and how many shall be permitted to enter. Liberal regimes may encourage or even threaten countries that produce refugees and unwanted immigrants to change the conditions which induce or force people to leave, but they are reluctant to press governments to prevent people from leaving or to force people to return home against their will. They do not want regimes to prevent political dissidents or persecuted minorities from leaving their country; rather, they want governments to stop their repression. Mass flight across international boundaries justifies actions by states or international organizations to provide incentives, inducements, withdrawal of assistance, or a variety of individual or collective sanctions (e.g., trade or investment restrictions) to change the conditions which create flight. . . .

For advanced industrial countries that admit immigrants there is a preference for a migration policy which creates the fewest domestic or international political problems. One policy option is to admit those who best satisfy the requirements of the receiving country: who have skills needed in the labor market, or capital to create new businesses, or relatives who would facilitate their integration into the society. The criteria for admission then become more meritocratic based upon an agreed upon point system.[9] It is more difficult, and morally contentious, to give preferences to those most acceptable by the home population, though "acceptable" can often mean education and skills rather than culture and race. Moreover, for a labor-short Western Europe, the

---

[9]Wattenberg, Ben J. and Karl Zinsmeister, "The Case for More Immigration," *Commentary*, 89 (4), 1990, 19–25, and Simon, Julian L., *The Economic Consequences of Immigration*, New York: Basil Blackwell, 1989.

incorporation of countries of Central and Eastern Europe into the European Community will be politically more palatable than opening borders to north Africans without raising awkward issues of culture and religion. But a limited, largely skill-based immigration policy will leave large numbers of people banging on the doors, seeking to enter as refugees or, failing that, as illegals.

An alternative policy based upon the needs of immigrants and refugees is more difficult to formulate, more difficult to implement, and legally and politically more contentious, but morally more attractive. But no policy, short of the obliteration of international boundaries and sovereign states, can deal with the vast numbers of people who want to leave their country for another where opportunities are greater. A moral case can be made for giving preference to those in flight, even at the cost of limiting the number of immigrants admitted to meet labor force needs or to enable families to reunite. If countries have a ceiling as to how many people they are willing to admit, there is a strong moral argument for providing admissions first to those who are persecuted or whose lives are in danger, and have few places to go. But for reasons indicated earlier only a narrow definition of what constitutes a refugee with a case-by-case review will enable states to put a cap on what they regard as potentially unlimited flows. We thus conclude with a paradoxical formulation, the large-scale unwanted mass population flows that threaten states require that states, individually or collectively through international organizations, seek ways to influence the domestic factors that force and induce people to leave their homeland, even though such interventions may themselves create international conflicts.

THE WAR OVER WATER

John K. Cooley

"Water is not necessary to life but rather life itself," the French poet and aviator Antoine de Saint Exupéry wrote on the basis of his vast experience in arid countries. His observation highlights a fundamental of Middle East politics that has lately been forgotten by nearly everyone except Israel and its Arab neighbors. Indeed, long after oil runs out, water is likely to cause wars, cement peace, and make and break empires and alliances in the region, as it has for thousands of years.

The constant struggle for the waters of the Jordan, Litani, Orontes, Yarmuk, and other life-giving Middle East rivers, little understood outside the region, was a principal cause of the 1967 Arab-Israeli war and could help spark a new all-out conflict. It is also a major aspect of the Palestinian question and of the struggle over the future of the West Bank. Since 1947 many an attempt has been made to write peace documents or draw new cease-fire agreements between Israel and its neighbors. Each time, the water question has helped to block agreement. While the need for a rational, overall water-sharing scheme steadily grows more apparent, it seems less attainable, as water issues are aggravated by political tensions and by the fact that, while its neighbors' consumptions are rapidly rising, Israel still consumes roughly five times as much water per capita as each of its less industrialized and less intensively farmed neighbors.

In 1967 Israel went to war against Syria and Syria's ally, Egypt, partly because the Arabs had unsuccessfully tried to divert into Arab rivers Jordan River headwaters that feed Israel. During that war Israel captured Syria's Baniyas River, the last of the important Jordan headwaters not under Israel's control. Israel also succeeded in destroying the foundations and thus halting construction of a giant new dam at Mukheiba on the Yarmuk River, which runs toward Israel between Jordan and Syria. This dam, still desired by Amman and enjoying American and World Bank (International Bank for Reconstruction and Development) backing, would have greatly augmented the water available to pre-1967 Jordan, including the West Bank, but might have deprived Israel of water supplies its planners coveted.

Today the threat of a war stems primarily from Israel's occupation of southern Lebanon. Launched ostensibly to drive out the Palestinian fighters, Israel's June 1982 invasion of Lebanon gave the Jewish state control of the lower reaches of a new river—Lebanon's Litani. The Litani has never flowed into Israel, and the invasion strengthened long-held Arab convictions that capturing its waters and diverting them into Israel has been an important long-term Israeli goal. Official Israeli government silence on the issue and continued expressions of interest in the Litani by Israeli hawks, such as former

John K. Cooley, "The War Over Water," *Foreign Policy* No. 54 (spring 1984). Copyright © 1984 by the Carnegie Endowment for International Peace. Reprinted with permission.

Defense Minister Ariel Sharon and Technology Minister Yuval Neeman, only serve to fuel Arab fears.

Meanwhile, as early as May 1983, Syrian officials informed the Lebanese government of President Amin Gemayel that Syrian troops would not leave Lebanon until Damascus had obtained, as part of an overall accord protecting Syrian interests in Lebanon, an ironbound water agreement. Syria wanted absolute guarantees that head-waters of the Orontes River, which rises in Lebanon's fertile Bekaa Valley, would never be seized by hostile forces. The Orontes irrigates much of Syria's best farm land and provides both drinking water and electric power for western Syria, the country's most populous region.

Meanwhile, the major project Israel has proposed to solve some of its own water and hydroelectric power problems poses some potentially serious difficulties for another neighbor, Jordan. This project, known as the Med-Dead Canal, would be a salt-water conduit linking the Mediterranean Sea near Gaza with the saline Dead Sea. The canal would use the drop of about 1,300 feet as the water flows east into the Dead Sea basin to drive electric turbines. Practical designs for the canal were drawn up by James Hayes and Joseph Cotton, American water consultants to the Water Planning Authority of Israel. At that time, Israeli Finance Minister Pinhas Sapir said the canal would "compensate the Dead Sea for the diversion of the Jordan River into the [Israeli] diversion system."

Yet the project has alarmed the Arab states, especially Jordan. They have studied delaying or halting the scheme. Specifically, Jordan fears that the rise in the level of the Dead Sea caused by the influx of Mediterranean water will destroy the phosphate extraction and other chemical industries Amman has built on its own side of the Dead Sea, opposite Israel's chemical and nuclear complexes at Arad and Dimona. This fear was heightened by the confirming findings of a 1981 Israeli parliamentary commission report. Jordanians have also feared for the last two generations that the Med-Dead Canal would ruin Jordan's already well-advanced plans for reclaiming for Jordanian agriculture much of the salt-saturated Wadi Araba region southeast of the Dead Sea and pollute much of the still-fresh waters of the Jordan Valley's streams and aquifers. Israel's economic planning already takes these effects into account; Jordan's economy would need to make costly adjustments.

RAINFALL AND POLITICS

The Middle East's problems of water and agriculture stem fundamentally from its climate, not from politics. Seasonal temperature variations are wide and rainfall is highly irregular. On the whole the region simply does not receive enough rainfall to support even subsistence agriculture without extensive irrigation. The scarcity of water has weighed upon the region's life since prehistoric times.

Permanent farms require at least eight inches of water a year—enough to sustain the grass needed to raise sheep, goats, donkeys, and camels. Somewhat more rainfall is needed to grow most vegetables and fruits. Wherever rainfall reaches these levels, villages and towns can be built. And where water supplies are supplemented by rivers and wells, cities such as Alexandria, Baghdad, Damascus, and Tehran have been able to grow. Inadequate or excessively erratic rainfall forces people to stay on the move and live as herdsmen or migrant farmers—like those of the American dust bowl of the 1930s. They seek the oases: islands in the desert where spring water or cisterns can be found. And if a season passes without restorative rain, desertification sets in. Indeed, Arab literature is filled with delighted, sensitive accounts of the coming of rain, a momentous event, and the Arabic language has a special verb—*shama*—that means "to watch for lightning flashes to see where rain will fall."

Despite all the talk of "making the desert bloom," cultivated land still represents no more than 5–7.5 per cent of the Middle East. The rest is mainly desert, mountain, or swamp. Yet a large percentage of the region's population—including a majority in Syria—depends directly on agriculture for its livelihood. Many others work as cotton and tobacco packers, fruit driers, or canners of vegetables, fruit, or olive oil. Paradoxically, however, agriculture represents less than half the gross national product of Egypt, Israel, Jordan, Lebanon, and Syria. Thus for most Middle Eastern countries food production for domestic consumption or export remains the least successful aspect of national economic development.

The Middle East's water problems are regional, deriving from common sources, and cannot be regarded solely as an Arab-Israeli problem. In fact, the Arab states have quarreled among themselves about water. But the water problem's Arab-Israeli dimension is vitally important and is rooted in Israel's original diversion of Jordan River waters after 1948. Since the Palestinian Arabs displaced during the Israeli war of independence and their Arab supporters considered the Israeli state to be illegitimate, they persistently decried the unilateral diversion of the Jordan as completely illegal and utterly nefarious. The Israelis responded that the surrounding Arabs were never willing to let Israel live in peace, that most remained in a state of war with Israel, and that Israel never intended to deprive Arab neighbors of water they needed.

The Jordan River rises in the hills and mountains that make up the Anti-Lebanon range in eastern Lebanon. As the Jordan flows south through the beginning of the Great Rift Valley, it is fed from underground sources and an intricate network of smaller rivers, rivulets, and streams at various points in Jordan, Israel, Syria, and Lebanon. The Jordan continues southward into the middle of the Jordan Valley, forming the border between East Jordan and Israeli-occupied West Jordan (Judaea and Samaria, in official Israeli parlance). The Jordan's main sources are the Hasbani River, which flows from Lebanon into Israel; the Yarmuk River, which rises near the Golan Heights and flows downward between Jordan and the Golan Heights; the Baniyas River, which also originates in Syria; and the Dan River, which rises and flows inside Israel.

The Litani flows entirely inside Lebanon. From its source in the north-central region of the country, it runs south through Lake Qir'awn to a point below steep cliffs where the 11th-century Crusader castle of Beaufort guards the Lebanese-Israeli frontier. The river then makes a sharp right turn in the gorges beneath Beaufort and empties into the Mediterranean. Along the way, it irrigates Lebanon's lush Bekaa Valley and many of the orchards, California-style truck farms, and tobacco fields of Lebanon's southwest.

As World War II still raged, the problem of accommodating the needs of the native Palestinian Jews and Arabs and the hundreds of thousands of new European Jewish immigrants crowding into Palestine became acute. Zionist leaders argued that exploiting the Jordan Valley's untapped water, electric power, and agricultural resources held the key to a peaceful future. One such scheme was proposed in 1944 by Walter Clay Lowdermilk, an American water engineer, in his book *Palestine: Land of Promise.* After extensive studies conducted in Palestine for the U.S. Department of Agriculture, Lowdermilk proposed using the waters of the Jordan, Yarmuk, Baniyas, Hasbani, Dan, and Zarqa (a river in East Jordan) in a comprehensive plan to irrigate the Jordan Valley, much of northern Galilee, and northern Palestine. Lowdermilk and other succeeding American consultants also suggested diverting the Litani in southern Lebanon to form an artificial lake in northern Palestine whose waters would be pumped southward to irrigate the Negev Desert. And Lowdermilk proposed an early version of the Med-Dead Canal as well.

The Arab-Israeli wars of 1947–1948, which surrounded Israel's creation, vastly complicated the task of those who sought a regional water solution. In particular, none of them could have foreseen that 420,000 Palestinian Arabs would flee eastward, to settle on either the Jordan River's West Bank, which Amman would soon annex, or on the East Bank, in Jordan proper.

The new state of Israel came to rely for most of its water on the diversion of between 50 and 75 percent of the Jordan River's flow, depending on whether one accepts Israeli or Arab figures. Israel's main diversion project is the National Water Carrier, a large conduit capable of channeling 11 billion cubic feet annually from the Sea of Galilee (Lake Tiberias) to Rosh Haayin, near Tel Aviv. To carry water from the Jordan and its headwaters as far as the Negev Desert, pipeline and canal systems such as the Yarkon-Negev project were built. These new waterways permitted cultivation of some additional desert land. But more important, they enabled Israelis to recultivate, by more intensive farming methods such as drip irrigation, the areas from which the Palestinian Arabs had fled.

According to early Israeli statistics, cultivated land increased from 400,000 acres in Israel's first full crop year, 1948–1949, to more than 1.1 million acres in 1977–1978, about 500,000 acres of which are irrigated. Since Operation Litani in 1978, Israel's first major invasion of southern Lebanon, which was intended to drive the forces of the Palestine Liberation Organization (PLO) back across the Litani, the Israeli government has not published full water and cultivation figures. The country's total 1980 water consumption, however, was authoritatively estimated at 64 billion cubic feet, of which about 42 billion cubic feet are used in agriculture.

It is impossible to say how much of this water Israel's less developed neighbors might have used in the past or could use in the future. What is certain is that all of the water development plans of the region's countries depend on tapping the region's rivers. Not surprisingly, to the Arabs in the 1950s the National Water Carrier became a symbol of Israel's aggressive expansionism. As early as 1953, Syrian artillery units opened fire on the construction and engineering sites behind the town and lake of Tiberias, forcing the Israelis to move the main pumping station.

The incident helped convince the United States that the water dispute both reflected and aggravated the political conflict sparked by the exodus of the Palestinian Arabs. President Dwight Eisenhower appointed motion-picture magnate Eric Johnston to perform the herculean labor of negotiating regional watersharing arrangements. Johnston presented a series of proposals based largely on the work of Charles T. Main, Inc., a Boston, Massachusetts, consulting firm. A fundamental tenet of international law underlay these proposals: Water within one catchment area should not be diverted outside that area—regardless of political boundaries—until all needs of those within the catchment area are satisfied. Since it was already clear that nothing would deter Israel from sending Jordan River water as far as the Negev Desert, U.S. negotiators focused on other ways of meeting the needs of both Arabs and Israelis in the catchment areas of Galilee, southern Lebanon, and western Syria.

The Johnston proposals began with a series of dams on the Hasbani, Baniyas, and Dan rivers in Lebanon, Syria, and Israel, which would feed a canal to water Galilee farm land. The Huleh swamps were to be drained, a project soon carried out by Israel. A high dam was to be built on the Yarmuk River, a project still in abeyance. Finally, smaller works were called for to irrigate both sides of the Jordan Valley. One of these projects was Jordan's East Ghor Canal, eventually built mainly with U.S. foreign assistance.

The American planners thought that the Johnston proposals would preserve the catchment area principle. Indeed, the Israeli National Water Carrier was not yet complete. The proposals allotted Syria 1.6 billion cubic feet of water a year; Jordan, 27.3 billion; and Israel, 13.9 billion. But all three states objected to the scheme. The Arab states wanted larger shares, especially for Syria. They also insisted on an international board to supervise the allocation of regional water resources. Israel, too, wanted much more water and rejected giving a board containing Arab members any control over Israeli water supplies. A major Israeli counterproposal was prepared by Cotton in 1954. It differed from the Johnston proposals primarily by reviving the idea of diverting Lebanon's Litani River into Israel.

Notwithstanding these changes favored by Israel, the original Johnston proposals seemed, at times, to be drawing Israel and the Arab states toward a technical accord on sharing water resources that might have paved the way to wider political agreements. President Gamal Abdel Nasser of Egypt became actively involved in the process because Johnston submitted another set of proposals designed to deal with the Arab-Israeli conflict and the Palestinian problem simultaneously. Along with U.N. officials, Johnston envisaged using a canal from the Nile River to irrigate the western Sinai Desert and resettling some of the 2 million Palestinian Arab refugees in the one-time wasteland.

When the late Egyptian President Anwar el-Sadat revived this idea after his historic 1977 trip to Jerusalem, his seemingly cavalier treatment of the country's most precious natural resource outraged many Egyptians. Western interest in this concept revealed a total lack of understanding of the Palestinian problem. The refugees' concern was recovering their homes, farm lands, and jobs, not helping to make the Sinai Desert bloom. However, Egypt's involvement in the regional water controversy undoubtedly helped to spur its own grandiose projects for developing the Nile Valley—plans that centered around the highly political question of whether the Soviets or the Americans would build the high dam at Aswan.

The Egyptians also participated directly in the discussions on the Johnston proposals for the Israel-Jordan area: Johnston himself disclosed that Egypt was urging Jordan, Lebanon, and Syria to accept them. Indeed, then Egyptian Foreign Minister Mahmoud Riyad headed an Arab League committee set up to prepare a far-reaching, pan-Arab, regional water plan, which Nasser hoped that Israel would have no choice but to accept. According to his diaries, throughout the early 1950s dovish Israeli Prime Minister Moshe Sharett favored working with the American proposals and discussed a number of water plans with his cabinet, including the Litani diversion. Sharett also sought ways to open both public and secret conversations with Nasser.

Riyad, however, insisted that Israel's inclusion of the Litani River ruined any hopes of a regional agreement, since the project would doom Lebanon's hopes for developing its underdeveloped south and sully Arab honor. By the time Israeli leaders told Washington in early 1955 that they would drop the Litani idea, political tensions were rising for other reasons. Israel had responded to the beginning of guerrilla attacks from Gaza with a massive raid on the area: Nasser had decided to buy Soviet arms through Czechoslovakia; and the West had organized friendly regimes in Iraq, Jordan, and Turkey into the Baghdad Pact. There was talk of an Arab water diversion project that would pump the Hasbani River in Lebanon into the Litani, to prevent any of the Hasbani from watering Israel.

At this point, Sharett left the Israeli government. Doves began to vanish from the Mideast scene. Hawks moved into the ascendant, and Nasser's mood became more defiant. In July 1956 the United States refused to finance the Aswan High Dam, which the Soviets then took over as their showcase project in the Arab world. Nasser dropped the Johnston proposals and all of their offshoots, consigning the mission to history.

WATER AND THE PLO

Arab-Israeli wars twice totally disrupted the economy and demography of Jordan, first in 1948, then again in 1967. The kingdom's annexation after the 1948 war of the 2,165 square miles of the West Bank, a rocky salient only partially suitable for irrigated cultivation, more than tripled its population, to 1.2 million. When Israel conquered the territory in 1967, about 300,000 of its inhabitants fled to unoccupied East Jordan. Today, about 1.9 million Arabs in the region are classified as refugees because their former homes or those of their parents were in Israel, Israeli-occupied territory, or pre-1948 Palestine.

Losing the West Bank in 1967 cost Jordan much of its foreign-exchange earning from tourism, which centered on East Jerusalem and the well-watered oasis region of Jericho; its grain production, which had helped to feed many of the Palestinians who had stayed on in their temporary or permanent homes in the West Bank; and worst of all, 80 per cent of its total fruit-growing and 45 per cent of its vegetable-growing land, both of which had become valuable sources of export revenues during the 1950s and 1960s.

Yet by 1948 it was already clear that the Arab refugees on both the East and the West Banks could subsist by their own efforts only if the Jordan's waters were augmented by waters from the Yarmuk River. The intensifying Arab-Israeli political conflict also made it clear that Jordan and Syria could not count on using water from the Sea of Galilee.

Enter Mills Bunger, a water expert on the U.S. Point Four aid team in Amman. In winter 1951, while flying over the Yarmuk River valley, Bunger spotted an intriguing basin he realized could be turned with the help of a dam into a natural reservoir to hold excess winter flood waters from converging rivers and streams. Soon, the U.S. and Jordanian governments and the U.N. Relief and Works Agency for Palestinian Refugees jointly planned a 480-foot high dam for the Yarmuk River at the site, named Maqarin, and allocated nearly $160 million for the venture. The dam was intended to store 18 billion cubic feet of water and feed canals that would water both the east and the west banks of the Jordan. A diversion dam would complete a system capable of irrigating both Jordanian and Syrian farm land without depending on Israel's Sea of Galilee.

To implement the Bunger plan, Syria and Jordan agreed in June 1953 on joint use of Yarmuk River water. But Israel, pushing to be included, laid claim to a share of the Yarmuk water. The Bunger plan quickly died, and the Syrians and Jordanians partially diverted the Yarmuk's flow for a brief time to irrigate farm lands in the eastern part of the Jordan Valley. The water controversy settled into a discouraging pattern for most of the decade. Local water projects went ahead, amid growing Arab anger over Israel's unilateral diversion of Jordan River waters and occasional military incidents that were sometimes raised in the U.N. Security Council.

But the Arabs also responded with their own diversion plans. As though to prove its Arab credentials, the Lebanese government showed an uncharacteristic zeal during the 1950s in attempting to thwart Israeli water plans. In 1959 the Arab League's technical committee called for boring a short tunnel to divert Lebanon's Hasbani River where it passed closest to the Litani, a place called Kaoukaba. Israel still takes this threat seriously. In 1982 Israeli invaders built a new road, a new bridge over the Litani, and a heavily fortified military camp, showing special vigilance over this area.

At this point, the water issue helped contribute to formation of the PLO. As long as the Israeli national water project was still under construction and Jordan River water was not actually flowing to the Negev Desert, Arab governments could oppose Israeli plans with safe rhetoric rather than potentially dangerous deeds. But Jordan's King Hussein and Nasser both realized the inherent threat they faced from the water problem. Action against the new Israeli water system might deprive Hussein, in the certain event of an Israeli counter-attack, of the West Bank (as it eventually did in 1967). Inaction could cost Nasser the claim to Arab leadership he had been so carefully carving out, following the embarrassing collapse in 1961 of his Egyptian-Syrian United Arab Republic after only three years. The Arab states needed a formula that would permit them to resist Israel's designs without provoking disastrous reprisals.

In January 1964 Arab representatives gathered in Cairo at Nasser's request for the first of a series of summit conferences to work out a joint strategy on water. Yet instead of fashioning a new water strategy, the conferees dumped the water issue and all the other Arab-Israeli political problems into the lap of the Palestinians. The Cairo conferees decided to create a "Palestinian entity" to mobilize the Palestinians themselves for the eventual "liberation of Palestine." The PLO became this entity's financial, political, and military expression. It was to be supported by all of the Arab participants in the summit meeting. But in 1964, when the ineffectiveness of the PLO's leadership and of its nascent "conventional" military arm, the Palestine Liberation Army, became apparent, Yasir Arafat decided to act. Arafat had already founded al-Fatah (the Palestine National Liberation Movement) in secret in 1959. In the groups' writings and indoctrination programs, Arafat and the other Fatah leaders laid great stress on Israel's usurpation of Arab land and water resources.

One of Arafat's closest associates, Dr. Nabil al-Shath, an American-trained engineer and business management specialist, told this writer in 1970, "The water issue was the crucial one. We considered our own impact on this to be the crucial test of our own war with Israel." Therefore, it was no accident that the first action of al-Assifa, Fatah's armed branch, was an unsuccessful attempt to sabotage the Israeli National Water Carrier on December 31, 1964.

Meanwhile, the Arab governments continued their own efforts to create an Arab counterdiversion project. Work aimed at diverting the Baniyas was begun on Syrian territory. But three times, in March and May 1965 and July 1966, the Israeli army and air force attacked the site. Nasser called another Arab summit meeting in Cairo, where he acknowledged that Arab states were unprepared to go to war with Israel and urged them to admit it and accept the consequences. Nasser evidently forgot his own advice in the months preceding the disastrous 1967 war.

The Syrian project and the Israeli attacks created what Harvard University political scientist Nadav Safran calls "a prolonged chain reaction of border violence that linked directly to the events that led to war" in June 1967. In that war Israel captured and bulldozed about 50 Syrian villages in the Golan Heights. The Israeli advance forced about 100,000 Syrians to flee eastward and become refugees in their own country. Victory enabled Israel not only to build a system of strategic Jewish settlements in the Golan but also to prevent the Baniyas diversion by capturing the site of its Golan Heights headwaters, a site that the Romans had garrisoned to protect their water supplies.

The Six-Day War led Mideast states to abandon finally regional water projects and focus on the resources within their own frontiers. For Israel, the central problem was husbanding its dwindling domestic supplies and efficiently using sources captured from Jordan and Syria. Water in the Arab farmers' wells in the West Bank became a key element in Israeli strategy to hold the West Bank, Golan Heights, and Gaza, as it has subsequently been in moves to annex and absorb them. Israeli journalists, military men, and water engineers have spoken and written often of the need to "protect Jewish water supplies from encroaching Arab water wells." Military government regulations now forbid West Bank Arabs from drilling new wells without special authorization, which is almost impossible to obtain. Many existing wells have been blocked or sealed by the occupation authorities, in some cases to prevent their use from draining nearby Jewish wells. Further, Arabs' access to water is determined by a rather restrictive consumption quota.

Israeli water experts explain that the ground water for northern and central Israel is supplied by two main aquifers. Both originate on the West Bank. They have apparently been augmented by another, originating from an underground lake, which extends beneath both banks of the Jordan.

Both of these aquifers drain westward toward the Mediterranean and are tapped by an elaborate system of wells along the coast between Haifa and Tel Aviv. Between these aquifers and the National Water Carrier, Israel draws its entire water consumption, although exact figures are closely guarded Israeli state secrets. Since 1967 the balanced functioning of the entire system has come to depend on a smooth, underground flow of water into Israel from the West Bank. The hydrological balance could be easily upset by interfering with the Hasbani, the Baniyas, the Dan, or the Yarmuk.

Keeping Tel Aviv, Haifa, and the other cities of the Israeli coastal plain from running dry depends on blocking Arab water development in the West Bank that could stop the aquifers' flow westward: hence the ban on Arab wells. Westward-flowing underground water also helps to stabilize pressure and prevent Mediterranean water from intruding into Israel's own coastal water wells. Some such saline pollution had befouled the Israeli coastal aquifers before the 1967 war and before the upper Jordan headwaters had been completely diverted.

The Golan Heights is as critical to Israeli water supplies as the West Bank's wells. About one-quarter of Israel's water is taken from the Sea of Galilee and channeled through the water carrier. Most of this water is used for consumption and industry in central and southern Israel. Syrian control of the Golan placed the upper Jordan basin's freshwater supplies beyond Israel's pre-emptive reach. Israel reversed this situation first by capturing the Golan Heights in 1967 and then by effectively annexing the region in 1981. Israeli leaders view maintaining access to this water largely as a military problem: Holding on to the territory is necessary to protect an intake system and pumping works embedded in rock cliffs just south of Kafer Nahum. The system can easily be hit by artillery on the Golan ridges overlooking the Sea of Galilee. . . .

Since the Israeli invasion, the old and well-known Israeli-American plans for diverting the Litani have placed several developments in a worrisome light in Lebanese eyes. For example, when they captured the dam and lake at Qir'awn in June 1982 after a short battle with the Syrians, the Israelis immediately seized all the hydrographic charts and technical documents relating to the Litani and its installation. The Israelis were openly augmenting the flow of the Hasbani across the frontier into Israel by laying surface pipes to catch the run-off and other water from the mountains and nearby springs.

Moreover, a watchful American military observer claims to have seen Israelis burying pipes deep in a hillside near Marj'Uyn after the Israeli incursion of 1978, indicating that the Israelis might be secretly siphoning water underground from the Marj Plain in southern Lebanon into Israel, without affecting the measured flow of the Litani. Such a diversion would tap the extensive underground aquifer, which is fed by seepage from both the Litani and the Hasbani rivers and by underground streams from the Mount Hermon region. The site where the pipes and pumping equipment seem to have been secretly buried is near a World War II airfield built by the British and repaved and extended in fall 1983 by the Israeli Defense Forces.

In interviews, Technology Minister Neeman, a brilliant physicist from the far-right Techiya Party who has vowed to work for the "sharing" of Litani water with Lebanon, freely acknowledged Israel's long interest in Litani water. And he confirmed that seismic sounding and surveys had been conducted at a spot on the Litani gorges called Deir Mimas—sounding that Lebanese Litani River Authority officials were certain had been undertaken to find the optimum place for the inlet of a diversion tunnel to be dug about three miles into Israel.

Norwegian officers and soldiers of the U.N.'s Lebanon force have described how, in January 1983, an Israeli military bulldozer cut a steep road into the face of the rocky gorge below Deir Mimas. An engineering party then inserted rods into the rock outcroppings to take the sounding. In investigating these reports ABC News teams and other reporters in southern Lebanon encountered Israeli land survey parties taking measurements on the hills and hairpin turns of the roads near the Litani. The Israelis may simply be planning new military roads or improving topographical maps. A number of Israeli families in the Metullah area, however, hold deeds or other claims to land in southern Lebanon—just as Lebanese still hold similar claims to land south of the border in Israel. Should Israel decide to go ahead with the Litani plan, this Israeli-claimed land could be used for the artificial lake or reservoir or other irrigation works.

Neeman contended that such diversion tunnels might have been interesting when the Cotton plan and other earlier schemes were proposed in the past, but no longer. Neeman relates that when Sharon, his political ally, returned from the Lebanon campaign, Neeman asked, "What do you think about the Litani?" "The Litani?" Sharon allegedly responded, "Have you seen the Litani? It's only a trickle, not worth the taking." This meager flow, acknowledged Neeman, results from the intensive Lebanese power and irrigation projects upstream. Neeman added, however, if the Lebanese ever cared to sell some of the Litani water, "We would be glad to buy this little water and make good use of it in northern Galilee."

Lebanese water engineers estimate that an Israeli downstream diversion effort could cost the Litani at least 3.5 billion cubic feet annually. This loss would rule out effective irrigation of the southern Lebanon panhandle and would ultimately turn much of the region into a desert. Moreover, diversion, at least under schemes advanced in 1943 and 1954, would also require Israel to stay on in Lebanon and hold at least the entire Bekaa Valley south of the Damascus road in order to control the river's flow, to preempt Lebanon's use of the water to irrigate the panhandle if it regains the region, and to protect the diversion system from any Syrian counterattack. Any long-term harnessing by Israel of Lebanon's water resources would also require control of both slopes of the Lebanon mountain range. Otherwise, enemy spotters in the Shuf Mountains to the west, where the Israelis have upgraded and now operate a long-range radar station at Dar Barouk, could direct artillery fire or air strikes on diversion projects.

Israelis avoid public discussion of the sensitive subject of water resources. Never once did the Litani question come up during all of the Israeli-U.S.-Lebanese talks leading to the May 1, 1983, troop withdrawal agreement, even though the Lebanese were prepared to discuss the matter had it been raised by the Israelis. The Saudis have privately assured Lebanon that they would fully finance irrigation of the area south of the Litani, if the United States could provide a guaranteed date for Israeli withdrawal.

Israel's own water needs have been rising rapidly. Recent Israeli Water Administration statistics show that from 1948 to 1978 Israel's cultivated area increased at a slower rate than population. Yet 900,000 additional acres remain potentially available for irrigated agriculture, while 400,000 more acres are potentially suitable for dry farming. Upon considering that Israel's efficient farming methods require 100,000 cubic feet of water each year for the average acre of irrigated land, Israel's great need for water becomes clear.

Moreover, Israeli planners privately admit that unless the country concentrates purely on expensive desalination plants, or finds a way to increase substantially the present recycling of used irrigation and waste water, present aquifers can scarcely meet the country's current needs or greater levels of consumption much beyond 1990. Another major water source will be needed. The hydraulic imperative, from the Israeli point of view, is capturing either the Litani or a much greater share of the Yarmuk. Whether Israel moves unilaterally or whether the region returns to the Eisenhower-Johnston concepts of finding ways to share the Earth's most precious resource for the common good will help determine the future political geography of the Middle East. . . .

ENVIRONMENTAL CHANGES AS CAUSES OF ACUTE CONFLICT

Thomas F. Homer-Dixon

How might environmental change lead to acute conflict? Some experts propose that environmental change may shift the balance of power between states either regionally or globally, producing instabilities that could lead to war.[1] Or, as global environmental damage increases the disparity between the North and South, poor nations may militarily confront the rich for a greater share of the world's wealth.[2] Warmer temperatures could lead to contention over new ice-free sea-lanes in the Arctic or more accessible resources in the Antarctic.[3] Bulging populations and land stress may produce waves of environmental refugees[4] that spill across borders with destabilizing effects on the recipient's domestic order and on international stability. Countries may fight over dwindling supplies of water and the effects of upstream pollution.[5] In developing countries, a sharp drop in food crop production could lead to internal strife across urban-rural and nomadic-sedentary cleavages.[6] If environmental degradation makes food supplies increasingly tight, exporters may be tempted to use food as a weapon.[7] Environmental change could ultimately cause the gradual impoverishment of societies in both the North and South, which could aggravate class and ethnic cleavages, undermine liberal regimes, and spawn insurgencies.[8] Finally, many scholars indicate that environmental degradation will "ratchet up" the level of stress within national and international society,

Thomas F. Homer-Dixon, "On the Threshold: Environmental Changes as Causes of Acute Conflict," *International Security* Vol. 16, No. 2 (fall 1991) pp. 76–116. © 1991 by the President and Fellows of Harvard College and of the Massachusetts Institute of Technology, and the Canadian Institute of International Affairs.

[1]For example, see David Wirth, "Climate Chaos," *Foreign Policy,* No. 74 (Spring 1989), p. 10.
[2]Robert Heilbroner, *An Inquiry into the Human Prospect* (New York: Norton, 1980), pp. 39 and 95; William Ophuls, *Ecology and the Politics of Scarcity: A Prologue to a Political Theory of the Steady State* (San Francisco: Freeman, 1977), pp. 214–217.
[3]Fen Hampson, "The Climate for War," *Peace and Security,* Vol. 3, No. 3 (Autumn 1988), p. 9.
[4]Jodi Jacobson, *Environmental Refugees: A Yardstick of Habitability,* Worldwatch Paper No. 86 (Washington, D.C.: Worldwatch Institute, 1988).
[5]Peter Gleick, "Climate Change," p. 336; Malin Falkenmark, "Fresh Waters as a Factor in Strategic Policy and Action," in Westing, *Global Resources,* pp. 85–113.
[6]Peter Wallensteen, "Food Crops as a Factor in Strategic Policy and Action," Westing, *Global Resources,* pp. 151–155.
[7]Ibid., pp. 146–151.
[8]Ted Gurr, "On the Political Consequences of Scarcity and Economic Decline," *International Studies Quarterly,* Vol. 29, No. 1 (March 1985), pp. 51–75.

thus increasing the likelihood of many different kinds of conflict and impeding the development of cooperative solutions. . . .[9]

Poor countries will in general be more vulnerable to environmental change than rich ones; therefore, environmentally induced conflicts are likely to arise first in the developing world. In these countries, a range of atmospheric, terrestrial, and aquatic environmental pressures will in time probably produce, either singly or in combination, four main, causally interrelated social effects: reduced agricultural production, economic decline, population displacement, and disruption of regular and legitimized social relations. These social effects, in turn, may cause several specific types of acute conflict, including scarcity disputes between countries, clashes between ethnic groups, and civil strife and insurgency, each with potentially serious repercussions for the security interests of the developed world. . . .

THE SALIENCE OF ENVIRONMENTAL ISSUES

. . . The environmental system, in particular the earth's climate, used to be regarded as relatively resilient and stable in the face of human insults. But now it is widely believed to have multiple local equilibria that are not highly stable.[10] In 1987, for example, geochemist Wallace Broecker reflected on recent polar ice-core and ocean sediment data: "What these records indicate is that Earth's climate does not respond to forcing in a smooth and gradual way. Rather, it responds in sharp jumps which involve large-scale reorganization of Earth's system. . . . We must consider the possibility that the main responses of the system to our provocation of the atmosphere will come in jumps whose timing and magnitude are unpredictable."[11]

A paradigm-shattering example of such nonlinear or "threshold" effects in complex environmental systems was the discovery of the Antarctic ozone hole in the mid-1980s. The hole was startling evidence of the instability of the environmental system in response to human inputs, of the capacity of humankind to significantly affect the ecosystem on a global scale, and of our inability to predict exactly how the system will change.

---

[9]"The disappearance of ecological abundance seems bound to make international politics even more tension ridden and potentially violent than it already is. Indeed, the pressures of ecological scarcity may embroil the world in hopeless strife, so that long before ecological collapse occurs by virtue of the physical limitations of the earth, the current world order will have been destroyed by turmoil and war." Ophuls, *Ecology,* p. 214.

[10]The development of chaos theory has contributed to this understanding. A chaotic system has nonlinear and feedback relationships between its variables that amplify small perturbations, thereby rendering accurate prediction of the system's state increasingly difficult the further one tries to project into the future. In chaos (not to be confused with randomness), deterministic causal processes still operate at the micro-level and, although the system's state may not be precisely predictable for a given point in the future, the boundaries within which its variables must operate are often identifiable. See James Crutchfield, J. Doyne Farmer, and Norman Packard, "Chaos," *Scientific American,* Vol. 255, No. 6 (December 1986), pp. 46–57; James Gleick, *Chaos: Making of a New Science* (New York: Viking, 1987).

[11]Wallace Broecker, "Unpleasant Surprises in the Greenhouse?" *Nature,* Vol. 328, No. 6126 (July 9, 1987), pp. 123–126.

This altered perception of the nature of the environmental system has percolated out of the scientific community into the policymaking community. It may also be influencing the broader public's view of environmental problems. Scientists, policymakers, and laypeople are beginning to interpret data about environmental change in a new light: progressive, incremental degradation of environmental systems is not as tolerable as it once was, because we now realize that we do not know where and when we might cross a threshold and move to a radically different and perhaps highly undesirable system. . . .

Angus MacKay examines the relationship between climate change and civil violence in the kingdom of Castile (much of modern-day Spain).[12] During the fifteenth century, there were numerous well-documented episodes of popular unrest in Castile, and some seem to have been produced directly by climate-induced food shortages. In March 1462, for instance, rioters rampaged through Seville after floods forced the price of bread beyond the means of the poor. Usually, however, the causal connections were more complex. An important intervening factor was the fabric of religious and social beliefs held by the people and promoted by preachers, especially those beliefs attributing weather fluctuations to the sin of someone in the community.[13] MacKay thus argues against a simplistic "stimulus-response" model of environment-conflict linkages and instead for one that allows for "culturally mediated" behavior.

Addressing a modern conflict, William Durham has analyzed the demographic and environmental pressures behind the 1969 "Soccer War" between El Salvador and Honduras.[14] Because of the prominence in this conflict of previous migration from El Salvador to Honduras, and because of the striking evidence of population growth and land stress in the two countries (most notably El Salvador), a number of analysts have asserted that the Soccer War is a first-class example of an ecologically driven conflict.[15] A simple Malthusian interpretation does not seem to have credibility when one looks at the aggregate data.[16] But Durham shows that changes in agricultural practice and land distribution—to the detriment of poor farmers—were more powerful inducements to

---

[12]Angus MacKay, "Climate and Popular Unrest in Late Medieval Castile," in T.M. Wigley, M.J. Ingram, and G. Farmer, *Climate and History: Studies in Past Climates and Their Impact on Man* (Cambridge: Cambridge University Press, 1981), pp. 356–376. For other historical case studies of climate–society interaction, see Hubert Lamb, *Weather, Climate and Human Affairs* (London: Routledge, 1988).

[13]Anger over food scarcity was sometimes turned against Jews and *conversos* (Jews who had converted to Christianity after Iberian pogroms in the late fourteenth century), and sometimes against small shopkeepers who were accused of the "sins" of creating shortages and overpricing food.

[14]William Durham, *Scarcity and Survival in Central America: The Ecological Origins of the Soccer War* (Stanford, Calif.: Stanford University Press, 1979).

[15]For instance, see Paul Ehrlich, Anne Ehrlich, and John Holdren, *Ecoscience: Population, Resources, Environment* (San Francisco: Freeman, 1977), p. 908.

[16]El Salvador was the most densely populated country in the Western Hemisphere (190 people per square kilometer in 1976; compare India at 186), with a population growth rate of 3.5 percent per year (representing a doubling time of about twenty years). Most of the country had lost its virgin forest, land erosion and nutrient depletion were severe, and total food production fell behind consumption in the mid-50s. Per capita farmland used for basic food crops fell from 0.15 hectares in 1953 to 0.11 hectares in 1971.

migration than sheer population growth. Land scarcity developed not because there was too little to go around, but because of "a process of competitive exclusion by which the small farmers [were] increasingly squeezed off the land" by large land owners.[17] Durham thus contends that ecologists cannot directly apply to human societies the simple, density-dependent models of resource competition they commonly use to study asocial animals: a distributional component must be added, because human behavior is powerfully constrained by social structure and the resource access it entails.[18]

Others have analyzed environment-conflict linkages in the Philippines. Although the country has suffered from serious internal strife for many decades, its underlying causes may be changing: population displacement, deforestation, and land degradation appear to be increasingly powerful forces driving the current communist-led insurgency. Here, too, the linkages between environmental change and conflict are complex, involving numerous intervening variables, both physical and social. The Filipino population growth rate of 2.5 percent is among the highest in Southeast Asia. To help pay the massive foreign debt, the government has encouraged the expansion of large-scale lowland agriculture. Both factors have swelled the number of landless agricultural laborers. Many have migrated to the Philippines' steep and ecologically vulnerable uplands where they have cleared land or established plots on previously logged land. This has set in motion a cycle of erosion, falling food production, and further clearing of land. Even marginally fertile land is becoming hard to find in many places, and economic conditions are often dire for the peasants.[19] Civil dissent is rampant in these peripheral areas, which are largely beyond the effective control of the central government.

While these studies are commendable, a review of all of the recent work on environmental change and conflict reveals a number of difficulties, some methodological and some conceptual. First, researchers often emphasize human-induced climate change and ozone depletion to the neglect of severe terrestrial and aquatic environmental problems such as deforestation, soil degradation, and fisheries depletion. Second, much of the recent writing on the links between environmental change and conflict is anecdotal. These pieces do not clearly separate the "how" question (how will environmental change lead to conflict?) from the "where" question (where will such conflict occur?). . . .

Third, environmental-social systems are hard to analyze. They are characterized by multiple causes and effects and by a host of intervening variables, often linked by inter-

---

[17]Durham, *Scarcity and Survival,* p. 54.

[18]The importance of variables intervening between population density and conflict is emphasized in Nazli Choucri, ed., *Multidisciplinary Perspectives on Population and Conflict* (Syracuse, N.Y.: Syracuse University Press, 1984); see also Jack Goldstone, *Revolution and Rebellion in the Early Modern World* (Berkeley, Calif.: University of California Press, 1991).

[19]Leonard notes that, around the planet, population growth, inequitable land distribution, and agricultural modernization have caused huge numbers of desperately poor people to move to "remote and ecologically fragile rural areas" or to already overcrowded cities. See Jeffrey Leonard, "Overview," *Environment and the Poor: Development Strategies for a Common Agenda* (New Brunswick, N.J.: Transaction, 1989), p. 5.

active, synergistic, and nonlinear causal relations. Empirical data about these variables and relations are rarely abundant. Although the underlying influence of environmental factors on conflict may be great, the complex and indirect causation in these systems means that the scanty evidence available is always open to many interpretations. Furthermore, understanding environmental-social systems involves specifying links across levels of analysis usually regarded as quite independent.

Fourth, the prevailing "naturalistic" epistemology and ontology of social science may hinder accurate understanding of the links between physical and social variables within environmental-social systems. In particular, it may be a mistake to conjoin, in causal generalizations, types of physical events with types of intentional social action. Fifth, researchers must acquire detailed knowledge of a daunting range of disciplines, from atmospheric science and agriculture hydrology to energy economics and international relations theory.

Sixth and finally, the modern realist perspective that is often used to understand security problems is largely inadequate for identifying and explaining the links between environmental change and conflict. Realism focuses on states as rational maximizers of power in an anarchic system; state behavior is mainly a function of the structure of power relations in the system. But this emphasis on states means that theorists tend to see the world as divided into territorially distinct, mutually exclusive countries, not broader environmental regions or systems. Realism thus encourages scholars to deemphasize transboundary environmental problems, because such problems often cannot be linked to a particular country, and do not have any easily conceptualized impact on the structure of economic and military power relations between states. Realism induces scholars to squeeze environmental issues into a structure of concepts including "state," "sovereignty," "territory," "national interest," and "balance of power." The fit is bad, which may lead theorists to ignore, distort, and misunderstand important aspects of global environmental problems.

MAPPING CAUSES AND EFFECTS

. . . The total effect of human activity on the environment in a particular ecological region is mainly a function of two variables: first, the product of total population in the region and physical activity per capita, and second, the vulnerability of the ecosystem in that region to those particular activities. Activity per capita, in turn, is a function of available physical resources (which include nonrenewable resources such as minerals, and renewable resources such as water, forests, and agricultural land) and ideational factors, including institutions, social relations, preferences, and beliefs. . . . Environmental effects may cause social effects that in turn could lead to conflict. For example, the degradation of agricultural land might produce large-scale migration, which could create ethnic conflicts as migratory groups clash with indigenous populations. There are important feedback loops from social effects and conflict to the ideational factors and thence back to activity per capita and population. Thus, ethnic clashes arising from migration could alter the operation of a society's markets and thereby its economic activity. . . .

The Range of Environmental Problems

Developing countries are likely to be affected sooner and more severely by environmental change than rich countries. By definition, they do not have the financial, material, or intellectual resources of the developed world; furthermore, their social and political institutions tend to be fragile and riven with discord. It is probable, therefore, that developing societies will be less able to apprehend or respond to environmental disruption.[20]

Seven major environmental problems might plausibly contribute to conflict within and among developing countries: greenhouse warming, stratospheric ozone depletion, acid deposition, deforestation, degradation of agricultural land, overuse and pollution of water supplies, and depletion of fish stocks. These problems can all be crudely characterized as large-scale human-induced problems, with long-term and often irreversible consequences, which is why they are often grouped together under the rubric "global change." However, they vary greatly in spatial scale: the first two involve genuinely global physical processes, while the last five involve regional physical processes, although they may appear in locales all over the planet. These seven problems also vary in time scale: for example, while a region can be deforested in only a few years, and severe ecological and social effects may be noticeable almost immediately, human-induced greenhouse warming will probably develop over many decades and may not have truly serious implications for humankind for a half century or more after the signal is first detected. In addition, some of these problems (for instance, deforestation and degradation of water supplies) are much more advanced than others (such as greenhouse warming and ozone depletion) and are already producing serious social disruption. This variance in tangible evidence for these problems contributes to great differences in our certainty about their ultimate severity. The uncertainties surrounding greenhouse warming, for example, are thus far greater than those concerning deforestation.

Many of these problems are causally interrelated. For instance, acid deposition damages agricultural land, fisheries, and forests. Greenhouse warming may contribute to deforestation by moving northward the optimal temperature and precipitation zones for many tree species, by increasing the severity of windstorms and wildfires, and by expanding the range of pests and diseases.[21] The release of carbon from these dying forests would reinforce the greenhouse effect. The increased incidence of ultraviolet radiation due to the depletion of the ozone layer will probably damage trees and crops, and it may also damage the phytoplankton at the bottom of the ocean food chain. . . .[22]

Four Principal Social Effects

Environmental degradation may cause countless often subtle changes in developing societies. These range from increased communal cooking as fuel-wood becomes scarce

---

[20]Gurr, "Political Consequences of Scarcity," pp. 70–71.

[21]WRI, et al., *World Resources 1990–91,* p. 111.

[22]Robert Worrest, Hermann Gucinski, and John Hardy, "Potential Impact of Stratospheric Ozone Depletion on Marine Ecosystems," in John Topping, Jr., ed., *Coping with Climate Change: Proceedings of the Second North American Conference on Preparing for Climate Change* (Washington, D.C.: The Climate Institute, 1989), pp. 256–262.

around African villages, to worsened poverty of Filipino coastal fishermen whose once-abundant grounds have been destroyed by trawlers and industrial pollution. Which of the many types of social effect might be crucial links between environmental change and acute conflict? This is the first part of the "how" question. To address it, we must use both the best knowledge about the social effects of environmental change and the best knowledge about the nature and causes of social conflict.

In thus working from both ends toward the middle of the causal chain, I hypothesize that four principal social effects may, either singly or in combination, substantially increase the probability of acute conflict in developing countries: decreased agricultural production, economic decline, population displacement, and disruption of legitimized and authoritative institutions and social relations. These effects will often be causally interlinked, sometimes with reinforcing relationships. For example, the population displacement resulting from a decrease in agricultural production may further disrupt agricultural production. Or economic decline may lead to the flight of people with wealth and education, which in turn could eviscerate universities, courts, and institutions of economic management, all of which are crucial to a healthy economy.

Agricultural Production   . . . Decreased agricultural production is often mentioned as potentially the most worrisome consequence of environmental change. . . . The Philippines provides a good illustration of deforestation's impact. . . . Since the Second World War, logging and the encroachment of farms have reduced the virgin and second-growth forest from about sixteen million hectares to 6.8–7.6 million hectares. Across the archipelago, logging and land-clearing have accelerated erosion, changed regional hydrological cycles and precipitation patterns, and decreased the land's ability to retain water during rainy periods. The resulting flash floods have damaged irrigation works while plugging reservoirs and irrigation channels with silt. These factors may seriously affect crop production. For example, when the government of the Philippines and the European Economic Community commissioned an Integrated Environmental Plan for the still relatively unspoiled island of Palawan, the authors of the study found that only about half of the 36,000 hectares of irrigated farmland projected within the Plan for 2007 will actually be irrigable because of the hydrological effects of decreases in forest cover.[23]

. . . Degradation and decreasing availability of good agricultural land [are] problems that deserve much closer attention than they usually receive. Currently, total global cropland amounts to about 1.5 billion hectares. Optimistic estimates of total arable land on the planet, which includes both current and potential cropland, range from 3.2 to 3.4 billion hectares, but nearly all the best land has already been exploited. What is left is either less fertile, not sufficiently rainfed or easily irrigable, infested with pests, or harder to clear and work.

For developing countries during the 1980s, cropland grew at just 0.26 percent a year, less than half the rate of the 1970s. More importantly, in these countries arable land per capita dropped by 1.9 percent a year. In the absence of a major increase in

---

[23]Christopher Finney and Stanley Western, "An Economic Analysis of Environmental Protection and Management: An Example from the Philippines," *The Environmentalist,* Vol. 6, No. 1 (1986), p. 56.

arable land in developing countries, experts expect that the world average of 0.28 hectares of cropland per capita will decline to 0.27 hectares by the year 2025, given the current rate of world population growth. Large tracts are being lost each year to urban encroachment, erosion, nutrient depletion, salinization, waterlogging, acidification, and compacting. The geographer Vaclav Smil, who is generally very conservative in his assessments of environmental damage, estimates that two to three million hectares of cropland are lost annually to erosion; perhaps twice as much land goes to urbanization, and at least one million hectares are abandoned because of excessive salinity. In addition, about one-fifth of the world's cropland is suffering from some degree of desertification. Taken together, he concludes, the planet will lose about 100 million hectares of arable land between 1985 and 2000. . . .[24]

Economic Decline . . . A great diversity of factors might affect wealth production. For example, increased ultraviolet radiation caused by ozone depletion is likely to raise the rate of disease in humans and livestock,[25] which could have serious economic results. Logging for export markets may produce short-term economic gain for the country's elite, but increased runoff can damage roads, bridges, and other valuable infrastructure, while the extra siltation reduces the transport and hydroelectric capacity of rivers. As forests are destroyed, wood becomes scarcer and more expensive, and it absorbs an increasing share of the household budget for the poor families that use it for fuel.

Agriculture is the source of much of the wealth generated in developing societies. Food production soared in many regions over the last decades because the green revolution more than compensated for inadequate or declining soil productivity; but some experts believe this economic relief will be short-lived. Jeffrey Leonard writes: "Millions of previously very poor families that have experienced less than one generation of increasing wealth due to rising agricultural productivity could see that trend reversed if environmental degradation is not checked."[26] Damage to the soil is already producing a harsh economic impact in some areas.

Gauging the actual economic cost of land degradation is not easy. Current national income accounts do not incorporate measures of resource depletion: "A nation could exhaust its mineral reserves, cut down its forests, erode its soils, pollute its aquifers, and hunt its wildlife to extinction—all without affecting measured income."[27] The

---

[24]Smil gives a startling account of the situation in China. From 1957 to 1977 the country lost 33.33 million hectares of farmland (30 percent of its 1957 total), while it added 21.2 million hectares of largely marginal land. He notes that "the net loss of 12 million hectares during a single generation when the country's population grew by about 300 million people means that per capita availability of arable land dropped by 40 per cent and that China's farmland is now no more abundant than Bangladesh's—a mere one-tenth of a hectare per capita!" See Vaclav Smil, *Energy, Food, Environment* (Oxford, U.K.: Oxford University Press, 1987), pp. 223, 230.

[25]Janice Longstreth, "Overview of the Potential Health Effects Associated with Ozone Depletion," in Topping, *Coping with Climate Change*, pp. 163–167.

[26]Leonard, *Environment and the Poor*, p. 27.

[27]Robert Repetto, "Wasting Assets: The Need for National Resource Accounting," *Technology Review*, January 1990, p. 40.

inadequacy of measures of economic productivity reinforces the perception that there is a policy trade-off between economic growth and environmental protection; this perception, in turn, encourages societies to generate present income at the expense of their potential for future income.

Population Displacement   Some commentators have suggested that environmental degradation may produce vast numbers of "environmental refugees." Sea-level rise may drive people back from coastal and delta areas in Egypt; spreading desert may empty Sahelian countries as their populations move south; Filipino fishermen may leave their depleted fishing grounds for the cities. The term "environmental refugee" is somewhat misleading, however, because it implies that environmental disruption could be a clear, proximate cause of refugee flows. Usually, though, environmental disruption will be only one of many interacting physical and social variables, including agricultural and economic decline, that ultimately force people from their homelands. For example, over the last three decades, millions of people have migrated from Bangladesh to neighboring West Bengal and Assam in India. While detailed data are scarce (in part because the Bangladeshi government is reluctant to admit there is significant out-migration), many specialists believe this movement is a result, at least in part, of shortages of adequately fertile land due to a rapidly growing population. Flooding, caused by deforestation in watersheds upstream on the Ganges and Brahmaputra rivers, might also be driving people from the area. In the future, this migration could be aggravated by rising sea-levels coupled with extreme weather events (both perhaps resulting from climate change).

Disrupted Institutions and Social Relations   The fourth social effect especially relevant to the connection between environment change and acute conflict is the disruption of institutions and of legitimized, accepted, and authoritative social relations. In many developing societies, the three social effects described above are likely to tear this fabric of custom and habitual behavior. A drop in agricultural output may weaken rural communities by causing malnutrition and disease, and by encouraging people to leave; economic decline may corrode confidence in the national purpose, weaken the tax base, and undermine financial, legal, and political institutions; and mass migrations of people into a region may disrupt labor markets, shift class relations, and upset the traditional balance of economic and political authority between ethnic groups. . . .

Cornucopians and Neo-Malthusians

Experts in environmental studies now commonly use the labels "cornucopian" for optimists like Simon and "neo-Malthusian" for pessimists like Paul and Anne Ehrlich. Cornucopians do not worry much about protecting the stock of any single resource, because of their faith that market-driven human ingenuity can always be tapped to allow the substitution of more abundant resources to produce the same end-use service. Simon, for example, writes: "There is no physical or economic reason why human resourcefulness and enterprise cannot forever continue to respond to impending shortages and existing problems with new expedients that, after an adjustment period, leave us better off than before the problem arose."[28] Neo-Malthusians are much more cautious. For renewable resources, they often distinguish between resource "capital" and its "income": the capital is the resource stock that generates a flow (the income) that can be tapped for human consumption and well-being. A "sustainable" economy, using this terminology, is one that leaves the capital intact and undamaged so that future generations can enjoy an undiminished income stream.

Historically, cornucopians have been right to criticize the idea that resource scarcity places fixed limits on human activity. Time and time again, human beings have circumvented scarcities, and neo-Malthusians have often been justly accused of "crying wolf." But in assuming that this experience pertains to the future, cornucopians overlook seven factors.

First, whereas serious scarcities of critical resources in the past usually appeared singly, now we face multiple scarcities that exhibit powerful interactive, feedback, and threshold effects. An agricultural region may, for example, be simultaneously affected by degraded water and soil, greenhouse-induced precipitation changes, and increased ultraviolet radiation. This makes the future highly uncertain for policymakers and economic actors; tomorrow will be full of extreme events and surprises. Furthermore, as numerous resources become scarce simultaneously, it will be harder to identify substitution possibilities that produce the same end-use services at costs that prevailed when scarcity was less severe. Second, in the past the scarcity of a given resource usually increased slowly, allowing time for social, economic, and technological adjustment. But human populations are much larger and activities of individuals are, on a global average, much more resource-intensive than before. This means that debilitating scarcities often develop much more quickly: whole countries may be deforested in a few decades; most of a region's topsoil can disappear in a generation; and critical ozone depletion may occur in as little as twenty years. Third, today's consumption has far greater momentum than in the past, because of the size of the consuming population, the sheer quantity of material consumed by this population, and the density of its interwoven fabric of consumption activities. The countless individual and corporate economic actors making up human society are heavily committed to certain patterns of resource use; and the ability of our markets to adapt may be sharply constrained by these entrenched interests.

These first three factors may soon combine to produce a daunting syndrome of environmentally induced scarcity: humankind will face multiple resource shortages that are interacting and unpredictable, that grow to crisis proportions rapidly, and that will be hard to address because of powerful commitments to certain consumption patterns.

The fourth reason that cornucopian arguments may not apply in the future is that the free-market price mechanism is a bad gauge of scarcity, especially for resources held in common, such as a benign climate and productive seas. In the past, many such resources seemed endlessly abundant; now they are being degraded and depleted and we are learning that their increased scarcity often has tremendous bearing on a society's well-being. Yet this scarcity is at best reflected only indirectly in market prices. In

---

[28]Julian Simon, *The Ultimate Resource* (Princeton: Princeton University Press, 1981), p. 345.

addition, people often cannot participate in market transactions in which they have an interest, either because they lack the resources or because they are distant from the transaction process in time or space; in these cases the true scarcity of the resource is not reflected by its price.

The fifth reason is an extension of a point made earlier: market-driven adaptation to resource scarcity is most likely to succeed in wealthy societies, where abundant reserves of capital, knowledge, and talent help economic actors invent new technologies, identify conservation possibilities, and make the transition to new production and consumption patterns. Yet many of the societies facing the most serious environmental problems in the coming decades will be poor; even if they have efficient markets, lack of capital and know-how will hinder their response to these problems.

Sixth, cornucopians have an anachronistic faith in humankind's ability to unravel and manage the myriad processes of nature. There is no *a priori* reason to expect that human scientific and technical ingenuity can always surmount all types of scarcity. Human beings may not have the mental capacity to understand adequately the complexities of environmental-social systems. Or it may simply be impossible, given the physical, biological, and social laws governing these systems, to reduce all scarcity or repair all environmental damage. Moreover, the chaotic nature of these systems may keep us from fully anticipating the consequences of various adaptation and intervention strategies. Perhaps most important, scientific and technical knowledge must be built incrementally—layer upon layer—and its diffusion to the broader society often takes decades. Any technical solutions to environmental scarcity may arrive too late to prevent catastrophe.

Seventh and finally, future environmental problems, rather than inspiring the wave of ingenuity predicted by cornucopians, may instead reduce the supply of ingenuity available in a society. The success of market mechanisms depends on an intricate and stable system of institutions, social relations, and shared understandings. . . . Cornucopians often overlook the role of *social* ingenuity in producing the complex legal and economic climate in which *technical* ingenuity can flourish. Policymakers must be clever "social engineers" to design and implement effective market mechanisms. Unfortunately, however, the syndrome of multiple, interacting, unpredictable, and rapidly changing environmental problems will increase the complexity and pressure of the policymaking setting. It will also generate increased "social friction" as elites and interest groups struggle to protect their prerogatives. The ability of policy makers to be good social engineers is likely to go *down,* not up, as these stresses increase. . . .

TYPES OF CONFLICT

. . . I hypothesize that severe environmental degradation will produce three principal types of conflict. These should be considered ideal types: they will rarely, if ever, be found in pure form in the real world.

Simple Scarcity Conflicts   [We would expect] simple scarcity conflicts . . . when state actors rationally calculate their interests in a zero-sum or negative-sum situation such as might arise from resource scarcity. We have seen such conflicts often in the past; they are easily understood within the realist paradigm of international relations theory, and they therefore are likely to receive undue attention from current security scholars. . . . I propose that simple scarcity conflicts may arise over three types of resources in particular: river water, fish, and agriculturally productive land. These renewable resources seem particularly likely to spark conflict because their scarcity is increasing rapidly in some regions, they are often essential for human survival, and they can be physically seized or controlled. There may be a positive feedback relationship between conflict and reduced agricultural production: for example, lower food supplies caused by environmental change may lead countries to fight over irrigable land, and this fighting could further reduce food supplies.

The current controversy over the Great Anatolia Project on the Euphrates River illustrates how simple scarcity conflicts can arise. By early in the next century, Turkey plans to build a huge complex of twenty dams and irrigation systems along the upper reaches of the Euphrates.[29] This $21 billion project, if fully funded and built, would reduce the average annual flow of the Euphrates within Syria from 32 billion cubic meters to 20 billion.[30] The water that passes through Turkey's irrigation system and on to Syria will be laden with fertilizers, pesticides, and salts. Syria is already desperately short of water, with an annual water availability of only about 600 cubic meters per capita. Much of the water for its towns, industries, and farms comes from the Euphrates, and the country has been chronically vulnerable to drought. Furthermore, Syria's population growth rate, at 3.7 percent per year, is one of the highest in the world, and this adds further to the country's demand for water.

Turkey and Syria have exchanged angry threats over this situation. Syria gives sanctuary to guerrillas of the Kurdish Workers Party (the PKK), which has long been waging an insurgency against the Turkish government in eastern Anatolia. Turkey suspects that Syria might be using these separatists to gain leverage in bargaining over Euphrates River water. Thus in October, 1989, then Prime Minister Turgut Ozal suggested that Turkey might impound the river's water if Syria did not restrain the PKK. Although he later retracted the threat, the tensions have not been resolved, and there are currently no high-level talks on water sharing.

Group-Identity Conflicts   Group-identity conflicts are . . . likely to arise from the large-scale movements of populations brought about by environmental change. As different ethnic and cultural groups are propelled together under circumstances of deprivation and stress, we should expect intergroup hostility, in which a group would emphasize its own identity while denigrating, discriminating against, and attacking outsiders. The situation in the Bangladesh-Assam region may be a good example of this process; Assam's ethnic strife over the last decade has apparently been provoked by migration from Bangladesh.[31]

---

[29]Alan Cowell, "Water Rights: Plenty of Mud to Sling," *New York Times,* February 7, 1990, p. A4; "Send for the Dowsers," *The Economist,* December 16, 1989, p. 42.

[30]On January 13, 1990, Turkey began filling the giant reservoir behind the Ataturk Dam, the first in this complex. For one month Turkey held back the main flow of the Euphrates River, which cut the downstream flow in Syria to about a quarter of its normal rate.

[31]Myron Weiner, "The Political Demography of Assam's Anti-Immigrant Movement," *Population and Development Review,* Vol. 9, No. 2 (June 1983), pp. 279–292.

As population and environmental stresses grow in developing countries, migration to the developed world is likely to surge. "The image of islands of affluence amidst a sea of poverty is not inaccurate."[32] People will seek to move from Latin America to the United States and Canada, from North Africa and the Middle East to Europe, and from South and Southeast Asia to Australia. This migration has already shifted the ethnic balance in many cities and regions of developed countries, and governments are struggling to contain a xenophobic backlash. Such racial strife will undoubtedly become much worse.

Relative-Deprivation Conflicts   Relative-deprivation [conflicts may arise] as developing societies produce less wealth because of environmental problems; their citizens will probably become increasingly discontented by the widening gap between their actual level of economic achievement and the level they feel they deserve. The rate of change is key: the faster the economic deterioration, it is hypothesized, the greater the discontent. Lower-status groups will be more frustrated than others because elites will use their power to maintain, as best they can, access to a constant standard of living despite a shrinking economic pie. At some point, the discontent and frustration of some groups may cross a critical threshold, and they will act violently against other groups perceived to be the agents of their economic misery or thought to be benefiting from a grossly unfair distribution of economic goods in the society. . . .

Conflict Objectives and Scope

Table 1 compares some attributes of the principal types of acute conflict that I hypothesize may result from environmental change. The table lists the objectives sought by actors involved in these conflicts (which are, once again, ideal types). There is strong normative content to the motives of challenger groups involved in relative-deprivation

TABLE 1

〰 **Comparison of Conflict Types**		
Conflict Type	*Objective Sought*	*Conflict Scope*
Simple scarcity	Relief from scarcity	International
Group identity	Protection and reinforcement of group identity	International or domestic
Relative deprivation	Distributive justice	Domestic (with international repercussions)

---

[32]Richard Ullman, "Redefining Security," *International Security,* Vol. 8, No. 1 (Summer, 1983), p. 143.

conflicts: these groups believe the distribution of rewards is unfair. But such an "ought" does not necessarily drive simple-scarcity conflicts: one state may decide that it needs something another state has, and then try to seize it, without being motivated by a strong sense of unfairness or injustice.

Table 1 also shows that the scope of conflict can be expected to differ. Although relative-deprivation conflicts will tend to be domestic, we should not underestimate their potentially severe international repercussions. The correlation between civil strife and external conflict behavior is a function of the nature of the regime and of the kind of internal conflict it faces. For example, highly centralized dictatorships threatened by revolutionary actions, purges, and strikes are especially prone to engage in external war and belligerence. In comparison, less centralized dictatorships are prone to such behavior when threatened by guerrilla action and assassinations.[33] External aggressions may also result after a new regime comes to power through civil strife: regimes born of revolution, for example, are particularly good at mobilizing their citizens and resources for military preparation and war.[34]

While environmental stresses and the conflicts they induce may encourage the rise of revolutionary regimes, other results are also plausible: these pressures might overwhelm the management capacity of institutions in developing countries, inducing praetorianism[35] or widespread social disintegration. They may also weaken the control of governments over their territories, especially over the hinterland (as in the Philippines). The regimes that do gain power in the face of such disruption are likely to be extremist, authoritarian, and abusive of human rights.[36] Moreover, the already short time horizons of policy makers in developing countries will be further shortened. These political factors could seriously undermine efforts to mitigate and adapt to environmental change. Soon to be the biggest contributors to global environmental problems, developing countries could become more belligerent, less willing to compromise with other states, and less capable of controlling their territories in order to implement measures to reduce environmental damage.

If many developing countries evolve in the direction of extremism, the interests of the North may be directly threatened. Of special concern here is the growing disparity between rich and poor nations that may be induced by environmental change. Robert Heilbroner notes that revolutionary regimes "are not likely to view the vast difference between first class and cattle class with the forgiving eyes of their predecessors."

---

[33]Jonathan Wilkenfeld, "Domestic and Foreign Conflict Behavior of Nations," *Journal of Peace Research,* Vol. 5 (1968), pp. 56–69.

[34]See Theda Skocpol, "Social Revolutions and Mass Military Mobilization," *World Politics,* Vol. 40, No. 2 (January 1988), pp. 147–168.

[35]"Praetorian" is a label used by Samuel Huntington for societies in which the level of political participation exceeds the capacity of political institutions to channel, moderate, and reconcile competing claims to economic and political resources. "In a praetorian system, social forces confront each other nakedly; no political institutions, no corps of professional political leaders are recognized or accepted as the legitimate intermediaries to moderate group conflict." Samuel Huntington, *Political Order in Changing Societies* (New Haven: Yale University Press, 1968), p. 196.

[36]Ophuls notes that ecological scarcity "seems to engender overwhelming pressures toward political systems that are frankly authoritarian by current standards." Ophuls, *Ecology,* p. 163.

Furthermore, these nations may be heavily armed, as the proliferation of nuclear and chemical weapons and ballistic missiles continues. Such regimes, he asserts, could be tempted to use nuclear blackmail as a "means of inducing the developed world to transfer its wealth on an unprecedented scale to the underdeveloped world."[37] Richard Ullman, however, argues that this concern is overstated. Third world nations are unlikely to confront the North violently in the face of the "superior destructive capabilities of the rich."[38] In light of the discussion in this article, we might conclude that environmental stress and its attendant social disruption will so debilitate the economies of developing countries that they will be unable to amass sizeable armed forces, conventional or otherwise. But the North would surely be unwise to rely on impoverishment and disorder in the South for its security.

---

[37]Heilbroner, *Inquiry,* pp. 39 and 95. These North-South disputes would be the international analogues of domestic relative-deprivation conflicts.
[38]Ullman, "Redefining Security," p. 143.

PART X

CONCLUSION: THE FUTURE BETWEEN CONTENDING FORCES

Aften every epochal conflict, optimists find new hope in the future. With each resurgence of large-scale violence, in contrast, pessimists find old reasons to believe that the future will be like the past. Thus after the Cold War, liberal theories for why modern states should be able to get along without war became popular again with many observers, and after the spread of disorder, ethnic violence, and civil wars in the wake of the Cold War, realist arguments resonated again with others. Analysts are no nearer a consensus on the future of conflict than they were a dozen years ago when the Red flag came down from the Kremlin.

This enduring theoretical debate may reflect the combination of insights and inattention in both theoretical traditions. Variants of both general approaches have a purchase on different aspects of the question of war and peace. Except at levels of generality so high as to be irrelevant, neither approach provides enough guidance that policymakers can risk dispensing entirely with the other. These theories help us to organize the problem and the range of potential solutions in our minds, and to decide which risks or opportunities should override others on average, but they do not provide reliable recipes for specific choices in particular cases. Sensible policymakers will continue to think about how to take the right direction without burning bridges—how to reduce causes of conflict without endangering national interests, and how to prepare against the worst potential threats without making it more likely that those threats will come to pass.

We end with a sample of perspectives on what elements of international strategic life in the post-Cold War era are new, and which of them imply solutions that are different from those of the past. If policymakers cannot yet assume that war is gone for good, how should they plan to cope with military conflict when it occurs? Eliot Cohen surveys the arguments for why and how technology has created a revolutionary situation in military planning—arguments that have been prominent within the defense community in the United States in the past decade, and have produced a widely used acronym: "RMA" (Revolution in Military Affairs). Assumptions that the RMA is either inevitable or desirable are not fully accepted, but they dominated debate about strategy in the

United States, at least until September 11.[1] The Betts essay addresses the uses of force that became prominent after the Cold War, criticizing assumptions prevalent in the 1990s that humanitarian and multilateral interventions should be conceived as something other than acts of war. It argues that to minimize carnage, interventions should not be both limited and impartial, but should aim to settle the question of who rules after the shooting stops.

On more general new trends that affect the context in which conflict or cooperation will occur, Robert Keohane and Joseph Nye discuss how the information revolution relates to their earlier arguments about interdependence and conflict. Benjamin Barber discusses two contending trends: the "globalization of politics," in which Western norms diffuse throughout the world, and the "Lebanonization of the world," in which parochial identities reassert themselves against globalization. The former reflects all the prominent liberal assumptions about progress and the substitution of efficient commerce for unprofitable conquest. The latter evokes the concerns of those who see vitality in nonliberal cultures as a challenge to such notions. Both tendencies collided vividly on September 11, 2001, when radical terrorists chose a prime symbol of economic globalization—the World Trade Center—as a prime target. That both trends can exist on a large scale in the contemporary world testifies to the unsettled question of what kind of a future war has.

—RKB

---

[1]For a strong criticism of arguments that an RMA is actually occurring, see Stephen Biddle "The Past as Prologue: Assessing Theories of Future Warfare," *Security Studies* Vol. 8, No. 1 (Autumn 1998). For other potential drawbacks in confidence in the RMA see Richard J. Harknett and the JCISS Study Group, "The Risks of a Networked Military," *Orbis* Vol. 43, No. 4 (Winter 2000) and Richard K. Betts, "The Downside of the Cutting Edge," *The National Interest* No. 45 (Fall 1996).

A REVOLUTION IN WARFARE

Eliot A. Cohen

TECHNOLOGY STRIKES AGAIN

For almost a decade American defense planners have foreseen an impending revolution in military affairs, sometimes described as the military-technical revolution. Such a transformation would open the way for a fundamental reordering of American defense posture. It might lead, for example, to a drastic shrinking of the military, a casting aside of old forms of organization and creation of new ones, a slashing of current force structure, and the investment of unusually large sums in research and development.

Such a revolution would touch virtually all aspects of the military establishment. Cruise missiles and unmanned aerial vehicles would replace fighter planes and tanks as chess pieces in the game of military power. Today's military organizations—divisions, fleets, and air wings—could disappear or give way to successors that would look very different. And if the forces themselves changed, so too would the people, as new career possibilities, educational requirements, and promotion paths became essential. New elites would gain in importance: "information warriors," for example, might supplant tankers and fighter pilots as groups from which the military establishment draws the bulk of its leaders.

The proponents of this view have turned to history to illustrate—and in some measure to create—their theory of radical change. It is, therefore, proper to ask whether the historical record substantiates their claims.

Most soldiers, in their heart of hearts, would agree with Cyril Falls, a military historian of an older generation, who noted in his 1953 work *A Hundred Years of War, 1850–1950:*

> Observers constantly describe the warfare of their own age as marking a revolutionary breach in the normal progress of methods of warfare. Their selection of their own age ought to put readers and listeners on their guard. . . . It is a fallacy, due to ignorance of technical and tactical military history, to suppose that methods of warfare have not made continuous and, on the whole, fairly even progress.

The cautious military historian (and even more cautious soldier) looks askance at prophets of radical change, although by no means at change itself. Unquestionably, military technology has never stood still. In the eighteenth century, for example, minor improvements in the design and manufacture of gun barrels and carriages, coupled with

---

Eliot A. Cohen, "A Revolution in Warfare," Reprinted by permission of *Foreign Affairs* Vol. 75, No. 2 (March/April 1996). Copyright 1996 by the Council on Foreign Relations, Inc.

the standardization of cannon calibers, laid the groundwork for the vastly improved cannonades of the armies of the French Revolution and Empire. At the same time, on closer inspection the apparently rapid rate of change in modern warfare may prove deceptive. Despite the attention the press lavished on "smart" bombs during the 1991 Persian Gulf War, for example, most of the ordnance in that conflict consisted of 1950s-technology unguided bombs dropped by aircraft developed in the 1960s or in some cases 1970s. This being so, whence comes the contention that the United States is undergoing a revolution in military affairs?

THE RUSSIANS SAW IT COMING

Beginning in the early 1980s Soviet observers led by Marshal Nikolai Ogarkov, then chief of the general staff, advanced the notion of an imminent technical revolution that would give conventional weapons a level of effectiveness in the field comparable to that of small tactical nuclear weapons. Armor on the march might find itself detected and attacked by conventional missiles showering self-guided antitank weapons, in an operation conducted from a distance of several hundred miles and with as little as 30 minutes between detection and assault. The Soviets found their reading of the military future profoundly disheartening, since it promised to thwart their strategy in case of war in Western Europe, which rested on the orderly forward movement of massed echelons of tanks and armored vehicles. They realized, moreover, that their country, incapable of manufacturing a satisfactory personal computer, could not possibly keep up in an arms race driven by the information technologies.

Soviet conceptions of a military-technical revolution seeped into the West, chiefly through the U.S. Department of Defense and its Office of Net Assessment. It gradually became clear that the Soviets had portrayed the revolution too narrowly. They had focused on one type of warfare in a single theater—armored conflict in Central Europe—and concentrated almost exclusively, as befitted the materialism of Marxist-Leninist thought, on technology and weapons rather than the organizational dimension of warfare. With the groundwork laid for an American assessment, the 1991 war with Iraq crystallized awareness among military planners in the United States on this momentous issue.

Many exponents of air power declared that in the Persian Gulf War the technology had finally caught up with the promise of air operations, first articulated in the period between the world wars; the revolution, they said, was in the realization of the 50-year quest for the decisive application of air power in war. Yet the conduct of the war against Iraq had very little to do with the kinds of operations envisaged by the original theorists of air warfare. No theorist in the 1920s imagined it would be possible to take down telecommunications systems or to conduct extensive attacks in densely populated areas without killing many civilians. The Gulf War showed air power off to great advantage but in extremely favorable circumstances: the United States brought to bear a force sized and trained to fight the Soviet Union in a global war, obtained the backing of almost every major military and financial power, and chose the time and place at which combat would begin in a theater ideally suited to air operations. Knowledgeable observers remained skeptical that a revolution had taken place.

A third version of the revolution has come from the American military. Admiral William Owens, vice chairman of the Joint Chiefs of Staff, has written of a "system of systems"—a world in which the many kinds of sensors, from satellites to shipborne radar, from unmanned aerial vehicles to remotely planted acoustic devices, will provide information to any military user who needs it. Thus a helicopter might launch a missile at a tank a dozen miles away based on information derived from airborne radar or satellite imagery. In this view the revolution in military affairs consists of the United States' astounding and unprecedented ability to amass and evaluate enormous quantities of information about any given battle arena—Owens has referred to a 200-mile-by-200-mile box—and make near-instantaneous use of it.

Ground soldiers are particularly dubious about the system of systems. They wonder whether any technologist can disperse what Carl von Clausewitz called the fog of war and ask what will happen when an opponent attempts to conceal its force or attacks the information systems that observe it. Even in naval warfare, where the system of systems originated, sea and storm can make it difficult to know all that goes on in a box of the kind described by Owens. The admiral's version of the military revolution focuses almost entirely on technology rather than on the less tangible aspects of warfare. As yet, it bespeaks an aspiration, not a reality, and it is predicated on the inability of other countries to systematically deny the United States the information its weapons systems need.

The Soviet, air power, and Owens versions of the revolution in military affairs all offer only partial insights into a larger set of changes. A revolution has indeed begun. But it will be shaped by powerful forces emanating from beyond the domain of warfare. It will, moreover, represent the culmination in modern military organizations of a variety of developments, some of them dating back decades. To understand it, one must begin with its origins.

REVOLUTION FROM THE OUTSIDE

From time to time dramatic changes in warfare occur as a consequence of forces endogenous to war. Military research and development programs gave birth to the nuclear revolution, and although space exploration has many civilian spinoffs, military resources drove it in its early phases. Submarine warfare, which gave weaker naval powers a tremendously potent tool against stronger ones, also originated in the military. Just as often, however, the driving forces behind a change in the conduct of war lie in the realms of political and economic life.

The transformation of warfare in the nineteenth century offers a particularly useful analogy for contemporary strategists. Describing the posture of Austria and Prussia at the outset of the French Revolution, Clausewitz noted in *On War* that the two countries resorted to the kind of limited war that the previous century had made familiar in Europe. However,

> they soon discovered its inadequacy. . . . People at first expected to have to deal only with a seriously weakened French army; but in 1793 a force appeared that beggared all imagination. Suddenly war again became the business of the people—a people of thirty millions, all of whom considered themselves to be citizens. . . . The resources and efforts now available for use surpassed all conventional limits; nothing now impeded the vigor with which war could be waged, and consequently the opponents of France faced the utmost peril.

The advent of broadly based conscription greatly enlarged armies and increased their durability. The secret of the success of the French revolutionary armies lay not in their skill on the battlefield—the reviews there are mixed—but in the new regime's ability to replenish its forces repeatedly after defeat and in the opening of military advancement to all classes of citizen. The age of the mass army had arrived.

Civilian technologies have also brought revolutionary change in warfare. The mass-produced rifle of the nineteenth century complicated the task of military tacticians enormously, while the appearance of the railroad and telegraph altered war even more. Generals could shuttle armies from one theater to another in weeks, a feat demonstrated in spectacular fashion during the Civil War when the Union shifted 25,000 troops, with artillery and baggage, over 1,100 miles of rail lines from Virginia to Chattanooga, Tennessee, in less than 12 days. Furthermore, the railroad, in conjunction with the mass army, made mobilization at the outset of war a critical element in the efficiency of a military organization.

The telegraph affected not only armies and governments but newspapers. It helped general staffs coordinate rapid mobilization and launch large military movements. Even more important, the rapid dissemination of news transformed the nature of civil-military relations in wartime, creating new opportunities for tension. Politicians discovered, to their consternation, that the literate publics of modern states could learn of events on the battlefield almost immediately from mass circulation newspapers. At the same time, generals discovered that political leaders could now communicate with them in the field, and would gladly do so. During the Civil War the Union established a military telegraph system, laying some 15,000 miles of wires, but placed it under civilian control rather than the Army Signal Corps'; Secretary of War Edwin M. Stanton made certain the lines terminated in his office, not that of the army's senior general. With knowledge came intervention—or interference, as many a Union general keenly felt it. As the wars of German unification went on, Field Marshal Helmuth Graf von Moltke felt the same way about the suggestions Bismarck telegraphed his subordinates, and attempted to restrict the information flowing over the wires to higher headquarters.

The contemporary revolution in military affairs, like those of the nineteenth century, has its origins in the civilian world, and in two developments in particular. The first is the rise of information technologies, which have transformed economic and social life in ways that hardly need elaboration. The consequences for military organizations are numerous; the development of intelligent weapons that can guide themselves to their targets is only one, and not necessarily the most important. The variety and ever-expanding capabilities of intelligence-gathering machines and the ability of computers to bring together and distribute to users the masses of information from these sources stem from the information revolution. Small wonder that a group of senior Marine Corps officers, led by the assistant commandant of the corps, visited the New York Stock Exchange recently to learn how brokers absorb, process, and transmit the vast quantities of perishable information that are the lifeblood of the financial markets.

The efflorescence of capitalism in the United States and abroad constitutes a second driving force. In the years after World War II, even Western nations spent a great deal of their national wealth on defense and created vast state bureaucracies to provide for every military need and function. Today very few states can successfully resist the pressures of postindustrial capitalism. Military dimensions include the sale of government-owned defense industries around the world and the increasing privatization of military functions; private contractors, for instance, handled much of the logistics for the U.S. operations in Haiti and Somalia. In a world where commercial satellites can deliver images of a quality that only a few years ago was the prerogative of the superpowers, military organizations are more and more willing to use civilian systems for military communications and even intelligence gathering rather than spend to develop their own. Furthermore, the end of the Cold War has freed up the markets in military goods and services. Countries can gain access to a wide spectrum of military capabilities for ready cash, including the services of skilled personnel to maintain and perhaps operate high-technology weapons. For much of this century armed forces could ignore the market, practicing a kind of military socialism in a sea of capitalism; no longer.

To know what the revolution in military affairs will look like, we need the answers to four questions. Will it change the appearance of combat? Will it change the structure of armies? Will it lead to the rise of new military elites? Will it alter countries' power position? Reflection on each of these suggests that this is the eve of a far-reaching change in warfare whose outlines are only dimly visible but real nonetheless.

THE FORMS OF COMBAT

A transformation of combat means change in the fundamental relationship between offense and defense, space and time, fire and maneuver. The advent of carrier-based warfare provides an example. Warfare in the age of battleships took place within visual range, between tightly drilled formations of ships of the line that battered each other with their big guns. Once carriers came on the scene, fleets struck at one another from hundreds of miles away, and their blows were not repeated salvos but massed air raids; fighting now depended on "one large pulse of firepower unleashed upon the arrival of the air wing at the target," as Wayne Hughes put it in his 1986 *Fleet Tactics*. The firepower revolution of the late nineteenth century rested on the adoption of the rifle and subsequent improvement of the weapon with smokeless powder, breechloading, and metal cartridges. In short order the densely packed battlefield of the early American Civil War gave way to the empty battlefield of modern times, in which small groups of soldiers scurry from shellhole to shellhole, eschewing the massed rush that dominated tactics for almost two centuries.

Today the forms of combat have begun a change no less dramatic. A military cliché has it that what can be seen on the modern battlefield can be hit, and what can be hit will be destroyed. Whereas at the beginning of the century this applied with deadly certainty only to front-line infantrymen, it now holds not only for machines on the front lines but for supporting forces in the rear. The introduction of long-range precision weapons, delivered by plane or missile, together with the development of intelligent mines that can be activated from a remote location, means that sophisticated armies can inflict unprecedented levels of destruction on any large armored force on the move. Fixed sites are also increasingly vulnerable.

The colossal maneuvers of the coalition armies in the deserts of Kuwait and Iraq in 1991 may in retrospect appear, like the final charges of cavalry in the nineteenth century, an anomaly in the face of modern firepower. Future warfare may be more a gigantic artillery duel fought with exceptionally sophisticated munitions than a chesslike game of maneuver and positioning. As all countries gain access to the new forms of air power (space-based reconnaissance and unmanned aerial vehicles), hiding large-scale armored movements or building up safe rear areas chock-a-block with ammunition dumps and truck convoys will gradually become impossible.

From the middle of the nineteenth century until very recently, platforms dominated warfare: the newest ship, plane, or tank outclassed its rivals and in most cases speedily rendered them obsolete. But this was not always the case. Until the 1830s, for example, naval technology remained roughly where it had been since the mid-eighteenth century. Nelson's *Victory* was laid down in 1759, launched in 1765, served brilliantly at Trafalgar in 1805, and was paid off only in 1835—a service life of 70 years. Steam propulsion and metal construction changed all that, and a period of near-constant technological change ensued, in which naval superiority seemed to shift rapidly from power to power depending on who had the most recently built warship.

The wheel has now turned again. The platform has become less important, while the quality of what it carries—sensors, munitions, and electronics of all kinds—has become critical. A modernized 30-year-old aircraft armed with the latest long-range air-to-air missile, cued by an airborne warning plane, can defeat a craft a third its age but not so equipped or guided. In a world dominated by long-range, intelligent precision weapons, the first blow can prove decisive; the collapse of the Iraqi air defense system in 1991 within a few hours of a sophisticated air attack is a case in point. As a result, incentives for preemption may grow. For two duelists armed with swords approaching each other from a dozen yards' distance, it makes little difference who unsheathes his weapon first. Give them pistols, however, and all odds favor the man quicker on the draw.

Furthermore, the nature of preemption itself may change. To the extent that information warfare, including the sabotage of computer systems, emerges as a new type of combat, the first blow may be covert, a precursor to more open and conventional hostilities. Such attacks—to which an information-dependent society like the United States is particularly vulnerable—could have many purposes: blinding, intimidating, diverting, or simply confusing an opponent. They could carry as well the threat of bringing war to a country's homeland and people, and thus even up the balance for countries that do not possess the conventional tools of long-range attack, such as missiles and bombers. How such wars initiated by information strikes would play themselves out is a matter of tremendous uncertainty.

THE STRUCTURE OF MILITARY ORGANIZATIONS

It is not merely the tools of warfare but the organizations that wield them that make for revolutionary change in war. The invention of the tank—itself a cluster of technologies—did not bring about the armored warfare revolution, nor did the acquisition of tanks in quantity allow countries to exploit the new technology equally. The raw conceptual ingredients for blitzkrieg existed as early as 1918, when J.F.C. Fuller devised Plan 1919 for the British army as it prepared its final assault into Germany. But it took armed forces more than 20 years to put the ideas into practice. The Germans had fewer (and in some respects inferior) tanks in 1940 than the British and French. They succeeded not because of material superiority but because they got several things right—supporting technologies such as tank radios, organization, operational concepts, and a proper climate or culture of command.

The construction of the Panzer division reflected a careful working out of the requirements of modern warfare. Whereas the French and British created armored divisions consisting almost exclusively of tanks, the Germans made theirs combined arms organizations built around the tank. The Germans saw the need for units of engineers and infantry to accompany the tanks, allowing them to develop their striking power to the fullest. To enable the new organizations to function, the German military had to cultivate a particular climate of command. An American liaison officer in the 1930s noted that the Germans made decisions with far less preparation than their American counterparts:

> The Germans point out, that often a Commander must make an important decision after only a few minutes' deliberation and emphasize, that a fair decision given in time for aggressive execution is much better than one wholly right but too late. They visualize rapidly changing situations in modern warfare and are gearing their command and staff operations accordingly.[1]

Fortunately for the Germans, the Panzer division fit well with pre-armored doctrine and military culture. The contemporary revolution in military affairs may require similar but more painful evolution. Armed forces do not know what the Panzer division of the future will look like, much less how to create it, but one can advance some tentative descriptions of the military of the next century. To begin with, the new military will rest primarily on long voluntary service. The balance between quality and quantity has shifted in favor of quality, and it is no mere drive for economy (because professional militaries are not cheap) that has led countries either to give up conscription or to create two separate militaries, one conscript and one professional, with ever more attention and resources going to the latter. At long last, after a reign of almost two centuries, the age of the mass military manned by short-service conscripts and equipped with the products of high-volume military manufacturing is coming to an end.

The new military will be an increasingly joint force—or perhaps, one might say, less and less a traditional, service-oriented force. In militaries around the world the traditional division into armies, navies, and air forces (and in only a few countries, marine corps) has begun to break down. Not only have air operations become inseparable from almost any action on the ground, but naval forces increasingly deliver fire against a wide range of ground targets. Quasi services have begun to emerge. In all militarily sophisticated countries special forces have grown, imitating the highly successful models

---

[1]Albert C. Wedemeyer, "Memorandum: German General Staff School Report," July 11, 1938, p. 12. This is one of the most insightful accounts of the temper and tone of the German army before World War II. See also the masterly survey in Herbert Rosinski, *The German Army,* London: Hogarth Press, 1939.

of the British Special Air Service and its American and Israeli counterparts. Even regular infantry formations have adopted the tactics of special forces—very small units, dispersion, and the extensive use of fire brought to bear from the air or rear areas. Other quasi services include organizations oriented toward space and information warfare and the horde of civilian contractors who fix airplanes, build bases, pay the troops, operate mess halls, and analyze operations.

Another structural change looms. Tack an organizational chart of an army corps on a wall, and next to it place a similar chart for a leading corporation of the 1950s—General Motors, say—and the similarities stand out. One would see in both cases a classical pyramid, small units reporting up to progressively smaller numbers of larger organizations. The organization of a corps has not changed much since then, but the cutting-edge corporation of today is not GM but Microsoft or Motorola, neither of which much resembles an army corps. The modern corporation has stripped out layers of middle management, reduced or even eliminated many of the functional and social distinctions between management and labor that dominated industrial organizations, and largely abolished the old long-term tenure and compensation systems, including company-based pensions. By and large, military organizations have not done this. "Management" still consists of commissioned and noncommissioned officers, and although the latter play a role quite different from that of even their World War II counterparts, they still operate within rank, deference, and pay structures of a bygone time. The radical revision of these structures will be the last manifestation of a revolution in military affairs, and the most difficult to implement.

THE NATURE OF COMMAND

In a period of revolutionary change in the conduct of war, different kinds of people—not simply the same people differently trained—rise to the top of armed services. For instance, air power gave birth to entirely new kinds of military organizations; unlike armies and navies, air forces consist of a tiny percentage of officer-warriors backed by an elaborate array of enlisted technicians. To take another example: in the late nineteenth century it became clear that the increasingly complex problem of mobilizing reservists and deploying them over a country's railroad network required a corps of technocratic experts. The American Civil War and the Franco-Prussian War demonstrated that dash and bravura could not compete with skill at scheduling large numbers of locomotives, handling loading manifests, and repairing damaged track. The logistical manager had become an indispensable member of a general staff and a well-trained general staff an essential feature of a military establishment.

A similar evolution is underway today. Even in the U.S. Air Force, an organization dominated by pilots (bomber pilots in the 1950s and 1960s, fighter pilots thereafter), the number of general officers in important positions who are not combat aviators has risen. The new technologies will increasingly bring to the fore the expert in missile operations, the space general, and the electronic warfare wizard—none of them a combat specialist in the old sense and a fair percentage of them, sooner or later, female. Military organizations still need, and will always need, specialists in direct combat. Indeed, both the lethality of direct combat and its physical and intellectual demands have grown. But the number of such fighters in military organizations, both in absolute terms and in proportion to the overall size of the militaries, has declined steadily since the beginning of the century and will continue to do so. The cultural challenge for military organizations will be to maintain a warrior spirit and the intuitive understanding of war that goes with it, even when their leaders are not, in large part, warriors themselves.

Different eras in warfare give rise to characteristic styles of military leadership. The age of industrial warfare has ended, and with it a certain kind of supreme command. Shortly after the mobilization against Austria in 1866, an aide found the Prussian chief of the general staff, Helmuth Graf von Moltke, lying on a sofa reading a novel. On the evening before D-Day, General Dwight D. Eisenhower, supreme commander of Allied forces, could be found on his sofa doing precisely the same thing. Despite the 80 intervening years, some features of supreme command remained constant: the general in chief and his staff assembled a vast force, planned its intricate movements, and then spent the next day or two letting the machine conduct its initial operations on virtual autopilot. Today, an aide would more likely find a field marshal pacing back and forth in an electronic command post, fiddling with television displays, talking to pilots or tank commanders on the front line by radio, and perhaps even peeking over their shoulders through remote cameras.

That the modern field marshal can sit invisibly in the cockpit with a pilot or perch cybernetically in the hatch of a tank commander raises a profound problem of centralization of authority. Although all military organizations pay lip service to delegation of maximum authority to the lowest levels of command, few military leaders can resist the temptation to dabble in their subordinates' business. The easier it is for them to find out what that business is, even though they are 10,000 miles away, the more likely they are to do so. Political leaders will have the same capability, and although for the moment most of them show little inclination to meddle, one can imagine situations in which they would choose otherwise.

THE POWER OF STATES

Few subjects exercise historians of early modern Europe more than the military revolution of the sixteenth and early seventeenth centuries. Yet all would agree that that period's remarkable set of changes profoundly altered the relative balance of power between Europe and the rest of the world in Europe's favor. The creation of modern military organizations—that is, armies led by professional officers, trained and organized according to impersonal standards of discipline and behavior—coupled with the appearance of governments that could mobilize both soldiers and financial resources, changed the international system. The rise of Holland and the decline of the Ottoman Empire represent the opposite extremes of the consequences of the revolution.

The contemporary revolution in military affairs offers tremendous opportunities to countries that can afford to acquire expensive modern weaponry and the skills to use it properly. An accurate measurement of Israel's power potential relative to its Arab neighbors, for example, would probably show a steep rise since 1973. Taiwan, Singapore, and Australia, to take just three examples, can do far more against potential opponents than would have been thinkable 30 years ago. As we have seen, the military leadership of the Soviet Union believed the revolutionary changes it saw coming would put it at a disadvantage. Indeed, only the United States, with its vast accumulation of military capital, better than four times the defense budget of the next leading power, and an unsurpassed ability to integrate large, complicated technological systems, can fully exploit this revolution.

Transformation in one area of military affairs does not, however, mean the irrelevance of all others. Just as nuclear weapons did not render conventional power obsolete, this revolution will not render guerrilla tactics, terrorism, or weapons of mass destruction obsolete. Indeed, the reverse may be true: where unconventional bypasses to conventional military power exist, any country confronting the United States will seek them out. The phenomenon of the persistence of older systems in the midst of revolutionary change occurs even at a tactical level. After the arrival of the carrier as the capital ship of naval warfare, for example, the venerable battleship did not disappear but instead acquired two important roles: shore bombardment platform and vast floating air defense battery. Battleships were part of the American fleet as recently as the Persian Gulf War, almost half a century after their day as the queens of naval warfare had passed.

To the extent that the revolution proceeds from forces in the civilian world, the potential will exist for new military powers to emerge extremely rapidly. A country like Japan or, in a few years, China will quickly translate civilian technological power into its military equivalent. An analogy might be Germany's acquisition of a modern air force in the space of less than a decade in the 1930s. At a time when civilian and military aviation technologies did not diverge too greatly, Germany could take the strongest civilian aviation industry in Europe and within a few years convert it into enormous military power, much as the United States would do a few years later with its automobile industry. After a long interval during the Cold War when military industry became an exotic and separate entity, the pendulum has begun to swing back, and economic strength may again prove easily translatable into military power.

THE CHANGING ORDER

Revolutionary change in the art of war stems not simply from the ineluctable march of technology but from an adaptation of the military instrument to political purposes. The subject of armored warfare languished in Great Britain and France between the world wars because those governments saw little need for an operationally offensive force on the continent. The powers that contemplated offensives to regain lost territories or to seize new ones—the Soviet Union and Germany—developed the armored instrument more fully than other states.

The United States may drive the revolution in military affairs, but only if it has a clear conception of what it wants military power for—which it does not now have. Indeed, when the Clinton administration formulated its defense policy in 1993 it came up with the Bottom-Up Review, which provided for a force capable of fighting simultaneously two regional wars assumed to resemble the Gulf War of 1991. By structuring its analysis around enemy forces similar to those of Iraq in that year—armor-heavy, with a relatively large conventional but third-rate air force—it guaranteed a conservatism in military thought at odds with the thorough reexamination promised by the administration early in its tenure. For this reason, among others, the revolution will take far longer to consummate than the Soviets predicted in the 1980s. Barring the pressure of a severe competition between the United States and some state capable of posing a real challenge to it, even available technologies are unlikely to be exploited fully. Military institutions in peacetime will normally evolve rather than submit to radical change.

World politics will also shape the revolution. One feature will certainly be the predominance of conventional warfare for limited objectives. Until the end of the Cold War, the possibility of total war, as in the great struggles of the first half of this century, dominated the planning of the American and Soviet military establishments, and perhaps others as well. With some exceptions, military action for limited ends seems more likely in the years ahead.

The most useful metaphor for the future military order may be a medieval one. During the Middle Ages, as at present, sovereignty did not reside exclusively in states but was diffused among political, civic, and religious bodies—states, but also sub- and supra-state entities. Warfare was not, as it has been in the modern period, an affair almost exclusively of states, but one that also involved private entities such as religious orders and other associations. Then, unlike during the past two centuries, military technology varied widely among combatants—an army of English bowmen and knights fought very differently from the Arab warriors of Saladin or the Mongol cavalry of Genghis Khan or the pike-wielding peasantry of Switzerland. Militaries defied comparison; their strength varied greatly depending on where and whom they were fighting.

Opacity in the matter of military power may prove one of the most troubling features of the current revolution. The wildly inaccurate predictions of casualties in the Gulf War from responsible and experienced observers (including military estimators, let it be noted) reflected not conservatism or incompetence but a disjunction between the realities of military power and conventional means of measuring it. Numbers of tanks, airplanes, and soldiers and more elaborate firepower-based measurements of military might were always questionable, but now they say almost nothing about real military effectiveness. As platforms become less important and the quality of munitions and, above all, the ability to handle information become more so, analysts will find it ever more difficult to assess the military balance of opposing sides. If Admiral Owens is right, the revolution in military affairs may bring a kind of tactical clarity to the battlefield, but at the price of strategic obscurity.

In the nineteenth and early twentieth centuries, God may not always have been on the side of the bigger battalions, as the saying went, but victory usually was. Future technologies, however, may create pockets of military capability that will allow very small states to hold off larger ones, much as companies of Swiss pikemen could stop armies sweeping through their mountain passes or a single, well-fortified castle could hold immensely larger forces at bay for months. Herein lies a potential challenge even for the United States, which will find itself attempting to project military power for limited purposes and at a low cost in materiel and lives. Other parties may well decide to inflict some hard, if not fatal, blows to stave off American intervention. For stymieing the American advantage in the megasystems of modern military power—fantastically expensive and effective aircraft carriers or satellites, for example—the microsystems of modern military technology, such as the cruise missile, may prove sufficient.

The predominance of warfare for limited objectives, the availability of vast quantities of centralized information, and the obscurity of military power may combine to make civil-military relations more awkward. Politicians will seek to use means they can readily see, as it were, but do not understand; generals will themselves be handling forces they do not fully comprehend and will be divided on the utility of various forms of military power.

In every previous period of revolutionary change in the conduct of war, military leaders made large mistakes. The human toll on European armies coming to terms with modern firepower in World War I reflected not only, or even primarily, the incompetence of generals but their bafflement in the face of new conditions of warfare. Less costly but no less time-consuming was the difficulty the U.S. Navy had developing the multi-carrier task forces that would ultimately enable it to sweep the Pacific clear of Japanese forces in World War II. The lesson of the 1942 Battle of Midway had appeared to be that the massing of carriers offered great advantages but posed no lesser vulnerabilities, should the defending side be caught while rearming its strike aircraft. As a result, the transformation of naval warfare by the carrier could not be realized until one side either felt overwhelming pressure to mass carriers despite the risks—the case in the early part of the war—or had enough carriers to make the risks bearable. For the United States the latter did not occur until almost two years after it entered the war, when the naval building program had produced the sheer numbers of vessels adequate for large-scale carrier operations.

A revolution in military affairs is under way. It will require changes of a magnitude that military people still do not completely grasp and political leaders do not fully imagine. For the moment, it appears to offer the United States the prospect of military power beyond that of any other country on the planet, now and well into the next century. Small wonder, then, that by and large American theorists have embraced the idea of a revolution in warfare as an opportunity for their country, as indeed it is. But revolution implies rapid, violent, and, above all, unpredictable change. Clio has a number of lessons to teach Mars, but perhaps none is more important than that.

THE DELUSION OF
IMPARTIAL INTERVENTION

Richard K. Betts

The United States, the United Nations, and the North Atlantic Treaty Organization (NATO) have had rocky experiences in humanitarian interventions in civil conflicts in the decade since the Cold War ended. Disastrous mistakes and shaky successes have outnumbered jobs solidly well done. By the end of the 1990s there was some evidence of learning from earlier errors, but not enough. The biggest such intervention—the war over Kosovo—will remain a subject of hot debate for many reasons, not least because there is no agreement about whether it should be counted a success or failure.[1] NATO's strategy in Kosovo did not make one of the two mistakes emphasized later in this essay (it was not impartial), but it did make the other (it was limited). In another big case—Bosnia—NATO intervention helped to put over a provisional peace settlement after the UN effort proved bankrupt. This was only achieved, however, by stipulating contradictory terms in the Dayton peace accords (in principle, reunification of three parts of the country, but in practice, partition). It is doubtful that this anomalous arrangement can last longer than the NATO occupation that papers over the contradiction. Despite some learning, many humanitarian interventionists still don't get it. This essay focuses on the misconceptions evident in the first half of the 1990s that still infect thinking among many who seek to use military instruments to relieve suffering and injustice in benighted countries.

Physicians have a motto that peacemakers would do well to adopt: "First, do no harm." Neither the United States nor the United Nations quite grasped this for most of the 1990s. After the end of the Cold War unleashed them to intervene in civil conflicts around the world, they did reasonably well in some cases, but in others they unwittingly prolonged suffering where they meant to relieve it.

How did this happen? By following a principle that sounds like common sense: Intervention should be both limited and impartial, because weighing in on one side of a local struggle undermines the legitimacy and effectiveness of outside involvement. This Olympian presumption resonates with respect for law and international cooperation. It has the ring of prudence, fairness, and restraint. It makes sense in old-fashioned UN

Richard K. Betts, "The Delusion of Impartial Intervention," in Chester A. Crocker, Fen Osler Hampson, and Pamela Aall, eds., *Turbulent Peace: The Challenges of Managing Global Conflict* (Washington, D.C.: U.S. Institute of Peace, 2001); revised version of article in *Foreign Affairs* Vol. 73, No. 6 (November/December 1994). Reprinted by permission.
[1]See Michael Mandelbaum's masterfully scathing criticism, "A Perfect Failure: NATO's War Against Yugoslavia," *Foreign Affairs* 78, no. 5 (September/October 1999) and the Clinton Administration rebuttal, James Steinberg, "A Perfect Polemic: Blind to Reality on Kosovo," *Foreign Affairs* 78, no. 6 (November/December 1999).

peacekeeping operations, where the outsiders' role is not to make peace, but to bless and monitor a cease-fire that all parties have decided to accept. But it becomes a destructive misconception when carried over to the messier realm of "peace enforcement," where the belligerents have yet to decide that they have nothing more to gain by fighting.

Limited intervention may end a war if the intervenor takes sides, tilts the local balance of power, and helps one of the rivals to win—that is, if it is not impartial. Impartial intervention may end a war if the outsiders take complete command of the situation, overawe all the local competitors, and impose a peace settlement—that is, if it is not limited. Trying to have it both ways (limited *and* impartial) usually blocks peace by doing enough to keep either side from defeating the other, but not enough to make them stop trying. And the attempt to have it both ways brought the United Nations and the United States—and those whom they sought to help—to varying degrees of grief in Bosnia, Somalia, and Haiti.

WHO RULES?

Wars have many causes, and each war is unique and complicated, but the root issue is always the same: Who rules when the fighting stops? In wars between countries, the issue may be sovereignty over disputed territory, or suzerainty over third parties, or influence over international transactions. In wars within countries the issue may be which group will control the government, or how the country should be divided so that adversaries can have separate governments. When political groups resort to war, it is because they cannot agree on who gets to call the tune in peace.

A war will not begin unless both sides in a dispute would rather fight than concede. After all, it is not hard to avert war if either party cares primarily about peace—all it has to do is let the other side have what it claims is its due. A war will not end until both sides agree who will control whatever is in dispute.

Is all this utterly obvious? Not to those enthusiasts for international peace enforcement who are imbued with hope for global governance, unsympathetic to thinking of security in terms of sovereignty, or viscerally sure that war is not a rational political act. They cannot bring themselves to deal forthrightly in the currency of war. They assume instead that outsiders' good offices can pull the scales from the eyes of fighting factions, make them realize that resorting to violence was a blunder, and substitute peaceful negotiation for force. But wars are rarely accidents, and it is no accident that belligerents often continue to kill each other while they negotiate, or that the terms of diplomatic settlements usually reflect results on the battlefield.

Others sometimes proceed from muddled assumptions about what force should be expected to accomplish. For instance, in a bizarre sequence of statements in spring 1994 (before the NATO intervention the following year), President Clinton threatened air strikes against the Bosnian Serbs, then said, "The United States is not, and should not, become involved as a partisan in a war." Next he declared that the United States should lead other western nations in ending ethnic cleansing in Bosnia, only to say a moment later, "That does not mean that the United States or the United Nations can enter a war, in effect, to redraw the lines . . . within what was Yugoslavia."

This profoundly confused policy, promulgated with the best of lawyerly intentions, inevitably cost lives on all sides in Bosnia. For what legitimate purpose can military forces be directed to kill people and break things, if not to take the side of their opponents? If the use of deadly force is to be legitimate killing rather than senseless killing, it must serve the purpose of settling the war—which means determining who rules, which means leaving someone in power at the end of the day.

How is this done without taking someone's side? And how can outside powers pretend to stop ethnic cleansing without allocating territory—that is, drawing lines? Yet for several years Clinton and UN Secretary General Boutros Boutros-Ghali did not make threats in order to protect recognized or viable borders, but to enforce naturally unstable truce lines that made no sense as a permanent territorial arrangement. In the early 1990s such confusion made intervention an accessory to stalemate, punishing either side for advancing too far, but not settling the issue that fueled the war.

Some see a method in the madness. There are two ways to stop a war: either one side imposes its will after defeating the other on the battlefield, or both sides accept a negotiated compromise. The hope for a compromise solution accounts for a misconceived impartiality. This is not to say that compromise never works. Indeed, after the turning point of 1995 in Bosnia, the Dayton accords emerged as a compromise, but one that embedded instability in the settlement, for reasons discussed later. To work, compromise must first be possible, and then it must prove durable.

When is compromise probable? When both sides believe that they have more to lose than to gain from fighting. Because leaders are often sensible, this usually happens before a war starts, which is why most crises are resolved by diplomacy rather than combat. But peaceful compromise has to seem impossible to the opponents for a war to start, and once it begins, compromise becomes even harder. Emotions intensify, sunk costs grow, demands for recompense escalate. If compromise was not tolerable enough to avert war in the first place, it becomes even less attractive once large amounts of blood and treasure have been invested in the cause.

If neither side manages to pound the other into submission and a stalemate emerges, does a compromise peace become more practical? Not for a long time, and not until many more lives have been invested in the contending quests for victory. Stalemates rarely seem solid to those with a strong stake in overcoming them. Belligerents conjure up one set of military stratagems and schemes after another to gain the upper hand, or they hope for shifts in alliances or outside assistance to tilt the balance of power, or they gamble that their adversary will be the first to lose heart and crack. Such developments often do break stalemates. In World War I, for example, trench warfare in France ebbed and flowed inconclusively for four years until the Russian capitulation. This allowed the Germans to move armies from the east and achieve a breakthrough that unglued the Western Front and almost brought them victory in the spring of 1918. Then the Allies rebounded, turned the tables with newly arrived American armies, and won the war six months later.

Stalemate is likely to yield to negotiated compromise only after it lasts so long that a military solution appears hopeless to both sides. In the Iran-Iraq War, where UN mediation was useful, the two sides had fought ferociously but inconclusively for eight years. The United Nations smoothed the way for both sides to lay down their arms, but it is hard to credit that diplomatic intervention with as much effect in bringing peace as the simple exhaustion and despair of war-makers in Tehran and Baghdad. Mediation is useful, but it helps peacemaking most where peacemaking needs help least.

In Bosnia, war among the Serb, Croat, and Muslim populations went on for nearly four years until the shocking disgrace at Srebrenica laid bare the bankruptcy of UN efforts. After the Security Council declared Srebrenica to be a "safe area," but refused to back up the declaration with the means to enforce it, the Dutch UN contingent stood by as the Serbs conquered the city, rounded up thousands of Muslims, and murdered them. NATO entered the fray, tilted decisively against the Serbs, bombed heavily in the "Deliberate Force" campaign, and stood by as the Croatian ground offensive cleansed the Krajina region of Serbs. Thus external intervention became more effective when it switched to being much less impartial and much less limited. But why did it take outside powers so long to get to that point?

COMPROMISES THAT KILL

If there is any place where peacemaking needed help most, and failed most abjectly, it was Bosnia in the early 1990s. There, the West's attempt at limited but impartial involvement abetted slow-motion savagery. The effort wound up doing things that helped one side, and counterbalancing them by actions that helped the other. This alienated both sides and enabled them to keep fighting.

The United Nations tried to prevent the Serbs from consolidating their victory, but without going all the way to provide consistent military support of the Muslims and the Croats. The main UN mission was humanitarian delivery of food and medicine to besieged communities, but this amounted to breaking the sieges—a military and political effect. It is hardly surprising that the Serbs interfered when they could get away with it. In line with the humanitarian rationale, the United Nations supported "safe areas"—pockets of Muslims and Croats hanging on in areas conquered by the Serbs. Apart from such limited action to frustrate the last phase of territorial rearrangement by force, UN and U.S. attempts to settle the war were limited to diplomatic mediation, an arms embargo, a "no-fly zone," and economic sanctions on Belgrade.

For over a year, the UN presence inhibited forceful reaction to Bosnian Serb provocations because French, British, and other units on the ground were hostage to retaliation. U.S. and UN threats were not just weak and hesitant; by trying to be both forceful and neutral, they worked at cross-purposes. First, after much dancing around and wringing of hands, the United Nations and NATO used force on behalf of the Bosnian government, albeit with only a few symbolic "pinprick" air raids against Serb positions. But the outside powers did this while refusing to let those they were defending buy arms to defend themselves. Given the awkward multilateral politics of the arms embargo, this may have been understandable; but as strategy, it was irrational, plain and simple.

Impartiality compounded the absurdity in August 1994, when the UN military commander also threatened the Bosnian government with attack if it violated the weapons exclusion zone around Sarajevo. UN strategy thus bounced between unwillingness to undertake any combat at all and a commitment to fight on two fronts against both belligerents. Such lofty evenhandedness may make sense for a judge in a court that can enforce its writ, but hardly for a general wielding a small stick in a bitter war.

Overall, UN pressures maintained a teetering balance of power between the belligerents; the intervenors refused to let either side win. Economic sanctions worked against the Serbs, while the arms embargo worked against the Muslims. The rationale was that evenhandedness would encourage a negotiated settlement. The result, however, was not peace or an end to the killing, but years of military stalemate, slow bleeding, and delusionary diplomatic haggling.

The desire for impartiality and fairness led outside diplomats to promote territorial compromises that made no strategic sense. The Vance-Owen plan mimicked the unrealistic 1947 UN partition plan for Palestine: a geographic patchwork of noncontiguous territories, vulnerable corridors and supply lines, exposed communities, and indefensible borders. If ever accepted, such a plan would have created a territorial tinderbox and a perpetual temptation to renew the conflict. Yet Washington said it was willing to thrust tens of thousands of American troops into the Bosnian tangle to enforce just such an accord.

As it turned out, the Dayton accords did not rest on a Vance-Owen-type patchwork. The agreement accepted a de facto three-way partition, where most of the territory controlled by each of the three factions was connected. At the same time the agreement embraced the principle that Bosnia should be a unitary, reintegrated, state. As long as outside forces continue to occupy Bosnia, this contradiction between integration in principle and partition in practice can function, and paper over the failure of the intervenors to establish a peace that the locals can make final on their own.

In Somalia in 1992–93, the United States succeeded laudably in relieving starvation. Then, fearful that food supply would fall apart again after withdrawal, Washington took on the mission of restoring civil order. This was less limited and more ambitious than the outside powers' "strategy" in Bosnia, but it stopped short of taking charge and imposing a settlement on the warring factions.

Incongruously, the international operation in Somalia worked at throwing together a local court and police organization before establishing the other essential elements of government, an executive or a legislature. Then U.S. forces set out to arrest General Mohammed Farah Aidid—who was not just a troublemaker but one of the prime claimants to governing authority—without championing any other contender. The U.S. attempts failed, but killed a large number of Somalis and further roiled the political waters in Mogadishu. Stung by casualties to U.S. forces, Washington pulled out and left UN troops from other countries holding the bag, maintaining an indecisive presence, and taking casualties of their own.

It may have been wise to avoid embroilment in the chaos of conflict among Somali clans. But it was then naive to think that intervention could help to end the local anarchy. As Michael Maren asked, "If the peacekeepers aren't keeping the peace, what are they doing?"—especially after the cost of the intervention topped $1.5 billion. The UN operation was not only indecisive, Maren argued, but it fueled the fighting by letting the feuding factions compete for UN jobs, contracts, and cash. In areas where UN forces were absent, the parties reached accommodation in order to reestablish commerce, rather than jockeying for UN resources.[2]

After early forceful rhetoric by President Clinton had raised expectations about U.S. action, experiences in Bosnia and Somalia helped to brake enthusiasm in New York

---

[2]Michael Maren, "Leave Somalia Alone," *New York Times,* July 6, 1994, p. A19.

and Washington for taking on other peace operations. It is indeed wise to be more selective than in the heady days of hope for collective security that followed the end of the Cold War, but it would be unfortunate if the Western powers and the United Nations abandon such missions altogether. Indeed, bad conscience over the failure to step in to stop genocide in Rwanda, and reinvigorated confidence from pseudo-success in Bosnia and Kosovo, has kept multilateral intervention alive into the twenty-first century. Without full recognition of the misconceptions of the early post-Cold War period the same problem—attempts to bring peace turning out to postpone peace—can arise again.

Of course, not all problems are due to impartiality. In Haiti, for example, the United States and the United Nations clearly did choose sides, supporting the exiled president, Jean-Bertrand Aristide; eventually the unmistakable U.S. willingness to invade forced the junta in Port-au-Prince to back down. Even there, however, suffering was prolonged by the initially limited character of the intervention.

For over a year after the junta reneged on the Governor's Island Agreement, Washington relied on economic sanctions against Haiti, a "trickle-up" strategy of coercion that was bound to hurt the innocent long before it touched the guilty. The blockade gradually devastated the health and welfare of the country's masses, who were powerless to make the policy changes demanded by Washington and on whose behalf the sanctions were supposedly being applied. Yet sanctions offered no incentive to Haiti's kleptocratic elites to cut their own throats, and sanctions were not what made the generals sign the accord brokered by former president Jimmy Carter. (The U.S. invasion force did that.) Instead, the many months during which sanctions were left to work were used by the junta to track down and murder Aristide supporters at a steady pace.

Meddling in the tragic saga of Haitian misgovernment was a dubious gamble for the United States, considering the formidable durability of Haiti's predatory political culture. While the relatively peaceful entry of the occupying U.S. forces was welcome, the fledgling Haitian experiment in democracy looked shaky, to say the least, when U.S. troops departed. The best that can be said is that, as of early 2000, things had turned out better than it appeared they might at the beginning of the occupation. The September 1994 agreement did not disband the Haitian military or even completely purge its officer corps, whose corruption and terror tactics had long been most of the problem. Even worse, the accord hinted that—for the first time in the crisis—Washington might have erred on the side of impartiality. American leaders spoke of the generals' "military honor," U.S. troops were ordered to cooperate with the usurpers' security forces, and many of the anti-Aristide gangsters were left free to plot to regain power. Deciding whether to intervene in Haiti was agonizing. Once that was done, however, picking a side was certainly wise. But that choice was weakened by dithering too long with sanctions, then appearing to waver in support for the chosen side when U.S. military force was finally applied.

Impartiality nonetheless remains a norm in many other cases. It has worked in cases that lie beyond traditional peacekeeping, such as the cease-fire mediation between Iran and Iraq or the political receivership of the United Nations Transitional Authority in Cambodia (UNTAC). When looking at the reasons for these successes, however, it becomes apparent that impartiality works best where intervention is needed least, where wars have played themselves out and the fighting factions need only the good offices of mediators to lay down their arms. Impartiality is likely to work against peace in the more challenging cases—where intervention must make the peace, rather than just preside over it—because it reflects deeper confusion over what war is about.

IMPERIAL IMPARTIALITY

If outsiders such as the United States, the United Nations, or NATO are faced with demands for peace in wars where passions have not burned out, they can avoid the costs and risks that go with entanglement by refusing the mandate—staying aloof and letting the locals fight it out. Or they can jump in and help one of the contenders defeat the other. But can they bring peace sooner than exhaustion from prolonged carnage would, if they remain impartial? Not with a gentle, restrained impartiality but with an active, harsh impartiality that overpowers both sides: an imperial impartiality. This is a tall order, seldom with many supporters, and it is hard to think of cases where it has actually worked.

The closest thing to a good example of imperial impartiality is the UN operation in Cambodia—a grand-scale takeover of much of the administrative authority in the country and a program for establishing a new government through supervised elections and a constituent assembly. Despite great obstacles, tenuous results, and eventual unraveling, UNTAC fulfilled most of its mandate; the final unraveling also left the country better off than it had been before the UNTAC operation. This success should be given its due. As a model to rescue the ideal of limited and impartial intervention, however, it falls short.

First, the United Nations did not nip a horrible war in the bud; as was the case with Iran and Iraq, it capitalized on fifteen years of exhaustion and bloody stalemate. The outside powers recognized that the main order of business was to determine who rules, but they did not act before the local factions were weary enough to agree on a procedure for doing so.

Second, UN intervention was limited only in one sense: it avoided direct enforcement of the transition agreement when local contenders proved recalcitrant. Luckily, such incidents were manageable, or the whole experiment would have been a fiasco. In other respects, the scale of involvement was too huge to provide a model. Apart from the wars in Korea and Kuwait, UNTAC was the most massive intervention in UN history. It involved thousands of personnel from a host of countries and billions of dollars in expenditures. The Cambodia operation proved so expensive, at a time when other demands on the United Nations were escalating dramatically, that it cannot be repeated much more than once in a blue moon. (The occupation of Kosovo is the next blue moon.)

Third, although UNTAC should count as a success—especially after the election it conducted against all odds in 1993—the operation's results were unstable. Despite a tremendous UN presence, the terms of the transition agreement were never faithfully followed by all the local combatants and continued to erode after UNTAC's departure. For example, because the Khmer Rouge reneged, none of the Cambodian factions disarmed to the degree stipulated in the agreement; after the election, the constituent assembly never seriously debated a constitution, but more or less rubber-stamped King Norodom Sihanouk's demands; and sporadic fighting between the Khmer Rouge and other parties continued before and after UNTAC left.

Fourth, and more to the point, the UN success in Cambodia was linked with impartiality only in principle, not in effect. The real success of the transition overseen by UN-TAC was not in fostering a final peaceful compromise among the parties in Cambodia, but in altering the balance of power among them and marginalizing the worst one. The transition did not compel an end to violent strife, but it did facilitate the realignment of parties and military forces that might bring it about. The old Cold War alignment of Sihanouk, Son Sann, and the Khmer Rouge against the Vietnamese-installed government in Phnom Penh was transformed into a new coalition of everyone against the Khmer Rouge. Any peace Cambodia could achieve had to come from a new balance of power. Ultimately the revised balance that facilitated the peace accord shifted altogether, as the Khmer Rouge were eliminated completely, and then the Hun Sen forces suppressed moderate opposition and took firm control of the country.

The least impartial and most imperial example of post-Cold War intervention was NATO's war against Serbian Yugoslavia for the purpose of protecting the Albanians of Kosovo. One may question that intervention on many grounds: the justification for starting the war (since greater crimes against humanitarian values were being perpetrated elsewhere, in places such as Sudan or Sierra Leone, without prompting such forceful intervention); or whether NATO's attack exacerbated the problem it was meant to cure (Belgrade did not begin mass expulsions of Albanians until after NATO bombing began); or whether NATO's insistence on limiting the military effort to aerial attack delayed resolution of the conflict and increased Albanian suffering; or whether the result represents a huge net improvement on the pre-war situation (in effect, ethnic cleansing of the Albanian majority by the Serb minority was traded for the reverse after Belgrade surrendered control of the territory); or whether the strategic costs in damage to relations with great powers—Russia and China—were outweighed by the humanitarian benefits; or whether there is any legitimate way that NATO can ever end its occupation of Kosovo (to get Yugoslavia to surrender NATO promised that Kosovo would remain under Belgrade's sovereignty, but this principle can never be turned into practice again without betraying the Kosovar Albanians). The fact remains, however, that the intervention did succeed in its primary purpose: removing Kosovo's Albanians from the oppression of the Serb central government. NATO did so by supporting unambiguously one side in the civil war, and by executing military operations that, while not unlimited, were massively destructive.

MEDDLING WITHOUT MUDDLING

The "peacekeeping" that has been the United Nations' forte can help fortify peace, but it does not create peace as "peace enforcement" is supposed to do. During the decade after the Cold War, the United States and the United Nations stumbled into several imbroglios where it was not clear which of the two missions they were pursuing, and there was much head scratching about the gray area between operations under Chapters VI and VII of the UN Charter. Washington and New York responded to rough experiences by remaining mired in indecision and hamstrung by half-measures (Bosnia to 1995), facing failure and bailing out (Somalia), acting only after a long period of limited and misdirected pressure (Haiti), or holding back from action where more awesome disaster than anywhere else called for it (Rwanda). UN performance was so frequently disappointing that great powers turned to another multilateral organization—NATO—when they wanted to use force effectively in Bosnia and Kosovo. In Kosovo, NATO almost avoided the delusion of impartiality. Indeed, it initiated a war against Belgrade explicitly on behalf of the Kosovar Albanians. NATO could not bring itself to own up to the logic of what it was doing, however, because it refused to endorse independence for the group for which it was fighting. This illogic may have eased the way for Slobodan Milosevic to capitulate, but it left the intervenors with no honorable way out of indefinite occupation of Kosovo.

If intervention is not to be foresworn, and is not to be undertaken arbitrarily, what is the alternative? To do better in picking and choosing, it would help to be clearer about how military means should be marshaled for political ends. The following points should be kept in mind.

Recognize That to Make Peace Is to Decide Who Rules

Making peace means determining how the war ends. If American or UN forces are going to intervene to make peace, they will often have to kill people and break things in the process. If they choose to do this, they should do so only after they have decided who will rule afterward.

If claims or capabilities in the local fracas are not clear enough to make this judgment, then they are not clear enough for intervention to bring peace. By the same token, international forces should not mix in the dangerous business of determining who governs without expecting deadly opposition. An intervention that can be stopped in its tracks by a few dozen fatalities, as the U.S. operation in Somalia was, is one that should never begin.

Avoid Half-Measures

If the United States or the United Nations wishes to bring peace to violent places before tragedy unfolds in full, gruesome detail, they should act decisively by either lending their military weight to one side or forcing both sides to compromise. In either case, leaders or outside powers should avoid what the natural instincts of successful politicians and bureaucrats tell them is sensible: a middle course.

Half-measures often make sense in domestic politics, but that is precisely because peace already exists. Contending interests accept compromises negotiated in legislatures, adjudicated in courts, and enforced by executives because the state has a monopoly on organized force; the question of who rules is settled. That is the premise of politics in peace; in war, that premise is what the fighting is all about. A middle course in intervention—especially a gradual and symbolic use of force—is likely to do little but muddy both sides' calculations, fuel their hopes of victory, or kill people for principles only indirectly related to the purpose of the war. If deadly force is to make a direct contribution to peace, it must engage the purposes most directly related to war—the determination of borders and the distribution of political power. (NATO used force less hesitantly and abstemiously in Bosnia in 1995 and Kosovo and Serbia in 1999 and, aided by ground action from Croatia in the first case and the Kosovo Liberation Army in the second, succeeded in defeating Serb forces. In neither of these later cases, however, did NATO go all the way to settling the terms of local government. It embraced the fantasy of re-creating integral multiethnic states, rather than reinforcing permanent partitions.)

Do Not Confuse Peace with Justice

If outside powers want to do the right thing, but do not want to do it in a big way, they should recognize that they are placing a higher premium on legitimacy than on peace. Most international interventions since the end of the Cold War were not driven by the material interests of the outside powers but by their moral interests: securing peace and justice. Peace and justice, however, are not natural allies, unless right just happens to coincide with might.

Outside intervention in a civil war usually becomes an issue when the sides are closely enough matched that neither can defeat the other quickly. When material interests are not directly involved, it is impractical to expect great powers or the United Nations to expend the resources for an overwhelming and decisive military action. So if peace should take precedence, intervention should support the mightiest of the rivals, irrespective of their legitimacy. If the United Nations had weighed in on the side of the Serbs when they were dominant in Bosnia in the early 1990s, or had helped Aidid take control in Mogadishu rather than trying to jail him, there might well have been peace in Bosnia and Somalia much earlier. If justice takes precedence, however, limited intervention may well lengthen a conflict. Perhaps putting an end to killing should not be the first priority in peacemaking, but interventionists should admit that any intervention involves such a choice.

Tension between peace and justice also arises in assessing territorial divisions like those proposed for Bosnia. If the aim is to reduce violent eruptions, borders should be drawn not to minimize the transfer of populations and property, but to make the borders coherent, congruent with political solidarity, and defensible. This, unfortunately, makes ethnic cleansing the solution to ethnic cleansing. Also, it will not guarantee against later outbreaks of revanchism, but it can make war less constant.

Do Not Confuse Balance
with Peace or Justice

Preventing either side from gaining a military advantage prevents ending the war by military means. Countries that are not losing a war are likely to keep fighting until prolonged indecision makes winning seem hopeless. Outsiders who want to make peace but do not want to take sides or take control themselves try to avoid favoritism by keeping either side from overturning an indecisive balance on the battlefield. This supports the military stalemate, lengthens the war, and costs more lives.

Make Humanitarian Intervention
Militarily Rational

Sometimes the imperative to stop the slaughter or save the starving should be too much even for the most hard-boiled realists, and intervention may be warranted even if it does not aim to secure peace. This was a motive in Bosnia and Somalia in the early 1990s, but intervention there involved presence in battle areas, constant friction with combatants or local political factions, and skirmishes that escalated without any sensible strategic plan. Bad experiences in those cases prevented rapid multilateral intervention in the butchery in Rwanda, intervention that could have saved many more lives.

Operation Provide Comfort, the U.S. humanitarian intervention in northern Iraq, and the unilateral French action in Rwanda provide better models. In these cases, the intervening forces carved out lines within which they could take command without fighting, but which they could defend if necessary—areas within which the intervenors themselves would rule temporarily. Then they got on with ministering to the needy populations and protecting them from assault. Such action is a stopgap, not a solution, but it is less likely to make the war worse.

In Bosnia, by contrast, the "safe areas," weapons exclusion zones, and towns supplied by American airdrops in the early 1990s were islands surrounded by hostile forces and represented messy territorial anomalies in what was effectively, at that point, a Serb conquest. It was no surprise that the Serbs would hover, waiting to pounce whenever they thought they might get away with it, probing and testing the resolve of the outsiders to fight, waiting for the international community to tire of the effort to keep the enclaves on life support.

Calling attention to mistakes, confusions, and uncomfortable choices is not intended to discredit intervention altogether. It is meant to argue for caution, because confusion about what is at issue can make such undertakings cause conflict rather than cure it. Doing it right is not impossible. The United States and the United Nations have collaborated successfully in peacemaking in the past, most notably in the wars over Korea and Kuwait. Enthusiasm for widespread involvement in local conflicts in the early 1990s was based on expectations that it would require a small proportion of the effort of those two huge enterprises. Unfortunately, this was probably true in some cases where the United Nations held back, as in Rwanda, and untrue in some cases where it jumped in, as in Bosnia. Peacemaking will not always cost as much as it did in Korea and Kuwait. The underlying issues, however, are much the same—who is in charge, and in what pieces of territory, after a war ends. Intervention that proceeds as if the issues are different—and can be settled by action toward the belligerents that is both evenhanded in intent and weak in capability—will more likely prevent peace than enforce it.

Scarcely better, if at all, are interventions that learn this lesson halfway, and use ample force and diplomatic legerdemain to secure peace agreements that do not really settle the question of who rules. This is what happened in Bosnia in 1995 and in Kosovo in 1999. Such interventions step up to the delusion of impartiality when they apply force, but then back away in the diplomatic aftermath. By pretending not to side decisively with one side against the other in a peace settlement, and pretending to support the reintegration of hopelessly riven polities, such interventions purchase peace at the price of an indefinite liberal, multilateral, imperium.

POWER, INTERDEPENDENCE, AND THE INFORMATION AGE

Robert O. Keohane and Joseph S. Nye

. . . The modernists of past generations were partly right. Angell's understanding of the impact of war on interdependence was insightful: World War I wrought unprecedented destruction, not only on the battlefield but by wrecking the sociopolitical systems and networks of economic interdependence that had thrived during the relatively peaceful years since 1815. As the modernists of the 1970s predicted, multinational corporations, nongovernmental organizations, and global financial markets have indeed become immensely more significant during the last quarter-century. But the state has been more resilient than modernists have expected. Not only do states continue to command the loyalties of a vast majority of the world's people; their control over material resources in most wealthy countries of the OECD, where markets are so important, has stayed at a third to half of gross domestic product (GDP).

The modernists of 1910 and the 1970s were right about the direction of change but simplistic about its consequences. Like some contemporary commentators on the information revolution, they moved too directly from technology to political effects, without sufficiently considering the continuity of belief systems, the persistence of institutions, or the strategic options available to leaders of states. They failed to analyze how holders of power could wield that power to shape or distort patterns of societal interdependence.

No longer is it sufficient to analyze flows of raw materials, goods, and capital across borders, or to understand how states construct territorial boundaries on the high seas. Cyberspace is itself a "place": everywhere and nowhere. But the prophets of a new cyberworld, like modernists before them, often overlook the fact that rules will be necessary to govern cyberspace—not only protecting lawful users from criminals but ensuring intellectual property rights. Rules require authority, whether in the form of public government or private or community governance. Classic issues of politics—who governs, on what terms? who benefits?—are as relevant to cyberspace as to traditionally physical space.

Traditionally, political activity has focused first at the local level, only extending to national and international spheres as the activity being regulated escaped jurisdictional boundaries. The contemporary information revolution, however, is inherently global, since "cyberplace" is divided on a nongeographical basis. The suffixes "edu," "org," and "com" are not geographical; and even where a country suffix appears in an address, there is no guarantee that the person being reached actually resides in that jurisdiction.

Information is power, as Frances Bacon wrote four hundred years ago. Undoubtedly, the information revolution has profound political implications. It therefore makes sense to seek to analyze some of these implications, using tools developed in studying the politics of interdependence. As traditionalists maintain, much will be the same: states will play important roles; vulnerability will lead to bargaining weakness and lack of vulnerability to power; actors will seek to manipulate cyberspace, as they manipulate flows across borders, to enhance their power. Yet as modernists insist, the information revolution is not "déjà vu all over again": cyberspace is truly global; it is harder to stop or even monitor the flow of information-carrying electrons than to do so for raw materials or goods; and dramatic reductions in the cost of information transmission make other resources relatively scarce. . . .

The information revolution itself can only be understood within the context of the globalization of the world economy. . . . Globalization was deliberately fostered by United States policy, and by international institutions, for half a century after the end of World War II. In the late 1940s the United States sought to create an open international economy to forestall another depression and contain communism. The resulting international institutions, formed on the basis of multilateral principles, fostered an environment that put a premium on information and were themselves affected by developments in the technologies of transportation and communications. It became increasingly costly for states to turn away from the patterns of interdependence that had been created.

The information revolution occurred not merely within a preexisting political context, but within one characterized by continuing military tensions and conflicts. Although the end of the Cold War removed one set of military-related tensions, it left some in place (as in the Middle East), and created situations of state-breaking and state-making in which violence was used ruthlessly to attain political ends—notably in Africa, the Caucasus, central Asia, and southeastern Europe. Even in East Asia, the scene until recently of rapid economic growth, political-military rivalries persist. At the same time, the military presence of the United States plays a clearly stabilizing role in East Asia, Central Europe, and—tenuously—the Balkans. Contrary to some early predictions after the end of the Cold War, NATO remained popular in Western and Central Europe. Markets thrive only with secure property rights, which depend on a political framework—which in turn requires military security.

Outside the democratic zone of peace, the world of states is not a world of complex interdependence: in many areas, realist assumptions about the role of military force and the hierarchy of issues remain valid. However, where the information revolution has had the most pronounced impact relates to the third assumption, about multiple channels of contact among societies. Here is the real change. We see an order of magnitude shift as a result of the information revolution. Now anyone with a computer is a desktop publisher, and anyone with a modem can communicate with distant parts of the globe at trivial costs. Barriers to entry into the world "information market" have been dramatically lowered.

Earlier transnational flows were heavily controlled by large bureaucratic organizations like multinational corporations or the Catholic Church, with the resources to establish a communication infrastructure. Such organizations remain important, but the vast cheapening of information transmission has now opened the field to loosely structured network organizations, and even individuals. These nongovernmental organizations and networks are particularly effective in penetrating states without regard to borders and us- ing domestic constituencies for agenda setting. By vastly increasing the number of chan- nels of contact among societies, the information revolution is changing the extent to which politics is approximating our model of complex interdependence.

However, information is not like goods or pollution, for which quantities flowing across borders are meaningful. The quantity of information available in cyberspace means little by itself. Philosophers could debate whether a Web page that no one ever looks at really exists; political scientists know that it would not be meaningful. As many observers have pointed out, the information revolution has made attention the scarce re- source. We used to ask: who has the capacity to transmit information? That question has become trivial, since the answer is: everyone with an Internet hookup. We now must ask: who has the capacity to attract others' attention to the information that he or she transmits? Getting others' attention is a necessary condition for using information as a political resource. . . .

INFORMATION AND POWER

Knowledge is power: but what is power? A basic distinction can be made between be- havioral power—the ability to obtain outcomes you want—and resource power—the possession of the resources that are usually associated with the ability to get the out- comes you want. Behavioral power, in turn, can be divided into hard and soft power. Hard power is the ability to get others to do what they otherwise would not do through threat of punishment or promise of reward. Whether by economic carrots or military sticks, the ability to coax or coerce has long been the central element of power. . . . Asymmetrical interdependence is an important source of hard power. The ability of the less vulnerable to manipulate or escape the constraints of an interdependent relation- ship at low cost is an important source of power. In the context of hard power, asymme- tries of information can greatly strengthen the hand of the less vulnerable party.

Soft power, on the other hand, is the ability to get desired outcomes because others want what you want; it is the ability to achieve desired outcomes through attraction rather than coercion. It works by convincing others to follow or getting them to agree to norms and institutions that produce the desired behavior. Soft power can rest on the ap- peal of one's ideas or culture or the ability to set the agenda through standards and insti- tutions that shape the preferences of others. It depends largely on the persuasiveness of the free information that an actor seeks to transmit. If a state can make its power legiti- mate in the eyes of others and establish international institutions that encourage others to define their interests in compatible ways, it may not need to expend as many of its costly traditional economic or military resources.

Hard and soft power are related, but they are not the same. Samuel P. Huntington is correct when he says that material success makes a culture and ideology attractive, and decreases in economic and military success lead to self-doubt and crises of identity. He is wrong when he argues that soft power is power only when it rests on a foundation of hard power. The soft power of the Vatican did not wane as the size of the papal states diminished. Canada, Sweden, and the Netherlands tend to have more influence than some other states with equivalent economic or military capability. The Soviet Union had considerable soft power in Europe after World War II but squandered it with the invasions of Hungary and Czechoslovakia even at a time when Soviet economic and military power were continuing to grow. Soft power varies over time and different domains. America's popular culture, with its libertarian and egalitarian currents, dominates film, television, and electronic communications in the world today. However, not all aspects of that culture are attractive to all others, for example conservative Moslems. In that domain, American soft power is limited. Nonetheless, the spread of information and American popular culture has generally increased global awareness of and openness to American ideas and values. To some extent this reflects deliberate policies, but more often soft power is an inadvertent by-product. For example, companies all over the world voluntarily subject themselves to the financial disclosure standards of the U.S. Securities and Exchange Commission because of the importance of American capital markets.

The information revolution is also affecting power measured in terms of resources rather than behavior. In the eighteenth century European balance of power, territory, population, and agriculture provided the basis for infantry, which was a crucial power resource, and France was a principal beneficiary. In the nineteenth century, industrial capacity provided the crucial resources that enabled Britain and, later, Germany to gain dominance. By the mid-twentieth century, science and particularly nuclear physics contributed crucial power resources to the United States and the Soviet Union. In this century, information capability broadly defined is likely to be the most crucial power resource. As Akihiko Tanaka puts it, "world politics" is becoming more important in world politics.

The new conventional wisdom is that the information revolution has a decentralizing and leveling effect. As it reduces costs, economies of scale, and barriers of entry to markets, it should reduce the power of large states and enhance the power of small states and nonstate actors. In practice, however, international relations are more complex than the technological determinism of the new conventional wisdom suggests. Some aspects of the information revolution help the small, but some help the already large and powerful. There are several reasons why. First, important barriers to entry and economies of scale remain in some aspects of power that are related to information. For example, soft power is strongly affected by the cultural content of what is broadcast or appears in movies and television programs. Large, established entertainment industries often enjoy considerable economies of scale in content production and distribution. The dominant American market share in films and television programs in world markets is a case in point.

Second, even where it is now cheap to disseminate existing information, the collection and production of new information often requires major costly investments. In many competitive situations, it is the newness of information at the margin that counts more than the average cost of all information. Intelligence collection is a good example. States like America, Britain, and France have capabilities for collection and production that dwarf those of other nations. In some commercial situations, a fast follower can do better than a first mover, but in terms of power among states, it is usually better to be a first mover than a fast follower.

Third, first movers are often the creators of the standards and architecture of information systems. The path dependent development of such systems reflects the advantage

TABLE 1

≋ **Effects of Information Technology on Power**		
	Hard power	*Soft power*
Benefit to large actors	• Revolution in military affairs • First mover and architecture • Technical intelligence collection	• Economies of scale in content production • Attention scarcity and marketing power
Benefit to small actors	• Commercial availability • Infrastructure vulnerability • Markets and economic intelligence	• NGOs and cheap interactive communication • Narrowcasting and new virtual communities

of the first mover. The use of the English language and the pattern of top-level domain names on the Internet provide relevant examples. Partly because of the transformation of the American economy in the 1980s (which was missed or misunderstood by the prophets of decline) and partly because of large investments driven by the Cold War military competition, the United States was often the first mover and still enjoys a lead in the application of a wide variety of information technologies.

Fourth, military power remains important in some critical domains of international relations. Information technology has some effects on the use of force that benefit the small and some that favor the already powerful. The off-the-shelf commercial availability of what used to be costly military technologies benefits small states and nonstate actors and contributes to the vulnerability of large states. Information systems add lucrative targets for terrorist (including state-sponsored) groups. Other trends, however, strengthen the already powerful. Many military analysts refer to a "revolution in military affairs" that has been produced by the application of information technology. Space-based sensors, direct broadcasting, high-speed computers, and complex software provide the ability to gather, sort, process, transfer, and disseminate information about highly complex events that occur in wide geographic areas. This dominant battlespace awareness combined with precision force provides a powerful advantage. As the 1991 Gulf War showed, traditional assessments of balances of weapons platforms such as tanks or planes become irrelevant unless they include the ability to integrate information with those weapons. Many of the relevant technologies are available in commercial markets, and weaker states can be expected to have many of them. The key, however, will not be the possession of fancy hardware or advanced systems, but the ability to integrate a system of systems. In this dimension, the United States is likely to keep its lead, and in terms of information warfare, a small edge makes all the difference. For instance, in Paul Dibb's assessment of the future balance of power in East Asia, he finds that the revolution in military affairs will not diminish, and may in some instances even increase, the American lead.

Contrary to the expectations of some theorists, the information revolution has not greatly decentralized or equalized power among states. If anything, thus far it has had the opposite effect. Table 1, on the next page, summarizes the effects of the information revolution on power. But what about reducing the role of governments and the power of all states? Here the changes are more likely to be along the lines the modernists predicted. But to understand these changes, we need first to explore a topic briefly noted earlier: how the information revolution, by minimizing the costs of transmitting information, has increased the relative significance of the scarce resource of attention, and the implications of this shift for what we call the politics of credibility.

THE PARADOX OF PLENTY AND THE POLITICS OF CREDIBILITY

A plenitude of information leads to a poverty of attention. Attention becomes the scarce resource, and those who can distinguish valuable signals from white noise gain power. Editors, filters, and cue-givers become more in demand, and this is a source of power. There will be an imperfect market for evaluators. Brand names and the ability to bestow an international seal of approval will become more important.

But power does not necessarily flow to those who can withhold information. As George Akerlof has argued, under some circumstances private information can cripple the credibility of those who have it. For instance, sellers of used cars have more knowledge about their defects than potential buyers. But an awareness of this situation and the fact that owners of bad cars are more likely to sell than owners of good ones lead potential buyers to discount the price they are willing to pay in order to adjust for unknown defects. Hence the result of the superior information of sellers is not to improve the mean price they receive, but instead to make them unable to sell good used cars for their real value. Unlike asymmetrical interdependence in trade, where power goes to those who can afford to hold back or break trade ties, information power flows to those who can edit and credibly validate information to sort out what is both correct and important.

Hence among editors and cue-givers, credibility is the crucial resource, and asymmetrical credibility is a key source of power. Reputation has always mattered in world politics, and it becomes even more important because of the "paradox of plenty." The low cost of transmitting data means that the ability to transmit it is much less important as a power resource than it used to be, but the ability to filter information is more so. Political struggles focus less on control over the ability to transmit information than over the creation and destruction of credibility.

One implication of the abundance of information sources, and the role of credibility, is that soft power is likely to become less a function simply of material resources than in the past. When ability to produce and disseminate information is the scarce resource, limiting factors include the control of printing presses, radio stations, and newsprint. Hard power, for instance using force to take over a radio station, can generate soft power. In the case of worldwide television, wealth can also lead to soft power. For instance, CNN was based in Atlanta rather than Amman or Cairo because of America's leading position in the industry. When Iraq invaded Kuwait in 1990, the fact that CNN was basically an American company helped to frame the issue, worldwide, as aggression (analogous to Hitler's actions in the 1930s) rather than as a justified attempt to reverse colonial humiliation (analogous to India's capture of Goa).

This close connection between hard and soft power is likely to be somewhat weakened under conditions of complex interdependence in an information age. Propaganda is not new. Hitler and Stalin used it effectively in the 1930s. Milosevic's control of television was crucial to his power in Serbia. In Moscow in 1993, a battle for power was fought at a TV station. In Rwanda, Hutu-controlled radio stations contributed to genocide in 1994. The power of broadcasting persists but is supplemented by multiple channels of communication, which are controlled by multiple actors that cannot use force to control one another. The issue is not only which actors own television networks, radio stations, or Web sites once a plethora of such sources exist, but who pays attention to which fountains of information and misinformation.

Soft power today can also be the legacy of yesterday's hard and soft power. Britain's resources over a half-century ago enabled it to construct the BBC, and the nature of British society and politics made the BBC what it has become: a relatively reliable and unbiased source of information worldwide. The BBC was an important soft power resource for Britain in Eastern Europe during the Cold War, as a result of the credibility it had established earlier. Now it has more competitors, but to the extent that it maintains credibility in an era of white noise, its value as a power resource may actually increase.

Broadcasting has long had an impact on public opinion. By focusing on some conflicts and human rights problems, broadcasters have pressed politicians to respond to some foreign conflicts rather than others—e.g., Somalia rather than Southern Sudan. Not surprisingly, governments have sought to influence, manipulate, and control television and radio stations and have been able to do so with considerable success, since a relatively small number of physically located broadcasting sites were used to reach many people with the same message. However, the shift from broadcasting to narrowcasting has major political implications. Cable and the Internet enable senders to segment and target audiences. Even more important for politics is the interactive role of the Internet; it not only focuses attention but facilitates coordination of action across borders. Interactivity at low cost allows for the development of new virtual communities: people who imagine themselves as part of a single group regardless of how far apart they are physically from one another.

These new technologies create opportunities for nongovernmental actors. Advocacy networks find their potential impact vastly expanded by the information revolution, since the fax machine and the Internet enable them to send messages from the most obscure corners of the world: from the oil platforms of the North Sea to the forests of Chiapas. The 1997 Landmine Conference was a coalition of network organizations working with middle power governments like Canada and some individual politicians and celebrities to capture attention and set the agenda. The role of NGOs was also important as a channel of communication across delegations in the global warming discussions. Environmental groups and industry competed in Kyoto in 1997 for the attention of the media from major countries, basing their arguments in part on the findings of nongovernmental scientists. Many observers have heralded a new era for NGOs as a result of the information revolution, and there seems little doubt that substantial opportunities exist for a flowering of issue advocacy networks and virtual communities.

Yet the credibility of these networks is fragile. Greenpeace, for instance, imposed large costs on Royal Dutch Shell by criticizing Shell's planned disposal of its Brentspar drilling rig. Greenpeace, however, itself lost credibility and membership when it later had to admit the inaccuracy of some of its factual claims. The findings of atmospheric scientists about climate change have gained credibility, not just from the prestige of science but from the procedures developed in the Intergovernmental Panel on Climate Change (IPCC) for extensive and careful peer review of scientific papers and intergovernmental review of executive summaries. The IPCC is an example of an intergovernmental information-legitimating institution, whose major function is to give coherence and credibility to masses of scientific information about climate change.

As the IPCC example shows, the importance of credibility is giving increasing importance to what Peter Haas has called "epistemic communities": transnational networks of like-minded experts. By framing issues where knowledge is important, epistemic communities become important actors in forming coalitions and in bargaining processes. By creating knowledge, they can provide the basis for effective cooperation. But to be effective, the procedures by which this information is produced have to appear unbiased. It is increasingly recognized that scientific information is socially constructed; to be credible, the information has to be produced through a process that is dominated by professional norms and that appears transparent and procedurally fair. Even if their information is credible, professional communities will not resolve contentious issues that involve major distributional costs. But they will become more significant actors in the politics of decision.

The politics of soft power do not depend only on the "information shapers," who seek to persuade others to adopt their practices and values. They also depend on the characteristics of their targets: the "information takers," or the targets of information flows. Of course, the shapers and takers are often the same people, organizations, or countries, in different capacities. Information shapers, as we have seen, require credibility. The takers, on the other hand, will be differentially receptive depending on the character, and internal legitimacy, of their own institutions. Self-confident information takers with internal legitimacy can absorb flows of information more readily, with less disturbance, than can institutions (governmental or nongovernmental) lacking such legitimacy and self-confidence.

Not all democracies are leaders in the information revolution, but, as far as countries are concerned, all information shapers are democracies. This is not accidental. Their societies are familiar with free exchange of information and their institutions of governance are not threatened by it. They can shape information because they can also take it. Authoritarian states, typically among the laggards, have more trouble. At this point, governments such as China's can control the access of their citizens to the Internet by controlling Internet service providers. It is possible, but costly, to route around such restrictions, and control does not have to be complete to be effective for political purposes. But as societies like Singapore reach levels of development where their knowledge workers want free access to the Net, they run the risk of losing their scarcest resource for competing in the information economy. Thus Singapore is wrestling with the dilemma of reshaping its educational system to encourage the individual creativity that the information economy will demand, and at the same time maintain existing social controls over the flow of information. Singapore's leaders realize they cannot hope to control the Internet in the long run. Closed systems become more costly.

One reason that closed systems become more costly is that it is risky for foreigners to invest funds in a country where the key decisions are made in an opaque fashion.

Transparency is becoming a key asset for countries seeking investments. The ability to keep information from leaving, which once seemed valuable to authoritarian states, undermines the credibility and transparency necessary to attract investment on globally competitive terms. This point is illustrated by the 1997 Asian financial crisis. Governments that are not transparent are not credible, since the information they offer is seen as biased and selective. Moreover, as economic development progresses and middle-class societies develop, repressive measures become more expensive not merely at home, but also in terms of international reputation. Both Taiwan and South Korea discovered in the late 1980s that repression of rising demands for democracy would be expensive in terms of their reputation and soft power. By having begun to democratize earlier, they have strengthened their capacity—as compared with, for instance, Indonesia—to cope with economic crisis.

Whatever the future effects of interactivity and virtual communities, one political effect of increased free information flows through multiple channels is already clear: states have lost much of their control over information about their own societies. States that seek to develop (with the exception of some energy suppliers) need foreign capital and the technology and organization that go with it. Geographical communities still matter most, but governments that want to see rapid development will find that they will have to give up some of the barriers to information flows that protected officials from outside scrutiny. No longer will governments that want high levels of development be able to afford the comfort of keeping their financial and political situations inside a black box. The motto of the global information society might become, "If you can't take it, you can't shape it."

From a business standpoint, the information revolution has vastly increased the marketability and value of commercial information, by reducing costs of transmission and the transaction costs of charging information users. Politically, however, the most important shift concerns free information. The ability to disseminate free information increases the potential for persuasion in world politics—as long as credibility can be attained and maintained. NGOs and other states can more readily influence the beliefs of people within other jurisdictions. If one actor can persuade others to adopt similar values and policies, whether it possesses hard power and strategic information may become relatively less important. Soft power and free information can, if sufficiently persuasive, change perceptions of self-interest, and therefore how hard power and strategic information are used. If governments or NGOs are to take advantage of the information revolution, they will have to establish reputations for credibility in the world of white noise that constitutes the information revolution.

In conclusion, the new conventional wisdom is wrong in its predictions of an equalizing effect of the information and communications revolutions in the distributions of power among states. In part, this is because economies of scale and barriers to entry persist in regard to strategic information, and in part because with respect to free information, the larger states will often be well-placed in the competition for credibility. On the other hand, the information revolution is altering the degree of control that all states can exert in today's world. Cheap flows of information have created an order-of-magnitude change in channels of information. Nongovernmental actors operating transnationally have much greater opportunities to organize and to propagate their views. States are more easily penetrated and less like black boxes. The coherence and elite maintenance of hierarchical ordering of foreign policy issues is diminished.

The net effect of the information revolution is to change political processes in a way where soft power becomes more important in relation to hard power than it was in the past. Credibility becomes a key power resource both for governments and NGOs, giving more open, transparent organizations an advantage with respect to free information. Although the coherence of government policies may diminish in more pluralistic and penetrated states, those same countries may be better placed in terms of credibility and soft power. . . .

JIHAD VS. MCWORLD

Benjamin R. Barber

Just beyond the horizon of current events lie two possible political futures—both bleak, neither democratic. The first is a retribalization of large swaths of humankind by war and bloodshed: a threatened Lebanonization of national states in which culture is pitted against culture, people against people, tribe against tribe—a Jihad in the name of a hundred narrowly conceived faiths against every kind of interdependence, every kind of artificial social cooperation and civic mutuality. The second is being borne in on us by the onrush of economic and ecological forces that demand integration and uniformity and that mesmerize the world with fast music, fast computers, and fast food—with MTV, Macintosh, and McDonald's, pressing nations into one commercially homogenous global network: one McWorld tied together by technology, ecology, communications, and commerce. The planet is falling precipitantly apart *AND* coming reluctantly together at the very same moment.

These two tendencies are sometimes visible in the same countries at the same instant: thus Yugoslavia, clamoring just recently to join the New Europe, is exploding into fragments; India is trying to live up to its reputation as the world's largest integral democracy while powerful new fundamentalist parties like the Hindu nationalist Bharatiya Janata Party, along with nationalist assassins, are imperiling its hard-won unity. States are breaking up or joining up: the Soviet Union has disappeared almost overnight, its parts forming new unions with one another or with like-minded nationalities in neighboring states. The old interwar national state based on territory and political sovereignty looks to be a mere transitional development.

The tendencies of what I am here calling the forces of Jihad and the forces of McWorld operate with equal strength in opposite directions, the one driven by parochial hatreds, the other by universalizing markets, the one re-creating ancient subnational and ethnic borders from within, the other making national borders porous from without. They have one thing in common: neither offers much hope to citizens looking for practical ways to govern themselves democratically. If the global future is to pit Jihad's centrifugal whirlwind against McWorld's centripetal black hole, the outcome is unlikely to be democratic—or so I will argue.

MCWORLD, OR THE GLOBALIZATION OF POLITICS

Four imperatives make up the dynamic of McWorld: a market imperative, a resource imperative, an information-technology imperative, and an ecological imperative. By

Benjamin R. Barber, "Jihad Vs. McWorld." Published originally in *The Atlantic Monthly* 1992 as an introduction to *Jihad Vs. McWorld* (Ballantine paperback, 1996), a volume that discusses and extends the theme of the original article. Reprinted by permission.

shrinking the world and diminishing the salience of national borders, these imperatives have in combination achieved a considerable victory over factiousness and particularism, and not least of all over their most virulent traditional form—nationalism. It is the realists who are now Europeans, the utopians who dream nostalgically of a resurgent England or Germany, perhaps even a resurgent Wales or Saxony. Yesterday's wishful cry for one world has yielded to the reality of McWorld.

The Market Imperative

Marxist and Leninist theories of imperialism assumed that the quest for ever-expanding markets would in time compel nation-based capitalist economies to push against national boundaries in search of an international economic imperium. Whatever else has happened to the scientistic predictions of Marxism, in this domain they have proved farsighted. All national economies are now vulnerable to the inroads of larger, transnational markets within which trade is free, currencies are convertible, access to banking is open, and contracts are enforceable under law. In Europe, Asia, Africa, the South Pacific, and the Americas such markets are eroding national sovereignty and giving rise to entities—international banks, trade associations, transnational lobbies like OPEC and Greenpeace, world news services like CNN and the BBC, and multinational corporations that increasingly lack a meaningful national identity—that neither reflect nor respect nationhood as an organizing or regulative principle.

The market imperative has also reinforced the quest for international peace and stability, requisites of an efficient international economy. Markets are enemies of parochialism, isolation, fractiousness, war. Market psychology attenuates the psychology of ideological and religious cleavages and assumes a concord among producers and consumers—categories that ill fit narrowly conceived national or religious cultures. Shopping has little tolerance for blue laws, whether dictated by pub-closing British paternalism, Sabbath-observing Jewish Orthodox fundamentalism, or no-Sunday-liquor-sales Massachusetts puritanism. In the context of common markets, international law ceases to be a vision of justice and becomes a workaday framework for getting things done—enforcing contracts, ensuring that governments abide by deals, regulating trade and currency relations, and so forth.

Common markets demand a common language, as well as a common currency, and they produce common behaviors of the kind bred by cosmopolitan city life everywhere. Commercial pilots, computer programmers, international bankers, media specialists, oil riggers, entertainment celebrities, ecology experts, demographers, accountants, professors, athletes—these compose a new breed of men and women for whom religion, culture, and nationality can seem only marginal elements in a working identity. Although sociologists of everyday life will no doubt continue to distinguish a Japanese from an American mode, shopping has a common signature throughout the world. Cynics might even say that some of the recent revolutions in Eastern Europe have had as their true goal not liberty and the right to vote but well-paying jobs and the right to shop (although the vote is proving easier to acquire than consumer goods). The market imperative is, then, plenty powerful; but, notwithstanding some of the claims made for "democratic capitalism," it is not identical with the democratic imperative.

The Resource Imperative

Democrats once dreamed of societies whose political autonomy rested firmly on economic independence. The Athenians idealized what they called autarky, and tried for a while to create a way of life simple and austere enough to make the polis genuinely self-sufficient. To be free meant to be independent of any other community or polis. Not even the Athenians were able to achieve autarky, however: human nature, it turns out, is dependency. By the time of Pericles, Athenian politics was inextricably bound up with a flowering empire held together by naval power and commerce—an empire that, even as it appeared to enhance Athenian might, ate away at Athenian independence and autarky. Master and slave, it turned out, were bound together by mutual insufficiency.

The dream of autarky briefly engrossed nineteenth-century America as well, for the underpopulated, endlessly bountiful land, the cornucopia of natural resources, and the natural barriers of a continent walled in by two great seas led many to believe that America could be a world unto itself. Given this past, it has been harder for Americans than for most to accept the inevitability of interdependence. But the rapid depletion of resources even in a country like ours, where they once seemed inexhaustible, and the maldistribution of arable soil and mineral resources on the planet, leave even the wealthiest societies ever more resource-dependent and many other nations in permanently desperate straits.

Every nation, it turns out, needs something another nation has; some nations have almost nothing they need.

THE INFORMATION-TECHNOLOGY IMPERATIVE

Enlightenment science and the technologies derived from it are inherently universalizing. They entail a quest for descriptive principles of general application, a search for universal solutions to particular problems, and an unswerving embrace of objectivity and impartiality.

Scientific progress embodies and depends on open communication, a common discourse rooted in rationality, collaboration, and an easy and regular flow and exchange of information. Such ideals can be hypocritical covers for power-mongering by elites, and they may be shown to be wanting in many other ways, but they are entailed by the very idea of science and they make science and globalization practical allies.

Business, banking, and commerce all depend on information flow and are facilitated by new communication technologies. The hardware of these technologies tends to be systemic and integrated—computer, television, cable, satellite, laser, fiber-optic, and microchip technologies combining to create a vast interactive communications and information network that can potentially give every person on earth access to every other person, and make every datum, every byte, available to every set of eyes. If the automobile was, as George Ball once said (when he gave his blessing to a Fiat factory in the Soviet Union during the Cold War), "an ideology on four wheels," then electronic telecommunication and information systems are an ideology at 186,000 miles per second—which makes for a very small planet in a very big hurry. Individual cultures speak particular languages; commerce and science increasingly speak English; the whole world speaks logarithms and binary mathematics.

Moreover, the pursuit of science and technology asks for, even compels, open societies. Satellite footprints do not respect national borders; telephone wires penetrate the most closed societies. With photocopying and then fax machines having infiltrated Soviet universities and *samizdat* literary circles in the eighties, and computer modems having multiplied like rabbits in communism's bureaucratic warrens thereafter, *glasnost* could not be far behind. In their social requisites, secrecy and science are enemies.

The new technology's software is perhaps even more globalizing than its hardware. The information arm of international commerce's sprawling body reaches out and touches distinct nations and parochial cultures, and gives them a common face chiseled in Hollywood, on Madison Avenue, and in Silicon Valley. Throughout the 1980s one of the most-watched television programs in South Africa was *The Cosby Show.* The demise of apartheid was already in production. Exhibitors at the 1991 Cannes film festival expressed growing anxiety over the "homogenization" and "Americanization" of the global film industry when, for the third year running, American films dominated the awards ceremonies. America has dominated the world's popular culture for much longer, and much more decisively. In November of 1991 Switzerland's once insular culture boasted best-seller lists featuring *Terminator 2* as the No. 1 movie, *Scarlett* as the No. 1 book, and Prince's *Diamonds and Pearls* as the No. 1 record album. No wonder the Japanese are buying Hollywood film studios even faster than Americans are buying Japanese television sets. This kind of software supremacy may in the long term be far more important than hardware superiority, because culture has become more potent than armaments. What is the power of the Pentagon compared with Disneyland? Can the Sixth Fleet keep up with CNN? McDonald's in Moscow and Coke in China will do more to create a global culture than military colonization ever could. It is less the goods than the brand names that do the work, for they convey life-style images that alter perception and challenge behavior. They make up the seductive software of McWorld's common (at times much too common) soul.

Yet in all this high-tech commercial world there is nothing that looks particularly democratic. It lends itself to surveillance as well as liberty, to new forms of manipulation and covert control as well as new kinds of participation, to skewed, unjust market outcomes as well as greater productivity. The consumer society and the open society are not quite synonymous. Capitalism and democracy have a relationship, but it is something less than a marriage. An efficient free market after all requires that consumers be free to vote their dollars on competing goods, not that citizens be free to vote their values and beliefs on competing political candidates and programs. The free market flourished in junta-run Chile, in military-governed Taiwan and Korea, and, earlier, in a variety of autocratic European empires as well as their colonial possessions.

The Ecological Imperative

The impact of globalization on ecology is a cliche even to world leaders who ignore it. We know well enough that the German forests can be destroyed by Swiss and Italians driving gas-guzzlers fueled by leaded gas. We also know that the planet can be asphyxiated by greenhouse gases because Brazilian farmers want to be part of the twentieth century and are burning down tropical rain forests to clear a little land to plough, and because Indonesians make a living out of converting their lush jungle into toothpicks for fastidious Japanese diners, upsetting the delicate oxygen balance and in effect puncturing our global lungs. Yet this ecological consciousness has meant not only greater awareness but also greater inequality, as modernized nations try to slam the door behind them, saying to developing nations, "The world cannot afford your modernization; ours has wrung it dry!"

Each of the four imperatives just cited is transnational, transideological, and transcultural. Each applies impartially to Catholics, Jews, Muslims, Hindus, and Buddhists; to democrats and totalitarians; to capitalists and socialists. The Enlightenment dream of a universal rational society has to a remarkable degree been realized—but in a form that is commercialized, homogenized, depoliticized, bureaucratized, and, of course, radically incomplete, for the movement toward McWorld is in competition with forces of global breakdown, national dissolution, and centrifugal corruption. These forces, working in the opposite direction, are the essence of what I call Jihad.

JIHAD, OR THE LEBANONIZATION OF THE WORLD

OPEC, the World Bank, the United Nations, the International Red Cross, the multinational corporation . . . there are scores of institutions that reflect globalization. But they often appear as ineffective reactors to the world's real actors: national states and, to an ever greater degree, subnational factions in permanent rebellion against uniformity and integration—even the kind represented by universal law and justice. The headlines feature these players regularly: they are cultures, not countries; parts, not wholes; sects, not religions; rebellious factions and dissenting minorities at war not just with globalism but with the traditional nation-state. Kurds, Basques, Puerto Ricans, Ossetians, East Timoreans, Quebecois, the Catholics of Northern Ireland, Abkhasians, Kurile Islander Japanese, the Zulus of Inkatha, Catalonians, Tamils, and, of course, Palestinians—people without countries, inhabiting nations not their own, seeking smaller worlds within borders that will seal them off from modernity.

A powerful irony is at work here. Nationalism was once a force of integration and unification, a movement aimed at bringing together disparate clans, tribes, and cultural fragments under new, assimilationist flags. But as Ortega y Gasset noted more than sixty years ago, having won its victories, nationalism changed its strategy. In the 1920s, and again today, it is more often a reactionary and divisive force, pulverizing the very nations it once helped cement together. The force that creates nations is "inclusive," Ortega wrote in *The Revolt of the Masses*. "In periods of consolidation, nationalism has a positive value, and is a lofty standard. But in Europe everything is more than consolidated, and nationalism is nothing but a mania . . ."

This mania has left the post-Cold War world smoldering with hot wars; the international scene is little more unified than it was at the end of the Great War, in Ortega's own time. There were more than thirty wars in progress last year, most of them ethnic, racial, tribal, or religious in character, and the list of unsafe regions doesn't seem to be getting any shorter. Some new world order!

The aim of many of these small-scale wars is to redraw boundaries, to implode states and resecure parochial identities: to escape McWorld's dully insistent imperatives. The mood is that of Jihad: war not as an instrument of policy but as an emblem of identity, an expression of community, an end in itself. Even where there is no shooting war, there is fractiousness, secession, and the quest for ever smaller communities. Add to the list of dangerous countries those at risk: In Switzerland and Spain, Jurassian and Basque separatists still argue the virtues of ancient identities, sometimes in the language of bombs. Hyperdisintegration in the former Soviet Union may well continue unabated—not just a Ukraine independent from the Soviet Union but a Bessarabian Ukraine independent from the Ukrainian republic; not just Russia severed from the defunct union but Tatarstan severed from Russia. Yugoslavia makes even the disunited, ex-Soviet, nonsocialist republics that were once the Soviet Union look integrated, its sectarian fatherlands springing up within factional motherlands like weeds within weeds within weeds. Kurdish independence would threaten the territorial integrity of four Middle Eastern nations. Well before the current cataclysm Soviet Georgia made a claim for autonomy from the Soviet Union, only to be faced with its Ossetians (164,000 in a republic of 5.5 million) demanding their own self-determination within Georgia. The Abkhasian minority in Georgia has followed suit. Even the good will established by Canada's once promising Meech Lake protocols is in danger, with Francophone Quebec again threatening the dissolution of the federation. In South Africa the emergence from apartheid was hardly achieved when friction between Inkatha's Zulus and the African National Congress's tribally identified members threatened to replace Europeans' racism with an indigenous tribal war. After thirty years of attempted integration using the colonial language (English) as a unifier, Nigeria is now playing with the idea of linguistic multiculturalism—which could mean the cultural breakup of the nation into hundreds of tribal fragments. Even Saddam Hussein has benefited from the threat of internal Jihad, having used renewed tribal and religious warfare to turn last season's mortal enemies into reluctant allies of an Iraqi nationhood that he nearly destroyed.

The passing of communism has torn away the thin veneer of internationalism (workers of the world unite!) to reveal ethnic prejudices that are not only ugly and deep-seated but increasingly murderous. Europe's old scourge, anti-Semitism, is back with a vengeance, but it is only one of many antagonisms. It appears all too easy to throw the historical gears into reverse and pass from a Communist dictatorship back into a tribal state.

Among the tribes, religion is also a battlefield. ("Jihad" is a rich word whose generic meaning is "struggle"—usually the struggle of the soul to avert evil. Strictly applied to religious war, it is used only in reference to battles where the faith is under assault, or battles against a government that denies the practice of Islam. My use here is rhetorical, but does follow both journalistic practice and history.) Remember the Thirty Years War? Whatever forms of Enlightenment universalism might once have come to grace such historically related forms of monotheism as Judaism, Christianity, and Islam, in many of their modern incarnations they are parochial rather than cosmopolitan, angry rather than loving, proselytizing rather than ecumenical, zealous rather than rationalist, sectarian rather than deistic, ethnocentric rather than universalizing. As a result, like the new forms of hypernationalism, the new expressions of religious fundamentalism are fractious and pulverizing, never integrating. This is religion as the Crusaders knew it: a battle to the death for souls that if not saved will be forever lost.

The atmospherics of Jihad have resulted in a breakdown of civility in the name of identity, of comity in the name of community. International relations have sometimes taken on the aspect of gang war—cultural turf battles featuring tribal factions that were supposed to be sublimated as integral parts of large national, economic, postcolonial, and constitutional entities.

THE DARKENING FUTURE OF DEMOCRACY

These rather melodramatic tableaux vivants do not tell the whole story, however. For all their defects, Jihad and McWorld have their attractions. Yet, to repeat and insist, the attractions are unrelated to democracy. Neither McWorld nor Jihad is remotely democratic in impulse. Neither needs democracy; neither promotes democracy.

McWorld does manage to look pretty seductive in a world obsessed with Jihad. It delivers peace, prosperity, and relative unity—if at the cost of independence, community, and identity (which is generally based on difference). The primary political values required by the global market are order and tranquillity, and freedom—as in the phrases "free trade," "free press," and "free love." Human rights are needed to a degree, but not citizenship or participation—and no more social justice and equality than are necessary to promote efficient economic production and consumption. Multinational corporations sometimes seem to prefer doing business with local oligarchs, inasmuch as they can take confidence from dealing with the boss on all crucial matters. Despots who slaughter their own populations are no problem, so long as they leave markets in place and refrain from making war on their neighbors (Saddam Hussein's fatal mistake). In trading partners, predictability is of more value than justice.

The Eastern European revolutions that seemed to arise out of concern for global democratic values quickly deteriorated into a stampede in the general direction of free markets and their ubiquitous, television-promoted shopping malls. East Germany's Neues Forum, that courageous gathering of intellectuals, students, and workers which overturned the Stalinist regime in Berlin in 1989, lasted only six months in Germany's mini-version of McWorld. Then it gave way to money and markets and monopolies from the West. By the time of the first all-German elections, it could scarcely manage to secure three percent of the vote. Elsewhere there is growing evidence that glasnost will go and perestroika—defined as privatization and an opening of markets to Western bidders—will stay. So understandably anxious are the new rulers of Eastern Europe and whatever entities are forged from the residues of the Soviet Union to gain access to credit and markets and technology—McWorld's flourishing new currencies—that they have shown themselves willing to trade away democratic prospects in pursuit of them: not just old totalitarian ideologies and command-economy production models but some possible indigenous experiments with a third way between capitalism and socialism, such as economic cooperatives and employee stock-ownership plans, both of which have their ardent supporters in the East.

Jihad delivers a different set of virtues: a vibrant local identity, a sense of community, solidarity among kinsmen, neighbors, and countrymen, narrowly conceived. But it also guarantees parochialism and is grounded in exclusion. Solidarity is secured through war against outsiders. And solidarity often means obedience to a hierarchy in governance, fanaticism in beliefs, and the obliteration of individual selves in the name of the group. Deference to leaders and intolerance toward outsiders (and toward "enemies within") are hallmarks of tribalism—hardly the attitudes required for the cultivation of new democratic women and men capable of governing themselves. Where new democratic experiments have been conducted in retribalizing societies, in both Europe and the Third World, the result has often been anarchy, repression, persecution, and the coming of new, noncommunist forms of very old kinds of despotism. During the past year, Havel's velvet revolution in Czechoslovakia was imperiled by partisans of "Czechland" and of Slovakia as independent entities. India seemed little less rent by Sikh, Hindu, Muslim, and Tamil infighting than it was immediately after the British pulled out, more than forty years ago.

To the extent that either McWorld or Jihad has a *natural* politics, it has turned out to be more of an antipolitics. For McWorld, it is the antipolitics of globalism: bureaucratic, technocratic, and meritocratic, focused (as Marx predicted it would be) on the administration of things—with people, however, among the chief things to be administered. In its politico-economic imperatives McWorld has been guided by laissez-faire market principles that privilege efficiency, productivity, and beneficence at the expense of civic liberty and self-government.

For Jihad, the antipolitics of tribalization has been explicitly antidemocratic: one-party dictatorship, government by military junta, theocratic fundamentalism—often associated with a version of the *Fuhrerprinzip* that empowers an individual to rule on behalf of a people. Even the government of India, struggling for decades to model democracy for a people who will soon number a billion, longs for great leaders; and for every Mahatma Gandhi, Indira Gandhi, or Rajiv Gandhi taken from them by zealous assassins, the Indians appear to seek a replacement who will deliver them from the lengthy travail of their freedom.

THE CONFEDERAL OPTION

How can democracy be secured and spread in a world whose primary tendencies are at best indifferent to it (McWorld) and at worst deeply antithetical to it (Jihad)? My guess is that globalization will eventually vanquish retribalization. The ethos of material "civilization" has not yet encountered an obstacle it has been unable to thrust aside. Ortega may have grasped in the 1920s a clue to our own future in the coming millennium.

"Everyone sees the need of a new principle of life. But as always happens in similar crises—some people attempt to save the situation by an artificial intensification of the very principle which has led to decay. This is the meaning of the 'nationalist' outburst of recent years. . . . things have always gone that way. The last flare, the longest;

the last sigh, the deepest. On the very eve of their disappearance there is an intensification of frontiers—military and economic."

Jihad may be a last deep sigh before the eternal yawn of McWorld. On the other hand, Ortega was not exactly prescient; his prophecy of peace and internationalism came just before blitzkrieg, world war, and the Holocaust tore the old order to bits. Yet democracy is how we remonstrate with reality, the rebuke our aspirations offer to history. And if retribalization is inhospitable to democracy, there is nonetheless a form of democratic government that can accommodate parochialism and communitarianism, one that can even save them from their defects and make them more tolerant and participatory: decentralized participatory democracy. And if McWorld is indifferent to democracy, there is nonetheless a form of democratic government that suits global markets passably well—representative government in its federal or, better still, confederal variation.

With its concern for accountability, the protection of minorities, and the universal rule of law, a confederalized representative system would serve the political needs of McWorld as well as oligarchic bureaucratism or meritocratic elitism is currently doing. As we are already beginning to see, many nations may survive in the long term only as confederations that afford local regions smaller than "nations" extensive jurisdiction. Recommended reading for democrats of the twenty-first century is not the U.S. Constitution or the French Declaration of Rights of Man and Citizen but the Articles of Confederation, that suddenly pertinent document that stitched together the thirteen American colonies into what then seemed a too loose confederation of independent states but now appears a new form of political realism, as veterans of Yeltsin's new Russia and the new Europe created at Maastricht will attest.

By the same token, the participatory and direct form of democracy that engages citizens in civic activity and civic judgment and goes well beyond just voting and accountability—the system I have called "strong democracy"—suits the political needs of decentralized communities as well as theocratic and nationalist party dictatorships have done. Local neighborhoods need not be democratic, but they can be. Real democracy has flourished in diminutive settings: the spirit of liberty, Tocqueville said, is local. Participatory democracy, if not naturally apposite to tribalism, has an undeniable attractiveness under conditions of parochialism.

Democracy in any of these variations will, however, continue to be obstructed by the undemocratic and antidemocratic trends toward uniformitarian globalism and intolerant retribalization which I have portrayed here. For democracy to persist in our brave new McWorld, we will have to commit acts of conscious political will—a possibility, but hardly a probability, under these conditions. Political will requires much more than the quick fix of the transfer of institutions. Like technology transfer, institution transfer rests on foolish assumptions about a uniform world of the kind that once fired the imagination of colonial administrators. Spread English justice to the colonies by exporting wigs. Let an East Indian trading company act as the vanguard to Britain's free parliamentary institutions. Today's well-intentioned quick-fixers in the National Endowment for Democracy and the Kennedy School of Government, in the unions and foundations and universities zealously nurturing contacts in Eastern Europe and the Third World, are hoping to democratize by long distance. Post Bulgaria a parliament by first-class mail. Fed Ex the Bill of Rights to Sri Lanka. Cable Cambodia some common law.

Yet Eastern Europe has already demonstrated that importing free political parties, parliaments, and presses cannot establish a democratic civil society; imposing a free market may even have the opposite effect. Democracy grows from the bottom up and cannot be imposed from the top down. Civil society has to be built from the inside out. The institutional superstructure comes last. Poland may become democratic, but then again it may heed the Pope, and prefer to found its politics on its Catholicism, with uncertain consequences for democracy. Bulgaria may become democratic, but it may prefer tribal war. The former Soviet Union may become a democratic confederation, or it may just grow into an anarchic and weak conglomeration of markets for other nations' goods and services.

Democrats need to seek out indigenous democratic impulses. There is always a desire for self-government, always some expression of participation, accountability, consent, and representation, even in traditional hierarchical societies. These need to be identified, tapped, modified, and incorporated into new democratic practices with an indigenous flavor. The tortoises among the democratizers may ultimately outlive or outpace the hares, for they will have the time and patience to explore conditions along the way, and to adapt their gait to changing circumstances. Tragically, democracy in a hurry often looks something like France in 1794 or China in 1989.

It certainly seems possible that the most attractive democratic ideal in the face of the brutal realities of Jihad and the dull realities of McWorld will be a confederal union of semi-autonomous communities smaller than nation-states, tied together into regional economic associations and markets larger than nation-states—participatory and self-determining in local matters at the bottom, representative and accountable at the top. The nation-state would play a diminished role, and sovereignty would lose some of its political potency. The Green movement adage "Think globally, act locally" would actually come to describe the conduct of politics.

This vision reflects only an ideal, however—one that is not terribly likely to be realized. Freedom, Jean-Jacques Rousseau once wrote, is a food easy to eat but hard to digest. Still, democracy has always played itself out against the odds. And democracy remains both a form of coherence as binding as McWorld and a secular faith potentially as inspiriting as Jihad.